Killer
Borland® C++ 4

Chris Corry

Mark Davidson

John M. Dlugosz

Michael R. Dunlavey

Greg Perry

Steve Potts

Namir Clement Shammas

Clayton Walnum

BORLAND C++

CW01424431

que

Killer Borland C++ 4

Copyright © 1994 by Que® Corporation

All rights reserved. Printed in the United States of America. No part of this book may be used or reproduced in any form or by any means, or stored in a database or retrieval system, without prior written permission of the publisher except in the case of brief quotations embodied in critical articles and reviews. Making copies of any part of this book for any purpose other than your own personal use is a violation of United States copyright laws. For information, address Que Corporation, 201 W. 103rd Street, Indianapolis, IN 46290.

Library of Congress Catalog No.: 94-66558

ISBN: 1-56529-685-0

This book is sold *as is*, without warranty of any kind, either express or implied, respecting the contents of this book, including but not limited to implied warranties for the book's quality, performance, merchantability, or fitness for any particular purpose. Neither Que Corporation nor its dealers or distributors shall be liable to the purchaser or any other person or entity with respect to any liability, loss, or damage caused or alleged to have been caused directly or indirectly by this book.

97   96   95   94   4   3   2   1

Interpretation of the printing code: the rightmost double-digit number is the year of the book's printing; the rightmost single-digit number, the number of the book's printing. For example, a printing code of 94-1 shows that the first printing of the book occurred in 1994.

Publisher: David P. Ewing

Associate Publisher: Michael Miller

Publishing Director: Joseph B. Wikert

Managing Editor: Michael Cunningham

Marketing Manager: Greg Wiegand

Composed in Utopia and MCPdigital by Que Corporation

Credits

Publishing Manager
Joseph B. Wikert

Acquisitions Editor
Angela J. Lee

Product Director
Bryan Gambrel

Production Editor
Thomas F. Hayes

Copy Editors
Danielle Bird
Geneil Breeze
Noelle Gasco
Lorna Gentry
Patrick Kanouse
Heather Kaufman
Jeanne Lemen
Susan Ross Moore
Andy Saff
Kathy Simpson

Technical Editor
Russ Jacobs

Acquisitions Coordinator
Patricia J. Brooks

Book Designer
Amy Peppler-Adams

Production Team
Stephen Adams
Jeff Baker
Angela Bannan
Claudia Bell
Cameron Booker
Ayrika Bryant
Dan Caparo
Stephen Carlin
Karen Dodson
Brook Farling
Joelynn Gifford
Dennis Clay Hager
Angela Judy
Debbie Kincaid
Jenny Kucera
Bob LaRoche
Elizabeth Lewis
Jamie Milazzo
Stephanie Mineart
Tim Montgomery
Aren Munk
Wendy Ott
G. Alan Palmore
Nanci Sears Perry
Linda Quigley
Ryan Rader
Beth Rago
Dennis Sheehan
Tonya R. Simpson
Sue VandeWalle
Mary Beth Wakefield
Elaine Webb
Dennis Wesner
Donna Winter
Lillian Yates

About the Authors

Chris Corry is an OS/2 and Windows developer working in the Center for Advanced Technologies at American Management Systems of Fairfax, Va. His predominate professional interests include object-oriented programming, user-interface design, and client/server technologies.

Mark Davidson has been developing with Borland products since Turbo Pascal for CP/M and has been using Borland C++ since it was Turbo C 1.0. He has been writing Windows applications since the days of Windows 2.0. Currently, he works for Sony Electronic Publishing, where he develops Windows as well as Macintosh applications.

John M. Dlugosz is currently senior software engineer at Tobias Associates, Inc. working on dedicated control equipment and embedded systems. He also is principal of Dlugosz Software, where he coauthored the C++ ViewPoint Graphics Library. He is a past member of the ANSI C++ committee, and was a reviewer of the C+ 2.0 specification from AT&T.

Michael R. Dunlavey was raised in Palatine, Illinois. He attended MIT, receiving a BS in Mechanical Engineering in 1966, and an MS in Mechanical and Civil Engineering in 1969. He received a Ph.D. in Computer Science from Georgia Institute of Technology in 1977. He has worked at Charles Stark Draper Laboratory, Bachman Information Systems, and is now head of Performance Software Associates, Inc. He taught Computer Science at Boston College from 1980-84. He lives with his wife, the former Mary Newman, and their four children in Needham, Massachusetts. He enjoys writing, sailing, snorkel diving, bicycling, and recreational programming. His professional interests lie in cross-fertilizing the industrial and academic worlds for the good of people.

Steve Potts received a degree in Computer Science from Georgia Tech. He has been designing and writing software systems for 12 years. He is a consultant in Windows-based technologies, and owns NoBoredom Classes, a computer education firm in Atlanta, Ga.

Greg Perry has been a programmer and trainer for the past 14 years. He received his first degree in computer science and then a masters in corporate finance. Greg Perry is the author of 30 other computer books. In addition, he has written articles for several publications, including *PC World*, *Data Training*, and *Inside First Publisher*. He has traveled in several countries, attending computer conferences and trade shows, and is fluent in nine computer languages.

Namir Clement Shammas is a full-time book author specializing in BASIC, Pascal, and C++ programming languages, as well as object-oriented programming. He is the author of more than 30 books on these topics.

Clayton Walnum has been writing about computers for a decade and has published more than 300 articles in major computer publications. He is the author of books, covering such diverse topics as programming, computer gaming, and application programs. His most recent book is *Creating Turbo C++ Games*, also published by Que. His earlier titles include *Borland C++ Object-Oriented Programming*, *Borland C++ Power Programming*, and *QBasic for Rookies* (Que); *PC Picasso: A Child's Computer Drawing Kit* and *The First Book of Microsoft Works for Windows* (Sams); *PowerMonger: The Official Strategy Guide* (Prima); and *C-manship Complete* (Taylor Ridge Books). Walnum is a full-time freelance writer and lives in Connecticut with his wife and their three children.

Trademark Acknowledgments

All terms mentioned in this book that are known to be trademarks or service marks have been appropriately capitalized. Que cannot attest to the accuracy of this information. Use of a term in this book should not be regarded as affecting the validity of any trademark or service mark. Trademarks indicated below were derived from various sources.

Borland is a registered trademark of Borland International.

Contents at a Glance

Contents

Contents   **xiii**

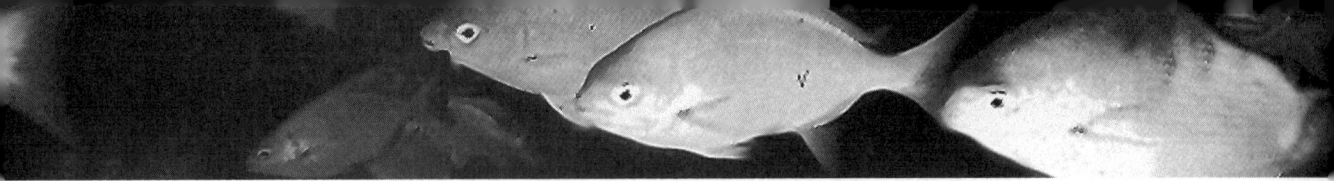

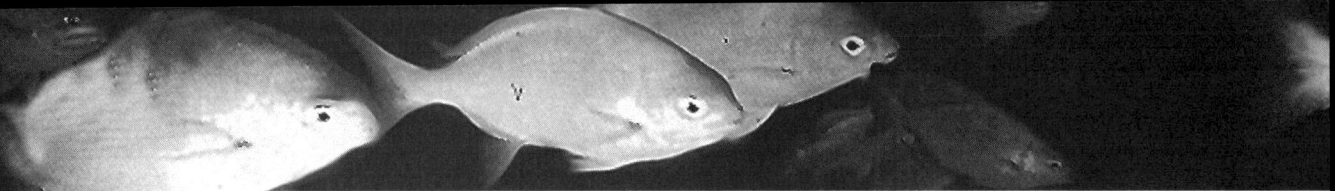

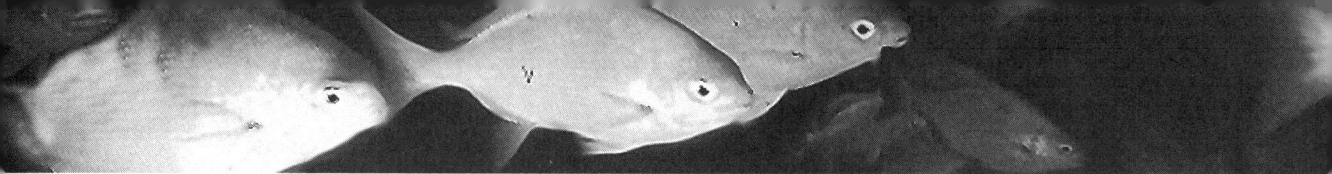

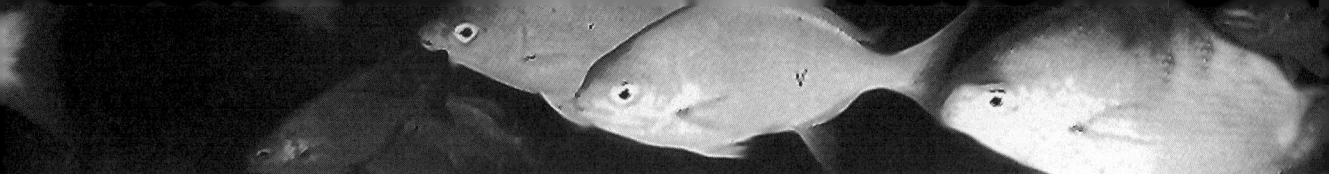

Introduction

Unlike most other books on Borland C++ which simply try to teach the fundamentals of the C/C++ languages, *Killer Borland C++ 4* focuses on the needs of the professional application developer. The topics covered in this book were selected because they have been given very light treatment in other Borland C++ books. In addition, we hand-picked a team of authors based on their expertise and insight into the Borland C++ professional programming market.

Who Should Read This Book?

This book is for developers who want to learn how to push the envelope with Borland C++ 4.x. This group includes developers who want to learn how to write mixed-language applications, write C++ routines to interface with database modules, optimize C/C++ code, etc.

Killer Borland C++ 4 also shows you how to write tighter, more efficient code with better use of pointers, recursion, and more. In addition, you learn how to enhance your code with some of the recent C++ language extensions including runtime type identification, templates, and exception handling.

What the Disk Contains

Also included with this book is a 3 1/2 inch disk containing the source code for every example program. This will save you hours of time that would normally be required to type and debug program listings. It also will help you learn the material quicker.

As a bonus, the book disk contains a number of VBX custom controls for use with the Resource Workshop. These special bonus custom controls enable you to add new features to your Windows dialog boxes that normally are not available through Windows. Several of the custom controls on the disk are special versions of commercial control packages that retail for hundreds of dollars.

The example programs are discussed throughout the book, and information about the custom controls is covered in chapters 21-25.

How This Book Is Organized

Each chapter of *Killer Borland C++ 4* covers a different advanced programming topic that may only receive partial attention in another C++ book. This approach enables you to read the material in any order, depending on your needs.

The first 20 chapters of the book deal with a wide variety of topics, ranging from writing portable code to third-party debugger alternatives to coding stylistics. The last five chapters of *Killer Borland C++ 4* explain how to utilize each of the commercial custom controls included on the companion disk.

How to Use This Book

How you approach this book depends on what sort of programming task you are trying to accomplish. If you are interested in code optimization, you should focus on chapters 2 through 5, which explain optimization techniques for pointers, recursion, and the C/C++ languages in general. If you need to write code that dovetails with other languages or database applications, you should review chapters 13-15, which discuss mixed-language programming and interfacing with database languages. Regardless of your specific interests and goals, you should find an assortment of valuable chapters in *Killer Borland C++ 4*.

Conventions Used in This Book

To get the most out of the book, you need to know something about how it is designed. The chapters contain italicized text, bulleted lists, numbered lists, figures, program listings, code fragments, and tables of information. All these design features should help you understand the material being presented.

Italic type is used to emphasize an important word or phrase. You should pay close attention to italicized text. It is also used to introduce new technical terms. An italicized term is followed immediately by a definition or an explanation.

Bulleted lists have the following characteristics:

➤ Each item in a bulleted list is preceded by a small black triangle (the bullet). The bullet is a special flag that draws your attention to important material.

➤ The order of items in a bulleted list is not mandatory. That is, the items represent related points you should understand, but not in a special sequence.

➤ The text for items in a bulleted list is often longer than the text you see in other kinds of lists. Items in bulleted lists contain explanations, not simple actions.

Numbered lists contain actions you should perform, or lists of items that must be kept in a particular sequence. When you see a numbered list, you should do the following:

1. Start at the beginning of the list. Don't skip ahead to later items in the list; order is important.

2. Make sure that you completely understand each item as you encounter it.

3. Read all the items in the list. Don't skip any of them—each item is important.

Figures are pictures or graphics that can help you understand the text. Each figure has a number in the form *c.n*: *c* is the chapter in which the figure appears, and *n* is the number of the figure in a sequence within the chapter. Figure 0.1, which is the first figure in the Introduction, shows how a figure will appear.

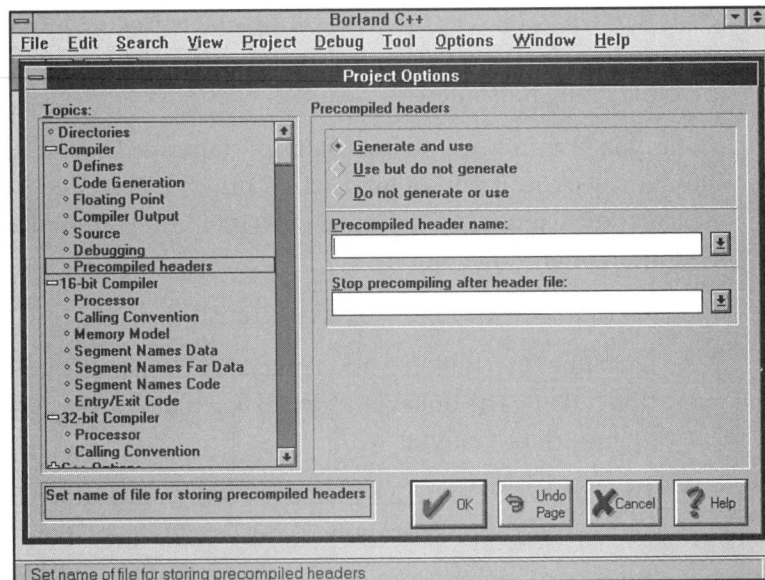

Fig. 0.1. A sample illustration.

The *syntax form* is a special kind of code fragment that shows you the general form used for writing a C statement or declaration. A syntax form looks like this:

```
void perror(const char *errMsg);
```

In a syntax form, the `italicized` characters are placeholders for names and labels of your own choosing, whereas the regular `monospace` items must be written exactly as you see them.

In code listings, lines that should be typed as one long line but are too long for the book page have been broken into two lines. Such cases are marked with the code-continuation icon, as in the following:

```
InitArray( lostTourists.coord, lostTourists.count,
         MAX_X, MAX_Y );
```

Tables appear where lists and columns of information are suitable. Tables also have their own headings and reference numbers—again, independent of the numbers for figures and program listings. Table 0.1 shows how a table is presented in this book.

Table 0.1. The Formatting Conventions Used in Killer Borland C++ 4

Format Convention	Use
Italic	An eye-catching type style used to emphasize important words or phrases.
Bulleted lists	A list of items with a bullet flagging each item; the sequence of items is not usually important.
Numbered lists	A list of items with numbers flagging each item; sequence is important.
Program listings	Complete programs that can be compiled.
Code fragments	A small number of C or C++ source code lines that illustrate a single point; code fragments cannot be compiled apart from other code.
Tables	Information arranged in columnar format; tables may or may not contain explanations or descriptions.

Writing Portable Code

by Chris Corry

C++, and its predecessor C, have a reputation for being *portable languages*. This means that, in theory, a C++ program built with one development system will recompile without error under another compiler, even if that compiler is running on a different type of computer or on a different operating system (OS).

Well, you can forget that fantasy. For a variety of reasons explored throughout this chapter, C++ programs rarely can be moved to other compilers (let alone other computers and operating systems) without a significant amount of work.

However, all hope is not lost. You can take proactive steps during the development of your C++ programs that help to minimize the difficulties inherent in moving code from one compiler to another. Using these techniques helps ensure that you write portable code.

When all is said and done, you may be a little disheartened to realize that if you faithfully follow all the advice in this chapter you are doomed to produce a program that is portable but probably not very interesting. The trickiest part of moving a C++ program between compilers and operating systems is determining where to make the compromises.

Who Really Cares about Portability?

Portability is not a requirement of writing bug-free, correct programs (although some argue that it should be). You can write a very effective and impressive application that doesn't have a prayer of being successfully moved to another compiler without a total rewrite.

Maybe this doesn't bother you. Not everyone develops programs that must run on three different hardware architectures and five separate operating systems. Be careful though, before adopting this philosophy wholesale. Even if you program in C++ simply as a hobby or write programs only for personal use, if you find one of your programs useful, there is a good chance that someone else will. The only problem is, in full accordance with Murphy's Law, more often than not that other person does not use the same sort of computer or operating system that you do. Before you know it, you are asked to migrate the program to the foreign computer.

If, on the other hand, you program in C++ as part of your job, you probably already know how important it is to ensure that your programs are portable. As users of computer software become increasingly sophisticated, more and more of them will expect your software to run in a variety of different computing environments. Achieving this goal is very difficult without designing portability into programs from the start.

If you write computer programs for a living, having your software available in many different environments is a competitive advantage. Some of the most successful applications on the market today offer seamless

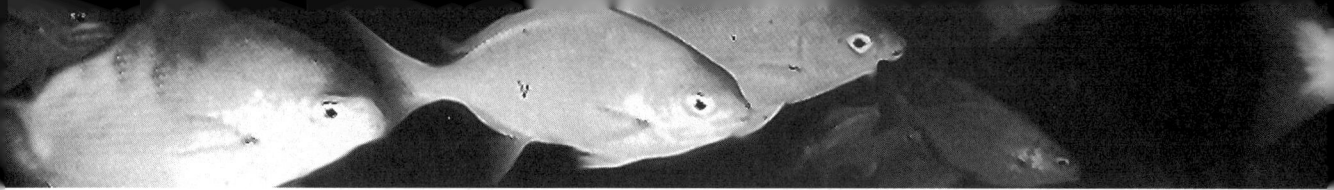

compatibility between different computers. An excellent example of this competitive advantage is the Photoshop image editing program from Adobe Systems. If a graphic designer working with Photoshop on the Macintosh needs to work at a location that has only the Microsoft Windows version of Photoshop, the designer can feel confident that the software can be used effectively, even if the user has very little experience working in the Windows environment. Photoshop is a program ported so competently that users familiar with one version can readily use and understand how to use the software on other platforms. Many large, corporate customers use Photoshop just because it can run on a variety of different hardware and software platforms.

So What Exactly Is a Port?

Before explicitly defining a port, it is advantageous to briefly lay down some terminology.

Throughout the chapter I often make references to the *codebase*. A codebase is a body of computer code that is part of your program. As you will see, however, it is not always possible (or even desirable) to port your entire codebase from one environment to another. Certain parts of your codebase may be identical from program port to program port, while other parts of your codebase may be specifically written or optimized for one computer or operating system. In this chapter, it's assumed that the codebase ported is written in C++, and that the Borland C++ 4.0 compiler is the specific variant of C++ used for code designed to run under DOS, Windows, or Windows NT.

The word *platform* is mentioned often. A platform refers to the totality of an operating environment in which a program executes. The computer chip architecture, operating system, development environment, and networking software are all unique aspects that help to define a system platform. An Apple Macintosh running programs written in Symantec ThinkC under the System 7.1 operating system is one platform, an Intel 80486-based computer running Borland-compiled programs under Windows for Workgroups 3.11 is another, and a

Hewlett-Packard PA-RISC workstation running UNIX-based X-Windows applications built with the HP SoftBench C++ compiler is yet a third. Obviously, the domain of possible platforms that a program supports can be very large indeed. Very few programs are capable of running on even a handful of different platforms. Because the platform has the most profound impact on the porting process, I revisit its various components in the section "Components of the Platform," later in this chapter.

Understanding the terminology, we can now define the process of *porting* as moving a codebase from one platform to another. As alluded to earlier, in many cases not every part of the codebase needs to be moved from platform to platform. Some programs, particularly those that rely on simple, character-based user interfaces can be comprehensively ported.

Porting versus Concurrent Development

You can approach the porting of an application from at least two different directions. While a port is typically associated with moving a completed codebase from one platform to another, the concept of *concurrent development* is a variation on the same theme. During concurrent development, code is completed in small chunks (sometimes as small as a single source file) and ported to the target platform. Porting occurs throughout development rather than all at once, when the entire application is completed.

It should be immediately apparent that concurrent development is really just porting applied on a scale with finer granularity. It is generally easier, if only psychologically, to port a small piece of code as opposed to a large piece of code. The main advantage of performing a port in lots of small pieces, rather than after all the code has been completed, is that most of your mistakes (that is to say, pieces of code written in a nonportable manner) are caught early in the development

process. Once you catch these mistakes, you probably will not make them again. On the other hand, if the code is already finished, one mistake in technique can be propagated over the entire codebase, and must be corrected in every place that it appears.

That said, concurrent development doesn't happen very often. While it is the most effective way to write portable applications, it can also be considerably more expensive in the short run. Concurrent development generally requires two different development teams working in tandem, or a single development team with extraordinary abilities and experience. With concurrent development, the initial release of a product is generally delayed because of the parallel development cycle. This is often unacceptable for organizations that absolutely need to get a version (*any* version) of their application delivered on schedule. It is far more commonplace to see a product initially developed on the most financially lucrative and convenient platforms (for example, Windows, DOS) before being ported to other platforms with smaller installed bases (for example, OS/2, Windows NT, UNIX). In the real world, most organizations build a single codebase that is as portable as possible, and port this code to other targeted platforms, one at a time. Only the largest companies can afford to commit the sort of financial resources and manpower necessary to support concurrent development.

Of course, if you are a programmer writing code just for yourself, you have no compelling reason or need to think about porting versus concurrent development. Instead, most programmers are interested in ensuring that their code is as portable as they can make it during the development of the initial version, so that if they decide at some later date to move their programs to another platform, the process is as painless as possible.

Regardless of whether you decide to write code concurrently on more than one platform or port your codebase only after it is complete, I refer to the process of writing code for multiple platforms as a *port*. Remember that even if you write code simultaneously on different platforms, you still port. The only difference is that you perform the

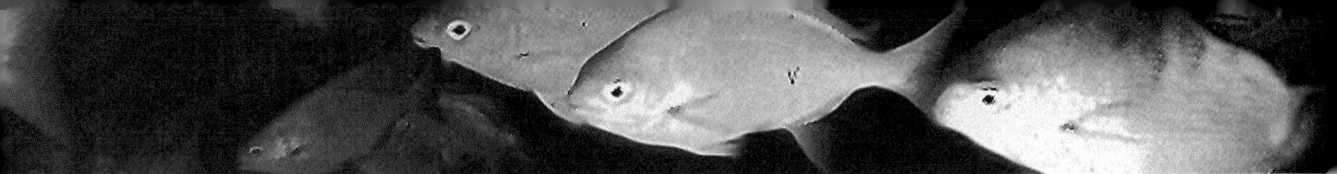

port in much smaller pieces. You do, however, still run into almost all the same problems that you encounter if you wait until your first version is finished before starting the port.

Components of the Platform

The main problem with writing portable C++ code is intimately related to the details of the platform to which you need to port. The platform defines the complexity, maturity, width, and breadth of system services available to a program. If a service is offered on one platform but not on others, the program becomes responsible for simulating or implementing a comparable service. It is precisely because of the lack of parity between different platforms that porting code can become a programmer's biggest headache.

The Hardware

From the standpoint of the C++ compiler writer, the hardware architecture is the most important aspect of the platform. Surprisingly, the hardware can also have equally profound implications for the C++ programmers that use the compiler. This is because the computer hardware often dictates a wide range of different compiler limitations and features, like the size of integral types and the way that aggregate types get packed into memory.

No matter how efficient and sophisticated a C++ compiler is, it cannot *and should not* completely shield the programmer from some of the most profound intricacies of the underlying hardware. Some CPUs, for example, cry out for the use of 32-bit unsigned long integers, while others support only 16-bit longs. If your program stores a variety of Boolean flags in the bits of a long integer, on some platforms you will have 16 possible flags, and on others you may have 32 or even 64. One thing is sure: if you assume that an unsigned long integer is 16 bits long, your program will simply not be portable.

Memory models, byte ordering schemes, CPU dependent optimizations, and much more conspire to make the porting of your code more difficult than it should be.

The Operating System

The operating system is the layer of software responsible for managing the execution of programs and for controlling the interactions of programs with the underlying hardware. It is a crucial part of the porting equation because the operating system is the primary provider of *system services*.

System services are features of an operating system that provide a benefit to executing programs, or users of executing programs. This is a broad definition, and rightly so. System services typically run the gamut from supplying display capabilities to managing network connections to providing a full range of input/output operations on connected hardware devices. In fact, virtually every operation of note performed by your program relies on a system service.

Almost all operating systems provide a common set of core functions. For example, DOS, Windows NT, OS/2, the Macintosh System 7, and UNIX all enable programs to read, write, and append information into files stored on a disk drive. Although this feature is not earth-shattering, a general purpose operating system that cannot do at least these simple operations is not likely to gain much of a market following. All these operating systems also provide the capability for programs to write character data to a display screen, and to send binary data to a connected hardware device (e.g., serial port, parallel port, SCSI device). If your program does not rely on services any more sophisticated than these, the process of porting your code will proceed quite smoothly.

Big problems start to crop up when your programs need system services offered by the operating system under which the program was initially developed, but that are not available under the operating system to which you want to port.

Take as an example the process of starting a separate strand of execution within one of your programs. This action is called *starting a thread*, where a thread is an element of simultaneous execution within the same program. To see the value of this feature, imagine a multithreaded program in which one thread updates the screen display while another thread concurrently spools output to a printer. DOS enables you to run other programs in a synchronous manner, but doesn't support threads. Windows isn't much better; you can spawn off programs in a synchronous or asynchronous manner, but, like DOS, Windows doesn't support multithreading as an operating system service. The same thing can be said about the Macintosh System 7. Even UNIX, a fully preemptive multitasking operating system, doesn't typically support multithreading (with notable exceptions, such as NextStep). Right now, the only mainstream operating systems to natively support multithreading are OS/2 and Windows NT (although Microsoft has publically asserted that future versions of Windows will have multithreading capabilities).

A program initially written under Windows NT will probably have to deal with the implications of porting multithreaded code to a platform running a nonthreading operating system. How does an application simulate, emulate, or even implement threads under DOS or Windows? This extremely difficult endeavor is not one that you are likely to have much success with (if it were easy to do, a developer would certainly be able to purchase this capability as some sort of third-party software product).

As a final aside, notice that the rest of this chapter refers to the Microsoft Windows 3.X environment as if it were an operating system. Many users (and even some programmers) are not aware that Windows is a graphical environment that runs on top of DOS. When discussing the topic of writing portable C++ code, however, one should treat Windows as an operating system for two reasons. First, Windows actually relies on DOS for only a small number of system services. Most of the time Windows interacts directly with the computer hardware and bypasses DOS completely. Second, future versions of Windows

will merge Windows and DOS into a single operating system product. When this happens, Windows will no longer be a program environment running on top of DOS. Instead, it will be a fully functional 32-bit operating system that supports the execution of programs originally built for DOS.

> **Note:** A final class of operating system bears at least a casual mention. Some operating systems, usually referred to as *embedded systems*, are designed for extremely specialized purposes. For example, some embedded systems were built for the sole purpose of controlling household appliances. Because there is a rather limited demand for microwave ovens that can interact with disk drives and modems (at least for now), you typically find the system services offered by these types of operating systems to be more limited than their general purpose counterparts. Embedded systems, however, are not necessarily less sophisticated than the operating systems you might find loaded on your PC. Indeed, many embedded systems must deal with a host of extremely challenging problems such as realtime processing, limited resources, and severely restricted memory spaces. Because few embedded system programs are written in C++, this chapter does not discuss them in more depth.

The Environment

In the context used here, *the environment* is a catch-all phrase that refers to all factors not addressed by the operating system and compiler. Note that while the operating system is the primary provider of system services, it is not necessarily the *only* provider of system services.

On some platforms it is very common to find programs and drivers that complement the operating system and augment the OS's native capabilities. Under DOS, these programs are typically referred to as

terminate-and-stay-resident programs (TSRs). The Mac has INITs and control panels, and Windows has virtual device drivers (VxDs). The Novell DOS client shell is just such an example. The Novell drivers and TSRs hook themselves into DOS and provide a variety of mechanisms (both programmatic and utility-driven) that enable PCs to access Netware-based local area networks (LANs).

Some products also offer system services, without hooking themselves into the operating system proper. For example, Sybase's OpenClient interface does virtually nothing by itself. Instead, it provides a generic programming interface that programs can use to access a Sybase SQL database, without concern for the communications protocols used or the location and platform on which the database runs. Programs written to the OpenClient interfaces only need to concern themselves with details that are pertinent to using the database, as opposed to accessing it. For the most part, communications configurations (TCP/IP versus Named-Pipes, for example) become administrative burdens instead of issues that need to be addressed by programmers.

> **Note:** Sometimes these products take an existing operating system service and make it more approachable through a convenient programming abstraction or development environment. These types of programs are often referred to as *middleware*.

It is by no means uncommon for C++ programs to use third-party products to enhance their functionality. In many, if not most, cases, using these products is the only realistic way that your programs can accomplish what they need to. C++ Windows programmers are not likely to sit down and build TCP/IP networking protocol support into their programs from scratch. Because the de facto standard in Windows TCP/IP communication revolves around the Winsock specification, most developers go to one of a half dozen vendors and purchase a Winsock dynamic-link library (DLL) that painlessly adds the functionality.

It's not fair or realistic to discourage this practice for the sake of portability. Most of these value-adding products are so useful and save the programmer so much time that it would be foolhardy not to take advantage of them. At the same time, it is important that software developers make informed decisions before marrying their programs to third-party products, especially if they are concerned with portability. As with a major operating system service, if the third-party product is not available for the platform that you are porting to, you can have a potentially major porting problem.

The Development Tools

In some circumstances, even the most simple C++ programs written with one compiler do not compile under another compiler, even if the other compiler operates on the same platform. There are a couple of reasons for this, but of greater importance is realizing that C++ is not yet a completely standardized and portable language. This leads to slightly differing interpretations of the language on issues that seem esoteric and obscure until you end up getting stung during a porting effort. A feature implemented by one compiler vendor may be implemented just differently enough on another compiler to break your code, or worse, to allow your code to compile without error, but execute differently.

Some development environments, including Borland C++ 4.0, add a variety of features that help speed up the development and debugging process. Conveniences such as project files, the class browser, precompiled headers, AppExpert, and ClassExpert all help speed up the development cycle. These features are also completely proprietary. Borland project files (.IDE) and precompiled header files (.CSW) do not work with development environments on other platforms. This is not so much a portability concern as it is an annoyance. Porting your application to other platforms certainly makes you appreciate the benefits of the Borland environment.

The ANSI Standardization Effort

C++ is not yet a standardized language. As of this writing, the ANSI/ISO X3J16 committee was hard at work trying to meet a draft standard deadline of September 1994. This committee's work has very real implications for any C++ programmer, since the ANSI standard will be the "official" specification used by compiler vendors when building their development environments.

To date, the unofficial standard used by almost everyone as the definitive word on the language is *The Annotated C++ Reference Manual* (or ARM) by Margaret A. Ellis and Bjarne Stroustrup (Addison-Wesley, 1990). This book was used by the ANSI committee as the starting point for the C++ standardization effort.

The ARM, however, shows its age, especially when considered alongside the bulk of additions and revisions already incorporated by X3J16.

The ARM is also not without its flaws. Many topics and discussions within the book are too vague, clearly ambiguous, or can lead to serious portability concerns. These flaws are not so much the fault of the authors, as they are artifacts of the considerable effort required to write a completely unambiguous language specification. The X3J16 committee has brooded over these issues for a couple of years and they are now readying their first public draft. Clearly, standardizing a language as sophisticated and potentially complex as C++ is a very difficult task!

The good news is that once the language standard has been frozen, the vast majority of new "clean" C++ will be readily portable from compiler to compiler. *Clean C++* means code that does not take advantage of keywords, capabilities, and features that are unique to a particular compiler or class of compilers (and, in doing so, ensure that they are not completely ANSI C++ compliant). The bad news is that the final standard cannot be expected for quite some time: late 1995 or early 1996 at the earliest. Although most compiler vendors are doing their best to make sure that their compilers conform to the current working draft of the standard proposal, there are likely to be pockets of incompatibility until the final standard document is ratified.

Using C++ Extensions

If you read the ARM from cover to cover you will note a number of language extensions referred to as "experimental." Virtually all these experimental extensions have been incorporated into the ANSI draft standard, although with varying degrees of adherence to the original ARM specifications. In addition, many new language characteristics have been added to the proposed ANSI version of C++ that have never been addressed by the ARM.

Examining Table 1.1 will help give you a good idea of the major extensions you can expect to find in the final ANSI/ISO C++ standard. The table also indicates whether the extension is supported by the Borland C++ 4.0 compiler.

Table 1.1. C++ Language Extensions Expected to Appear in the Final ANSI/ISO Standard

Extension	Supported by BC++ 4.0
Standard classes (for example, `string`, `xalloc`)	Yes
`Operator new[]()` and `operator delete[]()`	Yes
Specialty casts (for example, `const_cast`, `dynamic_cast`, `reinterpret_cast`, `static_cast`)	Yes
Templates	Yes
Exceptions	Yes
Runtime type information	Yes
Namespaces	No

As you can see, the Borland compiler provides excellent coverage of proposed C++ extensions. The only extension not supported by Borland is namespaces, and there are no major compiler vendors currently offering this feature on the same platforms that Borland supports.

Once again, you have a good news/bad news situation. The good news is that since the Borland coverage is so complete, you have a whole arsenal of advanced compiler features to use to make your programs smaller, faster, and more reliable. Your programs can be the first on the block to be fully RTTI, exception, and template enabled. The bad news is that, because your programs will be the first on the block to use these features, few compilers will be able to compile your code. Those features which make your program better will also conspire to make your programs less portable.

Actually, things aren't really that bad. Some of these extensions are more prevalent than others.

Template support, for example, is an almost common extension found in most contemporary C++ compilers. There are, however, notable exceptions. Microsoft Visual C++ does not have true template support, and the template support that it does have is nonstandard and rather inadequate. You can expect Microsoft to rectify this problem (and to offer full exception support) with the next release of the product.

Exception support is considerably more rare, although it is starting to make appearances in a number of new compiler releases. Many UNIX-based C++ compilers support exceptions, as does IBM's OS/2 compiler. The latest version of Borland's C++ compiler for OS/2 also supports exceptions (along with RTTI and the standard classes). Still, exception support is varied among compiler vendors and, from a portability standpoint, an element of risk is associated with using this feature.

Few compilers currently support runtime type information, the standard classes, new cast types, array new and delete operators, and namespaces. Again, you are probably more likely to see these

extensions in scattered UNIX compilers first, with Windows NT, Mac, and OS/2 compilers releasing support as soon as possible (for most vendors that means probably in the next version release).

When you get down to it, the question of using C++ extensions now is a problematic one. Many C++ gurus have made a point of discouraging extension use until the feature becomes more prevalent and mature. This is good advice, but it's hard medicine to swallow, especially after you've just ripped the shrink-wrap off your brand new Borland compiler.

This is one of those classic porting compromises. If portability is of limited importance to you right now, follow the rest of the advice in this chapter but don't hold back from using the extension support provided by the Borland product. If it looks like you will port code in the near future, however, you should probably steer away from most of these extensions for at least a little while.

An exception to this rule of thumb is templates. Template support is now becoming common enough that any platform you port to is bound to offer template-enabled compilers. Incompatibilies between different vendors' interpretations of the ARM or ANSI committee template specifications exist, so always look before you leap. If you decide to use templates, make sure that you code up a typical example of how your code will use the feature and try it on both compilers before beginning.

A Comment on International Language Support

The English language contains 62 alphanumeric characters and numbers (of mixed case). Add in the most commonly used special characters and punctuation marks and you're talking about a hundred or so characters needed to convey the vast majority of information that your program is likely to use. Because the minimal character type on almost every C++ platform is at least 8 bits (supporting 127 possible characters), there should be no portability issues associated with porting programs that communicate with their users in English. But what do you do if your users don't speak English?

The issue of extended character sets typically runs right up against the goals and aims of program portability. There are adequate (although seldom convenient) solutions to both problems, but combine the two and you have a first-class programming dilemma. It seems unfair and unrealistic that you should have to choose between making your code portable programmatically and making your code portable linguistically. Unfortunately, there currently is no efficient and portable way to write language-neutral code.

Some operating systems support nonportable mechanisms (for example, code pages, character maps) to achieve international language support. Theoretically, however, more portable ways to internationalize your programs exist. A full-blown discussion of these methods is out of the scope of this chapter, but the clearly emerging standard for foreign language support is Unicode. Unicode is a double-byte character set (referred to as DBCS by the acronym obsessed), which means that each character is represented using two bytes rather than one. Doing a little bit of Computer Science 101 math reveals that Unicode can represent more than 65,000 different characters. Now that ought to do it! (Of course, 16K of RAM once sounded like a lot of memory.) Many people are excited about Unicode; programmers who need to write foreign language-enabled code will hear a lot more about Unicode in the years to come.

Although it looks like Unicode will make portable, linguistically neutral programs easier to write, very few platforms currently support the Unicode standard. Windows NT (and its Win32 programming interface) is the only commercially viable operating system that understands Unicode. Sadly, it appears that it will be quite some time before Unicode supplants ASCII as the character set of choice. For these reasons, Unicode should be regarded as a portability breaker and should be avoided (for now). Unfortunately, because there are no other

alternatives, you will have to resign yourself to accepting the fact that those parts of your codebase that need to support multiple languages will need to be implemented using a nonportable (probably operating system dependent) mechanism. Do whatever you can to localize foreign language support in just a few objects, so that when you port to other platforms only those objects will have to be rewritten.

> **Note:** If you want to read more about Unicode, the specification is documented by The Unicode Consortium in *The Unicode Standard: Worldwide Character Encoding, Version 1.0* (Addison-Wesley, 1991).

Getting into the Code

So far we've talked a lot about some of the broader issues surrounding a porting effort, but now it's time to get into the specifics of how to make your C++ code more portable. It's difficult to be comprehensive about a topic as complex as portability (entire books about writing portable code exist), but this chapter includes a few suggestions about "gotcha"s that have stung me more than once. Using these guidelines should serve as a good starting point for writing portable code.

This section dwells on the generic, microscopic language issues of writing portable code. It discusses features of your programs that are not intimately related to an operating system or the environment, but are closely coupled to the chip architecture and the specifics of the development environment used. Later sections discuss how to encapsulate system services provided by the operating system and the rest of the platform environment, and how to approach the problem of graphical user interface design in a portable manner.

Don't Use Integral Types

Huh? How can you write a useful program that doesn't use any of C++'s built-in types? Well, you can't really, but you can make sure that your program only uses aliases to integral types. Using aliases provides you with the flexibility to change the meaning of integral types and other compiler-dependent definitions on a codebase-wide basis if you run into any severe porting problems. Using aliases wholesale, however, requires some advance planning.

The key is to create a port.h header file that is included by all source code modules. The job of port.h is to isolate all compiler dependencies using a network of preprocessor `#ifdefs`. Because many compilers contain keywords that are inherently nonportable, these keywords should be aliased in port.h. Listing 1.1 shows a simple port.h header file. Depending on the number of platforms that you want to support, your version of port.h can be considerably more complex.

Listing 1.1. PORT.H—A Simple port.h Header File

```
// Don't allow this header to be included more than once
#ifndef PORT_H
#define PORT_H

// The port flags define macros which will determine
// which areas of this file are activated. Port flags
// can be set inside of portflgs.h, by a makefile, or
// be passed in on a compiler command line. Macros
// specific to the porting include files that are prefixed
// with PORT_ (P_ is sometimes used as an abbreviated
// form).
#ifndef PORTFLGS_H
    #include <portflgs.h>
#endif

// Aliases for ANSI standard integral types only
typedef char            P_CHAR;
typedef char *          P_PCHAR;
typedef char            P_BYTE;
typedef char *          P_PBYTE;
typedef unsigned char   P_UCHAR;
typedef unsigned char * P_PUCHAR;
typedef int             P_INT;
typedef int *           P_PINT;
typedef unsigned int    P_UINT;
typedef unsigned int *  P_PUINT;
```

```
typedef short int              P_SHORT;
typedef short int *            P_PSHORT;
typedef unsigned short int     P_USHORT;
typedef unsigned short int *   P_PUSHORT;
typedef long int               P_LONG;
typedef long int *             P_PLONG;
typedef unsigned long int      P_ULONG;
typedef unsigned long int *    P_PULONG;
typedef float                  P_FLOAT;
typedef float *                P_PFLOAT;
typedef double                 P_DOUBLE;
typedef double *               P_PDOUBLE;
typedef long double            P_LDOUBLE;
typedef long double *          P_PLDOUBLE;
typedef void                   P_VOID;
typedef void *                 P_PVOID;

// Definitions common to all platforms placed here
// WARNING!! Be very careful about any other items
//           placed at this level of scope (I don't put
//           _anything_ else out here).

// What operating system are we using here?
#if defined(PORT_OS_WIN16)

    // ********************************************** //
    // **              16-BIT WINDOWS            ** //
    // ********************************************** //

    // Types which may vary by platform, compiler, or
    // your preference
    typedef unsigned char      P_BOOLEAN;
    typedef unsigned char *    P_PBOOLEAN;

    // Other common compiler definitions could appear here

    // What compiler are we using here?
    #if defined(PORT_COMP_BORLAND_CPP)

        // Compiler-specific items
        #define P_FAR           _far
        #define P_NEAR          _near
        #define P_HUGE          _huge
        #define P_CDECL         _cdecl
        #define P_PASCAL        _pascal
        #define P_FASTCALL      _fastcall
        #define P_OS_API_CALL   _far _pascal

        // These non-Win16 specific items are not defined.
        // This is so that any code which uses these
        // definitions will not compile, helping you
        // to catch non-portable code.
        // #define P_STDCALL
```

continues

Listing 1.1. Continued

```
                // #define P_SYSCALL
                // #define P_THREAD

                // Does this target use and support dynamic
                // linking?
                // WARNING! Portable only between Win16,
                //          Win32s, Win32, and OS/2
                #if defined(PORT_DYNAMIC_LINK)
                    #define P_EXPORT        _export
                    #define P_FUNC          _export
                #else
                    #define P_EXPORT
                    #define P_FUNC
                #endif

                // Basic aggregate keywords
                #define P_CLASS         class P_EXPORT
                #define P_STRUCT        struct P_EXPORT
                #define P_UNION         union P_EXPORT

        #elif defined(PORT_COMP_MICROSOFT_CPP)
                // Visual C++-specific items here

        #elif defined(PORT_COMP_SYMANTEC_CPP)
                // And so on and so on...

        #endif

#elif defined(PORT_OS_WINNT) || \
        defined(PORT_OS_CHICAGO)

        // ************************************************ //
        // **     32-BIT WINDOWS (Win32 and Win32s)     ** //
        // ************************************************ //

        // Types which may vary by platform, compiler, or
        // your preference
        typedef unsigned char       P_BOOLEAN;
        typedef unsigned char *     P_PBOOLEAN;

        // Other common compiler definitions could appear here

        // What compiler are we using here?
        #if defined(PORT_COMP_BORLAND_CPP)

            // Compiler-specific items
            #define P_FAR
            #define P_NEAR
            #define P_HUGE
            #define P_CDECL             _cdecl
            #define P_PASCAL            _pascal
```

```
#define P_FASTCALL         _fastcall
#define P_OS_API_CALL       _stdcall

// Use these at the risk of losing portability!
#define P_STDCALL           _stdcall
#define P_SYSCALL           _stdcall
#define P_THREAD            _thread

// Does this target use and support dynamic
// linking?
// WARNING! Portable only between Win16,
//          Win32s, Win32, and OS/2
#if defined(PORT_DYNAMIC_LINK)
    #define P_EXPORT         _export
    #define P_FUNC           _export
#else
    #define P_EXPORT
    #define P_FUNC
#endif

// Basic aggregate keywords
#define P_CLASS         class P_EXPORT
#define P_STRUCT        struct P_EXPORT
#define P_UNION         union P_EXPORT

#elif defined(PORT_COMP_MICROSOFT_CPP)
    // And so on and so on...

#endif

#elif defined(PORT_OS_OS2)

// *********************************************** //
// **        32-BIT OS/2 (Versions 2.X)       ** //
// *********************************************** //

// Types which may vary by platform, compiler, or
// your preference
typedef unsigned char       P_BOOLEAN;
typedef unsigned char *     P_PBOOLEAN;

// Other common compiler definitions could appear here

// What compiler are we using here?
#if defined(PORT_COMP_BORLAND_CPP)

    // Compiler specific items
    #define P_FAR
    #define P_NEAR
    #define P_HUGE
    #define P_CDECL          _cdecl
    #define P_PASCAL         _pascal
```

continues

Listing 1.1. Continued

```
#define P_FASTCALL          _fastcall
#define P_OS_API_CALL       _stdcall

// Use these at the risk of losing portability!
#define P_STDCALL           _stdcall
#define P_SYSCALL           _syscall

// Not supported under OS/2. Non-portable...
// #define P_THREAD

// Does this target use and support dynamic
// linking?
// WARNING! Portable only between Win16,
//          Win32s, Win32, and OS/2
#if defined(PORT_DYNAMIC_LINK)
    #define P_EXPORT        _export
    #define P_FUNC          _export
#else
    #define P_EXPORT
    #define P_FUNC
#endif

// Basic aggregate keywords
#define P_CLASS             class P_EXPORT
#define P_STRUCT            struct P_EXPORT
#define P_UNION             union P_EXPORT

#elif defined(PORT_COMP_IBM_CSET)
    // And so on and so on...

#endif

#elif defined(PORT_OS_UNIX_SYSTEM_V) || \
      defined(PORT_OS_UNIX_AIX)

// Types which may vary by platform, compiler, or
// your preference
typedef unsigned char       P_BOOLEAN;
typedef unsigned char *     P_PBOOLEAN;

// Items not used under UNIX
#define P_FAR
#define P_NEAR
#define P_HUGE
#define P_CDECL
#define P_PASCAL
#define P_FASTCALL
#define P_OS_API_CALL
#define P_STDCALL
#define P_SYSCALL
#define P_THREAD
#define P_EXPORT
#define P_FUNC
```

```
        #define P_CLASS        class
        #define P_STRUCT       struct
        #define P_UNION        union

        // Other common UNIX definitions could appear here

        // Specific UNIX implementations
        #if defined(PORT_OS_UNIX_SYSTEM_V)

            // ****************************************** //
            // **            UNIX SYSTEM V           ** //
            // ****************************************** //

        #elif defined(PORT_OS_UNIX_AIX)

            // ****************************************** //
            // **               IBM AIX              ** //
            // ****************************************** //

        #endif

    #endif

    #endif
```

This version of port.h is by no means all inclusive, and you can certainly add many useful and important items to improve it. The important thing is that you understand the structure of these porting include
files and that you use the PORT_ and P_ types and macros defined here.

The key to conditionally activating various parts of port.h is portflgs.h.
This file defines a variety of PORT_ macros that port.h uses to determine
various features of the platform on which the code is compiled. If you
have setup port.h correctly, the only porting file that will have to
change when moving to another platform is portflgs.h. If your compilers provide the appropriate predefined macros, you can even make
portflgs.h portable! Various parts of the portflgs.h header file shown in
Listing 1.2 do just that for the various Borland compilers. Finally, note
that you can set individual PORT_ macros from inside a makefile or
even from your compiler's command line.

Listing 1.2. PORTFLGS.H—The portflgs.h Header File

```
// Don't allow this header to be included more than once
#ifndef PORTFLGS_H
#define PORTFLGS_H

// PORT_OS_... values used to determine the operating
//            system being compiled for
//
// This block of statements is NOT all inclusive. It
// will merely pick up selected predefined macros that
// some compilers may define.
#if defined(__WIN32__)
    #define PORT_OS_WINNT
#elif defined(_Windows)
    #define PORT_OS_WIN16
#elif defined(__OS2__)
    #define PORT_OS_OS2
#endif
//
// Uncomment the appropriate value if the above block
// doesn't work for your compiler
// #define PORT_OS_WIN16
// #define PORT_OS_CHICAGO
// #define PORT_OS_WINNT
// #define PORT_OS_OS2
// #define PORT_OS_UNIX_SYSTEM_V
// #define PORT_OS_UNIX_AIX


// PORT_COMP_... values used to determine the operating
//              compiler being used.
//
// This block of statements is NOT all inclusive. It
// will merely pick up selected predefined macros that
// some compilers may define.
#if defined(__BCPLUSPLUS__)
    #define PORT_COMP_BORLAND_CPP
#elif defined(__IBMC__)
    #define PORT_COMP_IBM_CSET
#endif
//
// Uncomment the appropriate value if the above block
// doesn't work for your compiler
// #define PORT_COMP_BORLAND_CPP
// #define PORT_COMP_MICROSOFT_CPP
// #define PORT_COMP_SYMANTEC_CPP
// #define PORT_COMP_IBM_CSET

// PORT_DYNAMIC_LINK value used if the module being
//                   compiled is to be placed in a
//                   dynamic link library (DLL).
//
// WARNING! DLLs are available only to Win16, Win32,
//          Win32s, and OS/2 applications. Code relying
//          on DLL support will not be readily portable
```

```
//              to platforms which do not support the operating
//              systems listed.
//
// This block of statements is NOT all inclusive. It
// will merely pick up selected predefined macros that
// some compilers may define.
#ifdef __DLL__
    #define PORT_DYNAMIC_LINK
#endif
//
// Uncomment this value if the above block doesn't
// work for your compiler and you are using DLLs
// #define PORT_DYNAMIC_LINK

#endif
```

Remember that these header files are a starting point for your own versions of port.h and portflgs.h. It is possible to make these files very intelligent and sophisticated (not to mention complicated), if you want to invest the proper amount of time and effort. The more time spent in hiding compiler dependencies in these two files, the less time you spend changing your codebase when it is time to start a port. To see an example of how you might use these header files, study the following class definition.

```
#include <port.h>

P_CLASS ATestClass : public Base {
public:
    ATestClass(P_PCHAR P_FAR pszString);
};
```

This class definition is portable between a variety of different platforms, and will even export access to the class if it is placed into a DLL.

With these header files, you can write code in a fashion that ignores most differences between compilers. They do not, however, save you from having to write a full implementation. Under Windows, for example, you still have to worry about the segmented architecture of the Intel processors and use your compiler's non-ANSI keywords where appropriate (P_FAR, P_NEAR, P_HUGE, etc.). When moving to a platform that ignores or does not support these keywords, the code should compile without error.

To be truly useful to you, these header files will almost certainly have to be modified to fit the peculiarities of your environment and codebase. This in itself is not a portability concern; once these files have been tailored to your codebase, they should help to ease many aspects of the porting process.

> **Note:** Remember, these header files will do nothing for you unless you use their values exclusively over built-in integral types.

Don't Make Assumptions about Integral Type Sizes

Quick, how many bits are in a `char`? How many bytes are in an `int`? How many bytes are in an `unsigned long`?

The Windows programmer smiles wryly at these simple questions and confidently replies "8, 2, and 4. Don't waste my time!" The Windows NT programmer sneers condescendingly, "8, 4, and 4." The OS/2 programmer nods in agreement with the NT guru. A hotshot programmer helping to develop a new souped-up operating system for super-computers cries out, "8, 8, and 32... really!" For some reason these programmers are giving us different answers. So who's right?

Of course, they all are. The size and range of integral types in C++ can vary widely depending on the platform on which the code is written.

This fact has some pretty profound implications for any code you write that relies on the size of integral types. Listing 1.3, taken from a real codebase that had to be ported, is supposed to count the number of high (i.e., "1") bits in an unsigned long integer.

Listing 1.3. Counting the High Bits in an Unsigned Long Integer

```
// Return the number of high bits in an unsigned long
int NumHighBits(unsigned long ulLong)
{
    int iLoop = 0, iNumHighBits = 0;
    for (; iLoop < 32; iLoop++, ulLong >>= 1)
        iNumHighBits += (ulLong & 0x00000001);
    return iNumHighBits;
}
```

This code is an example of code that *might* be correct (depending on the platform on which it is compiled) but is nonportable because of assumptions made about the sizes of types. In this case, we can see that the programmer, knowing that unsigned long integers for his compiler are four bytes long, loops through the number and checks all 32 bits. For most compilers today this is a correct assumption, *but it is an unnecessary one.* The programmer also used the goofy numerical constant of 0x00000001 to check the low order bit, and there is definitely a better way to do that. Now, look at the corrected version in Listing 1.4.

Listing 1.4. A More Portable NumHighBits

```
#include <limits.h>
#include <port.h>

// Return the number of high bits in an unsigned long
P_INT NumHighBits(P_ULONG ulLong)
{
    P_INT iBitsInULong = sizeof(P_ULONG) * CHAR_BIT;
    P_INT iLoop = 0, iNumHighBits = 0;
    for (; iLoop < iBitsInULong; iLoop++, ulLong >>= 1)
        iNumHighBits += (ulLong & 1UL);
    return iNumHighBits;
}
```

This method is better. The number of bits in the `long` is now calculated and the weird constant has been replaced by something more succinct and readily understood.

The number of bits is calculated using the CHAR_BIT macro defined in the standard library header file limits.h. If you are not familiar with this header file, print out the versions that come with each of your compilers and walk through the listings. The ANSI C standard (of which the C++ standard will be a functional superset) dictates that numerical limits for a compiler implementation appear in the header files limits.h and float.h.

> **Tip:** Use these constants rather than make assumptions about type sizes.

Also, note that although the name of the macro used above is CHAR_BIT, the ANSI standard implies that CHAR_BIT really represents the number of bits in a byte. For this reason, code like that found in Listing 1.4 should be portable.

Avoid Anachronisms

Anachronisms are those language features that are outdated, or whose original intent or purpose is superseded by another language feature. Implicit in this definition is the fact that even though your new code should not use anachronistic features, you shouldn't forget about your old code. Most C++ compilers still support anachronistic features, if only because C++ hasn't been around long enough for these features to be worked out of existing codebases. Still, don't rely on the continued support of anachronisms by your compilers; ferret out code that uses these outdated constructs and fix them.

Use Base Class Names in Constructor Initializer Lists

Older C++ compilers enabled you to initialize base classes without actually specifying the base class name. Therefore, code such as the following used to be perfectly acceptable.

```
class Base {
public:
    Base(char *) { ... };
};

class Derived : public Base {
public:
    Derived() : ("Invisible Robot Fish") { ... };
}
```

This can obviously cause problems with those programs that use multiple inheritance, so the above syntax is now regarded as incorrect C++. Instead, use the base class name, like so:

```
class Derived : public Base {
public:
    Derived() : Base("Invisible Robot Fish") { ... };
}
```

Don't Use K&R-style Prototypes

Older C (and some C++ compilers) enabled function and class methods to be declared in the following manner.

```
void foo(a, b, c)
int a, b, c;
{
    Do something...
}
```

This is not correct C++ and, although the Borland 4.0 compiler compiles it, the default compiler settings flag this sort of prototype as a warning. Instead, use the ANSI style prototypes.

```
void foo(int a, int b, int c)
{
    Do something...
}
```

Scrutinize Overloaded Prefix and Postfix Operators

In older versions of C++, a program cannot overload the prefix for example, ++MyVar, −MyVar) and postfix (for example, MyVar++, MyVar−) operators separately. Programs instead wrote a single overloaded operator for both cases.

```
MyClass operator++(MyClass& AddValue) {
    // Increment the value somehow...
}

// Both of these lines used to call the same operator
MyClass MyInstance;
MyInstance++;
++MyInstance;
```

As of the 2.1 version of the AT&T cfront C++ specification, an overloaded increment or decrement operator that takes an additional
integer argument is defined as the *postfix operator*.

```
MyClass operator++(MyClass& AddValue) {
    cout << "In the prefix version\n";
    // Increment the value somehow...
}

MyClass operator++(MyClass& AddValue, int) {
    cout << "In the postfix version\n";
    // Increment the value somehow...
}

MyClass MyInstance;
MyInstance++; // Will display "In the postfix version"
++MyInstance; // Will display "In the prefix version"
```

Older code that overloads only the prefix version of these operators,
but uses the postfix operator, is nonportable. Make sure that these
programs either use the prefix operator exclusively, or add the definition of the postfix operator.

Use the ANSI Character-Handling Functions

Because portable code should make few (if any) assumptions about the
character set that the program uses, it is important that you avoid code
that relies on things like ordering properties or natural sorting behaviors. For example, the following function reads in a character from an
input stream and prints "Yes" to the console if the character is uppercase, and "No" otherwise.

```
P_CHAR CheckChar(istream& strm)
{
    P_CHAR b;
    strm >> b;
```

```
    cout << (b >= 'A' && b <= 'Z' ? "Yes" : "No") << "\n";
    return b;
}
```

While this code is not wrong, it contains some potential portability snags. This code will not function correctly if ported to a platform that utilizes a character set where alphanumerics are not consecutive.

> **Note:** The advice in this section may sound a little bit like overkill. After all, who uses a character set where the letters in the alphabet are not ordered consecutively? Actually, a lot of people do. The capital letters in IBM's Extended Binary Coded Decimal Interchange Code (EBCDIC) character set are represented by three noncontiguous ranges separating A-I, J-R, and S-Z. The reasons for this are historical and ultimately relate to the way that characters were ordered on mainframe punch cards. Because EBCDIC is the character set used on IBM mainframes, this example is not that obscure or reserved for the most portability paranoid.

Once again, the ANSI standard rescues us. The ctype.h header file defines functions designed to provide platform-independent character-testing functions. The version of CheckChar below is portable.

```
#include <ctype.h>

P_CHAR CheckChar(istream& strm)
{
    char b;
    strm >> b;
    cout << (isupper(b) ? "Yes" : "No") << "\n";
    return b;
}
```

Perform Bitwise Operations Only on Unsigned Data

On some platforms, the standard bitwise operators (i.e., &, |, ^, ~, >>, <<) can return inaccurate results if the type manipulated is signed. Under

many compilers the following code, for example, always evaluates to -1 regardless of the value of iNumShiftBits.

```
int iMyValue = ~0 >> iNumShiftBits;
```

This problem is easily solved by ensuring that the negation operator is applied to an unsigned 0. If the data type that you are working with is signed, a local cast to an unsigned type ensures the correct results. The following correction is unambiguous and should work without error on all platforms.

```
int iMyValue = ~((unsigned int) 0) >> iNumShiftBits;
```

These sort of portability bugs can be very tricky to find because a codebase can be moved to another platform and recompiled without errors, but still function incorrectly. Remember that all ported code, regardless of its previous history of reliability and robustness on other platforms, should be treated as if it were brand new.

Don't Cast Pointers to "Magic Addresses"

Try to guess what the following code fragment does under each of the following platforms: DOS, Windows, Windows NT, OS/2, System 7.1, and AIX.

```
unsigned char MysteryFunc()
{
    char far *info = (char far *) 0x00400088L;
    return ((*info & 0x0F) == 0x0F) ? 0 : 1;
}
```

The first time I looked at this code (which I was supposed to port to X-Windows) I had no idea what it was supposed to do. Even after it was explained to me and cleaned up, it became obvious that this code didn't have a prayer of being ported to any other platform.

```
// Constants
const P_ULONG VIDEO_ADDR = 0x00400088L;
const P_ULONG EGA_FLAG    = 0x0000000FL;

P_BOOLEAN CheckForEGA()
```

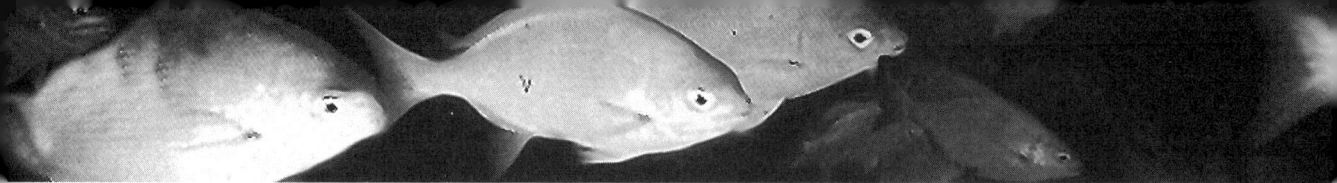

```
{
    P_CHAR P_FAR *info = (P_CHAR P_FAR *) VIDEO_ADDR;
    return (*info & EGA_FLAG) == EGA_FLAG ? FALSE :TRUE;
}
```

This function, on DOS-based platforms at least, checks to see if the display adapter installed supports the old-style EGA video standard. Who knows what will happen if you try to run this code on other platforms (it certainly will not check for EGA adapters)!

> **Caution:** If you need to hardcode addresses, the code you are writing is inherently nonportable. Don't do it unless you absolutely have to.

Most modern operating systems shield programmers from having to worry about details that require direct hardware interaction. If you find yourself writing code that uses magic addresses (or magic interrupt numbers, or magic service codes, and so on), stop for a second and ask yourself if there is another, more portable, way of accomplishing the same thing. In some cases there is not and you are stuck, but in most cases there is. If you are stuck, see the section entitled "Service Encapsulation" later in this chapter.

Don't Assume That Your Structures Are Packed

Run the short program from Listing 1.5 on your system. This program defines a structure and prints the offsets of each structure member using the ANSI standard offset() macro.

Listing 1.5. OFFSETS.CPP—Display the Offsets of a Structure's Members

```
#include <stddef.h>
#include <iostreams.h>
#include <port.h>
```

continues

Listing 1.5. Continued

```
typedef P_STRUCT {

        P_UINT    a;
        P_CHAR    b;
        P_LONG    c;
        P_SHORT   d;
        P_CHAR    e;
        P_CHAR    f;
        P_FLOAT   g;
        P_ULONG   h;

} StructType;

P_VOID main()
{
        // Where are the offsets?
        cout << "StructType offsets...\n";
        cout << "\toffset of \"a\" is "
             << offsetof(StructType, a);
        cout << "\n\toffset of \"b\" is "
             << offsetof(StructType, b);
        cout << "\n\toffset of \"c\" is "
             << offsetof(StructType, c);
        cout << "\n\toffset of \"d\" is "
             << offsetof(StructType, d);
        cout << "\n\toffset of \"e\" is "
             << offsetof(StructType, e);
        cout << "\n\toffset of \"f\" is "
             << offsetof(StructType, f);
        cout << "\n\toffset of \"g\" is "
             << offsetof(StructType, g);
        cout << "\n\toffset of \"h\" is "
             << offsetof(StructType, h);
}
```

Under Borland C++ 4.0, using the default project settings, this short
program displays the following information.

```
StructType offsets...
     offset of "a" is 0
     offset of "b" is 2
     offset of "c" is 3
     offset of "d" is 7
     offset of "e" is 9
     offset of "f" is 10
     offset of "g" is 11
     offset of "h" is 15
```

After you enter the project notebook and set the data alignment property to "Word" instead of "Byte," this program prints out something a little different.

```
StructType offsets...
        offset of "a" is 0
        offset of "b" is 2
        offset of "c" is 4
        offset of "d" is 8
        offset of "e" is 10
        offset of "f" is 11
        offset of "g" is 12
        offset of "h" is 16
```

Depending on the computer, operating system, compiler, and your compiler settings, your version of the same program may output exactly the same thing. On the other hand, it may not.

Structure alignment is one of those gray areas that can confuse you if you're not careful. On many CPUs, performance can be substantially increased simply by playing games with the way that structure data members are placed within the structure. Some compilers understand this and follow alignment strategies that help optimize program speed.

Don't get me wrong; this is generally a good thing. Because most compilers enable you to turn this behavior on and off, or specify exactly how the alignment is to take place, there's no real danger associated with the alignment process itself. In fact, some hardware platforms require it. On Motorola 68000-based computers, placing a long integer value at an odd address causes a hardware exception; in examples like this, structures cannot be packed and *have to be* even-byte aligned.

Usually structure alignment isn't a problem; look closely at Listing 1.6. This code places a `StructType` into a generic character buffer and digs into the structure to retrieve the StructType.d short-integer member. This sort of code is common in programs that need to read in data structures from a database file or from a byte stream coming from a network.

Listing 1.6. The Wrong Way to Dig into Structures

```
#include <stddef.h>
#include <iostreams.h>
#include <port.h>

typedef P_STRUCT {

        P_UINT    a;
        P_CHAR    b;
        P_LONG    c;
        P_SHORT   d;
        P_CHAR    e;
        P_CHAR    f;
        P_FLOAT   g;
        P_ULONG   h;

} StructType;

P_VOID main()
{
    P_BYTE Buffer[100];
    StructType TestStruct = { 123, 'c', 0, 234, 'k', 'c',
                              6.023, 0x00FF6534UL };

    // Copy the structure into our memory buffer
    memcpy(Buffer, &TestStruct, sizeof(StructType));

    // Point to the "d" structure member
    P_SHORT AShortInt = *((P_PSHORT)
                          (Buffer +
                           sizeof(P_UINT) +
                           sizeof(P_CHAR) +
                           sizeof(P_LONG)));

    // Display it
    cout << "AShortInt (\"d\") is " << AShortInt << "\n";
{
```

Once again, this program runs as you would expect (displaying a value of 234) when the data alignment property is set to "Byte" (i.e., packed structures). Although the code looks like it's written in a portable fashion, when using "Word" alignment this code displays the erroneous value of -5632. Using `sizeof()` is a good idea to help support portability; it just isn't enough in this case. To make this code portable, substitute the following line for the assignment of the `AShortInt` variable.

```
P_SHORT AShortInt = *((P_PSHORT) (Buffer +
                          offsetof(StructType, d)));
```

As you can probably tell, use of the `offsetof()` macro is crucial to ensure that your code is not dependent on a specific structure-packing strategy.

> **Tip:** By the way, don't use `offsetof()` to muck around inside aggregates that are not "pure" C-compatible types. Using `offsetof()` on classes, structures, and unions that contain items other than simple member data (i.e., methods) can be dangerous and nonportable.

Don't Try to Do Too Much

C++ programmers are notorious for writing code that is cryptic and terse to a fault. A programmer once showed me a single line of code designed to calculate the number of days in a given month, and it might as well have been written in Greek. Avoid writing code in this manner for many reasons. First and foremost, it is error-prone and indecipherable. If other people have to maintain your code, don't make things difficult for them. Consider the fact that, in most large companies at least, maintenance programmers are usually the youngest and most inexperienced programmers available.

Finally, realize that code that tries to do too much in a single line may not be portable. C and C++ make no promises about the order of evaluation of expressions except for the logical "and" (`&&`), the logical "or" (`||`), the ternary operator (`?:`), and the comma (`,`). In these cases (and these cases alone) the language guarantees that expressions are evaluated from left to right in the order in which they are encountered. Note that expression evaluation should not be confused with operator precedence, which is very well-defined for all operators.

These sorts of portability problems crop up most often when a variable is modified in an expression, but is used later in the same line of code. Here are two examples.

```
// MyVar is NOT guaranteed to be incremented
// before being added at the end of this line
P_INT iAnswer = (++MyVar == 2) + MyVar;

// Does Array1[Index] get Array2[Index+1]? Or does
// Array1[Index] get Array2[Index] before Index
// gets incremented?
Array1[Index++] = Array2[Index];
```

Code that works correctly on one compiler, using expression relationships like these, may break when ported to another compiler. Avoid these sorts of code fragments.

Use LINT

If you know what LINT is, you're probably cringing at this advice. If you don't know what LINT is, pay no attention to the previous sentence. LINT is a utility used to help ensure that C and C++ code is as portable as possible. Programmers feed their code into the utility and LINT outputs a list of potential portability errors. Unfortunately, the program has gotten a bad name from programmers who feel that LINT flags too much code unnecessarily.

As an example I wrote the following trivial (to say the least) program in C++ and then fed it through LINT. Notice that the program really does next to nothing and, at first glance, appears to be so simple and straightforward that it *has* to be portable.

```
#include <stdio.h>

void main()
{
  unsigned long a = 12345L;
  short b;

  b = a;

  printf("b is %d", b);
}
```

The following output is what the LINT utility spat out. Notice that the utility has flagged a number of things that most programmers regard as common practice (for example, not checking return codes from common runtime library functions). However, the first message about the conversion potentially losing accuracy is exactly the sort of coding error that can make for a painful and drawn-out porting process.

```
"tester.c", line 8: warning: conversion from long may lose accuracy
"tester.c", line 11: warning: main() returns random value to invoca-
➡tion environment
"stdio.h", line 200 ("llib-lc"): warning: function printf return value
➡is always ignored
```

Don't be disheartened when you run your code through LINT for the first time and it spits out a hundred portability warnings. Many of these warnings do not require source code modifications, unless you strive for the absolute highest level of portability possible. Of more importance is the fact that LINT often finds those big, important portability errors that you may overlook.

Remember that LINT output is not inscribed on stone tablets and passed down from on high. It is a tool that you should use to facilitate the development of code that causes you the fewest headaches later.

Dealing with Operating System Dependencies

It should be clear by now that there really is no such thing as a completely portable application. Once you factor in different operating systems, hardware, and compilers, maintaining a single codebase for all possible platforms becomes a nirvana that you will never reach.

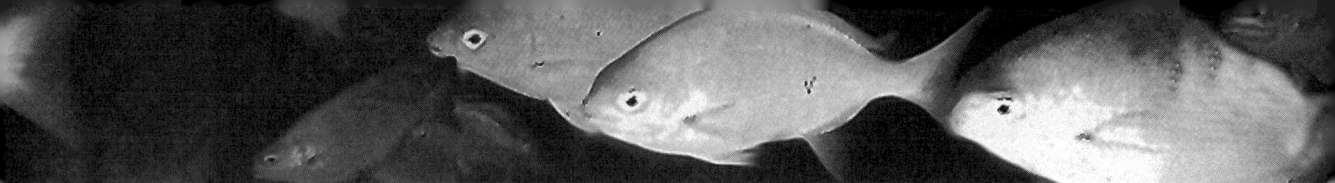

Rooms and Doors

The trick is to segregate your code into *rooms* and *doors* (also known as application and edge code, or implementation and interface code). *Room code* is that part of the codebase that is readily portable from platform to platform. Candidates for room code include algorithms, generic data structure objects, proprietary processes, and anything that has only high-level interactions with system services.

Door code is code that needs to interact with the operating system (or other parts of the environment) in a platform-specific example. Door code is the stuff that you probably will have to rewrite from scratch every time you move code from one platform to another. The `CheckForEGA()` function, presented in the section "Don't Cast Pointers to 'Magic Addresses,'" is an excellent example of door code.

Room code is the easier of the two code types to work with. As long as you follow the basic tenets of portability, development of C++ room code should proceed normally.

Door code is the tricky stuff. In C++, door code is usually provided through a generic interface provided by various door objects. The key is that interfaces to door objects need to be generic enough that the same interfaces can be used on a variety of potentially disparate platforms. If a given system service does not exist on a particular platform, it is the responsibility of the appropriate door object to implement, emulate, or simulate the system service in such a manner that the room code that uses the door object is unaware that the door object is not directly supported by the operating system.

Building a Door Object Layer

Building a door object usually is not a very difficult task. Building a door object in a truly platform-independent manner is usually much more difficult. Since a door object has to hide every last visage of the operating system from room code, a door object implementation needs to be carefully thought out.

As an example of the thought process you might go through when designing a door object, I present the steps you might take when designing a door object that starts up other programs.

For the sake of this example, we assume that our code needs to support DOS, Windows, Windows NT (i.e., Win32), OS/2, UNIX, and the Macintosh. Because this is only a design example, the actual coding of the door object is left as an exercise. Our door object, `Program`, is simple for the sake of brevity.

Isolating the System Service

Let's start at the very beginning. What is it exactly that we need our object to do? In this example, let's say that our object needs to do nothing more than spawn off another program. We'll assume that the program we start executes asynchronously (i.e., independent of and concurrent with the program that started it) and that control returns to the room code immediately after the spawned program is started.

Clearly, our object needs a method responsible for starting the program. `StartProgram` seems as good a method name as any. The only immediately obvious information a `Program` object would absolutely require is a program name.

Now we need to look at each of the operating systems that we will support and examine the interfaces to their "start a new program" system service APIs. This may seem a little backward at first. Because we are trying to arrive at a generic interface, it may not appear to make sense that we look at operating system interfaces before designing the object. Programmers, however, are mere mortals and can't be expected to get everything right the first time around. Perhaps, just maybe, there are other pieces of information that will be required by a `Program` object. Examining specific API calls helps us to determine if a program name is a generic and capable interface for our object.

Starting a Program under DOS

Borland C++ 4.0 provides a variety of different ways to start another DOS program. The most promising appear to be the `spawn()` family of runtime library functions, all of which provide a number of different programming interfaces to the task of starting a program. Even more promising is the fact that the Borland compiler supports the `spawn()` functions under DOS, Windows NT, and OS/2.

The `spawn()` functions take a fully qualified path name and an execution mode as their first two arguments. The path name represents the name of the program to start. The mode is a constant that indicates how the function behaves after the program is started. The `Program` object should hardcode this constant to `P_NOWAIT`, which introduces our first problem.

The `P_NOWAIT` mode indicates that the function should return immediately after starting the new program. This works fine under Win32 and OS/2, but DOS simply doesn't support concurrently executing programs. Because the `spawn()` functions under DOS can only be used to start a program that must complete before returning, the only valid mode that we can use is `P_WAIT`. We're stuck.

In cases like this, you can do a couple of things. If the requirement of asynchronous execution is absolute and inflexible, you have to decide whether the application that needs the services should really be ported to DOS in the first place. Here is where compromise comes in. If you need the DOS port, you can only have synchronous program spawning. If you must have asynchronous program spawning, then you can't have a native DOS port. Of course, in this particular instance there are some other options. Because Windows runs on top of DOS, and fully supports the asynchronous execution of programs, perhaps a Windows port will satisfy the requirements that necessitated a DOS port.

Later in this section, we explore some ways that we can write our room code so that, although the room code remains generic and platform independent, the door objects afford the maximum amount of flexibility and effectiveness.

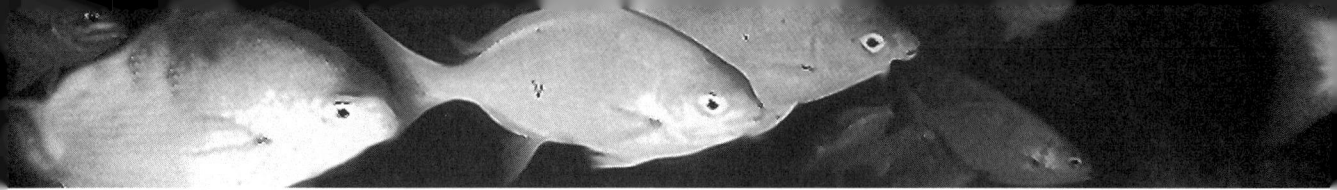

All `spawn()` functions vary in the way command-line arguments are passed on to the program started, but passing arguments is not part of our anticipated design. In this case, under DOS at least, we can just give our `Program` object the path name and use the `spawnl()` variant.

Starting a Program under Windows

Starting a new program under Windows isn't much more difficult than using the `spawnl()` function discussed above. The Windows API provides the function `WinExec()`, which requires a program name and some miscellaneous display details (which can be coded as constants for our purposes). The `WinExec()` API is inherently asynchronous, so we avoid the messy problems that cropped up under DOS.

Starting a Program under Windows NT and OS/2

We've already determined that the same `spawnl()` runtime function used by the DOS door object works under both Win32 and OS/2 2.X. Our `Program` door object, in this case, is actually portable between DOS, Win32, and OS/2, and has to be rewritten only for Windows, UNIX, and the Mac.

Note that this discussion assumes that only Borland compilers are used on each of these platforms. Because `spawnl()` is not an ANSI C/C++ function, it is quite possible that other compilers on these platforms do not support `spawnl()`. In these cases, it is necessary to create new door objects for Win32 and OS/2 that utilize the appropriate operating system API calls (i.e., `CreateProcess()` and `DosExecPgm()`, respectively).

Starting a Program under UNIX

Starting a program under UNIX, and implementing the specific behaviors that we want, is a little bit trickier than on the other platforms. This is because many UNIX implementations do not have a system service call analogous to the `spawnl()` function. Instead, our `Program` object must use a combination of the `execl()` and `fork()` functions.

The exec() family of functions is similar to the spawn() family of functions (and are, incidentally, supported by Borland compilers under DOS, Win32, and OS/2), except the program started is loaded into memory and overwrites the process making the execl() call. A successful call to execl() is the equivalent of a program committing suicide, and then rising Phoenix-like in the form of another program.

As far as our Program object is concerned, this approach appears to be a dead end. Yes, execl() starts a program, but is useless if it destroys the program currently executing. That's where fork() comes in. fork() does the inverse of execl(): it asynchronously starts a completely separate but identical instance of the program that makes the fork call. For our purposes, however, fork() also seems to be a dead end. It doesn't destroy the program making the call, but it enables a program to start a copy of itself only.

The solution, as you've probably guessed, is to use a combination of fork() and execl(). Our program can begin by using the fork() command to start a copy of itself. fork() provides an easy way to determine if a program is the original instance or the cloned instance, so that if the program senses that it is the clone, it can call the execl() function, with the name of the program that needs to be started.

Starting a Program on the Macintosh (System 7)

The Macintosh is discussed last because System 7.X application launching introduces a new problem to our design effort. Up to this point, the design has assumed that a room object can always indicate what program should be started by passing a character buffer into the Program object. We assumed that the contents and format of this buffer may vary wildly from platform to platform, but, as long as the information can be represented in a character string form, the interface to our object remains constant across platforms.

The Mac ruins this pretty picture. Under System 7.0 and later, programs use the LaunchApplication() function to start a new program. The LaunchApplication() API takes a single structure as its argument, which needs to be filled in by the calling program before making the API call.

The Mac file system is a hierarchical file system, just like those found under DOS, Windows NT, OS/2, and UNIX. The Mac file system, however, does not enable you to uniquely specify a particular file by simply generating a single character string. Instead, a program (or another operating system component like the Finder) needs to build a file system specification record. These records are typically referred to by their programmatic moniker, FSSpec. Once a program builds an FSSpec using the FSMakeFSSpec() function, or obtains an FSSpec from another source, the appropriate fields in a LaunchParamBlockRec structure can be filled in and passed on to the LaunchApplication() API.

This requires a change to the Program object's interface. It looks like there is no easy way to guarantee a portable mechanism for moving file specifications across platforms. Well, what did we do when we found that we couldn't guarantee a portable mechanism for starting programs across platforms? We designed the Program door object. If we can design a file specification door object, we can make the Program object's StartProgram() method require an instance of one of these file specification objects.

The Program Class Definition

For the sake of example, let's assume that this new class of door object is called FileSpec. Now we can code up a rough picture of what Program looks like initially.

```
P_CLASS Program {
public:
    ... Useful constructors and destructors here ...
    P_UINT StartProgram(const FileSpec&);
    ... Other useful public methods here ...

private:
    // Items placed here will probably vary from platform
    // to platform
    .. Private data and methods ...
};
```

This design now requires the room code to first obtain, through some mechanism that we do not define here, a FileSpec object before spawning off new programs. On many platforms, this FileSpec object is just a

wrapper around a character buffer, but some operating systems require support for a more elaborate file naming scheme. On the Mac, for example, the `FSMakeFSSpec()` function requires a volume reference number, a directory ID, and a path name.

The partial class definition for `Program` presented here doesn't look very exciting, but that's often a good sign. Portable solutions generally have simple interfaces, and this interface certainly qualifies.

Querying Door Object Capabilities

At this point you may be thinking, "Well that's all fine and good, but what about the hard cases? What if, for example, we want the `Program` door object to conditionally support either asynchronous or synchronous program execution as indicated by a passed-in argument to `StartProgram()`?"

Some platforms support this sort of behavior easily. Others require extra work by the `Program` object, but this work can be hidden from room objects that use `Program`. Still other operating systems, as we saw in the case of DOS, do not cooperate at all and cannot realistically support these features.

Yet, it doesn't make sense for a few problematic operating environments to spoil the party for everyone else. What if room objects query door objects to see if they support the desired behavior? If a door object does exactly what the room object wants, then program execution continues normally. Otherwise, the room object asks if the door object supports a level of functionality that is less than optimal, but still adequate.

Assuming that our `Program` door object is modified to conditionally take a program execution mode, a room object might interact with the door object as depicted in Listing 1.7.

Listing 1.7. Querying a Program Door Object's Capabilities

```
// Instantiate our door objects
Program    ProgStarter;
FileSpec   ProgramSpec;

... Fill in the ProgramSpec ...

// Ask the object if it can start our program
// asynchronously
if (!ProgStarter.QueryCapSupport(EXEC_ASYNCH)) {

    // Nope. Oh well, operate synchronously then
    ProgStarter.StartProgram(EXEC_SYNCH, ProgramSpec);
}

// Yes! Start things off asynchronously
else {
    ProgStarter.StartProgram(EXEC_ASYNCH, ProgramSpec);
}
```

Hiding Operating System Header Files

Your door objects need to include certain operating-system-specific include files in order to gain access to function prototypes, constants, data structures, and other relevant definitions. The number of source files dependent on these header files needs to be kept to a minimum, and access to these operating-system-specific files must be tightly regulated.

One way of doing this is to create an osinc.h header file. This file works in concert with the porting header files to ensure that the appropriate files get used according to the platform on which the codebase is built. Listing 1.8 shows an example of an osinc.h header file.

Listing 1.8. OSINC.H—An osinc.h Header File

```
// Don't allow this header to be included more than once
#ifndef OSINC_H
#define OSINC_H
```

continues

Listing 1.8. Continued

```
// Get our porting files
#ifndef PORT_H
    #include <port.h>
#endif

// Based on the operating system we are using,
// include certain files
#if defined(PORT_OS_WIN16)

    // Standard windows header file
    #include <windows.h>

    // Get OLE 2.X stuff (for example's sake)
    #include <ole2.h>

    // Get ODBC stuff (for example's sake)
    #include <sql.h>

#elif defined(PORT_OS_CHICAGO) || \
      defined(PORT_OS_WINNT)

    // Standard Win32 header file
    #include <windows.h>

#elif defined(PORT_OS_OS2)

    // Standard OS/2 header file
    #define INCL_PM
    #define INCL_DOSERRORS
    #define INCL_DOSSEMAPHORES
    #define INCL_DOSPROCESS
    #include <os2.h>

#endif

#endif
```

The osinc.h header file is the only header file that should include operating-system-specific header files. Door objects that use operating system services and rely on these include files should themselves include osinc.h only.

Door objects may, in their class definitions, need to reference operating-system-dependent definitions, even though their public interfaces do not depend on platform-specific declarations. This is really a glaring deficiency of C++. If a door object has a Windows-style HWND as a private data member, any room code that includes the door header file needs

to include the windows.h header file. In these sorts of situations, it is permissible to place an inclusion of osinc.h in a door header file that will be included by room code.

> **Caution:** It is of paramount importance that room code, although it may have access to platform-specific definitions, does not reference any operating-system-dependent definitions. *Code that does this will not port.*

Some Closing Words about Behavior Abstraction

Regardless of the approach that you adopt, it is crucial that door code completely and absolutely isolates room code from all parts of the operating system. The two most problematic aspects of porting revolve around compiler and operating system dependencies. Using the porting include files discussed earlier should help with compiler dependencies, and making effective use of door objects should help with the operating system side of the equation.

The Headaches of Porting a Graphical Application

It was only a decade ago that the Mac introduced us to a computing environment that was not based on cryptic commands, but instead relied on a virtual world populated by pictures and metaphors that really made sense. The Mac was the first practical implementation of a graphical user interface (GUI), and it changed the computer industry forever.

Today, of course, the tricks and images that amazed us ten years ago on the Macintosh are now old hat. Users think nothing of dragging file objects between windows, using tool palettes, and mousing around on

a virtual desktop all day. Indeed, many computer users have never had to use a computer that didn't provide them with an easy-to-use GUI. The future of computing is here, and it *is* graphical.

This dramatic ease of use has not come without a price. For users, it has meant that their computers had to be upgraded to faster, more capable machines with more memory and hard disk capacity. And for developers, it has meant learning a whole new way of programming.

GUI programming, quite simply, is difficult. Users expect their new programs to be graphical, and to run on the platforms that they use. The poor developer, on the other hand, is faced with API sets typically consisting of *thousands* of different function calls. The graphical super-programs of today rely on a new type of program coding technique called *event-driven programming*. Event-driven code is larger and more complicated (by several orders of magnitude) than more traditional code.

The biggest problem facing the programmer concerned with writing portable, graphical code is that no two GUI programming interfaces are alike. Windows is different from OS/2, which in turn is different from X-Windows, and so on and so on. The problem is really the same one faced by the programmer trying to encapsulate standard operating services, but on a much grander scale. Isolating a couple hundred system service API calls into a couple dozen door objects is a walk in the park compared to creating a door layer that provides graphical computing services across a wide range of different platforms.

Don't even try it. Creating a single virtual object layer that provides portable access to all GUIs is a task comparable to discovering the Unified Theory of Physics. It has been tried by many people with varying levels of success, and if you need to port graphical applications, I recommend that you don't try to do it all by yourself.

A variety of third-party C++ class libraries are for sale that purport to support a wide variety of graphical platforms. In some respects many of them succeed. The good news is that, in many cases, code written with one set of class libraries will port quite well to another platform.

The bad news is twofold. Most of the good C++ class libraries don't support more than two or three different platforms (hopefully, the ones that you need to develop for), and virtually all these libraries suffer from the least-common-denominator problem.

The least-common-denominator problem is this: There are a wide variety of different GUIs, and they are not all alike. OS/2, for example, has notebook and container controls that you will not find on the Mac. The Mac has, however, balloon-like help windows that you will not find under X-Windows, and X-Windows has a distributed graphical architecture that you will not find under Windows.

If you want to build a collection of C++ objects that provide a single generic interface to all these GUIs, you either have to select those features that are common to all of them, or provide the missing features on those platforms that are lacking some capabilities (does this sound familiar?). When you're talking about a scale as massive as a GUI interface, these tasks are daunting indeed. The least-common-denominator problem arises when a class library (for perfectly understandable reasons) supports only those graphical elements that every GUI supports. This leads to applications that look and act alike across different platforms, but it also leads to a blandness and stark uniformity that turns users off. These programs cannot take advantage of those GUI mechanisms and constructs that differentiate one platform from another.

Currently these problems have no real solutions, at least not yet. Right now, if you are concerned about porting a graphical application, you have a few courses of action available.

As already mentioned, don't reinvent the wheel. If you need to provide a graphical application, bite the bullet and commit yourself to a third-party C++ class library that is available on the platforms to which you need to port. Microsoft and Borland are currently fighting for market share with their OWL and MFC graphical class libraries. Both of these class libraries are available under Windows and Windows NT, and both of these libraries are highly portable in that respect. Although these products are the leaders in the Windows world, many, many other vendors are eager to provide GUI class libraries with wide platform interoperability. Shop around carefully before making your final decision.

From Here...

Porting affects almost every part of your code. The following chapters discuss features of programming with Borland C++ that will concern any programmer writing portable code.

> ➤ Sometimes optimization techniques work better on some platforms than on others. Investigate these issues carefully. Chapter 4, "Optimizing C," and Chapter 5, "Optimizing C++," should give you a good start.

> ➤ For techniques that apply to mixed language programming for one platform that typically cannot be used on other platforms, see Chapter 13, "Mixed Language Programming."

> ➤ Chapter 15, "Interfacing with Database Languages," describes database languages, even if they use a common language family (like SQL), that often require a different dialect from platform to platform.

> ➤ Chapter 16, "Runtime Type Identification," describes some compilers that do not support the RTTI features in the current ANSI standards draft. Be careful when using these extensions.

> ➤ Some compilers don't support templates, or do so in nonstandard ways. For a discussion of templates, see Chapter 17, "Mastering Templates." Exercise caution.

> ➤ Some compilers don't support exception handling. Make sure that if you use exceptions, the compilers you will be porting to support this extension. For a discussion of exception handling, see Chapter 18, "Exception Handling."

Turbocharging Pointers

by Clayton Walnum

Fact: You can truly understand C++ only when you fully understand pointers.

Anyone who has tried to decipher a professional programmer's C++ source code, which is inevitably filled with all kinds of esoteric pointer manipulations, will appreciate the truth of this statement. Although the basic concept of pointers—data items that hold the addresses of other data items—is fairly simple, C++ enables programmers to manipulate pointers in so many ways that their simplicity quickly becomes obscured by confusing pointer math, unclear syntax, and complex type casts. Even a seasoned programmer often must stop and think when he encounters pointers in a program. Except in the simplest cases, how a pointer is being used is rarely evident at a glance.

To help you better understand pointers, this chapter gives you a quick review of pointer basics, and then explores some advanced ways that you can use pointers in your programs. You learn how to use pointer math, implement variable argument lists, create vector tables, and use pointer casts to look at data in various ways.

A Quick Review

A pointer holds the address of an item in memory. As such, C++ usually needs to know the type of data to which the pointer points. Pointers can point to just about any kind of data, even derived types like structures and objects. So, to declare a pointer, you precede the pointer name with the data type, as in the following examples:

```
char *cPtr;
int *iPtr;
```

These two lines declare pointers to character and integer data types, respectively. The data types `char` and `int` are these pointers' reference types. The asterisk, called an indirection operator, tells the compiler that you want a pointer rather than a variable of the given type. If you omit the asterisks in these examples, you would have `char` and `int` variables rather than pointers to those data types.

One indirect way that you can declare a pointer is to declare an array. This is because an array's name is a pointer to the first element of the array. The following two lines both result in a pointer to an integer:

```
int *iPtr;
int array[10];
```

If you use the array name `array` without a subscript, it is a pointer. So, although `array[1]` refers to the second element of the array, `array` by itself is the address of the array, which also is the address of the first element of the array.

An uninitialized pointer is pretty useless. To make such a pointer useful, you must first assign it the address of a data item:

```
int *iPtr;
int x = 0;
int y;

iPtr = &x;
```

This example declares an `int` pointer named `iPtr`, an `int` variable named `x`, and an `int` variable named `y`. It then assigns the address of `x` to the pointer `iPtr`. Now, `iPtr` points to `x`, and `int` is `iPtr`'s reference data type.

Having the address of the integer variable `x` doesn't help much if you have no way to access that memory location. This is another reason that C++ provides the indirection operator, which enables you to dereference a pointer or access the location to which the pointer points:

```
y = *iPtr;
y = x;
```

When you execute both lines in this example, they are exactly equivalent: Both set `y` equal to the value of `x`. Using the indirection operator, you can also change the value of `x`:

```
*iPtr = 5;
x = 5;
```

These two lines also are equivalent. Both change the value of `x` to 5. Listing 2.1 demonstrates the basics of using pointers.

Listing 2.1. POINTER1.CPP—A Demonstration of Pointer Basics

```
//////////////////////////////////////////////////////////
// POINTER1.CPP: Pointer example program 1.
//////////////////////////////////////////////////////////

#include <iostream.h>
#include <conio.h>

int main(void)
{
   int x, y;
   int *iPtr;

   clrscr();
   x = 1;
   iPtr = &x;
   y = *iPtr;
   cout << "y = " << y << endl;
   *iPtr = 10;
   cout << "x now equals " << x << endl;
   return 1;
}
```

Listing 2.1 first declares two integer variables, x and y, and then declares iPtr, an integer pointer. The program then clears the screen, sets x equal to 1, sets iPtr equal to the address of x, and sets the value of y to the value of x by dereferencing iPtr on the right side of the assignment statement. The first call to the I/O stream object cout prints the value of y, proving that y now equals x. Finally, the program dereferences iPtr on the left side of an assignment statement, setting x to the value 10. The last call to cout proves that x is now equal to 10.

Pointers to Void

One special type of pointer is a void pointer, which is not exactly what it sounds like. Although a void pointer is void in the sense that you cannot dereference it, it does hold a perfectly valid address. The difference between a void pointer and a regular pointer is that the compiler has no idea what the pointer's reference type is. Until you give the compiler that reference type, you can't use the pointer to access memory.

Using Void Pointers

If you don't have much experience with pointers, void pointers may seem pretty useless. However, they are helpful in many circumstances. For example, before C++ introduced the new operator for allocating memory, you had to use a memory-allocation function such as malloc(). Because malloc() has no idea how you plan to use allocated memory, it returns a void pointer. It's up to your program to ensure that the void pointer is cast to the appropriate data type. For example, in the following line, (char *) is a type cast that tells the compiler that the pointer that malloc() returns should be interpreted as a char pointer:

```
char *ptr = (char *) malloc(1024);
```

The more modern C++ version of the preceding line is as follows:

```
char *ptr = new char[1024];
```

A void pointer also can be useful when you want to write a function that copies one array to another, regardless of the source and destination arrays' types. Listing 2.2 is such a program.

Listing 2.2. POINTER2.CPP—A Program That Copies an Array, Regardless of Type

```
/////////////////////////////////////////////////////////
// POINTER2.CPP: Pointer example program 2.
/////////////////////////////////////////////////////////

#include <iostream.h>
#include <conio.h>

// Function prototype.
void CopyArray(void *array1, void *array2, int bytes);

/////////////////////////////////////////////////////////
// main()
/////////////////////////////////////////////////////////
int main(void)
{
   int x;
   int array1[13];
   char array2[26] =
      { 'a', 'b', 'c', 'd', 'e', 'f', 'g', 'h', 'i',
        'j', 'k', 'l', 'm', 'n', 'o', 'p', 'q', 'r',
        's', 't', 'u', 'v', 'w', 'x', 'y', 'z' };

   clrscr();

   for (x=0; x<26; ++x)
      cout << array2[x];
   cout << endl;

   CopyArray(array1, array2, sizeof(array2));

   for (x=0; x<26; ++x)
      cout << ((char *) array2)[x];
   cout << endl;

   return 1;
}

/////////////////////////////////////////////////////////
// CopyArray()
/////////////////////////////////////////////////////////
void CopyArray(void *array1, void *array2, int bytes)
{
   unsigned char *ptr1, *ptr2;

   ptr1 = (unsigned char *) array1;
   ptr2 = (unsigned char *) array2;
   for (int x=0; x<bytes; ++x)
      *ptr1++ = *ptr2++;
}
```

Taking Apart POINTER2

The program in listing 2.2 generates the following output:

```
abcdefghijklmnopqrstuvwxyz
abcdefghijklmnopqrstuvwxyz
```

The program's `main()` function declares a 13-element `int` array and a 26-element `char` array. The program initializes the character array to the letters of the alphabet. Because integers take up two bytes and characters take up only one byte, both arrays are exactly the same length in memory. The only difference between them is the way that the compiler interprets the data they contain.

After clearing the screen, `main()` uses a `for` loop to display on-screen the characters contained in `array2[]`. The function then calls `CopyArray()` to copy `array2[]` into `array1[]`. `CopyArray()` receives the arrays' addresses as `void` pointers, which means that you can call `CopyArray()` with any type of array.

`CopyArray()` casts the `void` pointers to `char` pointers, which enables the function to handle the arrays byte by byte. The `for` loop copies the array pointed to by `ptr2` into the array pointed to by `ptr1`. After the `for` loop copies the arrays, `main()` displays the new contents of `array1[]`, casting `array1` to a character pointer, so that you can see that both arrays now contain the same data. Notice the parentheses that enclose the type cast and the array name `array2`. Without these parentheses, you would be trying to cast the contents of `array2[x]` to a `char` pointer.

Notice also the increment operators that `CopyArray()` uses to calculate the address of the next character in the array. These increment operators perform arithmetic operations on the pointers—which brings you to the subject of pointer math.

Pointer Math

A pointer isn't much different than any other value that you use in your C++ programs. That is, a pointer is just a number. You can use pointers, like integers or floating-point numbers, in mathematical expressions. However, you can use only three arithmetic operations

on pointers. You can increment a pointer, decrement a pointer, and subtract one pointer from another. How an arithmetic operation works with a pointer depends on the pointer's reference type.

For example, when you add 1 to the integer 5,245, you get 5,246. Similarly, when you add 1 to a `char` pointer that holds the address 8f99:0000, you get 8f99:0001. However, when you add 1 to an `int` pointer that holds the address 8f99:0000, you get 8f99:0002. This is because C++ knows that a character takes up only one byte of memory, and an integer takes up two. Although it makes sense to increment a `char` pointer one byte at a time, such incrementing makes no sense at all for an integer. Incrementing an `int` pointer by one byte leaves you with a pointer to invalid data.

Incrementing or Decrementing a Pointer

When you increment or decrement a pointer, the address stored in the pointer increments or decrements by a value equal to the size of the pointer's reference type. This includes derived data types, such as structures and objects. Listing 2.3 demonstrates how this pointer math works.

Listing 2.3. POINTER3.CPP—A Pointer Math Example

```
/////////////////////////////////////////////////////////
// POINTER3.CPP: Pointer example program 3.
/////////////////////////////////////////////////////////

#include <iostream.h>
#include <iomanip.h>
#include <dos.h>
#include <conio.h>

struct Strc
{
   char c;
   int i;
   long l;
};

// Function prototype.
void ShowData(char *cPtr, int *iPtr, long *lPtr, Strc *sPrt);
```

continues

Listing 2.3. Continued

```cpp
//////////////////////////////////////////////////////////
// main()
//////////////////////////////////////////////////////////
int main(void)
{
   char c;
   int i;
   long l;
   Strc s;

   clrscr();
   char *cPtr = &c;
   int *iPtr = &i;
   long *lPtr = &l;
   Strc *sPtr = &s;

   cout << "BEFORE INCREMENTING" << endl;
   ShowData(cPtr, iPtr, lPtr, sPtr);

   cPtr += 1;
   iPtr += 1;
   lPtr += 1;
   sPtr += 1;

   cout << "AFTER INCREMENTING" << endl;
   ShowData(cPtr, iPtr, lPtr, sPtr);

   return 1;
}

//////////////////////////////////////////////////////////
// ShowData()
//////////////////////////////////////////////////////////
void ShowData(char *cPtr, int *iPtr, long *lPtr, Strc *sPtr)
{
   unsigned segment, offset;

   segment = FP_SEG(cPtr);
   offset = FP_OFF(cPtr);
   cout << "cPtr = " << hex << segment << ':';
   cout << hex << offset << endl;
   segment = FP_SEG(iPtr);
   offset = FP_OFF(iPtr);
   cout << "iPtr = " << hex << segment << ':';
   cout << hex << offset << endl;
   segment = FP_SEG(lPtr);
   offset = FP_OFF(lPtr);
   cout << "lPtr = " << hex << segment << ':';
   cout << hex << offset << endl;
   segment = FP_SEG(sPtr);
   offset = FP_OFF(sPtr);
   cout << "sPtr = " << hex << segment << ':';
   cout << hex << offset << endl << endl;
}
```

The program shown in Listing 2.3 generates output similar to the following:

```
BEFORE INCREMENTING
cPtr = 8f99:fff
iPtr = 8f99:ffc
lPtr = 8f99:ff8
sPtr = 8f99:ff0

AFTER INCREMENTING
cPtr = 8f99:1000
iPtr = 8f99:ffe
lPtr = 8f99:ffc
sPtr = 8f99:ff7
```

As you can see, when you add 1 to a `char` pointer, the address moves forward one byte, which is the size of a character, but when you add 1 to an `integer` pointer, the address moves forward two bytes, which is the size of an integer. Similarly, adding 1 to a `long` pointer changes the address by four bytes, and adding 1 to the `Strc` pointer moves the pointer forward seven bytes, because that's the size of the `Strc` structure.

Decrementing a pointer works similarly, except that the new address is lower rather than higher.

Subtracting Pointers

Another arithmetic operation that you can perform on pointers is to subtract one pointer from another. This operation results in the number of data items between the two pointers. Listing 2.4 is a short program that shows how this works.

Listing 2.4. POINTER4.CPP—A Program That Subtracts Pointers

```
///////////////////////////////////////////////////////////
// POINTER4.CPP: Pointer example program 4.
///////////////////////////////////////////////////////////

#include <iostream.h>
#include <conio.h>

int main(void)
{
```

continues

Listing 2.4. Continued

```
    char c1[20];
    char *c2;
    int i1[20];
    int *i2;
    long l1[20];
    long *l2;

    clrscr();
    c2 = &c1[10];
    i2 = &i1[10];
    l2 = &l1[10];
    ptrdiff_t cDif = c2 - c1;
    ptrdiff_t iDif = i2 - i1;
    ptrdiff_t lDif = l2 - l1;
    cout << "The difference between c1 and c2 is ";
    cout << cDif << endl;
    cout << "The difference between i1 and i2 is ";
    cout << iDif << endl;
    cout << "The difference between l1 and l2 is ";
    cout << lDif << endl;
    return 1;
}
```

The output of this program looks like the following:

```
The difference between c1 and c2 is 10
The difference between i1 and i2 is 10
The difference between l1 and l2 is 10
```

This program first declares several 10-element arrays, one each for the char, int, and long data types. Because of the sizes of the data types, the char array is 10 bytes long, the int array is 20 bytes long, and the long array is 40 bytes long. The program then creates pointers that point to the tenth element (counting from 0, of course) of each array. It then subtracts the arrays' starting addresses from these new pointers, giving the number of data items between the pointers. The compiler knows the sizes of the reference data types, so, regardless of the number of bytes that any of the arrays consume, the number of data items between element 0 and element 10 is still 10.

Notice the data type ptrdiff_t in Listing 2.4. This data type is defined by Borland C++ and is used specifically for the results of pointer subtractions. The large, huge, and compact memory models define ptrdiff_t as a long int. Other memory models define this data type as an int.

Type Casts and Data

Ultimately, all data in a computer is in exactly the same form. Every memory location holds a single value; it's the way that you interpret each value that determines the data's type. For example, if you were to look into memory and see the value 32, what would you be looking at? Is it one byte of a two-byte integer value? Is it the ASCII representation of a space character? Is it part of an address? Until you give a memory location a data type, the values contained in memory mean nothing.

When you declare a variable, C++ reserves the appropriate amount of memory for the variable and assigns a data type to that memory. If you were to declare a character variable and place the value 32 into that memory location, you would definitely have a space character because 32 is the ASCII character value of a space. However, if you apply different data types to the memory locations, you can look at the value contained in a location in different ways. You can do this with type casts.

A Demonstration Type Casts

Actually, you have already seen type casting demonstrated in this chapter. The program in Listing 2.2 uses a `(unsigned char *)` type cast to interpret an integer array as a character array. You can do similar type casts for any data type. Listing 2.5 demonstrates how this is done.

Listing 2.5. POINTER5.CPP—Using Type Casts

```
//////////////////////////////////////////////////////////
// POINTER5: Pointer example program 5.
//////////////////////////////////////////////////////////

#include <iostream.h>
#include <conio.h>

// Function prototypes.
int DoMenu(void);
void DisplayData(int choice, void *ptr);
```

continues

Listing 2.5. Continued

```cpp
//////////////////////////////////////////////////////////
// main()
//////////////////////////////////////////////////////////
int main(void)
{
   int done, choice;
   int array[10] =
       { 0x2041, 0x4553, 0x5243, 0x5445, 0x4d20,
         0x5345, 0x4153, 0x4547, 0x2021, 0x2020 };

   clrscr();
   done = 0;
   do
   {
      choice = DoMenu();
      if (choice == 5)
         done = 1;
      else
         DisplayData(choice, array);
   }
   while (!done);

   return 1;
}

//////////////////////////////////////////////////////////
// DoMenu()
//////////////////////////////////////////////////////////
int DoMenu(void)
{
   int choice;

   cout << "CHOOSE A DATA TYPE:" << endl;
   cout << "————————" << endl;
   cout << "1. Integer" << endl;
   cout << "2. Long integer" << endl;
   cout << "3. Float" << endl;
   cout << "4. Character" << endl;
   cout << "5. Quit" << endl << endl;

   cin >> choice;
   cout << endl;
   return choice;
}

//////////////////////////////////////////////////////////
// DisplayData()
//////////////////////////////////////////////////////////
void DisplayData(int choice, void *ptr)
{
   int x;

   switch (choice)
```

```
    {
        case 1: for (x=0; x<10; ++x)
                    cout << ((int *) ptr)[x] << ' ';
                break;
        case 2: for (x=0; x<5; ++x)
                    cout << ((long *) ptr)[x] << ' ';
                break;
        case 3: for (x=0; x<5; ++x)
                    cout << ((float *) ptr)[x] << ' ';
                break;
        case 4: for (x=0; x<20; ++x)
                    cout << ((char *) ptr)[x];
                break;
    }
    cout << endl << endl;
}
```

This program declares an array of 10 integers, and then enables you to look at the contents of the array in various ways—as integers, long integers, floating-point numbers, or characters:

```
CHOOSE A DATA TYPE:
_____

1. Integer
2. Long integer
3. Float
4. Character
5. Quit
```

To view the array as integers, type **1**. The program then displays the following output:

```
8257 17747 21059 21573 19774 21317 16723 17735 8225 8224
```

To view the array as characters, type **4**, which results in this output:

```
A SECRET MESSAGE!
```

If you choose other data types, the program displays the array in the same format as the preceding example, except with the chosen data type. To end the program, type **5**.

Most of the program is straightforward C++. The function `DoMenu()` gets a data-type choice from the user, and then `DisplayData()` displays the data in the chosen format.

The real fun begins in the function `DisplayData()`. First, notice that `DisplayData()` receives the array address as a `void` pointer, which means

that the function can handle any type of array. The `switch` statement in `DisplayData()` determines, based on the value of `choice`, how to display the data. In each case, the program casts the array's address in `ptr` to the appropriate data type before calling the input-output object `cout` to display the data value.

Remember that an array name is actually a pointer to the array's first element. Similarly, you can use any pointer to reference an array of data objects. In `DisplayData()`, the pointer `ptr` is nothing more than a `void` pointer. However, by a combination of type casting and adding an array subscript to the pointer name, `ptr` references an array.

Putting Type Casts to Work

Although viewing a predefined array in your program can be instructive, it isn't very useful. You can, however, use the same technique to view any data, whether in your computer's memory or on a disk. Listing 2.6, which is a revised version of listing 2.5, uses the pointer type-casting technique to display the contents of part of the program's PSP (program segment prefix).

Listing 2.6. POINTER6.CPP—Another Example of Pointer Type Casting

```
//////////////////////////////////////////////////////////////
// POINTER6: Pointer example program 6.
//////////////////////////////////////////////////////////////

#include <iostream.h>
#include <conio.h>
#include <dos.h>

// Function prototypes.
int DoMenu(void);
void DisplayData(int choice, void *ptr);

//////////////////////////////////////////////////////////////
// main()
//////////////////////////////////////////////////////////////
int main(void)
{
    int done, choice;
    char *ptr;
```

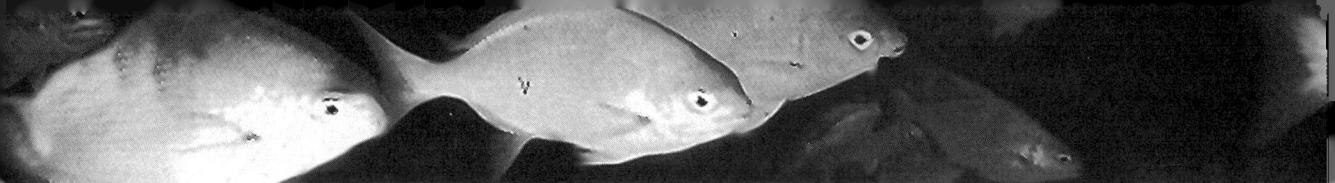

```
      clrscr();

      ptr = (char *) MK_FP(_psp, 0L);
      ptr += 0x82;

      done = 0;
      do
      {
         choice = DoMenu();
         if (choice == 5)
            done = 1;
         else
            DisplayData(choice, ptr);
      }
      while (!done);

      return 1;
}

//////////////////////////////////////////////////////////
// DoMenu()
//////////////////////////////////////////////////////////
int DoMenu(void)
{
   int choice;

   cout << "CHOOSE A DATA TYPE:" << endl;
   cout << "————————————" << endl;
   cout << "1. Integer" << endl;
   cout << "2. Long integer" << endl;
   cout << "3. Float" << endl;
   cout << "4. Character" << endl;
   cout << "5. Quit" << endl << endl;

   cin >> choice;
   cout << endl;
   return choice;
}

//////////////////////////////////////////////////////////
// DisplayData()
//////////////////////////////////////////////////////////
void DisplayData(int choice, void *ptr)
{
   int row, x;

   for (row=0; row<10; ++row)
   {
      switch (choice)
      {
         case 1: for (x=row*10; x<row*10+10; ++x)
                    cout << ((int *) ptr)[x] << ' ';
                 break;
```

continues

Listing 2.6. Continued

```
case 2: for (x=row*5; x<row*5+5; ++x)
            cout << ((long *) ptr)[x] << ' ';
        break;
case 3: for (x=row*5; x<row*5+5; ++x)
            cout << ((float *) ptr)[x] << ' ';
        break;
case 4: for (x=row*20; x<row*20+20; ++x)
        {
            if (((char *) ptr)[x] < 32 ||
                ((char *) ptr)[x] > 126)
                cout << '.';
            else
                cout << ((char *) ptr)[x];
        }
        break;
    }
    cout << endl;
    }
    cout << endl;
}
```

When you run the program shown in Listing 2.6, type the program's name along with some sort of command string. For example, you might run this program with the command POINTER6 TEST COMMAND. If you add a command string, you can then view the string in the program's PSP.

How does the program display the command string? Look at main(). After clearing the screen, main() creates a pointer to the program's PSP:

```
ptr = (char *) MK_FP(_psp, 0L);
```

MK_FP is a macro defined in DOS.H (a standard Borland header file) that enables you to create a far pointer from the segment and offset portions of an address. DOS.H also defines the global constant _psp, which holds the segment at which the program's PSP is located. So, the preceding code line creates a far pointer from the PSP's segment and the offset 0L. The returned pointer is type cast to char, so main() can access memory as a series of bytes.

After creating the far pointer to the program's PSP, main() adds 0x82 to the pointer so that it points to the area of the PSP that contains the program's command tail, which is the command string that you entered after the command POINTER6. The function DoMenu()

accomplishes the same task as in Listing 2.5, enabling you to choose the way that you want to view the data. If you choose character data (by typing **4**), the program's output looks like the following:

```
TEST COMMAND........
...................
...................
...................
...................
...................
.......3!...'..0.!..
....,....}...{...w..
....R..7u...........
.cc&8.u........u....
```

The program's command tail is on the first line, which is followed by other data in character form. Any value that cannot be expressed as a visible ASCII character is displayed as a dot.

Listing 2.6's version of `DisplayData()` works similarly to Listing 2.5's version. Now, though, the function displays 20 lines of data rather than one. In either case, the pointer gets type cast to the chosen data type before displaying the data for the current line.

Arrays of Function Pointers

Your computer's operating system has to keep track of many addresses. When an interrupt occurs, for example, the operating system must know where to find the address of the appropriate interrupt handler. The addresses of the interrupt handlers are stored in a vector table. Using an appropriate index, the operating system can quickly find in the table the address that it needs.

You can easily implement something like vector tables in your C++ programs by using pointers to functions.

Declaring a Function Pointer

A pointer to a function, of course, holds the address of a function. To declare such a pointer, you must list the return type of the function, the name of the pointer, and any parameters that the function accepts.

The following line, for example, declares a pointer to a function:

```
void (*ptr) (void);
```

The function to which the pointer points returns no value and accepts only the void parameter.

An alternative way to declare a similar pointer is to omit the argument list entirely. The following line declares a pointer to a function that returns no value and accepts no arguments (including void):

```
void (*ptr);
```

The next example declares a pointer to a function that returns an integer and accepts two integers as arguments:

```
int (*ptr)(int, int);
```

Initializing a Function Pointer

After you declare a function pointer, you must assign it the address of a function. You do this just as you would assign the address of an array: by using the function's name. The following line sets the function pointer ptr to the address of the function MyFunc():

```
ptr = MyFunc;
```

Notice that you do not include the function's parentheses and argument list with the function's name, just as you do not include an array's square brackets and subscript when getting the address of an array.

Dereferencing a Function Pointer

In most programs, knowing the address of a function isn't particularly useful. However, now that you have a function pointer, you can actually call the function simply by dereferencing the pointer. For example, assuming that ptr contains the address of MyFunc(), as in the previous example, the following line calls MyFunc():

```
(*ptr)();
```

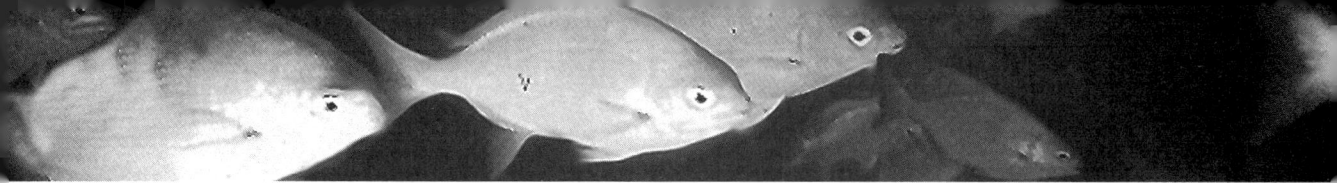

You also could use `ptr` to call the function like this:

```
ptr();
```

The first example is the non-ANSI method for calling a function with a function pointer. The second method complies with new ANSI standards.

Creating a Vector Table

Now that you know how to use a function pointer to call a function, you can take the idea one step further. You can define an array of function pointers and thus create a kind of vector table that you can use to call functions by accessing the array with an index. You can declare an array of function pointers simply by adding the size of the array within square brackets, just as you would with any array declaration.

The following line declares an array of function pointers:

```
void (*ptr[10]) (void);
```

This function pointer array can hold the addresses of 10 functions. You can call any of the 10 functions by dereferencing the appropriate array element, as follows:

```
(*ptr[4])()
```

This line calls the function whose address is stored in the fifth element of the function pointer array `ptr`.

Listing 2.7 demonstrates the use of a function pointer array in an actual program. This function pointer array calls a function based on the user's input.

Listing 2.7. POINTER7.CPP—A Program That Uses an Array of Function Pointers

```
///////////////////////////////////////////////////////////
// POINTER7.CPP: Example pointer program 7.
///////////////////////////////////////////////////////////
```

continues

Listing 2.7. Continued

```cpp
#include <iostream.h>
#include <stdlib.h>
#include <dos.h>
#include <conio.h>
#include <ctype.h>
#include <string.h>

// Function prototypes.
void PlayNumbers(void);
void PlayMemory(void);
void DoQuit(void);

/////////////////////////////////////////////////////////////
// main()
/////////////////////////////////////////////////////////////
void main(void)
{
   int choice;
   void (*games[3])(void);

   randomize();
   games[0] = PlayNumbers;
   games[1] = PlayMemory;
   games[2] = DoQuit;

   do
   {
      cout << "GAME MENU" << endl;
      cout << "——" << endl;
      cout << "1. Number Guess" << endl;
      cout << "2. Memory" << endl;
      cout << "3. Quit" << endl << endl;
      cin >> choice;

      if ((choice > 0) && (choice < 4))
         (*games[choice-1])();
   }
   while (1);
}

/////////////////////////////////////////////////////////////
// PlayNumbers()
/////////////////////////////////////////////////////////////
void PlayNumbers(void)
{
   int number, guess, turn;

   clrscr();
   turn = 0;
   number = random(100) + 1;
   cout << "Guess a number from 1 to 100" << endl;
   do
   {
```

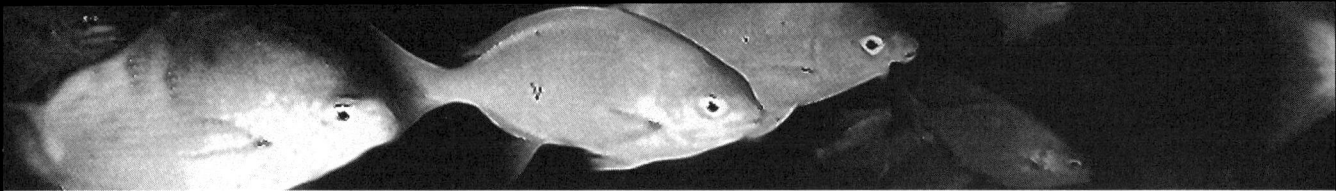

```
        cin >> guess;
        ++turn;
        if (guess < number)
            cout << "Too low" << endl;
        else if (guess > number)
            cout << "Too high" << endl;
        else
        {
            cout << "You guessed the number in ";
            cout << turn << " turns" << endl << endl;
        }
    }
    while (guess != number);
}


/////////////////////////////////////////////////////////////
// PlayMemory()
/////////////////////////////////////////////////////////////
void PlayMemory(void)
{
    char numbers[20];
    char guess[20];
    int turn, done;

    clrscr();
    done = 0;
    turn = 0;
    do
    {
        numbers[turn] = toascii(random(10)+48);
        numbers[turn+1] = 0;
        gotoxy(1, 2);
        cout << numbers;
        delay(2000);
        gotoxy(1, 2);
        cout << "                    " << endl;
        cout << "Enter the correct sequence: ";
        cin >> guess;
        if (strcmp(guess, numbers) != 0)
        {
            cout << "You were able to read and remember ";
            cout << turn << " digits" << endl << endl;
            done = 1;
        }
        else
        {
            gotoxy(28, 3);
            cout << "                 ";
        }
        ++turn;
    }
    while (!done);
}
```

continues

Listing 2.7. Continued

```
/////////////////////////////////////////////////////////////
// DoQuit()
/////////////////////////////////////////////////////////////
void DoQuit(void)
{
    cout << "Thanks for playing!" << endl;
    exit(0);
}
```

When you run this program, you see the following menu:

```
GAME MENU
‾‾‾‾‾‾‾‾‾
1. Number Guess
2. Memory
3. Quit
```

Selections 1 and 2 run simple text games, and selection 3 exits the program. In the Number Guess game, you try to guess a number from 1 to 100 with the fewest number of tries. In the Memory game, you must read and remember a growing list of digits.

In `main()`, the program declares a three-element array of function pointers:

```
void (*games[3])(void);
```

Then, after calling `randomize()` to seed the random-number generator, the program assigns function addresses to each element of the array:

```
games[0] = PlayNumbers;
games[1] = PlayMemory;
games[2] = DoQuit;
```

Finally, after printing the menu, `main()` accepts input from the user and then uses that input as an index into the function pointer array, calling the appropriate function:

```
if ((choice > 0) && (choice < 4))
    (*games[choice-1])();
```

Because of the infinite `do` loop, the games continue until `DoQuit()` is called.

Variable Argument Lists

You may have spent some time puzzling over functions like `printf()`, which can take any number of arguments. No matter how many arguments you supply, as long as your format string is in good order, `printf()` manages to sort things out and generate exactly the formatted output you want. You might think that you can accomplish such a programming trick only with assembly language, but in fact you can easily implement variable argument lists in your own program—without ever struggling with `mov`, `pop`, or `loopne` instructions.

Simulating a Variable Argument List with an Array

When you want to supply a variable number of values to a function, you can employ a couple of simple approaches—neither of which requires the use of variable argument lists. Instead, a simple pointer will do. For example, suppose that you want to write a function that sums a series of integer values, but you want to be able to call the function with a variable number of integers. To do this, you can create an array of integers and pass a pointer to this array to the function. Listing 2.8 is a program that demonstrates how you might do this.

Listing 2.8. POINTER8.CPP—A Program That Uses an Array to Pass a Variable Number of Values

```
///////////////////////////////////////////////////////////
// POINTER8.CPP: Pointer example program 8.
///////////////////////////////////////////////////////////

#include <iostream.h>
#include <conio.h>

// Function prototype.
int Add(int *ptr);

///////////////////////////////////////////////////////////
// main()
///////////////////////////////////////////////////////////
```

continues

Listing 2.8. Continued

```
int main(void)
{
    int array[] = { 1, 2, 3, 4, 5, -1 };

    clrscr();
    int total = Add(array);
    cout << "The total is " << total << endl;

    return 1;
}

//////////////////////////////////////////////////////////////
// Add()
//////////////////////////////////////////////////////////////
int Add(int *ptr)
{
    int i, sum = 0;

    i = 0;
    while (ptr[i] != -1)
        sum += ptr[i++];

    return sum;
}
```

This program first sets up an array of integers. You can have any number of integers in the array, but the last value must be a –1, which signals the end of the list. The `Add()` function accepts as its single parameter a pointer to this array of integers. In the function, the `while` loop iterates through the array, adding the values in the array until it gets to the –1, at which point the function returns the sum. You can probably immediately see the problem with this technique: You can never use –1 as a value to be summed. If you do, the function assumes that the –1 signals the end of the list. Listing 2.9 demonstrates a better way to handle the input array.

Listing 2.9. POINTER9.CPP—A Program That Uses an Argument Count with an Array

```
//////////////////////////////////////////////////////////////
// POINTER9.CPP: Pointer example program 9.
//////////////////////////////////////////////////////////////

#include <iostream.h>
#include <conio.h>
```

```
// Function prototype.
int Add(int *ptr);

//////////////////////////////////////////////////////////
// main()
//////////////////////////////////////////////////////////
int main(void)
{
   int array[] = { 5, 1, 2, 3, 4, 5 };

   clrscr();
   int total = Add(array);
   cout << "The total is " << total << endl;

   return 1;
}

//////////////////////////////////////////////////////////
// Add()
//////////////////////////////////////////////////////////
int Add(int *ptr)
{
   int count, sum = 0;

   count = ptr[0];
   for (int x=1; x<=count; ++x)
      sum += ptr[x];

   return sum;
}
```

In this version of the program, the first value in the source array is
not a number to be summed, but rather the number of values to be
summed. As before, the `Add()` function accepts as its single parameter a
pointer to the array. Now, however, it extracts the count from the first
element in the array, after which the `for` loop runs from 1 to `count`, sum-
ming the remaining values in the array.

If you need to work with a variable number of strings, you can use exactly the same technique as in Listing 2.8. Listing 2.10 shows just such
a program.

Note: In case you have forgotten, concatenating strings means to
join the strings together. For example, when you concatenate the
strings POLLY and CRACKER, you get POLLYCRACKER.

Listing 2.10. POINTR10.CPP—Concatenating a Variable Number of Strings

```
//////////////////////////////////////////////////////////
// POINTR10.CPP: Pointer example program 10.
//////////////////////////////////////////////////////////

#include <iostream.h>
#include <conio.h>
#include <string.h>

// Function prototype.
char *Join(char *ptr[]);

//////////////////////////////////////////////////////////
// main()
//////////////////////////////////////////////////////////
int main(void)
{
    char *array[] = { "THIS ", "IS ", "A ",  "TEST", 0};

    clrscr();
    char *str = Join(array);
    str = Join(array);
    cout << "The combined string: " << str << endl;

    return 1;
}

//////////////////////////////////////////////////////////
// Join()
//////////////////////////////////////////////////////////
char *Join(char *ptr[])
{
    int i = 0;
    static char s[81];

    s[0] = 0;
    while (ptr[i] != NULL)
        strcat(s, ptr[i++]);

    return s;
}
```

The source array in this program is an array of char pointers. The last value in the array is a NULL pointer, which signals the end of the list. The Join() function accepts as its parameter a pointer to this array. In the function, the while loop concatenates the strings pointed to by the pointers in the array. When the loop reaches the NULL pointer, the loop ends, and the function returns a pointer to the new string.

Programming a Variable Argument List

Although the examples shown in Listings 2.8 through 2.10 work well for simple applications, they are not really examples of variable argument lists, because each function has a set number of arguments: one. The fact that the argument happens to be an array of indeterminate length is just a technicality. The `printf()` function accepts a variable number of arguments, not just a single argument of variable length.

However, Borland C++ provides an easy way to implement variable argument lists. To take advantage of Borland's variable argument lists, you need to know about the `va_list` data type and three special macros: `va_start()`, `va_arg()`, and `va_end()`.

The `va_list` data type is defined in the STDARG.H header file as a `void` pointer. Before you can set up a variable argument list, you must declare a pointer of the `va_list` type:

```
va_list varList;
```

The `va_start()`, `va_arg()`, and `va_end()` macros also are defined in the STDARG.H header file, so you must `#include` this file in your program if you want to use variable argument lists.

The macro `va_start()` initializes the `va_list` argument pointer to the address of the argument list and notes the number of arguments in the list. You call the `va_start()` macro as follows:

```
va_start(varList, num);
```

In this example, `varList` is a `va_list` pointer, and `num` is the name of the last fixed parameter passed to the function, which, in the examples in this chapter, is the number of arguments in the list.

After you have called `va_start()` to set up the variable argument list, you can use `va_arg()` to retrieve arguments from the list:

```
va_arg(varList, type);
```

Here, `varList` is a `va_list` pointer, and `type` is the data type of the argument that you're retrieving. When you call `va_arg()`, not only does the macro return the argument that you requested, but it also changes the

variable list pointer so that it points to the next argument in the list. To retrieve all the arguments in the list, you call `va_arg()` the number of times indicated by the variable list count.

When you retrieve the last argument from the list, you must call `va_end()`. Otherwise, when you try to return from the function using the variable argument list, you may cause serious problems in your program. To call `va_end()`, you supply the `va_list` pointer, `varList`, as the macro's single argument:

```
va_end(varList);
```

If you're a little confused, Listing 2.11 should help you understand variable argument lists. This program uses variable argument lists to sum a series of integers and to concatenate a number of strings.

Listing 2.11. POINTR11.CPP—A Program That Uses Variable Argument Lists

```
/////////////////////////////////////////////////////////////
// POINTR11.CPP: Pointer example program 11.
/////////////////////////////////////////////////////////////

#include <iostream.h>
#include <conio.h>
#include <string.h>
#include <stdarg.h>

// Function prototypes.
int Add(int count, ... );
char *Join(int count, ... );

/////////////////////////////////////////////////////////////
// main()
/////////////////////////////////////////////////////////////
int main(void)
{
    clrscr();

    int total = Add(5, 1, 2, 3, 4, 5);
    cout << "The total is " << total << endl;

    total = Add(7, 1, 2, 3, 4, 5, 6, 7);
    cout << "The total is " << total << endl;

    char *str = Join(4, "THIS ", "IS ", "A ", "TEST");
    cout << "Joined string: " << str << endl;
```

```
    str = Join(5, "THIS ", "IS ", "THE ",
        "SECOND ", "TEST");
    cout << "Joined string: " << str << endl;

    return 1;
}

///////////////////////////////////////////////////////////
// Add()
///////////////////////////////////////////////////////////
int Add(int count, ...)
{
    va_list varList;
    int sum = 0;

    va_start(varList, count);
    for (int x=0; x<count; ++x)
        sum += va_arg(varList, int);
    va_end(varList);

    return sum;
}

///////////////////////////////////////////////////////////
// Join()
///////////////////////////////////////////////////////////
char *Join(int count, ...)
{
    va_list varList;
    static char s[81];

    va_start(varList, count);
    s[0] = 0;
    for (int x=0; x<count; ++x)
        strcat(s, va_arg(varList, char *));
    va_end(varList);

    return s;
}
```

This program includes two functions that use variable argument lists:
one that sums a series of integers, and one that concatenates a list of
strings. Notice the functions' prototypes near the top of the program.
The program declares the functions as you normally would, except that
it uses ellipses to indicate that the functions are to be called with a
variable number of arguments.

The main program calls these functions twice, both times with a different number of arguments, so you can see the variable argument lists in action. The program calls the `Add()` function like this:

```
int total = Add(5, 1, 2, 3, 4, 5);
```

The first argument is the number of arguments in the list. The remaining arguments are the values that the function should sum. You can have the function sum as many values as you want, as long as the first argument indicates the correct count. In `Add()`, the program declares a `va_list` pointer named `varList`, and then initializes the variable argument list by calling `va_start()`:

```
va_start(varList, count);
```

A `for` loop then retrieves each argument from the list, and sums the arguments as it goes:

```
for (int x=0; x<count; ++x)
    sum += va_arg(varList, int);
```

Finally, before returning the sum, the function calls `va_end()` to clean things up:

```
va_end(varList);
```

The main program calls `Join()`, which concatenates a variable number of strings:

```
char *str = Join(4, "THIS ", "IS ", "A ", "TEST");
```

Here, the first argument is the number of strings to concatenate, followed by the strings themselves. Again, the function can accept any number of arguments. As in `Add()`, `Join()` calls `va_start()` to initialize the variable argument list, and then loops until it has retrieved all the strings in the list (actually, the list consists of pointers to strings, not the strings themselves), concatenating them as it goes. The function then calls `va_end()` to clean up, and returns a pointer to the string. (Notice that the function declares the string as `static`. This ensures that the string is still around after the function exits.)

That's all you need to know about variable argument lists. You can even implement lists that contain different types of data. Just be sure that when you call `va_arg()` to retrieve an argument from the list, you get the correct data type.

From Here...

Pointers can be mysterious and perplexing if you don't understand exactly how to use them. But as you have seen, pointers provide C++ with immense power, enabling you to write programs that would be difficult, if not impossible, to write with some other programming languages. C++ is a high-level language that provides much of the flexibility of assembly language. The greater portion of that flexibility is due to pointers.

For additional information, use these tips:

➤ For information about using pointers to optimize your programs, see Chapter 4, "Optimizing C."

➤ For a discussion on the dangers of using null pointers in your programs, and ways of avoiding them, see Chapter 6, "Writing Bug-Free Code."

➤ For tips on debugging code containing pointers and checking for errors involving pointers, see Chapter 7, "Debugging Tips and Tricks."

➤ For information on pointers and the heap, see Chapter 9, "K&R Implementation Secrets."

➤ For a discussion of near pointers versus far pointers, see Chapter 10, "Extending K&R's C."

➤ For information on character pointers, see Chapter 17, "Mastering Templates."

Turbocharging Recursion

by *Clayton Walnum*

During your programming career, you've probably heard the words "divide and conquer" as often as a mouse hunts for food. This is because experienced programmers know that writing a large program can be a psychologically draining challenge. When you think about all that goes into a full-length program, it's easy to become overwhelmed by the magnitude of the job. So just as you read a book page by page or clean a house room by room, you write a program one function at a time. This way, you can understand a huge task that might otherwise be beyond your abilities to grasp.

You can adopt the divide-and-conquer strategy in several ways, including using object-oriented programming and structured programming. *Recursion*, the subject of this chapter, is another technique you can use to break complex tasks into their components. Using recursion, you can take a repetitive task and reduce it to a single step that is repeated again and again until you obtain the desired result.

In this chapter, you learn how recursion can be used to replace complex code with short and elegant functions. You also use recursion in a full-length program (a game!), thus applying what you've learned to a practical case. Finally, the chapter concludes with a more sophisticated example of recursion, a parser for solving complex mathematical expressions.

Recursion: Barrels within Barrels

You've probably run into recursion many times. You may not, however, have been sure how recursion can simplify a programming task. In this section, you learn how recursion works, the first step in applying recursion to your own programming problems. Later in this chapter, you apply what you've learned in a full-length program.

In general, recursive objects refer to themselves. For example, if someone asked you to define "irony" and you said "it's when something is ironical," you'd be giving a recursive definition, one that keeps looping back in on itself. It's recursive because a word in the definition leads right back to word you're trying to define.

In programming, a recursive function is simply one that calls itself. But just as the above definition of the word "irony" is useless, so too is a recursive function that keeps coming back to itself. You need some way, eventually, of breaking out of the recursive function.

You can sum all this up with the following definition of a recursive function:

> ➤ A recursive function calls itself.

> ➤ A recursive function must contain a conditional statement that breaks the recursive cycle.

Consider the value 10^3. The result of the exponentiation is calculated by multiplying 10 by itself three times: 10*10*10. You can use a `for` loop to calculate this value, but that's much too pedestrian for power

programmers. Instead, you can perform this multiplication operation recursively. Listing 3.1 includes a recursive function, `Power()`, which calculates the value of any integer raised to a positive integer exponent.

Listing 3.1. POWER.CPP—A Recursive Exponentiation Example

```cpp
/////////////////////////////////////////////////////////
// POWER.CPP: Simple recursion demonstration.
/////////////////////////////////////////////////////////

#include <iostream.h>
#include <conio.h>

// Function prototype.
int Power(int num, int exp);

/////////////////////////////////////////////////////////
// main()
/////////////////////////////////////////////////////////
int main(void)
{
  cout << Power(10,3) << '\n';
  getch();
  return 1;
}

/////////////////////////////////////////////////////////
// Power()
//
// This is a recursive function that returns the value of
// num to the power of exp.
/////////////////////////////////////////////////////////
int Power(int num, int exp)
{
  if (exp == 1)
     return num;
  else
     return num * Power(num, exp-1);
}
```

Examine this short program carefully. Although the `Power()` function is only a few lines long, a lot more is going on than may at first be apparent. Basically, this function repeatedly calls itself with smaller and smaller values of `exp`, until `exp` equals 1. At this point, instead of calling itself again, `Power()` simply returns the value `num`. (In the 10^3 example, `num` is 10.) Notice that no calculations are performed until the recursion is

as deep as it can go. Then it returns 10 to the previous invocation of `Power()`, which multiplies that return value by 10. The result (100) is passed on to the first invocation, which also multiplies it by 10, giving the final result of 1,000.

Confused? Figure 3.1 helps dispel the mystery. Starting at the top of the figure, `Power()` is called with the parameters 10 and 3. In the first call to `Power()`, the `if` statement examines `exp` and finds it to be 3, so the `else` statement executes. In the `else` statement, `num` is multiplied by the value returned from `Power(num, exp[nd]1)`.

The function can't perform the multiplication until it gets a return value from `Power()`, however, so it drops down to the second call to `Power()`, which gets the parameters 10 and 2. Again, the `if` statement is evaluated and program execution drops down to the `else` statement, which multiplies `num` by yet another call to `Power()`, this time with the parameters 10 and 1.

This brings the program to the third call to `Power()`, shown in the bottom box. This call gets the parameters 10 and 1. This time the `if` statement finds that `exp` is 1, so it immediately returns the value of `num`, which in this case is 10.

Notice that the program has performed no multiplication operations because it has had no result from `Power()`. Instead, it has simply called `Power()` `exp` times. The multiplication takes place as the program works its way back out of the recursions. The third recursion returns 10 to the second recursion, where this 10 is multiplied by `num`. The result of 100 is returned to the first call to `Power()`, which also multiplies the result by `num`. The result of 1,000 is finally returned to your original call.

Power (10,3);

```
int Power (int num,int exp)
{
    if (exp = 1) return num;
    else return num * Power(num,exp-1);
}
```
— 1000 —

Power (10,2);

```
int Power (int num, int exp)
{
    if (exp = 1) return num;
    else return num * Power(num,exp-1);
}
```
—100—

Power (10,1);

```
int Power (int num, int exp)
{
    if (exp = 1) return num;
    else return num * Power(num,exp-1);
}
```
—10—

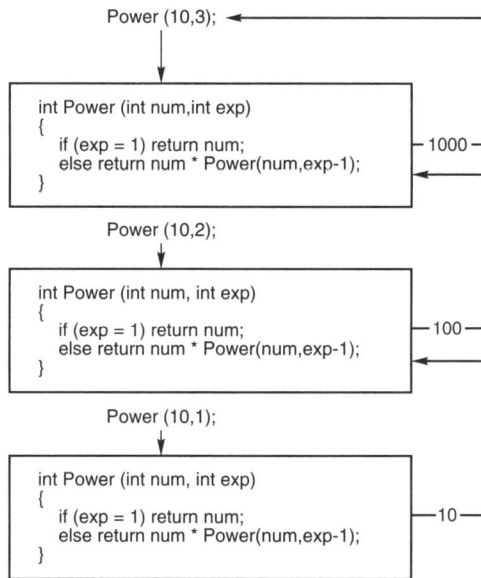

Fig. 3.1. Solving 10^3 recursively.

Caution: Always be aware that you place a lot of data on the stack when using recursive routines. Moreover, the more parameters required by the recursive routines, the fewer number of stack frames fit on the stack, which limits even further the number of recursive calls you can make. To avoid stack problems, recursive functions should use as few parameters as possible. Be especially careful of passing large data structures such as arrays as parameters in a recursive function. If you need to use a large data structure as a parameter to a recursive function, pass it by reference (which passes only the data's address) not by value (which passes the contents of the entire data structure).

An Example Application: Trap Hunt

That takes care of all the work. Now for a little fun. Listing 3.2 is a puzzle game called *Trap Hunt*, shown in figure 3.2. When you compile and run the program, the main screen appears with 400 buttons in a 25x16 grid. To win the game, you must find the 60 traps hidden under these buttons.

Listing 3.2. TRAPHUNT.CPP—The Trap Hunt Program

```cpp
/////////////////////////////////////////////////////////
// TRAP HUNT
// by Clayton Walnum
// Written with Borland C++
/////////////////////////////////////////////////////////

#include <stdlib.h>
#include <graphics.h>
#include <iostream.h>
#include <conio.h>
#include <dos.h>
#include "windw.h"
#include "event.h"
#include "mous.h"
#include "butn.h"

#define TRUE         1
#define FALSE        0
#define TRAP        -1    // Value for a trap square.
#define BLANK        0    // Value for a blank square.
#define TRAP_CNT    60    // # of traps on the board.
#define MAXCOLS     25    // # of columns on the board.
#define MAXROWS     16    // # of rows on the board.
#define XOFF        44    // Offset from left of first button.
#define YOFF        60    // Offset from top of first button.

// Game board array.
int board[MAXROWS][MAXCOLS];

// Numbers for marking numbered squares.
char *numbrs[5] = {"1", "2", "3", "4"};

int repeat,        // Controls main game loop.
    buttons_left,  // # of unpressed buttons on the board.
    butn_num,      // Total # of buttons on the board.
    mark_cnt,      // # of marked buttons.
    good_marks;    // # of correctly marked buttons.

EventMsg eventMsg;
```

```
// Function prototypes
int KeyEvent(void);
void GetEvent(EventMsg &eventMsg);
void DispatchEvent(EventMsg eventMsg);
void CheckButton(EventMsg eventMsg);
void ShowSquare(int x, int y);
void DoBlanks(int x, int y);
void Check4Blank(int x, int y);
void Init(void);
void Start(void);
void InitMouse(void);
void DrawScreen(void);
void PlaceTraps(void);
void PlaceCounts(void);
void DrawNumbers (int x, int y);
void DeleteButns(void);
void FallIntoTrap(int x, int y);
void ShowBoard(void);
void GameOver(void);
void DrawTrap(int c, int r);
void DrawNoTrap(int c, int r);
void MarkButn(int x, int y);
int CountTraps(int c, int r);

// Array of button pointers for game board.
Butn *butn[MAXCOLS*MAXROWS];

// Display windows and buttons.
CapWindw wnd1(0, 0, 639, 479, TRUE, FALSE, "TRAP HUNT");
Button butn1(528, 425, "^QUIT");
Button butn2(450, 425, "^START");

////////////////////////////////////////////////////////
// Main program.
////////////////////////////////////////////////////////
void main(void)
{
  // Initialize game, mouse, and screen.
  Init();

  // Repeat event loop until Quit.
  repeat = TRUE;
  while (repeat)
  {
    if ((buttons_left == 0) || (mark_cnt == TRAP_CNT))
      GameOver();
    GetEvent(eventMsg);
    DispatchEvent(eventMsg);
  }
  DeleteButns();
  closegraph();
}
```

continues

Listing 3.2. Continued

```cpp
//////////////////////////////////////////////////////
// Init()
//
// This function performs general program initialization.
// It initializes the graphics driver and mouse, then
// calls the Start() function, which initializes a
// new game.
//////////////////////////////////////////////////////
void Init(void)
{
  int gdriver = VGA, gmode = VGAHI, errorcode;

  errorcode = registerbgidriver(EGAVGA_driver);
  if (errorcode < 0)
  {
    cout << "Graphics not initialized: " << errorcode << '\n';
    cout << "Press any key.";
    getch();
    abort();
  }
  initgraph(&gdriver, &gmode, "");
  if ( (errorcode = graphresult()) != grOk)
  {
    cout << "Graphics not initialized: " << errorcode << '\n';
    cout << "Press any key.";
    getch();
    abort();
  }
  InitMouse();
  Start();
}


//////////////////////////////////////////////////////
// DispatchEvent()
//
// This function checks the current event message and
// branches to the function chosen by the user.
//////////////////////////////////////////////////////
void DispatchEvent(EventMsg eventMsg)
{
  mouse.ButtonUp();

  // Check whether START button was clicked.
  if (butn1.Clicked(eventMsg))
    repeat = FALSE;

  // Check whether QUIT button was pressed.
  else if (butn2.Clicked(eventMsg))
  {
    DeleteButns();
    Start();
  }
```

```
    // Cycle through all the buttons on the board,
    // to check whether one has been pressed.
    else
      for (int bn=0; bn<butn_num; ++bn)
        if ( !butn[bn]->Pressed())
        if (butn[bn]->Clicked(eventMsg))
          CheckButton(eventMsg);
}

//////////////////////////////////////////////////////////////
// GameOver()
//
// This function is called when the player finds all
// the traps on the board or marks the maximum number
// of buttons allowed. It displays a dialog box and
// then resets the variables buttons_left and mark_cnt
// to prevent main() from calling GameOver() again.
//////////////////////////////////////////////////////////////
void GameOver(void)
{
  // If all the buttons have been pressed or the number
  // of correctly marked buttons matches the number of
  // traps, the player has won the game.
  if ((buttons_left == 0) || (good_marks == TRAP_CNT))
  {
    OKWindw wndw("YOU WIN!", "Congratulations! You",
                 "found all the traps.");
    wndw.DrawWindow();
    wndw.RunWindow();
  }

  // Otherwise, the player loses, because he or she
  // has used up all marks without marking the
  // correct buttons.
  else
  {
    OKWindw *wndw = new OKWindw ("YOU LOSE",
           "You've marked the maximum",
           "number of buttons.");
    wndw->DrawWindow();
    wndw->RunWindow();
    delete wndw;
    ShowBoard();
  }

  // These variables are reset so the main game
  // loop will not re-call this function.
  buttons_left = MAXCOLS * MAXROWS;
  mark_cnt = 0;
}

//////////////////////////////////////////////////////////////
// Start()
```

continues

Listing 3.2. Continued

```
//
// This function initializes all variables needed to
// begin a new game, including setting the playing board
// to all blanks, calling the functions that place and
// count the traps, and calling the function that draws
// the main screen.
//////////////////////////////////////////////////////////
void Start(void)
{
  // Initialize the random-number generator.
  randomize();

  // Set the entire game board to blanks.
  for ( int col=0; col<MAXCOLS; ++col )
    for ( int row=0; row<MAXROWS; ++row )
      board[row][col] = BLANK;

  // Place traps and numbers on game board.
  PlaceTraps ();
  PlaceCounts ();

  // Draw game screen and init some variables.
  DrawScreen();
  buttons_left = MAXCOLS * MAXROWS;
  mark_cnt = good_marks = 0;
}


//////////////////////////////////////////////////////////
// CheckButton()
//
// This function checks to see what is beneath the
// selected button, calling the appropriate function
// to display the part of the puzzle chosen.
//////////////////////////////////////////////////////////
void CheckButton(EventMsg eventMsg)
{
  // Translate mouse-button coords to column and
  // row coords for the playing board.
  int x = (eventMsg.mx - XOFF) / 22;
  int y = (eventMsg.my - YOFF) / 22;

  // If right mouse button pressed, mark
  // clicked button for a trap...
  if (eventMsg.button == RIGHT)
  {
    butn[y*MAXCOLS+x]->MarkButton();
    buttons_left -= 1;
    mark_cnt += 1;
    if (board[y][x] == TRAP)
      good_marks += 1;
  }
```

```
  // ...or if button pressed hides a trap, end game...
  else if (board[y][x] == TRAP)
    FallIntoTrap(x, y);

  // ...or else show what's under the square.
  else ShowSquare(x, y);
}


//////////////////////////////////////////////////////////
// FallIntoTrap()
//
// This function is called when the player selects a
// button hiding a trap. It first displays a dialog
// box, informing the player of the mistake, then
// reveals all the squares on the board.
//////////////////////////////////////////////////////////
void FallIntoTrap(int x, int y)
{
  // Draw trap image.
  DrawTrap(x, y);

  // Display and run dialog box.
  OKWindw *wndw = new OKWindw ("YOU LOSE",
        "Whoops! You fell", "into a trap!");
  wndw->DrawWindow();
  wndw->RunWindow();
  delete wndw;

  // Reveal all the squares on the board.
  ShowBoard();
}


//////////////////////////////////////////////////////////
// ShowSquare()
//
// This function shows the contents of the selected
// square. If the square is blank, the recursive
// function DoBlanks() is called to show all the blank
// squares connected to the selected square.
//////////////////////////////////////////////////////////
void ShowSquare (int x, int y)
{
  int b = board[y][x];

  // If the square contains a blank, call the
  // function to show all connecting blanks.
  if (!b) DoBlanks(x, y);

  // Otherwise show the square's number.
  else DrawNumbers(x, y);
}
```

continues

Listing 3.2. Continued

```
//////////////////////////////////////////////////////
// ShowBoard()
//
// This function reveals all the squares on the board.
//////////////////////////////////////////////////////
void ShowBoard(void)
{
  // Cycle through all the buttons on the board.
  for (int c=0; c<MAXCOLS; ++c)
    for (int r=0; r<MAXROWS; ++r)
    {
        // If the square contains a trap and the
        // button was not marked, show the trap.
        if ((board[r][c]==TRAP) && (!butn[r*MAXCOLS+c]->Marked()))
        DrawTrap(c, r);

        // If the button is marked, but the square doesn't
        // contain a trap, display the error symbol.
        else if ((butn[r*MAXCOLS+c]->Marked()) &&
              (board[r][c]!=TRAP))
        DrawNoTrap(c, r);

        // If the square contains a number, show it.
        else if (board[r][c] > 0)
        DrawNumbers(c, r);

        // If the square contains a blank, show it.
        else if (board[r][c] == 0)
        butn[r*MAXCOLS+c]->PressButton();
    }
}


//////////////////////////////////////////////////////
// DoBlanks()
//
// This function reveals all the blank squares
// connected to a selected square.
//////////////////////////////////////////////////////
void DoBlanks (int x, int y)
{
  butn[y*MAXCOLS+x]->PressButton();
  buttons_left -= 1;

  // Move one square up.
  if (y != 0)
    Check4Blank(x, y-1);

  // Move one square up and to the right.
  if ((y != 0) && (x != MAXCOLS-1))
    Check4Blank(x+1, y-1);
```

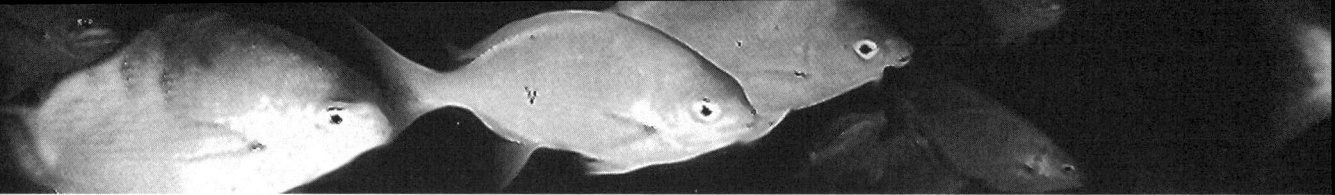

```
    // Move one square right.
    if (x != MAXCOLS-1)
      Check4Blank(x+1, y);

    // Move one square down and to the right.
    if ((y != MAXROWS-1) && (x != MAXCOLS-1))
      Check4Blank(x+1, y+1);

    // Move one square down.
    if (y != MAXROWS-1)
      Check4Blank(x, y+1);

    // Move one square down and to the left.
    if ((y != MAXROWS-1) && (x != 0))
      Check4Blank(x-1, y+1);

    // Move one square left.
    if (x != 0)
      Check4Blank(x-1, y);

    // Move one square up and to the left.
    if ((y != 0) && (x != 0))
      Check4Blank(x-1, y-1);
}


////////////////////////////////////////////////////////
// Check4Blank()
//
// This function checks the square at x,y for a blank.
// If it finds one, it makes a recursive call to
// DoBlanks() to traverse all the blank squares in the
// current direction. If the square is not a blank, it
// calls DrawNumbers() to reveal the contents of the
// square.
////////////////////////////////////////////////////////
void Check4Blank(int x, int y)
{
  if ((board[y][x] == BLANK) &&
      (!butn[y*MAXCOLS+x]->Pressed()))
    DoBlanks (x, y);
  else if ((!butn[y*MAXCOLS+x]->Pressed()) &&
           (!butn[y*MAXCOLS+x]->Marked()))
    DrawNumbers (x, y);
}


////////////////////////////////////////////////////////
// DrawTrap()
//
// This function draws the image that represents a trap.
////////////////////////////////////////////////////////
void DrawTrap(int c, int r)
{
  butn[r*MAXCOLS+c]->PressButton();
  setcolor(RED);
```

continues

Listing 3.2. Continued

```
      setfillstyle(SOLID_FILL, BLACK);
      setlinestyle(SOLID_LINE, 0, NORM_WIDTH);
      int sx = c*22+XOFF;
      int sy = r*22+YOFF;
      mouse.HideMouse();
      fillellipse(sx+10, sy+10, 6, 6);
      mouse.ShowMouse();
}


///////////////////////////////////////////////////////
// DrawNoTrap()
//
// This function draws the image that represents an
// incorrect trap-marked square.
///////////////////////////////////////////////////////
void DrawNoTrap(int c, int r)
{
  butn[r*MAXCOLS+c]->PressButton();
  setlinestyle(SOLID_LINE, 0, THICK_WIDTH);
  setcolor(RED);
  int sx = (c*22)+XOFF;
  int sy = (r*22)+YOFF;
  circle(sx+10, sy+10, 8);
  moveto(sx+4, sy+4);
  lineto(sx+16, sy+17);
}


///////////////////////////////////////////////////////
// DrawNumbers()
//
// This function is called when the player selects a
// square containing a number. It draws the square and
// its number.
///////////////////////////////////////////////////////
void DrawNumbers (int x, int y)
{
  butn[y*MAXCOLS+x]->PressButton();
  setcolor(BLUE);
  int n = board[y][x];
  int sx = (x*22) + XOFF;
  int sy = (y*22) + YOFF;
  mouse.HideMouse();
  outtextxy(sx+7, sy+7, numbrs[n-1]);
  mouse.ShowMouse();
  buttons_left -= 1;
}


///////////////////////////////////////////////////////
// DrawScreen()
//
// This function draws the main screen.
///////////////////////////////////////////////////////
```

```
void DrawScreen(void)
{
  // Draw main display.
  wnd1.DrawWindow();
  butn1.DrawWindow();
  butn2.DrawWindow();

  // Create and display all the game-board buttons.
  butn_num = 0;
  for (int y=0; y<MAXROWS; ++y)
    for (int x=0; x<MAXCOLS; ++x)
    {
      butn[butn_num] = new Butn(x*22+XOFF, y*22+YOFF);
      butn[butn_num]->DrawWindow();
      ++butn_num;
    }
}


///////////////////////////////////////////////////////
// PlaceTraps()
//
// This function places traps on an empty playing board.
// The traps are placed so that no more than four traps
// are adjacent to any square.
///////////////////////////////////////////////////////
void PlaceTraps(void)
{
  int n;

  // Loop for each trap on the board.
  for ( int z=0; z<TRAP_CNT; ++z )
  {
    int okay = FALSE;

    // The while loop will repeat until the
    // trap is properly placed.
    while (!okay)
    {
      // Get a random column and row for the trap.
      int c = random(MAXCOLS);
      int r = random(MAXROWS);

      // If there isn't already a trap at this
      // location, calculate the maximum and minimum
      // coordinates for every square adjacent to
      // this one.
      if (board[r][c] != TRAP)
      {
      int yl = r - 1;
      int yh = r + 1;
      int xl = c - 1;
      int xh = c + 1;
      if (xl == -1) xl = 0;
```

continues

An Example Application: Trap Hunt **105**

Listing 3.2. Continued

```
        if (xh == MAXCOLS) xh = MAXCOLS-1;
        if (yl == -1) yl = 0;
        if (yh == MAXROWS) yh = MAXROWS-1;

        okay = TRUE;

        // Count the traps surrounding every adjacent
        // square to be sure that no trap count goes
        // over four.
        for (int y=yl; y<yh+1; ++y )
          for (int x=xl; x<xh+1; ++x )
          {
            n = CountTraps(x, y);
            if (n > 3) okay = FALSE;
          }

          // If all trap counts are low enough,
          // place the trap.
          if (okay) board[r][c] = TRAP;
        }
      }
    }
}

//////////////////////////////////////////////////////
// PlaceCounts()
//
// This function counts the number of traps adjacent to
// each square on the board.
//////////////////////////////////////////////////////
void PlaceCounts(void)
{
    // Cycle through every square on the board,
    // counting adjacent traps.
    for ( int row=0; row<MAXROWS; ++row )
      for ( int col=0; col<MAXCOLS; ++col )
        if ( board[row][col] != TRAP )
          board[row][col] = CountTraps(col, row);
}

//////////////////////////////////////////////////////
// CountTraps()
//
// This function counts the traps adjacent to the square
// located at c,r.
//////////////////////////////////////////////////////
int CountTraps(int c, int r)
{
  // Calculate the minimum and maximum coords
  // for every square adjacent to the one you're
  // checking.
```

```cpp
  int yl = r - 1;
  int yh = r + 1;
  int xl = c - 1;
  int xh = c + 1;
  if (xl == -1) xl = 0;
  if (xh == MAXCOLS) xh = MAXCOLS-1;
  if (yl == -1) yl = 0;
  if (yh == MAXROWS) yh = MAXROWS-1;

  // Count all traps in adjacent squares.
  int count = 0;
  for (int y=yl; y<yh+1; ++y)
    for (int x=xl; x<xh+1; ++x)
      if (((x != c) || (y != r)) &&
          (board[y][x] == TRAP))
        ++count;
  return count;
}


//////////////////////////////////////////////////////////
// DeleteButns()
//
// This function deletes all buttons from the playing
// board.
//////////////////////////////////////////////////////////
void DeleteButns()
{
  for (int x=0; x<butn_num; ++x)
    if (butn[x] != NULL)
      delete butn[x];
}


//////////////////////////////////////////////////////////
// InitMouse()
//
// This function initializes the user's mouse.
//////////////////////////////////////////////////////////
void InitMouse(void) {
  if (!mouse.GotMouse()) {
    cout << "You have no mouse.\n";
    cout << "Press any key.";
    getch();
  }
  mouse.SetLimits(0,getmaxx(),0,getmaxy());
  mouse.ShowMouse();
}
```

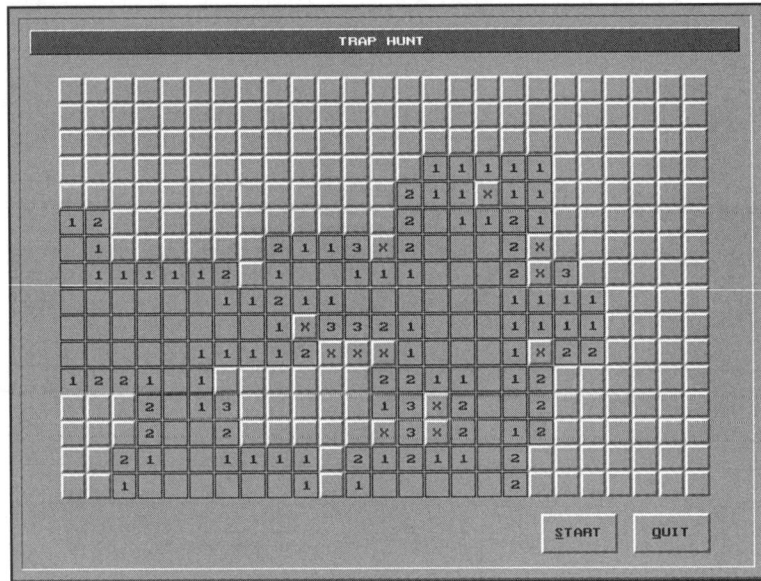

Fig. 3.2. The Trap Hunt game board.

Each square on the game board contains one of three things: a trap, a number, or a blank. To start, click a button on the game board with your left mouse button (*not* the right button). If the button you choose reveals a trap, you lose the game (whew, that was fast!), and the entire game board is revealed. If the button reveals a blank square, every blank square connected to it is shown, up to and including bordering number squares. If a button reveals a number, this number informs you of the number of traps adjacent to the selected button.

Try to locate all the traps by using the number clues. When you locate a trapped button, click it with the right mouse button (not the left button). This marks the button with a red X and locks the button so that it can no longer be clicked. You are apportioned only 60 markers, exactly enough for the traps, so you can't waste even one. If you use your markers before you've located all the traps, the game ends.

Note: The Trap Hunt program includes several source code files which, for the sake of brevity, are not all listed in this book. The additional files are EVENT.H and EVENT.CPP, which are a keyboard and mouse event handler; MOUS.H and MOUS.CPP, which are a C++ class for controlling a mouse in a DOS program; WINDW.H and WINDW.CPP, which are a library of DOS graphical windows and buttons; and BUTN.H and BUTN.CPP, which are a special button class inherited from the buttons defined in WINDW.CPP. These additional files are on this book's disk, along with TRAPHUNT.CPP. A quick reference for the WINDW library also can be found on this book's disk under the file name WINDW.TXT.

To compile Trap Hunt, you must be sure to include all the above .CPP files in your project, as well as EGAVGA.OBJ and GRAPHICS.LIB. EGAVGA.OBJ is included with the other Trap Hunt files. GRAPHICS.LIB comes with Borland C++ and can be found in the BC4\LIB directory.

At the bottom of the screen are the START and QUIT buttons. You can start a new game by clicking the START button, and you can exit the program by clicking the QUIT button. Neither button warns you before it performs its function, so you can't undo your action if you accidentally click one during a game.

Recursion and Trees

The Trap Hunt program contains an excellent example of recursion that you can study to get further insight into this handy and interesting programming technique. In a previous discussion of ways to use recursion, tree-traversal routines were mentioned. This is the type of recursion used in Trap Hunt.

What's a *tree*? A tree is a data structure that connects a collection of items, called *nodes*. A tree starts with a root node. Connected to the root are any number of child nodes. Each child node, too, can have any number of its own child nodes. This hierarchy continues down the tree until a child node has no children of its own.

Figure 3.3 shows a binary tree, which is a special type of tree that has left and right children for every node except the base nodes. Node A is the root node. Nodes B and C, which are called siblings because they are on the same level of the tree, are A's child nodes. Nodes B and C also have two child nodes each, the base nodes D, E, F, and G.

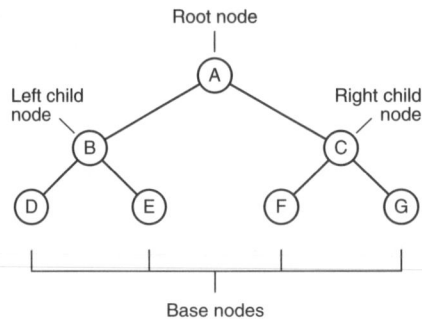

Fig. 3.3. A binary tree.

Recursion is particularly useful for traversing trees—that is, for following every path in the tree from the root to the base nodes. Listing 3.3 creates and traverses the binary tree shown in figure 3.3. The program's output follows:

```
At node A
At node B
At node D
At node E
At node C
At node F
At node G
```

Listing 3.3. TREE.CPP—Creating the Binary Tree Shown in Figure 3.3

```cpp
/////////////////////////////////////////////////////////
// TREE.CPP: An example of using recursion to traverse
//           a binary tree.
/////////////////////////////////////////////////////////

#include <stdlib.h>
#include <iostream.h>
#include <conio.h>

// Structure for a tree node.
struct Node
{
  char name;
  Node *left, *right;
};

// A pointer to the tree.
Node *tree;

// Function prototypes.
void AddNodes(Node *node, char c1, char c2);
void TraverseTree(Node *n);

/////////////////////////////////////////////////////////
// main()
/////////////////////////////////////////////////////////
int main(void)
{
  tree = new Node;
  tree->name = 'A';
  AddNodes(tree, 'B', 'C');
  AddNodes(tree->left, 'D', 'E');
  AddNodes(tree->right, 'F', 'G');
  TraverseTree(tree);
  delete tree;
  getch();
  return 1;
}

/////////////////////////////////////////////////////////
// AddNodes()
/////////////////////////////////////////////////////////
void AddNodes(Node *node, char c1, char c2)
{
  Node *n = new Node;
  n->name = c1;
  n->left = NULL;
  n->right = NULL;
  node->left = n;
  n = new Node;
```

continues

An Example Application: Trap Hunt **111**

Listing 3.3. Continued

```
    n->name = c2;
    n->left = NULL;
    n->right = NULL;
    node->right = n;
}

//////////////////////////////////////////////////////////
// TraverseTree()
//////////////////////////////////////////////////////////
void TraverseTree(Node *n)
{
  cout << "At node " << n->name << '\n';
  if (n->left)
  {
    TraverseTree(n->left);
    delete n->left;
  }
  if (n->right)
  {
    TraverseTree(n->right);
    delete n->right;
  }
}
```

The program implements a node as a `struct` containing the node's label
and pointers to the node's left and right children. In `main()`, the program first creates the tree's root node, which is appropriately named
`tree`. Then it calls the `AddNodes()` function to create two child nodes
for `tree`. The program also calls `Addnodes()` (indirectly by way of the
`tree->left` and `tree->right` pointers) for each of `tree`'s child nodes to
create their child nodes.

There should be no need to go into the details of the tree construction.
What you must examine closely, though, is the recursive procedure
that traverses the tree structure. In Listing 3.3, that function is
`TraverseTree()`.

Here's how the recursion works:

1. The program calls `TraverseTree()` from `main()` with `tree`, which is a
   pointer to the tree's root node.

2. In `TraverseTree()`, the function first prints a message, showing which node it's currently examining. In this case, the node is A.

3. Then the function checks node A's `left` pointer. If it's not NULL, A has a left child, so the function calls `TraverseNode()` recursively to check that left child, which is B.

4. This call initiates a second invocation of `TraverseNode()`, in which a message for node B is printed and node B's `left` pointer is checked.

5. Because node B also has a left child, the program calls `TraverseNode()` yet again, this time for node D. In this third invocation of `TraverseTree()`, the program prints D's message and checks its `left` pointer.

6. D has no left child, so the program drops out of the first `if` and checks D's `right` pointer. D has no right child either. So the third invocation of `TraverseTree()` ends, and the program is back to the second, where it last checked B's `left` pointer.

7. The program is now finished with B's left child, D, so it deletes it and checks B's `right` pointer, only to discover that it has a right child, E. This means the program must call `TraverseTree()` to examine node E.

8. Because node E, like node D, has no left or right children, the program promptly returns to B, where it deletes E and steps back to the first invocation of `TraverseTree()`.

9. The program had last checked A's `left` pointer, so it can delete that left child and move to A's right child, C.

10. The right side of the tree is traversed the same way the left side was, by visiting C, F, and finally G.

11. At the end of the traversal, the program returns to A with all nodes examined and all nodes deleted, except the root node. The root node, `tree`, is deleted in `main()`.

Trap Hunt's Trees

Trap Hunt uses trees. How? When the player selects a blank square, the program must reveal all blank squares connected to it, as well as any number squares adjacent to blank squares. It does this by forming a tree and traversing the tree recursively.

The first step in forming the tree is to select the tree's root. Trap Hunt makes the selected square the root of the tree. When the program has selected this root node, all other squares on the board fall logically into a tree pattern (not a binary tree), as you'll soon see. No matter which square the user selects, the remaining squares can be thought of as a tree structure with the selected square as the root.

The program then calls a recursive routine to traverse the tree, starting at the root. Any node in the tree can have as many as seven child nodes. A child node, in this case, is an unpressed button covering either another blank square or a number. Number squares are the tree's base nodes—that is, the traversal never goes past a number square.

This tree traversal is more complex than the first example. In the binary tree, the program had to examine only left and right pointers for each node in a tree. In the game-board tree, the program must examine nodes in *eight* directions: up, up-right, right, right-down, down, left-down, left, and left-up. Still, except for extra recursive calls to the additional directions, the process is identical to the one you used for binary trees.

Listing 3.4 shows two functions in the Trap Hunt program that accomplish the tree traversal, DoBlanks() and Check4Blank().

Listing 3.4. The Functions That Traverse Trap Hunt's Trees

```
void DoBlanks (int x, int y)
{
  butn[y*MAXCOLS+x]->PressButton();
  buttons_left -= 1;

  // Move one square up.
  if (y != 0)
    Check4Blank(x, y-1);
```

```
    // Move one square up and to the right.
    if ((y != 0) && (x != MAXCOLS-1))
      Check4Blank(x+1, y-1);

    // Move one square right.
    if (x != MAXCOLS-1)
      Check4Blank(x+1, y);

    // Move one square down and to the right.
    if ((y != MAXROWS-1) && (x != MAXCOLS-1))
      Check4Blank(x+1, y+1);

    // Move one square down.
    if (y != MAXROWS-1)
      Check4Blank(x, y+1);

    // Move one square down and to the left.
    if ((y != MAXROWS-1) && (x != 0))
      Check4Blank(x-1, y+1);

    // Move one square left.
    if (x != 0)
      Check4Blank(x-1, y);

    // Move one square up and to the left.
    if ((y != 0) && (x != 0))
      Check4Blank(x-1, y-1);
}

void Check4Blank(int x, int y)
{
  if ((board[y][x] == BLANK) &&
      (!butn[y*MAXCOLS+x]->Pressed()))
    DoBlanks(x, y);
  else if ((!butn[y*MAXCOLS+x]->Pressed()) &&
         (!butn[y*MAXCOLS+x]->Marked()))
    DrawNumbers(x, y);
}
```

Although this code performs a recursive traversal of your game board's tree, there are no calls to DoBlanks() inside DoBlanks() and no calls to Check4Blank() inside Check4Blank(). How, then, is this routine recursive? Easy! DoBlanks() calls Check4Blank(), which then calls DoBlanks(). This circular pattern is recursive because new calls to DoBlanks() are made before previous invocations of DoBlanks() have ended. Neither of these functions is recursive, but together they form a recursive routine.

The `if` statements in the `DoBlanks()` function check that the recursion doesn't overrun the boundary of the game board. `DoBlanks()` also makes sure that all eight directions are checked. `DoBlanks()` selects the next square in the traversal and passes it to `Check4Blank()`, which decides what to do with the square. If the square is a blank and its button hasn't been pressed, `Check4Blank()` calls `DoBlanks()` recursively for the new blank square. Otherwise, if the square's button hasn't been pressed or marked, `Check4Blank()` calls `DrawNumbers()` to reveal the square's number.

This is probably very confusing, not because the concept is difficult to understand, but because it is difficult to follow the many recursions needed to traverse the tree. To help you understand Trap Hunt's tree-traversal routine, try the exercise in figure 3.4, which shows the Trap Hunt game screen immediately after the player has selected a blank square.

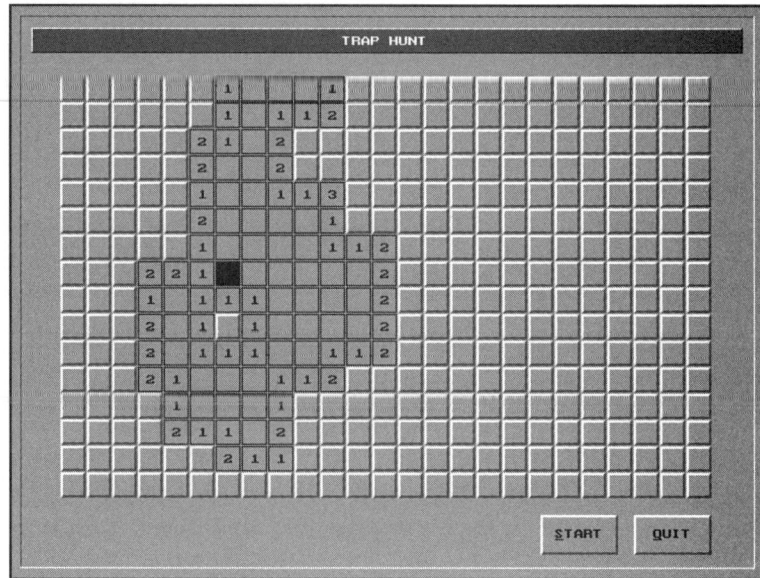

Fig. 3.4. Tree-traversal exercise.

At the point shown in the figure, the program has traversed the game-board tree, revealing blank squares and bordering number squares. The large black rectangle is the square the player originally chose. (During the game, there is no black rectangle. It was added to the figure for the exercise.) Get a pencil and draw the path that the traversal took to reveal the squares, using the source code for the `DoBlanks()` and `Check4Blank()` functions.

> **Tip:** Start the traversal by moving upward from the selected square. If you run into a numbered square, back up and try the next direction. Every new blank square you run into starts the process over again, because it results in a recursive call to `DoBlanks()`.

To get you started, figure 3.5 shows the first 14 squares in the traversal. The entire traversal is shown in figure 3.6.

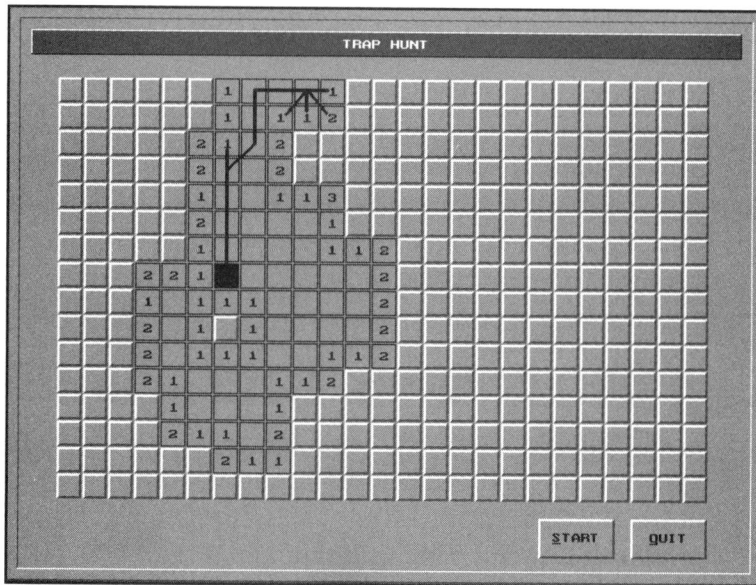

Fig. 3.5. The first 14 steps in the tree traversal.

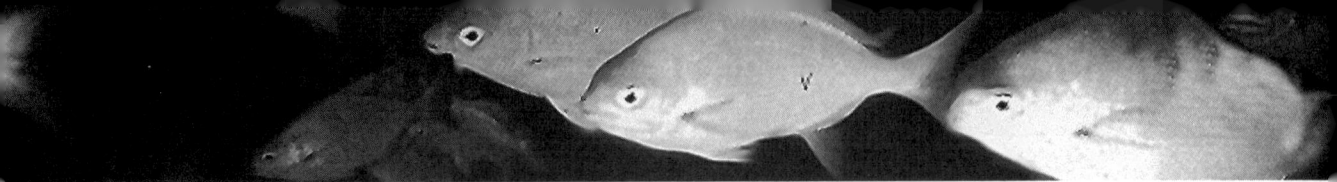

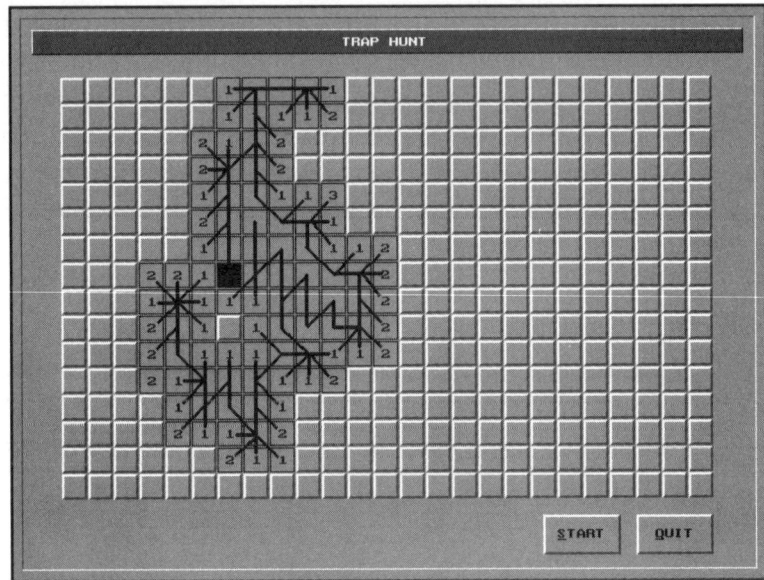

Fig. 3.6. The complete tree traversal.

The exercise in figure 3.4 may look like an immense task, but after you get the hang of it, you will be able to trace the traversal without even looking at the source code. When you can do that, you have a good understanding of how recursive tree traversal works (which is the whole point). And when you have that understanding, you are ready to tackle the next topic, which shows how recursion can be used to parse and evaluate mathematical formulas.

Using Recursion to Parse Formulas

Anyone who's ever written a program that must accept elaborate text input from a user knows how difficult it can be to change that input into usable data. *Parsing*—the process of analyzing text input and translating it into something the computer can understand—is a complex task. A complete tutorial on the subject of parsing could probably fill an encyclopedia. Unfortunately, this book doesn't have that much

space to dedicate to this important topic. This section, however, looks at one of the most useful forms of parsing: recursive descent parsing.

Look at this expression:

```
AVG(SQRT(7*ABS(AVG(-15,-20,-32.5))),SQRT(999))
```

What if your job was to write a program that could solve expressions like this? How would you go about it? Your first inclination might be to scan the characters comprising the expression, starting at the left and working your way to the right. However, because expressions like the preceding can contain any number of nested functions or operations, the process of keeping track of parentheses, not to mention the results of the operations within parentheses, would be clumsier than a blind date.

One solution to working with nested functions is to use a data structure like a stack as a temporary holding place, storing values to be used after operations with higher precedence have been solved. But there's a more elegant solution. Think about the structure of the example expression. It has expressions within expressions within expressions. Looks a lot like a recursion problem, doesn't it? You can use recursion to work your way to the deepest level of the expression and then solve the expression a step at a time as you work your way back out of the recursion.

Before you can solve an expression, though, you have to define exactly what an expression is.

Expressions as a Grammar

Your expressions can contain many types of functions and operations. This means you must develop a grammar for your expressions so that the user knows how your program expects an expression to be constructed. For example, if you were writing a spreadsheet program, your program, as well as the user, must know not only how basic mathematical operations are entered from the keyboard but also what built-in functions are available. Trying to write a parser without this information is like trying to make a cake without a recipe.

To define the syntax for expressions, you must think of expressions as language constructions. Just as a sentence is the expression of a concept in the English language, so an expression is the expression of a concept in a mathematical language. It's up to you, the author of the parser, to decide the rules of this mathematical language. To do this, you must identify the elements of the language and its hierarchical structure. After you've identified these important characteristics, you can define your language's formal rules, or *grammar*.

Think about what makes up an expression like the one you previously saw. First, it has a few built-in functions. `AVG()` returns the average of a list of numbers, `SQRT()` returns the square root of a number, and `ABS()` returns the absolute value of a number. Besides these functions, the example expression has multiplication (`*`), one of the basic mathematical operations that also includes addition, subtraction, and division (`+`,`-`, and `/`, respectively). The expression also contains parentheses for specifying operation precedence and enclosing function arguments. Finally, the expression contains values, which are expressed using a combination of digits, decimal points, and minus signs.

All of these items are the building blocks of an expression, but knowing them is not enough to define a grammar. You must know the proper way in which these elements can be combined to form valid expressions. In short, you must know the language's *syntax*. This syntax can be expressed in top-down, recursive form by using something called the *Backus-Naur Form*, explained in a section called "Backus-Naur Form" later in this chapter.

Defining Grammar Syntax

Every language is defined by its grammar. In the English language, you use letters to form words, words to form sentences, and sentences to form paragraphs. In addition, to organize these constructions, you use syntactical rules that define the way the elements of the language can be combined. Your mathematical language also can be defined as a grammar. You can identify the elements of your language and organize

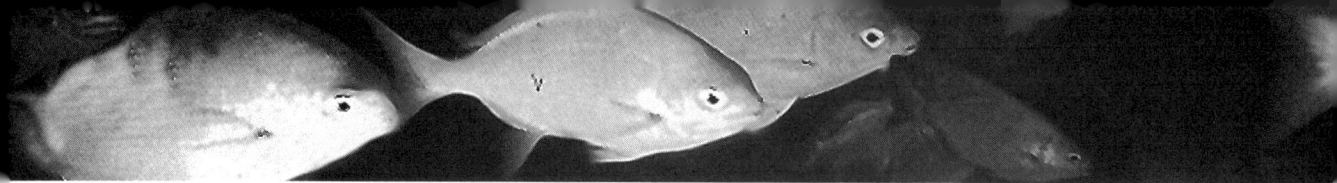

these elements into a hierarchy. Finally, you can develop rules for combining these language elements into expressions.

Assume that an expression is the mathematical equivalent of a paragraph in English. An expression, then, is the top of your grammatical hierarchy. Unfortunately, your expressions are not written in anything much like English—they don't have sentences or words. You must think of your grammar in mathematical terms before you can fully represent it in hierarchical form.

If an English paragraph contains sentences and punctuation, what does a mathematical expression contain? The answer is one or more terms combined with the + and - additive operators. An example of an expression might be

```
term + term - term
```

Guess what? You've just developed the first rule for your grammar. But before you define the complete syntax, you have to develop many similar rules. This means you must have a notation for specifying the rules of your grammar. There are many forms of grammar notation; this book uses the Backus-Naur Form.

Backus-Naur Form

With Backus-Naur Form, or BNF, a grammar is broken down into a set of rules. These rules—each of which defines one element of the grammar—are developed using a top-down approach. The first rule describes the entire grammar in general, the same way the `main()` function in a well-structured C program describes a program in general. Each subsequent rule is more specific, with the last rules defining grammar elements that can no longer be described generally.

For example, a grammar describing a simplified version of the Pascal programming language begins with a rule that defines a program. This rule might state that a program is the keyword `PROGRAM`, followed by a program name, the keyword `VAR`, a variable-declaration list, the keyword `BEGIN`, a statement list, and the keyword `END`. Program elements

such as the variable-declaration list and the statement list are defined in their own rules. Likewise, general elements of the variable-declaration list and the statement list are defined in their own rules, and so on until the entire grammar has been described.

To describe rules clearly and concisely, BNF grammars use special symbols, some of which (the ones you need for your formulas) are listed in Table 3.1. Basically, BNF rules consist of terminal symbols and nonterminal symbols organized using the symbols listed in the table. A *terminal symbol* is an element of the grammar that cannot be described in general terms. In other words, it has been described as specifically as possible. In the simplified Pascal grammar, the keywords PROGRAM, VAR, BEGIN, and END are all terminal symbols. *Nonterminal symbols* are the elements of the grammar that need to be further defined in other rules. In the Pascal example, the nonterminal symbols are the program name, the variable-declaration list, and the statement list. A nonterminal symbol is always enclosed in angle brackets, so it can't be confused with terminal symbols or other symbols used to define the grammar.

Table 3.1. BNF Symbols Used in a Formula Grammar

Symbol	Definition
<>	Identifies a nonterminal symbol (that is, <strg>)
::=	"is defined as"
{}	Identifies an item that is repeated 0 or more times (that is, { item })
|	"or"

So, the first rule in the simplified Pascal grammar might look like this:

```
<program> ::= PROGRAM <prgname> VAR <decl-list>
              BEGIN <stmt-list> END.
```

Here, the nonterminal symbol <program> is on the left of the ::= symbol, so it is the symbol being defined by the rule. (The ::= is read as "is

defined to be.") The nonterminal symbols on the right side of the `::=` symbol (in this case, `<prgname>`, `<decl-list>`, and `<stmt-list>`) are defined elsewhere in the grammar.

Defining an Expression

Now, getting back to your expression, the first grammar rule looks like this in Backus-Naur notation:

```
<expr> ::= <term> { <addop> <term> }
```

In this rule, the nonterminal symbol `<expr>` (expression) is being defined by the rule. Now, although you have a definition for `<expr>`, you don't have definitions for `<term>` and `<addop>` (additive operator). These nonterminal symbols must be defined in other rules, as you will do soon.

In a BNF rule, the items enclosed in the braces may be repeated zero or more times, but always as a complete set. In other words, based on the preceding rule, if you place an `<addop>` after the first `<term>` in an `<expr>`, you must follow that `<addop>` with another `<term>`. So, an `<expr>` is defined as a `<term>`, which may be followed by one or more sets of `<addop>` and `<term>`.

You've taken a step down your grammar's hierarchy, but you're a long way from finished. You now must define both `<term>` and `<addop>`. Defining `<addop>` is easy:

```
<addop> ::= + | -
```

This rule is read as "an additive operator is defined to be a plus or minus symbol." The plus and minus symbols in this rule are terminal symbols, because they require no further definition. The single, vertical line separating the terminal symbols is the symbol for "or." A nonterminal can have more than one definition, as long as you use the "|" symbol to separate each definition.

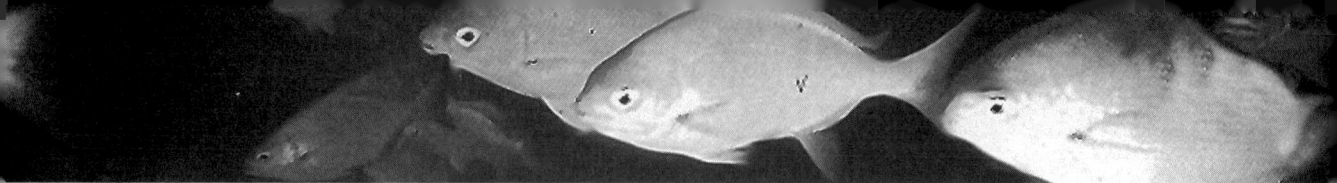

Defining a Term

Now you can tackle `<term>`. If an `<expr>` is any number of `<term>`s combined with additive operators, it's logical to say that a `<term>` can be any number of `<factor>`s combined with multiplicative operators. When you define the basic mathematical operations in this order, you retain the standard operator precedence, where multiplication and division must be performed before addition and subtraction.

> **Note:** In your recursive routines, you first find your way to the expression's deepest level and then work your way back up, solving expressions as you go. That is, the lowest items in the hierarchy are solved before higher ones. This is why placing the multiplicative operators lower in precedence than the additive operators assures that operator precedence is maintained.

Here's your rule for a `<term>`:

```
<term> ::= <factor> ( <multop> <factor> )
```

This rule is similar to the one for an `<expr>`, except here `<factor>` and `<multop>` are used instead of `<term>` and `<addop>`. The `<multop>` (multiplicative operator) nonterminal is easily defined as

```
<multop> ::= * | /
```

Defining a Factor

Now look at a `<factor>`. It must be something that yields a value you can multiply, divide, add, or subtract. So the most obvious way to define a `<factor>` is to say that it is a constant value, such as 0, 10, or 54.6746. If you were to stop there, however, you could parse only expressions that contain constant values and mathematical operations.

Luckily, a `<factor>` can be anything that results in a value, including functions. In addition, remember that your formulas can have nested functions. Moreover, you can use parentheses not only to enclose a function's arguments, but also to change the standard operator precedence. Somehow, you have to add a recursive element to your

definition of a `<factor>`, one that includes parentheses and, more important, brings you back to the top of the hierarchy. So, assume that a `<factor>` also can be an `<expr>` enclosed in parentheses. Your rule for a factor then is

```
<factor> ::= value | <func> | ( <expr> )
```

As you can see, this is where the recursion comes in. A formula that starts with `<expr>` (as all formulas must) can lead you back to `<expr>` any number of times. That is, an `<expr>` is a `<term>`, a `<term>` is a `<factor>`, a `<factor>` is an `<expr>`, an `<expr>` is a `<term>`, a `<term>` is a `<factor>`, a `<factor>` is an `<expr>`, and so on, until `<factor>` finally resolves into something other than an `<expr>`. This rule enables you to describe expressions that are nested any number of levels. This process is summarized in figure 3.7, using the expression (3) as an example.

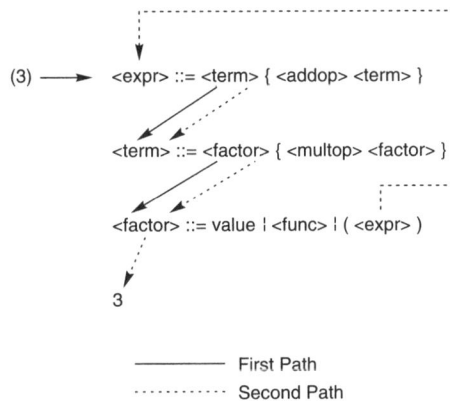

```
(3) ──▶   <expr> ::= <term> { <addop> <term> }

          <term> ::= <factor> { <multop> <factor> }

          <factor> ::= value | <func> | ( <expr> )

          3
```

────────── First Path
·············· Second Path

Fig. 3.7. Recursion in a formula.

Now you can define a `<func>` (function). Because you have two types of functions—one that takes only a single argument and one that takes a list of arguments—a `<func>` is defined as

```
<func> ::= <func1> | <func2>
```

where

```
<func1> ::= <fname1> ( <expr> )
<func2> ::= <fname2> ( <expr> { , <expr> } )
```

Notice that, even if a `<factor>` resolves into a `<func>`, you still may end up back at `<expr>` because any argument for a function is an `<expr>`!

Finally, to finish your grammar definition:

```
<fname1> ::= ABS | SQRT
<fname2> ::= AVG
```

You really don't need a separate rule for `<fname2>`, because you could have used the AVG terminal in the rule for `<func2>`. But by defining the single function name this way, you are remaining consistent with the definition for `<func1>`, and you can add a new function easily, by adding the | symbol and another function name.

The Finished Grammar

Here's the entire grammar in Backus-Naur Form. Look it over to be sure you understand how it works. Write a few formulas of your own, and trace them through the rules to see how they are derived.

```
<expr>   ::= <term> { <addop> <term> }
<term>   ::= <factor> { <multop> <factor> }
<factor> ::= value | <func> | ( <expr> )
<func>   ::= <func1> | <func2>
<func1>  ::= <fname1> ( <expr> )
<func2>  ::= <fname2> ( <expr> { , <expr> } )
<fname1> ::= ABS | SQRT
<fname2> ::= AVG
<addop>  ::= + | -
<multop> ::= * | /
```

A Recursive-Descent Parser

Developing the grammar for expressions, or for any type of language (especially programming languages), is a lot of work. The good news is that after the grammar is written, it can be used as an outline for the parser program itself.

To write the code for your parser, you need only follow the map you've developed. Each nonterminal in the grammar has a corresponding function. In other words, you start evaluating a formula with a function called `Expr()`. This function calls a function called `Term()`, `Term()` calls a

function called `Factor()`, and so on down the hierarchy, until you have a function for every nonterminal in the grammar (see fig. 3.8). This type of program is called a *recursive-descent parser* because it uses recursion to descend to the deepest level of the grammar it's parsing.

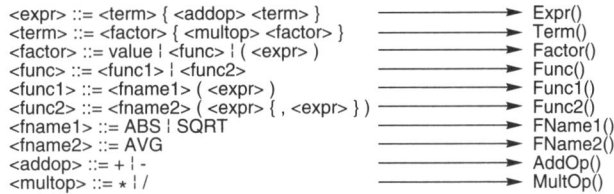

```
<expr> ::= <term> { <addop> <term> }            ──────────► Expr()
<term> ::= <factor> { <multop> <factor> }       ──────────► Term()
<factor> ::= value ¦ <func> ¦ ( <expr> )        ──────────► Factor()
<func> ::= <func1> ¦ <func2>                     ──────────► Func()
<func1> ::= <fname1> ( <expr> )                  ──────────► Func1()
<func2> ::= <fname2> ( <expr> { , <expr> } )     ──────────► Func2()
<fname1> ::= ABS ¦ SQRT                           ──────────► FName1()
<fname2> ::= AVG                                  ──────────► FName2()
<addop> ::= + ¦ -                                 ──────────► AddOp()
<multop> ::= * ¦ /                                ──────────► MultOp()
```

Fig. 3.8. Changing grammar rules to functions.

Listing 3.5 is the recursive-descent parser for the grammar you just developed. If you start at the top of the listing and work your way down, you'll see all the functions that represent the nonterminals in your grammar. Following these functions are several utility functions that help the nonterminal functions do their job. Notice that the comments at the beginning of each nonterminal function include the rule for the appropriate nonterminal.

Listing 3.5. PARSER.CPP—A Parser for Mathematical Expressions

```cpp
///////////////////////////////////////////////////////////
// PARSER.CPP: A parser for mathematical expressions.
///////////////////////////////////////////////////////////

#include <math.h>
#include <string.h>
#include "strng.h"

#define TRUE        1
#define FALSE       0

// Function prototypes.
void Expr(String &s, float &v);
void Term(String &s, float &v);
void Factor(String &s, float &v);
void Func(String &s, float &v);
int Func1(String &s, float &v);
int Func2(String &s, float &v);
```

continues

Listing 3.5. Continued

```cpp
int FName1(String &s, String &name);
int FName2(String &s, String &name);
int AddOp(String &s, String &op);
int MultOp(String &s, String &op);
int FindValue(String &s, float &v);
int GetFuncName(String &s, String &name);
float CalcValues(String &name, float *values, int indx);
int NumChar(String s, int indx);
float Do_SQRT(float v);
float Do_ABS(float v);
float Do_AVG (float *values, int indx);
int Expect(String &s, char *c);
float Evaluate(String formula);

///////////////////////////////////////////////////////
// Main program
///////////////////////////////////////////////////////
int main(void)
{
  char s[81];
  String formula("");

  while (formula != "QUIT")
  {
    cout << "Type Formula: ";
    cin >> s;
    formula = s;
    float answer = Evaluate(formula);
    cout << "Answer: " << answer << '\n';
  }
  return 1;
}

///////////////////////////////////////////////////////
// Expr()
//
// <expr> ::= <term> { <addop> <term> }
///////////////////////////////////////////////////////
void Expr(String &s, float &v)
{
  Term(s, v);
  float v1 = v;
  String op("");
  while (AddOp(s, op))
  {
    Term(s, v);
    if (op == "+")
      v += v1;
    else
      v = v1 - v;
    v1 = v;
  }
}
```

```
//////////////////////////////////////////////////////
// Term()
//
// <term> ::= <factor> { <multop> <factor> }
//////////////////////////////////////////////////////
void Term(String &s, float &v)
{
  Factor(s, v);
  float v1 = v;
  String op("");
  while (MultOp(s, op))
  {
    Factor(s, v);
    if (op == "*")
      v *= v1;
    else v = v1 / v;
    v1 = v;
  }
}

//////////////////////////////////////////////////////
// Factor()
//
// <factor> ::= value | <func> | ( <expr> )
//////////////////////////////////////////////////////
void Factor(String &s, float &v)
{
  if (s.GetSubStr(1,1) == "(")
  {
    Expect(s, "(");
    Expr(s, v);
    Expect(s, ")");
  }
  else
    if (!FindValue(s, v))
      Func(s, v);
}

//////////////////////////////////////////////////////
// Func()
//
// Func ::= <func1> | <func2>
//////////////////////////////////////////////////////
void Func(String &s, float &v)
{
  if (!Func1(s, v))
    Func2(s, v);
}

//////////////////////////////////////////////////////
// Func1()
//
```

continues

Listing 3.5. Continued

```
// <func1> ::= <fname1> ( <expr> )
//////////////////////////////////////////////////////
int Func1(String &s, float &v)
{
  int result = FALSE;

  String name("");
  if (FName1(s, name))
  {
    result = TRUE;
    Expect(s, "(");
    Expr(s, v);
    Expect(s, ")");
    if (name == "ABS")
      v = Do_ABS(v);
    else
      v = Do_SQRT(v);
  }
  return result;
}


//////////////////////////////////////////////////////
// Func2()
//
// <func2> ::= <fname2> ( <expr> { , <expr> } )
//////////////////////////////////////////////////////
int Func2(String &s, float &v)
{
  float values[10];

  int result = FALSE;
  String name("");
  if (FName2(s, name))
  {
    result = TRUE;
    Expect(s, "(");
    s.Insert(",",1);
    int indx = 0;
    while (s.GetSubStr(1,1) == ",")
    {
      Expect(s, ",");
      Expr(s, v);
      values[indx++] = v;
    }
    Expect(s, ")");
    v = Do_AVG(values, indx-1);
  }
  return result;
}


//////////////////////////////////////////////////////
// FName1()
```

```
//
// <fname1> ::= ABS | SQRT
//////////////////////////////////////////////////////
int FName1(String &s, String &name)
{
  GetFuncName(s, name);
  if ((name != "ABS") && (name != "SQRT"))
  {
    s.Insert(name, 1);
    return FALSE;
  }
  else
    return TRUE;
}


//////////////////////////////////////////////////////
// FName2()
//
// <fname2> ::= AVG
//////////////////////////////////////////////////////
int FName2(String &s, String &name)
{
  GetFuncName(s, name);
  if (name != "AVG")
  {
    s.Insert(name, 1);
    return FALSE;
  }
  else
    return TRUE;
}


//////////////////////////////////////////////////////
// AddOp()
//
// <addop> ::= + | -
//////////////////////////////////////////////////////
int AddOp(String &s, String &op)
{
  op = s.GetSubStr(1,1);
  if ((op == "+") || (op == "-"))
  {
    s = s.GetSubStr(2, s.Length()-1);
    return TRUE;
  }
  else
    return FALSE;
}


//////////////////////////////////////////////////////
// MultOp()
//
```

continues

Listing 3.5. Continued

```cpp
// <multop> ::= * | /
//////////////////////////////////////////////////////////
int MultOp(String &s, String &op)
{
  op = s.GetSubStr(1,1);
  if ((op == "*") || (op == "/"))
  {
    s = s.GetSubStr(2, s.Length()-1);
    return TRUE;
  }
  else
    return FALSE;
}


//////////////////////////////////////////////////////////
// Expect()
//////////////////////////////////////////////////////////
int Expect(String &s, char *c)
{
  String chr(c);
  if (s.GetSubStr(1,1) != chr)
    return FALSE;
  else
  {
    s = s.GetSubStr(2, s.Length()-1);
    return TRUE;
  }
}


//////////////////////////////////////////////////////////
// FindValue()
//////////////////////////////////////////////////////////
int FindValue (String &s, float &v)
{
  int result;

  result = TRUE;
  int indx = 1;
  if (s.GetSubStr(1,1) == "-")
    indx = 2;
  while ((indx <= s.Length()) && (NumChar(s, indx)))
    ++indx;
  if (indx == 1)
    result = FALSE;
  else
  {
    String ts = s.GetSubStr(1, indx-1);
    char c[81];
    ts.GetStr(c, sizeof(c));
    v = atof(c);
    s = s.GetSubStr(indx, s.Length()-indx+1);
```

```
  }
  return result;
}


/////////////////////////////////////////////////////////
// GetFuncName()
/////////////////////////////////////////////////////////
int GetFuncName(String &s, String &name)
{
  int found_open_paren = FALSE;
  int indx = 1;
  while ((indx <= s.Length()) && (!found_open_paren))
  {
    if (s.GetSubStr(indx, 1) != "(")
      ++indx;
    else found_open_paren = TRUE;
  }

  int result;
  if (indx > s.Length()) result = FALSE;
  else
  {
    name = s.GetSubStr(1, indx-1);
    s = s.GetSubStr(indx, s.Length()-indx+1);
    result = TRUE;
  }
  return result;
}


/////////////////////////////////////////////////////////
// NumChar()
/////////////////////////////////////////////////////////
int NumChar(String s, int indx)
{
  if (((s.GetSubStr(indx, 1) >= "0") &&
       (s.GetSubStr(indx, 1) <= "9")) ||
       (s.GetSubStr(indx, 1) == "."))
    return TRUE;
  else
    return FALSE;
}


/////////////////////////////////////////////////////////
// Do_ABS()
/////////////////////////////////////////////////////////
float Do_ABS(float v)
{
  return fabs(v);
}


/////////////////////////////////////////////////////////
// Do_AVG()
/////////////////////////////////////////////////////////
```

continues

Using Recursion to Parse Formulas   **133**

Listing 3.5. Continued

```
float Do_AVG (float *values, int indx)
{
  float sum = 0;
  for (int x=0; x<=indx; ++x)
    sum += values[x];
  return sum / (indx+1);
}


/////////////////////////////////////////////////////////
// Do_SQRT()
/////////////////////////////////////////////////////////
float Do_SQRT(float v)
{
  if (v > 0)
    return sqrt(v);
  else
    return 0;
}


/////////////////////////////////////////////////////////
// Evaluate
/////////////////////////////////////////////////////////
float Evaluate(String formula)
{
  String s(formula);
  float v;

  v = 0;
  Expr(s, v);
  return v;
}
```

Note: The parser program includes a couple of source code files which, for the sake of brevity, are not listed in this book. The additional files are STRNG.H and STRNG.CPP, which are a simple string-handling class included on this book's disk, along with PARSER.CPP. To compile Listing 3.5, you must be sure to include the STRNG.CPP file in your project.

Run the program and try it out. Enter an expression, and the parser returns the answer. Be careful not to make a mistake when entering your expression, though. To keep the workings of the parser as clear as possible, there is no error-checking. If, for example, you enter an

expression that results in a division-by-zero error, you'll crash the program. Ditto for something like requesting the square root of a negative number. Also, the parser isn't smart enough to handle lowercase characters, so enter all function names in uppercase. Don't include any spaces in your expression, either. To exit the program, type QUIT when prompted for an expression. Table 3.2 shows the steps involved in parsing an expression. You will want to refer to this table as you learn how the program works.

Table 3.2. Parsing a Formula

Contents of s before function call	Function trace	Terminals extracted	Value of v
4*(SQRT(10+15))	Enter Expr()1		0
4*(SQRT(10+15))	Enter Term()1		0
4*(SQRT(10+15))	Enter Factor()1	4	4
*(SQRT(10+15))	Exit Factor()1		4
*(SQRT(10+15))	Return to Term()1	*	4
(SQRT(10+15))	Enter Factor()2	(	4
SQRT(10+15))	Enter Expr()2		4
SQRT(10+15))	Enter Term()2		4
SQRT(10+15))	Enter Factor()3		4
SQRT(10+15))	Enter Func()1		4
SQRT(10+15))	Enter Func1()1		4
SQRT(10+15))	Enter FName1()1	SQRT	4
(10+15))	Exit FName1()1		4
(10+15))	Return to Func1()1	(	4
10+15))	Exit Func1()1		4
10+15))	Enter Expr()3		4
10+15))	Enter Term()3		4
10+15))	Enter Factor()4	10	10

continues

Table 3.2. Continued

Contents of *s* before function call	Function trace	Terminals extracted	Value of *v*
+15))	Exit Factor()4		10
+15))	Exit Term()3		10
+15))	Return to Expr()3	+	10
15))	Enter Term()4		10
15))	Enter Factor()5	15	15
))	Exit Factor()5		15
))	Exit Term()4		15
))	Return Expr()3		25
))	Exit Expr()3		25
))	Return to Func1()1	)	5
)	Exit Func1()1		5
)	Exit Factor()3		5
)	Return to Term()2		5
)	Exit Term()2		5
)	Exit Expr()2		5
)	Return to Factor()2	)	5
	Exit Factor()2		5
	Return to Term()1		5
	Exit Term()1		20
	Exit Expr()1		20

Note: The numbers following the functions identify the specific function call. For example, Factor()1 is the first call to Factor(), and Factor()2 is the second call to Factor(). This numbering scheme helps track recursive calls.

Now, you can see what makes the program tick. (Somewhere along the line, you might want to trace through Table 3.2, which shows a formula going through the parsing process.) Look at the main program first:

```
void main(void)
{
  char s[81];
  String formula("");

  while (formula != "QUIT")
  {
    cout << "Type Formula: ";
    cin >> s;
    formula = s;
    float answer = Evaluate(formula);
    cout << "Answer: " << answer << '\n';
  }
}
```

As you can see from Listing 3.5, there's a lot of string handling in this program, so a string class, `String`, is included in the program. Using this class greatly simplifies the parsing process. (Yes, I know Borland C++ has its own string class, but I'm accustomed to using mine.) In the main program, the `String formula` holds the formula to be parsed. However, because the `String` class doesn't include functions for accepting a string from an input stream, an 81-element character array is used to get the formula from the user. This character array is then converted to a `String` and passed on to the function `Evaluate()`:

```
float Evaluate(String formula)
{
  String s(formula);
  float v;

  v = 0;
  Expr(s, v);
  return v;
}
```

`Evaluate()` initializes the data needed by the parser, then calls `Expr()`, which begins the parsing process. See the `String s` and the floating point value `v`? At any point in the parsing process, `s` contains the portion of `formula` that has yet to be parsed. Each time a part of `s` is parsed, that part is removed from `s`. At the end of the parsing process, `s` contains an empty `String`. The value `v` is used to pass the value of the most recently evaluated expression between functions.

Now you can see how your grammar is converted into C++ functions, starting at the top of the hierarchy. As you examine these functions, you should compare them to the grammar you developed earlier.

```cpp
void Expr(String &s, float &v)
{
  Term(s, v);
  float v1 = v;
  String op("");
  while (AddOp(s, op))
  {
    Term(s, v);
    if (op == "+")
      v += v1;
    else
      v = v1 - v;
    v1 = v;
  }
}
```

According to the grammar rules, an `<expr>` must start with a `<term>`, so the first thing `Expr()` does is call `Term()`. After returning from `Term()`, there is a value in `v`, which is the result of parsing the first term in the expression. For example, if the first term were 10, `v` would be 10. If the first term were AVG(10,30,5), `v` would be 15.

Because it might use the result of the first term in an addition or subtraction operation, `Expr()` saves it in `v1`. (The variable `v` changes the next time you call `Term()`.) `Expr()` then creates a `String` to hold the additive operator, if there is one. Because, according to the grammar, the program must allow any number of `<term>` and `<addop>` pairs, `Expr()` sets up a `while` loop that iterates until there are no additive operators left in the expression. The function `AddOp()`, which is the loop's conditional expression, returns true if the next character in the formula is a plus or minus sign. It also returns the character in the `op String`:

```cpp
int AddOp(String &s, String &op)
{
  op = s.GetSubStr(1,1);
  if ((op == "+") || (op == "-"))
  {
    s = s.GetSubStr(2, s.Length()-1);
    return TRUE;
  }
  else
    return FALSE;
}
```

If `AddOp()` returns True, `Expr()` must call `Term()` to get a value for the next term in the expression. When `Term()` returns, the operator in `op` is checked. If it's a plus sign, `v1` is added to the new `v`. Otherwise, `v` is subtracted from `v1`. In any case, the result is stored in `v`, after which the program goes back to the top of the loop and checks `AddOp()` again. As long as `AddOp()` returns true, `Expr()` continues to add or subtract new terms.

Now, look at `Term()`:

```
void Term(String &s, float &v)
{
  Factor(s, v);
  float v1 = v;
  String op("");
  while (MultOp(s, op))
  {
    Factor(s, v);
    if (op == "*")
      v *= v1;
    else v = v1 / v;
    v1 = v;
  }
}
```

The `Term()` function is similar to `Expr()`, just as the rule for `<term>` is similar to the rule for `<expr>`. In fact, `Term()` works exactly like `Expr()`, except it evaluates factors and performs multiplication and division. To check mathematical operations, `Term()` calls `MultOp()` instead of `AddOp()`.

`Factor()`, on the other hand, is very different from `Expr()` and `Term()`:

```
void Factor(String &s, float &v)
{
  if (s.GetSubStr(1,1) == "(")
  {
    Expect(s, "(");
    Expr(s, v);
    Expect(s, ")");
  }
  else
    if (!FindValue(s, v))
      Func(s, v);
}
```

`Factor()` must allow for three types of factors: constant values, functions, or expressions enclosed in parentheses. First, `Factor()` checks whether the first character of the `String` s is an open parenthesis. If it is,

`Expect()` is called, which checks for a specific character and, if found, removes the character from the `String`:

```
int Expect(String &s, char *c)
{
  String chr(c);
  if (s.GetSubStr(1,1) != chr)
    return FALSE;
  else
  {
    s = s.GetSubStr(2, s.Length()-1);
    return TRUE;
  }
}
```

(`Expect()` also returns true or false, depending on whether it found the expected character. The return value isn't used here, but it's discussed in the "Returning Syntax Errors" section.) Then `Factor()` calls `Expr()` recursively to evaluate the expression enclosed in the parentheses. After `Expr()` returns, `Factor()` checks for the closing parenthesis.

If the first character in `s` is not a parenthesis, `Factor()` must check for a value or a function. Because a value is a terminal, there is no function called `Value()`. However, there is a utility function called `FindValue()` that returns true if the next characters in `s` form a constant. Also, the value of the constant is returned in `v`.

```
int FindValue (String &s, float &v)
{
  int result;

  result = TRUE;
  int indx = 1;
  if (s.GetSubStr(1,1) == "-")
    indx = 2;
  while ((indx <= s.Length()) && (NumChar(s, indx)))
    ++indx;
  if (indx == 1)
    result = FALSE;
  else
  {
    String ts = s.GetSubStr(1, indx-1);
    char c[81];
    ts.GetStr(c, sizeof(c));
    v = atof(c);
    s = s.GetSubStr(indx, s.Length()-indx+1);
  }
  return result;
}
```

Here, s is scanned one character at a time, until a character that is not part of a value is found (that is, it is not a decimal point or a digit from 0 to 9). The NumChar() function does this checking, returning True if it finds an appropriate character or false if it does not.

If no value is found, FindValue() returns False. If it does find a value, it not only returns True, but also converts the ASCII characters to a floating point value and removes the converted characters from s.

Getting back to Factor(), if a value isn't found, the only possible factor left is a function. Factor() checks for this with the Func() nonterminal function:

```
void Func(String &s, float &v)
{
  if (!Func1(s, v))
    Func2(s, v);
}
```

As with the rule for <func>, Func() first checks for a function of type <func1>. If it doesn't find one, it looks for a function of type <func2>. Both functions return True or False, as appropriate. Notice, however, that the program doesn't use the return value from Func2(). This is because this stripped-down parser doesn't check for errors and instead assumes that if it doesn't have a <func1>, it must have a <func2>. In a full program, you'd want to generate an error if both Func1() and Func2() returned False.

Now, move on to Func1():

```
int Func1(String &s, float &v)
{
  int result = FALSE;
  String name("");
  if (FName1(s, name))
  {
    result = TRUE;
    Expect(s, "(");
    Expr(s, v);
    Expect(s, ")");
    if (name == "ABS")
      v = Do_ABS(v);
    else
      v = Do_SQRT(v);
  }
  return result;
}
```

Here, the `FName1()` nonterminal function is first called, which checks for the function names `ABS()` and `SQRT()`. If it finds either, it returns true. It also returns the function name in the `name` reference variable. If a function name is found, `Func1()` then calls `Expect()` to get the function's opening parenthesis. It then makes a recursive call to `Expr()` to evaluate the function's argument, after which another call to `Expect()` gets the closing parenthesis. Finally, the function's value is calculated by calling `Do_ABS()` or `Do_SQRT()`, as appropriate.

`Func2()` works similarly, except it must handle an unknown number of arguments:

```
int Func2(String &s, float &v)
{
  float values[10];

  int result = FALSE;
  String name("");
  if (FName2(s, name))
  {
    result = TRUE;
    Expect(s, "(");
    s.Insert(",",1);
    int indx = 0;
    while (s.GetSubStr(1,1) == ",")
    {
      Expect(s, ",");
      Expr(s, v);
      values[indx++] = v;
    }
    Expect(s, ")");
    v = Do_AVG(values, indx-1);
  }
  return result;
}
```

As `Func2()` is written, you can have a maximum of 10 arguments for a `<func2>` function. If you like, you can increase this maximum by changing the declaration of the `values[]` array.

`Func2()` checks for function names just as `Func1()` did, except it calls the `FName2()` nonterminal function instead of `FName1()`. If it finds a function name of type `<fname2>`, it checks for and removes the open parenthesis, then inserts a comma into the beginning of `s`. The comma is added only so the function can get into the `while` loop, which iterates as long as it finds a comma in the first character of `s`.

Note: In the parser presented here, `<fname2>` can only be AVG, but you can add other functions of this type if you like. How about MIN and MAX, which return the minimum and maximum value, respectively, in a list of values?

In the loop, a call to Expect() gets the comma, after which Expr() is called recursively to evaluate the current argument. The value returned in v is saved in the values array. Finally, after processing all the arguments, the program breaks from the loop, checks for the closing parenthesis, and calls Do_AVG() to average the values stored in the values[] array.

The FName1() nonterminal function looks for function names of the type `<fname1>`:

```
int FName1(String &s, String &name)
{
  GetFuncName(s, name);
  if ((name != "ABS") && (name != "SQRT"))
  {
    s.Insert(name, 1);
    return FALSE;
  }
  else
    return TRUE;
}
```

First, the GetFuncName() utility function is called, which scans s, looking for and removing the function name. The name is returned in the name reference variable. This variable is checked against the function names ABS() and SQRT(). If it doesn't match, s is restored to its original state by reinserting name into the beginning of String, after which the function returns False. If an appropriate function name is found, FName1() returns true, with the function name stored in name.

The FName2() function is similar. The main difference is that this function looks for the name AVG(), rather than ABS() or SQRT():

```
int FName2(String &s, String &name)
{
  GetFuncName(s, name);
  if (name != "AVG")
  {
    s.Insert(name, 1);
```

```
      return FALSE;
   }
   else
      return TRUE;
}
```

The remaining functions in the program are fairly self-explanatory, so there's no need to explore them in any detail. However, before closing up shop for this chapter, you have to consider an important parsing topic: syntax errors.

Returning Syntax Errors

The program in Listing 3.5 does no error checking. It is assumed that the formula the parser receives follows the rules of the grammar. More important, there is no checking for illegal mathematical operations, which could crash the program if allowed to get through. The error checking was left out because the extra code would have made the source code much more difficult to follow.

Before you use a parser like Listing 3.5, you must add enough error checking to ensure that the program doesn't crash and that the values returned from the parser are always accurate. As the parser stands now, a return value of 0 may be the formula's result or may indicate an error in the formula. Obviously, this ambiguity cannot be tolerated in a finished program.

Where should you add the error checking? The first place to look is any function that performs mathematical operations. For example, in the `Term()` function, the statement `v = v1 / v` doesn't get far if `v` happens to be zero. You should not only check for this illegal value, but also display an error message and, probably, stop the parsing. Exiting the parser early is tricky because you have to back out of the recursion first. You could do this by setting an error flag that can be checked by each function. If an error is detected, each function does nothing but return.

Another type of error arises when the user types a formula that doesn't follow the rules of the grammar. For example, what if every open parenthesis can't be matched with a closed parenthesis? One place to

check for an error like this would be in the `Expect()` function. If the character `Expect()` is expecting doesn't exist, the function could return an error.

The error message you return to the user should be as helpful as possible. For example, if your error message indicates that a parenthesis is missing, the user knows at least what type of problem to look for.

This is how you might rewrite the `Factor()` function with error checking:

```
void Factor(String &s, float &v)
{
  if (s.GetSubStr(1,1) == "(")
  {
    Expect(s, "(");
    Expr(s, v);
    if (!error)
      if (!Expect(s, ")"))
        error = MISSINGPAREN;
  }
  else
    if (!FindValue(s, v))
      if (!Func(s, v))
        error = NOSUCHFUNC;
}
```

In this new version of `Factor()`, the function first checks for an open parenthesis. If it finds one, it calls `Expect()` to remove the parenthesis from `s`. `Expect()`'s return value is ignored because, if the program got past the `if` statement, it already knows it has the open parenthesis. Next, `Expr()` is called to evaluate the expression enclosed in the parentheses. By the time `Expr()` returns, an error condition may have been detected. So, before continuing, the program checks the `error` flag. If there is no error, it calls `Expect()` to look for the close parenthesis. If the parenthesis is missing, `error` is set to a constant that indicates the type of error discovered. At the end of the parsing process, the program can check `error`. If it's not zero, an appropriate error message should be printed rather than the value returned from the parser.

If the first `if` statement doesn't find an open parenthesis, it's safe to assume that the factor is a value or a function. Therefore, `FindValue()` is called. If `FindValue()` returns true, the constant value is in `v`. If `FindValue()` returns false, the only thing left to check for is a function. If `Func()` returns true, the value returned from the function is in `v`. If `Func()` returns

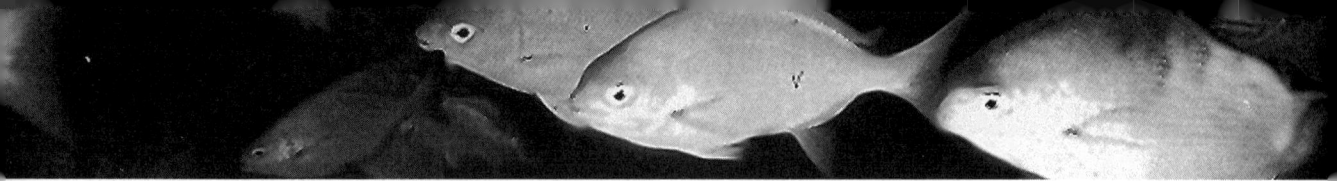

false, the program has discovered an error, because there is no other type of factor for which to check. To flag this error, `error` is set to `NOSUCHFUNC`.

You can check for other error conditions throughout the parser by adding similar code to the other functions. As you beef up the parser with error-checking routines, you discover why the errors you get from your C++ compiler don't always seem to make sense. Because C++ includes no mind-reading functions, it's often impossible to know exactly why something is wrong. All you can do is make an educated guess and hope the user can figure out the problem from the clues you supply.

From Here...

Recursion is a powerful programming technique that can simplify some complex programming chores. As you write programs, you will see numerous opportunities to use recursion in your own programs.

➤ Chapter 17, "Mastering Templates," discusses converting recursive code into macros without using recursion.

➤ For information on porting code from databases and other programming languages into your C++ programs, see Chapters 13, "Mixed Language Programming," Chapter 14, "Bare Metal Programming," and Chapter 15, "Interfacing with Database Languages."

➤ Recursive code is often the most difficult code to debug. For information on power-debugging and add-on debuggers, see chapter 6, "Writing Bug-Free Code," Chapter 7, "Debugging Tips and Tricks," and Chapter 8, "Third-Party Debugger Tools."

Optimizing C

by Michael R. Dunlavey

In software, a *slug* is like a bug, except that a slug only makes the program run slowly, not incorrectly. An example of a program with a slug is one that performs the same calculation many times instead of performing it once and reusing the result.

When a program is hindered by a slug, it's tempting to blame the program's author, who never should have written the slug in the first place. Maybe so, but the same can be said of normal software bugs, which never should be written either. Despite all the "shoulds," both bugs and slugs often plague software. The difference is that programmers are used to removing bugs, but not slugs. Nevertheless, deslugging is a crucial aspect of performance tuning. The bad news is that slugs exist; the good news is that removing them is easy and makes software run like blazes.

Performance tuning falls into two broad categories: synchronous and asynchronous. Most performance tuning is *synchronous.* When you perform synchronous performance tuning, you try to eliminate the invocation of subroutines. *Asynchronous* performance tuning is often necessary for software that has a significant amount of parallelism, such as real-time control or communications systems. When you perform asynchronous performance tuning, you try to eliminate spurious messages or to coordinate parallel activities. Whether you are performing synchronous or asynchronous performance tuning, you should always employ effective diagnostics, not guesswork.

Synchronous Tuning

Slugs and bugs are the same in one respect: You must find and fix both. Bugs are often hard to find. Sometimes you must trace the program's execution to find out where it goes wrong. Slugs, on the other hand, are easy to find. All you have to do is run the program, manually stop it with a hot key at random times, and take a good look at what the program is doing. You do this by examining the call stack. Suppose the program is spending 90 percent of its time executing a slug. When you halt execution, you have a 90 percent probability of catching the program while the slug is active, whether the slug is an unnecessary subroutine call or a hot spot. This is illustrated in figure 4.1. After you halt execution, the slug's code is somewhere on the call stack. Simply by fixing the slug, you can increase the program's speed as much as tenfold.

Alternative Techniques

The enduring popularity of relatively ineffective techniques can be amazing. This is particularly true of commonly used deslugging techniques.

In software, things happen on a time scale that spans eight orders of magnitude, from microseconds to minutes. So, counting how many times a program executes a statement or subroutine tells you nothing if you don't know how much time it takes to execute the statement or subroutine. Likewise, measuring the average execution time of a subroutine tells you nothing if you don't know how many times the

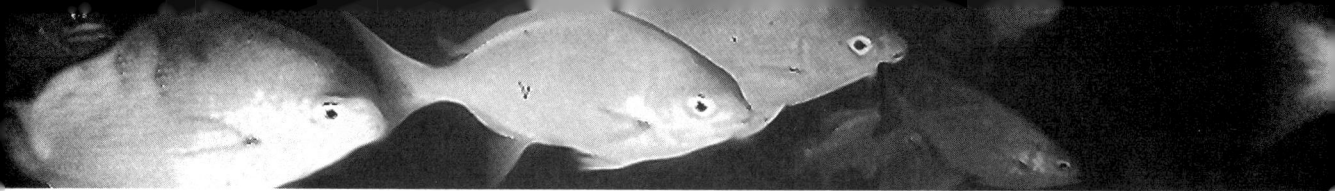

program executes it. And knowing how much total time is spent in a subroutine tells you little if you don't know how much time the subroutine spends in lower-level subroutines. Histogramming the program counter (or *profiling*) can tell you where slugs are, but only if they do not consist of subroutine calls. Getting statistics of "who-calls-who" tells you nothing if you don't know how much time is spent in the calls. You don't have to take numerous samples or have accurate timers, because precision is not your objective when you are deslugging. (To lose weight, you need not weigh your limbs with three-digit accuracy.) Finally, nothing is so discouraging as profiling a user-interface program and having your input-output wait time show up as a giant hot spot on a histogram, simply because you couldn't type fast enough.

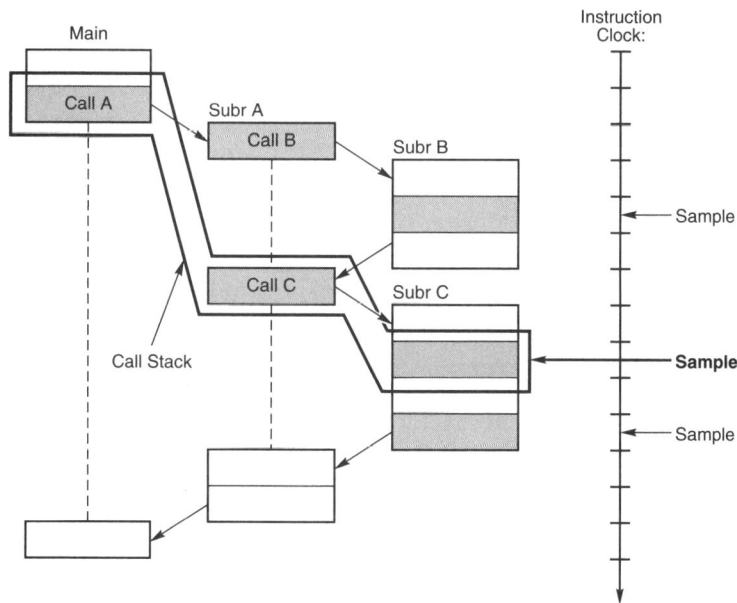

Fig. 4.1. Call instructions can cause a program to spend many cycles executing a slug. While executing a slug, these instructions are displayed on the call stack. You can usually find such call instructions by randomly halting the program's execution.

The results of these popular tools are usually disappointing. They work best on small demonstration programs that have a shallow call stack. When used with more substantial software, however, these tools usually yield only marginal improvement, after which they are quietly set aside.

By contrast, the technique of randomly halting execution and checking the call stack can greatly enhance a program's performance, whether the program's slugs are hot spots or unnecessary subroutine calls. Although this method is conceptually simple, it can be difficult to implement. This is because modern debugging environments added such features as the hot-key interrupt and the examination of the call stack only as an afterthought. Older debuggers actually provided better features for implementing this technique. Perhaps future releases of debugging environments will improve these features.

The following are a couple of personal experiences that have affirmed my faith in the value of randomly halting and checking the call stack.

Indexing Arrays

I was once involved in a project on a 68000 UNIX machine. The following program loop, which was indexing over an array of structures, seemed to be taking longer than necessary:

```
struct mystruct {
    ...
    };

struct mystruct aaa[];

...

int i;
...
while( ... ){
    ...
    ... aaa[ i ] ...
    ...
    }
...
```

Nothing obvious was slowing down this loop. Running it under the profiler told us only that the math library seemed to have a hot spot. However, we dismissed this evidence as anomalous, because the loop contained no math.

Next, we ran the program under the debugger and halted it manually (not with a breakpoint). The call stack looked like this:

```
... some location in the IMULT32 math library routine

CALL IMULT32 ... as part of computing "aaa[ i ]"

main()
```

As we examined the compiler-generated instructions for the expression `aaa[ i ]`, we noticed that, to determine the effective address, the program was multiplying the index by the size of an array element. The index variable `i` was declared `integer`, making it a 32-bit quantity (in that particular compiler). The 68000 has a 16-bit multiplication instruction, but not 32. Therefore, the compiler generated a subroutine call.

After we discovered this problem, fixing it was easy. We declared the index variable `short`, the subroutine call became a multiplication instruction, and the speed of the loop tripled.

You might learn from this tale that you should scrounge around the code looking for 32-bit variables used as array indexes—but that would be the wrong lesson. The right lesson is that you should run the code under a debugger, manually interrupt it, and see what the code is actually doing. In other words: *don't guess.* This simple advice is sometimes hard to follow, because it requires that you learn to use a debugger.

Printing Floating-Point Numbers

In another program, an 8086-based graphics display processor was supposed to paint floating-point numbers on-screen, but the painting seemed to be taking much too long. Guesswork yielded many possible explanations and fixes. However, when we ran the program under an

ICE (In-Circuit-Emulator), manually halted it, and traced the call stack, we discovered that it spent a lot of time in the floating-point math library (which seemed appropriate), but that the calls were from the following code (which was a surprise). It was printing the floating-point numbers by peeling off digits with the following loop:

```
float num, newnum;
char digit;

while(...){
    newnum = (int)(num / 10);
    digit = num - newnum * 10 + '0';
    num = newnum;
    ... store digit for output ...
    }
```

When we wrote the program, we had to write our own `printf()` function. (The code was actually in Pascal.) This simple-looking loop performs floating-divide, float-to-fix, fix-to-float, floating-multiply, floating-subtract, and float-to-fix on every single digit to be printed. A typical call to a floating-point library routine consumes 100 to 300 instructions, because it must unpack the operands, adjust the exponents, calculate the mantissa, and normalize and pack the result.

After we discovered this slug, fixing it was easy. We simply converted the number to fixed-point and handled it in that form. (Actually, the code would have been fine if it had been invoked only a few times every second. Its crime was that the program used it frequently.)

The Manufacturing Simulation Program

The following example chronicles an actual case of performance tuning an application. While demonstrating the deslugging process, this example also supports the following maxims:

➤ The larger the program is, the more you probably can speed it up.

➤ Faster software is not necessarily less maintainable. In fact, it can be much more maintainable than slower software.

➤ Aggressive performance tuning leads to a new style of code that may look quite unlike that of traditional programming. For example, the new style of code may include much less explicit data.

These cheeky assertions will be explained after this detailed example is described.

The Program to Be Deslugged

To see how the performance tuning process works, you'll examine a program that simulates a computer-integrated manufacturing (CIM) application. It is a bit large for a sample program, but quite small for a CIM application. The most interesting slugs appear when a program is large enough to need a few layers of subroutines. First you'll examine the design of the program. Then you'll see each stage in which the program is debugged. Finally, you'll see how to redesign the application so that it's not only much faster, but also much smaller and clearer.

The Problem to Be Solved

CIM cell-control applications often have four principal functions:

➤ *Schedule execution* (called ISCH in this program): This function takes requests for individual manufacturing jobs. A *job* consists of a sequence of *operations*. The function fits these jobs and operations into a schedule, allocates resources for them, and dispatches them for processing. When all operations of a job are done, it sends completion information back to the requester.

➤ *Task coordination* (called ITC in this program): This function takes requests for executing an operation for a job, and controls the execution of the operation. An operation consists of a series of *tasks*, such as the following:

- Command IMH (material handling) to move a part to the machining center.

- Command IDEV (device control) to start downloading the tool path file.

- Wait for both tasks to complete.

- Validate the bar code on the part.

- Instruct the machining center to begin cutting.

- Wait for the machining center to finish cutting.

- Upload the status information.

- Command IMH to move the part to storage.

➤ *Device control* (IDEV): This function takes requests for machine-related functions—such as tool path download, cycle start and stop, and status monitoring—and then gives orders to the machine that actually performs the action. In this simulation, this function is just a no-op. (That is, it does nothing except take a small amount of time.)

➤ *Material handling* (IMH): This function takes care of moving the parts from one location to another. It gives orders to the actual controllers. In this simulation, this function is just a no-op.

The Program Design

The data-flow diagram in figure 4.2 shows how you can design such a program. It contains the four main functional modules mentioned above. Each module receives requests and then issues an acknowledgment after it fulfills each request. Each module in turn sends requests to the module or modules below it and receives acknowledgments from those modules. Also, each module maintains a list of outstanding requests that keeps track of the status of those requests. The module uses this list to decide what to do next whenever something happens. The program is event-driven. Keep in mind, though, that this is only a demonstration program; a real one would have many more functional modules and message paths.

The main entry point consists of a message-dispatch loop, just as in Microsoft Windows. The loop takes each queued message in turn and passes it to the proper function module. That function will most likely put more messages in the queue.

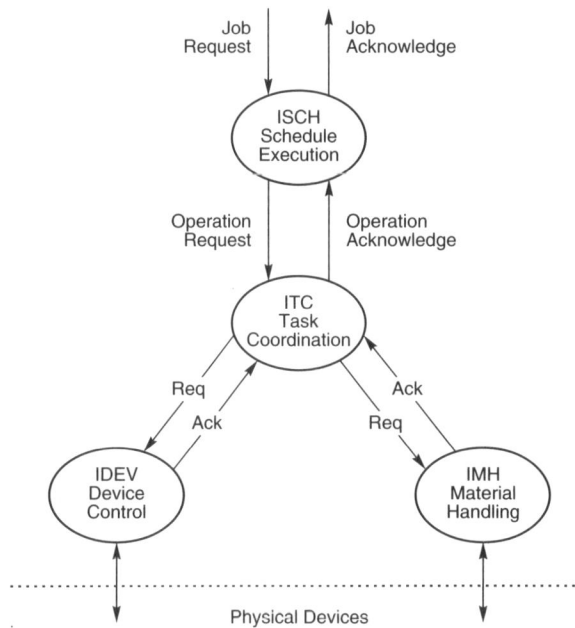

Fig. 4.2. A data-flow diagram of manufacturing simulation program.

In addition to the major function modules, some utilities are needed. The *cluster* paradigm, a state-of-the-art paradigm that is related to object-oriented programming, was used to design these utilities. In a cluster, you surround each data structure definition with accessor macros and subroutines so that its implementation can be changed without having to change the source code that uses it. Using this paradigm, the following utility clusters were created:

➤ *List cluster* (called ILST). This cluster includes primitives for creating linked lists, deleting them, appending to them, iterating over them, and so on.

➤ *Transaction cluster* (called ITRN). A transaction is a queued message. This cluster includes primitives for creating transactions, deleting them, sending them, receiving them, and so on.

The Program Code

Listing 4.1 is the manufacturing simulation program, which consists of about 800 lines of code.

Listing 4.1. The First Version of the Manufacturing Simulation Program

```
/* idev.h -------- device-handler specifics go here */
/* ignl.h -------- global definitions */

#define FALSE 0
#define TRUE  1

#define MALLOC malloc
/* ilst.h -------- list the cluster definitions */

typedef struct ilst_struct {      /* list the cell structure */
    struct ilst_struct * next;     /* pointer to the next cell */
    void * thing;                  /* pointer to thing in the cell */
    } * ILST ;

/* list the cluster-access macros */

#define ILST_CREATE (NULL)

#define ILST_APPEND(list,thing) ((list)=ilst_append((list),thing))

#define ILST_FIRST(list) (((ILST)(list))->thing)

#define ILST_NEXT(list,thing) (ilst_next((list),(thing)))

#define ILST_NTH(list,n) (ilst_nth((list),n))

#define ILST_LENGTH(list) (ilst_length(list))

#define ILST_DELETE(list,thing) ((list)=ilst_delete((list),thing))

/* list the cluster function externs */

extern ILST     ilst_append();
extern void *    ilst_next();
extern void *    ilst_nth();
extern int    ilst_length();
extern ILST     ilst_delete();
/* imh.h -------- material-handling specifics go here */
/* isch.h -------- schedule-execution statistics go here */
/* itrn.h -------- transaction definitions */

/* ITRN is the 'superclass' of all transactions */
typedef struct itrn_struct {
    int code;          /* the transaction code */
    } * ITRN;
```

```
/* externs of the transaction-processing cluster routines */

extern void itrn_put();              /* put a transaction in the queue */
extern ITRN itrn_get();              /* get a transaction from the queue */
extern ITRN itrn_examine();  /* get a transaction but leave it in queue */

typedef struct {      /* job-request transaction */
    int code;             /* transaction code */
    int jobid;            /* job ID */
    } itrn_reqjob_t;

typedef struct {      /* job-completion transaction */
    int code;             /* transaction code */
    int jobid;            /* job ID */
    } itrn_ackjob_t;

typedef struct {      /* operation-request transaction */
    int code;             /* transaction code */
    int jobid;            /* job ID */
    int opid;             /* operation ID */
    } itrn_reqop_t;

typedef struct {      /* operation-completion transaction */
    int code;             /* transaction code */
    int jobid;            /* job ID */
    int opid;             /* operation ID */
    } itrn_ackop_t;

typedef struct {      /* material-handling move-request transaction */
    int code;             /* transaction code */
    int mvid;             /* move ID */
    } itrn_reqmh_t;

typedef struct {      /* material-handling move-completion transaction
*/
    int code;             /* transaction code */
    int mvid;             /* move ID */
    } itrn_ackmh_t;

typedef struct {      /* device task-request transaction */
    int code;             /* transaction code */
    int tskid;            /* task ID */
    } itrn_reqtsk_t;

typedef struct {      /* device task-completion transaction */
    int code;             /* transaction code */
    int tskid;            /* task ID */
    } itrn_acktsk_t;
/* itrndef.h -------- transaction code definitions */
```

continues

Listing 4.1. Continued

```c
#define ISCH_REQJOB    101    /* job request */

#define ISCH_ACKJOB    102    /* job completion, */

#define ITC_REQOP    201    /* operation request */

#define ITC_ACKOP    202    /* operation completion */

#define IMH_REQMOVE    301    /* material-handling move request */

#define IMH_ACKMOVE    302    /* material-handling move completion
*/

#define IDEV_REQTSK    401    /* device task request */

#define IDEV_ACKTSK    402    /* device task completion */
/* idev.c -------- device-controller transaction handler */

#include <stdio.h>
#include "ignl.h"
#include "ilst.h"
#include "itrn.h"
#include "itrndef.h"
#include "idev.h"

#if 0
On request for processing on a device,
    queue up the request.
    If the device can handle the request now, initiate it.

On completion of processing on a device,
    signal operation completion to the requester.
    If any further request for the device can be served,
        initiate it.

#endif

int idev_hndlr(ptn) ITRN ptn;{
    int err = FALSE;
    switch(ptn->code){
    case IDEV_REQTSK:
        err = idev_reqtsk(ptn);
        break;
        }
    return(err);
    }

int idev_reqtsk(ptn) ITRN ptn;{
    int err = FALSE;
    ptn->code = IDEV_ACKTSK;
```

```
          itrn_put(ptn);
          return(err);
     }
/* ilst.c -------- list the cluster routines */

#include "callstk.h"

#include <stdio.h>
#include "ignl.h"
#include "ilst.h"

ILST ilst_append(list,thing) ILST list; void * thing;{
     ILST l = list;
     if (list==NULL){
          list = (ILST)MALLOC(sizeof(*list));
          list->next = NULL;
          list->thing = thing;
          return(list);
          }
     for (l=list; l->next != NULL; l = l->next);
     l->next = (ILST)MALLOC(sizeof(*list));
     l->next->next = NULL;
     l->next->thing = thing;
     return(list);
     }

void * ilst_next(list,thing) ILST list; void * thing;{
     for (; list != NULL && list->thing != thing; list = list->next);
     if (list==NULL) return(NULL);
     else if (list->next==NULL) return(NULL);
     else return(list->next->thing);
     }

void * ilst_nth(list,n) ILST list; int n;{
     for (; list!=NULL && n>0; list=list->next, —n);
     if (list==NULL) return(NULL);
     else return(list->thing);
     }

int ilst_length(list) ILST list;{
     int n;
     for (n=0; list!=NULL; list=list->next, ++n);
     return(n);
     }

ILST ilst_delete(list,thing) ILST list; void * thing;{
     ILST l;
     if (list==NULL) return(list);
     if (list->thing==thing){
          l = list->next;
          free(list);
          return(l);
          }
     if (list->next==NULL) return(list);
```

continues

Listing 4.1. Continued

```
        for (l=list; l->next!=NULL && l->next->thing!=thing; l=l->next);
        if (l->next!=NULL){
            ILST next = l->next->next;
            free(l->next);
            l->next = next;
            }
        return(list);
        }
/* imh.c -------- material-handling transaction handler */

#include <stdio.h>
#include "ignl.h"
#include "ilst.h"
#include "itrn.h"
#include "itrndef.h"
#include "imh.h"

#if 0
On request for mh move,
        queue up the request.
        If a cart can initiate the move, initiate it.

On cart transit completion,
        if this is the completion of an mh move request,
            send the completion request to the requester.
        See which move request should be handled next,
            and initiate the card transit.

#endif

int imh_hndlr(ptn) ITRN ptn;{
        int err = FALSE;
        switch(ptn->code){
        case IMH_REQMOVE:
            err = imh_reqmv(ptn);
            break;
            }
        return(err);
        }

int imh_reqmv(ptn) ITRN ptn;{
        int err = FALSE;
        ptn->code = IMH_ACKMOVE;
        itrn_put(ptn);
        return(err);
        }
/* isch.c -------- schedule-execution transaction handler */

#include "callstk.h"

#include <stdio.h>
#include "ignl.h"
#include "ilst.h"
#include "itrn.h"
#include "itrndef.h"
```

```
#if 0
On job request,
     receive the process plan,
     include it in the database,
     and create the job structure.

On batch-operation completion,
     determine the next batch operation to run
          and send the request to the task coordinator.
     If there are no more batch operations on the job,
          signal job completion.
#endif

ILST joblist;

typedef struct {
     int jobid;
     ILST boplist;
     int current_op;
     } job_t;

typedef struct {
     int triggered, complete;
     } bop_t;

job_t * isch_findjob(jobid) int jobid;{
     job_t * pjob;
     for (pjob = ILST_FIRST(joblist);
          pjob && pjob->jobid != jobid;
          pjob = ILST_NEXT(joblist,pjob)
          ){
          }
     return(pjob);
     }

int isch_hndlr(ptn) ITRN ptn;{
     int err = FALSE;
     switch(ptn->code){
     case ISCH_REQJOB:
          err = isch_reqjob(ptn);
          break;
     case ITC_ACKOP:
          err = isch_ackop(ptn);
          break;
          }
     free(ptn);
     return(err);
     }

#define NBOPS (rand()%5 + 10)
```

continues

Listing 4.1. Continued

```
int isch_reqjob(preq) itrn_reqjob_t * preq;{
    int err = FALSE;
    int nbops = NBOPS;
    job_t * pjob;
    int opid;
    bop_t * pbop;
    /* CREATE A JOB, WITH BATCH OPERATIONS */
    pjob = (job_t *)MALLOC(sizeof(job_t));
    pjob->jobid = preq->jobid;
    pjob->current_op = 0;
    pjob->boplist = ILST_CREATE;
    for (opid=0; opid<nbops; opid++){
        pbop = (bop_t*)MALLOC(sizeof(bop_t));
        pbop->complete - pbop->triggered = FALSE;
        ILST_APPEND(pjob->boplist,pbop);
        }
    ILST_APPEND(joblist,pjob);
    /* PERFORM SCHEDULE EXECUTION */
    isch_process();
    return(err);
    }

int isch_ackop(ptn) itrn_ackop_t * ptn;{
    int err = FALSE;
    job_t * pjob;
    bop_t * pbop;
    /* MARK THE COMPLETION OF THE CURRENT BATCH OPERATION */
    pjob = isch_findjob(ptn->jobid);
    if (pjob==NULL){
        /* ERROR */
        }
    if (ptn->opid != pjob->current_op){
        /* ERROR */
        }
    pbop = ILST_NTH(pjob->boplist,pjob->current_op);
    if (!pbop){
        /* ERROR */
        }
    pbop->complete - TRUE,
    /* PERFORM SCHEDULE EXECUTION */
    isch_process();
    return(err);
    }

ILST isch_free_boplist(list) ILST list;{
    ILST l;
    while(list!=NULL){
        l = list->next;
        free(list->thing);
        free(list);
        list = l;
        }
    return(NULL);
    }
```

```
isch_process(){
    job_t * pjob;
    bop_t * pbop;
    /* FOR EACH JOB */
    for (pjob=ILST_FIRST(joblist);
        pjob!=NULL;
        pjob=ILST_NEXT(joblist,pjob)
        ){
        /* IF CURRENT OP IS COMPLETE, INCREMENT TO NEXT OP */
        pbop = ILST_NTH(pjob->boplist,pjob->current_op);
        if (pbop && pbop->complete){
            pjob->current_op++;
            }
        /* IF THE JOB IS DONE */
        pbop = ILST_NTH(pjob->boplist,pjob->current_op);
        if (pbop==NULL){
            /* SEND THE ACKJOB TRANSACTION */
            itrn_ackjob_t * ptrn;
            ptrn = (itrn_ackjob_t*)MALLOC(sizeof(itrn_ackjob_t));
            ptrn->code = ISCH_ACKJOB;
            ptrn->jobid = pjob->jobid;
            /* DELETE THE JOB */
            isch_free_boplist(pjob->boplist);
            ILST_DELETE(joblist,pjob);
            itrn_put(ptrn);
            /* DON'T CHECK FOR TRIGGERING */
            free(pjob);
            continue;
            }
        /* IF CURRENT OP IS NOT YET TRIGGERED */
        if (!pbop->triggered){
            /* TRIGGER THE CURRENT OPERATION */
            itrn_reqop_t * ptrn;
            pbop->triggered = TRUE;
            /* SEND OPERATION REQUEST TO THE TASK COORDINATOR */
            ptrn = (itrn_reqop_t*)MALLOC(sizeof(itrn_reqop_t));
            ptrn->code = ITC_REQOP;
            ptrn->jobid = pjob->jobid;
            ptrn->opid = pjob->current_op;
            itrn_put(ptrn);
            }
        }
    }
/* itc.c -------- task-coordinator transaction handler */

#include <stdio.h>
#include "ignl.h"
#include "ilst.h"
#include "itrn.h"
#include "itrndef.h"
```

continues

Listing 4.1. Continued

```
#if 0
On completion of an mh move or a device operation,
     determine the next task to do and request it.
     If there is no next task in operation,
          signal that the operation is complete to schedule execution
          and that the record operation is complete in the database.

On start-operation request from schedule execution,
     determine the next task to do and trigger it
     and record the operation started in the database.

#endif

/* THERE IS A LIST OF OPERATIONS, EACH WITH A LIST OF TASKS */

ILST oplist;
int next_op;

typedef struct operation_struct {
     int id;
     int current_task;
     ILST tasklist;
     int jobid;
     } operation_t;

ILST itc_tree_tasks(list) ILST list;{
     ILST l;
     while(list!=NULL){
          l = list->next;
          free(list->thing);
          free(list);
          list = l;
          }
     return(NULL);
     }

typedef struct task_struct {
     int id;
     int type;
     int triggered, complete;
     } task_t;

int itc_hndlr(ptn) ITRN ptn;{
     int err = FALSE;
     switch(ptn->code){
     case ITC_REQOP:
          err = itc_reqop(ptn);
          break;
     case IMH_ACKMOVE:
```

```
                err = itc_ack_mh(ptn);
                break;
        case IDEV_ACKTSK:
                err = itc_ack_idev(ptn);
                break;
                }
        free(ptn);
        return(err);
        }

#define NTASKS 10

/* HANDLE START-OPERATION REQUEST */
int itc_reqop(preq) itrn_reqop_t * preq;{
        int err = FALSE;
        int i;
        operation_t * ptop;
        task_t * ptask;
        /* CREATE OPERATION REQUEST */
        ptop = (operation_t *)MALLOC(sizeof(operation_t));
        ptop->id = next_op++;
        ptop->tasklist = ILST_CREATE;
        ptop->current_task = 0;
        ptop->jobid = preq->jobid;
        for (i=0; i<NTASKS; i++){
                ptask = (task_t *)MALLOC(sizeof(task_t));
                ptask->id = i;
                ptask->type = i % 2;
                ptask->triggered = FALSE;
                ptask->complete = FALSE;
                ILST_APPEND(ptop->tasklist,ptask);
                }
        ILST_APPEND(oplist,ptop);
        /* DO TASK COORDINATOR PROCESSING */
        err = itc_process();
        return(err);
        }

int itc_ack_mh(ptn) itrn_ackmh_t * ptn;{
        int err = FALSE;
        operation_t * ptop;
        task_t * ptask;
        /* FIND THE RELEVANT OPERATION REQUEST */
        for (     ptop = ILST_FIRST(oplist);
                ptop != NULL;
                ptop = ILST_NEXT(oplist,ptop)
                ){
                if (ptop->id==ptn->mvid) break;
                }
        if (ptop==NULL){
                /* ERROR: INVALID OPERATION ID */
                }
```

continues

Listing 4.1. Continued

```c
        /* THE CURRENT TASK SHOULD BE AN MH MOVE */
        ptask = ILST_NTH(ptop->tasklist,ptop->current_task);
        if (ptask->type != 0){
            /* ERROR: TASK-TYPE MISMATCH */
            }
        /* MARK THE TASK COMPLETE AND ADVANCE TO THE NEXT */
        ptask->complete = TRUE;
        ptop->current_task ++;
        /* DO TASK-COORDINATOR PROCESSING */
        err = itc_process();
        return(err);
        }

int itc_ack_idev(ptn) itrn_acktsk_t * ptn;{
    int err = FALSE;
    operation_t * ptop;
    task_t * ptask;
    /* FIND THE RELEVANT OPERATION REQUEST */
    for (    ptop = ILST_FIRST(oplist);
        ptop != NULL;
        ptop = ILST_NEXT(oplist,ptop)
        ){
        if (ptop->id==ptn->tskid) break;
        }
    if (ptop==NULL){
        /* ERROR: INVALID OPERATION ID */
        }
    /* THE CURRENT TASK SHOULD BE A DEVICE OPERATION */
    ptask = ILST_NTH(ptop->tasklist,ptop->current_task);
    if (ptask->type != 1){
        /* ERROR: TASK-TYPE MISMATCH */
        }
    /* MARK THE TASK COMPLETE AND ADVANCE TO THE NEXT */
    ptask->complete = TRUE;
    ptop->current_task ++;
    /* DO THE TASK-COORDINATOR PROCESSING */
    err = itc_process();
    return(err);
    }

int itc_process(){
    int err = FALSE;
    operation_t * ptop;
    task_t * ptask;
    /* FOR EACH OPERATION REQUEST */
    for (    ptop = ILST_FIRST(oplist);
        ptop != NULL;
        ptop = ILST_NEXT(oplist,ptop)
        ){
        /* IF ALL TASKS DONE, SEND ITC_ACKOP AND DELETE OP */
        if (ptop->current_task >= ILST_LENGTH(ptop->tasklist)){
            itrn_ackop_t * p_ack;
            p_ack = (itrn_ackop_t *)MALLOC(sizeof(itrn_ackop_t));
```

```
                    p_ack->code = ITC_ACKOP;
                    p_ack->jobid = ptop->jobid;
                    p_ack->opid = ptop->id;
                    itrn_put(p_ack);
                    ptop->tasklist = itc_free_tasks(ptop->tasklist);
                    ILST_DELETE(oplist,ptop);
                    free(ptop);
                    }
            /* IF NEXT TASK CAN BE TRIGGERED, DO SO */
            else {
                    ptask = ILST_NTH(ptop->tasklist,ptop->current_task);
                    if (!ptask->triggered){
                        if (ptask->type==0){
                            itrn_reqmh_t * p_req;
                            p_req = (itrn_reqmh_t *)
[ccc]                       MALLOC(sizeof(itrn_reqmh_t));
                            p_req->code = IMH_REQMOVE;
                            p_req->mvid = ptop->id;
                            itrn_put(p_req);
                            }
                        else if (ptask->type==1){
                            itrn_reqtsk_t * p_req;
                            p_req = (itrn_reqtsk_t *)
                                MALLOC(sizeof(itrn_reqtsk_t));
                            p_req->code = IDEV_REQTSK;
                            p_req->tskid = ptop->id;
                            itrn_put(p_req);
                            }
                        ptask->triggered = TRUE;
                        }
                    }
            }
    return(err);
    }
/* itrn.c -------- transaction-cluster routines */

#include "itrn.h"
#include "ilst.h"

ILST trnque;

void itrn_put(ptrn) ITRN ptrn;{
    ILST_APPEND(trnque,ptrn);
    }

ITRN itrn_examine(){
    return(ILST_FIRST(trnque));
    }

ITRN itrn_get(){
    ITRN ptrn;
    ptrn = ILST_FIRST(trnque);
    ILST_DELETE(trnque,ptrn);
```

continues

Listing 4.1. Continued

```
        return(ptrn);
        }
/* main.c -------- */

#define IN_MAIN
#include <stdio.h>
#include "ignl.h"
#include "ilst.h"
#include "itrn.h"
#include "itrndef.h"

typedef int (*func_t)();

typedef struct itrn_tbl_struct {
        int code;
        func_t hndlr;
        } itrn_tbl_t;

extern int isch_hndlr();
extern int itc_hndlr();
extern int imh_hndlr();
extern int idev_hndlr();

int nextjob;
int jobs_started, jobs_completed;

#define in_process_jobs (jobs_started - jobs_completed)

#define MAXJOBS 100

int newjobs(){
        itrn_reqjob_t * preq;
        while(jobs_started < MAXJOBS && in_process_jobs < 10){
                preq = (itrn_reqjob_t*)MALLOC(sizeof(itrn_reqjob_t));
                preq->code = ISCH_REQJOB;
                preq->jobid = nextjob++;
                itrn_put(preq);
                jobs_started++;
                }
        }

int debug=1;

int main_hndlr(ptrn) ITRN ptrn;{
        int err = FALSE;
        if (ptrn->code==ISCH_ACKJOB){
                jobs_completed++;
                if (debug){
                        printf("Ack Job %d\n",((itrn_ackjob_t*)ptrn)->jobid);
                        }
                newjobs();
                }
        free(ptrn);
        return(err);
        }
```

```
itrn_tbl_t itrn_tbl[] = {
    {ISCH_REQJOB,      isch_hndlr},
    {ISCH_ACKJOB,      main_hndlr},
    {ITC_REQOP,       itc_hndlr},
    {ITC_ACKOP,      isch_hndlr},
    {IMH_REQMOVE,      imh_hndlr},
    {IMH_ACKMOVE,      itc_hndlr},
    {IDEV_REQTSK,      idev_hndlr},
    {IDEV_ACKTSK,      itc_hndlr},
    {0,NULL}
    };

ITRN ptrn;

main(argc,argv) char ** argv;{
    itrn_tbl_t * p;
    /* INITIALIZE THE TRANSACTION HANDLERS */
    /* REQUEST THE FIRST JOBS */
    newjobs();
    /* LOOP FOREVER */
    while(TRUE){
        /* GET THE NEXT TRANSACTION */
        ptrn = itrn_get();
        if (ptrn==NULL) break;
        /* IF THERE ARE NO MORE TRANSACTIONS, QUIT */
        /* DISPATCH TO THE PROPER HANDLER */
        for (pt = itrn_tbl; pt->code; pt++){
            if (pt->code==ptrn->code){
                if (pt->hndlr != NULL){
                    (*pt->hndlr)(ptrn);
                    }
                break;
                }
            }
        if (!pt->code){
            /* UNRECOGNIZED CODE */
            fprintf(stderr,"Error - unrec transaction code %d\n"
                ,ptrn->code
                );
            }
        }
    }
```

The First Deslugging Pass

The simulation program runs 100 simulated jobs. Each job has 10±5
operations, and each operation has 10 tasks, 5 device operations, and 5
material-handling operations. As each job completes, the program
prints the message Ack Job nn. Ultimately, the program must perform
100 jobs, about 1,000 operations, and 10,000 tasks.

Running on an AT-level PC, the program takes 48 seconds to complete. This is enough time to reflect on what it is doing. If it does 10,000 tasks (each of which is a no-op) in 50 seconds, it is doing about 200 tasks per second. If you are running the program on a 1-MIP machine, that is about one task every 5 milliseconds, or about 5,000 instructions per task.

What is it about a no-op task that takes 5,000 instructions to perform? What can you do to speed it up? Guesswork could lead you to suspect that the message-queueing mechanism is at fault. Should you replace it with something hand-coded in assembly language?

Resisting that temptation, you instead run the program under the debugger. While the program is running, you press Ctrl-Alt-SysReq to stop the execution. Figure 4.3 shows the screen that results.

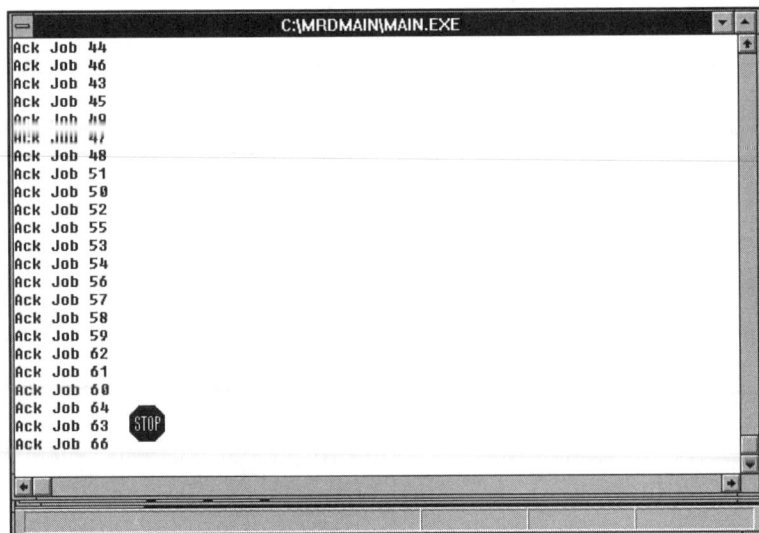

Fig. 4.3. You manually halt the program by pressing Ctrl-Alt-SysReq.

Then you display the call stack by selecting the **View** menu and then choosing **Call Stack**. Figure 4.4 shows a typical call stack display that appears in the Call Stack window.

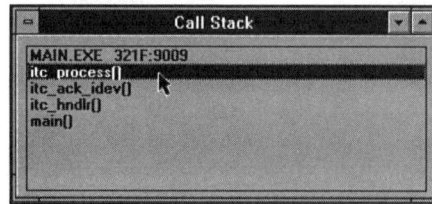

Fig. 4.4. The Call Stack window.

In this particular program, the first slug accounts for only about 55 percent of the execution time. So, you may have to take half a dozen samples before a pattern becomes apparent.

The program spends much of its time in the ILST cluster, in the functions ILST_NTH(), ILST_NEXT(), and ILST_LENGTH(). You might be tempted to optimize these routines, especially because they are kind of silly, always running down the list from the beginning. Or you might be tempted to scuttle the ILST cluster altogether—going around to all 50 or so places in which it is used and replacing it with something else. Or you might be tempted to rewrite the transaction cluster, because it is based on the ILST cluster.

However, for most of the time that the program spends in the ILST functions, the program is calling the functions from the routine itc_process(). The call stack displayed in figure 4.4 illustrates this point. As shown in figure 4.5, when you double-click a line displayed in the Call Stack window, another window displays the part of the listing that contains that particular code line.

If you examine the specific lines on the call stack, you can find one of the slugs. For example, note the statement:

```
/* IF ALL TASKS DONE, SEND ITC_ACKOP AND DELETE OP */
if (ptop->current_task >= ILST_LENGTH(ptop->tasklist)){
```

The operation variable current_task is the index of the next task to perform. The program performs this test solely to determine whether the operation is complete, and about 90 percent of the time it is not.

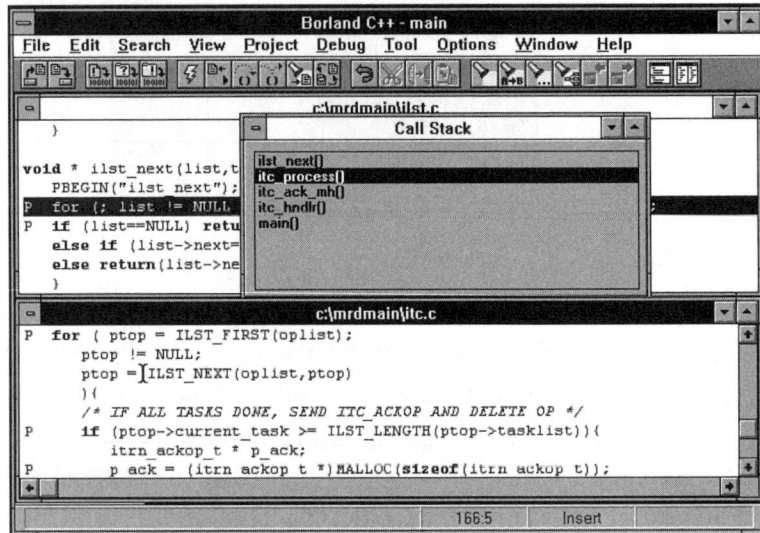

Fig. 4.5. You can access a slug directly from the call stack.

Right above this line is another slug:

```
/* FOR EACH OPERATION REQUEST */
for (      ptop = ILST_FIRST(oplist);
      ptop != NULL;
      ptop = ILST_NEXT(oplist,ptop)
      ){
```

The program calls the cluster operation `ILST_NEXT()` to iterate over the list of operation requests. This is an *n*-squared operation, because `ILST_NEXT()` searches from the beginning of the list. (If you double the length of the list, you quadruple the time that the loop spends searching because you have a loop-within-a-loop.)

A few lines below, the call stack points to another slug:

```
ptask = ILST_NTH(ptop->tasklist,ptop->current_task);
```

All this line does is extract from the task list a pointer to the current task.

You probably are wondering who would ever introduce such slugs into a program; they were not planted in the program just for the sake of

example. This program is a tiny example of an actual, state-of-the-art application. These slugs were all caused by the stilted way that the application's programmers designed and used the list cluster.

You also might think this example is a lesson in how not to use list clusters, but it is not intended to be. Instead, it is a lesson in how to find actual slugs. The slugs that you find in other software will be different, but the process that you use to find them is the same.

Fixing these slugs is easy. First, you remove the ILST_NEXT() in the iteration. Just step a pointer along in the normal way. Second, instead of keeping a numeric index of the next task in the list, keep a pointer to it. Then the program won't have to call the ILST_NTH() and ILST_LENGTH() primitives. (When the program runs off the end and becomes NULL, there are no more tasks.)

Just by making these changes, you decrease execution time to about 20 seconds—and you didn't have to hand-optimize anything. It is 2.4 times as fast as before, for a speedup factor of 2.4.

The Second Deslugging Pass

On the second pass, you once again run the program under the debugger and randomly halt the execution a few times. This time you will find some more slugs. (These slugs were in the program during the first pass, but were masked by the big one.) Now you find that the program still spends a lot of time in the ILST cluster, but this time in the ILST_APPEND() primitive. This routine moves down the list and tacks a new item to the end of the list. Should you make the list cluster more complex, by adding a pointer to both ends of the list?

Fortunately, the call stacks find a more effective fix. Some of the calls occur while the program is creating the task list of an operation. The tasks are appended to the list one at a time in the following line:

```
ILST_APPEND(ptop->tasklist,ptask);
```

This is an *n*-squared operation, because `ILST_APPEND()` runs the length of the list.

Another significant source of calls to `ILST_APPEND()` is this line in `ITRN_PUT()` in the transaction cluster:

```
ILST_APPEND(trnque,ptrn);
```

Now you are finally seeing some time spent in transactions.

The fix that you should make to correct this slug is twofold. First, to eliminate the time that the program spends appending tasks while building a task list, you simply put the tasks in a temporary array and then build the list all at once. Then add to the `ILST` cluster a routine that takes an array of pointers and creates an equivalent list. Second, you change the transaction cluster so that it uses a circular array, rather than a list, for the queue.

After you make these corrections, execution time decreases to 17 seconds (speedup factor: 2.8 times faster than the original program).

The Third Deslugging Pass

At this stage, the slugs become smaller, but you find more of them. You find that the program is spending time on list operations at the operation and job level. You also find the program spending significant time in transaction dispatching.

To fix these slugs, you make the following changes:

➤ In `ITRN`, change the cluster so that, instead of using indexes, it uses pointers into the queue.

➤ In `ITC`, change pointers `l` and `ptop` to register variables.

➤ In `ISCH`, stop using the `ILST` cluster on the operation lists, just as you did earlier on the task lists in `ITC`.

In `ITC`, the program is spending time in the following loop:

```
for (l=oplist; l; l=l->next){
    ptop = l->thing;
    if (ptop->id==ptn->tskid) break;
    }
```

```
if (ptop==NULL){
    /* ERROR: INVALID OPERATION ID */
    }
```

This loop conducts a linear search of the operation list whenever a task completion is received from IDEV. Replace it with the following code:

```
for (l=oplist
    ; l && ((operation_t*)l->thing)->id != ptn->tskid
    ; l=l->next){
    }
if (l==NULL){
    /* ERROR: INVALID OPERATION ID */
    }
ptop = l->thing;
```

This compiles into a faster loop. Make the same changes for the loop that receives material-handling acknowledgments.

The main() function handles transaction dispatching by conducting a linear table search. When the function finds the transaction code in the table, it knows which routine to send the transaction to. Replace that loop, hard-coding the search as a series of if statements.

> **Note:** Some programmers believe that a data structure should be used only to hold information that is variable at runtime. The transaction-dispatching table never changes, so you might as well hard-code it.

The result of these fixes is an execution time of 13 seconds (speedup factor: 3.7).

As you continue subsequent passes of deslugging, the slugs become much less obvious. The call stacks give you a pretty good idea of how the program is spending its time, but you can't find anything more that you can eliminate. The program spends the bulk of its time in two operations:

➤ Dispatching transactions

➤ Finding relevant operations when acknowledgments are received

Redesigning the Program

Let's go back to the original problem. The program has *jobs*, each job has *operations*, and each operation has *tasks*. In structured pseudocode, the problem looks like this:

> *To perform a job:*
> *For each operation of the job*
> *begin*
> *   Perform the operation.*
> *end*

> *To perform an operation:*
> *For each task of the operation*
> *begin*
> *   Perform the device task.*
> *   Perform material handling task.*
> *end*

> *To perform a device task:*
> *(Simulate a delay.)*

> *To perform a material-handling task:*
> *(Simulate a delay.)*

If the preceding code were executable, you would have an implementation. Nowhere does the problem state that you must have functional modules, transactions, events, and all that state-of-the-art stuff.

What you actually must do is implement the language that makes this statement run. On the other hand, if you want the program to maintain the same functionality as before, the basic time-sequence of activities must remain pretty much the same.

To do this, you can build a little language that uses some C macros. (It doesn't have to look pretty.) What kind of language? Because jobs run in parallel with each other, it must support parallel execution. However, you don't have to have a separate process for each job. You want

to keep things simple, small, and efficient. Also, you want each job to be a lightweight process. (Some operating systems provide lightweight processes, which are a simple form of parallel process of which you can have many instances within the same address space. But those are actually still too heavy, with their preemptive scheduling, context-switching, and so on.) In short, you really don't want the final program to behave any differently, you just want to simplify its source code.

Listing 4.2 shows the redesigned program. Some languages are interpreted, and some are compiled. This language's compiler consists of a few C macros that compile the source language into ordinary C. Just as normal compilers generate jump instructions to simulate structured programming, these macros generate `goto` statements to simulate the structured control constructs of the language.

The redesigned program is not only faster, it is startling in its brevity:

Listing 4.2. The Redesigned Manufacturing Simulation Program

```
/* fast.h ------- state machine-dispatch macros */

#define DISPATCH0

#define DISPATCH1 \
    if (p->state==1) goto L1;\
    DISPATCH0

#define DISPATCH2 \
    if (p->state==2) goto L2;\
    DISPATCH1

#define DISPATCH3 \
    if (p->state==3) goto L3;\
    DISPATCH2

#define DISPATCH4 \
    if (p->state==4) goto L4;\
    DISPATCH3
/* fast.c -------- the redesigned simulation program */

#include <stdio.h>
#include "fast.h"

#define STDVARS\
    int (*func)(); int state; struct machine_struct *caller
```

continues

Listing 4.2. Continued

```c
typedef struct machine_struct {
    STDVARS;
    } machine_t;

#define PROLOGUE(typ,f)\
    typ *p = (typ*)malloc(sizeof(*p));\
    extern int f();\
    p->caller = caller;\
    p->func = f;\
    p->state = 0;\
    (*p->func)(p);

#define BREAK(n,lab) p->state=(n); enque(p); return; lab:

#define CALL(n,lab,expr) p->state=(n); (expr); return; lab:

machine_t * ptcmp=NULL;
int retn_val=0;

#define RETURN(v)\
    ptemp=p->caller;\
    retn_val=(v);\
    free(p);\
    if (ptemp){(*ptemp->func)(ptemp);};

int onq=0, deq=0, ninq=0;
machine_t *queue[256];
enque(p) machine_t *p;{
    queue[enq++] = p;
    if (enq>=256) enq=0;
    ninq++;
    }

machine_t * deque(){
    machine_t *p = NULL;
    if (ninq){
        p = queue[deq++];
        if (deq>=256) deq=0;
        ninq--;
        }
    return(p);
    }

int jobs_started=0;
int jobs_completed=0;
#define NBOPS (rand()%5 + 10)
#define NTASK 10
#define NJOBS 100

main(){
    machine_t *p;
    /* REPEAT UNTIL ALL JOBS ARE COMPLETE */
    while(jobs_completed < NJOBS){
```

```
          /* RUN WHATEVER CAN BE RUN */
          if (ninq){
               p = deque();
               (*p->func)(p);
               }
          /* IF < 100 JOBS STARTED AND < 10 JOBS IN PROCESS */
          if (jobs_started<NJOBS
[ccc]     && jobs_started-jobs_completed < 10
[ccc]     ){
               /* START ANOTHER JOB */
               job(NULL);
               }
          }
     }

typedef struct {
     STDVARS;
     int jobid;
     int i;
     int nbops;
     } job_t;
job(caller) machine_t *caller;{
     PROLOGUE(job_t,job_func);
     }
job_func(p) job_t *p;{
     DISPATCH1;
     p->jobid = jobs_started++;
     p->nbops = NBOPS;
     /* FOR EACH OPERATION */
     for (p->i=0; p->i < p->nbops; p->i++){
          CALL(1,L1,opn(p));
          }
     jobs_completed++;
     printf("Ack Job %d\n",p->jobid);
     RETURN(1);
     }

typedef struct {
     STDVARS;
     int taskid;
     int ntask;
     } opn_t;
opn(caller) machine_t *caller;{
     PROLOGUE(opn_t,opn_func);
     }
opn_func(p) opn_t *p;{
     DISPATCH2;
     p->ntask = NTASK;
     /* FOR EACH OPERATION */
     for (p->taskid=0; p->taskid < p->ntask; p->taskid++){
          CALL(1,L1,dev_ctl(p));
```

continues

Listing 4.2. Continued

```
            CALL(2,L2,mh_ctl(p));
            }
        RETURN(1);
        }

typedef struct {
    STDVARS;
    } dev_ctl_t;
dev_ctl(caller) machine_t *caller;{
    PROLOGUE(dev_ctl_t,dev_ctl_func);
    }
dev_ctl_func(p) dev_ctl_t *p;{
    DISPATCH1;
    /* DO SOMETHING */
    BREAK(1,L1);
    RETURN(1);
    }

typedef struct {
    STDVARS;
    } mh_ctl_t;
mh_ctl(caller) machine_t *caller;{
    PROLOGUE(mh_ctl_t,mh_ctl_func);
    }
mh_ctl_func(p) mh_ctl_t *p;{
    DISPATCH1;
    /* DO SOMETHING */
    BREAK(1,L1);
    RETURN(1);
    }
```

This language consists of processes, and each process consists of an application data record, such as a job record, operation record, or task record. In the record is a pointer to a control procedure, and an integer state variable.

When a new job process begins, the program allocates and initializes the record of the process. Then the process resumes by calling the record's control procedure. The control procedure does whatever it needs to do and then returns, but first it sets the state variable. The next time that the process resumes, the state variable will cause the control procedure to do whatever comes next. No surprise—the process is just a finite state machine.

So, when the program starts a job, it simply creates a finite state machine. When the job starts an operation, that too is a finite state machine. Think of an operation as a subroutine of the job, because the job waits for the operation to finish before starting the next operation. In fact, to create the operation state machine record, you include a pointer to the job's state machine record. Then when the operation finishes, it simply deletes itself and resumes the job.

This scheme eliminates the following:

➤ The transaction to start an operation.

➤ The transaction that occurs when an operation finishes.

➤ The need to search for and find the job that requests the operation.

The same is true for the relationship between operations and tasks. Therefore, the only transactions that remain are those connected to simulated outside events: device and material-handling delays.

Note: This technique obviously is object-oriented, so you may wonder why you didn't use C++. But in fact, you can use either C or C++. C++'s syntax is a little neater, but not enough to claim great productivity benefits.

There's an underlying lesson in this example. Although both programs, before and after the redesign, have a very object-oriented flavor, the second one is much smaller and faster. It is hard to see how to solve the simulation problem *without* doing object-oriented programming (OOP). The lesson is: OOP is a property of the problem, regardless of the language in which it is programmed.

The following are the primitives of the language:

PROLOGUE(*type*, *f*) where *type* is the name of the application record as specified in a *typedef* statement, and *f* is the name of the control procedure. This statement is called from within the process-creation procedure. It expands into all the necessary setup code and resumes the process.

DISPATCH*n* where *n* is the number of states in the process. This is the first statement inside the control procedure of a process. Whenever the process resumes, the state variable causes the control procedure to jump to the proper statement.

BREAK(*n*) where *n* is a unique state number within the control procedure. This statement causes the nonpreemptive release of control to a global process queue. It puts the process in a global queue and then gives up control. Later, when the global dispatcher resumes it, the DISPATCH statement sends control to the statement that follows the BREAK statement.

CALL(*n*, *expr*) where *n* is a unique state number, and *expr* creates another process (passing itself as the first argument). This statement does the lightweight-process equivalent of a subroutine call. The statement creates and resumes a subordinate process. When that process completes, it deletes itself and resumes the current process. The subordinate can return a value.

RETURN(*v*) This primitive affects a lightweight process return, resuming the calling process and passing it the value *v*. The process knows who the caller is because that was its first argument when it was created.

Note: You can put BREAK statements anywhere, such as deep inside loops or conditional statements. For example, if you want to poll for some condition to be true, you could code the following:

```
while (... condition is FALSE ...){
    printf("I'm still waiting\n");
    BREAK(3);
    }
```

BREAK(3) expands into

```
p->state = 3;
enque(p);
return;
L3:;
```

and DISPATCH*n* expands into

```
if (p->state==1) goto L1;
if (p->state==2) goto L2;
if (p->state==3) goto L3;
... up to n ...
```

Is this language structured? It certainly is easy to maintain. Suppose that you suddenly realize that you must have the state machine wait for one more thing. Just insert a BREAK statement at the right spot and renumber the states.

The application in Listing 4.2 is one-fourth the size of the first version, even including the definitions of the process macros. It now gets the job done in 10 scconds (speedup factor: 4.8).

Deslugging the Redesigned Program

Now that you've redesigned the program, it's time to deslug it. The redesigned program has hot spots in the enque() and deque() routines. Simply replace these routines with inline macros, and you decrease the time of execution to 7 seconds (speedup factor: 6.9).

The next iteration shows that the program spends most of its time printing the hundred Ack Job nn messages. Commenting out the printf statement reduce the execution time to 4 seconds (speedup factor: 12).

On the sixth pass, you increase the number of jobs to 1,000, which makes the program run long enough to enable you to observe and analyze its execution. You then see that the program spends a large percentage of time in the `_malloc()` and `_free()` functions as it creates and destroys objects. To fix this, you recycle used objects in special stacks. Also, in each process, you make the self pointer `p` a register variable. The execution time that results is 26 seconds, or 2.6 seconds for 100 jobs (speedup factor: 18.5).

The Final Revision

On the next iteration, the bulk of the time goes into the CALL and RETURN statements. Because operations and tasks are serialized within each job, you need not make them separate processes. Instead, you recode them, as indicated in the following pseudocode:

> *To perform a job:*
>   *For each operation of the job*
>   *begin*
>   *for each task of the operation*
>   *begin*
>   *(Simulate device task delay.)*
>   *(Simulate material handling task delay.)*
>   *end*
>   *end*

This final revision of the manufacturing simulation program eliminates the CALL statements, as shown in Listing 4.3. The result is an execution time of 11 seconds, or 1.1 seconds per 100 jobs (speedup factor: 43.6).

Listing 4.3. The Final Version of the Manufacturing Simulation Program

```
/* fast.c ------- the final simulation program */

#include <stdio.h>
#include "fast.h"
```

```
#pragma check_stack(off)

#define STDVARS int state; int (*func)(); struct machine_struct
*caller

typedef struct machine_struct {
    STDVARS;
    } machine_t;

/* STACK STRUCTURES FOR CACHING USED STATE MACHINES */
struct mstk_struct {
    int n;
    struct machine_struct *stk[64];
    };
#define M_ALLOC(mstk,size,p) {\
    if (mstk.n <= 0) p = (struct machine_struct*)malloc(size);\
    else p = mstk.stk[-mstk.n];\
    }
#define M_FREE(mstk,p) {\
    if (mstk.n >= 64) free(p);\
    else mstk.stk[mstk.n++] = p;\
    }

#define PROLOGUE(typ,f,stk)\
    register typ *p;\
    extern int f();\
    M_ALLOC(stk,sizeof(*p),p);\
    p->caller = caller;\
    p->func = f;\
    p->state = 0;\
    (*p->func)(p);

#define BREAK(n,lab) p->state=(n); ENQUE(p); return; lab:

#define CALL(n,lab,expr) p->state=(n); (expr); return; lab:

machine_t * ptemp=NULL;

int retn_val=0;

#define RETURN(v,stk)\
    ptemp=p->caller;\
    retn_val=(v);\
    M_FREE(stk,p);\
    if (ptemp){(*ptemp->func)(ptemp);};

unsigned int ninq=0;
machine_t *queue[256];
machine_t **enq = queue, **deq = queue;

#define ENQUE(p)\
    {*enq++ = p; if (enq>=(queue+256)) enq=queue; ninq++;}
```

continues

Listing 4.3. Continued

```
#define DEQUE(p)\
    {p = *deq++; if (deq>=(queue+256)) deq=queue; ninq-;}

int jobs_started=0;
int jobs_completed=0;
#define NBOPS (rand()%5 + 10)
#define NTASK 10
int njobs = 1000;

main(){
    register machine_t *p;
    /* REPEAT UNTIL ALL JOBS ARE COMPLETE */
    while(jobs_completed < njobs){
        /* RUN WHATEVER CAN BE RUN */
        if (ninq){
            DEQUE(p);
            (*p->func)(p);
            }
        /* IF < 100 JOBS STARTED AND < 10 JOBS IN PROCESS */
        if (jobs_started < njobs
[ccc]       && jobs_started - jobs_completed < 10
[ccc]       ){
            /* START ANOTHER JOB */
            job(NULL);
            }
        }
    }

struct mstk_struct jobstk;
typedef struct {
    STDVARS;
    int jobid;
    int i;
    int nbops;
    int taskid, ntask;
    } job_t;
job(caller) machine_t *caller;{
    PROLOGUE(job_t,job_func,jobstk);
    }
job_func(p) register job_t *p;{
    DISPATCH2;
    p->jobid = jobs_started++;
    p->nbops = NBOPS;
    /* FOR EACH OPERATION */
    for (p->i=0; p->i < p->nbops; p->i++){
        p->ntask = NTASK;
        /* FOR EACH TASK */
        for (p->taskid=0; p->taskid < p->ntask; p->taskid++){
```

```
                /* DO DEVICE CONTROL */
                BREAK(1,L1);
                /* DO MATERIAL HANDLING */
                BREAK(2,L2);
                }
        }
    jobs_completed++;
    RETURN(1,jobstk);
    }
```

Summary of the Manufacturing Simulation Example

The original state-of-the-art program took 48 seconds to execute.
That 48 seconds consisted of the following:

Seconds	Action
28	ITC use of list processing
3	Processing and building transaction-queue lists
4	More random list processing and searching
3	Handling request and acknowledgment transactions, and searching for IDs after acknowledgments
3	Processing enque() and deque() subroutines
3	Printing messages on-screen
1.4	Processing _malloc() and _free() functions
1.5	Processing CALL and RETURN statements
1.1	"Real meat"; that is, processing actions that actually solve the original problem.

Figure 4.6 shows these results in a pie graph.

Notice that the redesigned program is not only faster, but also four
times smaller, as shown in figure 4.7.

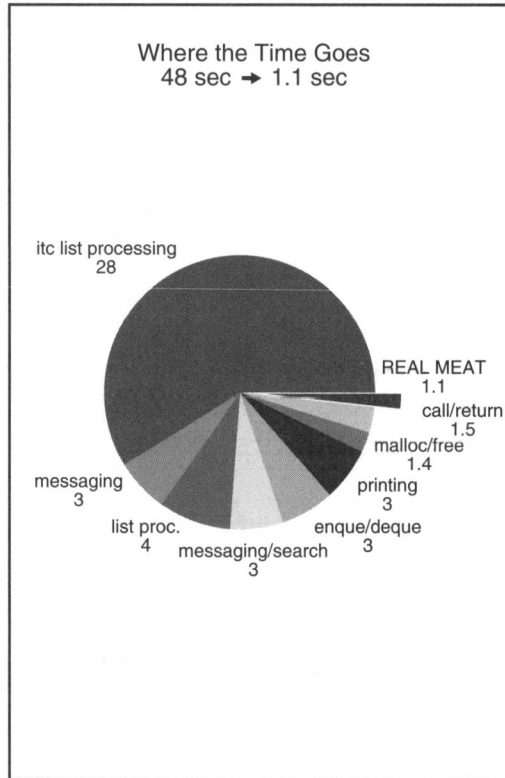

Fig. 4.6. The original execution time of 48 seconds consists of many slugs. By removing them, you reduce the time to 1.1 seconds, a speedup factor of more than 40 times.

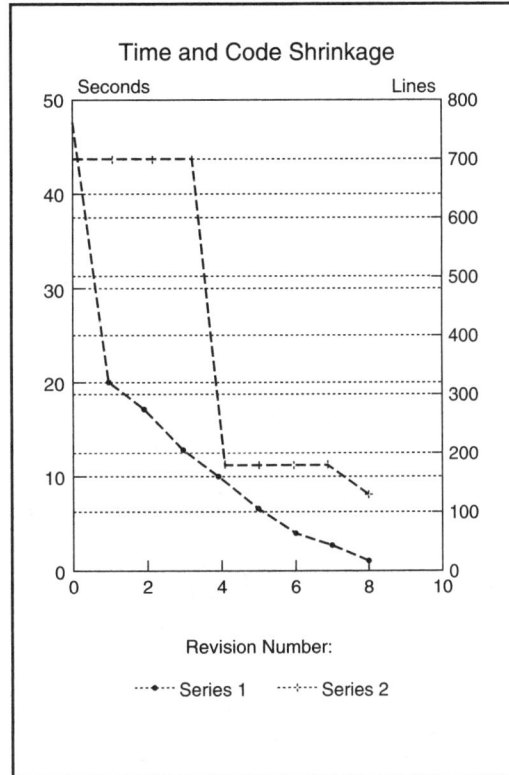

Fig. 4.7. Revision history of the example. Deslugging the original
program reduces the execution time by a factor of about 4.

This example illustrates some intriguing points:

➤ Larger programs tend to be slower and provide greater opportunities for speeding up the execution time. You can see this in the average depth of the call stack during execution. The deeper the call stack is, the more call instructions are on it, and each of these instructions is a possible slug.

➤ This example contradicts the common wisdom that more efficient code is necessarily less maintainable. In the redesigned program, you can more easily make functional changes, at least after you've learned how to do so.

➤ The redesigned, high-speed code looks unlike traditional programming. It contains less explicit data structure, and favors polling and direct invocation over event-mediated methods. This is not an isolated phenomenon. Although polling methods theoretically have lower performance, many programs spend most of their cycles managing a data structure whose ultimate justification was to support an event-driven style. And the justification for the event-driven style ostensibly was higher performance!

Although this case study is lengthy, it shows you how the deslugging process actually works. As you have seen, performance tuning is like wringing water out of a towel: You can always get more if you keep working at it. The example also demonstrates the importance of analysis and diagnosis, and why guesswork doesn't work. Finally, the example demonstrates that redesigning the software not only improves performance, but also can improve maintainability.

Macros That Help Display the Call Stack

As mentioned previously, modern development environments do not adequately support the capability to sample the call stack randomly. However, you can work around this deficiency somewhat by adding certain things to the source code. For example, by adding a small

amount of code, the application program can keep track of its own call stack so that you don't have to rely on being able to read the system's call stack. This section describes a set of macros that enable an application program to keep track of its own call stack, shown in Listing 4.4.

Listing 4.4. Macros That Allow a Program to Monitor its Own Call Stack

```
/* callstk.h */

#define MAX_CALLSTK 50

struct callstk_struct {
    char * name;
    long line;
    };

#ifdef IN_MAIN
int ncallstk = 0;
struct callstk_struct callstk[MAX_CALLSTK];
#else
extern int ncallstk;
extern struct callstk_struct callstk[];
#endif

#define PBEGIN(sbrname)\
    struct callstk_struct * pcallstk = callstk+ncallstk;\
    int save_ncallstk = (\
        pcallstk->name = sbrname,\
        pcallstk->line = __LINE__,\
        ncallstk++)

#define PLINE\
    (ncallstk=save_ncallstk+1, pcallstk->line = (long)__LINE__)

#define P PLINE;
```

This code declares a global array called `callstk[]`. Each element of the array holds a subroutine name `char * name`, and a line number `long line`. A global variable called `int ncallstk` stores the current number of entries that the program is using. As the program enters each application routine, it pushes the routine's name and the current line number on the call stack, using the macro `PBEGIN(subrname)`. Before and after each subroutine or function call, the program truncates the stack to the proper level and stores the line number in the stack. This is done by the macro PLINE, which is abbreviated as P. As a result, the array callstk always contains the name and current line number of each active subroutine. If you halt the program, you can display this array instead of depending on the debugger's possibly unreliable capability to display the call stack. Another advantage of this display capability is that it is transparent to system routines, such as those in Windows, that would otherwise appear on the stack. The CPU overhead of the macros is negligible.

Listing 4.5 gives an example of how you can insert the macros into an application routine.

Listing 4.5. An Example of Inserting Macros Into an Application

```
/* itc.c task-coordinator transaction handler */

#include "callstk.h"

        . . . .

int itc_process(){
        PBEGIN("itc_process");
        int err = FALSE;
        operation_t * ptop;
        task_t * ptask;
        /* FOR EACH OPERATION REQUEST */
P       for (    ptop = ILST_FIRST(oplist);
            ptop != NULL;
            ptop = ILST_NEXT(oplist,ptop)
            ){
            /* IF ALL TASKS DONE, SEND ITC_ACKOP AND DELETE OP */
P           if (ptop->current_task >=
[ccc]          ILST_LENGTH(ptop->tasklist)
[ccc]          ){
                itrn_ackop_t * p_ack;
P               p_ack = (itrn_ackop_t *)
[ccc]           MALLOC(sizeof(itrn_ackop_t));
P               p_ack->code = ITC_ACKOP;
P               p_ack->jobid = ptop->jobid;
P               p_ack->opid = ptop->id;
P               itrn_put(p_ack);
P               ptop->tasklist =
[ccc]           itc_free_tasks(ptop->tasklist);
P               ILST_DELETE(oplist,ptop);
P               free(ptop);
                }
            /* IF NEXT TASK CAN BE TRIGGERED, DO SO */
            else {
P               ptask = ILST_NTH(ptop->tasklist,
```

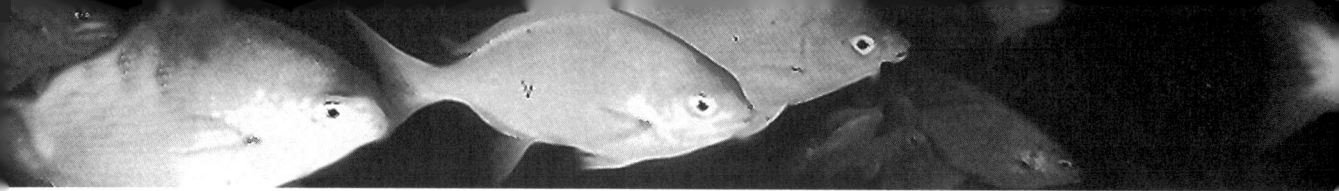

```
[ccc]                ptop->current_task);
P                if (!ptask->triggered){
P                    if (ptask->type==0){
                         itrn_reqmh_t * p_req;
P                         p_req = (itrn_reqmh_t *)
[ccc]                     MALLOC(sizeof(itrn_reqmh_t));
P                         p_req->code = IMII_REQMOVE;
P                         p_req->mvid = ptop->id;
P                         itrn_put(p_req);
                     }
                    else if (ptask->type==1){
                         itrn_reqtsk_t * p_req;
P                         p_req = (itrn_reqtsk_t *)
[ccc]                     MALLOC(sizeof(itrn_reqtsk_t));
P                         p_req->code = IDEV_REQTSK;
P                         p_req->tskid = ptop->id;
P                         itrn_put(p_req);
                     }
P                    ptask->triggered = TRUE;
P                }
P            }
P        }
P    return(err);
    }
```

The result is that you can display part of the call stack in the Watch window, showing both routine names and line numbers, as shown in figure 4.8.

A Prototype Tool for Performance Analysis

Included here is a prototype of a tool that assists in performance analysis. Since the tool only works for DOS programs, it is not included on the disk. The tool is presented here so that you can see how such a tool functions. The tool is a TSR (terminate-and-stay-resident) DOS program called YAPA (Yet Another Performance Analyzer). While the application program runs, you can take as many as 20 samples of the call stack by pressing both Shift keys simultaneously. The program emits an audible signal to confirm that it has taken each sample. When the application program finishes, YAPA's user interface displays the results in a format, shown in figure 4.9, that enables you to find slugs quickly.

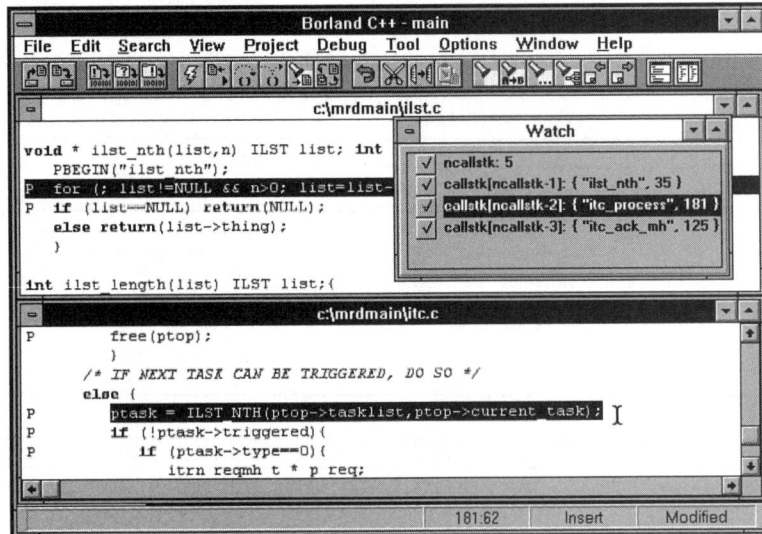

Fig. 4.8. Using the macros, the source code can keep track of its own call stack in a global array called `callstk`. You can query this call stack or display in it in the Watch window.

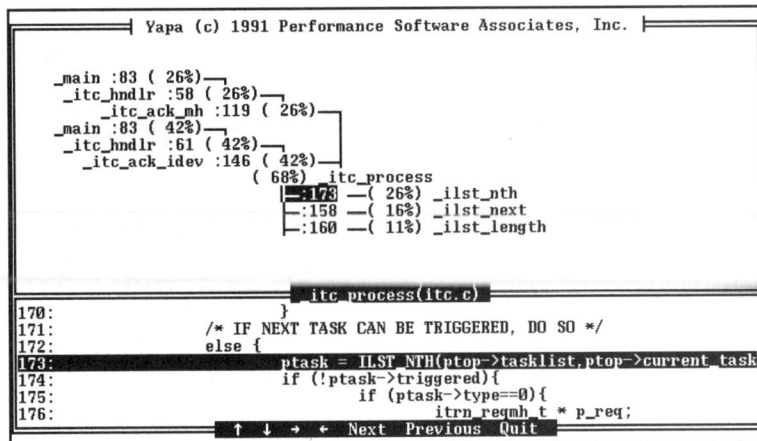

Fig. 4.9. The user interface of a prototype deslugging tool, YAPA.

The display is split into two parts. The upper half shows the name of a particular subroutine, along with the percentage of time that it was on the call stack. Above it is an ancestry tree of its callers. Below it is the call tree that descends from it, complete with the line numbers of the call instructions. As you move the cursor from one line to another, the window in the lower half of the interface displays the source code for that line. In figure 4.9, this window displays the first slug found in the main program.

Asynchronous Tuning

Many modern systems pass queued messages among multiple processes or separate pieces of equipment. Practically every cash register, teller machine, lottery terminal, travel agent terminal, manufacturing robot, and similar system is online to one or more other computers. Determining what such systems are doing can be difficult, because you cannot stop all the processes at once and figure out what each is doing and why. Instead of analysis, you often hear such excuses as "The system can't go any faster because it's waiting for the terminal to respond."

Although there is no easy technique for analyzing such systems, there is a difficult one. (It has never been said that performance tuning is easy—but it can be effective.) The technique is to run the software and collect time-stamped logs of events that are occurring on as many interacting processes as possible. You then merge these logs into a common time line, as shown in figure 4.10. (You can use whatever kind of graph paper you want.) Then look for delays between the time that a message is sent and the time that the message is received and processed. By tracing the message flows required to accomplish typical transactions, you can determine whether there are any unnecessary delays or messages. On the graph, such delays are indicated by slanting lines. This technique is not for the lazy, but it can result in quick responses on real-time systems.

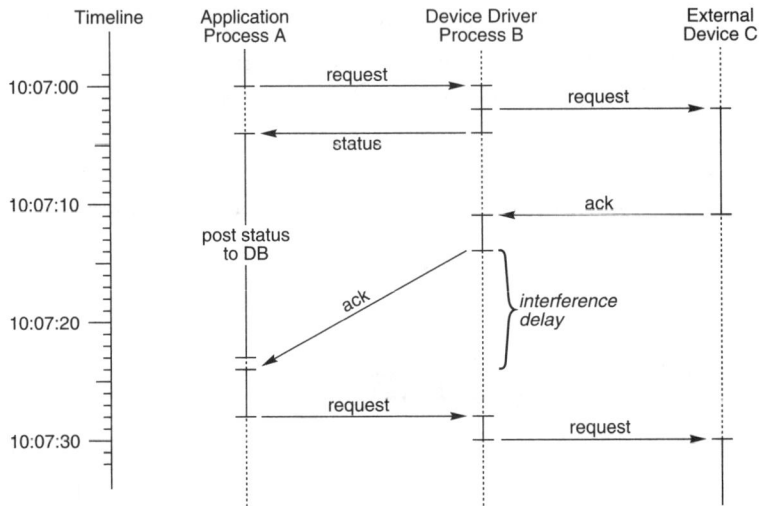

Fig. 4.10. You can analyze asynchronous processes by creating an event time line.

From Here...

Deslugging is only a small part of creating an efficient program. There are many other ways to make your programs the most effective they can be.

➤ There are many ways to optimize your use of pointers. For a lengthy discussion, see Chapter 2, "Turbocharging Pointers."

➤ There also are many ways you can optimize your use of recursion. For a discussion on this, see Chapter 3, "Turbocharging Recursion."

➤ For tips on writing code with as few errors as possible, see Chapter 6, "Writing Bug-Free Code."

➤ For a discussion on getting the most out of K&R's guide to C, see Chapter 9, "K&R Implementation Secrets."

➤ For an in-depth discussion on elements of C that K&R did not include, see Chapter 10, "Extending K&R's C."

➤ For tips and programming hints on getting the most out of templates, see Chapter 17, "Mastering Templates."

Michael R. Dunlavey, Ph.D., is the author of Building Better Applications: A Theory of Efficient Software Development, *Van Nostrand Reinhold, New York, 1994.*

Optimizing C++

by Steve Potts

The efficiency of any program can vary greatly, depending on how the program is written. C, which has been the language of choice in the system software community, is known for its efficient use of the computer. A number of very effective techniques for speeding the execution of C programs have been published and are in widespread use. Almost all of the traditional techniques of C code optimization can be applied to a C++ program as well. Because of its object-oriented nature, however, C++ presents a unique set of performance challenges (a.k.a. insurmountable opportunities) for the professional software developer.

Object-oriented languages were designed around the concept of user-defined data types. These data types, known as classes in C++, are used to declare objects. Much of the power of C++ comes from its treatment of these user-defined data types. When written properly, C++ can make a class behave as naturally as the languages built-in data types (in effect, `integer`, `double`). This means that the programmers who use the class may not understand the behavior of the class during execution. When an object is declared, the program calls an initialization function, known as a *constructor*. When that object goes out of existence, a complimentary function known as a *destructor* is executed. These routines can be complex, and often consume considerable resources. The fact that these routines execute implicitly, and not as the result of a direct function call, makes them (and the resources that they consume) easy to forget.

Much of this chapter is devoted to a discussion of the behavior of objects during the execution of C++ programs. As you become more aware of the code that the compiler generates, you will be in a better position to design classes that perform well. This chapter discusses a number of language features and the effect that they have on the performance of your software.

Efficient C++ Programs

In most people's estimation, an efficient program is one that responds quickly to user input. This definition is useful, if somewhat muddy. Before you can begin to optimize well, you need to understand the definitions of a few terms. A program normally is called *efficient* if the customer considers its execution time for important functions to be "good." Although the program may be very wasteful, if the customers are happy, so are the programmers. If your team is writing an ODBC driver for a new client-server DBMS, every nanosecond of execution time is precious. Even in that driver, inefficiencies in some non-critical parts of the program may not be discernible to the naked eye. The theorist in you may hate inefficiency in all of its perverted forms. This obsession must be tempered with wisdom, however, to avoid allocating your coding resources poorly.

Programs are composed of *hot* spots, or areas that execute frequently while the program is running. If you concentrate in these areas and ignore the *cold* spots (areas that rarely execute), you get the highest return on your investment of time. A slightly inefficient hot spot can destroy system performance, but even a highly inefficient cold spot in a program is of no real concern.

Not all programs need to be optimized for performance. If you are writing a program to keep track of your company's golf league scores, execution time is not important. If you are writing for a target operating system that can load only those programs smaller than 512K, the most efficient program must still fit in 512K. All of these considerations are important for making wise decisions about what you will tune, and how much time you will spend on the effort.

C++ is a relatively new language. Because of this, few programmers understand the nature of the code that the compiler generates. It is not clear in the mind of the everyday C++ programmer where the inherent inefficiencies of the language lie. As a result, many innocent errors are made that affect performance adversely. Every object created in C++ causes the invocation of a constructor function at its birth, and a destructor function at its death. This fact is wonderfully powerful, and makes program design fun again. However, it greatly increases the cost of creating objects.

Most programmers grew up in a world where they knew, with a degree of certainty, what memory structures their programs allocated and what functions they called. In an object-oriented world, much of the processing occurs behind the scenes, caused by object creation, both implicit and explicit. In this brave new object-oriented world, you need to be cognizant of every object our software creates.

There is no magic potion that you can apply to the code to get it to run faster; but there are a number of techniques that, when used properly, can yield remarkable results. Some of these techniques are rules of thumb in the form of "always do this," or "never do that." Others are algorithms which avoid some of the high cost associated with programming convenience. Serious programmers must learn how to make their systems perform at an acceptable level.

Class Design and Declaration

The best way to obtain good performance from an application is to design the system in the most natural way. In C++, this design

approach means that the classes you create must be well-designed and implemented. C++ programs, contrary to myth, need not be slower, take up more space, or take longer to develop than the equivalent C programs. Although some of the most useful features of C++ (such as virtual functions) can consume considerable resources at runtime, the average C++ program is more modular and contains fewer lines of code. If you fail to consider the trade-offs, your strategy to improve performance may produce undesirable results. Designing well using C++ takes time. This investment can be recouped numerous times if a truly useful class is the result. Consider how much time that you have saved by using the ostream class object, cout.

To design a class well, you must consider a number of issues:

➤ Is it a new class entirely, or is it inherited from another class?

➤ What operators and functions do you provide the users of this class?

➤ What kind of state variables are required to support these functions?

➤ What is the set of all legal values for each state variable?

➤ Will other classes be derived from this one?

➤ What kind of access will you allow on the state variables?

➤ How will objects of this type be created and destroyed?

➤ Will these objects be built in static or dynamic memory?

When you know the answers to these questions, you are well on your way to creating a new data type for your software universe. Entire books have been written on the subject of designing classes. In this limited space, you examine the issues primarily from the standpoint of application performance, and concentrate on areas of potential inefficiency.

When designing a class, you need to determine what the interface looks like. You should strive to create function calls that provide all

required operations, without unnecessarily burdening the interface. This design often is referred to as the complete and minimal interface.

According to most pundits in the field of object-oriented design, all of the state variables of a class should be *private*. When values are needed, function calls should retrieve them. When values must be changed, different function calls are made. These function calls, taken as a set, form the interface of the class. This approach allows the programmer to validate all data that is passed to the object for update. The programs that use the interface don't even know the names of the state variables. The reason for this secrecy is the desire to separate a software objects implementation (internal workings) from its behavior (function calls). This encapsulation empowers the owner of the class to change the object when necessary, perhaps to make it more efficient or more complete. The owner can do a better job if he/she has total freedom from all external constraints. The downside of this arrangement is the introduction of a new layer of function calls. Whereas in C, a programmer referred to a variable by name, the programmer now must call a function.

Function calls, by their very nature, carry with them considerable overhead. Because of this overhead, it is critical that the interface be rich enough to provide for common operations. If a function is part of the interface of the object, it has private (therefore efficient) access to its state variables. Objects normally are designed with certain routines that query and update the state variables. A poor design can force the user of the class to overuse these routines, and this overuse can hurt performance. Listing 5.1 illustrates such a design.

Listing 5.1. A Program to Calculate the Volume of a Cube

```
// Example 1.1  cubevol1.cpp
// Program to calculate the volume of a cube

#include <iostream.h>

class Cube    {
    int height, width, depth;
public:
    Cube(  int high, int wide, int deep )
```

continues

Listing 5.1. Continued

```
        {
            height  =  high;
            width = wide;
            depth = deep;
        }
        int get_height( )
        {
            return height;
        }

        int get_width( )
        {
            return width;
        }

        int get_depth( )
        {
            return depth;
        }
    };

main()
{
    Cube base_cube( 10, 20, 30 );
    int volume;
    volume - base_cube.get_height()*base_cube.get_width()*base_cube.get_depth();
    cout << "The volume is " << volume;
}
```

Is this a good interface or a bad one? The answer is both. From the standpoint of being minimal, this interface is good. The interface certainly can't be accused of having an overabundance of functions. It keeps all of the private data members properly hidden from unauthorized access. Let's look, though, at the calculation of the volume. Because of the tight encapsulation of the variables in the Cube class, they cannot be accessed by the `main()` function. They must be retrieved using the class's interface in the following statement:

```
volume = base_cube.get_height()*base_cube.get_width()*base_cube.get_depth();
```

To calculate the volume of the cube, you had to call three functions and then take the product of the three return values. How else can you approach it? An alternative would be to create a new function called `cube_volume()`. If you make the new function a member function of the

`Cube` class, then it will have direct access to the private state variables (`height`, `width`, and `depth`). This new function yields the same answer, while reducing by three the function call total. If this function is called frequently, then performance could improve considerably. Listing 5.2 shows this new program.

Listing 5.2. Revision of Listing 5.1

```
// Example 1.1 Revised cubevol2.cpp
// Program to calculate the volume of a cube
#include <iostream.h>

class Cube     {
    int height, width, depth;
public:
    Cube(  int high, int wide, int deep )
    {
        height  =  high;
        width = wide;
        depth = deep;
    }
    int cube_volume()
    {
        return height * width * depth;
    };

    int get_height( )
    {
        return height;
    }

    int get_width( )
    {
        return width;
    }

    int get_depth( )
    {
        return depth;
    }
};

main()
{
    Cube base_cube( 10, 20, 30 );

    cout << "The volume is " << base_cube.cube_volume();
}
```

Observe that the volume variable and the calculation of its value have been moved up into the class definition proper.

What about other similar types of calculations? Should a "moment of inertia" member function be added to the interface? The answer is a definitive "it depends." Such a function certainly belongs in a mechanical engineering simulation program. If, on the other hand, you are writing an art package for kids, such a function would be an unnecessary complication. What (you ask with a shocked expression)! How could a richer interface not be better? The reason is simple. An interface is written for programmers to use. If the interface is too complicated, it can scare off potential users; if it causes the code size of the executable to grow disproportionately, your customer is better off without it. The moral of the story is "to be a good class designer, you have to be a fanatic about moderation."

Inline Functions

While on this crusade against function calls, take a moment to consier a valuable C++ feature called "inline functions." Inline functions are called exactly like other functions in your code. However, because of the insertion of the word *inline,* as in

```
inline     int cube_volume()
    {
        return height * width * depth;
    };
```

the compiler is instructed to copy the actual source code in place of the function call. This arrangement removes the overhead associated with calling a function. It does not, however, make your code any more complicated or harder to maintain. Thus, the line

```
cout << "The volume is " << base_cube.cube_volume();
```

is replaced by the machine language equivalent of

```
cout << "The volume is " << (height * width * depth);
```

Because of the direct reference to the private state variables, (height, width, and depth), the code generated by the compiler for inline functions can be very efficient.

Do inline function calls make the program larger? Maybe not! Remember that the output of the compiler is a file of machine code instructions. Every source code statement is replaced by one or more statements in the assembler language of the target machine. If the code contains function calls, the compiler adds code to jump to the entry point of that functions code, and then to return to the instruction immediately following the call. If arguments are being passed, then they are put on a stack. All of that adds to the size of the executable file. If the inline function's body is small enough, the compiler generates fewer instructions to include it inline than are necessary to produce the function call. In larger functions though, declaring functions inline increases the size of the executable.

Another advantage of *inlining* (as it is called by afficionados) is that it can help your compiler to do optimization. Optimizing compilers do well in stretches of code that are unmarred by function calls. By using inline functions, you can create exactly that situation.

Inlining can work against you in two situations. If you are writing for a target operating system with a fixed memory space, you must proceed with caution. If the inlining causes your code to outgrow that space, your program will not run. You safely can try to run it, because you get a clear message that you have a size problem.

The other situation is more subtle and requires a discussion of virtual memory. Virtual memory is a software device that is built into some operating systems. Virtual memory enables programs to be executed even if they are larger than physical memory. The device accomplishes this magic by dividing your program into sections called pages. The operating system tries to load all of your programs pages into physical memory. If the program is too big, it places the extra pages in a special file called the *swap file*. If your program tries to execute an instruction that is physically located in the swap file, then the operating system "swaps out" one page from real memory into the swap file . The system then reads or "swaps in" the needed page of code into the vacated spot in real memory (called a *page frame*). The program can then execute that instruction. The entire process of removing a page from memory

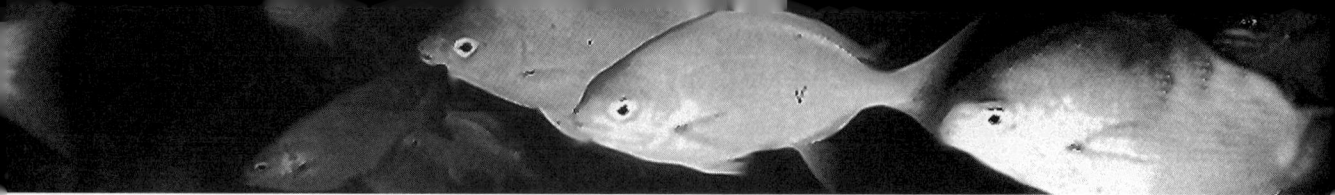

and replacing it with another is called a *page fault*. Your program never knows that the swap has occurred. You, as a programmer, never have to concern yourself with the virtual memory routines—they are invoked automatically.

The only problem with page faults is that they consume CPU resources. When a page fault occurs, the operating system takes control of the computer. It performs an I/O operation to bring the needed page into memory. It then updates several tables that keep track of where the pages now are located. In other words, it executes a ton of code.

Because most programs follow the 80:20 rule (20% of the code is running 80% of the time), this scheme works. The 20% finds its way into real memory, and the 80% goes out to disk. The program executes almost as well as it would with five times as much memory.

In the case where the 20% (called the *working set*) is larger than physical memory, serious problems can occur. The program then is making frequent references to addresses that are not in physical memory. These references cause the rate of page faulting to become too rapid, and the system is said to be *thrashing*.

If inlining causes your program to grow to the point of thrashing, then performance will suffer. The reason for the poor performance will not be obvious.

So, if you do not have a program size problem, you may be able to use inlining often, even if it causes your program to grow. Inlining generally speeds execution.

Friend Functions

As stated earlier, state variables in a class definition should be private. Private variables enable the class to maintain its own integrity via input validation. In theory, this works well. Unfortunately, very few salaries are paid to theorists. Most of us have to earn our daily bread in the real world. In this world of real applications, some systems are dominated

by performance concerns. In Listing 5.1, you saw the expense of obtaining the current value of a private variable. You solved the problem in that case by enhancing the class's interface by adding a function. This solution may not be appropriate in all cases; Listing 5.3 illustrates this point:

Listing 5.3. An Airplane Engine Thrust-Leveling Program

```
// Example 1.2 airplan1.cpp
// An airplane engine thrust leveling program
#include <iostream.h>

class Engine {
    int rpm;
public:
    Engine(int speed)
    {
        rpm = speed;
    }
    int get_rpm()
    {
        return rpm;
    }
    int update_rpm( int revs)
    {
        rpm = revs;
        return 0;
    }
};

// Function prototypes
int calc_engine_rpm(int, int, Engine&);
int get_wind_speed();
int get_wind_dir();


main()
{
    int new_rpm;
    int wind_speed;
    int wind_dir;
    int fly = 1;

    //Instantiate 4 engines
    Engine engine1(4000);
    Engine engine2(4000);
    Engine engine3(4000);
    Engine engine4(4000);

    while (fly)
    {
```

continues

Listing 5.3. Continued

```
        // obtain wind information
        wind_speed = get_wind_speed();
        wind_dir = get_wind_dir();

        //Calculate the speed of engine1
        new_rpm = calc_engine_rpm(wind_speed, wind_dir, engine1);
        engine1.update_rpm(new_rpm);

        //C alculate the new_rpm of engine2
        new_rpm  = calc_engine_rpm(wind_speed, wind_dir, engine2);
        engine2.update_rpm(new_rpm);

        //Calculate the new_rpm of engine3
        new_rpm  = calc_engine_rpm(wind_speed, wind_dir, engine3);
        engine3.update_rpm(new_rpm);

        //Calculate the new_rpm of engine4
        new_rpm  = calc_engine_rpm(wind_speed, wind_dir, engine4);
        engine4.update_rpm(new_rpm);
        fly = 0;
    }
    return (0);
}

int calc_engine_rpm(int wnd, int wnd_dir, Engine& eng)
{
    return ((wnd*1.1) + (wnd_dir - 180)  + eng.get_rpm() );          //
    ➥Fictional rpm

                                             // calculation
}
int get_wind_speed()
{
    return 300;
}
int get_wind_dir()
{
    return 45;
}
```

This program is a simple version of a flight control system. The
premise is that as the wind speed and direction change, the engine
rpms must be adjusted to compensate, and each engine must be computed individually. The new_rpm calculation is based on the rpm value for
each engine. The class definition is:

```
class Engine {
    int rpm;
public:
    Engine(int speed)
```

```
        {
            rpm = speed;
        }
        int get_rpm()
        {
            return rpm;
        }
        int update_rpm( int revs)
        {
            rpm = revs;
            return 0;
        }
    };
```

This class is designed in the orthodox way. The state variable, `rpm`, is declared to be private (by default) and hence, not available to outsiders. A function, `get_rpm()`, is provided to allow outside routines to access the `rpm` value. Another function, `update_rpm()`, enables the value to be modified. In theory, all access to `rpm` is to be via this interface. The reason for controlling updates to the private variables is plain. Why do you want to keep outsiders from seeing the variables in a read-only mode? The class designer needs to retain control over the internals of his class. If other programmers have written programs based on these internal details, implementation changes may cause errors in code. If the programs are written against the interface, the class designer need only honor it, and is free to alter the internals.

So why be tempted to violate the interface in this case? In the `calc_new_rpm()` function

```
    int calc_engine_rpm(int wnd, int wnd_dir, Engine& eng)
    {
        return ((wnd^1.1) + (wnd_dir - 180)  +  eng.get_rpm() );
    }
```

you see a call to the `get_rpm()` function executed once for each engine during each iteration of the `while` loop. Suppose that the handling characteristics of this airplane improve in direct proportion to the frequency of the thrust leveling (my apologies to any aerospace engineers in the audience) For this program, the faster the better.

So what can be done to speed up the program? As stated earlier, function call elimination is generally beneficial—so get rid of a few function calls. You could add the `calc_engine_rpm()` routine to the user interface, but that routine is not really part of the engine object. This calculation involves the wind speed, wind direction, and assumptions about the airframe to which it is attached. Adding this routine would clearly violate the common sense practice of keeping the interface focused on the object itself. You could make the `rpm` a part of the public interface, but then the whole world would have access to it. This program begs for a way to access private variables directly, but only in special cases. The logical way to enable such access is with a *friend* function.

A friend function has the special privilege of reading and writing the private data members of a class. In the airplane example, a friend function is ideal. If you declare the function `calc_engine_rpm()` to be a friend of the class Engine, you can improve the performance of the example significantly while preserving most of the integrity of the class. The revised program is shown in Listing 5.4.

Listing 5.4. Revision of Listing 5.3

```
// Example 1.2 Revised Airplan2.cpp
// An airplane engine thrust leveling program
#include <iostream.h>

class Engine {
    int rpm;
public:
    Engine(int speed)
    {
        rpm = speed;
    }
    int get_rpm()
    {
        return rpm;
    }
    int update_rpm( int revs)
    {
        rpm = revs;
        return 0;
    }
    friend int calc_engine_rpm(int, int, Engine&);
};

// Function prototypes
int get_wind_speed();
int get_wind_dir();
```

```
main()
{
    int retco;
    int wind_speed;
    int wind_dir;
    int fly = 1;

    //Instantiate 4 engines
    Engine engine1(4000);
    Engine engine2(4000);
    Engine engine3(4000);
    Engine engine4(4000);

    while (fly)
    {
        // obtain wind information
        wind_speed = get_wind_speed();
        wind_dir = get_wind_dir();

        //Calculate the speed of engine1
            retco = calc_engine_rpm(wind_speed, wind_dir, engine1);


        //Calculate the new_rpm of engine2
            retco = calc_engine_rpm(wind_speed, wind_dir, engine2);


        //Calculate the new_rpm of engine3
            retco = calc_engine_rpm(wind_speed, wind_dir, engine3);


        //Calculate the new_rpm of engine4
            retco = calc_engine_rpm(wind_speed, wind_dir, engine4);

        fly = 0;
    }
    return (0);
}

int calc_engine_rpm(int wnd, int wnd_dir, Engine& eng)
{
    eng.rpm = ((wnd*1.1) + (wnd_dir - 180)  + eng.rpm);
    return 0;
}
```

The prototype for the `calc_engine_rpm()` function has moved into the
class declaration and the keyword `friend` has been added to empower
this routine to access private variables:

```
friend int calc_engine_rpm(int, int, Engine&);
```

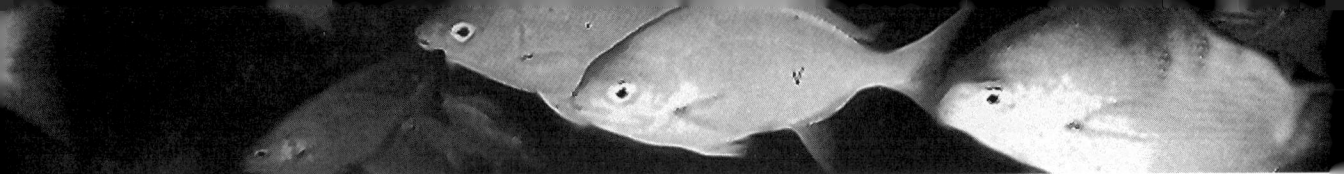

The function itself has changed in two ways. First, you have removed the function call to `get_rpm()`. Second, the actual update of the private variable `rpm` is moved into this function to take advantage of the `friend` status of this function.

```
int calc_engine_rpm(int wnd, int wnd_dir, Engine& eng)
{
    eng.rpm = ((wnd*1.1) + (wnd_dir - 180)  + eng.rpm);
    return 0;
}
```

Those changes simplify the logic used to update the rpms of each engine to:

```
//Calculate the new_rpm of engine2
    retco = calc_engine_rpm(wind_speed, wind_dir, engine2);
```

The score for the exercise can be measured by the number of function calls avoided, because they consume considerable resources. The "Before" column represents the number of times that the function was called in the original design. The "After" column represents the number of times that the function was called after the changes were made.

Table 5.1. Before and After Comparison

Function called	Before	After
Calc_engine_rpm()	4	4
get_rpm()	4	0
update_rpm()	4	0
get_wind_speed()	1	1
get_wind_dir()	1	1
	14	6

By judicious use of a `friend` function, you have eliminated over half of the function calls in the sample program. Because this type of program typically executes in a continuous loop for the duration of a flight, the savings is seven function calls per cycle. That figure represents a considerable return on your investment. True, the encapsulation of the `Engine` class has suffered to a degree, but in this case it was worth it.

The value of a well placed `friend` function can yield material improvements in performance, as you have just seen. How can you realize these gains, but still protect your classes from corruption? A little advice is in order:

➤ Use `friend` functions instead of `friend` classes. A `friend` class gives permission to every `member` function of that class to access `private` variables. This permission extends to `member` functions yet unwritten. How can this arrangement be good? It can't. Even if you currently "own" both classes, you may not own them forever. Award `friend` status with a bit of stinginess, and you will be glad that you did.

➤ Keep `friend` functions in the same source code module as the "infiltrated" class. Wouldn't it be great to know absolutely that no code outside the present module has access to the state variables? When that is true, the side effects caused by a change to a state variable can be localized with certainty.

Passing Objects as Parameters

Those of you with a keen eye will certainly have noticed that the object parameter in Listing 5.4 was passed by reference rather than by value. The declaration of the `calc_engine_rpm()` function was:

```
int calc_engine_rpm(int wnd, int wnd_dir, Engine& eng)
```

Most of you know the virtue of passing by reference rather than by value. You learned in C programming that a copy of a structure was made every time you called the function. This consumed precious resources, but yielded little or no advantage. The advantage of passing by reference in C++ is even more pronounced, due to the existence of constructor and destructor functions.

When a function receives a parameter (from a calling function) by value, it immediately makes a copy of that parameter at a new location in memory. If the parameter is an object, then the copy is made by invoking the copy constructor of that objects class. This process is illustrated in figure 5.1.

Pass by Value

Pass by Reference

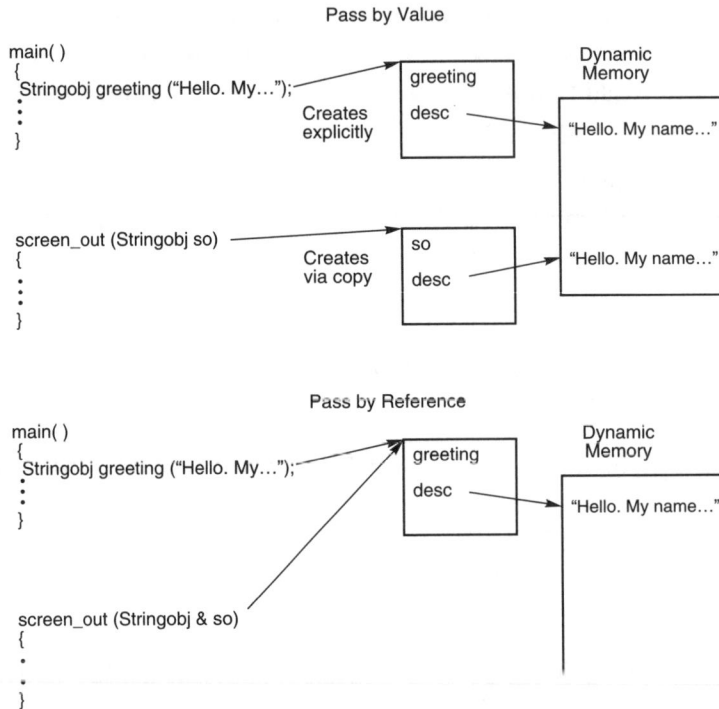

Fig. 5.1. Passing a parameter by value.

Listing 5.5 passes an object to a function, which then prints that object.

Listing 5.5. Call by Value

```cpp
// Example 1.3 string1.cpp
//  Call by value

#include <iostream.h>
#include <string.h>

// ---------------- Stringobj class
class Stringobj
{
     char *desc;
public:
     Stringobj( char *); // constructor
     ~Stringobj();       // destructor
```

```
        Stringobj(Stringobj&); // copy constructor
        display();
};

// --------------- Constructor function
Stringobj::Stringobj(char *s)
{
        cout << "Constructor callcd\n";
        desc = new char[strlen(s)+1];
        strcpy(desc, s);
}

// --------------- Copy Constructor function
Stringobj::Stringobj(Stringobj& st)
{
        cout << "Copy Constructor called\n";
        desc = new char[strlen(st.desc)+1];
        strcpy(desc, st.desc);

// --------------- Destructor function
}
Stringobj::~Stringobj()
{
        cout << "Destructor called\n";
        delete desc;
}
Stringobj::display()
{
        cout << desc << "\n";
        return 0;
}
// --------------- Prototype for functions
        int screen_out( Stringobj );

main()
{
        Stringobj greeting("Hello. My name is James.I will be your server
        ➥tonight.");
        screen_out( greeting );
        return 0;
}

screen_out( Stringobj so )
{
        cout << "screen_out called\n";
        so.display();
        return 0;
}
```

The function is defined to accept the object by value, because no & is appended to the end of the class name Stringobj.

The output of Listing 5.5 is as follows:

```
Constructor called
Copy Constructor called
screen_out called
Hello, my name is James.T will be your server tonight
Destructor called
Destructor called
```

Notice that only one object of type `stringobj` was ever created explicitly. The copy constructor was called implicitly when the compiler observed that the program passed an object by value. Having been created, the object had to be destroyed when it went out of scope. The destructor was called the first time when the `screen_out()` function ended. At this point there was no longer a need for the copied object. The second invocation of the destructor occurred when the program was terminating.

You change the `screen_out()` routine to expect a reference to an object. The changed routine eliminates the creation of the temporary copy of the object. The function is changed to:

```
screen_out( stringobja so)
{
    cout << "screen_out called\n";
    so.display();
    return 0;
}
```

Observe that no changes were made to the code in the body of the function. The output of this program now looks like this:

```
Constructor called
screen_out called
Hello. My name is James. I will be your server tonight.
Destructor called
```

Notice that a call to the copy constructor is avoided. Because the object is never constructed, it need not be destroyed. The copy constructor contains a call to the new dynamic memory allocation, which is an expensive call. Likewise, a call to the delete routine generally causes the operating system to do a considerable amount of work. (It has to record the location of the newly freed memory in its own tables. Otherwise, the space would be rendered useless.) The score for this example is in Table 5.2. The "Before" column represents the number of times

that the function was called in the original design. The "After" column represents the number of times that the function was called after the changes were made.

Table 5.2. Before and After Comparison—Call by Value

Function called	Before	After
Constructor	1	1
Destructor	2	1
Copy Constructor	1	0
screen_out()	1	1
new	2	1
delete	2	1
	9	5

In case you are not completely in awe, consider the case where the object being called contains other objects. For each one of the other objects, you must add:

1. A call to a copy constructor function.

2. A call to the destructor function.

3. A call to the new function inside the constructor function.

4. A call to the delete function inside the destructor function.

In conclusion, unless you have a compelling reason to do so, avoid passing objects by value.

Virtual Functions

The virtual function is perhaps the most useful feature that C++ added to the C language. Unfortunately, virtual functions have received an undeserved reputation for being a performance drain. This chapter explores whether you should altogether avoid using virtual functions.

Virtual functions enable you to declare a linked list of objects of different types (but of a common base type). You then can traverse and call the same member function for each element on the list. This same member function, however, can be implemented differently based on the class of the individual object. This sounds impossible, but it isn't. You get all of the programming convenience of linked list processing, without ignoring the uniqueness of each object.

In figure 5.2, you see a class hierarchy whose objects can be treated this way. The primitive object class is a base class. All of the classes in the hypothetical CAD system are derived from it. Because all objects must be drawn, this base class has a member function called `draw()`. Further, because each object is either a circle, square, or polygon, the `draw()` function must be capable of drawing each of these objects in its turn. The function also must be capable of drawing any new primitive object types created by developers of the system. These requirements clearly suggest a virtual function. For this reason, `draw()` is declared to be a pure virtual function in the base class `Primitive`. A pure virtual function requires that the derived classes supply the implementation of the function. In an ordinary virtual function, an implementation is declared which can be overridden by the derived class.

In figure 5.3, we see a linked list of objects that represents a CAD drawing.

Your purpose in declaring this list is to refresh the screen. The program will traverse the linked list and call the `draw()` member function for each element in turn. Because `draw()` is declared to be a pure virtual function in the base class, the program runs the version of the `draw()` function that is defined in each of the derived classes, when an object of that class is being told to draw.

Figure 5.4 shows us a layout in memory that most compilers use to implement this processing. The compiler knows `draw()` must be overidden during execution, because it is a pure virtual function. The compiler also knows that the object pointed to can be different each time. (This fact prevents the compiler from translating the virtual function call into a static function call.) Because of this uncertainty, when the running program encounters the call, it must follow the pointer to

the virtual table, look up the address of the actual member function in the derived class definition, and execute that function.

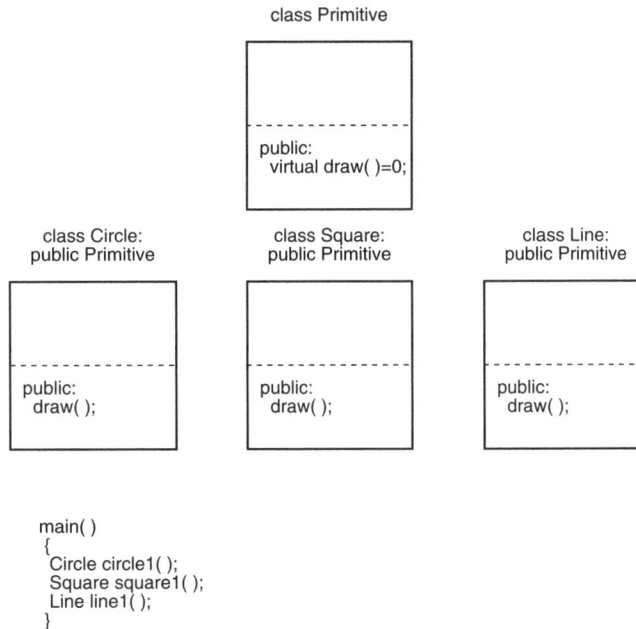

Fig. 5.2. A class hierarchy with a pure virtual function.

See if you can improve on this approach. What will you gain if you re-write the program using static function calls? In a static call, the address of the function is stored in the place of the function call. In the virtual function, the address of the virtual function table is stored in the generated code. You have a table lookup, and then a call to a pointer-to-function instead of a simple jump statement. This extra lookup could make the call slower. In both cases though, you still execute circle-drawing code for circles and square-drawing code for squares. If the static code uses a switch statement, the logic starts to look a lot like the virtual table processing code. In addition, your code may be less efficient than the virtual function processing. In the end, you have saved some processing time by giving up considerable programming convenience. You may not save enough processing, however, to pay for the inconvenience.

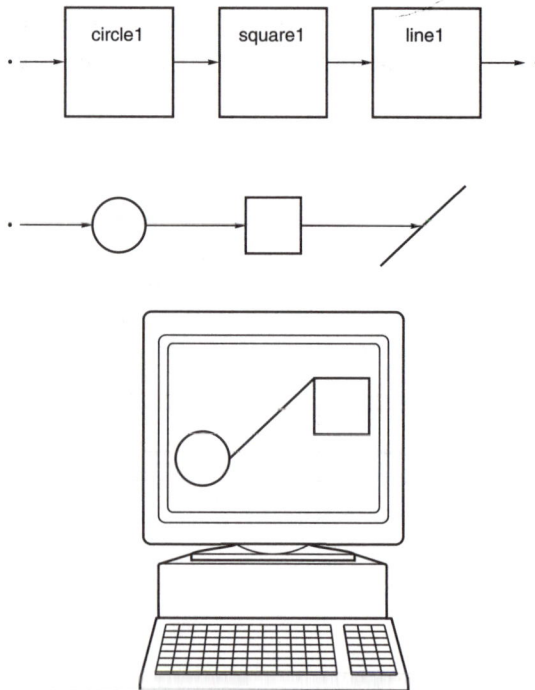

Fig. 5.3. A linked list of objects.

Not all virtual functions require a lookup. Some virtual functions are no longer virtual by runtime. When the compiler encounters a virtual function, it attempts to determine the type of the object that is to be declared at runtime. If the compiler can determine that the virtual function call is to be replaced 100% of the time by the same function, then the virtual function call is replaced by a garden-variety static function call. This virtual call has exactly the same runtime cost as the static function call. In these cases, the programmer enjoys the convenience of virtual functions and the performance of static-bound functions.

In some cases, virtual function calls are wasteful. If your code will always resolve a call to the same member function, then call the member function, not the virtual function. Depending on the program logic, the compiler may not be able to determine that the static call would work without your help.

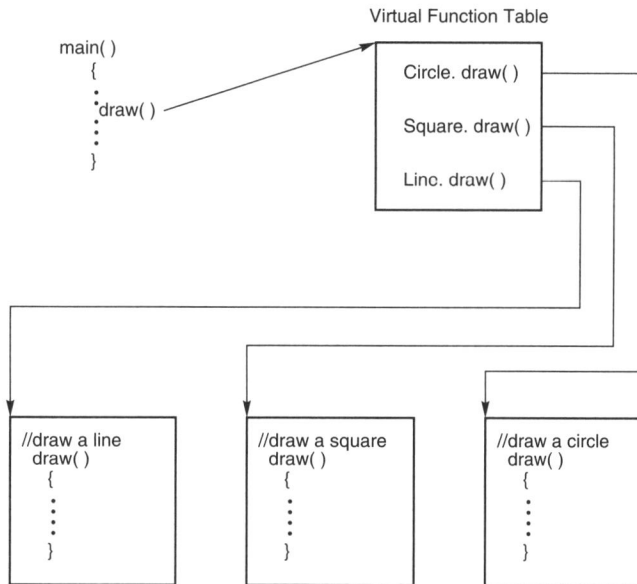

Fig. 5.4. A memory layout for virtual functions.

Each potential use of virtual functions has to be evaluated individually. You would be incorrect to conclude that you should always avoid virtual functions. As mentioned earlier, virtual functions are valuable from the standpoint of programming utility. If you use virtual functions with understanding, they can be a net gain and not a drain.

Eliminating Unnecessary Object Creation

Creating and deleting objects unnecessarily has an adverse effect on the performance of the system—this statement is common sense. The extent of the performance deterioration depends, of course, on the number and size of the objects. In the earlier discussion of pass-by-reference, you saw a case where an injudicious passing of an argument to a function caused extra objects to be created.

Thoughtlessly declaring objects at the top of the function can cause extra objects to be created. In C, programmers always declare variables at the top of the function. C++, however, doesn't require this arrangement. You can move the declarations down as far as possible in the code. You can avoid the execution of the constructor and destructor functions if you never arrive at that declaration because of program logic.

Consider the `StringObj` class again. Creating an object of this class consumes significant resources, because dynamic memory is allocated, as shown in Listing 5.6.

Listing 5.6. Creating Unnecessary Objects

```
// Example 1.4 string2.cpp
#include <iostream.h>
#include <string.h>

// --------------- Stringobj class
class Stringobj
{
      char *desc;
public:
     Stringobj( char *);
     ~Stringobj();
     Stringobj(Stringobj&);
     display();
};

// --------------- Constructor function
Stringobj::Stringobj(char *s)
{
     cout << "Constructor called\n";
     desc = new char[strlen(s)+1];
     strcpy(desc, s);
}

// --------------- Copy Constructor function
Stringobj::Stringobj(Stringobj& st)
{
     cout << "Copy Constructor called\n";
     desc = new char[strlen(st.desc)+1];
     strcpy(desc, st.desc);

// --------------- Destructor function
}
Stringobj::~Stringobj()
{
     cout << "Destructor called\n";
     delete desc;
}
Stringobj::display()
{
```

```
            cout << desc << "\n";
            return 0;
    }

    main()
    {
        int restaurant = 0;
        int garage = 1;
        int store = 0;

        Stringobj greeting1("Hello. My name is James.I will be your
        ➥server tonight.");
        Stringobj greeting2("Hello. What kind of trouble are you having
        ➥with your car?");
        Stringobj greeting3("Ring that up for you ma'am.?");

        if ( restaurant)
        {
            greeting1.display();
        }

        if ( garage )
        {
            greeting2.display();
        }

        if ( store )
        {
            greeting3.display();
        }
        return 0;
    }
```

The output of this program is:

```
Constructor called
Constructor called
Constructor called
Hello. What kind of trouble are you having with your car?"
Destructor called
Destructor called
Destructor called
```

In this example, the three `Stringobj` objects are created, but two of them
are never used. If you change the `main()` to:

```
main()
{
    int restaurant = 0;
    int garage = 1;
    int store = 0;
```

```
if ( restaurant)
{
Stringobj greeting1("Hello, my name is James.I will be your
➥server tonight.");
greeting1.display();
}

if ( garage )
{
Stringobj greeting2("Hello, what kind of trouble are you having
➥with your car?");
greeting2.display();
}

if ( store )
{
    Stringobj greeting3("Ring that up for you ma'am.?");
greeting3.display();
}
return 0;
}
```

the output becomes:

```
Constructor called
➥"Hello, what kind of trouble are you having with your car?"
Destructor called
```

This result is much better. Although this example would have been coded differently in a real application, it illustrates the point.

Another advantage of declaring objects just before they are needed in the program is in the area of assignment. Consider the following code:

```
// An airplane engine thrust leveling program
#include <iostream.h>

class Engine {
    int rpm;
public:
    Engine(int speed)
    {
        rpm = speed;
    }
    int get_rpm()
    {
        return rpm;
    }
    int update_rpm( int revs)
    {
        rpm = revs;
        return 0;
    }
    friend int calc_engine_rpm(int, int, Engine&);
};
```

```
main()
{
    int revs_per_min;
    Engine eng(0);
      revs_per_min = 3000;
      eng.update_rpm( revs_per_min );
}
```

This code looks quite normal. The code declares the object of class
`Engine`, but because the value of the `rpm` setting is unknown, the value is
set to 0. This value passes through the constructor function, as always.
The code then makes an assignment via the `update_rpm()` member function. The end result is an engine running at 3000 rpms. You can change
things slightly, as in this example:

```
main()
{
    int revs_per_min;
    revs_per_min = 3000;
    Engine eng(3000);
}
```

This code declares the object of type `Engine` after the initial value is
known. This placement allows you to provide the constructor function
with a value, and thereby avoid the call to `update_rpm()`.

Another kind of program plagued by unnecessary object creation and
deletion is in a system where objects have a short life. In many cases,
the objects are very important for a short period of time but then die a
rapid death. An assembly line in a fast food restaurant is a good analogy for such a program.

Consider the scenario where a customer places an order. This order is
a good candidate for an object declaration. The object is the life blood
of the company, but for less than three minutes. In the first pass at a
system for this kind of company, you could perform the traditional `new`
command in the constructor and a `delete` in the destructor. As you have
already seen, `new` and `delete` are very expensive operations. You notice
that a `new` is being done about as often as a `delete`. If you can find a way
to recycle the object used on one of the old orders, then you can be a
software environmentalist. The way to accomplish this task is through
the use of a *free list*, and the place to use the free list is in an overloaded
`new` function. Figure 5.5 illustrates this approach.

Dynamic Memory (heap)

New order objects
are created if
the free list is empty.

Free list

| Empty | Empty | Empty | Empty |

An object from the free list
becomes the new foodorder [m]

Completed orders
are put on the
free list

foodorder [49]

Burger
Fries
Shake

foodorder [73]

Hot dog
Cola

foodorder [53]

Salad
Milk

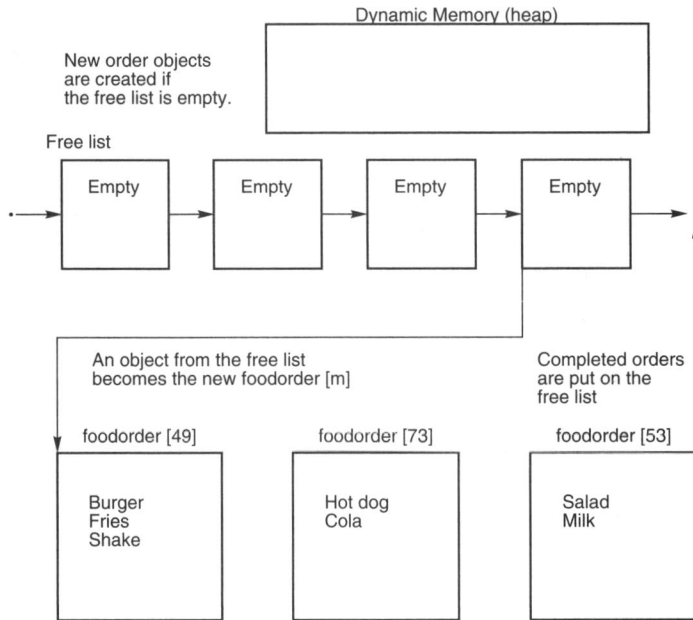

Fig. 5.5. Implementing the free list.

When the list is empty, a call to the new operator actually requests
space from the heap. As soon as an object is sent to the overloaded
delete, it erases the objects values and puts it on the free list. The next
invocation of the overloaded new operator finds an object on the list
and recycles it using the copy constructor. In a very short time, a working set of objects is in existence, and an actual allocation of memory
from the heap nearly ceases. To further enhance the efficiency, you can
pre-allocate *n* objects and load them on the free list at system start-up
(where *n* is a number that is close to the natural working-set size for
the application).

In a typical restaurant or factory application, this change yields a big
return. Suppose that a restaurant processes 800 orders per day. Further
suppose that at the busiest time of the day, 40 orders are in process.
Table 5.3 compares the effect. The "Before" column represents the
number of times that the function was called in the original design.
The "After" column represents the number of times that the function
was called after the changes were made.

Table 5.3. Before and After Comparison—Free List Used

Function called	Before	After
Constructor	800	40
Destructor	800	40
Copy Constructor	0	800
new	800	40
delete	800	40
	3200	960

Even though free-list processing creates extra work for the programmer, it can significantly improve the overall performance of some systems.

Using Reference Counts

A related method involves the use of a reference count. In some systems the copying of objects can become very common. For this example, consider a restaurant where an order object is created for each customer. This object contains a pointer to the recipe object for each item entered. When an order is placed, the constructor looks in a database and declares objects of the recipe class to hold the recipe.

This declaration is a great help for the cooks—particularly the new ones—but results in numerous copies of the same recipe residing in memory at the same time. Intuitively, you want to somehow make all of the references to the same recipe point to the same object in memory. Making copy after copy of the same recipe seems wasteful. You don't want to load every recipe in memory permanently though, because the demand for certain recipes changes with the hour of the day. You also don't want the order object to delete the recipe object if another order needs it.

The solution to the above is to call a reference count. A reference count is a field in an object that indicates how many other objects are pointing to it. Figure 5.6 illustrates the use of reference counts.

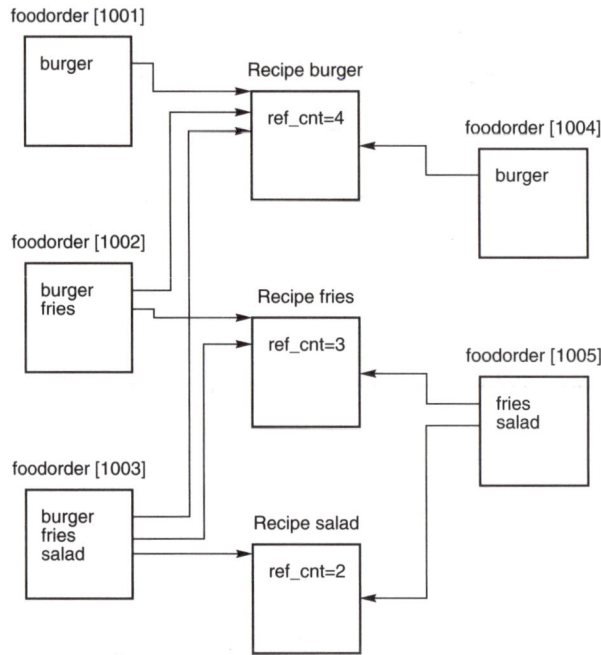

Fig. 5.6. Reference counts control object destruction.

When an `Order` object is constructed, it declares an instance of the `Recipe` class. Instead of declaring it right away, the `Order` class object traverses the list of orders to determine whether an identical recipe object already exists. If an identical recipe object exists, the `Order` object assigns its pointer to that `Recipe` object and calls a `Recipe` member function called `update_ref_count()`. Whenever an `Order` class object goes out of existence, its destructor function tries to delete its recipe objects. If this order is the last one that points to the recipe object, then the deletion takes place. If other `Order` objects still need this recipe, its reference count is greater than one; if not, the dying `Order` object decrements the reference count and self-destructs.

Memory Leaks

Many commercial applications leak memory. You know that this is true if the performance of the system deteriorates over time as you use

it. If, after you terminate and restart the program, you return to a better performance mode, the program is likely to be suffering from a memory leak. Occasionally, you may experience programs that just lock up after an hour or so of continuous use. This situation also can be caused by leaking memory. When your program has a memory leak, memory doesn't drip out the side of the computer—but it's just as lost as if it had. Memory leaks when it no longer is addressable by your program. Because your program has no way to address this memory, the program uses other memory instead. Over time, less and less memory is available, and your program either thrashes around in the limited memory left, or stops completely. The negative effect of memory leak varies with the host operating system. In a fixed memory operating system like DOS, the results can be a fatal OUT OF MEMORY error. Even on a virtual memory system like Windows NT, the result is a gradual slowdown of the system as the memory allocation routines in the operating system have to work harder and harder to satisfy *new* requests.

How can this memory leak happen? A common way to leak memory is for a mismatch to occur between the new and delete operators, as shown in Listing 5.7.

Listing 5.7. Memory Leaks

```cpp
// Example 1.5 memleak1.cpp
// Memory leaks

#include <iostream.h>

class Person {
  char *name;
public:
    Person(const char *n=0);
    ~Person();
};

main()
{
    Person *person_array = new  Person[10];
    delete person_array;
};
```

On the surface, this program looks correct, but it has a problem in `delete`. What does the program delete? It deleted the first element in `person_array`. The other nine elements are returned to the heap for reallocation, and they are not available when asked for in a future `new` statement. In the previous example, the memory has leaked.

The solution is simple:

```
delete  [] person_array;
```

The brackets tell the compiler that you want to delete the entire array, not just the first element.

Using <iostream.h>

Using <iostream.h> is much more convenient than using <stdio.h>. Surprisingly, <iostream.h> also is more efficient. Consider the following example:

```
printf(%d, xyz );
```

Executing this statement at runtime requires the parsing of the `%d` string and a call to another function to print the integer. Conversely, the C++ sentence

```
cout << xyz;
```

is analyzed at compile time where the decision is made to call the integer version of the overloaded `<<`. If you browse the iostream.h file you can see how many overloaded functions it requires to implement the `cout` `<<` construct. Much of the ostream class is implemented as inline functions, hence they perform well. The `printf()` function, on the other hand, is not written in macros (the closest C equivalent to inline functions) because it is a variable-argument function. The result of this is that C++ is likely to compile more slowly but run faster. This tradeoff favors C++ in almost every case.

Strategy for Optimization

This chapter previously defined *efficient* as fully meeting the performance requirements set by the customer (the boss, funding organization, client, and so on). *Efficient,* in this sense, means *making very good use of the resources consumed.* Because people also are a resource, how wise is it to consume 60 hours of a software engineer's time to achieve a 5% reduction in the time required to print a report in an overnight batch system? We have optimized the use of the CPU, but we have wasted another resource and lowered the overall efficiency of the project.

Every programmer has received a set of requirements from his boss (who typically is incapable of coding his or her way out of the proverbial wet paper bag) that sounds something like this: "We want this system done in six weeks. It has to be lightning fast, and must load in a very small memory space. I can only give you two of the four programmers that you said you needed. By the way, neither of them has any experience with C++, but they are willing to learn. Oh—and the system must be easy for others to maintain, because I'm sending you to Finland for a two-year assignment as soon as you are done." No one would expect an automotive engineer to design a new Lincoln that seats eight, costs less than $10,000, and gets 45 miles to the gallon. In the software development game, you may be asked to do something analogous to this on nearly every project.

You have seen a number of techniques in this chapter that require extra code, but speed execution. In addition, a plethora of techniques for speeding C programs exist which work on C++ programs as well. Which ones should you use? Should you use them during initial coding, or during QA? There are many schools of thought on this subject, and good systems have been produced using all of them. The following approach is based on a dozen years of software development experience on projects ranging from database management systems to factory control systems:

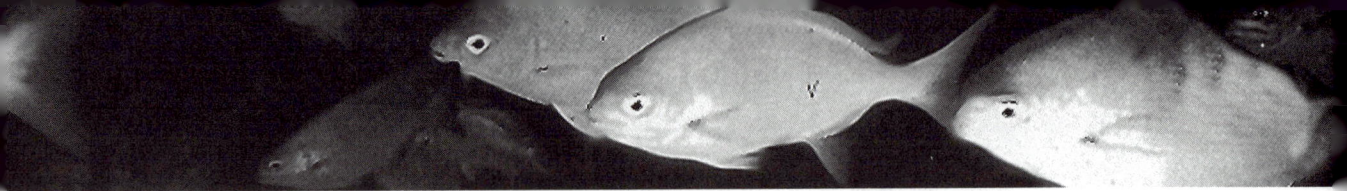

1. Design the system; don't just code it.

   By its very nature, C++ begs you to design your programs, and not just throw them together. The most dramatic performance improvements come from using the correct data structures and developing the most natural design for the interfaces to the objects. A colleague of mine once remarked, "I would rather hire one excellent programmer than three very good ones. Excellent people deliver the same functionality with far fewer lines of code." They write less code because they think about a program for a long time before starting to write it. Recall the really good code designers that you know. Weren't they always asking for others to critique their designs? How long did they evaluate competing algorithms before deciding which one was right for a specific application? How many conversations did they have with other respected designers about what they were trying to accomplish? How many alternative designs did they put in the trash along the way? If you are going to succeed like them, then you must act like them.

2. Build in efficiency by avoiding wasteful and inefficient practices; avoid wasteful operations.

   This chapter pointed out several wasteful operations. Many of the performance problems in C++ can be traced to these constructs. Be aware of the hidden objects and invisible function calls that are a fundamental part of the C++ language.

3. Use comments to mark places in your code that you suspect will be bottlenecks.

   Don't do any extra programming—just mark the potential problems. If you suspect that an area of code would be a good place for a reference count, or for a free list of objects, put that in the comments. Later, when you are measuring the performance of the system, you can measure these areas. In a large system, it is difficult to predict. Later, when you are sure of the payback, you can add code to speed up these areas. Spending three weeks on a

piece of code that is right in the middle of a cold spot is a waste of time. You may be surprised to discover where the hot spots really are.

4. Code for maintainability.

   As a business person (which you should be), you must consider the poor slob that is going to have to enhance the system many years after you have gone on to your next high-visibility assignment. Think of them when you are tempted to use some obscure programming technique. If no one but you can understand your program, you will be getting calls about it until the day that you resign from the company. Save all of the weird stuff until you are sure that it is required.

5. Obtain the true performance requirements from your customers.

   If you have thousands of customers, then ask your marketing department to provide the numbers. Remember, you want their requirements, not their wish list. You must know:

   ➤ How fast is fast enough;

   ➤ How small is small enough;

   Without this information, you will not know when to stop changing the program.

6. Run benchmarks against these requirements to discover where your program is too slow or too large.

7. Run a performance monitor against your code in the areas where the benchmark indicated a problem.

   Look first at the area where your program spends most of its time. Programs always follow the 80:20 rule, if not the 90:10. Make changes one at the time until you pass the benchmarks. If you add a special function that complicates your code, save the old code in a commented block, and explain in detail why you are making these changes. If you don't see a measurable improvement in the next benchmark, delete the complex code and restore the simple code.

8. Refine your code to make it faster if there is any time left.

   Go through and find the places that you marked during the initial coding phase. Experiment with alternative algorithms, then rerun the benchmarks. Retain the changes that help, but remove all tricks that don't improve performance.

This approach will ensure that the programming resources are being applied where they can produce the greatest benefit.

From Here...

This chapter has taught you the essentials for fine-tuning and getting the most out of your C++ applications, but this information is only the beginning. Here are some other areas you might look into:

➤ If you will be writing programs that involve database programs, see Chapter 15, "Interfacing with Database Languages."

➤ You can make your C++ programs more efficient by writing part of your programs in assembler (see Chapter 14, "Bare Metal Programming") or other languages (see Chapter 13, "Mixed Language Programming").

➤ You can save yourself hours in the debugging process by learning to write programs that are nearly bug-free. For pointers, see Chapter 6, "Writing Bug-Free Code."

➤ No matter how hard you try, your programs will always have some bugs. Learn how to perform "power debugging" in Chapter 7, "Debugging Tips and Tricks."

➤ If the standard debugger with Borland C++ 4 isn't powerful enough for you, there are other add-on debuggers available. For more information, see Chapter 8, "Third-Party Debugger Alternatives."

Writing Bug-Free Code

by John Dlugosz

The goal of writing bug-free code is a quest for perfection. Because ultimate perfection is impossible, the programmer's job is to produce a better product—programs that have no complaints from users and are easy to maintain and enhance.

Techniques for writing bug-free code fall into the following three categories: *antibugging*, *abugging*, and *debugging*. In addition, proper *design*, *documentation*, and *testing* are required to successfully write good code.

A Systematic Approach

To understand why programs are buggy and what techniques can be applied to prevent bugs, a systematic approach is necessary. Each idea can be classified and compared with other ideas. Ideas can be tested,

measured, and rated in effectiveness. Only then can you consider approaches to design and coding and decide that a potential technique or idea has merit, how it compares with other techniques, what it might do for you, and how it might be applied to the task at hand.

You are undoubtedly familiar with debugging, which involves diagnosing and removing bugs. Debugging, however, is merely the last line of defense—a last resort when all else fails. You should employ other techniques long before debugging becomes necessary.

Antibugging is the first line of defense. Antibugging techniques prevent bugs from appearing in the first place. Under antibugging, a mistake is conceptually impossible.

Abugging is when bugs are caught and reported (and perhaps even rendered harmless) automatically. C++ provides constructs that support antibugging and abugging—detailed in the following sections.

Applied abugging techniques make the computer automatically find bugs for you. This is done by exploiting the language to generate errors if you call a function wrong, or by inserting runtime tests at strategic points.

Applied antibugging techniques are difficult to notice; they are not something you see in the code, but a conceptual approach to design. In fact, most of the hype about *object-oriented design* concerns antibugging techniques. You can think of antibugging as simply not making any mistakes in the first place. The difference between antibugging and abugging is how they are applied. Imagine walking through the park and saying to your companion, "Hey, have you ever noticed that this is not a mine field?" A good design is not something you notice; you only notice the problems. Abugging puts fences around the buried mines in the park; antibugging builds a park without buried land mines.

Simply knowing and applying these concepts helps you to design and write better code. Identifying standard antibugging issues when you study a proposed design can help you judge the design against contenders, improve the design, or know where you may need abugging

attention. Identify standard abugging issues when implementing, and you can recognize and classify the needs of a function, weigh the issues, and code appropriately.

As an analogy, consider an electrical plug and socket. If they are symmetrical, the plug can be inserted upside down. This might cause bad things to happen, and someone using such plugs and sockets to assemble a complex machine might make a mistake, even if the plugs are clearly labeled.

If inserting the plug upside down trips a circuit breaker, this is a runtime check, analogous to a C `assert()` statement and a runtime abugging technique. If the plug were asymmetrical and an attempt to plug it in upside down were fruitless, this is analogous to strong type checking in a function call and is an early abugging technique.

If, instead, it did not matter which way the plug and socket connect or if there were no need for a plug, there would be no such mistake to make. Instead of having to catch that mistake in some way, it simply does not exist. This is antibugging.

Antibugging doesn't prevent mistakes. Instead, it prevents the causing of mistakes.

Antibugging

The C++ language is rich with support for antibugging. A main reason for inventing C++ was to have a language that supports a higher level of abstraction than C. The whole idea behind this "paradigm shift" is that C++ supports things that C simply allows.

C allows you to write code that embodies an object-oriented design, and sticking to it requires programming conventions. With C++, the language directly supports many of the concepts involved. In short, the compiler understands and enforces your rules, instead of having programming conventions.

Copy Semantics

The support for copy semantics is one of C++'s best features, which is not found in other languages such as SmallTalk and Turbo Pascal. This section discusses how copy semantics help you create a design that is missing a whole class of places in which the user could make mistakes.

For a simple example, consider a user-defined type that contains some pointers, as in the following:

```
struct person {
    char* name;
    unsigned long ssn;
    };
person p1, p2;
```

If you assign one `person` record to another, the name field needs to be duplicated. If this is something that needs to be done on occasion, in C you might have a `copy_person()` function. The documentation says that if you want to assign a `person` record, you should use the `copy_person()` function. Naturally, someone might forget and write `p1=p2;` instead. It is a perfectly natural thing to do, and the compiler permits it without complaint.

This is a potentially serious and difficult-to-detect bug. At some future time, secondary effects will occur when one `person` aliases another's `name` string or a corrupted heap when both are freed. This problem will not be easy to find.

In C++, you have a better way. Instead of writing a `copy_person()` function and documenting the need to use it instead of assignment, you can give the class an `operator=()` (assignment operator) that the compiler uses. Now, writing `p1=p2;` is correct. The design eliminates the possibility of a particular mistake, compared with the other design. In general, C++'s capability to define the copy semantics for a type is an important and valuable antibugging technique. Objects are copied correctly, and the compiler makes sure that the defined copy semantics are *always* applied. When an object's existence has side effects (such as the dynamic memory allocation in the `person` example), copy semantics ensure proper treatment.

Instead of telling the user that objects of a specific type must be initialized by calling a certain function, you provide a constructor. The user does not have to deal with the issue at all. Likewise, the destructor cleans up. Not only does the destructor make sure that the object is cleaned up with the proper function, but also that all objects are destroyed properly. The destructor works no matter how the block containing those variables are exited. A whole class of housekeeping details is no longer the user's problem.

Resource Acquisition Is Initialization

Besides dynamic memory, as seen in the preceding section, *any* resource management can be handled by objects of types specifically designed to encapsulate that resource. Resource acquisition is done with constructors, and resource relinquishment is done with destructors. Consider the following example of a file class:

```
class file {
    int handle;  //operating system file handle
    void operator=() const;  //never defined
    file(file&);   //never defined
public:
    file (string filename);
    ~file();
    // other members to read and write...
    }
```

Note a couple of things. The constructor opens a file; the destructor closes the file. If a file is in use, *any* exit from the scope containing that file ensures that the file is properly closed. Meanwhile, look at the copy constructor and assignment operator. They are private, meaning code cannot duplicate a file object. The operation makes no sense for this type, and the compiler prevents you from trying to do this. Making the destructor model file closing is an application of antibugging; the mistake of leaving a file open on some return path simply cannot be made. Making the assignment operator private is abugging because if you try to copy a file object by mistake, the compiler catches it.

In general, special rules should be made automatic, so that the user of the class never has to deal with them.

A Well-Defined Interface

If the program uses object-oriented techniques, a set of code is encapsulated as a class. This presents a formal public interface that users of this code can use. Besides constructors, destructors, and assignment discussed earlier, all functionality is described by a formal interface. Objects should be designed to take care of themselves. Instead of giving users of functions and structures free reign, hopefully following any instructions provided, you have full control over access to a class. If the class is written correctly, certain classes of errors are impossible. The user cannot tamper with internal data, call functions he or she is not supposed to, or perform incomplete modifications to an object.

Special Instructions

You can identify a need for antibugging when the class's and function's documentation gives usage instructions to the user of the code. The whole idea of antibugging is to eliminate the need for such instructions and usage restrictions. Contrast this with abugging, which codes the functions to catch and report misuses. When designing your code (you do design it before writing it, don't you?), treat such instructions to the user in the design as warning flags, and rework the design. Any time the documentation says "don't do that" or "you must do this," you are marking the land mines on the map of the park. Treat such wordings as warnings of potential bugs. Either dig up the land mines by reworking the design (antibugging), or put fences around the mines by having the code enforce the instructions as well (abugging).

For example, consider a buffer class. This was designed to fill a specific need in a program, where a lump of binary data is read from a disk file and then broken up into component objects that contain both fixed size primitives (such as `int`s) and variable length strings.

```
class read_buffer {
    //... implementation details...
public:
    read_buffer (size_t size);
    ~read_buffer();
    byte* buffer();  //fetch internal buffer, for filling
    // various functions for extracting data
```

```
void read (void* dest, size_t bytecount);
int read_int();  //calls read()
//... others
};
```

The use of the class is this: Create an instance of the class, and the constructor has a parameter that gives the buffer's size. Then use the `buffer()` member to access the buffer, which the constructor had allocated, and load the file data into it. Then use the read commands, which pull bytes out of the buffer and advance the current position. The destructor frees the buffer. This class must be used carefully, as the `buffer()` command cannot be used after you start reading its contents. It must be used immediately after construction.

The inverse class was even worse:

```
class write_buffer {
    //...   implementation details...
public:
   write_buffer();
   ~write_buffer();
   // various functions for storing data into the buffer
   void write (const void*, size_t);
   void write (int);  //write an int, calls general form
   //... others
   // functions to eject the filled buffer
   const void* get_first (size_t& chunksize);
   const void* get_next (size_t& chunksize);
   };
```

Here, you create the buffer and write things to it with the various forms of `write()`. The problem is with ejecting the now filled buffer. First, you call `get_first()`, which returns the first part of the data. The pointer to the data is returned, and the size is placed in the reference parameter. After this call is made, you cannot call `write()` again or bad things will happen. You read the rest of the buffer, in chunks, with repeated calls to `get_next()`. The size will be zero when all chunks are returned.

The use of these classes is overly complex, as identified by antibugging issues in the documentation. Telling users what they can and cannot do identifies these issues. In the first class, a better design allows `buffer()` to be called at any time (completes the functionality), trips an error if `buffer()` is called at the wrong time (abugging), or best of all, simplifies the initialization process so that it can somehow be done in one step rather than two (antibugging).

When reading this design, you can compare it to other contending designs by noting how many antibugging flags are raised in your mind while you study it. When you do accept a design, any issues not resolved with antibugging should be resolved with abugging.

In short, identify potential problems at the earliest point. Fix things in the design if you can; harden the code against mistakes if you can't.

In the preceding example, think about slight improvements to the existing design. Why not implement it so that the `buffer()` function can be called at any time? Why not eliminate the first/next fetch functions on the writer and just have one function? Can anything be done about the second return value found in the pass-by-reference parameter?

Consider how the class is used. An instance is created, filled, dumped, and destroyed all in a single short passage of code. If use of a single buffer object were more widespread throughout the code, having separate fill/purge modes would be more problematic. If you decide a program is not worth the trouble of redesigning it, turn toward abugging.

The remaining issues, primarily watching for the distinct mode change of switching from filling to purging, can be guarded against misuse with runtime checks in the code. Calling a function from the wrong side of the cycle can cause an error.

Note the overall process: First, examine the specification and documentation for antibugging issues. Next, see if all such flaws form an overall pattern that can be fixed in the design. Failing that, address individual issues one at a time. Deal with any remaining issues in the abugging stage.

Complete the Functionality

Sometimes a function appears to be more general than it really is. That is, in some cases it does not work. This can be simple, as the input parameters have a greater range than the function can actually use, or subtle, when multiple conditions in the object's state conspire to form an unusual condition. These unhandled cases might not be a worry in the program because they will never happen.

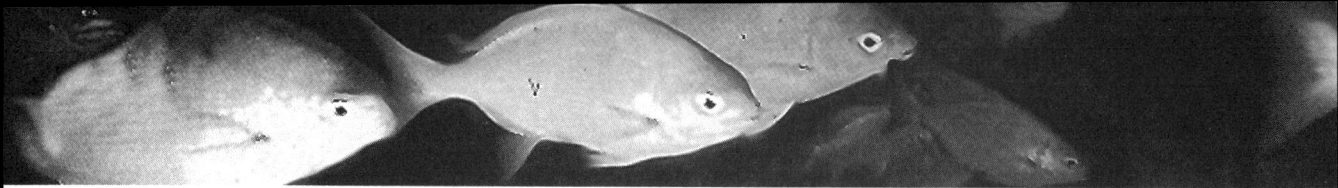

However, things change. Maintenance will be performed on the program. The program might be enhanced or altered, and the code may get reused elsewhere. The unhandled cases can cause bugs—bugs that are hard to find. Code that works "well enough" is the enemy of code reuse. Beware of functions and modules that work as currently used, but do not handle everything that their parameters and documentation imply. And do not just consider reusing the function in other programs or again in this program—consider future maintenance of the existing program.

At the very least, *identify* the unhandled cases. Include comments in the function as to what it can't handle, and why. Better yet, include code in the function to catch the unhandled cases. (This is covered again under abugging.)

However, the best solution of all is to complete the functionality. In some cases, it may be easier to provide for the unhandled cases than to explain in a comment what the function didn't like. Clearly, making the function better than it has to be at this time is sometimes the best solution overall. This thinking ahead promotes effective code reuse.

If you do complete the functionality of a function or subsystem, make sure that you test the complete supported range of input. Because the full range of functionality is not needed in the actual program, it might go untested if you rely on integration testing or whole-application testing to exercise the function. If the extra functionality is buggy, it can be worse than not handling the extra capability at all!

Restrictions on Domains

Consider a function `int foo (int n);`. If *n* must be between 1 and 200, the documentation will contain a "you must not..." clause that indicates an antibugging issue. On the other hand, if any integer value will do, you cannot call the function with an illegal argument.

Some languages offer subrange types. Unfortunately, C++ does not. You might use a class type rather than an `int` for the parameter, but in

most cases that is overkill. For a small range of choices with fixed meanings, it is a good idea to use an enumerated type rather than an `int`.

For values that are never negative, you might make the parameter an unsigned type. However, that is generally fruitless and more trouble than it is worth.

The issues concerning restricted domains follow the typical pattern: First, clearly document the restrictions. Second, try to eliminate them. Failing that, include abugging code in the implementation.

Prerequisites

The documentation might tell you that before a certain function can be used, another function must first be called to initialize things. For class-based code, this might just be a simple constructor issue. If the function is a member, clearly the class instance it operates on will have been initialized first. If your documentation contains instructions such as this, perhaps that module ought to be a class. That makes the special instructions easy to remove and makes it easier to use.

Sometimes, though, the situation is more complex. Perhaps you cannot create any instance of several classes before the entire system is initialized. This might happen in a library, for example. There may be a simple way around this. To initialize the library, a global object with a constructor can be placed in the library, and the constructor (called automatically before `main()`) initializes the system. Other times it is not that simple. You may need to initialize something on first use instead of simply initializing at the beginning of the program. If that's the case, then do so! Instead of telling the user to do something before using the system for the first time, have it be done automatically on first use. Here are examples of both ideas.

Suppose that a library contains several classes and even some non-member functions. The documentation says that a certain function must be called before the library can be used.

If the initialization is simple (just a single function call), it can be done automatically, with a static variable. Instead of having the documentation tell you that "you must call `lib_init()` before using any of this," the library can contain a dummy class whose constructor calls `lib_init()`, and a global variable of this class is in the library.

```
class lib_init_object_t {
public:
    lib_init_object_t() { lib_init(); }
    ~lib_init_object_t() { lib_shutdown(); }
    };
lib_init_object_t lib_init_object;
```

This provides for global initialization. Sometimes this is not good enough. Instead, you must ensure that one thing occurs before something else can occur. That "something else" might itself be done in a constructor for a global object, so order is important.

Here is a simple way to ensure that an object is constructed before it is used, when it can be used at any time. This example is for a program's setting file, which reads a disk file (or comes up with defaults) and is most definitely used by other initialization code.

The secret is to make a function access the object, instead of making the object itself global.

```
settings_t& get_settings()
{
static settings_t settings;
return settings;
}
```

This ensures that `settings` is constructed the first time `get_settings()` is called, and the same object is reused each time `get_settings()` is called again.

Above all, remember that when antibugging can't address a specific issue, use abugging. This issue is covered again in the abugging section.

Use a String Class (For Example)

A string class is attractive for several reasons. The first reason is a direct result of the advice in this chapter. C-style `char*` parameters and return values are an antibugging nightmare. C-style strings are prone to misuse. When a function takes strings as input or produces strings as output, who is responsible for freeing the memory, and who allocates it? In a string used for output, how much memory is available?

To minimize the problems, careful specification and many abugging techniques are needed. However, it is far better to apply antibugging and eliminate the source of the problem.

The second problem with C-style strings has to do with exception handling. In a function that allocates memory, you must take care that an exception does not cause a memory leak. This is covered in detail in Chapter 19, "Writing Interrupt Handlers and TSR Programs."

These problems apply not only to character strings, but to any place where resources are managed. Resource use should be encapsulated into classes.

Graceful Failure Modes

The specification of a function should cover error conditions. Just what happens if an operation does not work correctly? Even if the result is undefined, document that. Better yet, make any kind of error do something defined, whether it be returning a flag value, not doing anything, or throwing an exception. Someone using the function should know what to expect, not only in the normal case, but in an abnormal case.

When you are covering abnormal cases, think about what happens when an error occurs. An `assert()` that terminates the program is rather abrupt. A *graceful failure mode* is one that shuts down that part of the program in a calm way. For example, consider a file class. A file object may be closed or open to a specific file. If an error occurs in the `open()` function, it is natural to make that object `closed`.

Implementation versus Specification

The specification of a function (module, subsystem, or class) should state how it is supposed to work. This is what is in the documentation. The implementation of the function contains details that are not in the specification.

To rely on the implementation details that are not in the specification is a bad idea. Doing so is not "correct" but just "happens to work." This greatly hinders reusability and maintainability.

For example, consider the `strcmp()` function in ANSI/ISO C. The specification states that it returns a negative number, zero, or a positive number to indicate that the strings have a greater-than, equal-to, or less-than relationship. If you happen to know that the implementation of that function in your library computes this value by subtracting the first pair of non-matching characters, then you might be tempted to write code that uses the return value of `strcmp()` as a distance between the non-matching characters. The program is non-portable because another compiler (or a different version of the same compiler) may implement that function differently. The function is only supposed to return some negative number or some positive number. The details are *purposefully* left vague in the specification. You should respect that.

As another example, consider a member of a collection class called `contains()`. It is documented to return zero if the value indicated in the parameter is not present in the collection; and true (anything non-zero) if the element is present. However, you happen to know that the function actually returns the index at which the element is stored, if present. Using this knowledge is bad. Besides breaking encapsulation (you have to know that the collection is implemented as an array), what happens if maintenance is performed on this class and now `contains()` always returns 1, if present? You just broke some other code, even though what you did was well within the specification of the function. In short, it doesn't do much good to have a specification and to implement functions within a specification if the code that calls the function ignores the specification.

Abugging

Antibugging prevents mistakes from occurring, whereas abugging causes the computer to catch mistakes automatically. It is clearly less desirable to have mistakes automatically detected as opposed to not having mistakes in the first place. However, abugging can go further than antibugging. Antibugging only prevents usage mistakes by the programmer in the use of program components. Abugging can catch misuse of the program by the operator as well. In general, abugging can consider complex situations and discover anomalies that involve a complex combination of events. Even when the situation is not complex, some problems are not caused by mistakes, but are due to system environmental limitations, such as running out of memory or disk space. Abugging should be used to catch these conditions.

Abugging techniques fall into two major categories. Early abugging catches mistakes at compile time or link time, before the program is ever run. A fuzzy line exists between antibugging and early abugging. Runtime, or late abugging, catches things while the program is running. C++ provides constructs for both tasks.

The Bug Avalanche

A bug is like an avalanche; it starts out small with a simple and very subtle anomaly in the program's state. You might not be able to tell if the complex data structure is inconsistent or incorrect even if you were to inspect it. But this problem causes functions to be called with incorrect values, and the problem spreads. Code may not do any real damage yet, but just makes its own internal state worse and worse. Eventually, the problem becomes fatal. This is the "mortal wound" that you notice. A stray pointer writes to memory and clobbers something, a file is opened with a garbage name, or otherwise the problem is seen at a level where actual machine resources are being dealt with.

The first cause of a bug might be something nobody would ever think of, so naturally no one is watching for it. The problem spreads due to

the "domino effect" and is eventually felt on a primitive level. If the primitive level has good checking, a problem can be caught before it causes a fatal error, such as crashing the program or writing out a bad file.

Keep an Eye Out Where It Counts

The most common form of runtime abugging is to include explicit tests for error conditions in your code. Some tests, like running out of disk space, *must* be included or your program is in error. Other tests add extra safety and can catch program bugs. The former are mandatory, as they watch for things that can happen in a program functioning properly. The latter are for identifying where and when a program is not running correctly.

Low-Level Checks

As explained in the preceding section, a good place to insert runtime checks is at the lowest level, where primitive resources are managed. Memory and files are the most common examples. When resource acquisition or manipulation fails, the program needs to deal with it. This is covered in more detail in Chapter 18, "Exception Handling."

You *must* check the resources' behavior outside the control of your program. This is not optional; if you don't include such tests, that itself is a bug. Examples include running out of disk space, errors when reading from files, and running out of memory. This mandatory testing can be done at any level, but it is best to catch it at the lowest level to make sure that nothing slips through. A problem with a primitive resource should be caught immediately after manipulation of that resource.

Other low-level tests are not strictly necessary because a correctly running program does not encounter such a condition. This is the case of "Garbage in, garbage out." With extra testing, you get "Garbage in, error." The point is that these tests help you detect an incorrectly running program. If you are strongly opposed to extra checking on the

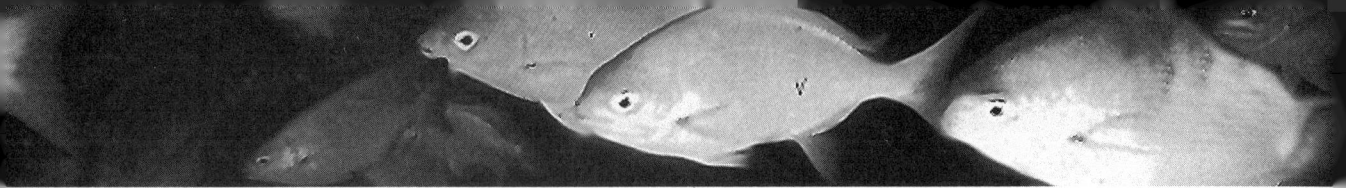

grounds that it slows down the program, you are not receptive to the thesis of this chapter. Keep an open mind and wait for the upcoming section, "How Much Testing Do You Need?"

The following is an example of extra testing:

```
void foo (const char* filename)
{
char temp[13];
strcpy (temp, filename);
...
```

Under DOS, file names are limited to 12 characters, and presumably the caller of this function (itself being non-buggy) never calls `foo()` with a string that is too long. The `strcpy()` call is considered a low-level manipulation of resources because it alters memory and can potentially crash or otherwise corrupt the program.

This test is not necessary because the tested-for condition never happens in a properly running program. But a test could be added as applied abugging, here to catch errors in the caller of `foo()` or elsewhere. Such checking will be welcome during maintenance or modification of the program. You will get an immediate error, not a subtle bug to track down.

Mid-Level Checks

Mid-level checks test for conditions not on the lowest, most primitive level of the program. Although low-level checks can conceptually catch anything, they are not always used because of concern that they reduce the efficency of the code. Suppose that the preceding function `foo()` was called many times. If the caller checks the parameters once beforehand, then you really would know that the test inside `foo()` is not necessary. Thus, mid-level checks are more efficient and can be used to circumvent the need for low-level checks.

In addition, mid-level checks can give better diagnostic information. If a test in `foo()` encounters an error with its parameter, the report would not give any indication as to the larger context of the part of the program in which the error occurred.

Understand the difference, and don't use mid-level checks when you actually need low-level checks. Conversely, use mid-level checks when you need higher-level diagnostic information or when low-level checks will seriously impair the efficiency of the code. Remember, low-level checks catch things for which you did not think of putting in mid-level checks.

High-Level Checks

Sometimes, a simple test of a value against an allowed range is not what is needed to detect an error state. Consider a vast, complex, linked data structure. Looking at a value in any one part, you cannot tell if that value is legal. The whole structure needs to be considered and checked for consistency. High-level checks do just this.

Use high-level checks when reading files that build a complex state in the program. Never trust the data coming in—check it up front and then the program can proceed with confidence.

High-level checks can be built-in as members of classes. They are like a fire department, ready to be called if you suddenly find the need to insert abugging statements into your program to locate a problem.

Prerequisites

In a beginner's programming class, *preconditions* are defined as conditions assumed to be true when a function begins its execution; *postconditions* are things that should be true when a function is finished and about to return. Part of the design process should be to understand what your preconditions and postconditions are.

The concept of late abugging is inserting run-time checks in the code. Taken to an extreme, this can be used to verify the preconditions and postconditions of every function.

Preconditions are prerequisites for a function or passage of code. The code is written with the implicit assumption that some things are so.

Take the following simple (and contrived) example:

```
int get_length (node* p)
{
return p->length;
}
```

The preceding line of code is simply not going to work if p does not point to a valid object of type node. Specifically, using a null pointer will be an error. Some things worth testing are in fact this simple. Other times, a precondition is more subtle, such as testing the relationship between several parameters.

The value of testing preconditions has been recognized for a long time. Even K&R C provided a simple and succinct mechanism designed for testing preconditions. Yet surprisingly, many C programmers have never heard of assert().

So You Test—Then What?

You identify things that can go wrong, and insert tests for these cases. What do you do when that test succeeds?

Assertions

The assert macro tests that a condition is true and aborts the program if it is not. Conditional compilation can render the assert statement dormant, while leaving it in place as a comment documenting the code's assumptions.

```
char* list::lookup (int n)
{
assert (n>=0 && n<max);
return data[n];
}
```

The assert is good for things that you never expect to happen. It enables you to put in tests without specifically having to design the program to accommodate failures in your function.

Exceptions

Aborting a program is not always the best choice; C++ provides better ways to react to an error. A mechanism similar to `assert` can be used that throws an exception instead of aborting the program.

```
#if defined NDEBUG
# define verfiy ((void)0)
#else
#define assert(b) \
    ((b) ? (void)0 : \
    throw xmsg ( "Verify failed: \
    " #b " at file" __FILE__ "line" QUOTE(__LINE__))
#endif
```

For new code without any need to imitate the `assert()` macro, more explicit use of exceptions might be more straightforward. An exception offers an emergency exit and, hopefully, controlled recovery of the program. The preceding function might be rewritten as:

```
char* list::lookup (int n)
{
if (n<0 || n>=max)  throw range_error;
return data[n];
}
```

Instead of aborting the program, strategic use of `catch` can allow the program to abort just the operation. For example, it can take you back to the last menu, clean up after the operation that failed, and enable you to try something else. Exceptions are covered in more detail in Chapter 18.

Repairs

Instead of just being warned when something goes wrong, you can treat or correct an error on the spot. This renders the problem a non-error, because you also should change the function's documentation to allow these cases. For example, the `lookup()` function might become the following:

```
char* list::lookup (int n)
{
if (n<0)  n= 0;
else if (n>=max)  n= max-1;
return data[n];
}
```

Meanwhile, the documentation for the function would state that values for `n` are clamped to `0` and `max-1`.

Surprisingly, this approach (sometimes called *defensive programming*) is generally considered bad. Look at the preceding example again. In some cases, clamping the input range makes perfect sense for the problem and makes the function better for the caller, which would have done something similar anyway. But most of the time, this just hides bugs instead of catching them. If there were a bug in which the caller is off-by-one (sometimes called a *fence post error*), it would go unnoticed here and yet may cause problems in other parts of the program.

Do not confuse repairing the error with completing the functionality.

Defensive programming is the correct thing to do when coding fault-tolerant input functions. If reading a complex file that represents the state of a job (think of a spreadsheet or word processor "document" file), you must check the input for sanity (this is described in more detail later in the section "Check the Input"). Here, it might be better to accept a slightly incorrect file (repairing simple problems) rather than refusing to load a file with any kind of error in it. The user would be much more pleased to get a spreadsheet with his fonts reverted to the default than to get an "error loading file" message!

How Much Testing Do You Need?

As pointed out earlier, some testing, such as for things outside the control of your program, is mandatory. You need to watch for a hostile outside environment. Other tests are useless in a correctly running program but can inform you if the program is running incorrectly. Unfortunately, these tests consume CPU cycles.

First, understand that checking can be conditional. You can have conditional compilation remove some checking, so that you have all the benefit of misuse detection when doing maintenance work and get rid of them for the shipping version. You also can build in conditional run-time checking, such as an on-demand trace.

Conditional Compilation

You can use the preprocessor to optionally include or remove passages of source. To do so, use the `#if`, `#elif`, `#else`, and `#endif` proprocessor directives. Besides creating different versions of a program for different configuration options, the mechanism can be used to produce a debug version of a program for testing. The ANSI C standard using the symbol NDEBUG to remove extra debugging code. You can use conditional compilation to remove extra checking when NDEBUG is defined.

You should leave some checking in place, however, even for the shipping version of your program. Programs are not perfect. It is said that each new user discovers a new class of bug. That is, different users use the programs in different ways and might come up with something totally unexpected that slipped through the testing process. Programs *do have latent bugs*, no matter how much work is put into testing and verification. They might not be blatant and overt, but rather are very subtle and, in fact, are design issues.

So how much checking should you leave in? The answer is not simple. It depends on the intended purpose and usage of the program. In a compiler, if something goes wrong and ruins the object file, it is not a big deal. The source file is still intact. In an accounting program, messing up the customer's data files is serious.

Some programs are simple utilities that have a runtime of a few seconds or minutes. Some programs are left running for days or weeks on end. In such long-running programs, any rare bugs have a better chance of showing up. Any latent problem such as a memory leak or a stray pointer has a long time to incubate and eventually cause problems. The long-running program needs much more serious internal checking.

Instead of asking how much to leave in, ask how much you should take out. Is the extra code too big, pushing the program size over the limit?

Does the high-level checking require large data structures that take up too much memory? Does the extra checking slow down the program? The speed issue is the most common consideration.

Instead of deciding on the minimum to leave in, decide what must be taken out because of the problems being caused. If the program is not too slow, why take out the tests? Perhaps mid-level checking can be used to speed up the program and still retain the safety. Profiling can give surprising answers as to what is really the slow part of a program.

Sometimes tests come for free. Consider this function, excerpted from an actual program:

```
int C::value (int n) const
{
if (n<0 || n > 4 || !(valid&(1<<n)))
    throw range_error (n, FNAME, __LINE__)
if (n == Reference)  return reference();
switch (mode) {
    case Absolute:
        return raw_values[n];
    case Delta:
        return reference() + raw_values[n];
    case Percentage:
        {
        int ref= reference();
        return ref+(raw_values[n]*ref+50)/100;
        }
    default:  //should never happen
        throw gerror ("bad mode", FNAME, __LINE__);
    }
}
```

The first test, checking the valid range of n, consumes some cycles. The second test, the default of the switch statement, is free. In fact, without the default case, the compiler complains about a missing return. The compiler doesn't know that the switch spans all possible values of mode. And the compiler is right! A funny value for mode would make this code malfunction. The default case is almost always a good idea.

Suggested Abugging Techniques

Now that you understand the concepts of abugging and how to recognize and apply abugging mechanisms, here are some suggestions on just where to use it.

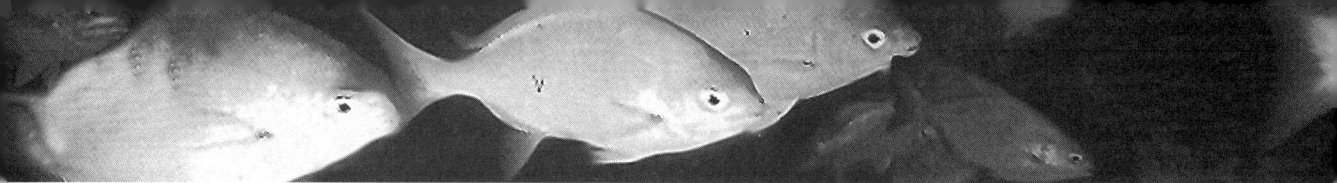

Strong Type Checking

The simplest form of early abugging is the programmer's best friend. If you've ever encountered a compile-time error, you might wonder how anyone ever accomplished anything before strong type checking. *Strong type checking,* when the compiler finds errors in usage of your functions, is a very effective tool. Most of you use it casually and might not even notice when the compiler informs you of errors. But next time you get a compiler error, think about what life would be like without it. With such a valuable tool, anything that helps its effectiveness is a powerful ally.

Avoid Casts

An explicit typecast is inherently dangerous. The compiler trusts what you say and does it. If you make a mistake, there is no error. Worse yet, you may have made other changes that render an existing cast incorrect. Here is an example:

```
void foo (const int* p)
{
//...other stuff
int* np= (int*) p;  //make a no-const version
}
```

Suppose that later, during maintenance or porting, the parameter p is changed from an `int` pointer to a `short` pointer. Now the cast is incorrect and can generate entirely wrong results.

The best advice is simply to avoid casts. Never use redundant casts or unnecessary explicit type conversions—let the compiler do these things for you. When you do need a potentially dangerous cast such as in the preceding example, isolate it.

```
inline int* noconst (const int* input)
{
return (int*)input;
}
void foo (const int* p)
{
//...other stuff
int* np= noconst (p);  //make a no-const version
}
```

Here, the cast is moved into an inline helper function. With no loss of efficiency, you gain some clarity and more important add strong type checking.

Instead of turning `p`, whatever it is, into an `int*`, you can verify that only a `const int*` gets turned into an `int*`. The compiler complains if you change the type of `p` and don't update the other parts of this function that need updating.

This is so important that the ANSI/ISO C++ committee saw fit to provide entirely new and safer casting forms. At this writing, they are not officially in the draft working paper yet, but this is how it is implemented in Borland C++ 4.0. In this example, you could use the `const_cast` operator. The `const_cast` only enables you to cast to the same type with different `const` and volatile modifiers and rejects a `cast` that actually changes the type.

```
void foo (const int* p)
{
//...other stuff
int* np= const_cast<int*> (p);   //make a no-const version
}
```

Null Pointers

Hopefully, a stray pointer never gets this far, but a null pointer might get used somewhere by accident. Writing to a null pointer can be bad; calling a virtual function on a null pointer can be disastrous. The following is a way to check for null objects in virtual function calls:

```
class Base {
    virtual void v_foo();
public:
    void foo();
    };
void Base::foo()
{
assert (this);
v_foo();
}
```

The user calls `foo()`, which is not virtual. This performs a test and calls `v_foo()`, which is the actual virtual function. To the caller, `foo()` behaves

exactly as if it had been the virtual function all along. To derived classes, they have to know to override `v_foo()` rather than `foo()`.

The abugging technique of catching uses of null pointers can be superseded with the antibugging technique of not having that null pointer in the first place. Many uses of null pointers simply go away if the pointer variable does not exist except when actually needed. Don't declare the variable until it is needed, and don't let it continue in scope after its use has ended. Other uses of null pointers can be eliminated by fine-tuning the algorithm manipulating pointers.

If you do have a pointer that may be null, *check it* before using it.

Check the Input

Even if the program is flawless, the program has no control over some things. In particular, problems can start with bad input. A robust program is paranoid about its input.

Bad input is like poison to a program. If the program has no internal error checking, the initial bad values can spread like a toxin throughout the system. If good checks are in place on a low level, they will be tripped. But low-level tests only tell you that the program is in trouble. Testing (and rejecting) the original input would have prevented the trouble.

When reading files, the program generally builds a complex network of data. This should be checked for consistency and correctness as it is created. User input tends to be more problematic. You never know what the user is going to type. The kind of testing necessary depends on the nature of the input and the user interface. But in general, it should be friendlier about reporting errors than you need to be for file input, and it should do more primitive checking on the correctness of the input before accepting the values.

Note that not all user input is what we would call *values*. Menu choices and commands are input too. Make sure that the user doesn't do something impossible or bizarre. Typically, a menu-driven program grays out inapplicable items.

Complete the Functionality

Under antibugging, you should identify situations that a function cannot handle. If there are holes in the functionality, the best thing to do for maintainability and reuse is to plug them and make the function handle those cases. However, this is sometimes impractical.

If holes exist, it can be a serious problem for future maintenance. Users might think they are using a function correctly, only to trace a bug to that function. It is important to trap these cases. Even with a simple `assert()`, you can save yourself a difficult bug hunt in the future.

Design

"A program is never finished—just shipped." The person who first said this is unknown, and perhaps it was meant as a joke. But most programmers find this statement to be serious and accurate. A program that is never again modified stagnates and dies. Successful programs are like living things, constantly evolving to meet the needs of their users.

Consider the design of a program; obviously, every program has one. The design may not be good or even written down anywhere, but every program does have a design.

Programs get added onto and modified over time. If an original design did exist, it is lost. Losing any appearance of good design and organization is the death of a program. All programs are that way to an extent, but those designed better in the first place have a much longer cycle.

The bottom line is if you want to write good code, you must design it first. You can't code it until you know what it is supposed to do. If you just make it up as you go along, it will be well along in its "maintained to death" cycle before it is even finished. Programs should be born young, not old. Designing well is beyond the subject of this chapter, which discusses the aspects of design that influence the writing and maintaining of bug-free code.

Characteristics of a Good Design

A program has a good design if it is easy to modify and extend and can be easily adapted to accept new enhancements. The design is especially good if such changes do not work against the original design, but with it. In a nutshell, if a program can be easily written (and maintained) without introducing bugs, it is a good design. The design helps or hinders the writing of bug-free code.

In C++, good design means that a program is hierarchically arranged and parts are well encapsulated. Components should be reusable and should exist in isolation.

Hierarchical Arrangement

A program of any length and complexity should be arranged hierarchically. A *high level* is responsible for the overall flow of the program and distinguishes this program from others that use all the same libraries and low-level code. A *low level* consists of functions and classes specific to a purpose. Low-level routines include `strcpy()`, file management, and other primitives. The word *primitive* is the key.

In a small program, `main()` is the high level, and the standard library is the low level. In a large program, the organization should be a smooth and logical extension of this idea. The highest-level functions call more primitive functions, which themselves call more primitive functions, continuing for several stages.

Components Should Exist in Isolation

Low-level components are reusable by their very nature—or at least, they should be. A low-level routine does not draw upon high-level modules, and this makes that routine transportable. Move it to a new program, and you won't get complaints from missing components. However, to be properly reusable it should be general purpose as well as primitive. A function can be self contained, but still have implicit assumptions about the program that will use it. The true primitives should not have this knowledge. You can use parameters to customize

the behavior to suit. Besides making that function more reusable, it makes the program that contains it more maintainable. Uses may change as the program evolves.

High-level components are trickier. High-level objects in a program should still take care of themselves and not be unduly affected by what other parts of the program are doing. Not doing so can be a very serious hindrance to maintaining the program, more so than the low-level components are.

For example, I once inherited a program that had a large and complex structure at the heart of it. That structure used global data for some things. This caused a problem when two instances of this structure were needed. They kept fighting over that global object. The program was written to very carefully pass it back and forth (it worked most of the time, anyway), but it made modification next to impossible. The use of this object was highly restricted, as doing some things with it would mess up the workings of other things.

In general, having an object contain an internal state that reflects its current usage is a bad idea. A simple example is a *current item* variable in a collection. Only one thing at a time can use that collection. Worse, the collection might make assumptions about how its user uses it. Naturally, that makes it difficult to maintain and modify the code that uses the collection.

If the object exists in isolation, it should not know or care how it is being used. This provides a "fire break" for maintenance.

Components Should Be Reusable

The encapsulation, arrangement, and isolation of parts of the program are an aid to comprehension, but also directly influence the reusability of the code. This leads to an interesting and very powerful concept: Reusable code is inherently maintainable. Reusable code and maintainable code are one and the same.

This is easy to see. When you modify a program, you are in fact changing the way some components are used. If those components don't

object, you have no secondary changes to make, and the program's change was easy. If you make an addition to the program, the new code can draw upon existing low-level (and mid-level) code, which is reused within the same program.

Home-Grown versus Bought

If a program component is not quite right, you can change it. An existing function, for example, might be nearly identical to what is suddenly needed elsewhere. The difference may be such that adding a parameter makes the function work for both places. With home-grown code, this is commonplace.

With purchased components, changing it might be more difficult or impossible. This means that code designed (by whoever sold it to you) for reuse as a complete work is very difficult to design. It must consider everything; it must consider the needs of other users, not just this program. It is, by its nature, more complex. Consider the preceding function: There might be an extra parameter that you don't need because someone else does or might.

When writing a program as a set of simpler modules, don't go overboard in making it general purpose. If designed well, it can be changed when needed. Design in flexibility, not just in use but in its own maintainability. This is preferred to thinking of everything in advance.

To summarize, writing bug-free code requires well-designed code. Code should be designed before it is implemented. As discussed in the first half of this chapter, the design should be examined for antibugging issues. That is where it all begins.

Documentation

Documentation can be produced during the design state, but design and documentation are not synonymous. Just because a program has a design doesn't mean it's written down anywhere. Likewise, documenting a poor design doesn't make it better. Documentation is not a substitute for design. Rather, documentation is an aid to understanding the design and the implementation.

Documenting the Design

Having a design document is a good thing. In a major development effort, the quest for writing bug-free code begins with the design document. For each component, this should contain two parts. First is an informal essay on what the component is for, what it does, and so on. The component should have a well-defined purpose, and you must first state the purpose.

The second part is a technical reference. You should document your class before coding it. In C++, classes form the backbone of the program's organization. The public interface should be specified, and the functions documented just as if this were a preexisting library that you just bought.

Higher levels of organization (such as a group of related classes) need the first part, at the very least. Explain what this subsystem does, and introduce the component systems.

Now that you have a technical reference manual, review it. Think about the higher-level parts of the program that this will be used in, and see if this library does what you need of it. Pretend you are evaluating the library prior to purchase. What would you say to the vendor? Are there reasons you don't like it, things you need that are not supplied? Vent it all. You may consider walk-through, which is basically doing the same thing as a group. Above all, think about using this interface. Make sure that it meets your needs.

Using other people in this stage has mixed results. It is difficult to get someone else to find things wrong with it. On the other hand, explaining it to someone else helps you to understand it and spot things in the documentation that are unclear. (As you find them, fix them!)

The best way to get someone else involved is to give it to someone else to implement. You quickly will be asked about unclear areas and inconsistencies.

Documenting the Implementation

Documenting the functions before they are implemented and documenting the functions while they are being implemented produces strikingly different results. The former is a design document that explains what things do on a high level and how they interact. The latter explains how the functions themselves work. Sometimes it explains so well how the functions work that it fails to explain what the function *does*. Clearly, this is a different kind of document.

An implementation document serves a different purpose from a design document. A design document should be used before the code is written to debug the specification and finally to drive the implementation. Later, it is used as a technical reference when these functions and classes are used by other code.

The implementation document is used by maintenance programmers maintaining that class itself, not using it in a larger context. Both uses are valid and aid in writing and keeping code bug-free. However, they serve two different audiences, and an attempt to make one description serve everyone instead serves no one.

A design document should exist as a separate document from the source code, and in fact predates it. With the implementation document, you have more freedom. It can be separate or maintained in the actual source file with the code. Good self-documenting code *is* implementation documentation, as are block comments and such. But besides documenting individual functions, make sure that you document the overall approach of how they work together to implement the whole design. Also, create reference documentation on the internal functions, not in the design document.

Good Documentation

Good documentation is hard to come by, but is worth its weight in gold. It is important to have a good technical reference for your classes and functions. This provides a road map for future maintenance. It must be clear what a function does, how it should be called, what it returns, and any outside effects it may have.

If you don't have complete documentation for a function, the only way to find out what it actually does is to try it or inspect the code. This does not tell you what the designer necessarily had in mind, but does tell you about the implementation. As pointed out earlier, it is important for future maintenance to make a clear distinction between specification and implementation.

Notice that documentation does not have to be particularly good from a grammatical point of view. It should contain hard information and facts, not golden prose. You're a programmer, not necessarily a writer. Don't worry about making nice transitions between paragraphs. Just list the information.

Testing

Test things well, and test things often. The only way to tell that something really does work is to try it.

After you make a change, verify that it works. By testing frequently, you know that any problem was just introduced in the last change. A correct test not only gives feedback that you are doing this correctly, but also verifies that you have not broken anything else in the process.

Code can be tested at several layers. Unit testing is for small parts. Integration testing makes sure that they fit together properly, and whole-application testing verifies the end product.

Each testing layer should be approached with different techniques. You can bang on the keyboard and see if anything goes wrong, you can verify that things work correctly in normal use, you can see what happens with atypical or improper usage, and you can use your knowledge

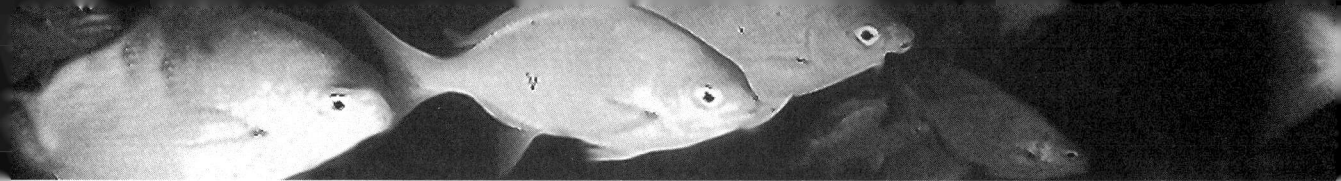

of the implementation to try and find weak points. Each approach has its advantages.

Unit Testing

Unit testing is a verification on a single component, be it a function, class, subsystem, or module. The component (of whatever size) is supposed to perform a well-defined role, and it should be tested to see if it in fact fulfills its role.

Unit testing generally involves the creating of test code along with the actual component. For this reason, it is often neglected.

If implementation is proceeding bottom-up, and low-level components are being created before being fit together into the final program, you definitely need to write a test program to try out this component. Don't wait until it is finished. You should be testing it along the way as you develop the component.

The scaffolding may grow into the next higher-level code. Or, it may be discarded or fall out of date. In general, the problem is that primitive code's test scaffolding goes away. This means that if the code ever needs to be retested with unit testing, new test code has to be developed. For components meant to be reused across multiple programs (such as a commercial library of code), test code should be maintained and provided along with the library.

If adding a component to an existing program, the test code can be a modified part of the main program rather than a separate test program. The issues are the same: The test code regrettably has a temporary nature. Do not get lazy and neglect to perform unit testing. Do write the test code and verify components. The benefits are worth the trouble.

Unit testing should test the complete functionality of the component. Even if the main program doesn't exercise the component fully, the test code should. This is why you may need to modify a part of the

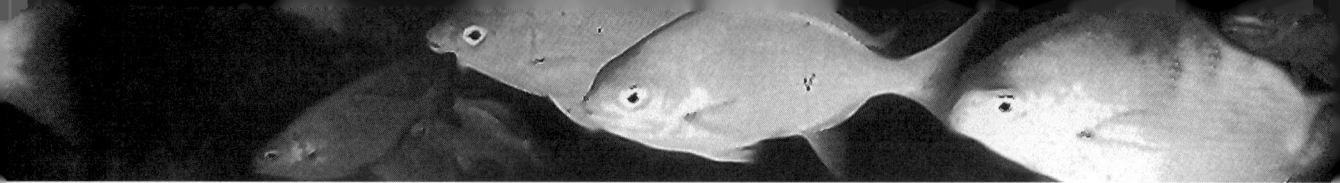

main program to test a new component instead of just sliding it in place and seeing how it works. The latter is whole-application testing and integration testing only, not unit testing. Unit testing should be a very complete check-out.

Black-box testing makes sure that a component meets its specification, period. In w*hite-box* testing, you use knowledge of how the component is implemented and try to identify weak points. You use this knowledge to design particularly difficult tests.

Both approaches are needed. You need to make sure that the component adheres to the specification. You also can use your implementation knowledge to know just where to stress it, in addition to trying some normal cases.

Integration Testing

After you know that individual components work properly and you can trust them, you can proceed to the next step. *Integration testing* is when you make sure that components work together properly, and that they are put together correctly.

At this point, you should be able to assume that the individual components can handle anything you throw at them. If an illegal condition occurs, you are alerted with an error. Any problems at this stage have to be with the communication between modules, not with the already-tested modules themselves. A problem at this point should be easy to identify and fix.

If several components are brought together into a larger assembly, this can become a unit-test of the larger assembly. However, make sure that you maintain the distinction. Proper integration testing, which specifically tests the connections between the subassemblies, should be done before unit testing the new assembly.

If you change one of the components, make sure that you retest that component using unit testing before reintegrating it. This is often

overlooked. Suppose that very primitive components A, B, and C get put together into a larger component D. A, B, and C were all well tested, and now that D is working, you test it too. Some later time, you decide to alter A. That problem is that you no longer have any viable test code for A. It is all too common to just retest D and assume that if D exercises A well, then A must be good. This is not true, and you have lost the benefits of unit testing.

Whole-Application Testing

Whole-application testing is very important. This tests the final product, which is what the customer finally sees.

Integration testing of the final assembly of major components and whole-application testing are two different things. The integration testing should be done first. The whole-application testing specifically runs the program, examining it from a user's point of view. This generally is black-box style testing, whereas integration testing is necessarily white-box style.

In whole-application testing, you test not only for implementation errors, but for overall usability. A cryptic, poorly documented, or difficult-to-use feature will probably be misused. This can involve debugging on a fundamentally different level from the normal debugging of components.

Application testing can often be done by personnel other than the developers. Technical support people and salespeople make good candidates. Treat them as users, and see if they discover anything.

Outside personnel, however, rarely are good at stress-testing the program, purposefully trying things that you are not supposed to do or using the program in ways you never intended. Only real customers can do that.

Debugging

This chapter is on writing bug-free code, not fixing buggy code. However, some debugging is still necessary. This chapter focuses on healing the code rather than just patching over it. For more information on debugging, see Chapter 7, "Debugging Tips and Tricks."

Debugging concerns the detection of problems. Problems can be misuses of program components in the code, design flaws, or sensitivities to conditions in the environment. You can do a number of things to make debugging easier, and certain practices help to make debugging a successful endeavor.

The preceding sections tell you how to prevent bugs from occurring. This section discusses finding a bug, if one does exist.

Don't Let It Happen Again

When a problem does occur that requires debugging, make sure that you understand it completely before fixing it. Then don't fix it yet. Instead, harden the program against it, adding abugging to the program that prevents this mistake from ever happening (or the environmental issue from going uncaught) again. The program should report the current bug. Test with some variations and finally remove the bug. In short, never make the same mistake twice.

In a real-life example, a program I am currently writing kept suffering from the same mistake: a set of configuration options was being accessed before the configuration file was loaded. A programmer making modifications to the program's startup sequence would inevitably make this mistake.

When I found out about it, I was able to improve the situation. A test was added to the code that accessed the settings information that would render the request harmless and alert the user. This is abugging. A better fix would be to load the information on first use (an anti-bugging technique), but that may not always be a practical option due to other considerations.

Think through Changes

When contemplating a change, you should understand how it affects the rest of the program. If you make something better or more powerful, follow through with other changes that may be needed to take advantage of it.

Often, a change in one place can require that other code be changed as well. In a poorly designed program, apparently unrelated things may need to change, and it is difficult to locate all the places. As discussed earlier, minimizing this effect is the defining property of good design.

In general, two kinds of changes exist. The good kind is an interior change to a component's implementation. The "ripple effect" of changes *will stop* at the component's boundaries.

Changing a component's interface, on the other hand, is really a design change that requires changing both the implementation of that component and all code that uses it. Often, such changes can be made to be downward compatible, or purposefully made incompatible so that the compiler spots any old, unupdated uses.

If, instead of the preceding, a change that should be simple actually affects a great deal of code, the program is suffering from improper encapsulation. If no proper and well-defined interface to a component exists, any change might in reality be an interface change. In short, the whole of the implementation details becomes the interface, and modifications are nearly impossible.

When contemplating a modification, consider the nature of the change. Keeping these general rules in mind helps you understand how changes affect the overall program.

The Debugger's Mindset

The debugger's mindset should be totally different from the programmer's mindset. To be successful, you have to mentally shift gears.

A programmer normally thinks like an engineer, or sometimes like an artist. The debugger must think like a scientist and a sleuth. He must become a Sherlock Holmes of programming, accepting the information of facts while keeping an open mind to hidden possibilities. The programmer must be creative; the debugger must be methodical.

Approach to Debugging

To track down a bug, you must use the scientific method. Start by making observations. Seek out new observations by trying test cases, instrumenting the program with debugging statements, or tracing through it with a debugger program. Formulate a hypothesis and then check to see if the hypothesis is true.

Most bugs are trivial to deduce from the observations. Good encapsulation only enhances the effect. Even so, some bugs are more difficult. If you can't deduce the nature of a bug, you don't change your methods. Rather, you make better observations.

Generally, you trace through a program and inspect values at certain points or make sure that conditional statements are branching the right way. This is not looking for the bug; this is looking for an effect closer to the cause. If you encounter a point where you know the program is behaving incorrectly, the quest is to prove that the program is behaving incorrectly at an earlier time. Your goal is to find the earliest point in time at which the program starts to behave incorrectly.

Cause and Effect

Recall the "domino effect" as explained in the section "The Bug Avalanche." A single and subtle anomaly grows into a noticeable effect in the program's behavior. This has a corollary: For any noticeable effect, there is an ultimate cause.

An effect is separated from its cause both in time and in space—by different parts of the source code. Worse, if a bug is not noticed early, you may have the "domino effect" and can find that the cause of the *observed* bug is itself an effect whose cause you need to find.

The idea of abugging is to reduce the space and time separation between cause and effect. Consider a program that produces a report and contains a bug noticed as incorrect output on that report. After much searching, the ultimate cause is found to be a field in an input file that is too wide, which messes up the extraction of the fields from that line and provides incorrect data to the heart of the program. This in turn provides incorrect data to the report generator, all without causing any kind of alarm. The fundamental cause and the originally observed effect are as widely separated both in space and in time as is possible.

On the other hand, if the program performed proper validation of its input, the bug would be noticed when the program diagnoses the error. If the program were designed to consider the possibility of bad input as a normal situation, it would offer a readable and clear diagnosis explaining what was wrong with the file. If this possibility were dismissed as impossible because another program was producing that input file, but an abugging test is put in anyway to catch internal errors, it may print a cryptic message and abort. You would have to look to see what is making the program abort. Even so, the bug (program aborts) is very close to the ultimate cause, both in space and time. It would be much easier to find and fix.

From Here...

➤ For information on making your programs more efficient (as opposed to fixing errors), see Chapter 4, "Optimizing C."

For helpful hints on debugging code containing errors, see Chapter 7, "Debugging Tips and Tricks."

➤ If the Borland C++ debugger does not provide the features you need or is not powerful enough for your needs, see Chapter 8, "Third-Party Debugger Tools."

➤ For information on debugging errors involving heap management, see Chapter 9, "K&R Implementation Secrets."

Debugging Tips and Tricks

by Clay Walnum

C and C++ programming is much like assembly language programming in that both languages provide the programmer much power. Of course, with this power comes an equal portion of responsibility. The more power the programmer has, the more wonderful things he can do. However, with that increased power also comes an increased likelihood of serious program bugs.

Every programmer must debug his programs. Unfortunately, instead of learning to use sophisticated debugging tools, programmers often resort to old-fashioned debugging techniques, like adding print statements to a program to trace the program's flow and to check the value of variables.

These tried-and-true techniques work well for obvious logic errors and other easy-to-find programming critters, but sooner or later you will encounter a problem that's not so easy to find. In such cases, you should use the sophisticated debugging tools supplied with Borland C++ 4.0. Both Turbo Debugger for DOS and Turbo Debugger for Windows are powerful tools that can do anything from locating an uninitialized variable to tracing through a function-call stack, and can even provide information about the state of the processor.

In this chapter, you learn some helpful techniques for tracking down slippery program bugs. You can apply the general debugging tips with both DOS and Windows programs. Later in the chapter, you get some specific advice for finding bugs in your Windows applications. As you soon see, spending a couple of hours learning to use Turbo Debugger can save you weeks or months in the long run.

General Debugging Techniques

Most program bugs are easy to find. Usually you can find whatever problem you're looking for simply by stepping through a program while watching the values of key variables. For these quickie debugging jobs, the Borland C++ compiler provides built-in debugging services, including those that step through a program, set breakpoints, watch variables, and modify variables. You can find these debugging functions in the Debug menu, shown in figure 7.1.

Unfortunately, the built-in debugging tools work only for Windows programs. If you're building a DOS application, you must load Turbo Debugger for DOS to perform any debugging. Still, thanks to Borland's smart menus, loading the debugger is just a matter of selecting Turbo Debugger from the Tool menu. When you do, Borland automatically loads the debugger that's appropriate for your current project.

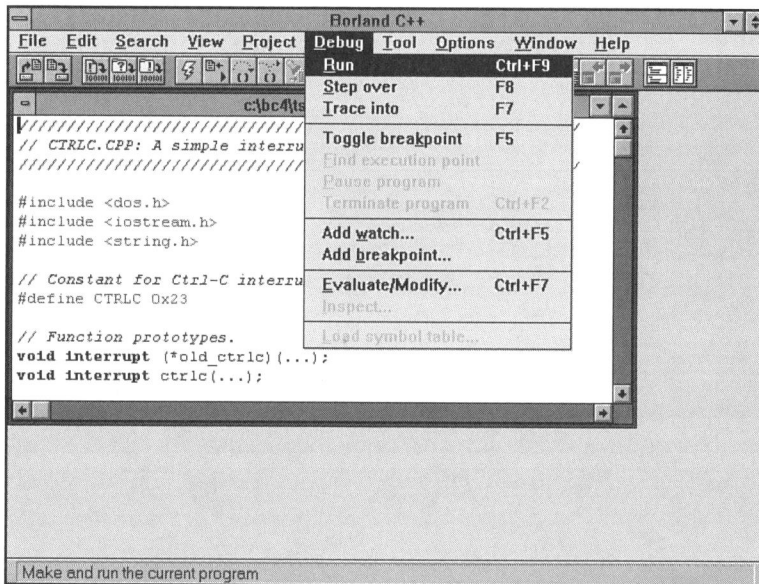

Fig. 7.1. Borland's Debug menu.

Stepping Through a Program

You can locate probably 90 percent of program errors by using some form of the step command. For this task, Turbo Debugger provides the Trace Into command, which steps through a program line by line, and can jump to functions when the program calls them. Turbo Debugger also includes the Step Over command, which enables you to treat a function call as a single line of code. That is, if the instruction arrow is pointing to a function call and you select the Step Over command, the debugger runs the function call without stepping through the function line by line.

Listing 7.1 is a simple C++ program that accepts five names from the user and then displays the names on the screen. Compile the program as a DOS application and then run it.

Listing 7.1. DEBUG1.CPP—A Program That Displays Five Names On-Screen

```cpp
///////////////////////////////////////////////////////////
// DEBUG1.CPP: CONTAINS BUGS!
///////////////////////////////////////////////////////////

#include <stdio.h>
#include <iostream.h>
#include <string.h>
#include <conio.h>

// Function prototypes.
void GetNames(char *names[]);
void ShowNames(char *names[]);
void DeleteNames(char *names[]);

///////////////////////////////////////////////////////////
// main()
///////////////////////////////////////////////////////////
int main(void)
{
    char *names[5];

    GetNames(names);
    ShowNames(names);
    DeleteNames(names);
    gotch();
    return 1;
}

///////////////////////////////////////////////////////////
// GetNames()
///////////////////////////////////////////////////////////
void GetNames(char *names[])
{
    char s[81];

    for (int x=0; x<5; ++x)
    {
        sprintf(s, "Enter name #%d: ", x+1);
        cout << s;
        cin >> s;
        names[x] = new char[strlen(s)+1];
        strcpy(names[x], s);
    }
    cout << endl;
}

///////////////////////////////////////////////////////////
// ShowNames()
///////////////////////////////////////////////////////////
void ShowNames(char *names[])
{
```

```
    char s[81];

    cout << "The names you entered are:" << endl;
    for (int x=0; x<5; ++x);
    {
        sprintf(s, "Name #%d: ", x+1);
        cout << s << names[x] << endl;
    }
}

///////////////////////////////////////////////////////////
// DeleteNames()
///////////////////////////////////////////////////////////
void DeleteNames(char *names[])
{
    for (int x=0; x<5; ++x)
        delete names[x];
}
```

When you run the program shown in Listing 7.1, enter the names as you are prompted. When you finish, you should see output similar to the following:

```
Enter name #1: Stephen
Enter name #2: Justin
Enter name #3: Chris
Enter name #4: Lynn
Enter name #5: Clay

The names you entered are:
Name #6:
```

Obviously, the program isn't working as it's supposed to. The error in this program is one that's insidiously easy to make and difficult to spot. However, stepping through the program reveals the problem almost immediately. To debug the program in Listing 7.1, follow these instructions:

1. Run Turbo Debugger for DOS by choosing Turbo Debugger from the Tool menu. Turbo Debugger runs the program, stopping the program's execution on the first line, as shown in figure 7.2.

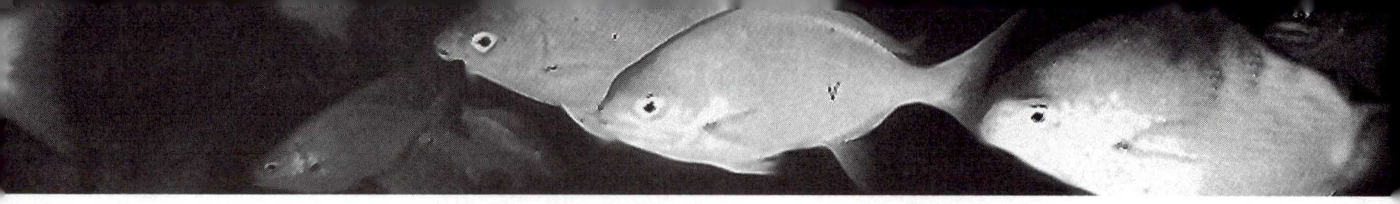

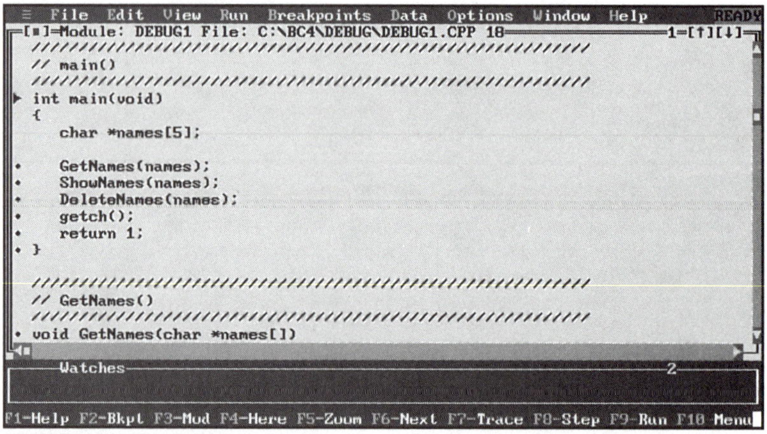

Fig. 7.2. Running a program with Turbo Debugger for DOS.

2. Choose <u>T</u>race Into from the <u>R</u>un menu, or press F7. The program's execution moves forward one step, stopping on the call to the function `GetNames()`.

3. Choose <u>S</u>tep Over from the <u>R</u>un menu, or press F8. The debugger then executes the `GetNames()` function without stepping through it. Then enter the names as prompted.

4. The instruction arrow should now point to the call to `ShowNames()`. Because Listing 7.1 seems to be having trouble displaying the names, press F7 to step through that function.

5. Press F7 twice more so that the instruction arrow points to the start of the `for` loop, as shown in figure 7.3.

6. Because `x` is the loop's control variable, it might be a good idea to watch its value as you step through the loop. To do this, click on the Watches window at the bottom of the screen, type **x**, and press Enter. The current value of `x` (which is garbage because `x` has not yet been initialized) appears in the Watches window.

7. Press F7 to start tracing through the for loop. The value of `x` jumps instantly to 5.

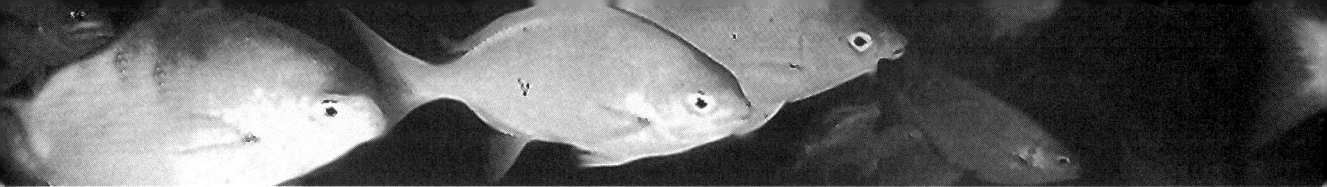

```
≡  File  Edit  View  Run  Breakpoints  Data  Options  Window  Help        READY
┌[■]─Module: DEBUG1 File: C:\BC4\DEBUG\DEBUG1.CPP (modified) 55════1=[↑][↓]┐
│ //////////////////////////////////////////////////////////////////////
│ // ShowNames()
│ //////////////////////////////////////////////////////////////////////
│•void ShowNames(char *names[])
│ {
│     char s[81];
│
│•    cout << "The names you entered are:" << endl;
│▶    for (int x=0; x<5; ++x);
│     {
│•        sprintf(s, "Name #%d: ", x+1);
│•        cout << s << names[x] << endl;
│     }
│•}
│
│
│ //////////////////////////////////////////////////////////////////////
│ // DeleteNames()
│ //////////////////////////////////////////////////////////////////////
│◄■                                                                    ▶
├────Watches──────────────────────────────────────────────────2────────
│
└──────────────────────────────────────────────────────────────────────
 F1-Help F2-Bkpt F3-Mod F4-Here F5-Zoom F6-Next F7-Trace F8-Step F9-Run F10-Menu
```

Fig. 7.3. Tracing through a *for* loop.

If you continue pressing F7, you'll notice that the program executes the body of the loop only once. But you already know that something is wrong in the first line of the for loop, because x is not supposed to jump from its uninitialized value all the way up to 5. A close examination of that line reveals that a semicolon follows the for statement, which makes this an empty for loop. The compiler is treating the lines that follow the for statement as simply another statement block rather than the body of the loop, because the looping is over before it reaches those lines. Remove the semicolon and then rerun the program. The program should now run correctly.

> **Note:** When you want to see the value of a variable, you don't have to include the variable in the Watches window. To take a quick look at a variable's value, place the blinking text cursor on the variable's name and press Enter. A small window appears, displaying the variable's address, data type, and value, both in hex and decimal. Remember that Turbo Debugger can display only those variables currently in scope.

When you ran DEBUG1.CPP the first time, you probably already had a good idea where to find the problem. You really didn't need to trace through the whole program to find it, you just needed to trace through the ShowNames() function. Therefore, you could have debugged this program more quickly by using the Go To Cursor command, which runs a program until it reaches the line that contains the cursor. To try this debugging method, follow these steps:

1. If you haven't done so already, terminate the program from the last debugging session by choosing Program Reset from the Run menu, or press Ctrl-F2. This command enables you to rerun the DEBUG1.CPP program from the beginning.

2. Use your keyboard's arrow keys to position the blinking text cursor on the first line of the ShowNames() function, as shown in figure 7.4.

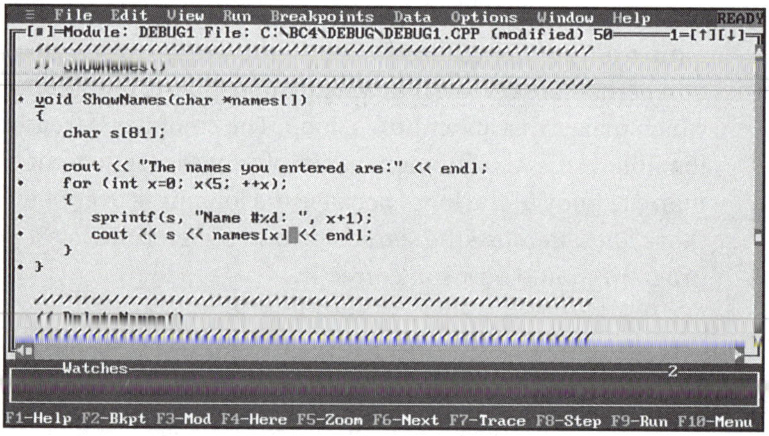

Fig. 7.4. The text cursor on the first line of *ShowNames()*.

3. Choose Go To Cursor from the Run menu, or press F4. The program begins to execute.

4. Enter the names as prompted. When you do, the program halts on the first line of the ShowNames() function.

5. Press F7 to step through the function, as you did in the previous debugging session.

Another way to stop program execution on a particular line is to set breakpoints. To set a breakpoint, simply click on the dot to the left of the line where you want the program to stop. The line turns red, indicating that the breakpoint is set. You can also set a breakpoint by moving the blinking text cursor to the breakpoint line, and then choosing Toggle from the Breakpoints menu or pressing F2.

Inspecting Data

Often, the information that the Watches window supplies about a piece of data isn't enough to enable you to solve a problem. Take Listing 7.2, for example. This program contains another hard-to-find program bug.

Listing 7.2. DEBUG2.CPP—A Program That Matches First and Last Names

```
/////////////////////////////////////////////////////////////
// DEBUG2.CPP: CONTAINS BUGS!
/////////////////////////////////////////////////////////////

#include <iostream.h>
#include <conio.h>
#include <string.h>

char *name1[10] =
    { "LUCY", "SAM", "FRED", "TEDFORD", "MARIA"
      "ALICE", "HARVEY", "LOUIS", "HEATHER", "RALPH" };

char *name2[10] =
    { "SMITH", "GRAYSON", "WALTERS", "WHITE", "PALMER",
      "DAVIS", "BENSON", "GREEN", "WEAVER", "KING" };

/////////////////////////////////////////////////////////////
// main()
/////////////////////////////////////////////////////////////
int main(void)
{
    int index, x;
    char s[81];

    cout << "Enter first name: ";
    cin >> s;
    strupr(s);
```

continues

Listing 7.2. Continued

```
index = -1;
x = 0;
do
{
    if (strcmp(s, name1[x]) == 0)
        index = x;
    ++x;
}
while ((index == -1) && (x != 10));

if (index == -1)
    cout << "Name not found" << endl;
else
    cout << "Last name is " << name2[index] << endl;
getch();

return 1;
}
```

When you run this program, enter one of the names found in the name1[] array. The program then matches the name that you entered with the appropriate last name, which it finds in the name2[] array.

When you enter **LUCY**, **SAM**, **FRED**, or **TEDFORD**, the program works fine, matching the name that you enter with the appropriate last name. However, when you enter **MARIA** or any of the names that follow it in the name1[] array, the program matches the person's first name with the wrong last name.

Tracing through this program a line at a time does not reveal the problem. The loop that matches up the names seems to work fine. You can get a clue to the problem, though, by using the Watches window, and then find the real problem by examining the program's data with Turbo Debugger's Inspect command. To debug DEBUG2.CPP, follow these steps:

1. After compiling DEBUG2.CPP as a DOS application, choose Turbo Debugger from Borland C++'s Tool menu.

2. Press F7, which is the hotkey for the Trace Into command, to begin tracing through the program.

3. Click the Watches window to activate it. Then type **x** and press Enter, type **s** and press Enter, and type **name1[x]** and press Enter. Turbo Debugger adds these three data items to the Watches window, as shown in figure 7.5.

```
≡  File  Edit  View  Run  Breakpoints  Data  Options  Window  Help        READY
   ─Module: DEBUG2 File: C:\BC4\DEBUG\DEBUG2.CPP 25───────────────1───
    int index, x;
    char s[20];

►   cout << "Enter first name: ";
•   cin >> s;
•   strupr(s);

•   index = -1;
•   x = 0;
    do
    {
•       if (strcmp(s, name1[x]) == 0)
            index = x;
•       ++x;
    }
•   while ((index == -1) && (x != 10));

─[■]─Watches──────────────────────────────────────────2─[↑][↓]─
name1[x]                    char far * 2E2E:2E5D                       ▲
s char [81] "\xE4\n\xE4\x0F\xC0L\x07\x91\b\x0B\xE4\n\xC6\x0Fz\x1B\x9E\x98R\rz\
x                           int 2788 (0xAE4)                           ▼
◄■►                                                                    ↕
F1-Help F2-Bkp■ F3-Mod F4-Here F5-Zoom F6-Next F7-Trace F8-Step F9-Run F10-Menu
```

Fig. 7.5. The Watches window after you enter *x, s,* and *name1[x].*

4. Press F7 twice, and then enter the name **maria**. In the Watches window, s should now show the string maria, followed by garbage bytes.

5. Continue pressing F7 while watching the results in the Watches window. In the Watches window, s continues to show the string that you entered (except that it is displayed in all uppercase letters) and name1[x] shows the string to which the program is comparing the string that you entered.

6. When x becomes 4, notice that name1[x] in the Watches window points to the string "MARIAALICE". Clearly, there's some sort of problem with the character pointers in the name1[] array.

7. Click the Watches window, and then type **name1** and press Enter. Turbo Debugger displays the name1[] array in the Watches window.

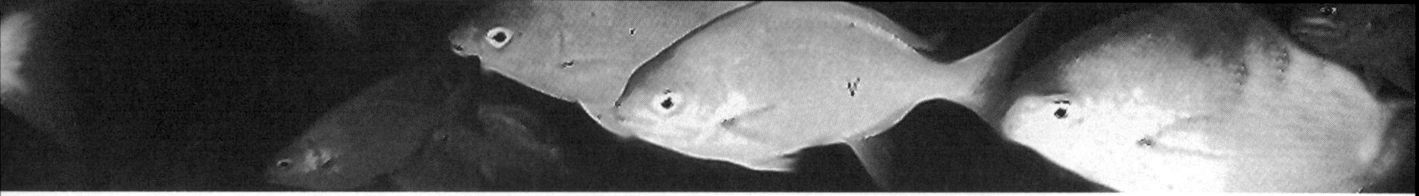

8. Use your keyboard's right-arrow key to scroll the Watches window so that you can see all the pointers stored in name1[]. You discover that only the first nine pointers are valid. The tenth pointer is null, as shown in figure 7.6.

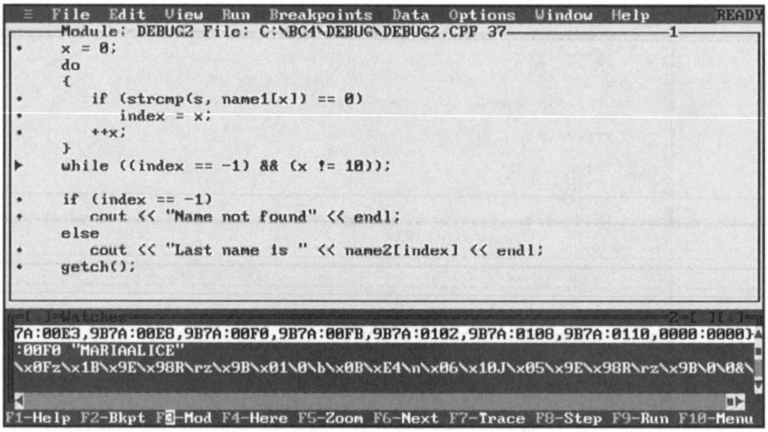

```
≡ File  Edit  View  Run  Breakpoints  Data  Options  Window  Help      READY
┌─Module: DEBUG2 File: C:\BC4\DEBUG\DEBUG2.CPP 37──────────────1─┐
•     x = 0;
      do
      {
•         if (strcmp(s, name1[x]) == 0)
•             index = x;
•         ++x;
      }
►     while ((index == -1) && (x != 10));

•     if (index == -1)
•         cout << "Name not found" << endl;
      else
•         cout << "Last name is " << name2[index] << endl;
•     getch();


┌─1─Watches───────────────────────────────────────────2─[↓][↑]─┐
│7A:00E3,9B7A:00E8,9B7A:00F0,9B7A:00FB,9B7A:0102,9B7A:0108,9B7A:0110,0000:0000│▲
│:00F0 "MARIAALICE"                                              │
│\x0Fz\x1B\x9E\x98R\rz\x9B\x01\0\b\x0B\xE4\n\x06\x10J\x05\x9E\x98R\rz\x9B\0\0&│▼
│◄                                                              ►│
└F1-Help F2-Bkpt F3-Mod F4-Here F5-Zoom F6-Next F7-Trace F8-Step F9-Run F10-Menu┘
```

Fig. 7.6. A null pointer in the *name1[]* array.

9. Activate the Module window again, and, using your mouse or your keyboard's arrow keys, place the blinking text cursor on any occurrence of name1 in the displayed source code. Press Enter, and Turbo Debugger displays the Inspecting box (see fig. 7.7). (You also can activate this box by selecting Inspect from the Data menu.) This box shows the address of the name1[] array, the addresses stored in the array, and the strings to which those addresses point.

10. Use the down-arrow key on your keyboard to scroll through the pointers in the Inspecting box. As you can see, for some reason the program combined the strings MARIA and ALICE, leaving the last pointer in the array null.

Have you discovered the problem yet? Examine Listing 7.2 closely, where the name1[] array is defined. Still don't see the problem? Notice that a comma is missing after the string "MARIA". Borland C++ is combining the strings MARIA and ALICE because a comma does not separate them. Insert a comma after "MARIA", and the program should work fine.

Fig. 7.7. Inspecting *name1[]*.

Changing a Variable's Value

Not only can you view any of the variables in your program, you can
also change their values. For example, consider Listing 7.3. This program calculates the profit on an item, based on the number of items
sold, the cost of the item, and the selling price of the item.

Listing 7.3. DEBUG3.CPP—A Profit-Calculating Program

```
////////////////////////////////////////////////////////////
// DEBUG3.CPP: CONTAINS BUGS!
////////////////////////////////////////////////////////////

#include <iostream.h>
#include <conio.h>

////////////////////////////////////////////////////////////
// main()
////////////////////////////////////////////////////////////
int main(void)
{
    int unitsSold, costPerUnit, sellingPrice;
    int totalCost, grossSales, profit;

    cout << "Enter number of units sold: ";
    cin >> unitsSold;
    cout << "Enter cost per unit: ";
    cin >> costPerUnit;
```

continues

Listing 7.3. Continued

```
cout << "Enter selling price of unit: ";
cin >> sellingPrice;
totalCost = sellingPrice * unitsSold;
grossSales = sellingPrice * unitsSold;
profit = grossSales - totalCost;
cout << "Your profit: " << profit << endl;
getch();

return 1;
}
```

Suppose that as you wrote this program, you accidentally used the wrong variable in one of the formulas. The seventh line of code should read

```
totalCost = costPerUnit * unitsSold
```

rather than

```
totalCost = sellingPrice * unitsSold
```

Now, as you use Turbo Debugger to trace through the program, you're just about to execute the line that calculates the value of profit when you notice the mistake in the seventh line. Because totalCost contains an invalid value, the formula for profit will not yield a correct result. What do you do? You could exit the debugger, fix the problem, recompile the program, and then rerun the debugger. Or, you could take the easy way out and change the value of totalCost so that the formulas that use it later in the program work correctly.

To make this modification to totalCost, follow these steps:

1. Place the blinking text cursor on totalCost, and choose Evaluate/Modify from the Data menu. You then see the Evaluate/Modify dialog box, as shown in figure 7.8. The variable that you selected with the text cursor should be highlighted in the Exp   ression box.

2. Choose the Eval button to select the variable and to display its current value in the Result box.

3. Click on the New value box, type the new value for the variable, and press Enter.

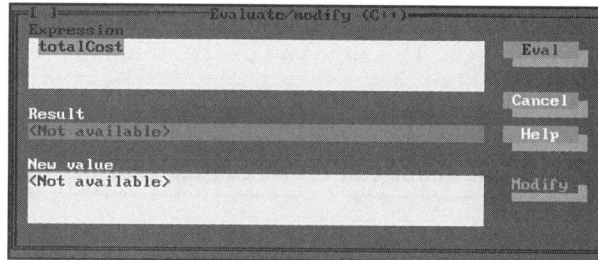

Fig. 7.8. The Evaluate/Modify dialog box.

Now you can continue with your debugging session as if nothing were wrong. Just remember to fix your source code when you return to the compiler.

Using Conditional Breakpoints

Computer programs are fast. Before you can blink an eye, they can complete millions of instructions. This speed is wonderful for the program's user, but it can be a nightmare for a programmer trying to find a bug in a piece of code that performs thousands of operations.

One solution to this sort of problem is Turbo Debugger's conditional breakpoint commands. These commands monitor your computer's memory, watching for given changes or conditions to occur.

The Changed Memory Global command watches an address in memory and halts the program when that area of memory is changed. This is a great debugging command to use when your program is changing the value of a variable "behind your back;" that is, when some error in your program—like a bad pointer or an invalid array index—is writing to memory where it shouldn't.

The Expression True Global command causes Turbo Debugger to watch for a given expression to become true. This command can also help you isolate places in your program where memory is being assigned invalid values. The Expression True Global command also enables you to halt loops at certain points and to halt the program after it calls a function a particular number of times.

Listing 7.4 is yet another buggy program that you can explore with Turbo Debugger. This time you use conditional breakpoints to solve the problem.

Listing 7.4. DEBUG4.CPP—A Program That Displays Customer Data

```cpp
/////////////////////////////////////////////////////////
// DEBUG4.CPP: CONTAINS BUGS!
/////////////////////////////////////////////////////////

#include <string.h>
#include <iostream.h>
#include <conio.h>
#include <stdio.h>
#include <stdlib.h>

// End-of-line character.
const EOL = 10;

// Structure type for a customer record.
struct Customer
{
   char firstName[10];
   char lastName[10];
   int custNumber;
};

// Function prototype.
void ReadString(char *s, FILE *f);

/////////////////////////////////////////////////////////
// main()
/////////////////////////////////////////////////////////
int main(void)
{
   Customer customer;
   FILE *file;
   int recCount, x;
   char s[3];

   if ((file = fopen("CUSTOMER.DAT", "rt")) != NULL)
   {
      ReadString(s, file);
      recCount = atoi(s);
      for (x=0; x<recCount; ++x)
      {
         ReadString(s, file);
         customer.custNumber = atoi(s);
         ReadString(customer.firstName, file);
         ReadString(customer.lastName, file);
         cout << "FIRST NAME: ";
         cout << customer.firstName << endl;
```

```
        cout << "LAST NAME: ";
        cout << customer.lastName << endl;
        cout << "CUSTOMER #: ";
        cout << customer.custNumber << endl << endl;
      }
    }
    else
      cout << "Couldn't open file" << endl;

    getch();

    return 1;
}


/////////////////////////////////////////////////////////////
// ReadString()
/////////////////////////////////////////////////////////////
void ReadString(char *s, FILE *f)
{
    int i = 0;
    char ch = 0;
    while ((ch = getc(f)) != EOL)
      s[i++] = ch;
    s[i] = 0;
}
```

When you run this program, it reads a customer data file (which is included on your companion disk) and displays the data that it finds there. The output looks like this:

```
FIRST NAME: Phil
LAST NAME: Martinson
CUSTOMER #: 12

FIRST NAME: Thomas
LAST NAME: Wendell
CUSTOMER #: 45

FIRST NAME: Sandy
LAST NAME: Albertanson
CUSTOMER #: 110

FIRST NAME: Alfred
LAST NAME: Thompson
CUSTOMER #: 36

FIRST NAME: Gregory
LAST NAME: Adams
CUSTOMER #: 29

FIRST NAME: Andrea
LAST NAME: Levitzabutsky
CUSTOMER #: 27507
```

The customer numbers are not supposed to be larger than 99, so there's obviously a problem somewhere in the program. Sandy Albertanson has a customer number of 110, and Andrea Levitzabutsky has a customer number of 27507. The problem is not in the data file; you won't find a 110 or a 27507 anywhere in it.

Assume now that you're a programmer for a big company that maintains a customer file that is continually changing. Because the customer file is changing frequently, you cannot be sure that the bug that you discovered when processing the current customer file will happen at the same place again. You need to catch the bug the instant it happens. Thanks to Turbo Debugger, this is no problem.

To use conditional breakpoints to debug the program in Listing 7.4, compile the program and then follow these steps:

1. Choose Turbo Debugger from Borland's Tool menu. Turbo Debugger loads and then displays the source code for DEBUG4.CPP.

2. Press F7, which is the hotkey for the Trace Into command, to start tracing the program.

3. Choose Expression True Global from the Breakpoints menu. The Enter Expression for Conditional Breakpoint box then appears. Type **customer.custNumber > 99**, as shown in figure 7.9, and press Enter.

4. Choose Evaluate/Modify from the Data menu. Then change the value of `customer.custNumber` to 0. (If you don't make this change, the conditional breakpoint will probably trigger immediately, because `customer.custNumber` is not initialized and probably contains a garbage value greater than 99.)

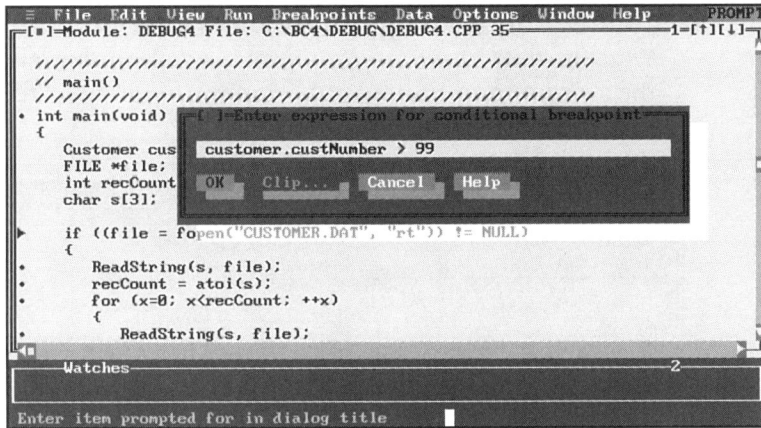

Fig. 7.9. Setting a conditional breakpoint.

5. Choose <u>R</u>un from the <u>R</u>un menu, or press F9. The program runs (much more slowly than usual) and halts when `customer.custNumber` becomes greater than 99. You then see the dialog box shown in figure 7.10.

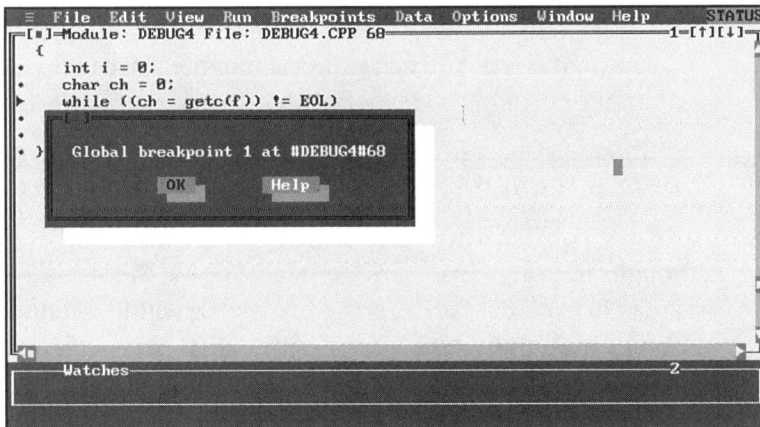

Fig. 7.10. A conditional breakpoint halts the program.

6. Click the Watches window, type **s**, and press Enter. In the Watches window, Turbo Debugger displays the current value of `s`, the string that was being read when the program halted, as shown in figure 7.11.

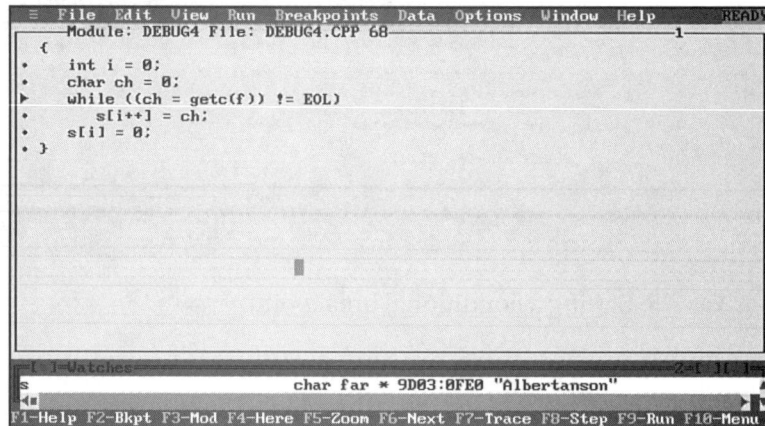

```
≡ File  Edit  View  Run  Breakpoints  Data  Options  Window  Help        READY
┌─Module: DEBUG4 File: DEBUG4.CPP 68──────────────────────────────────1─┐
│   {                                                                    │
│ •    int i = 0;                                                        │
│ •    char ch = 0;                                                      │
│ ▶    while ((ch = getc(f)) != EOL)                                     │
│ •        s[i++] = ch;                                                  │
│ •    s[i] = 0;                                                         │
│ • }                                                                    │
│                                                                        │
│                                                                        │
│                                                                        │
│                              █                                         │
│                                                                        │
│                                                                        │
│                                                                        │
│                                                                        │
│                                                                        │
│─[ ]─Watches═══════════════════════════════════════════════2═[ ][ ]═══│
│ s                         char far * 9D03:0FE0 "Albertanson"          ▲│
│◄█                                                                  ►▼│
└─F1-Help F2-Bkpt F3-Mod F4-Here F5-Zoom F6-Next F7-Trace F8-Step F9-Run F10-Menu┘
```

Fig. 7.11. Examining s in the Watches window.

7. Press F7 three times to trace out of the `ReadString()` function and return to `main()`. You can now see that the last call to `ReadString()` got the customer's last name and stored it in `customer.lastName`.

8. Choose **I**nspect from the **D**ata menu, type **customer**, and press Enter. The Inspecting box then appears, showing the current contents of the `customer` structure, as shown in figure 7.12.

Although checking `s` in `ReadString()` showed that the string `"Albertanson"` was read in from the file okay, the Inspecting window shows that `customer.lastName` is set to `"Albertanso"`. The final "n" is missing. If you remember your ASCII, the value 110 that has appeared seemingly by magic in the `customer.custNumber` element is actually the ASCII value of "n." Obviously, the `customer.lastName` character array is not large enough to hold all the last names in the database. If you change the sizes of the character arrays to 20, as follows, the program should run fine:

```
struct Customer
{
    char firstName[20];
    char lastName[20];
    int custNumber;
};
```

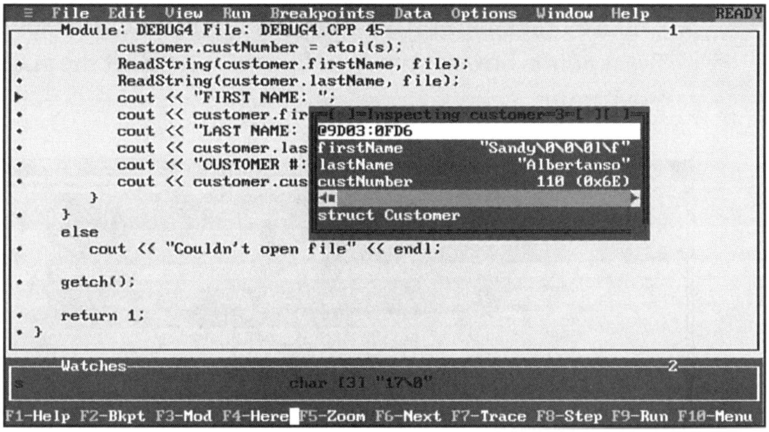

```
≡  File  Edit  View  Run  Breakpoints  Data  Options  Window  Help        READY
┌──Module: DEBUG4 File: DEBUG4.CPP 45───────────────────────────────1─┐
│ •      customer.custNumber = atoi(s);                                │
│ •      ReadString(customer.firstName, file);                         │
│ •      ReadString(customer.lastName, file);                          │
│ ▶      cout << "FIRST NAME: ";                                       │
│ •      cout << customer.fir ┌─[•]=Inspecting customer=3=[ ][ ]─┐     │
│ •      cout << "LAST NAME:  │ 09D03:0FD6                       │     │
│ •      cout << customer.las │ firstName          "Sandy\0\0\01\f" │  │
│ •      cout << "CUSTOMER #: │ lastName            "Albertanso"  │    │
│ •      cout << customer.cus │ custNumber          110 (0x6E)    │    │
│ •    }                      │ ◄■                              ► │    │
│ •    else                   ├───────────────────────────────────┤   │
│ •        cout << "Couldn't open file" << endl;  struct Customer │    │
│ •                           └───────────────────────────────────┘   │
│ •    getch();                                                        │
│ •                                                                    │
│ •    return 1;                                                       │
│ •}                                                                   │
├──Watches──────────────────────────────────────────────────────2─┐   │
│ s                 char [3] "17\0"                                │   │
└──────────────────────────────────────────────────────────────────┘  │
F1-Help F2-Bkpt F3-Mod F4-Here F5-Zoom F6-Next F7-Trace F8-Step F9-Run F10-Menu
```

Fig. 7.12. Inspecting the customer structure.

Logging Breakpoints

When you use conditional breakpoints to debug a program, the program runs slower than a turtle in quicksand. This is because Turbo Debugger must continually check the conditions that you set. The more conditional breakpoints you set, the slower the program runs.

One way to overcome this speed problem is to use a log file to record the results of expressions, instead of having Turbo Debugger constantly check the expressions. To use this method to debug DEBUG4.CPP (refer to Listing 7.4), follow these steps:

1. Reset the program by choosing Program Reset from the Run menu, and then clear all the breakpoints by choosing Delete All from the Breakpoints menu.

2. Set breakpoints on the following lines:

   ```
   ReadString(customer.firstName, file)

   cout << "FIRST NAME: "
   ```

To do so, either click the dot to the left of the line, or place the blinking text cursor on the line and press F2. The first line immediately follows the line in which `customer.custNumber` gets its original value; the second line is at the point where the program completely fills the `customer` structure with the current customer's data.

3. Choose Breakpoints from the View menu. You then see the Breakpoints box, as shown in figure 7.13. Select the #DEBUG4#43 breakpoint.

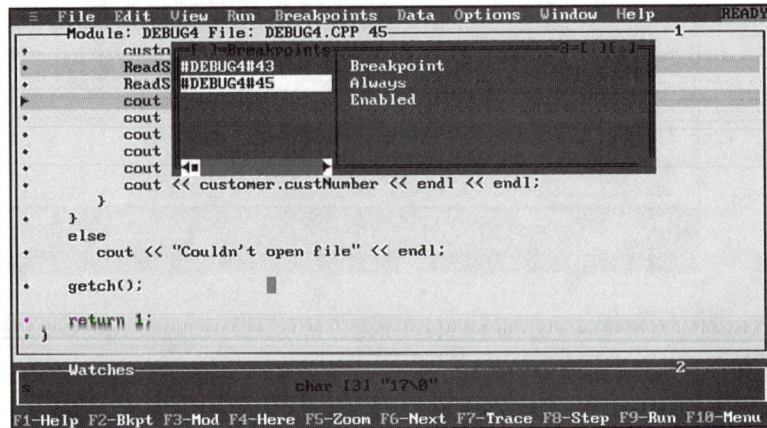

Fig. 7.13. The Breakpoints box.

4. Press Ctrl-S to display the Breakpoint Options box, and then choose the Change button, which displays the Conditions and Actions box (see fig. 7.14).

5. Click Log in the Action options box to toggle that option on. Then type **customer.custNumber** in the Action Expression box, and press Enter twice to return to the Breakpoints box.

6. Select the #DEBUG4#45 breakpoint, and set it to log `customer.custNumber` just as you did with #DEBUG4#43, and then press Enter three times to return to the main screen.

7. Run the program by pressing F9.

8. When the program finishes, choose Log from the View menu. You then see the Log box, as shown in figure 7.15.

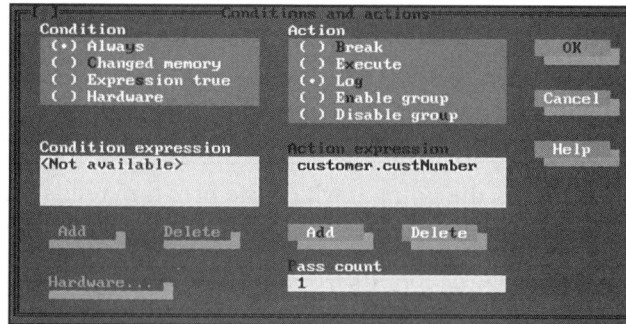

Fig. 7.14. The Conditions and Actions box.

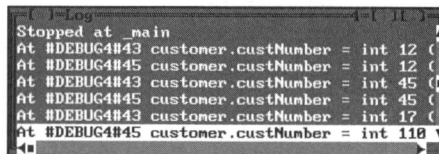

Fig. 7.15. The Log box.

Now you can examine the values in the Log box. Notice that, although `customer.custNumber` always starts with the right value, after the program reads data into the other elements of `customer`, `customer.custNumber` changes. This almost certainly indicates that `customer.custNumber` is getting overwritten when the program reads other data elements into the structure.

Using Pass Counts with Breakpoints

When you run the program in Listing 7.4, you can see that the third and sixth records are causing problems. Instead of stepping through the program to that point, you can set a breakpoint and then tell Turbo Debugger to halt the program only after passing the breakpoint a given number of times, called a *pass count*. This technique is particularly valuable when things go wrong in a long loop, because it enables you to halt the loop exactly where you want without having to set slow conditional breakpoints.

For example, you can use this method to debug DEBUG4.CPP. After you delete all breakpoints and reset the program, follow these steps:

1. Set a breakpoint on the line

```
cout << "FIRST NAME: "
```

   which is the point at which the program reads the current customer's entire record into the `customer` structure.

2. Choose Breakpoints from the View menu, press Ctrl-S to display the Breakpoint Options dialog box, and then choose the Change button to display the Conditions and Actions dialog box.

3. Choose the Pass Count box and type **3.** Then press Enter three times to return to the main screen.

4. Run the program by pressing F9. The program halts on the third pass through the loop, right before it displays the third customer record.

Now that you have halted the program at the problem point, you can inspect the data. You then discover, of course, that the `customer.lastName[]` character array is overwriting `customer.custNumber`.

Debugging Windows Programs

Windows programs present new challenges to bug-hunting programmers. Not only are Windows programs typically more complex than their DOS counterparts, but they also must deal with hundreds of messages passed to and from the application. Often, traditional debugging methods fail under Windows because the root of the problem may appear only when certain messages are processed or under conditions over which your program has little control.

When you use the ObjectWindows Library (OWL) to write your Windows applications, you add even more complexity to an already meaty stew. First, because you derive most of your classes from OWL classes, which themselves derive (sometimes multiply) from other OWL classes, your class hierarchies can become massive, comprising not

only the data members and member functions that you wrote, but also all the functions inherited from the base classes. Second, to trace into an OWL program, you have to know how to do a few tricks with Turbo Debugger for Windows. This is because you can't ordinarily trace into OWL.

A Simple ObjectWindows Program with Bugs

To examine some of these problems and see how to get around them, take a look at Listings 7.5 through 7.7, which make up a simple ObjectWindows application. When this application is working properly, it enables you to make simple line drawings in various colors and line thicknesses.

Listing 7.5. PAINT.CPP—A Simple Drawing Program

```
//////////////////////////////////////////////////////////
// PAINT.CPP: A simple OWL application. THIS LISTING
//            CONTAINS BUGS!
//////////////////////////////////////////////////////////

#include <owl\owlpch.h>
#include <owl\applicat.h>
#include <owl\decframe.h>
#include <owl\toolbox.h>
#include <owl\buttonga.h>
#include "paint.rc"

// The application class.
class TApp : public TApplication
{
public:
    TApp(): TApplication() {}
    void InitMainWindow();
};

// The frame window class.
class TWndw : public TDecoratedFrame
{
protected:
    TToolBox *toolBox;

public:
    TWndw(TWindow *parent, const char far *title,
```

continues

Listing 7.5. Continued

```cpp
          TWindow *client);

protected:
    void CmLine(WPARAM Id);
    void CmColor(WPARAM Id);

    DECLARE_RESPONSE_TABLE(TWndw);
};

DEFINE_RESPONSE_TABLE1(TWndw, TDecoratedFrame)
    EV_COMMAND_AND_ID(CM_LINE1, CmLine),
    EV_COMMAND_AND_ID(CM_LINE2, CmLine),
    EV_COMMAND_AND_ID(CM_LINE3, CmLine),
    EV_COMMAND_AND_ID(CM_LINE4, CmLine),
    EV_COMMAND_AND_ID(CM_BLACK, CmColor),
    EV_COMMAND_AND_ID(CM_BLUE, CmColor),
    EV_COMMAND_AND_ID(CM_RED, CmColor),
    EV_COMMAND_AND_ID(CM_GREEN, CmColor),
    EV_COMMAND_AND_ID(CM_YELLOW, CmColor),
    EV_COMMAND_AND_ID(CM_PURPLE, CmColor),
END_RESPONSE_TABLE;

// The client window class.
class TCWndw : public TWindow
{
protected:
    int lineWidth, lineColor;
    BOOL button;
    TPen *pen;
    TClientDC *lineDC;

public:
    TCWndw(TWindow *parent, const char far *title);

protected:
    void EvLButtonDown(UINT, TPoint &point);
    void EvLButtonUp(UINT, TPoint &point);
    void EvMouseMove(UINT, TPoint &point);
    LRESULT PmChangeColor(WPARAM color, LPARAM);
    LRESULT PmChangeLine(WPARAM width, LPARAM);

    DECLARE_RESPONSE_TABLE(TCWndw);
};

DEFINE_RESPONSE_TABLE1(TCWndw, TWindow)
    EV_WM_LBUTTONUP,
    EV_WM_MOUSEMOVE,
    EV_MESSAGE(PM_CHANGECOLOR, PmChangeColor),
    EV_MESSAGE(PM_CHANGELINE, PmChangeLine),
END_RESPONSE_TABLE;

//**********************************************************
// The TWndw class's implementation.
//**********************************************************
```

```
///////////////////////////////////////////////////////
// TWndw::TWndw()
//
// This is the main window's constructor.
///////////////////////////////////////////////////////
TWndw::TWndw(TWindow *parent, const char far *title,
        TWindow *clientWnd) :
        TDecoratedFrame(parent, title, clientWnd)
{
    TButtonGadget *b;
    TSeparatorGadget *s;

    // Add the menu to the main window.
    AssignMenu(MENU_1);

    // Add gadgets to the toolbox.
    b = new TButtonGadget(BMP_LINE1, CM_LINE1,
        TButtonGadget::Exclusive,
        TRUE, TButtonGadget::Down);
    toolBox->Insert(*b);
    b = new TButtonGadget(BMP_LINE2, CM_LINE2,
        TButtonGadget::Exclusive,
        TRUE, TButtonGadget::Up);
    toolBox->Insert(*b);
    b = new TButtonGadget(BMP_LINE3, CM_LINE3,
        TButtonGadget::Exclusive,
        TRUE, TButtonGadget::Up);
    toolBox->Insert(*b);
    b = new TButtonGadget(BMP_LINE4, CM_LINE4,
        TButtonGadget::Exclusive,
        TRUE, TButtonGadget::Up);
    toolBox->Insert(*b);

    s = new TSeparatorGadget(10);
    toolBox->Insert(*s);
    s = new TSeparatorGadget(10);
    toolBox->Insert(*s);

    b = new TButtonGadget(BMP_BLACK, CM_BLACK,
        TButtonGadget::Exclusive,
        TRUE, TButtonGadget::Down);
    toolBox->Insert(*b);
    b = new TButtonGadget(BMP_BLUE, CM_BLUE,
        TButtonGadget::Exclusive,
        TRUE, TButtonGadget::Up);
    toolBox->Insert(*b);
    b = new TButtonGadget(BMP_RED, CM_RED,
        TButtonGadget::Exclusive,
        TRUE, TButtonGadget::Up);
    toolBox->Insert(*b);
    b = new TButtonGadget(BMP_GREEN, CM_GREEN,
        TButtonGadget::Exclusive,
        TRUE, TButtonGadget::Up);
    toolBox->Insert(*b);
    b = new TButtonGadget(BMP_YELLOW, CM_YELLOW,
```

continues

Listing 7.5. Continued

```
          TButtonGadget::Exclusive,
          TRUE, TButtonGadget::Up);
      toolBox->Insert(*b);
      b = new TButtonGadget(BMP_PURPLE, CM_PURPLE,
          TButtonGadget::Exclusive,
          TRUE, TButtonGadget::Up);
      toolBox->Insert(*b);

      // Add the toolbox to this window.
      Insert(*toolBox, TDecoratedFrame::Left);

      // Position and size this window.
      Attr.X = 50;
      Attr.Y = 50;
      Attr.W = GetSystemMetrics(SM_CXSCREEN) / 1.5;
      Attr.H = GetSystemMetrics(SM_CYSCREEN) / 1.5;
  }


  /////////////////////////////////////////////////////////////
  // TWndw::CmLine()
  //
  // This function responds to any of the toolbox's line
  // buttons by posting a message to the client window. The
  // message informs the client window that the pen's
  // thickness must be changed.
  /////////////////////////////////////////////////////////////
  void TWndw::CmLine(WPARAM Id)
  {
      PostMessage(PM_CHANGELINE, Id-100, 0);
  }


  /////////////////////////////////////////////////////////////
  // TWndw::CmColor()
  //
  // This function responds to any of the toolbox's color
  // buttons by posting a message to the client window. The
  // message informs the client window that the pen's color
  // must be changed.
  /////////////////////////////////////////////////////////////
  void TWndw::CmColor(WPARAM Id)
  {
      PostMessage(PM_CHANGECOLOR, Id-200, 0);
  }


  //***********************************************************
  // The TCWndw class's implementation.
  //***********************************************************


  /////////////////////////////////////////////////////////////
  // TCWndw::TCWndw()
  //
  // This is the client window's constructor.
  /////////////////////////////////////////////////////////////
  TCWndw::TCWndw(TWindow *parent, const char far *title):
        TWindow(parent, title)
```

```
{
    // Initialize variables.
    lineWidth = 1;
    lineColor = 0;
    button = FALSE;
    pen = NULL;
    lineDC = NULL;
}


/////////////////////////////////////////////////////////////
// TCWndw::EvLButtonDown()
//
// This function responds to WM_LBUTTONDOWN messages, which
// Windows sends to the application when the user clicks
// the left mouse button within the client window.
/////////////////////////////////////////////////////////////
void TCWndw::EvLButtonDown(UINT, TPoint &point)
{
    // If this is a new button press...
    if (!button)
    {
        // Get a device context and a custom pen.
        lineDC = new TClientDC(HWindow);
        pen = new TPen(lineColor, lineWidth, PS_SOLID);
        lineDC->SelectObject(*pen);

        // Direct all mouse input to the window.
        SetCapture();

        // Set the line's start to the mouse coordinates.
        lineDC->MoveTo(point);

        // Set the mouse-button flag.
        button = TRUE;
    }
}


/////////////////////////////////////////////////////////////
// TCWndw::EvLButtonUp()
//
// This function responds to WM_LBUTTONUP messages, which
// Windows sends to the application when the user releases
// the left mouse button.
/////////////////////////////////////////////////////////////
void TCWndw::EvLButtonUp(UINT, TPoint&)
{
    // Release device context.
    delete lineDC;
    lineDC = NULL;

    // Delete custom pen object.
    delete pen;

    // Turn off button flag.
    button = FALSE;
```

continues

Debugging Windows Programs **305**

Listing 7.5. Continued

```
      // Release mouse capture.
      ReleaseCapture();
}


/////////////////////////////////////////////////////////////
// TCWndw::EvLButtonUp()
//
// This function responds to WM_LBUTTONUP messages, which
// Windows sends to the application when the user releases
// the left mouse button.
/////////////////////////////////////////////////////////////
void TCWndw::EvMouseMove(UINT, TPoint &point)
{
   // If the left mouse button is pressed,
   // draw a line to the new point.
   if (button)
      lineDC->LineTo(point);
}


/////////////////////////////////////////////////////////////
// TCWndw::PmChangeColor()
//
// This function responds to the user-defined
// PM_CHANGECOLOR message by setting the new line color.
/////////////////////////////////////////////////////////////
LRESULT TCWndw::PmChangeColor(WPARAM color, LPARAM)
{
   lineColor = color;
   return 1;
}


/////////////////////////////////////////////////////////////
// TCWndw::PmChangeLine()
//
// This function responds to the user-defined PM_CHANGELINE
// message by setting the new line thickness.
/////////////////////////////////////////////////////////////
LRESULT TCWndw::PmChangeLine(WPARAM width, LPARAM)
{
   lineWidth = width;
   return 1;
}


//***********************************************************
// The TApp class's Implementation.
//***********************************************************


/////////////////////////////////////////////////////////////
// TApp::InitMainWindow()
//
// This function creates the application's main window.
/////////////////////////////////////////////////////////////
void TApp::InitMainWindow()
{
```

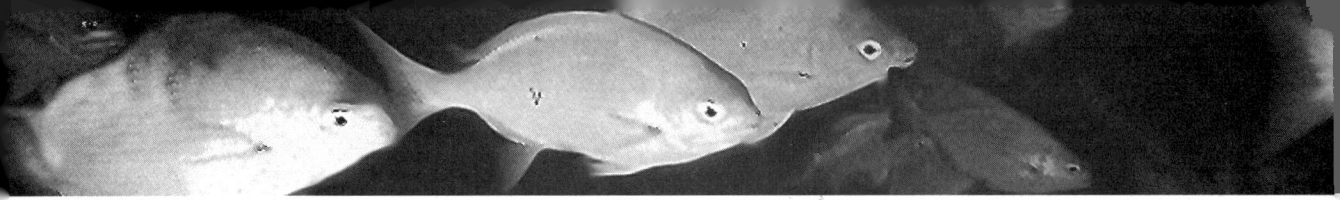

```
   // Construct the client window.
   TWindow *client = new TCWndw(0,0);

   // Construct the frame window.
   TDecoratedFrame *frame =
       new TWndw(0, "Mini Paint App", client);
}


//////////////////////////////////////////////////////
// OwlMain()
//////////////////////////////////////////////////////
int OwlMain(int, char*[])
{
   return TApp().Run();
}
```

Listing 7.6. PAINT.RC—The Resource File for PAINT.CPP

```
//////////////////////////////////////////////////////
// PAINT.RC
//////////////////////////////////////////////////////

#ifndef WORKSHOP_INVOKED
#include "windows.h"
#endif

#define MENU_1      100
#define CM_EXIT     24310
#define BMP_LINE1   1
#define BMP_LINE2   2
#define BMP_LINE3   3
#define BMP_LINE4   4
#define BMP_BLACK   5
#define BMP_BLUE    6
#define BMP_RED     7
#define BMP_GREEN   8
#define BMP_YELLOW  9
#define BMP_PURPLE  10
#define CM_LINE1    101
#define CM_LINE2    102
#define CM_LINE3    103
#define CM_LINE4    105
#define CM_BLACK    200
#define CM_BLUE     204
#define CM_RED      201
#define CM_GREEN    202
#define CM_YELLOW   203
#define CM_PURPLE   205
#define PM_CHANGECOLOR WM_USER
#define PM_CHANGELINE  WM_USER + 1

#ifdef RC_INVOKED
```

continues

Debugging Windows Programs   **307**

Listing 7.6. Continued

```
MENU_1 MENU
{
 POPUP "&File"
 {
   MENUITEM "E&xit", CM_EXIT
 }

}

BMP_LINE1 BITMAP "line1.bmp"
BMP_LINE2 BITMAP "line2.bmp"
BMP_LINE3 BITMAP "line3.bmp"
BMP_LINE4 BITMAP "line4.bmp"
BMP_BLACK BITMAP "black.bmp"
BMP BLUE BITMAP "blue.bmp"
BMP_RED BITMAP "red.bmp"
BMP_GREEN BITMAP "green.bmp"
BMP_YELLOW BITMAP "yellow.bmp"
BMP_PURPLE BITMAP "purple.bmp"

#endif
```

Listing 7.7. PAINT.DEF—The Definition File for PAINT.CPP

```
NAME PAINT
DESCRIPTION 'Simple OWL paint program by Clayton Walnum'
EXETYPE WINDOWS
STUB 'WINSTUB.EXE'
CODE PRELOAD MOVEABLE DISCARDABLE
DATA PRELOAD MOVEABLE MULTIPLE
HEAPSIZE 1024
STACKSIZE 8192
```

Fixing a General Protection Exception

When you run this program, it immediately halts with a General Protection Exception. After you close the dialog box that reports the exception, Borland C++ highlights the line that caused the error, as shown in figure 7.16.

```
                    c:\bc4\debug\paint.cpp
    // Add the menu to the main window.
    AssignMenu(MENU_1);

    // Add gadgets to the toolbox.
    b = new TButtonGadget(BMP_LINE1, CM_LINE1,
        TButtonGadget::Exclusive,
        TRUE, TButtonGadget::Down);
    toolBox->Insert(*b);
    b = new TButtonGadget(BMP_LINE2, CM_LINE2,
        TButtonGadget::Exclusive,
        TRUE, TButtonGadget::Up);
    toolBox->Insert(*b);
    b = new TButtonGadget(BMP_LINE3, CM_LINE3,
        TButtonGadget::Exclusive,
        TRUE, TButtonGadget::Up);
```

Fig. 7.16. The line that caused the General Protection Exception.

General Protection Exceptions are often caused by bad pointers, so the object pointer toolBox is immediately suspect. You need to discover where toolBox is getting initialized. To do this, follow these steps:

1. Place the text cursor on toolBox and choose Inspect from Borland C++'s Debug menu. The Inspect Expression dialog box then appears, showing toolBox in its text control.

2. Press Enter to inspect toolBox. The Inspect dialog box then appears. The toolBox object's data members are listed on the left, and the data members' values are listed on the right. The object's member functions are listed in the bottom pane of the window. All the data members, including the objects HWindow handle, are null, which indicates that this window object is not yet constructed.

3. Choose Terminate Program from the Debug menu. To learn more about toolBox, you need to use Turbo Debugger for Windows, so choose Turbo Debugger from the Tool menu. Turbo Debugger for Windows then loads, with the program's source code in its module window.

4. Set a breakpoint on the first code line of the TWndw constructor and run the program by pressing F9. Because toolBox is a data member of the TWndw class, you cannot access it until it is in scope. It first comes into scope in the constructor of the class.

5. Choose Changed Memory Global from the Breakpoints menu. The Enter Memory Address box then appears. Type **toolBox** and press Enter. Now, when the program tries to change `toolBox`, the program halts.

6. Press F9 to run the program. Turbo Debugger reports an Exception 13, which shows that `toolBox` is never assigned a value. If it had been assigned a value, the program would have halted before the exception, thanks to the breakpoint you set in step 5, which would have triggered if the program modified `toolBox`.

Because `toolBox` is never assigned a value, PAINT.CPP is probably not constructing a `TToolBox` object. If you examine the `TWndw` constructor, you'll see that this is true. To fix the problem, return to the compiler and add the following lines to the program, in the `TWndw` constructor and right before the comment `// Add gadgets to the tool box`:

```
// Create a new toolbox object.
toolBox = new TToolBox(this);
```

Finding and Fixing an OWL Exception

Now that you have fixed one bug, run the program again. This time the program generates an OWL exception. Because the program's main window never appears on the screen, you can be relatively sure that the bug that causes the exception happens early in the program's execution. (Also, the OWL Exception window gives you a hint by telling you that the program has an invalid main window.)

You may think that a simple F7 trace is in order. Go ahead and try it. You quickly discover one of the problems that occur when you try to debug an OWL program. You can't trace into OWL, so Turbo Debugger runs the single line found in `OwlMain()` (where program execution begins) just as though you had selected the Step Over command. Because this one line is the entire main program, you didn't get a chance to look at even one other line of code.

Before you can debug OWL and Windows programs, you have to understand how such programs work. For example, to track down the second bug in PAINT.CPP, you must set a breakpoint somewhere in the code so that you can single-step from that point. To set a useful breakpoint in an OWL program, you must know the order in which the program performs certain functions. The first function in Listing 7.5 that is called after `OwlMain()` is `TApp::InitMainWindow()`, because that is the function in which the program constructs its main and client windows. Obviously, the program isn't going to get very far if it hasn't first constructed at least its main window.

So, to find the second bug, follow these steps:

1. Place the text cursor on the first code line of `TApp::InitMainWindow()`.

2. Choose Go To Cursor from the Run menu or press F4 to run the program. The program halts at the line on which you placed the cursor.

3. Choose the Step Over command of the Run menu or press F8 to bypass the construction of the client window (the call to the `TCWndw` constructor). The program returns to `InitMainWindow()` without generating an error, which indicates that the client window was probably constructed correctly.

4. Choose Step Over or press F8 to execute the construction of the main window (the call to the `TWndw` constructor). The program again returns to `InitMainWindow()` with no errors.

5. Press F8 again. The program exits from `InitMainWindow()` and the OWL error appears.

Both the client and frame windows were presumably constructed without errors, so the program's problem probably doesn't lie in those constructors. As soon as the program exits from `InitMainWindow()`, though, you still get the OWL error, which indicates that `InitMainWindow()` might be the trouble. Do you see a problem? Although `InitMainWindow()` constructs its main window, it doesn't assign the window object's address to `TApp`'s `MainWindow` pointer.

To fix this bug, add the following lines to the end of `InitMainWindow()`:

```
// Set the main window to the frame window.
SetMainWindow(frame);
```

With the fix in place, run the program again. At last, the program's main window appears on the screen, as shown in figure 7.17.

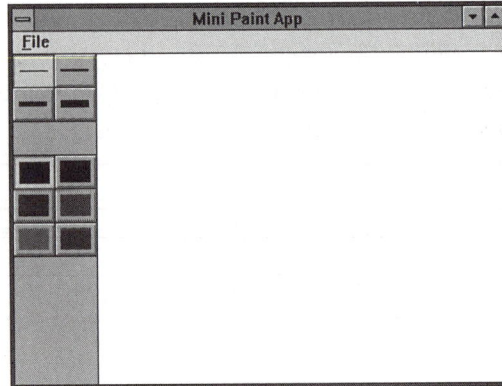

Fig. 7.17. The Paint application, running at last.

Fine-Tuning Mouse Messages

To use the program, you first select line widths and colors from the tool box on the left; then, to draw a line, you hold down the left mouse button in the window's client area. Unfortunately, when you try to draw, you discover that, although the program compiles without error, it still does not work properly. When you try to draw, no lines appear in the window's client area.

To be capable of drawing, the program must respond to mouse messages. After all, pressing the left mouse button initiates the drawing action, and releasing the left button terminates the drawing action. So, you must be sure that the program receives the mouse messages properly.

The mouse messages to which this program is designed to respond are `WM_LBUTTONDOWN`, `WM_MOUSEMOVE`, and `WM_LBUTTONUP`. To begin drawing, the user presses the left mouse button, so you should start looking for problems there:

1. Find the message-response function `TCWndw::EvLButtonDown()`. Then set a breakpoint on the first code line in that function by placing the text cursor on the line and pressing F5.

2. Run the program.

3. Try to draw a line in the main window's client area.

Nothing happens, because the breakpoint at the beginning of `EvLButtonDown()` did not stop the program. Therefore, you know that the window is not responding to `WM_LBUTTONDOWN` messages properly, because otherwise the program would halt when you press the left mouse button. When a program doesn't dispatch Windows messages to the proper functions, often there's a problem with the window class's response table. If you examine `TCWndw`'s response table closely, you'll see that it is missing the `EV_WM_LBUTTONDOWN` macro. Add this macro to the table, and then compile and run the program. You can now draw in the main window's client area.

Tracing User-Defined Messages

Now the program can draw a line, but you can't change to a new line width or color. To fix this toolbox bug, follow these steps:

1. Find the function `TWndw::CmLine()`, which is the function that responds to the toolbox's line buttons. Set a breakpoint on this function's single code line.

2. Run the program.

3. When the program's main window appears, click on one of the line buttons. The program halts on the breakpoint that you set, which means that the function responds properly to the line button.

4. Turn off the breakpoint in `CmLine()`.

5. Find the function `TCWndw::PmChangeLine()`, which is the function that responds to the user message `PM_CHANGELINE` that the function `CmLine()` sends. Set a breakpoint on the first code line in the function.

6. Run the program, and click on one of the line buttons. The breakpoint does not stop the program, which means that the PM_CHANGELINE message is not reaching the PmChangeLine() function.

You've found more message-passing problems, this time with a private, user-defined message rather than a regular Windows message. The first place to look for the problem is, of course, TCWndw's response table, in which you find this line:

```
EV_MESSAGE(PM_CHANGELINE, PmChangeLine),
```

No problems here. The response-table entry for the PM_CHANGELINE message is correct. So, it's back to TWndw::CmLine(), where you discover a mistake in the function's single line:

```
PostMessage(PM_CHANGELINE, Id-100, 0);
```

If you've been using OWL for more than an hour or two, you know that OWL features its own versions of Windows API calls. The preceding call to PostMessage() is one of these OWL look-alikes. The Windows API version of PostMessage() requires as an argument the handle of the window to which you want to post the message. The OWL version always uses the current window object's handle. Therefore, a window class that sends a message with the OWL version of PostMessage() always sends a message to itself. But you want to send the PM_CHANGELINE message to the client window, not the main window. The call to PostMessage() should look like this:

```
ClientWnd->PostMessage(PM_CHANGELINE, Id-100, 0);
```

This line calls ClientWnd's PostMessage() function rather than the main window's, which is exactly what the program is supposed to do. After you fix this mistake in CmLine() and CmColor() (you simply add ClientWnd-> to each PostMessage() call), the program should run perfectly, enabling you to draw different lines of different colors, as shown in figure 7.18.

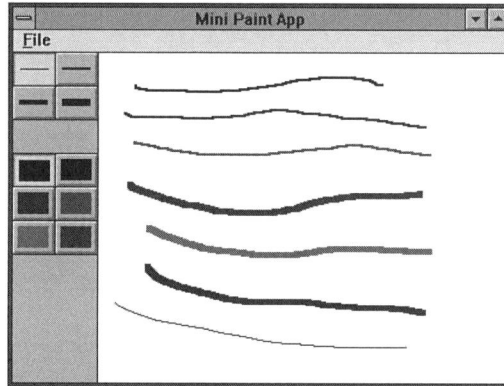

Fig. 7.18. The debugged Paint application.

Using WinSight

Hundreds of different messages pass to and from a running Windows program. Keeping track of all this message traffic is enough to give even the most seasoned Windows guru terrible headaches. For this reason, Borland C++ includes a handy tool called WinSight (see fig. 7.19) that can make tracing Windows messages if not easy, at least easier.

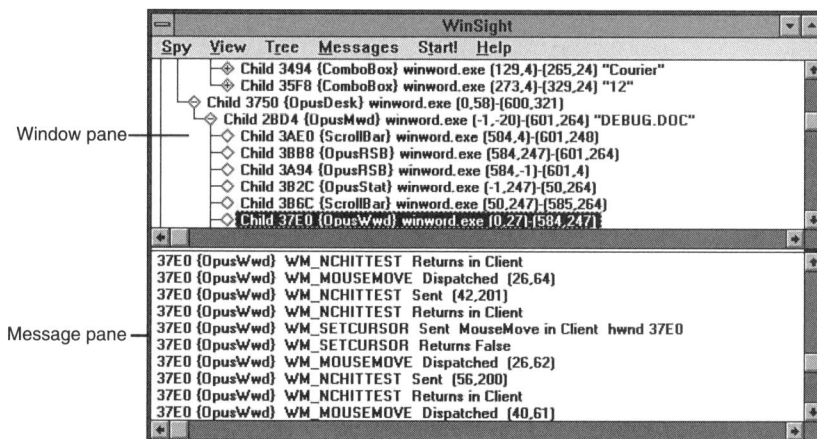

Fig. 7.19. WinSight in action.

When you run WinSight, it installs itself right in the middle of Windows' message highway and reports on everything that it finds there. You can tell WinSight exactly which windows to report on and which messages to trace. Then you can actually watch the message traffic as it happens, and even log the results to a disk file for later examination.

WinSight's window pane displays a list of all currently open windows, giving each window's handle, class, module, position, and title. Choosing a window to trace is simply a matter of selecting the window from the list. Or, to have WinSight find the window for you, you can select the Find Window command in the Spy menu. When the Find Window command is active, you need only place the mouse pointer over the window that you want to trace; WinSight then outlines the window on-screen and highlights it in the list.

After selecting a window to trace, you can choose the types of messages that you want to watch for, as shown in figure 7.20 (select the Options command from the Messages menu), and then set the message-tracing into action. WinSight then gathers all the messages being sent to and from the selected window so that you can view them both during and after a trace. Using WinSight, you can see exactly what's happening to the messages that your application is supposed to handle.

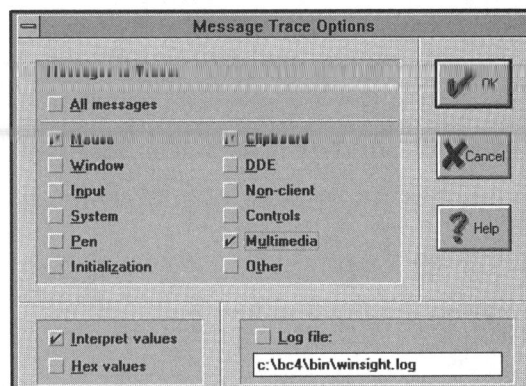

Fig. 7.20. Choosing message types.

Using Third-Party Debugging Tools

If you want to get really serious about program debugging, you can look into purchasing additional tools from third-party software developers. Such tools are often expensive, but they can make debugging a more pleasant task. One of the best Windows debugging tools is The Periscope Company's WinScope (see fig. 7.21).

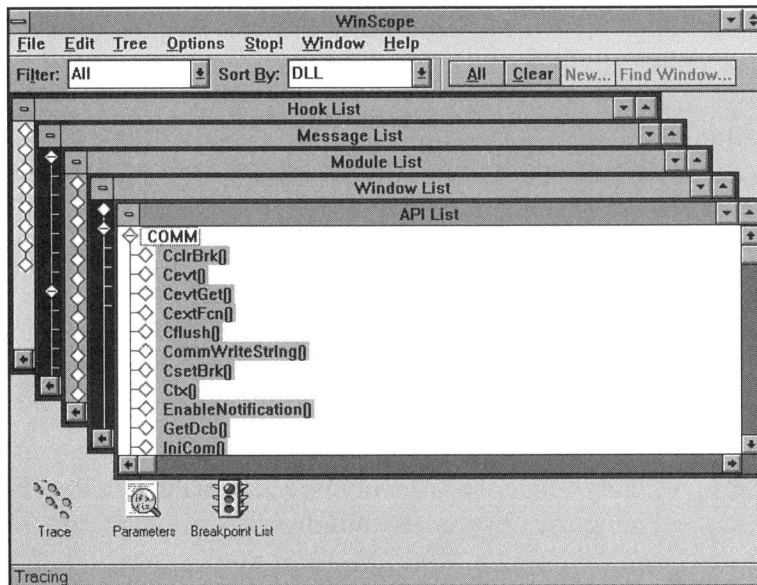

Fig. 7.21. WinScope's main window.

WinScope is essentially an advanced version of WinSight, capable of providing you with more options and supplying far more information about an application than WinSight. Not only can you display a list of active windows and trace messages sent to those windows, but you can also see exactly which Windows API calls a program makes. This capability makes WinScope more than just a debugging tool; it can actually help you write more powerful and professional programs, by tracing other programs to see how they do what they do.

Several other third-party debugging products that you can use with Borland C++ are also available, including Bounds-Checker for Windows (Nu-Mega Technologies, $250) and SafeWin (SeaBreeze Software Systems, $250). WinScope costs $150.

From Here...

In addition to the material covered in this chapter, there are several other places you can turn to for help in debugging your C programs:

➤ For those times when the built-in debugger just doesn't seem powerful enough, you can turn to add-on debuggers. See Chapter 8, "Third-Party Debugger Alternatives."

➤ If you're program contains code from other languages, this can make debugging more difficult. For information on assembler code, see Chapter 14, "Bare Metal Programming." For information on other languages, see Chapter 13, "Mixed Language Programming."

➤ Writing C programs that interface with databases can be an entirely different beast. For more information on database programming, see Chapter 15, "Interfacing with Database Languages."

➤ You can save yourself debugging time in many ways. See Chapter 6, "Writing Bug-Free Code," for information on avoiding common bugs. See Chapter 18, "Exception Handling," for help on building routines to "catch" exceptions that otherwise might lead to bugs. For information on writing efficient code in C or C++, see Chapter 4, "Optimizing C," or Chapter 5, "Optimizing C++."

Third-Party Debugging Tools

by Mark Davidson

You're all prepared. You've got *Killer Borland C++ 4* on your desk.
You've installed all 78 megabytes of Borland C++ 4.0 on your hard
drive. You've got a hot new IDE, a powerful class library, a built-in
debugger, and more. You're ready to write the next "killer app." You
can handle any programming and debugging problems that pop up.
You don't need anything else.

Or do you? While each new release of all the major compiler vendors'
development systems grows in size by leaps and bounds each year,
they can't provide you with every single tool you could possibly need.
Even if they do provide you with all the tools you need, it's a sure bet
that someone out there has a better version of a tool.

The development tools business is a funny business. It wasn't that long
ago that buying a C compiler got you pretty much that. Remember
Lattice C? For a while it was the de facto C compiler for the PC. In fact,

it was so standard that mighty Microsoft even licensed it and sold it under its own label. If memory serves, Lattice C came with a multi-pass compiler, a librarian, a linker, and a runtime library. No profiler. No class libraries. No support for Windows (this was back before Windows was a real product). No debugger. Even with as little as that, Lattice was the compiler to beat.

As the years went by (and the C compiler market got more competitive), vendors started adding more tools to their offerings to try and entice developers over to their product. When Borland released Turbo C, it bowled people over. Pretty soon all the vendors had to match what Borland offered. Many vendors disappeared. When a company offered some unique feature that made programmers more productive, they usually jumped on it. And, more often than not, it was Borland that offered the hottest new features.

Why Even Think about Other Tools?

Today, compilers seem to come with everything but the kitchen sink. With all the tools they provide, there still is a large market for add-ons. Companies offer all sorts of libraries to let you access databases, work with custom controls, plot graphs; in short, just about anything you can think of. The same is true of debugging tools.

While Turbo Debugger (TD) has evolved into a powerful, flexible debugging tool, there are several situations where Turbo Debugger can be of no help at all. In fact, it can get in the way. For example, let's say you're working on some code that lets you use the mouse to drag bitmaps around the screen. Your program is processing WM_LBUTTONDOWN to click a bitmap, WM_MOUSEMOVE to drag the bitmap around, and WM_LBUTTONUP to drop the bitmap. However, when you drag the bitmap around, you leave junk on the screen where you're not painting correctly. What do you do?

It becomes obvious that TD just isn't going to cut it. Having a break point fire every time you move the mouse makes it very difficult to track what is happening since you're always dropping into the debugger.

Or, let's say that you're finished with your program and you're testing it. Everything seems to run fine, but you notice that your Free System Resources drops by a few percentage points every time you exit your program. Obviously, you're not deleting something you created. How do you find out where it is? If you're lucky, you've got the debugging version of Windows, which can tell you that you haven't deleted, say, several bitmaps. Now that you know *what* you didn't delete, how do you find out exactly *what bitmap* you didn't delete? After all, the debugging kernel only tells you that you didn't delete something; it doesn't tell you how to find the object you forgot to delete.

What if you're getting really adventuresome and are working on a TSR that talks to a Windows program? How do you debug that?

Hopefully, this chapter will give you some guidelines on tools that help you solve thorny debugging problems. We'll look at four tools that help you find problems either before or after you compile your code. That's right, not all the tools are designed to replace Turbo Debugger. In fact, none of them are. Instead, they are additions to tools like Turbo Debugger.

The first tool, PC-Lint from Gimpel Software, is a source code checker. It looks at code just like the compiler does, but it goes over it with a fine-toothed comb to find all sorts of potential problems in your code. It's designed to look for those "gotchas" that you don't think about.

The second tool, Bounds Checker for Windows from nu-Mega, is (for want of a better term) a "parameter checker." Bounds Checker runs your program for you while thoroughly checking parameters you pass to Windows, looking for invalid pointer values, memory leaks, and much more. However, "parameter checker" is something of a misnomer since Bounds Checker does a lot more than look for stray pointers.

Soft-Ice for Windows, also from nu-Mega, is a low-level debugger that can debug even the lowest-level Windows code. It can debug *any* program under Windows, including the Windows startup code. Since it actually runs before Windows, it is always available. It also understands much of Windows itself, so it can be used to get a look at the internals of Windows.

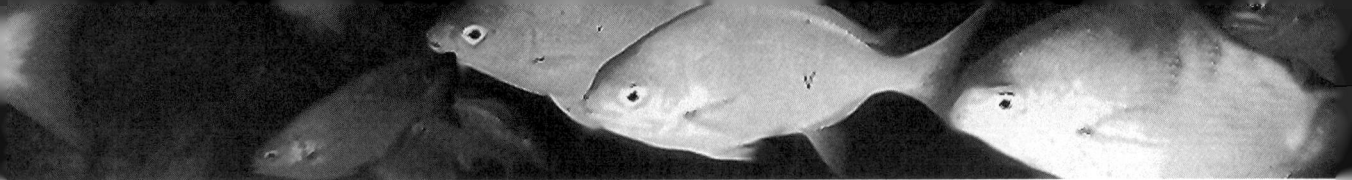

WinScope, from The Periscope Company, is a "message debugger" that allows you to watch Windows from a "high-level" viewpoint. Much like Spy (which is included with the Windows SDK) or WinSight (included with Borland C++), it lets you look at the messages that Windows is sending around the system.

The purpose of this chapter is to tell you about these tools and why you might want to consider adding one (or all) of them to your programming toolbox. Each tool serves a specific purpose for the Windows developer. Now, keep in mind that this a not a review. While installation and usage of each product will be covered, in the end it is up to you to decide if a tool is right for you. I'll just try to show you why each of these tools is considered top-notch.

PC-Lint

It's one thing to have your code compile without warnings or errors. But even code that compiles cleanly may or may not be correct. Both C and C++ contain many syntactical "gotchas" that can be perfectly legal code, but cause frustrating side effects. In these cases, the compiler isn't going to help you, and while TD can let you see what's going on, it doesn't always help you find out why.

What Exactly Is Lint?

Gimpel's PC-Lint for C/C++ is unique among the tools covered in this chapter in that it doesn't work with your program while your code is executing. In fact, PC-Lint doesn't even care about object code. Instead it works with your source code directly in order to point out potential problems.

So what exactly is PC-Lint? Perhaps a bit of history is in order here. The original C compilers developed by Brian Kernighan and Dennis Ritchie ran under the UNIX operating system. If you've ever used UNIX for development, you know that the operating system ships with an enormous number of tools that not only aid in program development, but

also in writing documentation, maintaining the system, and a number of other tasks. One of the tools that helped programmers to develop C programs was a little utility called *lint*.

Lint was designed to catch "fluff" in your code. While the C compiler looked for obvious problems, like syntax errors, it didn't do much checking of your code. For example, if you had a function called `mumble()` that looked like this:

```
int mumble(long marg)
{
        .
        .
        [ code for mumble ]
        .
        .
        return (some_value);
}
```

you knew that `mumble` expected a variable of type `long` to be passed to it and that it would return an integer. However, one night you are coding away and (due to too much coffee and not enough sleep) you pass `mumble()` the wrong value:

```
long l;
int i;

l = mumble(i);
```

All of a sudden your program stops working. Obviously, today's compilers would catch this kind of problem since the call to `mumble()` wouldn't match the prototype you created for `mumble()` (you *do* usc prototypes, don't you?). However, back then there was no ANSI C standard and C++ was still a gleam in Bjarne Stroustrop's eye. C compilers wouldn't catch this kind of problem. Thus, you would be destined to spend a while in the debugger trying to find the problem.

It was for this reason that lint was created. Lint would take a look at all the modules in your program and search for all the little inconsistencies that the C compiler would accept quietly but that would cause all sorts of problems later on.

Most of the companies developing C compilers for the PC didn't bother with producing lint-like tools. Instead, most companies tended

to beef up their parsers to catch problems like the one mentioned above. With the ANSI standard for C, a lot of these problems were caught because the "looseness" in the original K&R C definition was tightened up.

However, there are a lot of cases where modern C and C++ compilers still can't catch every bugaboo in your code. One main reason for this is that the compiler only looks at one source file at a time. It still relies on you to create proper prototypes to help it catch problems. Modern compilers also don't check for "obvious" problems, such as loss of precision or mismatched #defines. If they do look for these kinds of problems (Borland C++ does), then they don't always do the best job of telling you exactly what the problem *is*. For example, Borland's parser is great at telling you that an assignment is going to cause a loss of precision, but it does a lousy job of telling you *why*.

Gimpel's PC-Lint is an implementation of the UNIX lint utility for MS-DOS. However, that's not exactly a fair comparision since PC-Lint does much more than the original UNIX lint. It also is available in a version that can check C++ code for problems that can send many C++ programmers up the wall.

Installing and Configuring PC-Lint

PC-Lint has one of the least intrusive install procedures ever created. It doesn't modify any .INI files, nor does it touch AUTOEXEC.BAT or CONFIG.SYS. Instead, it creates a subdirectory on your hard drive and places several batch files in that directory. It then looks at your PATH and places a batch file called LIN.BAT in a directory of your choice (that exists in your PATH). LIN.BAT is responsible for invoking PC-Lint from the directory into which you installed it.

The installation program also asks you several questions about your development environment. First, it gives you the option to turn off several messages PC-Lint issues when dealing with certain code constructs. These constructs are usually innocuous, but as you will see, PC-Lint will usually find a LOT of problems with your code, so this

gives you the option of turning off some of the common messages PC-Lint may produce. The second set of questions deals with what compiler and libraries you use. PC-Lint supports no less than 25 different C and C++ compilers, running the gamut from Borland C++ to cross compilers like the Franklin 8051 C cross compiler. PC-Lint also knows about several C and C++ libraries, including OWL (from Borland), zApp from Inmark, Zinc from Zinc Software and the Windows SDK libraries. If you use any of these libraries, PC-Lint can adjust its behavior to compensate for "problems" in these libraries.

The result of this installation is the creation of several batch files, a file called STD.LNT and a file called OPTIONS.LNT. The first batch file, LCOPY, copies the contents of the PC-Lint distribution disk to the directory into which you've told the installation program to install PC-Lint. This allows you to customize which files will be copied to your hard drive. By default, LCOPY will copy all of PC-Lint's configuration files to your hard drive. Obviously, you can go back later and get rid of any you won't need, but you do have the chance to modify LCOPY if you like.

The second batch file, LSET, is only copied if you've told PC-Lint you don't have environment variables like INCLUDE set up. If you use Borland's IDE, you probably don't have INCLUDE or LIB set up since your IDE project files tell the compiler where to look for #include files and libraries. While PC-Lint can hook into the Borland IDE as a Tool, it is normally run from the DOS command line. Thus, it needs to know where to look for #include files. Remember, PC-Lint is doing the same job as the C++ compiler's preprocessor and parser. It needs this information just like BCC.EXE does.

The last two files, OPTIONS.LNT and STD.LNT, are configuration files for PC-Lint. OPTIONS.LNT is created by the installation program and contains any options that were turned on (or off) in response to the "common message" questions. If your answers to the questions don't cause any options to be changed, then OPTIONS.LNT is created as an empty file, which you can later add to if you have any favorite configuration options you want to set. STD.LNT is PC-Lint's "standard" configuration file. It is referenced by LIN.BAT as the main configuration file to process.

STD.LNT and OPTIONS.LNT are useful mostly because PC-Lint has *so* many options you can specify. There are over 150 different command line options available, which makes specifying options on the command line nearly impossible. Since PC-Lint's .LNT files can be nested, the installation procedure takes advantage of this fact in order to set up PC-Lint the way you want. For example, let's say you installed PC-Lint and told it you were using Borland C++ 4.0, the Windows SDK, and Zinc Software's Zinc class library. You also told the installation program that you wanted to suppress warnings about "Boolean test of assignment," which will occur when you have code that looks like this:

```
if (a = b)
{
    .
    .
}
```

The installation program will create an OPTIONS.LNT file that looks like this:

```
// Please note -- this is a representative set of error suppression
//                 options.  Please adjust to suit your own policies
//                 See PC-lint for C/C++ manual (chapter LIVING WITH LINT)
//                 for further details.



    -e720
```

The **-e720** command tells PC-Lint not to generate message #720, which is the "Boolean test of assignment" Information message.

Of course, you can add other options to OPTIONS.LNT to control PC-Lint's output. This is the whole reason for OPTION.LNT's existence.

STD.LNT will then reference this file. STD.LNT looks like this:

```
// Standard lint options

co-bc4.lnt  options.lnt  lib-win.lnt lib-zinc.lnt
```

The batch file used to invoke PC-Lint (LIN.BAT) then passes STD.LNT to PC-Lint for processing.

```
c:\lint\lint  +v   ic:\lint\  std.lnt  %1 %2 %3 %4 %5 %6 %7 %8 %9 >_lint.tmp
type _lint.tmp | more
@echo off
echo ---
echo PC-lint for C/C++ output placed in _LINT.TMP
```

As you can see, LIN.BAT simply invokes PC-Lint, telling it to look in
C:\LINT\ for option files and to process STD.LNT and any files passed
on the command line. The output from PC-Lint is put in a file called
"_lint.tmp," which is then piped to MORE for viewing.

STD.LNT just references other .LNT files. In this case, there is a .LNT
file specifically for Borland C++ 4.0, one for the Windows SDK libraries,
and one for Zinc. Since OPTIONS.LNT also is referenced, any options
you place there also are processed.

Using PC-Lint

Once you have PC-Lint installed and configured, using it is really easy.
You have two choices as to which version of PC-Lint you run. The first
version, LINT.EXE, is bound with Phar Lap's 386 DOS extender, so it
can use all the memory in your machine. Obviously, you must have an
80386 or higher processor to use this executable. If you don't, or your
machine has trouble with DOS extenders, you can use LINT2.EXE,
which is a "bound" executable that can run on either DOS or OS/2. It
doesn't use an extender, so it can't use all of your machine's memory,
but it's nice to have if you can't get LINT.EXE to run. By default,
LIN.BAT references LINT.EXE.

If all of your source code is in one directory, you can just go to that
directory and execute LIN on all the .C or .CPP files. However, if you
keep all your source code in different directories, you can create a .LNT
file that tells PC-Lint where all your source code is located. This also is
useful if you want to specify the location of #include files without setting
an INCLUDE environment variable. For example, let's say that we have a
program that consists of four modules and also uses Zinc. However, we
normally use the IDE so our INCLUDE variable isn't set. We could create a
.LNT file that looks like this:

```
-ic:\zinc
-ic:\bc4\include
module1.cpp
module2.cpp
module3.cpp
module4.cpp
```

This tells PC-Lint the names of our modules and also where to look for our include files. When we want to check the entire project, we just invoke LIN and pass it the name of our .LNT file.

```
LIN module.lnt
```

Again, we don't have to do this. For such a small project, we also could just pass all this to LNT directly:

```
LIN -ic:\zinc -ic:\bc4\include *.cpp
```

PC-Lint in Action

Let's look at PC-Lint in action. We'll run it on a C++ program. Since everyone here should be using Borland C++ 4.0 (or at least contemplating it), our C++ program will be one of the C++ programs given to you by Borland as an example. Since it's distributed with the compiler, we won't reproduce the code here (see \BC4\EXAMPLES\WINDOWS\WHELLO), but only pieces of code to point out problems. Please note that it is mostly due to lack of space that only one example is given. As mentioned previously, PC-Lint can produce a LOT of output, especially on C code. On C++ code, it tends to produce less because valid C++ code has to be more robust for the compiler not to generate an error. While PC-Lint will flag syntax errors, it really should be used to catch "gotchas" that the compiler doesn't complain about.

Invoking PC-Lint on WHELLO.CPP produces about 4K of output, shown here. The idea behind showing you this is to point out the kind of problems that PC-Lint can find. The _s, located above each line of code, point out where PC-Lint thinks the problem is.

```
--- Module:   whello.cpp
a                                             _
            MessageLength = strlen( Message );
whello.cpp   108   Info 713: Loss of precision (assignment) (unsigned int to int)
```

`strlen()` is defined to return a value of type `size_t`, which is `typedef`'d in stdio.h to be *unsigned int*. However, `MessageLength` is a variable of type `int`, so PC-Lint complains about a possible loss of precision. While Borland C++ will complain about losses of precision, it doesn't tell you what type is causing the problem. PC-Lint does.

```
            LineMessage = new far char [MessageLength+1];
whello.cpp  109  Info 1732: new in constructor for class LINEFUNCDATA which has
    no assignment operator
whello.cpp  109  Info 1733: new in constructor for class LINEFUNCDATA which has
    no copy constructor
whello.cpp  109  Info 737: Loss of sign in promotion from int to unsigned int
```

Here we have one line of code that generates several messages. In this case, the problem is in the definition of a class. The defintion for the class looks like this:

```
struct LINEFUNCDATA
{
    HDC hDC;
    char FAR *LineMessage;
    int MessageLength;
    LINEFUNCDATA( char *Message )
    {
        hDC = 0;
        MessageLength = strlen( Message );
        LineMessage = new far char [MessageLength+1];
        lstrcpy( LineMessage, Message );
    };
    ~LINEFUNCDATA( void ) { delete LineMessage; }
};
};
```

The constructor for the class LINEFUNCDATA contains a call to the C++ `new()` operator, but the class has no assignment operator or copy constructor. If, at some point in this program, we were to attempt to assign an instance of LINEFUNCDATA to another instance of LINEFUNCDATA, the pointer allocated by the call to `new()` would be duplicated. If at some later point one of these "copies" were to be deleted, the destructor would delete the memory allocated by `new()`, which would leave the second copy with a pointer that points to deallocated memory.

```
            lstrcpy( LineMessage, Message );
whello.cpp  110  Warning 534: Ignoring return value of lstrcpy(char far *,
    const char far *) (compare with line 1046, file d:\bc4\include\windows.h)
```

Here, PC-Lint notices that the code ignores the return value from `lstrcpy()`, which is not normally a problem. However, it is interesting to note that PC-Lint tells you where the original prototype for `lstrcpy()` occurs, so that you know where to look.

```
    ~LINEFUNCDATA( void ) { delete LineMessage; }
whello.cpp  112  Warning 619: Loss of precision (arg. no. 1) (pointer to pointer)

    };
```

This message is a little obscure. PC-Lint is complaining because the destructor for LINEFUNCDATA calls `delete()` without a cast on the parameter LineMessage. Since LineMessage was allocated with *new far char*, it needs to be deleted with *delete far LineMessage*.

```
whello.cpp  113  Info 1712: default constructor not defined for class
    'LINEFUNCDATA'
```

Generally, C++ classes should always have default constructors (constructors that take no arguments). However, LINEFUNCDATA only has one constructor and it requires a parameter.

```
    wndclass.lpfnWndProc   = ::WndProc;
whello.cpp  55  Error 64: Type mismatch (assignment) (ptrs to qualification)
```

Here, PC-Lint is complaining because the type of `::WndProc` doesn't match the definition of `lpfnWndProc` in the structure `wndclass`.

```
    Show( Main::nCmdShow );
whello.cpp  91  Warning 534: Ignoring return value of Window::Show(int)
    (compare with line 32)

    TranslateMessage( &msg );
whello.cpp  126  Warning 534: Ignoring return value of TranslateMessage(const
    struct tagMSG far *) (compare with line 2834, file d:\bc4\include\windows.h)

    DispatchMessage( &msg );
whello.cpp  127  Warning 534: Ignoring return value of DispatchMessage(const
    struct tagMSG far *) (compare with line 2835, file d:\bc4\include\windows.h)
```

Again, PC-Lint is pointing out that the return values from several functions are being ignored, since the function prototypes specify that these functions return values. This is a case where you probably don't care about the return value, but PC-Lint doesn't know this. There's an easy way to turn these messages off, which is described below.

```
        return msg.wParam;
whello.cpp  129  Info 713: Loss of precision (return) (unsigned int to int)
```

Here we have the problem of a function returning a value that doesn't match the type specified for the function. In this case, there is the possibility of a sign bit coming into play when an unsigned int value is coerced into an int.

```
        BeginPaint( hWnd, &ps );
whello.cpp  142  Warning 534: Ignoring return value of BeginPaint(const struct
    HWND__ near *, struct tagPAINTSTRUCT far *) (compare with line 3425, file
    d:\bc4\include\windows.h)

        SetTextAlign( ps.hdc, TA_BOTTOM );
whello.cpp  145  Warning 534: Ignoring return value of SetTextAlign(const
    struct HDC__ near *, unsigned int) (compare with line 1743, file
    d:\bc4\include\windows.h)
```

Again, more functions whose return values are being ignored.

```
{
whello.cpp  153  Error 18: MainWindow::LineFunc(int, int, char far *)
    redeclared (qualification) conflicts with line 44
```

In this case, PC-Lint is complaining that the one definition of LineFunc doesn't match another. The original defintion of LineFunc was static void FAR PASCAL, while the function was actually defined as void FAR PASCAL _export.

```
            lpLineFuncData->LineMessage, lpLineFuncData->MessageLength );
whello.cpp  156  Warning 534: Ignoring return value of TextOut(const struct
    HDC__ near *, int, int, const char far *, int) (compare with line 1684,
    file d:\bc4\include\windows.h)

        SetWindowWord( hWnd, 0, (WORD) pWindow );
whello.cpp  185  Warning 534: Ignoring return value of SetWindowWord(const
    struct HWND__ near *, int, unsigned short) (compare with line 3164, file
    d:\bc4\include\windows.h)

            pWindow = (Window *) lpcs->lpCreateParams;
whello.cpp  231  Warning 643: Loss of precision in pointer cast

        return pWindow->WndProc( iMessage, wParam, lParam );
whello.cpp  241  Warning 525: Negative indentation from line 226
```

One thing that PC-Lint checks for is indentation in your source code that "makes sense." This is usually done to warn you about problems with "if..then..else" constructs that may line up correctly, but in reality don't do what you expect because of improper brace placement.

```
        }
    whello.cpp  275  Info 715: lpszCmdLine (line 256) not referenced
```

When PC-Lint is done with a module, it reports any inconsistencies in that module, such as #include files that are never used, or (as in this case) variables declared that are never referenced.

```
    --- Global Wrap-up

    Info 1714: Member function Window::GetHandle(void) (line 30, file whello.cpp)
        not referenced
    Warning 1526: Member function Window::WndProc(unsigned int, unsigned int,
    long)
        (line 35, file whello.cpp) not defined
```

After PC-Lint is through processing all the modules you specified, it then reports on inconsistencies that occur *across* all modules. This is where it can find problems that the compiler can miss, since the compiler only looks at one source file at a time. For example, if you have #defines that conflict with each other (in different modules), or global variables whose types don't match up across modules, PC-Lint will tell you here.

Specifying Options Internally

You probably noticed that PC-Lint complained about some "problems" that aren't really problems. Specifically, it noticed that the code was ignoring the return values from functions like TranslateMessage() and BeginPaint(). Obviously, this is what you meant to do. So how do you tell PC-Lint that it's ok and that it shouldn't complain about it?

The obvious solution is to pass the command-line option **-e534** to PC-Lint, which will prevent it from issuing *any* warning 534s. However, this is probably not what you want since it would keep PC-Lint from complaining about any function whose return value is ignored.

There are two ways around this. You can specify options for PC-Lint in your source code that control its behavior. For example, the call to BeginPaint could be modified to look like this:

```
BeginPaint( hWnd, &ps );                          //lint !e534
```

This suppresses message 534 for this one line of code only. Another solution (if you have several lines of code that generate this message) is to "blanket" the code with a pair of PC-Lint options:

```
//lint -save -e534
BeginPaint(hWnd, &ps);
    .
    .
[other code]
    .
    .
//lint -restore
```

This saves PC-Lint's state and lets the "**-e534**" take effect. The **-restore** option sets PC-Lint's state back the way it was.

One final way to handle this is to tell PC-Lint once and for all that BeginPaint is always going to generate this message and you don't care. You can give PC-Lint a list of "symbols" and essentially tell it not to generate a specific message for that symbol:

```
//lint -esym(534,BeginPaint,SetTextAlign)
```

Other PC-Line Options

PC-Lint currently checks for several hundred potential problems. In addition, its behavior can be adjusted for just about any C or C++ compiler. You also can control the format of its output. This is why it cannot only be used as a stand-alone tool, but also can hook into Borland's IDE and run as a tool. With this setup, you can run PC-Lint on the source code in an editor window and have it generate output that can be parsed by the IDE filter tools. You then get a message window whose contents (the output of PC-Lint) track automatically in the editor!

It should be obvious that PC-Lint can find some very obscure problems with code. Not only is it an unobtrusive tool, it is easy to install and configure. If you're not using it, you should be—especially with C++.

Bounds Checker 2.0

Bounds Checker for Windows (BCHKW) is somewhat difficult to pin down. It isn't exactly a debugger, since it doesn't let you set breakpoints or modify the value of variables while a program runs. What it does do is let you track down some very hard to find bugs in your program.

BCHKW runs your program for you, setting hundreds of invisible breakpoints in your code. It looks at each call to the Windows API, checking to make sure that each parameter you send to Windows is valid. It also checks return values from Windows calls, stopping your program if an API call returns an error code. Additionally, it checks for memory overwrites and writes through null pointers.

BCHKW also acts like an API "logger," capturing events as Windows generates them. These events can either be viewed in memory or optionally written out to disk in a special format understood by nu-Mega's TVIEW utility.

In addition, BCHKW keeps track of how much stack space your application uses, how much GDI and USER heap space is used, and whether or not your program (and its DLLs) are leaking memory and resources.

The amazing thing about BCHKW is that it requires no special macros, libraries, or header files. Instead, it "understands" the debug information Borland C++ placed in your .OBJ and .EXE files. Preparing your program for BCHKW is as simple as turning on the debugging options when you build your executable file.

Once installed, BCHKW is a snap to use. However, describing how BCHKW works won't do the program justice. Instead, let's look at a session with BCHKW so that you can see what it does for you.

First of all, we need a program to check. We'll use another one of Borland's example programs, HDUMP (located in \BC4\EXAMPLES\WINDOWS\HDUMP), which displays the contents of a file in hex, along with an ASCII dump of each line (much like a debugger displays a memory dump). See figure 8.1 for an example of HDUMP in action.

HDUMP runs fine, so it doesn't have any obvious errors. But, it does make two Windows API calls that can fail, so it's a good way to show BCHKW at work. This is an appropriate time to point out that not all "error" return values from a Windows API function are actual problems. In this case, HDUMP doesn't crash or act strange because of these problems. BCHKW doesn't know this (unless we tell it), so it pops up when these calls fail.

Fig. 8.1. HDUMP in action.

To test a program with BCHKW, we simply double-click BCHKW's icon. Under the File menu, we pick Load… and select HDUMP.EXE. BCHKW will load HDUMP and then bring up a list of DLLs that

HDUMP uses. You can either let BCHKW load the DLLs (for checking) or tell it to ignore them. BCHKW only concerns itself with DLLs that aren't part of Windows (in other words, you won't see USER, GDI, or KERNEL in the list). In HDUMP's case, the only DLL it references is BC40RTL.DLL, Borland C++'s runtime library. After this, BCHKW will start executing HDUMP. Remember, as part of the loading process, BCHKW put breakpoints all throughout HDUMP's code so that it can check Windows API parameters and return values, along with the status of memory while HDUMP runs.

While your program is running, BCHKW minimizes itself in order for your program to have all the screen real estate it needs. You can pop BCHKW up at any time if you want to stop your program while it is running.

If the program you want to check loads in response to some event, you can have BCHKW wait in the background and watch for it to load, taking control when the program actually loads and runs. This is accomplished through the External Load... menu item.

After HDUMP starts, we can make one of the errors occur by selecting Open from the File menu. HDUMP makes a call to `DlgDirSelect()`, which returns a value of 0 because the file name that was selected is not a directory. Since, by default, BCHKW looks for `DlgDirSelect()` to return a nonzero value, it pops up at this point with an `*** API Failure ***` message.

When BCHKW pops up to inform you of a problem, it gives you several options. You can stop the program BCHKW is checking, log the error and continue, ignore the error and continue, or stop validating at this address. At this point, HDUMP (along with all other currently executing programs except BCHKW) is stopped.

If you select Stop, BCHKW will enter an interactive mode to let you see what code caused the problem. If you do this, BCHKW is currently operating in what is called *hard mode*, which means that it has complete control and no other application is getting any time from Windows. You can tell BCHKW to go into *soft mode* (via the Action menu) to let other programs run. While BCHKW is in hard mode, no

applications get any messages, whatsoever. This means that if you minimize BCHKW to look at the status of your app, it will not be getting any WM_PAINT messages. BCHKW gets around this problem by saving a copy of the screen and blitting it for you when you minimize BCHKW.

Selecting "Log the error and continue" writes a message to the log file for HDUMP (which you'll see later) explaining what the problem is, where the problem occurred, and the current call stack.

Selecting "Ignore the error and continue" simply lets HDUMP go on its merry way, logging nothing about the error.

Finally, selecting "Stop validating at this address" tells BCHKW not to pop up any more if an error occurs at this address.

In this case, "Stop" was selected. At this point, BCHKW shows you the current state of HDUMP so you can see what happened. Figure 8.2 shows several of BCHKW's seven windows that can be viewed.

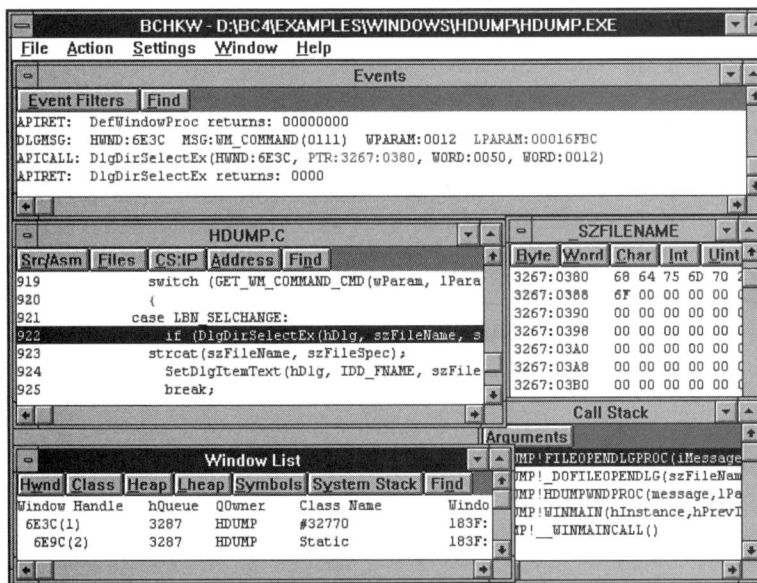

Fig. 8.2. Bounds Checker after selecting "Stop."

BCHKW has seven windows that it uses to show you the current state of an application. On a 640x480 screen, this can get a little crowded, so only five are shown in figure 8.2. BCHKW doesn't always pop up all these windows whenever it activates. Instead, you can customize BCHKW to show only those windows in which you are interested; this information is then recorded in an .INI file.

The top window (Events) keeps a record of the last 1,024 events that were both sent and received by HDUMP. If you want more than 1,024 events, BCHKW can write the events to a Trace (.TRC) file that can be viewed by the TVIEW utility, shown later in this section. The "Event Filters" button allows you to hide different event types to make it easier to read the event list. The Event window is discussed in more detail later in this section.

The next window, the Code window (labelled HDUMP.C here), shows the code that caused BCHKW to stop and complain. Since the problem occurred in HDUMP, the source code for HDUMP.C is shown, with the offending line highlighted. If the problem had occurred in the Borland runtime library (or in a module with no debugging information), you'd see assembler code in this window. The Code window lets you switch between source code (if available) and assembler via the "Src/Asm" button. The "Files" button lets you look at other source code files associated with the current program. "CS:IP" is used to move back to the current execution point (in case you've switched to another module and want to jump back quickly). "Address" lets you look at a particular address by either typing an absolute address or using symbols available through the Borland debug information. Finally, "Find" lets you search for specific strings in the Code window.

The other windows are shown in more detail.

Figure 8.3 shows the Events window expanded somewhat so you can see more detail. Each message (both for windows and dialogs) is shown, along with the actual message value, the window handle, and the values of `wParam` and `lParam`. Windows API calls also are shown, along with their parameters. The lines marked "APIRET" show the return values from the corresponding API call. It's not obvious here, but this heirarchy allows you to see if an API call generates any messages to your code, since the messages would be sandwiched between the corresponding "APICALL" and "APIRET" lines.

```
┌─                              Events                          ▼ ▲┐
│ Event Filters   Find                                           ▲│
│APICALL: DefWindowProc(HWND:6D50, MSG:WM_ENTERIDLE(0121), WORD:0000, DWORD:00006E3C)│
│APIRET:  DefWindowProc returns: 00000000                        │
│DLGMSG:  HWND:6E3C  MSG:WM_PARENTNOTIFY(0210)  WPARAM:0201  LPARAM:0090005C│
│DLGMSG:  HWND:6E3C  MSG:WM_MOUSEACTIVATE(0021)  WPARAM:6E3C  LPARAM:02010001│
│DLGMSG:  HWND:6E3C  MSG:WM_SETCURSOR(0020)  WPARAM:6FBC  LPARAM:02010001│
│DLGMSG:  HWND:6E3C  MSG:WM_USER+0000(0400)  WPARAM:0000  LPARAM:00000000│
│DLGMSG:  HWND:6E3C  MSG:WM_COMMAND(0111)  WPARAM:0010  LPARAM:02006EE4│
│DLGMSG:  HWND:6E3C  MSG:WM_COMMAND(0111)  WPARAM:0012  LPARAM:00046FBC│
│DLGMSG:  HWND:6E3C  MSG:(0131)  WPARAM:0002  LPARAM:00240058│
│DLGMSG:  HWND:6E3C  MSG:WM_CTLCOLOR(0019)  WPARAM:0B9E  LPARAM:00026FBC│
│DLGMSG:  HWND:6E3C  MSG:WM_CTLCOLOR(0019)  WPARAM:0B9E  LPARAM:00016EE4│
│DLGMSG:  HWND:6E3C  MSG:WM_CTLCOLOR(0019)  WPARAM:0B9E  LPARAM:00016EE4│
│DLGMSG:  HWND:6E3C  MSG:WM_CTLCOLOR(0019)  WPARAM:0B9E  LPARAM:00016EE4│
│WNDMSG:  HWND:6D50(hdump)  MSG:WM_ENTERIDLE(0121)  WPARAM:0000  LPARAM:00006E3C│
│APICALL: DefWindowProc(HWND:6D50, MSG:WM_ENTERIDLE(0121), WORD:0000, DWORD:00006E3C)│
│APIRET:  DefWindowProc returns: 00000000                        │
│DLGMSG:  HWND:6E3C  MSG:WM_COMMAND(0111)  WPARAM:0012  LPARAM:00016FBC│
│APICALL: DlgDirSelectEx(HWND:6E3C, PTR:3267:0380, WORD:0050, WORD:0012)│
│APIRET:  DlgDirSelectEx returns: 0000                           ▼│
│◄ ───────────────────────────────────────────────────────────► │
└────────────────────────────────────────────────────────────────┘
```

Fig. 8.3. The Events window.

Since this picture is not in color, you can't see that the MSG: entries and API calls themselves (like `DlgDirSelectEx()`) are blue. As part of its installation procedure, BCHKW hooks into the Windows help system, using the help files supplied with Borland C++. Thus, you can double-click Windows API functions in the Event window and have help come up for that function.

Figure 8.4 shows several of the windows in more detail. As you can see, the Call Stack window shows you where you are and how you got there. The entries that are prefixed with # are modules for which BCHKW has source code. In this case, all the source code is in HDUMP.C. The first entry (HDUMP!_WINMAINCALL()) is the startup code for HDUMP. Since it has no debug information compiled into it, BCHKW doesn't flag it as having source code available. The "Arguments" button at the top of the Call Stack window lets you view either variable names (which is what the window is currently showing) or absolute addresses and values.

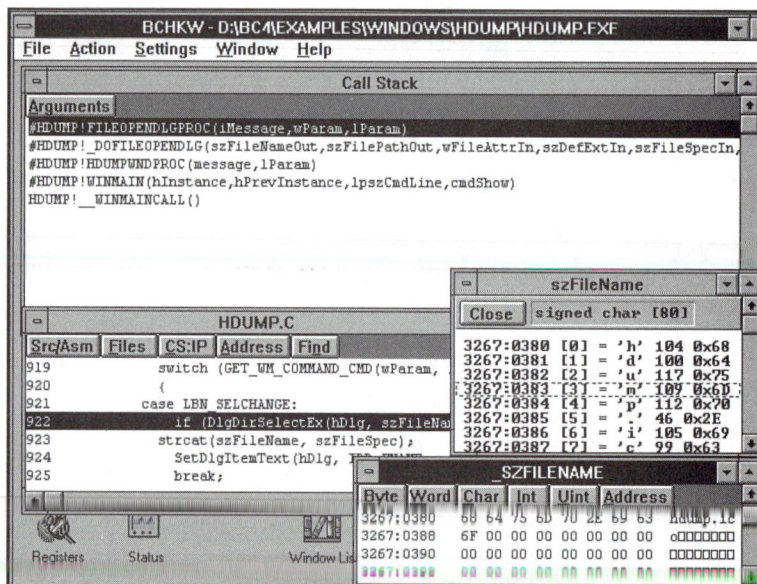

Fig. 8.4. The Call Stack and data windows.

The Data window shows the contents of the variable "szFileName." As you can see, it is a simple hex dump of the variable contents (in this case, showing the file name that was clicked). The buttons "Byte," "Word," "Char," "Int," and "Uint" let you change the format of the data being displayed. The "Address" button lets you select another address to view.

Double-clicking a variable name brings up an inspector (shown above the Data window). You can have as many inspectors open as you like. Inspectors let you see the value of variables or structures in the same format as they are declared. In this case, we're looking at `szFileName`. The Inspector (labelled "szFileName") shows it as an array of chars, displaying the address of each element, the offset of each element in the array, and the contents in character form, decimal and hexadecimal.

Figure 8.5 shows the remaining windows, along with some of the alternate views of the Call Stack and the Code windows. As mentioned previously, the Call Stack window also can show the arguments for each function call as absolute addresses and values. Similarly, the Code window can show assembler as well as C or C++ source. Notice that the call to `DlgDirSelectEx()` has been modified slightly by BCHKW in order for it to get control.

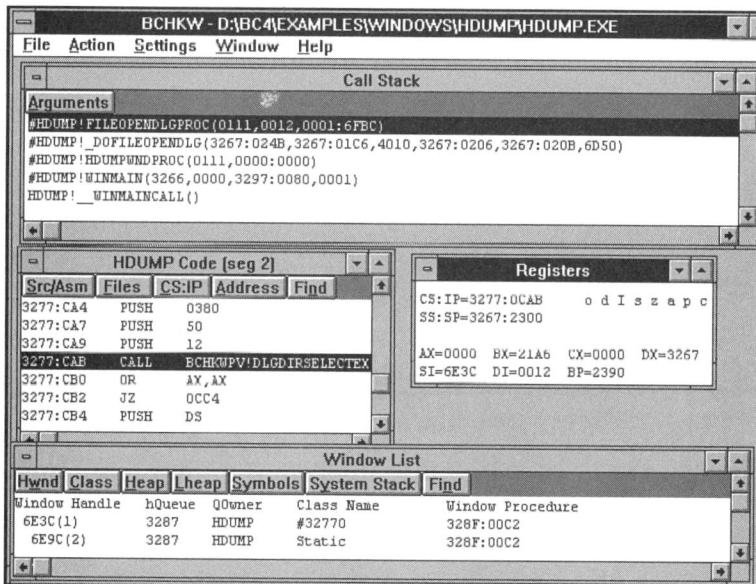

Fig. 8.5. Bounds Checker's remaining windows.

The last two windows are the Register window and the Window List window. The Register window simply shows the contents of the CPU registers. While not visible here, all of the segment registers are shown.

The window labelled "Window List" in figure 8.5 is actually the Info window. The Info window can show you several pieces of information depending on which button you click at the top of the window. Here, the "Hwnd" button was clicked, causing the window title to change to "Window List" and showing all the windows created by HDUMP. As you can see, each line shows the window handle along with the queue for that window, the owner, the class name of the window, and the address of the window procedure. What's not obvious from figure 8.5 is that the Window List shows the parent/child relationship of each window and its contents. The first line refers to the dialog box generated by HDUMP when we selected Open from the File menu. The dialog box has a class name of #32770, because HDUMP refers to the dialog box in the .RC file via a resource id and not a name. The second line, slightly indented, is the first control of that dialog box.

The Info window also can show what classes HDUMP has registered (via the "Class" button), the contents of HDUMP's heap (via the "Heap" button), the local heap, and even the system stack (the stack as seen by Windows and not just your application). Finally, you also can see any symbols declared by HDUMP, including what was linked in with it. Like all the other windows, if a symbol has a value that can be shown, BCHKW will open an Inspector if you double-click an entry in the Symbols list.

When your program exits, BCHKW brings up a log window to show you how much stack space your program used (and how much remained), how much GDI and USER heap space were used and any memory/resource leaks that occurred in your code. Again, it's easier to show you this than explain it, so Listing 8.1 contains the log file generated by the run of HDUMP. It's interesting to see that while HDUMP has no memory or resource leaks, BC40RTL.DLL allocates memory but never releases it!

Listing 8.1. Log File Generated for HDUMP.EXE

```
D:\BC4\EXAMPLES\WINDOWS\HDUMP\HDUMP.LOG created 03:17 PM  Tuesday March 29

-------------------------------------------------------------------------------
D:\BC4\EXAMPLES\WINDOWS\HDUMP\HDUMP.EXE loaded 03:17 PM  Tuesday March 29

---------- 03:18 PM  Tuesday March 29 ----------

***** API Failure *****

  Procedure:  FILEOPENDLGPROC   (0009FH)
     Module: HDUMP
Source File:  HDUMP.C
Line Number:  00922

DlgDirSelectEx failed: 0000


CALL STACK
----------
#HDUMP!FILEOPENDLGPROC(iMessage,wParam,lParam)
            (0111,0012,0001:6FE8)
#HDUMP!_DOFILEOPENDLG(szFileNameOut,szFilePathOut,wFileAttrIn,szDefExtIn,szFileSpecIn,hWnd)
            (31D7:024B,31D7:01C6,4010,31D7:0206,31D7:020B,6CFC)
#HDUMP!HDUMPWNDPROC(message,lParam)
            (0111,0000:0000)
#HDUMP!WINMAIN(hInstance,hPrevInstance,lpszCmdLine,cmdShow)
         (31D6,0000,33B7:0080,0001)
HDUMP!__WINMAINCALL()

---------- 03:18 PM  Tuesday March 29 ----------

***** API Failure *****

  Procedure:  FILEOPENDLGPROC   (002B3H)
     Module: HDUMP
Source File:  HDUMP.C
Line Number:  00995
DlgDirList failed: 0000


CALL STACK
----------
#HDUMP!FILEOPENDLGPROC(iMessage,wParam,lParam)
              (0111,0001,0000:7070)
#HDUMP!_DOFILEOPENDLG(szFileNameOut,szFilePathOut,wFileAttrIn,
➥szDefExtIn,szFileSpecIn,hWnd)
              (31D7:024B,31D7:01C6,4010,31D7:0206,31D7:020B,6CFC)
#HDUMP!HDUMPWNDPROC(message,lParam)
              (0111,0000:0000)
```

continues

Listing 8.1. Continued

```
#HDUMP!WINMAIN(hInstance,hPrevInstance,lpszCmdLine,cmdShow)
            (31D6,0000,33B7:0080,0001)
HDUMP!__WINMAINCALL()


*****************************************************************************
                        YOUR PROGRAM'S data usage
*****************************************************************************

   Stack Usage:
         stack space available           stack space used
         ---------------------           ----------------
         07980                           02272

HDUMP
   Memory used (in bytes):
         Local Heap                      Global Heap
         ----------                      ----------
         00081                           00288


BC40RTL
   Memory used (in bytes):
         Local Heap                      Global Heap
         ----------                      ----------
         00060                           05878


   Local leaks:
         Function Name              Size        Program location
         -------------              ----        ----------------
         KERNEL!LOCALALLOC          00060       0001:0459

   Global leaks:
         Function Name              Size        Program location
         -------------              ----        ----------------
         KERNEL!GLOBALALLOC         00001       0001:05A3
         KERNEL!GLOBALALLOC         04096       0001:BF7E
         KERNEL!GLOBALALLOC         00891       0001:05A3

   Resource leaks:
         Windows Function           Program location
         ----------------           ----------------
         KERNEL!LOADLIBRARY         0001:E7C5


*****************************************************************************
                  GDI data usage on your program's behalf
*****************************************************************************

   Memory used (in bytes):
         Local Heap                      Global Heap
```

```
          ----------                              -----------
          02168                                   41920

****************************************************************************
                    USER data usage on your program's behalf
****************************************************************************

     Memory used (in bytes):
          Local Heap                         Global Heap
          ----------                         -----------
          01080                              01536
```

It should be obvious that BCHKW can help you find those kinds of problems with your Windows code that are almost impossible to find by just looking it over. The fact that it requires absolutely no changes to your code in order to work makes it easy to use.

Now, let's look at BCHKW's Trace View Utility, TVIEW. You will recall that BCHKW shows you the last 1,024 "events" that your program generated. While 1,024 is a lot, if you have a program that generates a lot of events, you may want to see more. Or, you may want BCHKW to simply log all errors to a log file during a run (or just ignore them altogether). BCHKW can optionally write all the events generated during a run to a .TRC file, which TVIEW can interpret. However, TVIEW organizes the information for you and lets you see the message hierarchy of a run of your program. Figure 8.6 shows TVIEW processing the .TRC file generated by the run of HDUMP.

TVIEW shows the path of messages and API calls generated and processed during the lifetime of a program's execution. As figure 8.6 shows, API calls (and the return from the API call) are connected with vertical lines. The default is for TVIEW to show the parameters passed during the API call and the return value resulting from the call. The icons on the left let you see the hierarchy in a slightly different form. The large diamond on the left of the APICALL lines tell you that this APICALL is expanded fully. TVIEW lets you expand and collapse portions of the tree to hide or show as much detail as you like.

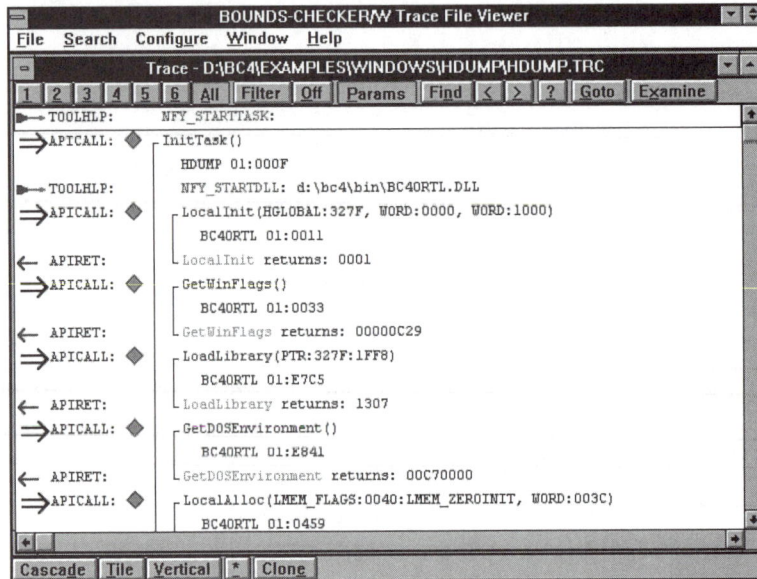

Fig. 8.6. TVIEW processing HDUMP's .TRC file.

TVIEW's windows have several buttons to also help you understand
the information being shown. The numbered buttons (1 through 6)
and the "All" button let you collapse and expand the entire display to
a certain level. For example, pressing 1 shows you only the first level
of calls. Figure 8.7 shows this in action.

At level 1, you only see the "top-level" events. In this case, you see all
the APICALLs that were made, along with the addresses of parameters
passed to each APICALL. The icons on the left have changed from green
diamonds to either red filled circles or circles with a red dot. The red
circles indicate that the corresponding APICALL has hidden details. The
circles with red dots indicate that only an APIRET is hidden. Double-
clicking an individual line will expand that line only.

The "Params" button turns on or off the display of the parameter
information. The "Find," "<," and ">" buttons allow you to search
for specific text in the tree. Keyboard shortcuts allow these buttons
to jump from an APICALL to the corresponding APIRET and vice versa.

The "?" button performs a Windows API lookup in the Windows help file supplied with Borland C++. "Goto" simply takes you to the line you specify. Finally, "Examine" opens up a parameter inspection window, which is covered shortly.

The button bar at the bottom of figure 8.7 helps you control the layout of TVIEW's child windows. "Cascade," "Tile," and "Vertical" let you quickly rearrange open windows. The "*" button takes the current window and makes it as large as possible. This is especially helpful if you have one window that you want to be as large as possible. If you rearrange all the other windows and then click "*" while the last window has the focus, it will enlarge as much as it can without disturbing any other open windows. "Clone" simply duplicates the current window, allowing you to see multiple views of the same data.

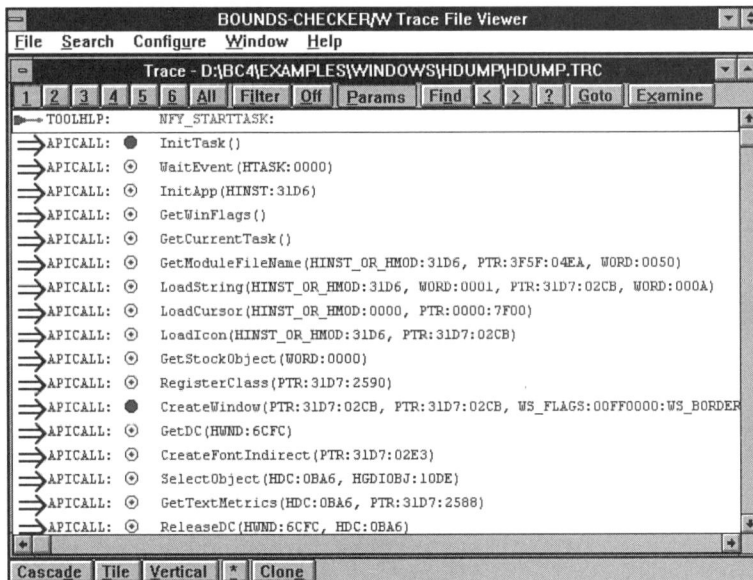

Fig. 8.7. Tree shown at level 1.

If you don't want to look at all the detailed lines TVIEW shows you, you can use TVIEW's filters to hide certain types of messages. Figure 8.8 shows you what you can turn on and off.

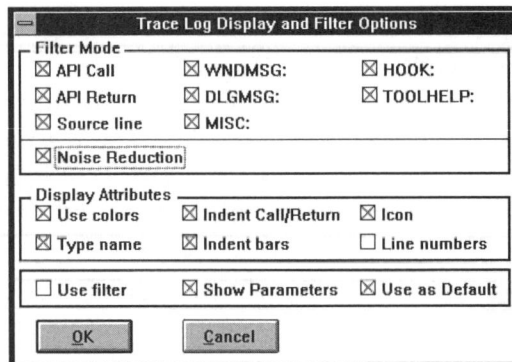

Fig. 8.8. Filtering options.

All of these should be fairly obvious. One option that deserves mention is the "Noise Reduction" option, which tells TVIEW to filter out "noise" in the trace window, which hides calls to GetMessage(), DispatchMessage(), TranslateAccelerator() and any of the DefWindowProc() code; in other words, anywhere Windows provided default processing.

The information in the .TRC file also lets you see how your code handled a specific message. For example, if we wanted to see what HDUMP did when it received a WM_PAINT message, TVIEW will show us. Figure 8.9 gives us the details.

As you can see, TVIEW flags the processing of the WM_PAINT message with a small icon respresenting a window. Following this is the list of API calls that HDUMP executed in response to the WM_PAINT message, along with all the parameters to each call.

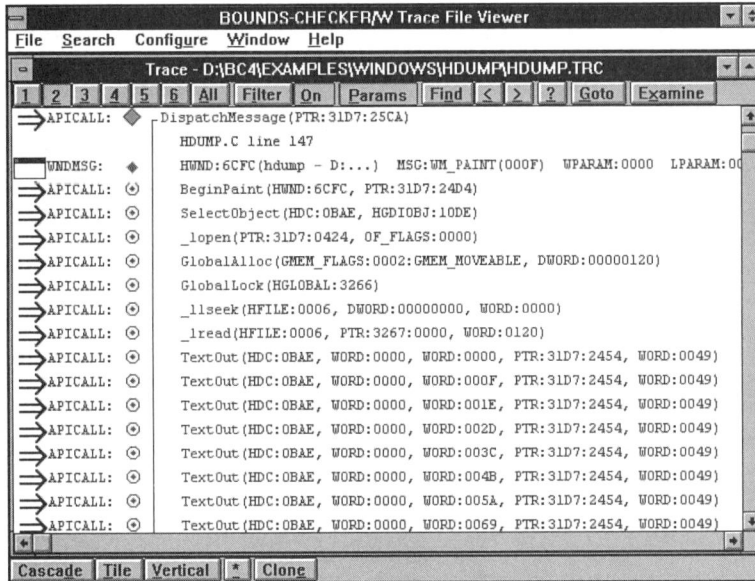

Fig. 8.9. How HDUMP handles *WM_PAINT*.

Finally, TVIEW keeps track of *all* values sent to a Windows API call. This means you can use TVIEW's "parameter pane" to view the contents of variables (see fig. 8.10).

By typing Ctrl-S (or selecting "Parameter pane" from the Window menu), we can ask TVIEW to open a small subwindow. Clicking an APICALL shows the values of parameters passed to that APICALL. In figure 8.10, the BeginPaint() call was clicked and TVIEW shows the parameter values and their types. If we click a particular parameter (for example, lpps), TVIEW will open an inspector just like BCHKW's.

As you can probably guess by now, BCHKW is a powerful program for developers. It can help you track down bugs that would otherwise be impossible to find. Furthermore, it can show how other Windows programs work, even if you don't have debug information. Curious about what message Taskman (the Windows task manager/switcher) works? Run BCHKW on it and capture the messages to a .TRC file. TVIEW does know about undocumented messages and functions and will dutifully point them out to you.

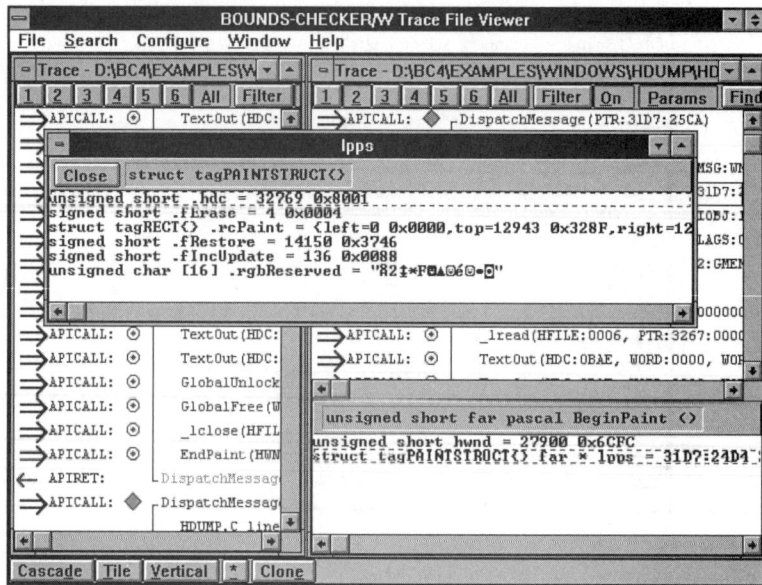

Fig. 8.10. TVIEW's parameter pane.

BCHKW also knows about Soft-Ice for Windows, another nu-Mega product. If BCHKW can't find the problem, you can always pop into Soft-Ice/W for low-level debugging.

It's always possible that if you don't use BCHKW, then your customers might. And wouldn't that be embarrassing? "Hello, Mr. Davidson? Yes, we're using your Mumble application and it's leaking resources. Would you please change the code to delete those bitmaps you are allocating in mumble.cpp? Thanks so much!"

You have been warned.

Soft-Ice for Windows

At the beginning of this chapter, I mentioned that none of these products really take the place of good old Turbo Debugger. That was only partially true. While none of these products fit into the integrated environment as well as TDW (and especially Borland's new integrated debugger), Soft-Ice for Windows (Soft-Ice/W) certainly comes close.

In fact, short of a hardware emulator, no product can give you the debugging power that Soft-Ice/W can give you. Not only can you debug your C and C++ programs at the source level, you can literally debug anything for Windows, including device drivers, virtual device drivers (VxD's), DOS TSRs in DOS boxes, and even Windows itself. Want to watch Windows start itself up? Soft-Ice/W will let you. Want to debug a TSR that loaded before Windows? You can do that too. Writing a Windows VxD and want to debug it at the source level? Yep. You can even debug multiple Windows programs at the same time!

All of this power comes at a price. Soft-Ice/W can be difficult to learn. It doesn't have a pretty graphical interface. It can be difficult to set up for your video card. But it can let you debug your programs using the powerful features of your 386, 486, or Pentium without slowing your program down at all.

While writing this chapter, I had to use two different releases of Soft-Ice/W since nu-Mega had to come out with a new version to handle Borland C/C++ 4.0's new debug format. While both were functionally the same, there are some caveats on installing the two versions. Both will be discussed.

Soft-Ice/W 1.4 (the most current as of this writing) installs via a standard Windows installation program. It is interesting to note that for a program with as much internal knowledge of Windows as Soft-Ice/W has, it makes absolutely no modifications to any of your system files. The previous version, 1.3, had no installation program at all. You simply copied the contents of the distribution disk to your hard drive and ran a small program called ICONS to create the Soft-Ice/W program group.

The step that probably causes people the most grief comes next — making Soft-Ice/W work with your video card. You see, Soft-Ice/W actually debugs *Windows itself,* and therefore is executed before Windows starts. In fact, you don't run Windows and then Soft-Ice/W. You run Soft-Ice/W and it starts Windows for you. This means that it is available at any point during your Windows session. To initially get to Soft-Ice/W, you just press Ctrl-D and it pops up.

When Soft-Ice/W pops up, nothing else is happening on your computer. No programs are running and no messages are being sent. Since Soft-Ice/W has such absolute control, it must handle all devices itself. Since there is no telling what state DOS is in, Soft-Ice/W performs no disk input/output. It also handles all keyboard and video input/output by itself. Working at such a low level means that Soft-Ice/W must intimately deal with your video card.

Version 1.3 uses a program called VIDMODE to handle talking to your video card. If you run WINICE (Soft-Ice/W's main program), let Windows start up, and then press Ctrl-D, you should see a screen similar to figure 8.11. Soft-Ice/W runs in text mode, not graphics mode. You can then press Ctrl-D again, and you should be back in Windows. If one (or both) of these steps doesn't produce a readable screen, you then can try using VIDMODE to help Soft-Ice/W talk to your video card.

VIDMODE allows you to tell Soft-Ice/W to trap all input/output calls done to the video driver in Windows. Soft-Ice/W then writes out a configuration file that helps it handle the transition between text and graphics modes. If you're running the standard Windows VGA driver, you probably won't have any problems. However, if you are running an SVGA card at 1,024 x 768 with 256 colors, you'll probably have to use VIDMODE. The thing to remember is that VIDMODE has to be run every time you change display drivers.

Version 1.4 takes a new approach. Instead of VIDMODE, Soft-Ice/W uses video driver VxDs to handle the transition. At this time, version 1.4 only came with two VxDs: one for standard VGA and one for the ET4000 chipset. However, the configuration file generated by VIDMODE also can be used if no VxD is available. nu-Mega plans to

make available several VxDs for popular video cards. They also include the necessary source files to write your own if you are fortunate enough to own the Windows DDK (Device Driver Kit).

```
EAX=00000000   EBX=80541000   ECX=00000001   EDX=00013ED0   ESI=0000FBA6
EDI=000002CC   EBP=80010C44   ESP=80010C30   EIP=8006515C   o d I s Z a P c
CS=0028   DS=0030   SS=0030   ES=0030   FS=012F   GS=0030   DS:80066304=80062382
─────GDI.Alloc ──────────────────────────────────byte──────PROT──(0)──
0897:000002E3 4E 17 10 F6 5D 71 2B 3C-FD 3C F4 3C 10 5D 71 2B   N...]q+<.<.<.]q+
0897:000002F3 F6 5D 71 2B ED 3C 10 3C-00 3F 3C 3F 3F ED 11 39   .]q+.<.<.?<??..9
──────────────────────────────────────────────────────────────PROT32─
0028:8006515B  RET
0028:8006515C  JMP      [80066304]
0028:80065162  PUSH     EAX
0028:80065163  PUSHFD
0028:80065164  CLI
0028:80065165  CALL     80064897
0028:8006516A  AND      AL,[800662BB]
0028:80065170  AND      AH,[800662C3]
0028:80065176  OR       AL,AH
0028:80065178  JZ       8006519A
0028:8006517A  CMP      DWORD PTR [8006630C],+00
VxD-Name──Address──Length──Code──Data──Type──ID──DDB──────────────
VMM          80001000  00012E14  0028  0030  0001  0001  80011A74
VMM          80280000  00004328  0028  0030  0002
SDVXD        80013E14  00000113  0028  0030  0001  0000  80013E74
SDVXD        80284328  00000028  0028  0030  0002
WINICE       80013F28  0003E6B5  0028  0030  0001  0202  80034FEC
WINICE       80284350  00000004  0028  0030  0002
VDDVGA       800525E0  00007B10  0028  0030  0001  000A  80056EFC
VDDVGA       80284354  00000618  0028  0030  0002
VMCPD        8005A0F0  000001EC  0028  0030  0001  0011  8005A28C
VMCPD        8028496C  000000E0  0028  0030  0002
PHARLAP      8005A2DC  0000087C  0028  0030  0001  28A1  8005AA7C
PHARLAP      80284A4C  000001B0  0028  0030  0002
MMD          8005AB58  00000700  0028  0030  0001  1025  8005B1B4
MMD          80284BFC  0000001C  0028  0030  0002
CV1          8005B258  0000034F  0028  0030  0001  0102  8005B4EC
WINDPMI      8005B5A8  000027C4  0028  0030  0001  EEEE  8005DC14
WINDPMI      80284C18  00000210  0028  0030  0002
TDDebug      8005DD6C  000001C4  0028  0030  0001  001D  8005DEE8
TDDebug      80284E28  00000004  0028  0030  0002
VMD          8005DF30  00000B28  0028  0030  0001  000C  8005E9F8
VMD          80284E2C  00000263  0028  0030  0002
EBIOS        8005EA58  000000B5  0028  0030  0001  0012  8005EAC8
EBIOS        80285090  0000011C  0028  0030  0002
VKD          8005EB10  00002168  0028  0030  0001  000D  8006099C
VKD          802851AC  00000898  0028  0030  0002
VTDAPI       80060C78  000004A0  0028  0030  0001  0442  800610B0
VTDAPI       80285A44  00000044  0028  0030  0002
VPICD        80061118  00001C14  0028  0030  0001  0003  8006244C
VPICD        80285A88  000003D8  0028  0030  0002
VTD          80062D2C  00000D20  0028  0030  0001  0005  80063954
         Any Key To Continue, Esc To Cancel
```

Fig. 8.11. Soft-Ice/W in action.

You also have to be careful with certain memory managers that have the capability to "hide" the video BIOS from Soft-Ice/W. Products like 386^{Max} from Qualitas and QEMM from Quarterdeck provide extra upper memory by playing around with the BIOS in your computer. If this happens, you'll have to disable that functionality because it will cause Soft-Ice/W to not be able to switch back and forth.

Once your video has been set up, using Soft-Ice/W is fairly straightforward (notice that I didn't say *easy*). As you can see from figure 8.11, Soft-Ice/W's screen looks like most any powerful debugger. The area at the top of the screen contains the register window. It shows you all the 386 registers (remember, we're in protected mode, so the registers are the true 32-bit registers). Below this is one of Soft-Ice/W's data windows. Right below this is the code window, which in figure 8.11 is showing code at some location inside Windows itself. At the top of the code window (on the far right) is the string "PROT32," which means that this code is located in a 32-bit protected-mode segment, probably a Windows VxD.

The bottom section of the screen is where you give commands to Soft-Ice/W. Soft-Ice/W has a lot of commands, most of which should be familiar to anyone who has used low-level debuggers like DEBUG or SYMDEB. However, many of the commands deal with Windows itself. As you have probably guessed, Soft-Ice/W knows a lot about Windows.

Before we look at Soft-Ice/W's commands, let's look at how we would tell Soft-Ice/W to debug a C++ program. Again, we'll use the HDUMP example that ships with Borland C++. Like BCHKW, Soft-Ice/W understands the debugging information the compiler and linker generate, so it's just a matter of compiling HDUMP with debugging information turned on. Next, run WLDR, which Soft-Ice/W uses to load programs for debugging. WLDR also handles the task of getting your program's source code and symbols to Soft-Ice/W. Remember, Soft-Ice/W can't do file input/output when it's popped up, so it gets your symbol information while it can and saves it off in memory. After WLDR is finished, Soft-Ice/W kicks in and positions you at the start of your program (see fig. 8.12).

Once Soft-Ice/W has your program loaded, you can use it like a normal debugger. For example, you can press F8 to step through your code a line at a time. You can use one of Soft-Ice/W's many data display commands to look at the values of variables. You can set breakpoints and let your program run until a breakpoint fires.

```
EAX=00000000    EBX=00002000    ECX=00001000    EDX=00000000    ESI=00000000
EDI=000009BE    EBP=00000000    ESP=000025F0    EIP=00000000    o d I s Z a P c
CS=327F    DS=09BF    SS=09BF    ES=0CB7    FS=0000    GS=0000
────GDI.Alloc──────────────────────────byte────────────────PROT──(0)──
0897:000002E3 4E 17 10 F6 5D 71 2B 3C-FD 3C F4 3C 10 5D 71 2B    N...]q+<.<.<.]q+
0897:000002F3 F6 5D 71 2B ED 3C 10 3C-00 3F 3C 3F 3F ED 11 39    .]q+.<.<.?<??..9
────HDUMP.C────────────────────────────────────────────────PROT16──
00001:// Borland C++ - (C) Copyright 1991, 1992 by Borland International
00002:
00003://****************************************************************
00004://
00005:// program - Hdump.c
00006:// purpose - a windows program to dump a file in hex.
00007://
00008://****************************************************************
00009:
00010:#define  STRICT
00011:#include <windows.h>
───────────────────────────HDUMP───────────────────────
:src
:d cursfont
:stack
__WINMAINCALL at 2E9F:00B1 [?]
WINMAIN at 0887:001E [00141]
 [BP+000E] hInstance
 [BP+000C] hPrevInstance
 [BP+0008] lpszCmdLine
 [BP+0006] cmdShow
 [BP-0014] msg
_INITHDUMP at 0887:00A2 [00200]
 [BP+000E] cmdShow
 [BP+000A] lpszCmdLine
_INITHDUMPEVERY at 0887:01CA [00286]
 [BP+0008] cmdShow
 [BP-0022] tm
=> BC40RTL(01) at 371F:61F8 [?] through 371F:61E6
:g
Break Due to LDR
:task
TaskName    SS:SP        StackTop  StackBot  StackLow  TaskDB  hQueue  Events
NHOOKEXE    235F:20AC    0308      2232      1D40      25DF    24CF    0000
NAVTSRW     2487:49A2    2B5C      4A66      32E8      24AF    2497    0000
SYMEVNTX    2197:281A    0124      288E      219E      21BF    21A7    0000
MSWORD      29CF:92E0    576D      9364      753A      2F67    3467    0000
CLOCK       232F:1916    02E4      1A4E      1070      2357    233F    0001
NDW         1777:455A    067A      45E4      3728      0617    079F    0001
WLDR        0A57:3C20    2B42      3EAC      373A      0B47    0ACF    0001
HDUMP     * 09BF:25DA    0000      0000      0000      09EF    0000    0001
:
      Enter A Command Or ? For Help
```

Fig. 8.12. Soft-Ice/W after loading HDUMP.EXE.

The real power of Soft-Ice/W comes into play when you want to do things like watch a section of memory and stop when it changes, or if your program causes Windows to die unexpectedly. Soft-Ice/W's breakpoints are handled by the 386 itself. Your program runs at full speed until the breakpoint fires, which is not true under Turbo Debugger.

One of the more interesting uses of Soft-Ice/W is that you can (if you want to) debug multiple programs at the same time. As you can see in figure 8.12, Soft-Ice/W's `task` command lists all of the programs currently running under Windows (the current program, HDUMP, has an '*' after its name). There is nothing to prevent you from loading several programs with WLDR and setting breakpoints in each of them. Soft-Ice/W will keep track of what program is active and bring up the proper source code when any program stops.

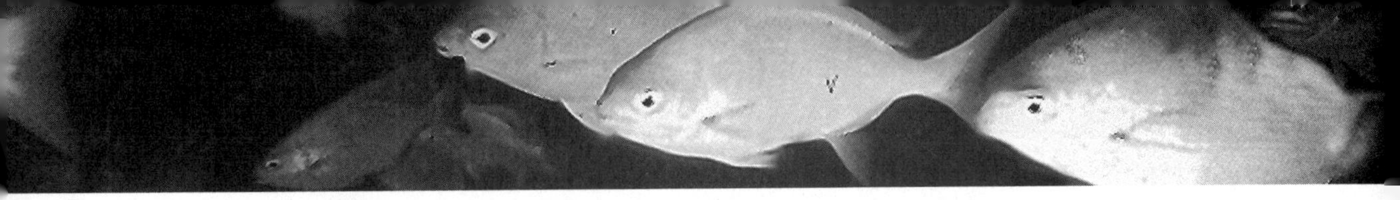

Like Turbo Debugger for Windows, Soft-Ice can work in either C/C++, assembly language or mixed mode. As figure 8.13 shows, you use the `src` command to toggle which mode you want. Figure 8.13 also shows that Soft-Ice/W knows about not only the globals in your code, but also throughout the Windows system. This brings up an important point: Remember that Soft-Ice/W is debugging *Windows*, not just your program. Everything in Windows is available to you, no matter what level it is at.

```
EAX=00000B96    EBX=00002D28    ECX=00003117    EDX=00000000    ESI=00000B96
EDI=00000896    EBP=000025AA    ESP=00002584    EIP=0000017C    o d I s z a P c
CS=0887   DS=0897   SS=0897   ES=3117   FS=0000   GS=0000   DS=02E3=0000
─────────────────────────────────────────────────byte──────PROT──(0)─
0030:00000000 8A 10 1C 01 F4 06 70 00-16 00 10 0D F4 06 70 00   ......p.......p.
0030:00000010 F4 06 70 00 54 FF 00 F0-52 EB 00 F0 A6 EA 00 F0   ..p.T...R.......
──────_INITHDUMPEVERY+0049────────────────────────────────PROT16─
0887:0000017A  MOV      SI,AX
00273    cursfont.lfHeight        = 14;
0887:0000017C  MOV      WORD PTR [_CURSFONT],000E
00274    cursfont.lfWidth         = 9;
0887:00000182  MOV      WORD PTR [_CURSFONT+02(02E5)],0009
00275    cursfont.lfEscapement    = 0;
0887:00000188  MOV      WORD PTR [_CURSFONT+04(02E7)],0000
00276    cursfont.lfOrientation   = 0;
0887:0000018E  MOV      WORD PTR [_CURSFONT+06(02E9)],0000
00277    cursfont.lfWeight        = FW_NORMAL;
0887:00000194  MOV      WORD PTR [_CURSFONT+08(02EB)],0190
────────────────────────────HDUMP(02)────────────────────
    0887:005C _INITHDUMPADDED
    0887:0078 _INITHDUMP
    0887:00AE _INITHDUMPFIRST
    0887:0131 _INITHDUMPEVERY
    0887:0233 _CLOSEHDUMP
    0887:024A ABOUT
    0887:0290 HDUMPWNDPROC
    0887:07C3 _SETUPSCROLL
    0887:08A4 _HDUMPPAINT
    0887:0A2B SNAPLINE
    0887:0B6B _DOFILEOPENDLG
    0887:0C0C FILEOPENDLGPROC
GLOBALS(0000)
    2E9F:0066 __INITAPPCALLED
    2E9F:00B1 __WINMAINCALL
    2E9F:00BC __CLEANUP
    2E9F:00CE __CHECKNULL
    2E9F:00CF __RESTOREZERO
    2E9F:00D0 __TERMINATE
    2E9F:00E5 __GETDGROUP
    2E9F:016E __ABORT
    2E9F:0186 _ABORT
    2E9F:0198 _ATEXIT
    2E9F:01CA _CHDIR
    2E9F:01E8 __DOS_GETFILEATTR
    2E9F:020E __DOS_SETFILEATTR
    2E9F:0232 ___ERRORMESSAGE
    2E9F:02CD _EXIT
:src
:
    Enter A Command Or ? For Help
```

Fig. 8.13. Another view of HDUMP's source code.

Tip: Some of Soft-Ice/W's commands are worth going over, since they will give you an idea of what kind of information and capabilities are available to you.

The BP commands allow you to set breakpoints on bytes, words, or double words, with the breakpoint firing if the location is read, written, or executed. Similarly, the BPR command allows you to set a breakpoint on a memory range. If you want to set a breakpoint on a code segment in a Windows program, you can use BPRW. You also can set breakpoints to occur on input/output port access (BPIO) or if a software interrupt occurs (BPINT). You can even set a breakpoint to occur if a certain Windows message (or range of messages) is sent to a window (BMSG).

Like most low-level debuggers, there are commands for displaying memory in a variety of formats and editing the contents of memory. Soft-Ice/W also knows about all the tables that Windows uses. Thus, you can look at the Global Descriptor Table (GDT), the Local Descriptor Table (LDT), a map of the current VxDs (VXD), and even a list of current window handles (HWND), window classes (CLASS), and virtual machines (VM). Figure 8.14 shows an example of a window handle list.

If you don't want to run Soft-Ice/W on one screen, you also can debug over a serial port or make use of a second monitor. If you do want to debug over a serial port, nu-Mega provides a program to control the debugging session from another PC.

Soft-Ice/W also is very configurable. Through a simple text-based configuration file, you can set up Soft-Ice/W the way you like. You also can reconfigure the keyboard to handle command strings the way you want. You can even configure whether or not Soft-Ice/W starts Windows for you automatically.

One thing must be mentioned about Soft-Ice/W, and that is its documentation. Like most products of this type, Soft-Ice/W's manual is fairly hard core. It tells you all you need to know, but it takes some time for the implications of what you can do with this tool to sink in.

nu-Mega drafted noted Windows programmer/columnist Martin Heller to write a 95-page book to accompany Soft-Ice/W that takes you on a knowledge-filled journey through the capabilities of Soft-Ice/W. It's both a great introduction and a helpful tutorial to this powerful product.

```
EAX=00000B96   EBX=00002D28   ECX=00003117   EDX=00000000   ESI=00000B96
EDI=00000896   EBP=000025AA   ESP=00002584   EIP=0000017C   o d I s z a P c
CS=0887  DS=0897   SS=0897   ES=3117   FS=0000   GS=0000   DS=02E3=0000
─────────────────────────────────────────────byte─────────PROT──(0)──
0030:00000000 8A 10 1C 01 F4 06 70 00-16 00 10 0D F4 06 70 00   ......p.......p.
0030:00000010 F4 06 70 00 54 FF 00 F0-52 EB 00 F0 A6 EA 00 F0   ..p.T...R.......
──HDUMP.C───────────────────────────────────────────────────────PROT16─
00267:                    );
00268:
00269:       // Get the display context.
00270:       hDC = GetDC(hWndMain);
00271:
00272:       // Build fixed screen font. Needed to display hex formated dump.
00273:       cursfont.lfHeight       =   14;
00274:       cursfont.lfWidth        =   9;
00275:       cursfont.lfEscapement   =   0;
00276:       cursfont.lfOrientation  =   0;
00277:       cursfont.lfWeight       =   FW_NORMAL;
─────────────────────────────────HDUMP────────────────────────────────
  1E00(1)      079F     NDW      QuickAccessGroup   282F:0D96
  20B0(2)      079F     NDW      QuickAccessDispl   158F:035C
  1834(1)      079F     NDW      QuickAccessGroup   282F:0D96
  1944(2)      079F     NDW      QuickAccessDispl   158F:035C
  15BC(1)      079F     NDW      QuickAccessGroup   282F:0D96
  1894(2)      079F     NDW      QuickAccessDispl   158F:035C
  178C(1)      079F     NDW      QuickAccessGroup   282F:0D96
  17E4(2)      079F     NDW      QuickAccessDispl   158F:035C
  017O(1)      079F     NDW      #32772             0457:6CA0
  18E4(1)      079F     NDW      QuickAccessGroup   282F:0D96
  19F4(2)      079F     NDW      QuickAccessDispl   158F:035C
  14DC(1)      079F     NDW      NFMWClass          282F:0D96
  154C(2)      079F     NDW      NGButtonBar:2      11BF:0000
  1E98(1)      24CF     NHOOKEXE NHOOKEXE           24DF:08FA
  174C(1)      079F     NDW      PROGMAN            1527:01B4
  16D0(1)      079F     NDW      QuickAccess        155F:02AA
  12DC(1)      079F     NDW      #00042             1FD7:0236
  1994(1)      2497     NAVTSRW  #32772             0457:6CA0
  1410(1)      2497     NAVTSRW  #32770             06E7:0429
  1A44(2)      2497     NAVTSRW  Static             06E7:2313
  1A8C(2)      2497     NAVTSRW  Static             2467:2B0A
  1AD4(2)      2497     NAVTSRW  Static             2467:2B0A
  1B1C(2)      2497     NAVTSRW  Static             2467:2B0A
  1B64(2)      2497     NAVTSRW  Static             2467:2B0A
  1BAC(2)      2497     NAVTSRW  Static             2467:2B0A
  1BF4(2)      2497     NAVTSRW  Button             2467:1CEA
  1C38(2)      2497     NAVTSRW  Button             2467:1CEA
  1D48(1)      233F     CLOCK    #32772             0457:6CA0
  1D9C(1)      233F     CLOCK    Clock              2337:1B9E
:
     Enter A Command Or ? For Help
```

Fig. 8.14. Soft-Ice/W listing of the current window hierarchy.

Soft-Ice/W is one of those tools that you wonder how you've lived without once you really need it. It's like having a powerful, low-level debugger that understands much of the high-level information you need. The fact that it doesn't get in the way of your program makes it a piece of cake to find those elusive, Windows-killing bugs. When

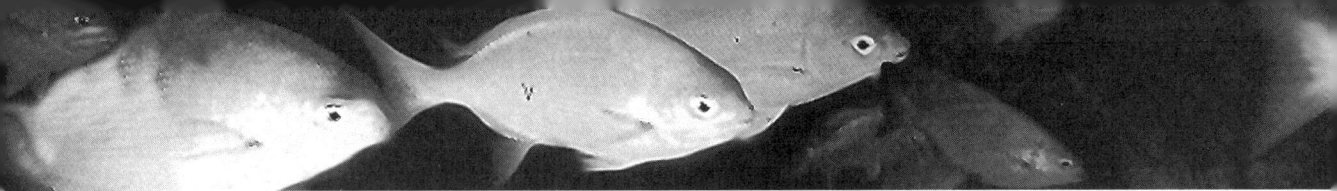

combined with a tool like Bounds Checker for Windows, it makes it possible to produce programs that simply don't have those annoying bugs. It's easy to see why nu-Mega gets so much praise for its tools.

WinScope

WinScope's purpose is fairly simple. It was designed to hook into Windows and capture events and API calls while an application runs. "Hey!" you say. "Doesn't TVIEW that comes with Bounds Checker do that? For that matter, don't Spy and Winsight do that?" Well, yes. But WinScope offers much more than Spy or Winsight. It also differs from Bounds Checker's TVIEW in several ways.

WinScope is designed *only* for watching events and API calls. Thus, it doesn't have some of the overhead that Bounds Checker does. Remember, it takes time for Bounds Checker to verify all that information it's processing. Secondly, WinScope also can act like a profiler, collecting information about how long each part of your program takes to work. Thirdly, it is much easier to tell WinScope what information to collect than it is with Bounds Checker. WinScope offers a very intuitive interface for controlling its collection of information. WinScope also is unique in that it lets you set breakpoints that fire when specific Windows events occur. If you are using a debugger (like Turbo Debugger), WinScope can transfer control when the breakpoint fires. Finally, WinScope offers *scripts,* which allow you to tell WinScope about your DLLs and data types. With scripts, WinScope can display your data the way you like.

WinScope installs with a standard Windows installation program. It has an optional VxD that it can install in your SYSTEM.INI file. However, according to the manual, this VxD is only used for the collection of timing information. It is not necessary for it to be installed for collecting information.

WinScope takes advantage of information Borland C++ has already placed in your .OBJ and .EXE files. Thus, it requires no special macros or libraries.

Like Bounds Checker for Windows, WinScope can either load your program for you or wait for your program to run. However, WinScope is unique in that it doesn't have to track an *executable* file. You can have it look for the creation of a specific window class.

WinScope is an MDI application, sporting eight different windows. However, six of these windows are used for specifying what you want WinScope to do. The remaining two windows are for the display of information about your program. Let's look at WinScope in action and make this a little clearer.

Figure 8.15 shows WinScope after running a trace on HDUMP.

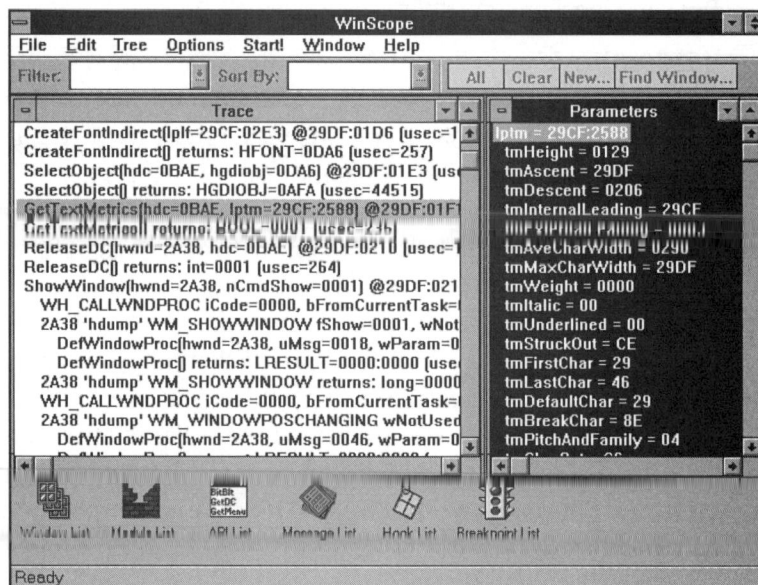

Fig. 8.15. WinScope displaying information about HDUMP.

Here, WinScope is showing the Trace and Parameter windows. The Trace window shows all events that WinScope was told to capture while a program executed. As you can see, the information is presented in a tree-like fashion, with messages and calls resulting from other calls indented below the call that started the whole process. For example, when HDUMP called the ShowWindow() function in the Windows API, this

resulted in a WH_CALLWNDPROC message, which allows applications to hook into the message chain before a message is sent to a window. Next, the window with handle 0x2A38 (HDUMP's main window) was sent a WM_SHOWWINDOW message, which HDUMP turned around and handed off to the default window procedure DefWindowProc(). The actual message chain goes on for quite a while, but you can see how WinScope is formatting this information for you.

The Parameter window shows the contents of any far pointers referenced in the Trace Window. In figure 8.15, we've clicked the GetTextMetrics() line, which causes WinScope to display the contents of the variable lptm. lptm happens to be a far pointer to a TEXTMETRIC structure, which WinScope knows how to display.

> **Note:** A TEXTMETRIC structure is a structure Windows uses to communicate information about fonts.

If you look closely at figure 8.15, you see that the lines of text are followed by the string (usec = nnnn). Unless told differently, WinScope keeps track of how long each message or function call takes to execute and how much time elapsed between one function call and the next. Figure 8.16 shows this a little better.

Take a look at the call tree for processing the UpdateWindow() call. The first line says that UpdateWindow() was called with a window handle of 0x2B9C. The code for UpdateWindow() is located at address 0x28EF:0225, and it's been 97 milliseconds since the last event occurred, in this case, since ShowWindow() returned.

Where did the value 97 come from, since the line clearly says 116 milleseconds? The times reported by WinScope are actually in units of 838 nanoseconds instead of milleseconds, so you must calculate the actual figure. In addition, if you are not running with the WinScope VxD installed, the times reported will be 20 percent too high. However, the relativeness of the times are accurate no matter what, so you can get a good idea of where your code is spending time.

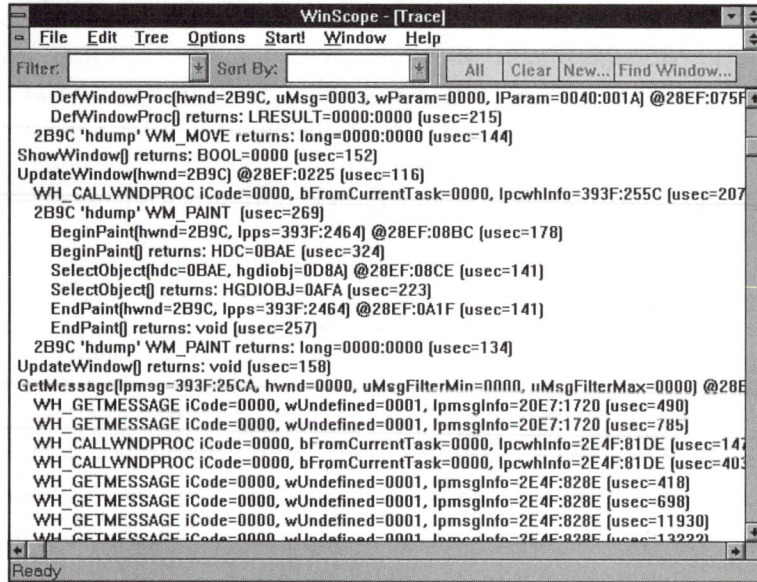

```
                              WinScope - [Trace]
   File   Edit   Tree   Options   Start!   Window   Help
 Filter:               |    Sort By:            |  |  All  | Clear | New... | Find Window...
          DefWindowProc(hwnd=2B9C, uMsg=0003, wParam=0000, lParam=0040:001A) @28EF:075F
          DefWindowProc() returns: LRESULT=0000:0000 (usec=215)
       2B9C 'hdump' WM_MOVE returns: long=0000:0000 (usec~144)
     ShowWindow() returns: BOOL=0000 (usec=152)
     UpdateWindow(hwnd=2B9C) @28EF:0225 (usec=116)
          WH_CALLWNDPROC iCode=0000, bFromCurrentTask=0000, lpcwhInfo=393F:255C (usec=207
       2B9C 'hdump' WM_PAINT (usec=269)
          BeginPaint(hwnd=2B9C, lpps=393F:2464) @28EF:08BC (usec=178)
          BeginPaint() returns: HDC=0BAE (usec=324)
          SelectObject(hdc=0BAE, hgdiobj=0D8A) @28EF:08CE (usec=141)
          SelectObject() returns: HGDIOBJ=0AFA (usec=223)
          EndPaint(hwnd=2B9C, lpps=393F:2464) @28EF:0A1F (usec=141)
          EndPaint() returns: void (usec=257)
       2B9C 'hdump' WM_PAINT returns: long=0000:0000 (usec=134)
     UpdateWindow() returns: void (usec=158)
     GetMessage(lpmsg=393F:25CA, hwnd=0000, uMsgFilterMin=0000, uMsgFilterMax=0000) @28E
          WH_GETMESSAGE iCode=0000, wUndefined=0001, lpmsgInfo=20E7:1720 (usec=490)
          WH_GETMESSAGE iCode=0000, wUndefined=0001, lpmsgInfo=20E7:1720 (usec=785)
          WH_CALLWNDPROC iCode=0000, bFromCurrentTask=0000, lpcwhInfo=2E4F:81DE (usec=147
          WH_CALLWNDPROC iCode=0000, bFromCurrentTask=0000, lpcwhInfo=2E4F:81DE (usec=403
          WH_GETMESSAGE iCode=0000, wUndefined=0001, lpmsgInfo=2E4F:828E (usec=418)
          WH_GETMESSAGE iCode=0000, wUndefined=0001, lpmsgInfo=2E4F:828E (usec=698)
          WH_GETMESSAGE iCode=0000, wUndefined=0001, lpmsgInfo=2E4F:828E (usec=11930)
          WH_GETMESSAGE iCode=0000, wUndefined=0001, lpmsgInfo=2E4F:828E (usec=13222)
 Ready
```

Fig. 8.16. A better view of the Trace window.

The times reported are delta times referring to the last "event" of that type. Thus, calls to functions show the time since the last call *returned*, but the return from a call shows how much time the call took to execute. Thus, at the end of the processing of `UpdateWindow()` (when `UpdateWindow()` returns), 132 milliseconds have passed (158 * .838).

Obviously, it takes time for WinScope to collect and store this information. Since what WinScope is doing can take time away from your program, you have several options to control *how* WinScope actually does this. WinScope captures tracing information to an in-memory buffer. You can specifiy how big this buffer is. When this buffer fills up, WinScope can do one of three things. First, it can page the buffer to disk. This lets you save as much tracing information as WinScope can generate, but at the cost of taking time away from your program while WinScope writes to disk. Second, it can reuse the buffer, which will cause the oldest events to be wiped. Finally, it can stop tracing.

WinScope provides several clues to let you know what it is doing. While it is capturing events, its icon background turns yellow to let you know

tracing information is being collected. When you stop capturing information (or WinScope fills up its buffer and has to stop), the icon's background turns blue. You can start and stop the capture of information with a simple keystroke; WinScope will beep to let you know it received the keystroke.

Telling WinScope what information you are interested in is extremely easy. WinScope uses several Windows to let you pick what messages, windows, API calls, and so on, you are interested in. They are organized in a logical, tree-like fashion. Let's look at this. Figure 8.17 shows the Window List; figure 8.18 shows the Module List.

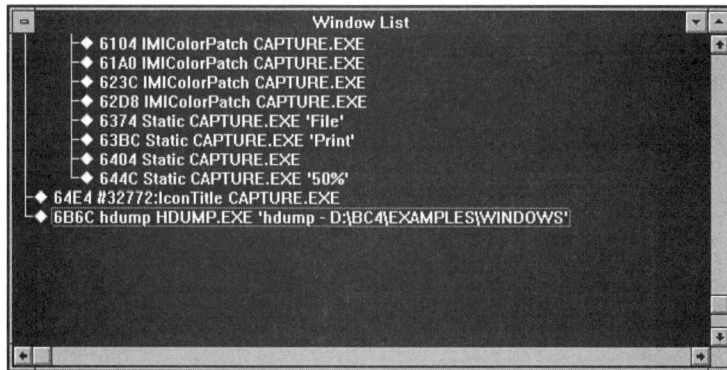

Fig. 8.17. WinScope's Window List.

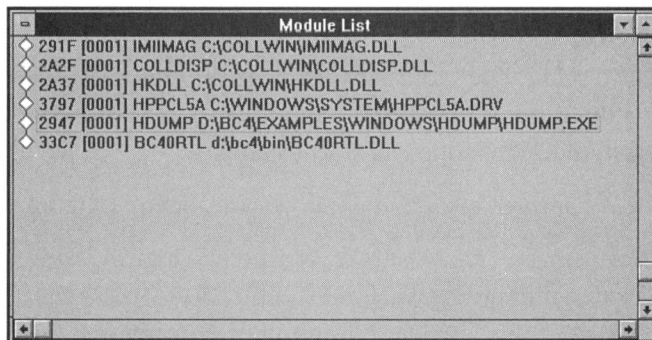

Fig. 8.18. WinScope's Module List.

As figure 8.17 shows, the Window List shows each window currently in the Windows system, with child windows indented under the parent window. Like all of WinScope's selection windows, when an entry is selected, it is highlighted to show that it is active. For each window, WinScope shows the window handle, the window class, the name of the program that created it, and the caption of the window. To select a window for tracing, you just click it. Clicking a parent window will select all the child windows.

For each of WinScope's selection windows, the buttons and combo-boxes below WinScope's menu bar control the display of information and allow you to select information on a global scale. The Filter control lets you select what information you want to see. In this case, it either can be "All" or "Selected." Similarly, the "Sort By" control lets you either view the list in "Parent-Child" format or sorted by window class.

The buttons are a little different. "All" lets you select all the entries in a window. This probably isn't very useful for the Window List, but it is definitely useful for windows like the Message window. The "Clear" button does the opposite: It turns off highlighting on all entries in a window. "Find" lets you search for a specific entry.

"New" is used to specify an entry that doesn't exist yet and is only available for the Window and Module Lists. For example, if you wanted to watch HDUMP when it loads (and you haven't told WinScope to load it), you can specify "New" and create an entry in the Module List. WinScope will then wait for that particular module to load and then start tracing. The same is true for the Window List; you can specify a specific window class to watch for. As soon as that window class gets registered, WinScope will start tracing.

The other three selection windows are shown in figure 8.19.

As you can see, each list is organized in a logical fashion and can be sorted in different ways. For example, The Message List can be sorted by "Msg Group," which differentiates messages by their "type" (Mouse, Non-Client, Clipboard, Combobox, etc.), "Message Class" (which orders them the same way they are ordered in the Windows SDK

manuals), by message value, or alphabetically. Similarly, the API list can be sorted by DLL, ordinal number, call class (where functions are sorted by what they "do"), and so on.

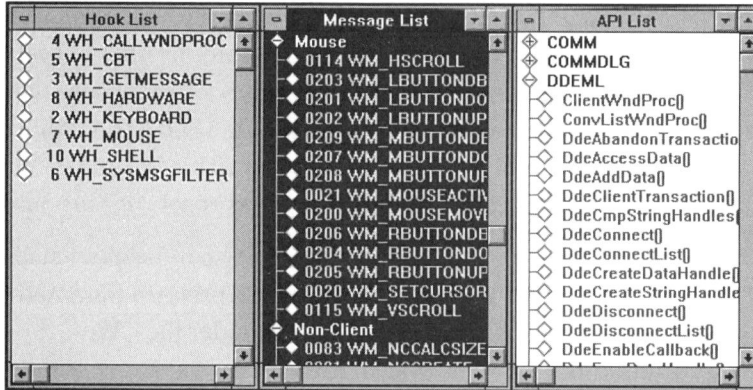

Fig. 8.19. WinScope's Hook, Message and API Lists.

These lists make selecting what you want to trace extremely easy. Want to only trace mouse messages? Just use the "Clear" button to deselect all messages and then scroll down to the "Mouse" section and select one line. WinScope won't bother to collect information about any other messages or API calls.

WinScope also allows you to set breakpoints, so that it will gain control when certain events occur. Figure 8.20 shows the Breakpoint List and the dialog that lets you specify where a breakpoint should fire.

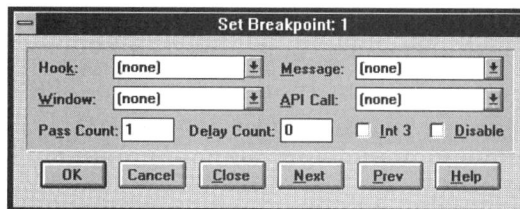

Fig. 8.20. WinScope's Breakpoint List.

WinScope allows you to set up to 16 breakpoints. You can specify a breakpoint to fire when a certain message occurs to a window, when an API call occurs, or when a hook gets control. You also can specify a "Pass Count," which is how many times the breakpoint should occur before it actually "fires" and returns control to WinScope. The "Delay Count" field is used to specify that a certain number of events should occur after a breakpoint fires before WinScope stops tracing and returns control to you. If you check the "Int 3" box, the WinScope issues an INT 3 to pass control to your debugger. This is quite useful since it can be difficult to set these kinds of breakpoints in Turbo Debugger.

WinScope can be extended through the use of *scripts*, which are little programs that tell WinScope how to interpret API parameters and message values. Scripts look a little like C header files. WinScope ships with several scripts that describe all the Windows messages and DLLs (although you don't get the source to these scripts). Two utilities are provided with WinScope to handle scripts: the Script Extractor and the Script Compiler.

The Script Compiler does just what its name implies. It takes a script file and turns it into a binary form that WinScope understands. The Script Extractor takes a given .EXE or .DLL and extracts the necessary information to help you build a script. It can only extract the information about what functions are in a module; it is up to you to describe any custom messages or data types that are used by your module.

These two utilities are unique in one sense: they are both DOS and Windows programs. That is, you can run them as a Windows app from Program Manager or as DOS utilities from the DOS command line. The Periscope Company took advantage of the ability to link a DOS executable on the front of a Windows executable and produced utilities that can be run no matter where you are.

You can think of WinScope as a "Windows Message Debugger." It's not a low-level utility designed to help you find bugs in your code. Rather, it enables you to see how your program reacts to Windows messages and what happens when you call the Windows API. It also enables you

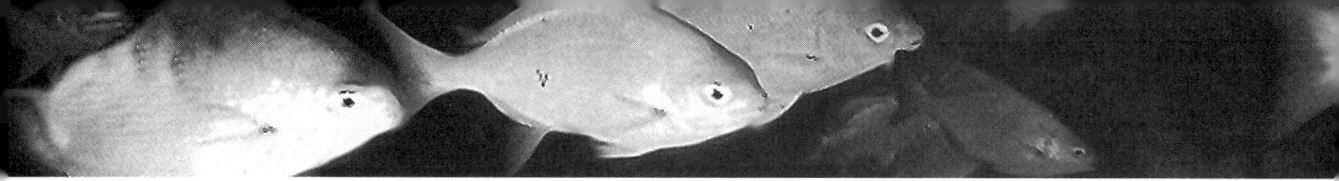

to see where your programs are spending their time. Its user interface is quite intuitive and it manages to be very "hidden" while it is working away. In short, it's easy to see why it won a *PC Magazine* Technical Excellence award.

Where Can I Get These Tools?

Here are the addresses for all vendors listed in this chapter. The version number specified is current as of this writing.

PC-Lint v6.00 is available from

> Gimpel Software
> 3207 Hogarth Lane
> Collegeville, PA 19426
> (610) 584-4261

Bounds Checker for Windows 2.02 and Soft-Ice for Windows 1.4 are available from

> nu-Mega Technologies
> P.O. Box 7780
> Nashua, NH 03060
> (603) 889-2386

WinScope v1.1 is available from

> The Periscope Company
> 1475 Peachtree Street, Suite 100
> Atlanta, GA 30309
> (404) 888-5335

From Here...

The process of finding bugs in your program is a never-ending one. While innovations in integrated environments can help reduce the work it takes to find bugs, it is still true that the process of bug finding is a learning experience. Each time you get a little better at it.

➤ For information on writing nearly bug-free C code, see Chapter 4, "Optimizing C."

➤ For tips on designing C++ programs that are the most efficient possible, see Chapter 5, "Optimizing C++."

➤ For help on using the Turbo Debugger more efficiently, see Chapter 7, "Debugging Tips and Tricks."

➤ For information on handling common exceptions within your code, see Chapter 18, "Exception Handling."

K&R Implementation Secrets

by Greg Perry

This chapter discusses *K&R*, the nickname for the most famous C reference manual named *The C Programming Language*. K&R contains a reference for the complete C programming language, but many of the more detailed implementation details are left out for brevity.

One of the most important C topics is dynamic memory allocation. This chapter explores some of the more esoteric aspects of dynamic memory allocation and explains several of the lesser-known memory allocation elements, such as error-checking and reallocation.

You'll also learn how Borland C++'s defined macros expand on those described in K&R and you'll see code examples that use many of those macros. Finally, you will learn some header file techniques and explanations that K&R does not explain.

K&R Belongs on Every Programmer's Shelf

Without argument, the pinnacle of C reference books, the epitome of C programming, and the book every student of C first hates and then loves, is Brian W. Kernighan and Dennis M. Ritchie's *The C Programming Language*, now in its second printing. Without one wasted word, *The C Programming Language* provides C programmers with a complete description of the ANSI C programming language, along with many of C's recommended usages and suggested elements of style.

The brevity of K&R (as it is known throughout the C programming community) is its strength. When you want a solid, straight-to-the-point, concrete answer to a question about C, K&R gives you just that. K&R leaves little room for ambiguity, a welcome relief from most compiler reference manuals that seem to raise as many questions as they answer.

Although K&R readers promote the strengths of K&R, they also know that K&R does not take the time to dive into some of the extended nuances of the language. If K&R supplied an example of every aspect of C and gave tutorials on each command, function, and header file, the book would quickly lose its focus and grow to a tremendous length. That is why C programmers still need the help of other books, magazines, journals, classes, and programmers' advice from time to time.

> **Note:** K&R concentrates solely on the C programming language. Therefore, C is this chapter's primary focus. When needed, the chapter makes references to C++. Chapters 11 and 12 concentrate solely on the C++ language by describing C++'s K&R equivalent: Bjarne Stroustrup's *The C++ Programming Language*.

This chapter expands upon some of the aspects of C that K&R did not take a lot of time to tell you about. Most agree that a solid foundation of K&R is the prerequisite to a solid foundation of C. (Most also agree that a solid foundation in C is the prerequisite to a solid foundation in C++.)

If you look at the bookshelves of any bookstore today, you will see scores of books on C. There is no way to expand on all of K&R's subjects here, and there is no need to. This chapter selects a few key topics covered in K&R and expands on those topics, giving you some additional insight that might prove helpful as you write programs with Borland C++.

> **Note:** Some of this chapter's topics, such as the in-memory formats of C's data types, may not directly change the way you now program. Nevertheless, knowing what is going on under the hood helps improve programming decisions you often make, such as deciding between efficiency, limited memory, and storage space.

A Heap of Memory

If you've written many C programs (as this book assumes), you've often allocated and deallocated heap memory. The heap seems to affect programmers differently depending on their stage of programming expertise. Scc if you agree with the following:

> ➤ The heap frustrates beginners because of its reliance on pointers and its replacement of standard arrays and other variables for many purposes.

> ➤ The heap elates intermediate C programmers by giving them power they may have never had in other programming languages.

> ➤ The heap frustrates experts because a large number of errors appear in programs that use the heap, especially advanced programs that rely on huge amounts of heap allocations. Bugs introduced because of incorrect heap management are some of the least obvious and most difficult to trace.

This section shows you ways to use and manage the heap that K&R could not go into. You explore the heap's inner-workings and learn how you can manage the heap more skillfully.

What Exactly Is the Heap?

If you've been using the heap for a while, you understand what the heap is and how to allocate and deallocate its memory. Even though you've used the heap for your applications, however, there are some underlying aspects of the heap that you should know about. Knowing more about the heap will help you debug program problems that arise from time to time.

> **Note:** Believe it or not, you'll look long and hard before you'll find the word heap mentioned in K&R. K&R calls the heap your operating system memory from which you can dynamically request blocks of memory for your application

As figure 9.1 shows, the heap is the free RAM memory your computer has left over once the operating system (including any add-on environments such as Windows), the user's program, the program's static data areas (for global variables and the like), and the stack consume their memory. Actually, the heap and the stack both share the free space because, as with the heap, the stack grows and shrinks over time. An extremely large stack (built through lots of local variables and many layers of function calls) can take away free heap space and a largely allocated heap takes away from stack space.

Figure 9.1 is rather simplistic so that we can focus on the heap. The user's program area might be shared by more than one program at any one time, depending on whether you've got TSRs (*terminate-and-stay-resident programs*) loaded or if you're running more than one task from within Windows. Each program then has its own static area for variables. Also, the operating system area consists of more than just operating system code; it includes device drivers and environment variables. The memory model you choose might also affect the exact layout and order of the heap. Chapter 10, "Extending K&R's C," discusses the specific differences of Borland C++'s memory models.

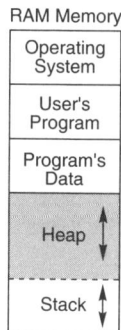

Fig. 9.1. The heap is left-over free RAM memory.

To keep such stack and heap conflicts from occurring, and to ensure that every attempt you make to allocate memory works, be sure to check your allocation function's return values. One of the advantages C++ brings to the programmer's table is the `set_new_handler()` function (supported by Borland C++), which decreases the amount of tedious error checking you have to perform. Nevertheless, the foundation of a good C program is extensive, and sometimes tedious, memory allocation error-checking. A later section entitled "Watch Out" describes some of the ins and outs of proper allocation error-checking.

No free() Lunch!

Use the heap for allocating and deallocating (*freeing*) memory as needed. If every function in your program needs to use the same 100-value floating-point array, there is no advantage to using the heap. As a matter of fact, the heap requires more overhead than a static (global) or dynamic (local) array would take. Every time you allocate a section of heap memory, C stores hidden overhead information about that section so that a subsequent `free()` properly deallocates every byte needed and not one byte more.

Use the heap only when a portion of your program needs storage so that you allocate that memory only when you need it. Dynamic allocation takes execution time and the overhead just described consumes extra storage. The heap is *great* when you need its on-the-fly expanding storage ability and efficiency. Overhead should be a secondary consideration in most cases instead of a primary fear of using the heap.

Tip: Use dynamic heap memory when you want to allocate more than 50 array elements. Fewer than 50 elements require allocation time overhead, and you spend a lot of extra bookkeeping memory relative to the few bytes you allocate. Arrays over 50 elements easily justify the overhead of dynamic allocation. Of course, if you need the array to be static, you have to use a regular global or local array variable.

Allocating Issues

In a perfect world, the runtime system would keep your heap defragmented. C has never been accused of being perfect (one can be likable without being perfect). In a program that allocates and deallocates frequently, holes quickly appear in the heap. C does not clean up the heap. It's true that if you allocate three sets of 100 doubles and deallocate those three sets at the same time, you'd *probably* be left with a defragmented heap. Rarely, however, does your application

allow such clean allocation order. Often, you allocate several sets of memory, all different sizes, and deallocate pieces of memory in a different order.

As figure 9.2 shows, you can end up with a heap that has a large number of bytes free, but not one section large enough to satisfy a single `malloc()` request. In effect, such a heap is full and there is little you can do about the situation.

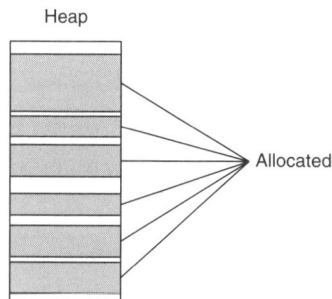

Fig. 9.2. Memory, memory everywhere, and not a byte to `malloc()`.

> **Note:** Suppose the designers of a C compiler decide to give you a constantly defragmented heap. In doing so, they violate ANSI C, but that's secondary to the fact that they are also giving you a lesser C product. C's strength lies in its efficiency. Defragmenting C's heap (as QBasic does, inefficiently, with its string space) slows your programs down. Depending on the amount of fragmentation, your C programs could come to a virtual halt at times. The spirit of C is then violated, which is a harsher crime than the ANSI C violation.

Tip: You can write your own allocation function that initially (the first time it's called) allocates a huge section of the heap. Your array of pointers can then dole out sections of that area as the rest of the program requests the memory. If needed, you can perform your own fragmentation in this way. This is not really a *tip* but a *hindrance* because such routines can be error-prone and probably waste much more of your time in programming than you'll benefit in runtime efficiency, except in rare instances where you allocate and free many different sizes of heap memory many times within the same program.

You cannot know what is in the allocated heap space if you use `malloc()` to allocate memory. For example, consider the following section of code:

```
ptr = (int *)malloc(40 * sizeof(int));
for (cnt=0; cnt<10; cnt++)
  {
    ptr[cnt] = cnt;
  }
free(ptr);
ptr = (int *)malloc(40 * sizeof(int));
  /* You DON't know what's in the heap memory
     pointed to by ptr! */
```

Despite the fact that `free()` just freed a block of the heap that was immediately allocated again with an identical `malloc()`, your program cannot rely on knowing what *any* of the allocated heap's values contain. The operating system or another task may have accessed the heap between the `free()` and the second `malloc()`.

Note: The `ptr` pointer is known as a *dangling pointer* once you free the heap memory. `ptr` still contains a valid address because `free()` does not change `ptr`. `free()` simply releases the pointed-to memory back to the deallocated heap store. The only way to use `ptr` safely after the previous code's `free()` is to use `ptr` with another memory allocation function call, as done at the end of the code.

If you were to make successive calls to `malloc()` (or a mixture of `malloc()`, `calloc()`, and any other allocation functions), there is no guarantee that each of those allocated sections appear back-to-back in memory. Therefore, these three sequential calls to `malloc()`:

```
p1 = (float *)malloc(100 * sizeof(float));
p2 = (float *)malloc(100 * sizeof(float));
p3 = (float *)malloc(100 * sizeof(float));
```

do *not* do the same thing as a single `malloc()` that allocates three hundred `float`s like this:

```
pLarge = (float *)malloc(300 * sizeof(float));
```

In the first trio of statements, three separate and possibly non-contiguous sections of the heap are allocated, making a total of three hundred floating-point allocated positions somewhere on the heap. The last statement also allocated three hundred floating-point allocated positions on the heap, but those three-hundred positions are guaranteed to be contiguous.

There is a way to know what the heap contains when you allocate the heap. The `calloc()` (*clear allocate*) initializes your newly allocated heap memory to zero. `calloc()` acts just like `malloc()`, but `calloc()`'s arguments differ a bit. Here is the prototype for `calloc()`:

```
void * calloc(size_t nobj, size_t size);
```

Consider the following simple program:

```
#include <stdio.h>
#include <stdlib.h>
main()
{
  int * cPtr;
  int cnt;
  cPtr = (int *)calloc(45, sizeof(int));
  for (cnt=0; cnt<45; cnt++)
    {
      printf("Value %2d: %1d\t", cnt, *(cPtr + cnt));
    }
  return 0;
}
```

The `calloc()` ensures that C initializes each allocated integer to zero. If you were to run this program, here are the results you'd get:

```
Value  0: 0      Value  1: 0      Value  2: 0      Value  3: 0      Value  4: 0
Value  5: 0      Value  6: 0      Value  7: 0      Value  8: 0      Value  9: 0
Value 10: 0      Value 11: 0      Value 12: 0      Value 13: 0      Value 14: 0
Value 15: 0      Value 16: 0      Value 17: 0      Value 18: 0      Value 19: 0
Value 20: 0      Value 21: 0      Value 22: 0      Value 23: 0      Value 24: 0
Value 25: 0      Value 26: 0      Value 27: 0      Value 28: 0      Value 29: 0
Value 30: 0      Value 31: 0      Value 32: 0      Value 33: 0      Value 34: 0
Value 35: 0      Value 36: 0      Value 37: 0      Value 38: 0      Value 39: 0
Value 40: 0      Value 41: 0      Value 42: 0      Value 43: 0      Value 44: 0
```

You might wonder why `calloc()` requires two arguments when `malloc()` requires only one. With `malloc()`, you must supply the total number of heap bytes to allocate. With `calloc()`, you must supply the size of each *object* you want to allocate (via the `nobj` argument) and then you supply the number of those objects (via the `size` argument).

> **Caution:** Don't think the term *object* here necessarily coincides with the C++/OOP term *object*. *Object* in `calloc()`'s can be a variable of an intrinsic data type (such as `int` or `double`) or a `struct` that you've defined.

The starting address boundary of the allocated data can affect performance and sometimes cause obscure bugs to slip into your code. Be very careful to follow `calloc()`'s requested arguments faithfully. For example, if you were allocating 350 2-byte integers using `calloc()`, you could do this:

```
pInt350 = (int *)calloc(350, 2);
```

It's strongly suggested that you use `sizeof()` instead of hardcoding a data type's storage requirement as done with the second argument, 2. Nevertheless, a case can be made that if you're using your own compiler, Borland C++, and you know that regular `signed int`s consume two bytes each (they do), you are free to allocate using this knowledge.

The following seems to be equivalent; the problem is that sometimes such a statement *is* equivalent:

```
pInt350 = (int *)calloc(2, 350);
```

Both of these `calloc()` calls appear to perform the same allocation, but there is a possibility that the second lays out the allocated data differently. Although you won't get into trouble with integers, memory boundaries might get you into sizing trouble when you allocate structures. The bottom line is that you should always send, as `calloc()`'s first argument, the number of values you want allocated, and as the second argument, the size of the data type of those values.

> **Note:** As with `malloc()`, `calloc()` returns NULL if the allocation request failed. See the section named "Watch Out" for more details on allocation failures.

Always be aware of a function's requested arguments as just shown. Notice K&R's prototype for `malloc()`:

```
void *malloc(size_t size);
```

As you can see, `malloc()` can return a section of allocated memory as large as `size_t`. `size_t` is defined by Borland C++ as an `unsigned int` (16 bits wide). Therefore, you can allocate a maximum amount of approximately 64K of memory with a single `malloc()`. (It's interesting to note that ANSI C defines `size_t` so as to allow only 32,767 bytes.) That 64K limit decreases the more stack-based data that your program consumes. Also, the memory model you use affects how much heap space is available.

If you ever allocate memory with `malloc()`, and then subsequent data-entry or disk file contents require that you expand the size of that allocated memory, `realloc()` reallocates heap memory for you. The following program first allocates ten integers, fills those integers with the values from 1 to 10, and then reallocates the heap space to double the size of the integer area.

```
#include <stdio.h>
#include <stdlib.h>
main()
{
  int * iPtr;
```

```
int cnt;
iPtr = (int *)malloc(10 * sizeof(int));
for (cnt=0; cnt<10; cnt++)
    {
        iPtr[cnt] = cnt+1;
    }

/* Now that they're filled, reallocate */
iPtr = realloc(iPtr, 20 * sizeof(int));

/* Print the first ten values of the new space */
printf("After the reallocation:\n");
for (cnt=0; cnt<10; cnt++)
    {
        printf("%d ", iPtr[cnt]);
    }

/* Fill the remaining ten spaces */
for (cnt=10; cnt<20; cnt++)
    {
        iPtr[cnt] = cnt+1;
    }

/* The next ten values */
printf("\nThe second ten values:\n");
for (cnt=10; cnt<20; cnt++)
    {
        printf("%d ", iPtr[cnt]);
    }

return 0;
}
```

Here is the program's output:

```
After the reallocation:

1 2 3 4 5 6 7 8 9 10

The second ten values:

11 12 13 14 15 16 17 18 19 20
```

Each call to `realloc()` must contain, as `realloc()`'s first argument, a pointer you used previously in `malloc()`. C (and, of course, C++ if you use these functions) does let you specify NULL for `calloc()`'s first argument. If you specify NULL, C allocates a new section of the heap just as if you'd called `malloc()`.

`realloc()` does *not* expand the space previously occupied by the original `malloc()` or `calloc()`. `realloc()` only *seems* to do so. The pointer returned

by `realloc()` is completely different from its original value before `realloc()`. However, as the previous code shows, `realloc()` copies all data from the old section to the new section. (If you use `realloc()` to shrink the size of allocated memory, C copies all of the original values up to the cut-off point for the new size.) `realloc()` returns a null pointer if the reallocation fails.

Is the memory limit, `size_t`, imposed by Borland really a limit? You rarely need to allocate more heap space than that. Although you could conceivably need that much space, you will not often need more than 64K allocated all at once. Instead, you are wiser to allocate in smaller blocks each time you need a little more.

What if you did run into that special occasion when `size_t` wouldn't allow enough heap memory for a single allocation? (This limit is not imposed in the large memory models; see the next tip for details.) Borland C++ goes beyond K&R (and ANSI C) to provide `farmalloc()` for such a large allocation. Here is the prototype for `farmalloc()`:

```
void far * farmalloc(unsigned long);
```

A *far pointer* is a pointer not limited to the 8088's segmented architecture. To reach a particular address, PCs combine two values, a *segment address* and an *offset address*, to form a single address because the original PCs did not contain registers large enough to hold a complete memory address. By using a far pointer, you are not limited to a 64K pointer addressing scheme (the size of a segment).

> **Tip:** If you compile using a compact, large, or huge memory model, using `far` is redundant because the compact, large, and huge pointers consume four bytes of memory and can hold complete unsegmented addresses.

Borland's `farmalloc()` lets you allocate, in a single step, as much RAM memory as is available at the time you call `farmalloc()`. You must use far pointers to point to such heap memory, which means that you simply define your pointers with the `far` qualifier.

Caution: Don't compile in Borland's tiny memory model if you want to use `farmalloc()`. The tiny memory model does not allow `farmalloc()` calls.

Consider the following section of code:

```
float far * pValues; /* Defines a far floating-point pointer */
pValues = (float far *) farmalloc(10000UL * sizeof(float));

    /* pValues now points to a 10,000 value
       floating-point array on the heap */

farfree(pValues);
```

As you can see, when defining the pointer to point to the heap, you need to declare the `far` keyword in the pointer's definition. `farmalloc()` requires an `unsigned long` argument, so the `UL` constant qualifier ensures that the `10000` constant formed the correct data type. (C converts the product, the answer to `10000UL * sizeof(float)`, to `unsigned long` due to the `UL`.)

What about the `farfree()` in the code? Borland C++ requires that you use `farfree()`, not simply `free()`, to free *far heap* memory. The *near heap* is the heap that lies outside your program's default data segment and is accessible with the regular pointer variables you are used to. The far heap is the heap memory that lies outside your program's default data segment, depending on your compiler's memory model (small, compact, large, or whatever). When you need access to more than 64K, as just discussed, you are accessing the far heap.

There also are far heap equivalent function calls, `farcalloc()` and `farrealloc()`, that work like their `calloc()` and `realloc()` near heap cousins.

The following *bottom-line* rules exist for `farfree()` and `free()`:

➤ When using `calloc()`, `malloc()`, and `realloc()`, use `free()` to free the memory.

➤ When using Borland's `farcalloc()`, `farmalloc()`, and `farrealloc()`, use `farfree()` to return the memory to the heap.

➤ If you use the compact, large, or huge memory models, your choice of heaps is not relevant because Borland C++ automatically uses the far heap (and far pointers).

Watch Out

`malloc()`, `free()`, and the related memory allocation functions require extensive error checking. Don't allocate without making sure the allocation worked. K&R states that `malloc()` returns the NULL value (defined in `stdio.h`) if `malloc()` fails.

There are rare instances when checking the return value of `malloc()` against NULL can cause problems. Some programmers recommend that you always compare `malloc()`'s (and `calloc()`'s and `realloc()`'s) value to `0`, not NULL. NULL pointers aren't always implemented in all compilers consistently. Even though you're using Borland C++ now with this book, and NULL seems to work consistently with Borland C++, you'll be developing better habits for the future if you compare against `0` (the *false* condition).

> **Note:** By the way, `free()` does not return a value. If you attempt to free memory by using a previously freed pointer or an invalid pointer (one not pointing to properly allocated memory), subsequent allocation attempts fail or produce runtime errors.

You also must be extremely careful not to write past the end of your allocated heap. In other words, if you allocate 100 bytes on the heap, don't write to the 101st byte. This warning is obvious to most programmers. Nevertheless, the warning is always justified in light of the fact that Borland C++ does not tell you if you've written outside the allocated memory's bounds. The heap is yours to do with what you please.

In the same way that K&R's C doesn't care if you write outside an array's boundaries, K&R's `malloc()`, as well as Borland's, doesn't care if you write to the heap using a pointer that allocated a different area of heap space.

> **Note:** If Borland C++ spent a lot of its runtime checking your array bounds and your heap allocation boundaries, every time you accessed memory, your programs would slow to a crawl. The lack of bounds checking is worth the efficiency trade-off, as long as you are a careful programmer.

Although the debugger is extremely useful for checking heap contents, there is also a runtime function named `heapcheck()` (prototyped in alloc.h) that returns a heap verification value. Here is the prototype for `heapcheck()`:

```
int heapcheck(void);
```

`heapcheck()` returns one of the three values listed in Table 9.1. The `heapcheck()` function is only available for DOS, Win 32, and OS/2 Borland C++ applications.

Table 9.1. The heapcheck() Return Values

Return Value	Description
_HEAPEMPTY	You have yet to allocate heap memory.
_HEAPOK	The heap is valid.
_HEAPCORRUPT	You've corrupted the heap by writing outside allocated memory.

The following program demonstrates the `heapcheck()` function. The program calls `heapcheck()` before allocating memory, after allocating memory, and after corrupting the heap to show the three return values. The `heapMsg()` function receives `heapcheck()`'s return value and prints an appropriate message, as determined by the `switch` statement. See if you can spot why the heap was corrupted.

Listing 9.1. The heapcheck() Function Monitors the Heap

```c
#include <alloc.h>
#include <stdio.h>
void heapMsg(int);    /* heapcheck()'s message function */
main()
{
  float *heapPtr;
  int heapRet;      /* heapcheck()'s return value */
  int cnt;

  /* Before allocating, check the heap */
  heapRet = heapcheck();
  heapMsg(heapRet);

  /* Allocate and then check the heap */
  heapPtr = (float *)malloc(50 * sizeof(float));
  heapRet = heapcheck();
  heapMsg(heapRet);

  /* Corrupt and then check the heap */
  for (cnt=0; cnt<=50; cnt++)
      {
          *(heapPtr+cnt) = (float)cnt;
      }
  heapRet = heapcheck();
  heapMsg(heapRet);
  return 0;
}
/****************************************************/
void heapMsg(int heapVal)
{
  switch (heapVal)
      { case _HEAPEMPTY :
            printf("There are no values yet on the heap.\n");
        break;
         case _HEAPOK :
         printf("The heap is fine.\n");
         break;
        case _HEAPCORRUPT :
         printf("The heap now has a problem.\n");
         break;
      }
  return;
}
```

Here is the program's output:

```
There are no values yet on the heap.

The heap is fine.

The heap now has a problem.
```

Notice that `malloc()`'s return value was checked for an error despite the fact that the program uses `heapcheck()` later to verify the heap. `heapcheck()` does not replace `malloc()`'s return value checking, and you should check `malloc()`'s (and `calloc()`'s and `realloc()`'s) return value to ensure that your specific heap request was satisfied.

Do you see how the heap was corrupted? Only 50 floating-point values were allocated on the heap, but the program wrote 51 floating-point values to the heap. The `for` loop's `cnt<=50` reads `cnt<50`. The 51st value triggered the last `heapcheck()`'s return value.

Using Common Macros

Table 9.2 describes five common, but seldom-used, macros that Borland calls *predefined global identifiers* and that K&R calls *predefined names*.

Table 9.2. Predefined Global Identifiers

Macro Name	Data Type	Description
__DATE__	String	The date that the current file was compiled.
__FILE__	String	Name of the current file being compiled.
__LINE__	Decimal	The line number of the source file being compiled.
__STDC__	1	Defined as 1 if, and only if, you compile using the ANSI keywords option. Undefined otherwise.
__TIME__	String	The time that the current file was compiled.

The reason these are called *predefined* global identifiers is because you don't have to include any header files to use these constants.

Tip: Use the data type column so you know just how to use these values. In other words, if you need to print the value of the `__TIME__` constant using `printf()`, you use the `%s` conversion character.

It's important that you realize these constants contain values that were valid *at the time the source code containing these constants was compiled.* Therefore, if you print the value of `__TIME__`, you won't see the current time. C replaces these constants with their actual values upon compilation. If you want a current system date or time, you must use a date or time function to return the current date or time.

Programmers often use these identifiers as debugging aids. There is another less-obvious reason for using `__TIME__` and `__DATE__` that you should tuck away for future reference. Sometimes, you write time-sensitive code that contains facts applicable to the current date, but which could change in the future. For example, the following printed messages describe a state of affairs that may need changing at a later time:

```
The following inventory figures were calculated using
accounting principles in effect on Jun 14 1995.

For purposes of international time zone calculations, the
following lab results were computed at 14:08:09.
```

If new accounting principles go into effect that require changing the inventory figures, or if the lab results require later chemicals, the source code *has* to be updated with new calculations and recompiled. There is no question about the date of the programs' code that produced these output lines. Use the predefined macros for debugging.

When debugging, the `__DATE__` and `__TIME__` values let you determine the time and date that you compiled executable programs. In today's programming world, with project makefile capabilities such as those that Borland C++ contains, you may not use `__DATE__` and `__TIME__` as much as programmers did when they had to track more of their own source code versions and recompiles.

The __LINE__ macro displays the source code at the point of the __LINE__'s location. In other words, the following three statements:

```
printf("%d\n", __LINE__);
printf("%d\n", __LINE__);
printf("%d\n", __LINE__);
```

always print three sequential numbers and those numbers correspond to the location of each `printf()` in the source code. Consider the following output:

```
Your printer doesn't seem to be responding. If you need
help, call Jim at x321 and tell him that line 5323 of
AR320.C produced this error.
```

In a business with computer support personnel, such error messages help both the user and the support people who must fix the user's problems. Such messages tell the user, in simple language, about the problem. The user might know enough to figure out that the printer is out of paper or is off-line. However, the user also might *not* know that much. Therefore, the user is then told exactly who to call for help. A __LINE__ macro tells the support person which line triggered the problem, and the __FILE__ macro tells the support person which compiled source code the user was running at the time of the error. Given all this help, user's problems should not be as frustrating as they otherwise could be.

__STDC__ is useful if you need to know about the target compiler's settings. The __STDC__ macro is only defined if ANSI C compiler settings are in effect. It is the compiler vendor's responsibility to ensure that __STDC__ is defined and that Borland does support __STDC__. Therefore, you cannot arbitrarily test __STDC__ with an `if` like this:

```
if (__STDC__)       /* Invalid! */
   { /* Here if ANSI C settings */ }
```

because __STDC__ may not even be defined, and you get a compile error if __STDC__ is not defined. You must use preprocessor directives to see if __STDC__ is defined like this:

```
#ifdef STDC
  printf("ANSI C in effect\n");
#endif
```

Although most of today's computers are capable of clearing their screens, ANSI C still does not believe it. Therefore, if you write programs for good old Borland C++, but you also want to port those programs to a minicomputer that does not recognize Borland's language extensions, the following section of code uses either Borland's clear screen function or prints 25 blank lines to scroll the screen to a blank state:

```
#ifdef STDC
  for (i=0; i<25; i++)
    { printf("\n"); }
#else
#include <conio.h>
  clrscr();   /* Borland's extension */
#endif
```

Here is a simple program that uses the rest of the predefined global identifiers, just to show you a sample of their use:

```
#include <stdio.h>
main()
{
  printf("At the time of this program's compile:\n");
  printf("\n__TIME__ is %s\n", __TIME__);
  printf("__DATE__ is %s\n", __DATE__);
  printf("__LINE__ is %d\n", __LINE__);
  printf("__FILE__ is %s\n", __FILE__);
  return 0;
}
```

A sample output from the program follows. The name of the source code that produced this program is MACRO.C, as you can see from the last line of output. If you run this program once a day for several days (without recompiling), the output remains the same.

```
At the time of this program's compile:

__TIME__ is 11:09:32
__DATE__ is Dec 6 1994
__LINE__ is 7
__FILE__ is MACRO.C
```

Borland supplies lots of other predefined macros, some C++-related and some general C/C++-related. Tables 9.3 and 9.4 offer two lists of these macros. Although many Borland C++ programmers don't use them (or even know about many of them), glance through the tables to familiarize yourself with Borland's offerings. Although K&R doesn't contain them, you want to use many of them yourself.

Table 9.3. Borland-Specific Memory Model Predefined Global Identifiers

Macro Name	Description
__COMPACT__	Defined if the program was compiled using the compact memory model.
__LARGE__	Defined if the program was compiled using the large memory model.
__MEDIUM__	Defined if the program was compiled using the medium memory model.
__SMALL__	Defined if the program was compiled using the small memory model.
__TINY__	Defined if the program was compiled using the tiny memory model.
__HUGE__	Defined if the program was compiled using the huge memory model.

Note: Only one of these constants is defined for any single compile. Check with `#ifdef` if you need to test for one and act accordingly in your code.

Tip: You can check for the definition of __COMPACT__, __LARGE__, or __HUGE__ to determine if you can use farmalloc() in your programs.

Table 9.4. Borland-Specific Predefined Macros

Macro Name	Value	Description
__BCOPT__	1	Defined if you use a Borland compiler with optimizations set.

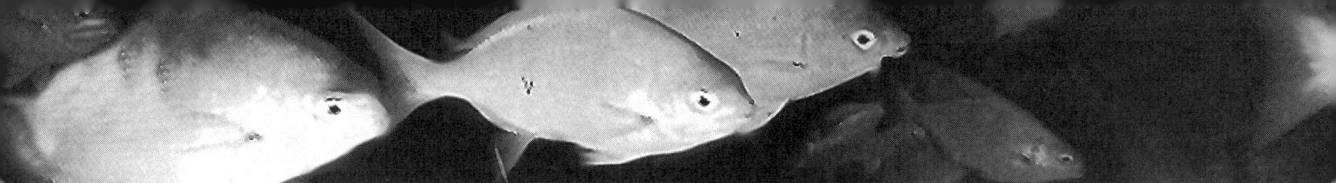

Macro Name	Value	Description
__BCPLUSPLUS__	0x310	Defined only if you use a C++ compiler. The value is subject to change in future releases.
__BORLANDC__	0x410	The version number of the compiler.
__CDECL__	1	Only defined if you've set the compiler's calling conventions to c (versus another calling convention such as Pascal).
__CONSOLE__	1	Only defined for 32-bit versions of Borland C++. If the program is compiled for console input-output (to and from the screen and keyboard) as opposed to a GUI application (to and from windows), __CONSOLE__ is defined.
__cplusplus__	1	Defined if you use a C++ compiler (to maintain compatibility with Stroustrup).
__DLL__	1	Defined if you use Windows DLL compile options.
__MSDOS__	1	Defined if you compile under the PC's MS-DOS operating system.
__OVERLAY__	1	Defined if you compile using overlay support.
__PASCAL__	1	Only defined if you've set the compiler's calling conventions to PASCAL (versus another calling convention such as c).
__TCPLUSPLUS__	0x310	Compiler version number.
__TEMPLATES__	1	Defined if you're using a Borland C++ compiler, Version 4.0 or later, that supports templates.
__TLS__	1	Defined when you compile using the 32-bit compiler.

continues

Table 9.4. Continued

Macro Name	Value	Description
__TURBOC__	0x410	Increases with each release of Borland's Turbo C++ compiler to reflect the version number.
__WIN32__	1	Defined when you compile using the 32-bit compiler.
_WINDOWS	1	Defined when compiling a 16-bit or 32-bit Windows program.

Some of the macro names in Table 9.4 are redundant and perform the same operation as another macro name.

Data Storage

A subject students of programming often wonder about is how the various data types are stored internally. If they knew, their programming tactics would hardly change because knowing the internal storage layout of variables and constants is not a prerequisite for writing good programs. Nevertheless, knowing how Borland C++ stores floats and ints satisfies their curiosity and also makes them more aware of the overhead required when accessing in-memory data of different types.

Each of the following sections takes a closer look at Borland C++'s internal storage for the following primary data types:

char (signed and unsigned)

int (signed, unsigned, and long)

float

double

Before looking closer at each of these data types, take a moment to study the output from the following simple Borland C++ program:

```
#include <stdio.h>
main()
{
```

```
char          c = 'a';
unsigned char uc = 'b';
signed char   sc = 'c';
int           i = 5;
unsigned int ui = 10;
signed int    si = 15;
long int     li = 20;
float         f = 100.5;
double        d = 4054.214;
long double  ld = 2934.21121;

printf("The size of a char is %d\n", sizeof(c));
printf("The size of an unsigned char is %d\n", sizeof(uc));
printf("The size of a signed char is %d\n", sizeof(sc));
printf("The size of an int is %d\n", sizeof(i));
printf("The size of an unsigned int is %d\n", sizeof(ui));
printf("The size of a signed int is %d\n", sizeof(si));
printf("The size of a long int is %d\n", sizeof(li));
printf("The size of a float is %d\n", sizeof(f));
printf("The size of a double is %d\n", sizeof(d));
printf("The size of a long double is %d\n", sizeof(ld));
return 0;
}
```

Here is the program's output:

```
The size of a char is 1
The size of an unsigned char is 1
The size of a signed char is 1
The size of an int is 2
The size of an unsigned int is 2
The size of a signed int is 2
The size of a long int is 4
The size of a float is 4
The size of a double is 8
The size of a long double is 10
```

If you compile and run this program, you receive several compiler warning messages letting you know that you never use the variables for anything. Actually, you do use the variables (you print their sizes), but simply printing their sizes does not please the compiler. You can safely ignore those warnings.

The following sections look at how those 1, 2, 4, or 8 bytes of storage appear in internal RAM memory.

Note: The `sizeof()` operator produces a data type of type `size_t`, so it would be proper to typecast `sizeof()` with an `(int)` typecast before printing, using the `%d` conversion character like this:

```
printf("The size of a float is %d\n", (int)sizeof(f));
```

The `sizeof()` values produced by the preceding program, however, are too small to warrant such a typecast. All of the values produced by these `sizeof()` operators easily fit within %d's range.

The char Data Storage

Not all compilers store character data in 1 byte. You learned early that in computers, a *byte* is a *character*, a *byte* is *8 bits*, a *character* is a *byte*, and a *character* consumes *8 bits*. Nevertheless, compiler vendors sometimes use two bytes to store character data. (Borland did this with early versions of Turbo C.)

The vendors are not trying to change the definition of a character. They are trying to closely tie the link between integers and characters and the easiest way to implement such a link is by using the same number of bytes to hold each. As you know, the following statements are valid in C and C++:

```
char c = 70;     /* Stores an F in the variable */
int i = 'F';     /* Stores a 70 in the variable */
```

C++ contains requirements that make the distinction between character data and integer data more important. Although the previous assignment statements still work in C++, C++ and most vendors whose C++ compilers compile C code (such as Borland C++) now store character data in a single byte as shown in the previous program.

In spite of the fact that character data does not seem to need a sign bit, there is one, as described below, for the `char` and the `signed char` data types.

Note: `char` and `signed char` are equivalent by default but Borland C++ gives you the option to change this default state. Therefore, if you want a `signed char` value, you only need to specify `char`. Unless you specify `unsigned char`, C always uses one bit for the sign bit when storing character data.

Character data provides some of the easiest memory layouts to understand. Figure 9.3 shows the memory layout of the three types of character data.

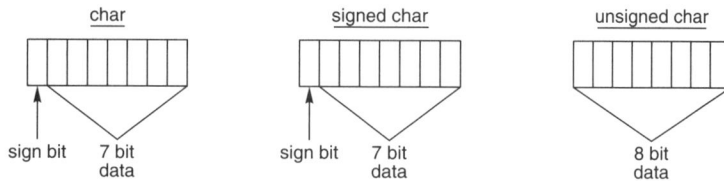

Fig. 9.3. Storing character data.

It's important to note that the sign bit is 0 or 1 to indicate whether or not the value is positive or negative. There are not any negative characters; the numeric range (if you know binary) possible in signed 8-bit memory is -128 to $+127$ and the range of values for an unsigned 8-bit value is 0 to 255, as K&R points out. However, what's the point in storing a character such as a P with a positive or negative sign?

If you were to store -128 in a `signed char` variable, here is the bit pattern stored:

```
1 1 1 1 1 1 1 1
```

That's the same bit pattern for 255 if you were to store 255 in an unsigned 8-bit value. Therefore, if you assigned `255` to a `char` variable and to an `unsigned char` variable, you won't get an error. The same bit pattern goes into the variable. However, if you printed the value's integer result, you'd see `-128` printed for the `char` variable and `255` printed for the unsigned char.

As far as C is concerned, it really doesn't care what `char` data type you store a value in, either `signed` or `unsigned`. However, if you need to store ASCII values higher than 127 in a character value, you should hold such high ASCII values in an `unsigned char` data type. As just described, it takes a full 8-bits to represent values higher than 127.

> **Tip:** Borland C++ distinguishes between `char`, `signed char`, and `unsigned char`, when needed, for overloaded argument lists, even though `char` is always stored the same as one of the other two data types, depending on which default option you have set.

The int Data Storage

Borland C++ requires two memory locations for each integer stored. As K&R clearly points out, you can never rely on data storage sizes, so you should rely on `sizeof()` to determine the width of storage on whatever machine you use. However, you're using Borland C++ with this book, and it is safe to assume that each int consumes two bytes of memory.

> **Caution:** You can assume that `int`s require two bytes *now*, but future versions of Borland C++ might change that requirement. Therefore, even if you are a Borland-only programmer, don't make assumptions about your data values. If K&R says the size is open to change, assume that somebody will change the storage size in the future and write your code with that in mind.

There are several integer data types. The fundamental `int` data type can be modified with the `signed`, `unsigned`, and `long` data types. A `signed int` is identical with `int`. Figure 9.4 shows the internal representation of integers.

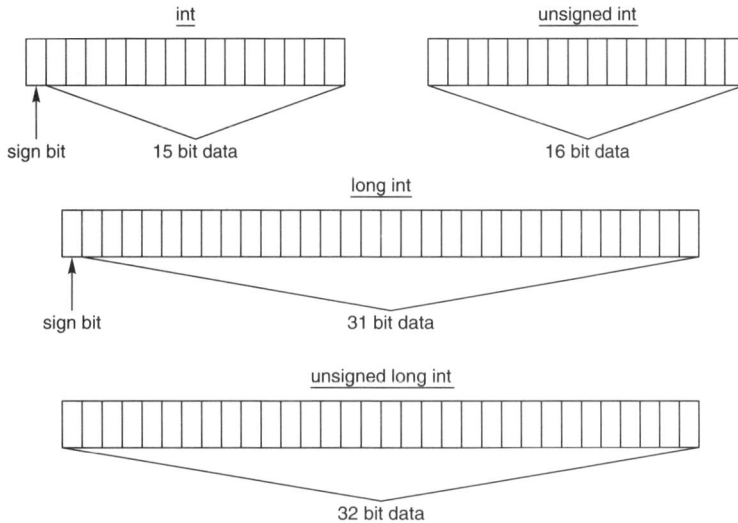

Fig. 9.4. Storing integer data.

The data portion of the integer, called the magnitudes in binary, determines the value stored in the memory. The computer uses *two's complement* to store all integer data. Two's complement is a common method used to represent signed values in today's computer systems. Although the details are not important here, the two's complement method is responsible for giving negative numbers one more extreme value (such as –32,768) than positive values (such as 32,767).

As with the character data types, C uses the first bit of the unsigned integer data types for data, not for a sign bit. That is why the positive range of unsigned values can go higher than the range for signed values. Borland C++ is capable of storing the range –32,768 to 32,767 in ints (and, therefore, signed ints) and the range 0 to 65,535 in unsigned int variables.

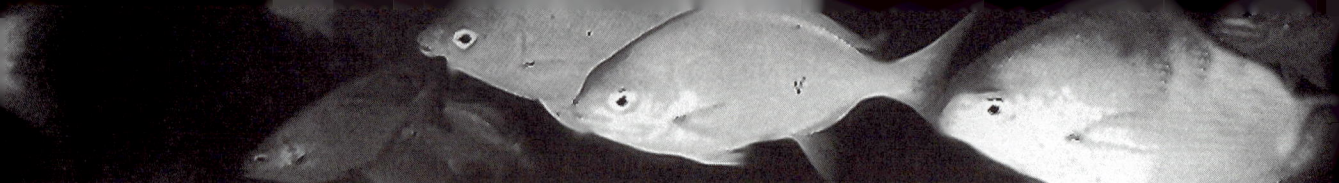

Don't Use Too Much

If nothing else, this section shows you how much more memory is consumed with the longer data types. You are limited in the range of values that the smaller data types hold. Therefore, if you need to store extreme values, you have to use the larger data types to do so (unless adding `unsigned` gives you the room you need, in which case you cannot store negative values).

If you don't need the large value ranges, though, don't waste memory or processing power by defining the larger data types. You'll know your application's data well enough to be able to predict your data needs. There's nothing wrong with using `long` `integer`s when you need them, but the computer takes much longer storing, accessing, and interpreting `long` `int`s than it takes for regular `int`s.

With the doubling of storage size in `long` integers, the range for `signed` `int`s goes from –2,147,483,648 to 2,147,483,647. The range for `unsigned` `long` `int`s goes from 0 to 4,294,967,295.

Caution: The integer 4,294,967,295 is the largest integer constant allowed in a program. If you use a larger integer, Borland C++ truncates the value and produces an incorrect result.

One point to note is that `int` and `short int` are equivalent sizes (16 bits) in Borland C++'s 16-bit programming modes. In the 32-bit programming modes (such as WIN32), `int` and `long` are the same size (32 bits).

A `short int` is identical to `int` in 16-bit programming. In 32-bit programming (such as WIN 32 programming), a `short int` is stored as a 16-bit integer whereas an `int` is the same as a `long int`.

The float Data Storage

C represents floating-point values in a slightly different method than that used for integer values. C must keep track of the following two portions on either side of the decimal point:

> The *exponent*: The power of the number on the left side of the decimal point.

> The *mantissa*: The value on the right side of the decimal point.

Figure 9.5 shows the breakdown of a `float` value in memory. The decimal point separates the parts of a floating-point value and C must keep track of these two values. Many combinations of exponent and mantissa binary values work together to store the values from approximately –3.4E+38 to 3.4E+38. A `long float` is identical to the `double` data type.

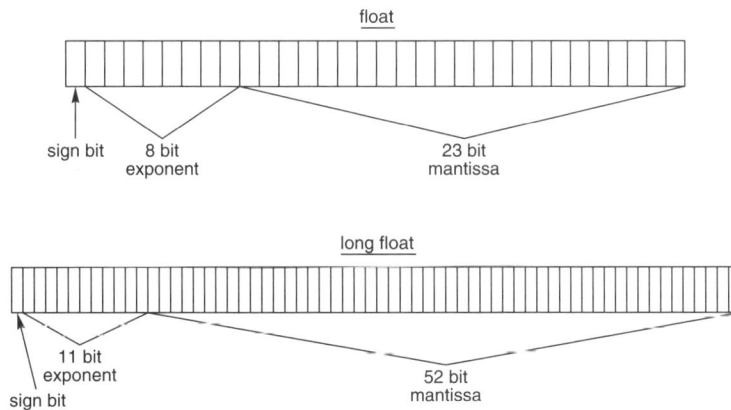

Fig. 9.5. Storing floating-point data.

Caution: Do not use an `unsigned` modifier before `float` or `double` because C does not allow for unsigned floating-point variables.

The double Data Storage

If you really want high precision, the `double` and `long double` data types give you high precision. The `double` data type looks just like the `long double` in memory, as figure 9.6 shows. `double` offers more room for the number's mantissa, so as many as 15 decimal positions can be maintained. The `double` allows for numbers in the approximate range of −1.7E+308 to 1.7E+308. `long double`'s 80 bits of precision allow for a range of −3.4E+4932 to 3.4E+4932, a rather large range of values indeed.

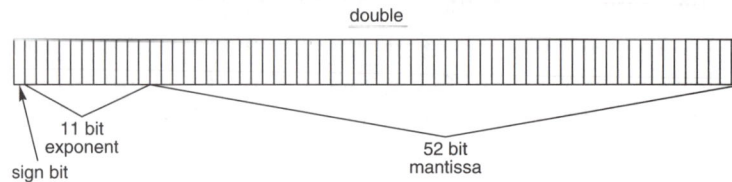

Add 12 more bits for long double, 3 more for the exponent and 12 more for the mantissa (1 bit is reserved)

Fig. 9.6. Storing double floating-point data.

Automatic Conversion

When you mix data types in expressions without explicitly specifying typecasts, Borland C++ closely follows K&R. For example, assuming that `i` is an integer and `x` is a floating-point, the following statement's *rvalue* (the expression on the right side of the assignment) produces a floating-point value and not an integer value:

```
x = i * x;
```

Most of the time, this automatic type conversion works the way you think it should. For instance, if Borland C++ converts the product to `i`'s lower integer data type, the answer loses precision (whatever value is to the right of the decimal point).

K&R suggests that C compilers perform a conversion from the smaller data types to the larger data types. In the previous expression, `i` is the smaller data type and `x` is the larger. Therefore, C first typecasts `i` to a floating-point before performing the multiplication.

> **Note:** Of course, the automatic type conversion lasts only as long as the expression needs it. `i` does not remain typecast to floating-point past the multiplication.

Borland follows K&R's suggestion closely. Table 9.5 lists some important conversions that you should be aware of when programming. Borland attempts to be as safe as possible, protecting the integrity of your data when you combine the data.

Table 9.5. Borland's Important Data Type Conversions

Combination	Result of expression
All `char`s and `short`s except `unsigned short` `unsigned short` and `int`s	`int` `unsigned int` (so as to not lose the positive quantity)
`unsigned` integers and any smaller `int`s	All integers are converted to any `signed unsigned`.
`long double` and any smaller data types	The remaining types are converted other type to `long double`.
`double` and any smaller data types	The remaining types are converted type to `double`.
`float` and any smaller data types	The remaining types are converted type to `float`.
`unsigned long` and any smaller data types	The remaining types are converted smaller `int` or `char` to `unsigned long`.

continues

Table 9.5. Continued

Combination	Result of expression
long and any smaller `int`	The remaining types are converted or char to `int`.

Caution: You can explicitly typecast to override these rules, but your values lose precision.

If a C compiler did not follow K&R's suggestion, you would get suspect results similar to the following expression's answer:

```
int i = 10;
float x = 56.789;
float ans;

ans = (int)x * i;
```

As you can probably guess, after the multiplication, ans holds `560.000000` and not `567.890000`, as it would without the down-typing of the variable `x`.

Tip: To be as safe as possible, don't leave conversions to chance. Explicitly typecast every value in your expressions that you combine with other data types so that Borland C++ performs the conversions you want.

Explicit typecasting can make a difference.

There are occasions, especially when dividing values of different data types, when you should be careful about overriding the default type conversion rules. There are times when you do not want the default conversion rules followed, but you must be careful about your typecast placements.

Remember that you can typecast expressions, as well as individual variables and values. Here is a typecast applied to an expression:

```
netSales = (float)(numSold * price);
```

Study the following short program to see how different typecasting can change an answer:

```
#include <stdio.h>
main()
{
  int hi = 10.0, lo = 6.0;
  float ans;

  ans = (float)(hi / lo);
  printf("ans = (float)(hi / lo) produces %.1f\n", ans);

  ans = (float)hi / (float)lo;
  printf("ans = (float) hi  / (float) lo produces %.1f\n", ans);

  return 0;
}
```

Here is the program's output:

```
ans = (float) (hi / lo) produces 1.0
ans = (float) hi / (float) lo produces 1.7
```

Attribute the difference in output to the fact the C computes the first hi / lo using integer division because of the individual typecasts. The second calculation converts hi and lo to float *before* the division so that C uses floating-point division and, therefore, the more accurate answer.

A Little about Header Files

Header files comprise an integral part of the C language. Header files hold defined constants, enumerated constants, function prototypes, `extern` declarations, and more. There are many header files supplied by your compiler (both ANSI C/K&R specific and Borland-specific header files).

As described in K&R, supplied header files use the following scheme to ensure that they are included only once in a program:

```
#ifndef __STDIO_H
#define __STDIO_H
/* Body of header
   file goes here */
#endif /* __STDIO_H */
```

The first `#infdef` tests to see if the constant `__STDIO_H` is defined already for the current compilation. If a `__STDIO_H` appears in the name space, the result is false and the entire body of the header file is ignored in the compilation. If, however, there is no `__STDIO_H` in the compiler's name space, the `#define` directive defines the constant and the body of the header file is compiled, along with the source code that included the header file. The `#define` ensures that if *another* part of the source code includes `__STDIO_H`, then *its* inclusion will be ignored because `__STDIO_H` will be defined already.

> **Tip:** If such a double-inclusion prevention is good for supplied header files, it's good for the header files you write as well. Follow this `#ifndef` practice with the header files that you write.

Often, programmers who work on a large data processing staff write programs in teams. As one programmer finishes a section of code, that section is combined with others until the final product is finished. Companies often develop their own company-wide header files with special company defined constants and `extern` data values. Each programmer working on a group of functions must include all headers needed to compile and test those specific functions. When the system coordinator combines the programmer's set of functions into the

overall team's program, clashes occur if any of the programmers failed to include the header file protection, and a multiple inclusion is attempted.

Design an agreed-to constant for each header file to ensure consistency. If you follow C's standard, append a double underscore __ to the beginning of the filename and use a single underscore where the extension's dot appears in the file name. Therefore, cname.h's `#define` constant is `__CNAME_H` and cdata.h's `#define` constant is `__CDATA_H`.

> **Caution:** If you don't make sure that everybody on the programming staff knows the named constant's naming convention, you can include the same header file twice and the compilation fails. Such a bug is sometimes difficult to track if you're not expecting it.

Don't rely on other programmers to include the headers that your code needs. If you work on a team, include at the top of your code *all* `#include <header.h>` files that your code needs. Following the previous discussion's technique for eliminating double-inclusion ensures that you will not inadvertently include a header that's already been included in the current compilation session.

> **Tip:** If you write header files specific to individual source code files, store those header files in the same directory as the source files, not in the regular `include` directory used by Borland C++. Also, include the file inside quotation marks like this:
>
> ```
> #include "myhdr.h"
> ```
>
> to ensure that the current directory is searched. You can keep your header files and related source code together so they are easier to maintain.

Some Header File Considerations

K&R describes all the ANSI C header files, but due to the brevity of K&R, the understanding of some of them may elude you. You know that __STDIO_H includes prototypes and support for common input-output routines, __MATH_H includes support for common (and not so common) math requirements, and so on. Nevertheless, there are a few points to make about header files that you may not have thought of before.

Precompiled Header Files

K&R did not mention *precompiled header files*, but K&R had no way of predicting what vendors would put in their C/C++ compilers after K&R went to print. By using precompiled header files, you might speed up your compilation time considerably. There are three ways to request precompiled header files:

1. Set Borland's compiler settings with Options Project Precompiled headers. Figure 9.7 shows the Project Options screen.

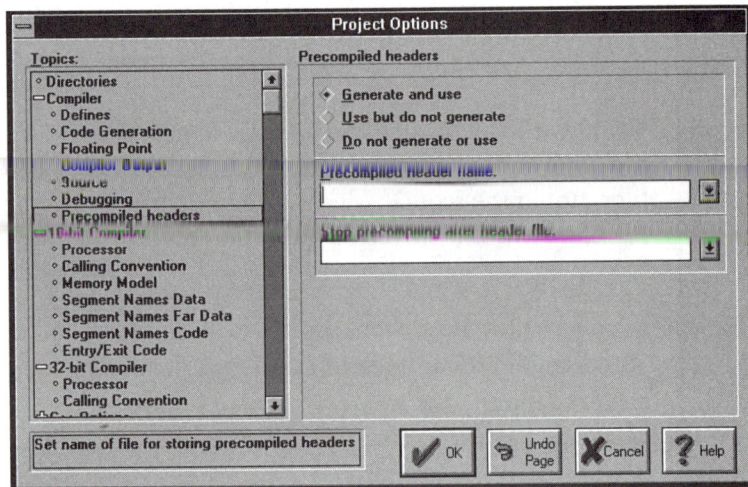

Fig. 9.7. Specifying precompiled headers.

If you select Generate and use, Borland C++ attempts to find your header files and generate compiled headers, if possible, for use in the next compilation. If you select Use but do not generate, Borland C++ uses whatever precompiled headers are already precompiled, but does not generate new precompiled headers. If you use Do not generate or use, Borland C++ does not use precompiled header files.

2. If you use Borland's command-line compiler, the options -H, -Hu, and -H- correspond to the three generate-and-use conditions described in #1. If you do not specify an option, Borland C++ cannot generate or use precompiled headers.

3. You can use the hdrfile and hdrstop pragma statements inside your code. Place the hdrfile pragma right before the first header file in your source that you want precompiled. Specify a precompiled header file name after hdrfile. Place hdrstop at the end of the list of headers you want precompiled. For example, in the following code, the header file named myhdr1.h is not precompiled, but myhdr2.h, mrhdr3.h, and myhdr4.h are precompiled:

```
#include "myhdr1.h>
#pragma hdrfile "precomp.sym"
#include "myhdr2.h"
#include "myhdr3.h"
#include "myhdr4.h"
#pragma hdrstop
```

> **Note:** If you do not specify a precompiled header file name, Borland C++ defaults to using tcdef.cym for the location of DOS precompiled headers and bcwdef.cym for Windows-based precompiled headers.

Not all header files can be precompiled, and you may not want to use precompiled header files. Precompiled header files consume disk space that can sometimes be a precious commodity. Also, not all header files are eligible for precompilation. You might be surprised to learn that it doesn't take much to force a regeneration of your header files. If you simply rearrange the order of `#include` statements, Borland C++ might decide to generate a new set of precompiled headers all over again.

> **Tip:** If you are short on disk space, you can delete any and all .sym precompiled header files. The only difference you'll notice is a possible slowdown the next time you compile.

Unusual Headers

This section of the book does not go into a comprehensive rundown of every header file and its contents. Nevertheless, there are a few header files that warrant some discussion. These header files sometimes separate the *C experts* from the *intermediate programmers*.

The C experts, for example, often use the assert.h header file and its important `assert()` macro due to its ease of use. Other C programmers often ignore `assert()` because of `assert()`'s cryptic nature or because of its seemingly primitive method of handling runtime errors. Nevertheless, the primitive nature of `assert()` is often the very reason you see C journals and books using `assert()`; `assert()` can save a lot of debugging hassle at times.

The assert.h header file contains the prototype for a single function-like macro named `assert()`. `assert()` aids in debugging code. `assert()` requires a single conditional expression; that condition determines whether or not the assertion takes place.

Suppose that you are getting ready to divide a sales record by a user-entered factor to produce a net sales amount. Company requirements dictate that the factor must be .75 or greater. The following `assert()` call before the division quickly ensures that the user entered an appropriate value:

```
assert(saleFactor >= .75);   /* Check for proper factor */
```

As long as the `saleFactor` is `.75` or more, there is no problem and the division takes place. If, however, the `saleFactor` is less than `.75`, the program terminates and the following error message appears on-screen:

```
Assertion failed: saleFactor >= .75, file sale.c, line 412

Abnormal program termination
```

Surely, all will agree that users will have a problem with these kinds of heart-stopping blatant and cryptic error messageS. But, assertion testing is not meant to be active in final user's production programs. Instead, you use `assert()` for debugging your programs during development and testing.

The biggest advantage that `assert()` brings to the table is that you can disconnect `assert()` when you no longer need it. `assert()` deactivates if the NDEBUG named constant is defined. Therefore, if you insert this statement before the `#include <assert.h>`:

```
#define NDEBUG
```

any and all `assert()` macros in the rest of the file will not expand and will no longer have any effect on the code. It's a lot easier to insert the simple `#define` to turn off the assertion testing than it is to remove all `if` statements.

Here is a simple program that uses the `assert()` just described after the user's input, so you can see for yourself just how `assert()` works:

```c
/* To eliminate the assertion, remove
   this comment and leave the #dcfine
#define NDEBUG
*/

/* Assume this source file is named sale.c */
#include <assert.h>
#include <stdio.h>
main()
{
  float sales, saleFactor;
  float adjSales;
  printf("What were the sales? ");
  scanf(" %f", &sales);
  printf("What is today's sales factor? ");
  scanf(" %f", &saleFactor);
```

```
/* Here comes the assertion */
assert(saleFactor >= .75); /* Check for proper factor */
adjSales = sales / saleFactor;
printf("The adjusted sales are $%.2f\n", adjSales);
return 0;
}
```

Here is a run that triggers the assertion:

```
What were the sales? 43223.45
What is today's sales factor? .62
Assertion failed: saleFactor >= .75, file sale.c, line 19
Abnormal program termination
```

Here is a run that works properly (due to the user's correct input):

```
What were the sales? 43223.45
What is today's sales factor? .81
The adjusted sales are $53362.28
```

You can see from the comment at the top of the program exactly how to eliminate the assertions when you want to turn off the assertion testing.

Note: The assertion code does nothing if you define the NDEBUG constant. The next time you compile the program, don't worry about removing `assert()` code, even if you're compiling for the final time. The assertion code does not add noticeable executable space if you define NDEBUG. By leaving the assertion testing in the code, you can turn it back on easily by removing the NDEBUG definition or commenting out the definition.

Caution: Be careful where you place `assert()` functions. `assert()` expands to a macro that becomes a time-consuming `if` statement, if you insert `assert()` inside loops. Efficiency dramatically evaporates if you are not careful.

The limits.h header file contains some interesting features that you may not need to know about right away but veteran C programmers

study for a while. The contents of the limits.h header file differ with almost every C/C++ compiler, and with almost every computer that supports the C and C++ language. Yet, limits.h, despite the fact that it is different in almost every language implementation, remains ANSI C compatible and keeps its respect proffered in K&R.

Integer sizes and ranges differ on each computer, and limits.h contains these ranges. An earlier section of this chapter described how different integer data types can support different ranges of data. There are lots of defined constants in limits.h that you can use, if needed, in your own programs so that you can write *portable code*. Although the next chapter further discusses the portability of code, you should know that you endanger your program's future if you rely too much on your compiler's limits today.

For example, in the future, Borland C++ version *13.0* might run on computers with 256-bit registers and bus sizes that contain hundreds of gigabytes of RAM. There is no good reason, on such a computer, to retain 16-bit integers when 256-bit integers will process just as efficiently (perhaps more so). However, if you write a program today that's still in use when Borland releases version 13.0 of Borland C++, you severely limit your program's ability if you write for the data sizes of today.

If you ever want to make your program take advantage of the limits provided by whatever compiler compiles the program, check out the limits.h header file. Here is a sample from Borland C++ Version 4.0's limits.h header file:

```
#define CHAR_BIT       8                  /* number of bits in a char */
#define MB_LEN_MAX     2                  /* max. # bytes in multibyte char */

#define SCHAR_MIN     (-128)              /* minimum signed   char value */
#define SCHAR_MAX      127                /* maximum signed   char value */
#define UCHAR_MAX      255                /* maximum unsigned char value */

#if ('\x80' < 0)
#define CHAR_MIN       SCHAR_MIN          /* minimum char value */
#define CHAR_MAX       SCHAR_MAX          /* maximum char value */
#else
#define CHAR_MIN       0
#define CHAR_MAX       UCHAR_MAX
#endif
```

```
#define SHRT_MIN      (-32767-1)        /* minimum signed   short value */
#define SHRT_MAX      32767             /* maximum signed   short value */
#define USHRT_MAX     65535U            /* maximum unsigned short value */

#define LONG_MIN      (-2147483647L-1)  /* minimum signed   long value */
#define LONG_MAX      2147483647L       /* maximum signed   long value */
#define ULONG_MAX     4294967295UL      /* maximum unsigned long value */
```

These defined constants are available to any program that includes
limits.h. For example, if you want to make sure that high-order ASCII
characters are available, you can check to see if CHAR_BIT is defined as 7
or 8. The header file also verifies that 32767 is the maximum value that
signed short can hold. The negative values appear in parentheses so that
the negative signs are evaluated as negative signs, and not interpreted
as a decrement operator, in statements such as this one:

```
if (32767-SCHAR_MIN)
```

which would incorrectly expand to this:

```
if (32767-128)
```

without the parentheses in the header file.

> **Caution:** If you want to load any header file from the include direc-
> tory to study the file's contents, be sure that you don't inadvert-
> ently change anything in the file, or you may have to reinstall
> Borland C++.

The float.h header file contains similar limit values for floating-point
data. You can ensure, when needed, that your mathematical statements don't exceed the floating-point limits of your computer and
produce calculated overflow. Here is a section from float.h:

```
#define DBL_DIG           15
#define FLT_DIG           7
#define LDBL_DIG          19

#define DBL_MANT_DIG      53
#define FLT_MANT_DIG      24
#define LDBL_MANT_DIG     64

#define DBL_EPSILON       2.2204460492503131E-16
#define FLT_EPSILON       1.19209290E-07F
#define LDBL_EPSILON      1.084202172485504E-19L
```

```
/* smallest positive IEEE normal numbers */
#define DBL_MIN          2.2250738585072014E-308
#define FLT_MIN          1.17549435E-38F
#define LDBL_MIN         _tiny_ldble

#define DBL_MAX          _huge_dble
#define FLT_MAX          _huge_flt
#define LDBL_MAX         _huge_ldble

#define DBL_MAX_EXP      +1024
#define FLT_MAX_EXP      +128
#define LDBL_MAX_EXP     +16384

#define DBL_MAX_10_EXP   +308
#define FLT_MAX_10_EXP   +38
#define LDBL_MAX_10_EXP  +4932

#define DBL_MIN_10_EXP   -307
#define FLT_MIN_10_EXP   -37
#define LDBL_MIN_10_EXP  -4931
```

Many of the values defined in Borland C++'s float.h are x86 processor specific.

Finally, the header file named math.h also contains many named constants that you might find a use for, especially if you write scientific and mathematical programs. Here is a section from Borland C++'s math.h:

```
#define M_E        2.71828182845904523536
#define M_LOG2E    1.44269504088896340736
#define M_LOG10E   0.434294481903251827651
#define M_LN2      0.693147180559945309417
#define M_LN10     2.30258509299404568402
#define M_PI       3.14159265358979323846
#define M_PI_2     1.57079632679489661923
#define M_PI_4     0.785398163397448309616
#define M_1_PI     0.318309886183790671538
#define M_2_PI     0.636619772367581343076
#define M_1_SQRTPI 0.564189583547756286948
#define M_2_SQRTPI 1.12837916709551257390
#define M_SQRT2    1.41421356237309504880
#define M_SQRT_2   0.707106781186547524401
```

Such defined constants eliminate the need for your own `#define` statements such as these:

```
#define PI 3.14159
```

The named constant `M_PI` is already defined for math's *pi* constant, and `M_PI` provides much more precision than you'll probably apply to your own `#define`s. The other named constants, such as the value of *e*, the square root of 2, and *pi* divided by 2 and 4 are supply-common values for the mathematical programmers who need to work with such values.

> **Note:** Borland C++'s mathematical, trigonometric, and logarithmic functions are prototyped in math.h along with the named constants.

From Here...

➤ Chapter 1, "Writing Portable Code," demonstrates the importance of writing clear, concise, K&R and ANSI-approved code when you want to write programs for several different kinds of computers.

➤ Chapter 10, "Extending K&R's C," shows how a K&R C programmer can extend the knowledge of K&R C to write more powerful programs using the compiler's extended library routines.

➤ If you liked the approach taken here on expanding upon Kernighan & Ritchie's C, and you program in C++, read Chapter 11, "Stroustrup Implementation Secrets."

Extending K&R's C

by Greg Perry

This chapter describes some of the ways that Borland C++ moves beyond K&R by extending parts of the language. You will read about why languages such as Borland C++ choose to supersede K&R and the ANSI C standard. Deviating from K&R and ANSI is not always a bad thing to do, especially if you want to take advantage of today's common computing environments.

There are two methods you can use to deviate from ANSI, but still remain compatible with the spirit of ANSI C: using ANSI device driver codes and the `#pragma` directive. The ANSI device driver codes for I/O let you clear the screen, control the cursor, and display colorful text. Certainly, such powerful screen control is not part of the ANSI C standard; the many differences in hardware would dictate that ANSI include too many hardware-specific commands and functions. The `#pragma` preprocessor directive lets your compiler vendor add additional non-ANSI features to their C language, without losing computability with other ANSI C compilers.

This chapter concludes with discussions on data representations. The new international wide character set takes C into a worldwide computing environment that the previous C data types do not allow. Finally, you learn how Borland C++ implements internal data types, and you explore Borland's memory models to see how to structure your own compilers.

Overview of ANSI C

Starting with the book's second edition, K&R's "The C Programming Language" began promoting and describing only those language elements that are ANSI C compatible. The ANSI (American National Standards Institute) people formed a committee named *X3J11* that began working on the C standard in 1983 and approved the finalized language standard in 1989.

> **Note:** The C standard developed by ANSI is officially known as the "ANSI Programming Language C, X3.159-1989." There is another standard, known as ISO C, defined by the International Standards Organization that is virtually identical with ANSI C.

One of the interesting and little-known facts about C is that there was an industry C standard before the ANSI committee formed its standard. That industry standard *was* the first edition of K&R's "The C Programming Language!" Until ANSI C, K&R's C (also known as *Classic C*) was followed by most programmers and compiler writers. The ANSI committee focused on more accurately defining and refining K&R's original publication and adding ANSI C requirements for function declarations that contain parameter descriptions.

Perhaps the ANSI committee could have improved upon K&R's C by greatly changing the language. Changing the language, however, was not and is not the committee's goal. The committee's goal was to standardize the language, keeping as much of the previous C language

intact, so that programs written before the standard compiled relatively easy under an ANSI C compiler.

Here are the two primary refinements firmed by the ANSI committee:

➤ Parameter data types were added to function declarations.

➤ The Standard C Library was defined for I/O and math routines (as defined in header files, such as stdio.h and math.h). K&R C did not define a standard library.

Due to the prevalence of ANSI C, many of today's C programmers who were trained after 1987 may be unaware of the original K&R function parameter declaration syntax. Suppose that you were writing a pre-ANSI C function that accepted a character parameter, an integer parameter, and a floating-point parameter. Here is such a function:

```
int myFunction(c, i, f)
char c;
int i;
float f;
{
  /* Body of function goes here */
}
```

The first line (the declaration line) of the function did not include the parameter data types. As you can see here, the prototype for the myFunction() function specified only the return value, not the arguments:

```
int myFunction();   /* Prototype */
```

Here is an ANSI C version of the same function:

```
int myFunction(char c, int i, float f)
{
  /* Body of function goes here */
}
```

The prototype for this ANSI C function looks like this:

```
int myFunction(char c, int i, float f);
```

Because the prototype now matches the function's first line, the C compiler has an easier time of accurately checking for proper parameters.

Note: You can now tell directly from the prototype the type of parameters your functions require, instead of having to wade through code looking for the parameter definitions.

Perhaps the only arguable advantage to the old function definitions was the ability to comment each parameter. The parameters appeared on separate lines, giving you the ability to document each parameter's purpose, as shown here:

```
char c;    /* The user's initial */
int i;     /* Value of the loop counter that calls this function */
float f;   /* Adjustment factor entered earlier by user */
```

The parameter type-checking that the compiler can now perform, however, far outweighs any documentation advantage of the K&R standard. The biggest danger in K&R was the bad data types that programmers could send to a function. Instead of automatic typecasting and data promotion of arguments, K&R's C had no way of deciphering incorrect arguments, whereas ANSI C can check for proper arguments.

Suppose that a `double` variable was sent as the second argument in `myFunction()`, instead of the expected `int` argument. Even if that `double` variable contained a small number such as `6.0`, the compiler would not properly convert the `double` to `int` in most implementations. An eight-byte `double` is sent, being stored on the stack along the way, and the receiving `myFunction()` retrieves only two of those eight bytes because of the (probable) two-byte integer size. The third argument, even if correctly sent, would probably be damaged by the incorrect state of the stack.

Tip: If you want to ensure ANSI C compatibility of your compiler, use the `__STDC__` predefined global identifier described in the previous chapter.

ANSI-Compatible: To Be or Not To Be

Compiler vendors know the importance of being labeled *ANSI C compatible,* and compiler vendors know the bad press that a lack of such compatibility would provide. Therefore, there are few, if any, C compilers still sold that do not read *ANSI C compatible* somewhere on the box or in the manuals.

Virtually every C programmer is taught the importance of writing ANSI C compatible code. Threats of the *boogeyman* storming into the programmer's chamber late at night can probably be heard coming from C instructors' mouths! Once the C programmer leaves the classroom and sits in front of a compiler such as Borland C++, ANSI C compatibility quickly flies out the window.

Here are some questions to ponder:

> ➤ Should programmers use ANSI C when working on their own compilers at home, outside a classroom, or away from work?

> ➤ Despite the huge advances made in the C programming language libraries and support tools, such as those provided by Borland C++, should programmers always maintain ANSI C compatibility to promote easy maintenance and future language changes?

> ➤ Should programmers adopt a quasi-ANSI C standard, using much of the ANSI definition but throwing in well-documented deviations, such as screen clearing functions, available in almost all C language packages since the mid-1980s?

> ➤ Is either K&R's or the ANSI committee's goals actually in alignment with the typical programmer's goals?

It is important to realize that, when a C compiler does deviate from the ANSI C standard, the core ANSI language remains virtually 100 percent intact. Compiler vendors often deviate only in the library routines added to the language's library. Therefore, the language compatibility is honestly maintained and it lies on the programmer's shoulders to decide which non-ANSI functions to use and which to ignore.

Caution: One standard deviated from by Borland C++ (and most other compiler vendors today) is the allowance of the C++-style // comment to the right of C statements in C programs. The new comment is not approved by ANSI, at this time, so using it could be dangerous. Borland, or any other vendor supporting the C // comment could, at any point in the future, *remove* that feature from the language. If the feature was not ANSI C to begin with, the vendor is under no obligation to maintain the feature. It's a shame that ANSI C does not support the // comment, but a standard cannot contain everything.

The ANSI C standard consists of the 32 keywords found in Table 10.1. You'll rarely find compilers that don't support these keywords exactly as ANSI intended them to be used.

Table 10.1. The ANSI C Keywords

auto	long
break	register
case	return
char	short
const	signed
continue	sizeof
default	static
do	struct
double	switch
else	typedef
enum	union
extern	unsigned
float	void
for	volatile
goto	while
if	

Portability and ANSI C

You learned about the importance of portable code in Chapter 1, "Writing Portable Code." Perhaps the safest and easiest way to ensure portable code, when you need to develop the same program for several platforms, is to stick to the ANSI C standard.

Portability was the primary concern of the ANSI C committee members as they pondered the standard. One of the main reasons to standardize was that the same programs had to be rewritten for each different compiler that was without portability and standards. Many languages were considered portable across different machines, but virtually all languages required more modifications than C to move between hardware (especially when porting from one class of computer to another, such as a PC to a minicomputer, a PC to a mainframe, or a minicomputer to a mainframe).

The previous compatibility questions are answered very easily: when programmers begin writing outside a classroom situation, ANSI flies out the window to be replaced by modern library routines. Given today's hardware advances, there is simply no way to write programs that have the power now expected without using non-ANSI library routines.

Consider the simple requirement that a program will clear the screen. Borland's `clrscr()` function will never appear in any ANSI C standard. As far as ANSI is concerned, if you want to erase the contents of your screen, the following code will do nicely:

```
for (ctr=0;ctr<25;ctr++)
  { printf("\n"); }
```

Such output looping code may suffice in the old teletype days, but window environments demand more advanced techniques. DOS-based text mode users also need more than the archaic looping provides.

Visiting the ANSI Driver

PC users can take advantage of ANSI-approved screen-manipulation routines that do not violate the standard, even though they are not part of the ANSI C standard. The *ANSI device driver codes*, for example, are a set of screen-manipulation codes defined by ANSI several years ago, which are still supported today. Here are the three primary jobs of the ANSI device driver codes:

1. To clear the screen and position the cursor in the upper-left hand corner (the *home* position).

2. To control cursor placement.

3. To specify text colors.

The ANSI driver has nothing to do with graphics, only text.

> **Note:** To take advantage of the ANSI codes, you must include the ANSI.SYS driver in CONFIG.SYS. On most systems, this means that the following line must appear somewhere in your CONFIG.SYS file:
>
> ```
> device=c:\dos\ansi.sys
> ```
>
> As with all DOS commands, you can specify any or all of this command in uppercase or lowercase letters. If DOS is stored in a directory other than C:\DOS, then change the path to the correct DOS directory.

The biggest advantage that the ANSI screen codes have to offer is that you can write programs for your PC, and give those programs more screen control (such as full-screen editing) than `printf()` and the other input/output functions would allow, without the ANSI codes. Those same programs will compile and work—screen-manipulation and all—on any other kind of computer, even a mainframe, as long as that computer also conforms to the ANSI device codes. (Most terminals connected to minicomputers and mainframes do conform to ANSI or have switches to make them conform.)

Here is the way the ANSI device driver codes work: When a program sends a specific stream of characters to the screen, and the screen's host is set up for ANSI, the terminal checks to see if the pattern matches one of the ANSI patterns of characters. There is a different combination of characters for each screen function supported by ANSI. If a stream of characters does not conform to one of the ANSI device driver codes, the ANSI device driver simply routes those characters to the screen as-is, without performing one of the screen-manipulation operations.

Table 10.2 offers a listing of ANSI device driver codes. Even though Borland C++ does not endorse or support these codes, your Borland C++ program can easily manipulate the screen with these codes (assuming you write for a DOS text mode environment). Each of the ANSI device driver codes are called *escape sequences* because they all begin with an escape character (ASCII value 33).

Table 10.2. The ANSI Device Driver Escape Sequences

Escape Sequence	Description
/033[2J	Clears the screen
/033[K	Erases the text from the cursor's position to the end of the line
/033[30m	Sets the foreground to black
/033[31m	Sets the foreground to red
/033[32m	Sets the foreground to green
/033[33m	Sets the foreground to orange
/033[34m	Sets the foreground to blue
/033[35m	Sets the foreground to magenta
/033[36m	Sets the foreground to cyan
/033[37m	Sets the foreground to white
/033[40m	Sets the background to black
/033[41m	Sets the background to red
/033[42m	Sets the background to green

continues

Table 10.2. Continued

Escape Sequence	Description
/033[43m	Sets the background to orange
/033[44m	Sets the background to blue
/033[45m	Sets the background to magenta
/033[46m	Sets the background to cyan
/033[47m	Sets the background to white
/033[#;#H	Moves the cursor to row # and column #
/033[#A	Moves the cursor up # rows
/033[#B	Moves the cursor down # rows
/033[#C	Moves the cursor # columns to the right
/033[#D	Moves the cursor # columns to the left
/033[S	Stores the cursor's current position
/033[U	Restores the previously-stored position

The cursor-movement codes require either row number, column number, or both arguments for the cursor to go to the position that you want.

The program in Listing 10.1 uses some of these codes by first defining with #define to ease subsequent printf() calls.

Listing 10.1. Using the ANSI Device Control Drivers

```
/* Utilizing the ANSI device driver */
#include <stdio.h>

#define CLS "\033[2J"
#define WHITEFG "\033[37m"
#define BLUEBG "\033[44m"
#define MOVECUR "\033[%d;%dH"

main()
{
  printf(CLS);
  printf(WHITEFG);
  printf(BLUEBG);
  printf(MOVECUR, 5, 5);
```

```
    printf("Hi!");
    printf(MOVECUR, 10, 10);
    printf("There!");
    printf(MOVECUR, 15, 15);
    printf("Bye!");
    printf(MOVECUR, 20, 20);
    printf("There!");
    return 0;
}
```

Caution: Be sure to type these codes *exactly as shown*, sticking to the uppercase and lowercase letters in each code. The codes are cumbersome by design; if the letters `cl` made the screen clear, the screen would clear every time a program attempted to print the word `cloud`.

Figure 10.1 shows the output of the program as it appears on a PC's text screen.

```
Hi!

             There!

                          Bye!

                                        There!
```

Fig. 10.1. Controlling the cursor.

Tip: If your program does not behave as this program is described, be sure that your CONFIG.SYS loads the ANSI.SYS driver. Without the ANSI.SYS device driver, you would see something like the following output:

```
2J 37m 44m 5;5HHi!  [10;10HThere!  [15;15HBye!  [20;20HThere!
```

If you plan to write exclusively for the PC, using Borland C++, and you will not be compiling the program using a different compiler, consider ignoring these ANSI-compatible codes. Use the built-in screen-manipulating functions and ignore ANSI compatibility for screen-control (see the next section). The ANSI codes are cryptic and slow. If, however, you'll ever have to write for a different platform, you may have to use the ANSI codes if you don't want a conversion nightmare later.

More Compatibility Issues

Not only do today's environments require more extensive and power-ful routines, programmers will be going back into time trying to maintain ANSI C compatability instead of taking advantage of the compiler's non-ANSI features. You simply have *got* to go above and beyond the ANSI standard if you want to achieve your programming goals. Today's data processing shops have incredible programming backlogs, and you've got to take advantage of all the power of the compiler.

However, when you use an ANSI C compatible compiler, you can en-sure that the core language that you use retains the standard, while using library functions that add the efficiency, productivity, and pizzazz that users want and need.

The ANSI C committee meets every so often to update the standard. In updating the standard, a high priority is placed on conforming to pre-vious standards, so that the large volume of programs already in exist-ence aren't made obsolete. The committee doesn't want to violate its own standard.

People often asked why the standards committee doesn't add now-common routines to the language, such as screen-clearing and color setting functions. After all, relatively few (if any) of today's video screens do not support erasing the screen. Most PCs sold today sup-port color and advanced cursor control capabilities. If a user were to buy a monochrome screen, then any color functions executed would

have no effect on the monochrome screen. Members of the ANSI C committee state that their standard is not necessarily an attempt to conform to hardware's lowest common denominator (LCD). If they wrote to the LCD, their standard would immediately be out of date because of guaranteed technological improvements that continually raise the LCD.

The Standards committee would have an extremely difficult task if it attempted to add more elegant and eclectic functions to the Standard C library. It has yet to deal with text-based video, and now GUI video is the norm. Does it bypass a more exotic text-based standard now? Which GUI does it support: X/Windows (a UNIX-based GUI operating environment), Windows, OS/2, Windows NT, or all of the above? The Standard C library may perhaps *never* adopt such video standards. It simply cannot because technology is constantly changing.

Given the fact that the standard may never support what you need, you cannot stick to the standard. You must deviate, hopefully in a well-structured and well-documented way, from the standards, knowing that the programs you write today may not work on tomorrow's compilers. Borland C++ offers no guarantee (other than strong market forces of existing installations) that `clrscr()` will remain the screen-clearing function in future versions. If you wrote OWL-based windows programs with OWL 1.0, you have no doubt seen what problems face you as you tediously convert to OWL 2.0.

The bottom line is that if you want functionality, you've got to stray from these boring text-based modes of the Standard C library, take advantage of everything your compiler has to offer, and realize that you'll have maintenance work ahead of you with future versions and with hardware advances.

#pragma: Non-Standard but ANSI C

The #pragma is an interesting preprocessor directive. The ANSI C standard fully supports the #pragma directive, and any programmer who uses #pragma is following ANSI C. Yet, virtually every compiler supports different versions of the #pragma directive! In a way, #pragma gives programmers a back door into writing ANSI-approved, but non-standard code. #pragma is, in effect, a standard way for being non-standard.

The idea behind #pragma is fairly straightforward. With #pragma, a compiler writer is free to add any implementation-dependent preprocessor directives. (Remember that a preprocessor directive provides instructions to the compiler—they are not language commands.)

When a compiler vendor, such as Borland, wants to implement its own compiler-specific preprocessor directives, instead of creating a brand new set of non-standard directives, the vendor adds new #pragma directives. Compilers that support those #pragma directives will follow the directives, and compilers that don't support those #pragma directives ignore the #pragmas. Therefore, if you use a Borland-specific #pragma but then move your application to a Microsoft compiler, the Microsoft compiler will ignore any #pragmas it finds and does not recognize. If Borland had written its own specific directives, without following the #pragma standard, Microsoft would have little choice but to issue compiler errors until the non-standard directives were removed.

The Format of #pragma

Here is the general format for the #pragma directive:

```
#pragma directiveName
```

Table 10.3 lists the directiveNames supported by Borland C++. In a way, all of these directives are Borland-specific non-ANSI C processor directives. Preceding them with #pragma, as in #pragma option instead of #option, ensures that other compilers will not abort the surrounding program's compilation.

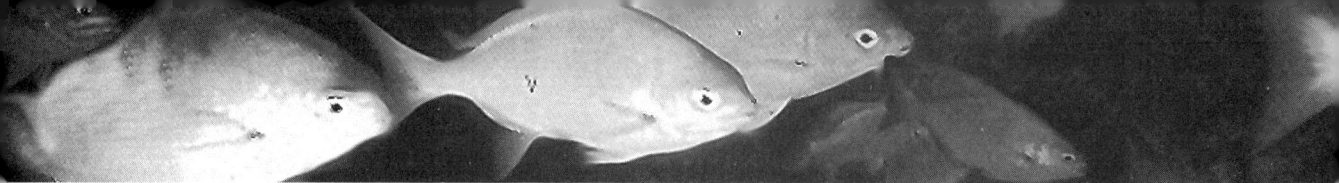

Table 10.3. The #pragma directiveNames

Pragma Name	Description
argsused	Removes warning for unused arguments.
codeseg	Specifies the segment in which the compiler is to allocate functions.
comment	Specifies an .OBJ object file comment record.
exit	Specifies which function should be called right before the program terminates.
hdrfile	Specifies the filename that will hold precompiled headers, if you use precompiled headers.
hdrstop	Signals the end of the header files to be included in the precompiled headers.
inline	Tells the compiler that your program contains inline assembly code.
intrinsic	Generates inline code for the following functions to speed up your program's execution and increase your program's size: alloca(), fabs(), memchr(), memcmp(), memcpy(), memset(), rotl(), rotr(), stpcpy(), strcat(), strchr(), strcmp(), strcpy(), strlen(), stncat(), strncmp(), strncpy(), strnset(), strrchr().
option	Specifies which of the command-line compiler options should be in effect for the source code's compilation. All command-line options except the following are allowed: -B, -c, -dname, -Dname=string, -efilename, -E, -Fx, -H, -Ifilename, -Lfilename, -Ixset, -M, -o, -P, -O, -S, T, Uname, V, -X, -Y.
saveregs	When calling a huge function from assembly language, the #pragma saveregs ensures that all register values are preserved.
startup	Specifies function to run first, prior to MAIN().
warn	Lets you control command-line options in effect and change the warnings in the Options dialog boxes.

Some #pragma Examples

Some of the `#pragma` directives are relatively obscure and available to programmers in extremely rare situations. If a `#pragma` directive were common, perhaps Borland would have thought to add a library routine to do the same. Nevertheless, this section will show you a few examples of `#pragma` just to give you a feel for its use.

In Listing 10.2, it appears that the function named `happy()` is unnecessary and that it never executes. Despite what you've always thought about `main()`, `main()` is *not* always the first function called! The `#pragma startup` tells the compiler to execute `happy()` before `main()` ever begins.

Listing 10.2. main() Doesn't Execute First

```
/* Demonstrates #pragma startup */
#include <stdio.h>

void happy(void);

/* This next directive tells Borland C++
   to execute happy() even BEFORE main() */
#pragma startup happy
main()
{
  printf("Just entered main()...\n");
  printf("About to exit main()...\n");
  return 0;
}
/************************************************************/
/* Despite the fact that main() never calls happy(), happy()
   is the first function called by the runtime system */
void happy(void)
{
  printf("Happy birthday!\n");
  return;
}
```

> **Caution:** Notice that you must prototype the `happy()` function before specifying the `#pragma startup` directive. The function cannot have arguments or a return value because no function calls the startup function and, therefore, no function exists to receive its return value.

Here is the output from Listing 10.2 to show that `happy()` does indeed execute before `main()`:

```
Happy Birthday!
Just entered main()...
About to exit main()...
```

In a like manner, you can specify an ending function that will execute by adding a `#pragma exit` directive. Listing 10.3 ensures that `happy()` executes after everything else in the program concludes.

Listing 10.3. happy() Executes before the Program Terminates

```
#include <stdio.h>

void happy(void);

/* This next directive tells Borland C++
   to execute happy() after main() */
#pragma exit happy
main()
{
  printf("Just entered main()...\n");
  printf("About to exit main()...\n");
  return 0;
}
/*************************************************************/
/* Despite the fact that main() never calls happy(), happy()
   is the last function called by the runtime system */
void happy(void)
{
  printf("Happy birthday!\n");
  return;
}

Just entered main()...
About to exit main()...
Happy Birthday!
```

You may find yourself specifying more than one startup and exit function, especially when coding debugging routines and writing flag-setting conditions in embedded programming (such as the programs inside computer chips in your car). If you have more than one startup or exit function, you can add a priority to the end of the `#pragma startup` and `#pragma exit` directives to let the compiler know your preferred execution order.

The priority values can range from 64 to 255, with 64 being the highest priority. The C libraries use the first 64 priorities from 0 to 63.

> **Note:** If you don't specify a priority, Borland C++ assumes a priority of 100. If two or more functions exist with the same priority, the first `#pragma startup` and the last `#pragma exit` determine which function executes first and last.

Listing 10.4 contains two `startup` functions, `happy()` and `happy2()`. The priorities ensure that `happy()` executes before `happy2()`, and that both execute before `main()` ever begins.

Listing 10.4. main() Executes Last

```c
#include <stdio.h>

void happy(void);
void happy2(void);

/* This here directive tells Borland C++
   to execute happy() then happy2() before main() */
#pragma startup happy2  101
#pragma startup happy   100

main()
{
  printf("Just entered main()...\n");
  printf("About to exit main()...\n");
  return 0;
}
/************************************************************/
/* Despite the fact that main() never calls them, happy() and
   happy2() are the first functions called by the runtime system */
void happy(void)
{
  printf("Happy birthday!\n");
  return;
}
void happy2(void)
{
  printf("And many more!\n");
  return;
}
```

Here is the output from Listing 10.4:

```
Happy Birthday!
And many more!
Just entered main()...
About to exit main()...
```

Some programmers like to write in a *top-down* fashion, meaning they prefer to write main() as a high-level program-controlling function that does little more than call other functions. Each of the other functions in turn call still more detailed functions, and so on. As you develop such programs, you might want to compile along the way, even though some functions are still only shells of their final form.

If you pass a function an argument, and the function accepts the argument in a parameter list, you'll get a compiler warning if you don't use every argument in the list. Consider the simple program in Listing 10.5. The function named get2() receives two arguments, but only uses one in the body of the function.

Listing 10.5. Not Using All Parameters Generates a Warning

```c
#include <stdio.h>
void get2(int i, int j);

main()
{
  int i=6;
  int j=8;
  get2(i, j);
  return 0;
}
/*************************************************************/
void get2(int i, int j)
{
  printf("i is %d\n", i);
  return;
}
```

Here is the warning you'll get when you compile this program:

```
Parameter 'j' is never used
```

This warning can be critical, especially if you've told the compiler to stop compiling after any warnings. You can turn off the display by placing the following #pragma directive before the function:

```
#pragma argsused
```

> **Caution:** You must use a separate #pragma argsused before each function whose argument warning message you want the compiler to suppress.

You learned in the previous chapter that you can control, from the source file, the name of the precompiled header file using the #pragma hdrfile directive. The following directive instructs Borland C++ to store the precompiled headers named myhdr2.h, myhdr3.h, and myhdr4.h in the precompiled header file named precomp.sym, but neither myhdr1.h nor myhdr5.h are precompiled:

```
#include "myhdr1.h>
#pragma hdrfile "precomp.sym"
#include "myhdr2.h
#include "myhdr3.h"
#include "myhdr4.h"
#pragma hdrstop
#include "myhdr5.h"
```

The #pragma hdrstop header tells the compiler when to stop adding header files to the separate compiled header file. Borland C++ will not include any headers that follow #pragma hdrstop. If a header file is extremely large, you might not want to include it in the list of precompiled headers. By excluding it, you can save precompiled header file disk space. Include such headers after the #pragma hdrstop directive.

This section attempted to give you some insight into some of the more common #pragma directives. Again, all of these directives are acceptable under ANSI C rules.

Wide Characters in a Global Environment

One new addition to C, an addition that the ANSI committee is working on perhaps more than they'd like, is support for wide characters and larger character sets. As of February 1990, the ANSI committee added support for wide characters in response to global requirements. Borland C++ now supports wide characters.

A wide character is a character that will not fit within the 8 bits that regular `char` data fits in. Borland C++ stores wide characters in 2 bytes, or 16 bits of storage, giving a total of 65,536 characters, as opposed to the 256 limit imposed on 8-bit characters.

International character sets, such as the Kanji character set, require more characters than allowed by 7- or 8-bit ASCII code. Although you might not think (or care) that you'll need such wide characters, someday you may want to write programs to *sell* to countries that need wide character programs. For now, simply take a cursory look at wide characters so that you'll know what's being supported.

> **Note:** The ANSI committee admits that they've only just begun. Support for larger character sets, including I/O and better character-mapping routines, are on the horizon for ANSI C.

Use the `wchar_t` data type (defined in STDLIB.H) to declare wide character variables. Once you declare a wide character variable, you can store a 2-byte character value by prefacing the value with the `L` qualifier. As you know, you can append `u` and `l` to the end of numeric literal to indicate `unsigned` and `long` literals. The `L` qualifier indicates a wide character. Why didn't the committee choose `w`? Who knows!

Listing 10.6 contains a short demonstration program that accomplishes these three actions:

➤ Prints the size of a wide character

➤ Prints the value stored in a wide character variable

➤ Prints the wide character variable size again, after storing the value to show that the size is not affected by the value stored (as is true about any variable)

Listing 10.6. Printing Sizes and Values of Wide Character Variables

```
#include <stdio.h>

/* Be sure to include the next header file that
   supports the wide characters */
#include <stdlib.h>

main()
{
  char *c1, *c2;
  wchar_t wideC;
  printf("The size of a wide character is %d\n", sizeof(wideC));

  wideC = L'YN';    /* Notice the single quotes */
  c1 = (char*)&wideC;       /* Set up pointers for each char */
  c2 = c1 + 1;
  printf("The characters stored are %c", *c1);
  printf(" and %c\n", *c2);

  /* Of course, the contents of the wide character
     variable has no bearing on the storage size */
  printf("The size of wideC is STILL %d\n", sizeof(wideC));

  return 0;
}
```

The assignment of the 2-byte YN value is accomplished with the following statement:

```
wideC = L'YN';    /* Notice the single quotes */
```

Notice that the value is enclosed in single quotes. That makes sense when you remember that a wide character is just that, a single *character,* and single quotes always enclose single characters.

When foreign C compilers supply true wide character sets, in which each individual character requires more than 8 bits, that wide character also would go inside single quotes.

> **Note:** You also can declare wide-character strings. Precede string literals with the L qualifier, as in wchar_t wideTitle = L"Killer C";, and each character in the string will consume two bytes of memory.

Here is the output from the program:

```
The size of a wide character is 2
The characters stored are Y and N
The size of wideC is STILL 2
```

There is a lot more work to be done with extensive character sets. The wide-character data type sets the stage for further development. Functions have to be added to display wide characters and make them behave more like 1-byte characters.

Superset of ANSI C

So often, people learning and using C feel that the ANSI standard does not go far enough—especially in light of today's hardware, large memory, *x86* PCs, video screens, mouse support, and so forth. The way that a compiler vendor, such as Borland, differentiates its product *has* to be in the non-ANSI C functions provided! All C compiler vendors know that they must support the ANSI standard. They must add pizzazz to the standard, creating a superset of the standard, to sell their product.

Borland's Variations on a Standard

Does the ANSI standard go far enough? Are there any elements of the C language that are open to interpretation *and* that still follow the ANSI committee's requirements? There is no way that ANSI can offer a set of requirements, for all aspects of the C language, that all vendors must

follow. There are simply too many versions of hardware and too many elements of the programming language still open to interpretation.

This section describes the ways that Borland C++ handles many of the unspecified elements of the ANSI C standard. It is interesting to look through some areas to see just how unspecific the standard can be. It is also interesting to note how different vendors might adhere to the ANSI C standard, while implementing different versions of that standard.

> **Caution:** The following sections discuss the unspecified ANSI issues that might apply to programmers as they write ANSI C code with Borland C++. There are other unspecified ANSI differences among compilers, such as the direction of truncating when rounding floating-point values. For an exhaustive list, check out the *Borland C++ Programmer's Guide* that comes with Borland C++.

ANSI Command-Line Issues

The ANSI C standard is an extremely long document. Many items address elements of C that the average programmer may never face or need to know about. For example, the ANSI C standard dictates how error messages are to be displayed. ANSI requires that the words `Fatal`, `Error`, or `Warning` appear before an error or warning diagnostic.

> **Note:** Among other things, ANSI figured that consistent diagnostic formats help with batch processing of program compiles.

To ensure that Borland C++ displays an ANSI-required diagnostic prefix, you must compile with the command-line compiler options found

in Table 10.4. This table lists the options that you *must* specify to ensure that the compiler precedes all command-line compile errors with `Fatal`, `Error`, or `Warning`.

> **Note:** When using Borland's IDE, you have no need for the diagnostic prefix because you won't do batch compiles inside the IDE; the Project Manager takes care of compiles.

Table 10.4. Command-Line Compiler Options Needed for ANSI Diagnostics

Option	Description
`-A`	Enables only ANSI keywords.
`-C-`	Does not allow nested `/* */` comments.
`-i32`	Allows for a minimum of 32 characters in identifiers.
`-p-`	Uses C calling conventions.
`-w-`	Turns off all warnings except those appearing in the rest of this table.
`-wbei`	Turns on warning about inappropriate initializers.
`-wbig`	Turns on warning about constants that are too large.
`-wcpt`	Turns on warning about inappropriate initializers.
`-wdcl`	Turns on warning about nonportable pointer comparisons.
`-wdup`	Turns on warning about duplicate, but nonidentical, macro definitions.
`-wext`	Turns on warning about variables declared with both `extern` and `static`.
`-wfdt`	Turns on warning about defining functions with `typedef`.
`-wrpt`	Turns on warning about nonportable pointer conversion.

continues

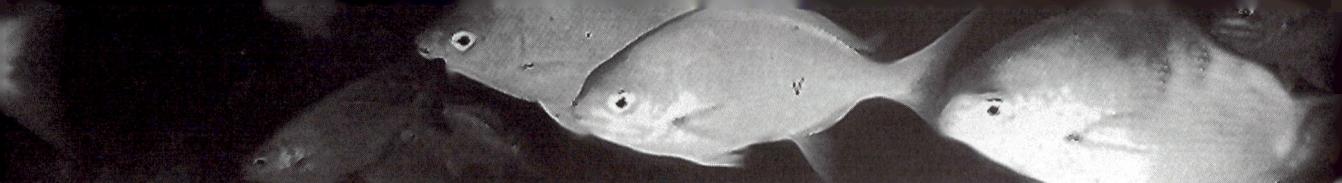

Table 10.4. Continued

Option	Description
-wstu	Turns on warning about undefined structures.
-wsus	Turns on warning about suspicious pointer conversion.
-wucp	Turns on warning about mixing pointers to signed and unsigned char.
-wvrt void	Turns on warning about returning values from functions.

Table 10.5 lists the command-line options that you *cannot* have set when you wish to conform to the ANSI diagnostics.

Table 10.5. Command-Line Compiler Options Unavailable for ANSI Diagnostics

Option	Description
mo!	Stack segment must be the same as the data segment when compiling in small memory models.
-mm!	Stack segment must be the same as the data segment when compiling in medium memory models.
-mt!	Stack segment must be the same as the data segment when compiling in tiny memory models.
-zGxx	You cannot change the BSS group.
zDint	You cannot change the data group name.

If you are compiling a program and you want to ensure that the ANSI diagnostic format appears, use all of Table 10.4's options and none of Table 10.5's. Here is an example of such a command-line compile:

```
C:\>bcc -A -C- -i32 -p- -w- -wbei -wbig -wcpt -wdcl -wdup -wext -wfdt
-wrpt -wstu -wsus -wucp -wvrt c:\try.c
```

Note: Command-line options that are not found in either Table 10.4 or Table 10.5 will not affect the appearance of ANSI diagnostics.

When compiling from either the IDE or from the command-line, you can specify command-line arguments. These arguments are passed to `main()` when your program first begins. The first argument, `argv[0]`, is open to interpretation by the ANSI standard. By convention (and as stated in K&R), `argv[0]` contains a pointer to the program name. This holds true for the vast majority of people running DOS versions since the introduction of 3.0. Users who run a compiled Borland C++ program on DOS versions prior to 3.0 (there are still some XT systems in use that do), `argv[0]` points to a null byte, so programs containing command-line arguments may not work on these systems.

Character Standards

There are several ANSI issues related to character data. This section describes some of the ways that Borland C++ handles character data in light of the ANSI standard.

Obviously, a PC-based product such as Borland C++ uses the ASCII table for *collating sequence.* A collating sequence is the sorting order used by such functions as `strcmp()`.

Not all computers are based on ASCII. Most mainframes are based on a similar, but slightly different, 8-bit character set named *EBCDIC* (pronounced *eb-si-dik*). The ANSI committee must let the compiler vendor use whatever collating sequence the compiler's hardware supports.

Borland C++ supports the 8-bit extended ASCII character set, meaning that C recognizes all ASCII values from 128 to 255. These characters, known as *higher-order ASCII* characters, contain many graphics and foreign characters.

Note: The only character that you cannot specify in string literals, character constants, or comments is Ctrl-Z.

The link editor supplied with Borland C++ (named *Turbo Link*) will distinguish between uppercase and lowercase characters in filenames. In a UNIX environment, where the operating system distinguishes between cases (the files abc.DAT and ABC.dat are different to UNIX, whereas they are the same to MS-DOS), the case can be significant. When using Borland C++, however, you can request that the linker suppresses the case distinction with the -I-c command-line option.

Borland C++ does not, by default, pad structures. Therefore, the size of a structure is the sum of the data types within that structure. By omitting the padding, Borland C++ stores data in the most efficient manner for memory savings. A program with lots of structure data, however, may slow down when no padding appears.

By specifying the -a command-line compiler option (n is 1 for Byte alignment [the default], 2 for Word alignment, or 4 for Double Word alignment), or setting the same alignment through the Options pull-down menu, you let Borland C++ pad between a structure's members, if the padding helps with the alignment. By forsaking the memory loss with the padding, you gain runtime speed efficiency.

When compiling with the 16-bit compiler, the program always reads 2-byte chunks of memory at once, and those 2-byte chunks always fall on even address boundaries. As Figure 10.2 shows, when a 16-bit program accesses a 2-byte int, only a single memory access is required because that data always falls on an even boundary. Borland C++ pads structures, if necessary, to ensure the even boundary of each data item. When byte-alignment is used (no padding of structures takes place) and a data item falls on an odd address boundary, Borland C++ must make two accesses to read the single 2-byte value. (For 32-bit compilations, Borland C++ accesses memory in 4-byte segments.)

Fig. 10.2. Alignment consumes extra memory at the price of speed.

Bit Field Considerations

As defined by Borland C++, a bit field might straddle word boundaries, if you don't specify word or double word alignment. Nevertheless, bit fields never consume more than two adjacent bytes of memory at once.

Be sure to specify `unsigned int` for all bit fields, unless you specifically want a `signed int`. If you designate a bit field as `int`, Borland C++ assumes that you mean `signed int`. (Everywhere in Borland C++ that you specify `int`, Borland C++ assumes `signed int`.)

The `char` data type is never aligned to even byte boundaries, due to the 1-byte length of all `char` data in Borland C++'s compiler.

Numeric Representations

Different computers and compilers support different integer sizes because of the differences in hardware register and bus sizes. Therefore, each C vendor is allowed to set its own exact numeric limits. Table 10.6 lists the integer limits that Borland C++ uses for both the 16-bit and 32-bit versions of the compiler.

Note: Table 10.6 also discusses the `char` data types, due to the similarities between `char` and `int` data types.

Table 10.6. Borland C++ integer Limits

Data Types	16-Bit Compiler Minimum	Maximum	32-Bit Compiler Minimum	Maximum
signed char	-128	+127	-128	+127
unsigned char	0	255	0	255
signed short	-32,768	+32,767	-32,768	+32,767
unsigned short	0	65,535	0	65,535
signed int	-32,768	32,767	-2,147,483,648	+2,147,483,647
unsigned int	0	65,535	0	4,294,967,295
signed long	-2,147,483,648	+2,147,483,647	-2,147,483,648	+2,147,483,647
unsigned long	0	4,294,967,295	0	4,294,967,295

Borland C++ uses the *IEEE* format for storing floating-point values. The *Institute of Electrical and Electronics Engineers* developed the IEEE format for Intel math co-processors. Borland C++ uses the 32-bit IEEE format for `float` values, the 64-bit IEEE format for `double` values, and the 80-bit IEEE for `long double` values. Other compiler vendors may use a different internal format, for floating-point data types, that is more efficient for other hardware.

Miscellaneous Issues

You might be interested to read about a few other unspecified ANSI standards. While this section does not cover all the remaining issues, several of the issues are worth mentioning, due to the possibility that they may occur in your own programming. As with all of these unspecified ANSI issues, you should watch out if you write programs for Borland C++ that others might compile and run on other vendors' compilers. This is because the other vendors may not support these features exactly as Borland does.

Address Formats

Different computers address memory in different ways. As discussed in the previous chapter, the PC uses a segmented memory architecture. Generally, addresses are specified using the following notation:

`BBBB:0000`

where `BBBB` represents an address's base address portion (the segment where the address resides) and `0000` represents the offset from the start of that segment, where the address actually appears. Both `BBBB` and `0000` always appear in hexadecimal.

Mapping Segmented Addresses to Real Addresses

To convert a segmented address to its real address, you must multiply the base by sixteen and add the offset. Multiplying hexadecimal values by 16 is easy because you only need to add a trailing zero. In other words, the segmented value `4F97:0443` represents the actual hex address `4FDB3` because of the following formula:

    4F970 (The zero was added to multiply by 16)
     0443 (The offset)

    4FDB3 (The actual hex address)

Non-PCs generally do not use the segmented addressing. The ANSI standard does not define the way the `%p` conversion character outputs addresses in functions such as `printf()`. When using a `near` data model (tiny, small, or medium models), `%p` outputs only the offset, because the segment will always be the starting address of the data segment. When using a compact, large, or huge memory model, Borland C++ outputs all `%p` addresses using the `BBBB:0000` format.

Note: The `%p` is useful for printing addresses of pointers. When using the IDE's debugger, all addresses appear in the `BBBB:0000` format.

Caution: If you ever request an address from the user, using functions such as `fprintf()` or `scanf()`, the `%p` format requires the same format of user input as `%p` outputs with the output function. In other words, the user must enter the `0000` address in a near memory model. Be sure to tell the user exactly what format your program expects for the input.

Bug Handling Issues

The `perror()` function is useful for outputting runtime error messages when writing ANSI C programs. The format of `perror()` is

```
void perror(const char *errMsg);
```

The `errMsg` is whatever error message you want displayed to the user. The message does not really have to be an error. The message might be instructions on whom to call in technical support or what to do to quit the program. There are several conditions in C, such as an attempt at opening a non-existing file, that don't produce immediate error messages, but which set a system macro named `errno` to an appropriate error number. `perror()` prints your message (the `errMsg` argument), followed by a colon, and the system error message for whatever error last occurred.

In the following code, if the disk drive x does not exist, and it probably will not on most systems, the `fopen()` fails and `perror()` executes because of the true `if` condition.

```c
#include <stdio.h>
int main(void)
{
    FILE *fp;

    fp = fopen("x:perror.dat", "w");
    if (!fp)
        perror("Call Technical Services at x304");
    return 0;
}
```

Here is the message generated:

```
Call Technical Services at x304: No such file or directory
```

Table 10.7 lists the `perror()` messages generated by Borland C++. Different compiler vendors might supply different messages because the different hardware might warrant a different set of errors. The ANSI standard cannot dictate exactly what `perror()` messages each compiler should produce.

Table 10.7. Borland C++ perror() Messages

Arg list too big

Attempted to remove current directory

Bad address *

Bad file number

Block device required *

Broken pipe *

Cross-device link

Error 0

Exec format error

Executable file in use *

File already exists

File too large *

Illegal seek *

Inappropriate I/O control operation *

Input/Output error *

Interrupted function call *

Invalid access code

Invalid argument

Invalid data

Invalid environment

Invalid format

Invalid function number

Invalid memory block address

Is a directory *

continues

Table 10.7. Continued

Math argument

Memory arena trashed

Name too long *

No child processes *

No more files

No space left on device *

No such device

No such device or address*

No such file or dircctory

No such process *

Not a directory *

Not enough memory

Not same device

Operation not permitted *

Path not found

Permission denied

Possible deadlock *

Read-only file system *

Resource busy *

Resource temporarily unavailable *

Result too large

Too many links *

Too many open files

* WIN 32 generates only these `perror()` messages.

By the way, if either `fgetpos()` and `ftell()` fails in any way, the `errno` macro is set to the `Bad file number` error message. According to ANSI, compiler vendors are able to handle these functions' `errno` values however they please.

Caution: `perror()` does not terminate the program! If you want a program to stop after a `perror()` executes, you must call `abort()`, `exit()`, or your own terminating routine.

C programmers sometimes use the `abort()` function to handle extreme errors. `abort()` produces the following message:

```
Abnormal program termination
```

After displaying the message, `abort()` terminates the program. ANSI leaves any cleaning up that `abort()` might do to each compiler writer. Borland C++'s `abort()` does just that: aborts whatever program is executing. Borland C++ will *not* close any files that are open or flush any remaining data to buffers.

The ANSI C `exit()` function *will* safely clean up loose ends from your program (when possible) by:

➤ Calling any and all functions registered with `atexit()`

➤ Flushing open stream buffers

➤ Closing open stream buffers

➤ Removing temporary files, if any exist

➤ Returning a code, signaling the program's result

You will always want to use `exit()` instead of `abort()` because of `exit()`'s cleaner nature. Nevertheless, you should understand `abort()` and how Borland C++ handles the function. The `assert()` macro calls `abort()` when the assertion is true, so you could trigger the `abort()` function through `assert()`, without realizing that `abort()` will not take care of a program's loose ends for you. Of course, `assert()` is more of a debugging than a runtime error-trapper, so the clean up should not lose a lot of valuable data.

ANSI C does provide for a uniform `exit()` return value. Instead of passing your own numeric value, you can pass the defined constants

`EXIT_SUCCESS` or `EXIT_FAILURE` as in:

```
exit(EXIT_SUCCESS);     /* Good termination */
```

If you port your source code to other ANSI C compilers, they should recognize these macros and handle them accordingly. If you pass something other than `0`, `EXIT_SUCCESS`, or `EXIT_FAILURE` to `exit()`, Borland C++ passes your value onto the receiver of the value (usually the operating system).

> **Note:** Borland C++ always treats the `exit()` return value as a `signed char`.

Making Sense of Memory Models

Sometimes, a C programmer begins to use a memory model and sticks with it, just for the reason that the model works for the job at hand. Often, newcomers to C choose a larger memory model than they should. They slow down their programs and consume larger amounts of memory than necessary.

If you've never taken the time to study the models and learn their differences, perhaps a review of the memory model concepts will help you make better decisions about your Borland C++ setup.

> **Note:** In the previous chapter, you saw references to the memory models as they affected the heap.

Here are the memory model sizes supported by Borland C++:

- Tiny
- Small
- Medium
- Compact

➤ Large

➤ Huge

The reasons that memory models are so vital to the PC world is because of the segmented memory architecture discussed in the previous chapter. If the original IBM PC's internal registers were wider than 16 bits, they could hold large addresses without the segment/offset scheme that had to be developed. 16 bits hold values from 0 to 64K, so a 64K segment value has to be combined with another register's 64K offset to form a true memory location.

To change the memory model that you use with Borland C++, you'll have to select the dialog box screen shown in Figure 10.3. You display this dialog box by selecting Options Project Memory Model. Change the options under the heading `Mixed Model Override`.

> **Note:** To retain the memory model settings across compiler sessions, choose Options Save and press Enter.

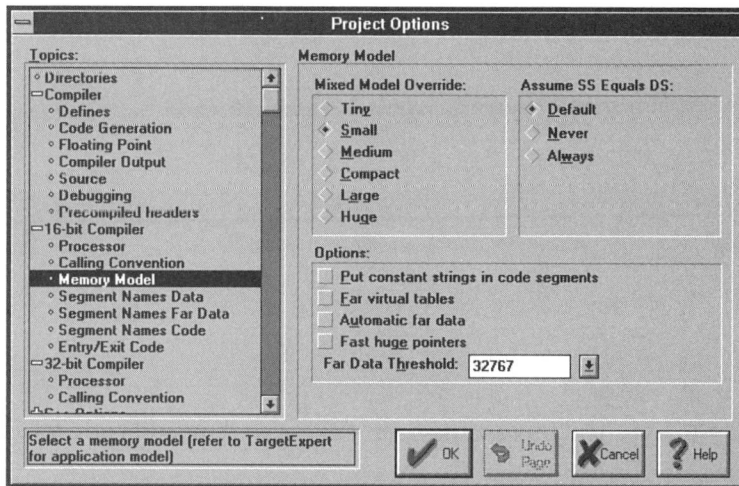

Fig. 10.3. Selecting the memory model.

The primary differences between memory models lie in the way Borland C++ stores a program's data and code. While reading through the following descriptions, keep in mind that a program's data occupies the heap and stack sections of memory.

> **Tip:** Table 9.3, in the previous chapter, described the predefined constants that are defined for each of the memory models. By testing the presence of a constant (using `#ifdef`), you can determine which memory model is in effect. Doing so may eliminate future runtime errors, if you know in advance which memory models are required for your code and data.

The Tiny Memory Model

The tiny memory model stores both data and code in one 64K segment. The tiny size of a single segment means that a program loads and executes quickly. Figure 10.4 shows how a program is stored using the tiny memory model.

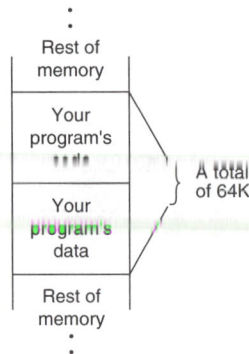

Fig. 10.4. The tiny memory model forces data and code into a tiny 64K segment.

There are several limits to a tiny model. Obviously, a program's data size is limited because both the program and data must share the same small section of memory. Despite the fact that 64K computers were common not too many years ago, today 64K is considered crippling for all but the smallest of programs.

> **Caution:** You can only create DOS-based non-Windows programs using the tiny memory model.

> **Note:** Although .COM executable programs are rare these days, Borland C++ lets you create .COM programs if you compile with the tiny option and specify the -t option.

By the way, the data area discussed throughout these memory models is the data area where the static, stack, *and* heap data goes. Therefore, the tiny memory model leaves you with very little room for code. Although your computer physically has more available memory, the tiny, small, and medium memory models provide access to a small data area due to their use of 2-byte near pointers for data.

The Small Memory Model

The small memory model gives you more data and program room by giving the code its own 64K segment and the data its own 64K segment, as figure 10.5 shows.

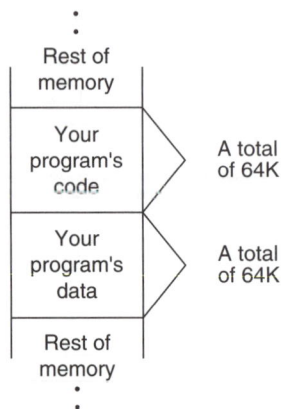

Fig. 10.5. The small memory model gives data and the code their own segment spaces.

The 64K space is enough room for most common DOS-based programs and some Windows programs. The programs run quickly because all pointers are near pointers (by default) and the larger 4-byte far pointers aren't necessary. No reference takes place outside a single segment.

The Medium Memory Model

The medium memory model gives preference to code, but does not expand the data space over the small memory model's structure. You can have several segments worth of code so that extremely large programs run in memory, but those programs will always run slower than identical ones that fit within the small memory model.

Figure 10.6 shows how Borland C++ sets up the medium memory model. The number of code segment sizes can add up to a total of one megabyte.

```
        ·
        ·
        ·
   Rest of
   memory

   A code          A total
   segment    >    of 64K

   Another
   code       >    A total
   segment         of 64K
        ·
        ·
        ·
   Another
   code       >    A total
   segment         of 64K

   Your            A total
   program's  >    of 64K
   data

   Rest of
   memory
        ·
        ·
        ·
```

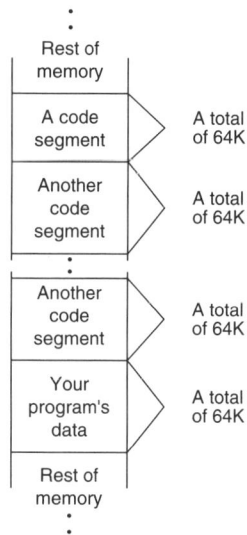

Fig. 10.6. The medium memory model gives data only 64K, but the code can occupy several segments.

Tip: The medium memory model is great for programs that keep very little data in memory. Disk access programs that don't load large amounts of data at once are good candidates, if you need the code room.

The Compact Memory Model

The compact memory model acts as a reciprocal to the medium memory model. Whereas the medium memory model gives code lots of room (one megabyte) but only one segment for the data, the compact memory model gives your code a single segment, but gives your data as many segments as needed.

Figure 10.7 shows the memory layout of compact memory models. When a program requires lots of room for in-memory data sorting,

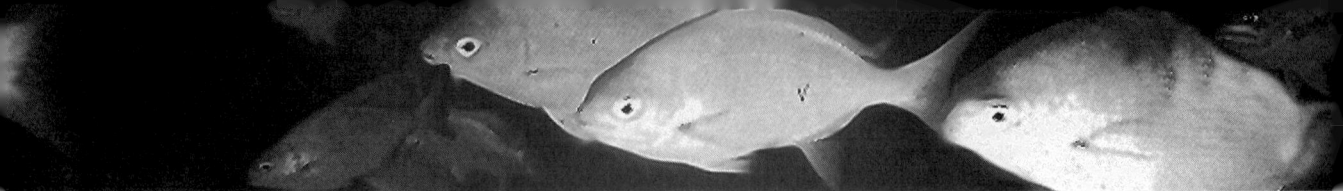

searching, and processing, and you want to achieve as much execution speed as possible, choose the compact memory model.

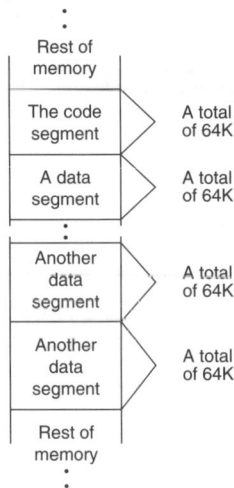

Fig. 10.7. The compact memory model gives code only 64K, but the data can occupy several segments.

Note: Borland C++ uses near pointers for all code execution to speed the program, but far pointers are needed for all the data access. If you need a lot of room for in-memory data, you'll be forced to convert to the slower access of the compact model.

The Large Memory Model

The large memory model is yet another step towards providing you with ample in-memory room for both code and data. You have up to one megabyte of memory for code and one megabyte of memory for data, as shown in figure 10.8.

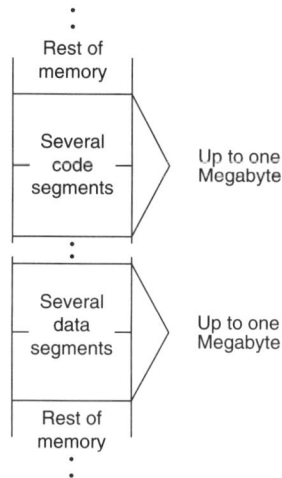

Fig. 10.8. The large memory model gives you lots of room for both data and code.

If you are unsure about your memory model requirements, try compiling and testing your program under the medium or compact models before using the large model. Of course, test under extreme data conditions — you don't want a user to run into a memory bottleneck after installing the program.

Caution: You'll notice decreases in both the program's execution and data access speeds if you use the large memory model. The compiler must use 4-byte pointers to access the code and data. Every time you call a function or declare variables, the 4-byte pointers will take longer to process than the 2-byte pointers available in other memory models.

Don't let the fear of slow program execution deter you from using the large memory model if you need the room. Computers get faster every day, not slower. Therefore, you have some solace in knowing that your program will speed up as it's run on newer computers in the future.

Also, some programmers will not notice any slowdowns, due to the type of data-access and computer processor that they use.

The Huge Memory Model

When developing applications, you might need to allocate a lot of static data, such as an array, that occupies more than 64K. The compact and large memory models give you the freedom to work with in-memory data that consumes more than 64K; however, each individual array or heap allocation must still fall within a 64K limit.

Therefore, use the huge memory model when you need to allocate arrays on the heap larger than 64K each. Be sure to compile your program using the huge memory model to support such large amounts of data.

From Here...

- ➤ Chapter 2, "Turbocharging Pointers," explains how Borland C++ supports the use of pointers. You can see how Borland extends the power of ANSI C by supporting pointer manipulation using many different operators and functions.

- ➤ Chapters 4 and 5, "Optimizing C" and "Optimizing C++," explain how and why older ANSI C-style coding techniques no longer suffice when you need extremely fast speed.

- ➤ Chapter 9, "K&R Implementation Secrets," gives the background for the genesis of ANSI C. It also explains why the ANSI committee adopted its standard, and why it works on a new standard for C++ today.

- ➤ Chapters 11 and 12, "Stroustrup Implementation Secrets" and "Extending Stroustrup's C++," give you the background on standardizing the C++ language. There is as yet no ANSI C++ standard, although the committee is working diligently on such a standard now.

Stroustrup Implementation Secrets

by Greg Perry

This chapter discusses Bjarne Stroustrup, the most important person connected to the C++ programming language. Without Mr. Stroustrup, there would not be a C++ language, because in 1979, Stroustrup designed the first version of C++ to improve on the C language.

This chapter explores the brief history of C++ and explains some of Stroustrup's intents for C++. In addition, perhaps you can get an insight into the current state of the language so that, in the next chapter, you can see where Borland C++ expands on the current C++ standard and hints at future C++ standard trends.

One of the most important C++ topics is the input-output stream class library, one of the few components of C++ that is open to debate as to what is "standard" and what is not. This chapter explains the input-output stream library from a specific viewpoint: Giving you practical specific tips and explanations that you may not have seen before. Like K&R's "C Programming Language," Stroustrup's books on the C++ language offer complete references on every aspect of C++, and yet, practical uses of C++ components such as the input-output stream class library are often buried in rich but sometimes terse explanations.

C++ lets you extend the behavior of the input-output streams and this chapter discusses that extensibility. One of the ways you can take advantage of C++'s extensibility is writing your own input-output manipulators to supplement those supplied by the standard C++ classes. This chapter explores the way that Borland C++ programmers can add their own input-output manipulators to C++ programs.

Many C++ programmers "cut their programming teeth" on string classes. One of the best ways to learn C++ is to start using the language as soon as possible. One of the ways that beginning C++ programmers tackle their first C++ project is by writing their own string class to make up for C's and C++'s lack of an intrinsic string data type. This chapter takes beginning string classes one step further by exploring some of the efficiency gains and trade offs of common string classes and describes how to develop a string class using *reference counting* to achieve high efficiency.

Finally, this chapter provides you with a miniature handbook of C++ tips and dangers, broken down by language topic. The format of this tip section's text gives you a tool that you will use often when implementing various elements of Stroustrup's C++.

A Brief History of Stroustrup's C++

In the mid-1970s, Mr. Bjarne Stroustrup worked on his doctoral thesis, writing simulation routines in the *Simula* programming language.

Simula, a simulation language (hence its name), contains a class structure that became a fundamental component of C++, extensive type checking, and a simulated co-processing feature that lets programs appear to model simultaneous events.

Although Stroustrup was greatly impressed with Simula, he could not complete his project using the Simula language due to Simula's difficulties with large projects. The language was not only slow, but consumed too many resources as the project grew. Stroustrup ended up completing the project in the BCPL language due to BCPL's high efficiency. That efficiency, however, added grief to Stroustrup's effort due to the low-level nature and tedious programming burdens that BCPL required. Nevertheless, Stroustrup's association with Simula and BCPL would impact the creation of C++. Although Stroustrup had yet to decide to develop a new programming language, he began to chart the features that he'd like to see in one someday.

Stroustrup joined Bell Labs and hung around such languages gurus as Kernighan and Ritchie (remember them?). K&R's impact on Stroustrup would both be praised and cursed by budding C++ programmers from the time of their first meeting. Although Stroustrup also began enjoying the abilities of the Algol68 language (more generically known as *Algol*), K&R's new C language hit Stroustrup with the most punch. C was based on Algol and the efficiency of C provided the vehicle that Stroustrup was looking for in his search for a language on which to base his language requirements. In 1979, Stroustrup began to develop his optimum language that was later to become C++. In Stroustrup's own tongue-in-cheek words, he wanted C++ to be "As close as possible to C, but no closer."

C++'s early versions (and some are still strongly used today) were not compilers but were interpreters. Stroustrup developed the *Cfront* interpreter for his new language called *C with Classes*.

> **Note:** That's right, C++ did not begin as *C++*. Stroustrup's original intent was to improve on C (which he did), but not to create a fully separate language.

As shown in figure 11.1, the UNIX-based Cfront processor took source code from C with Classes (shown in the figure as source code with the .CPP extension) and converted that code into straight C so that, in theory, any standard C compiler could compile the code. Stroustrup wanted to keep C's efficiencies but improve the programmer's prospective of the language. In 1983, Stroustrup's efforts took solid form when C with Classes was renamed C++ and finally considered enough of a stand-alone language to warrant its title as a separate language. (Not only did C++ have a new name, but many of the language's primary features such as virtual functions and references were added to C++.) Many say that Stroustrup's desire to compile his new language with available C compilers gave the language to enough programmers to spur its initial and needed growth.

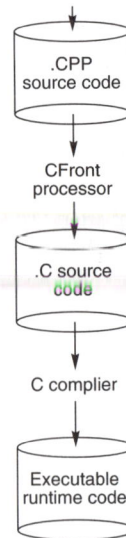

Fig. 11.1. Originally, a C compiler was used to compile "C with Classes" programs.

C++ became such an improvement over C—even the nonobject oriented aspects of C++—that the ANSI C committee added several C++ features to C, such as prototyping and the `const` declaration.

In 1985, Stroustrup published the *K&R* for C++. *The C++ Programming Language* was published and solidified many elements of C++ and was the primary language standard for a few years. During those years, the Cfront processors and the C++ language compilers went through several evolutionary steps until 1989 when version 2.0 of Cfront was released by Bell Labs. The version became known as *AT&T version 2.0.*

Stroustrup says that with AT&T 2.0, his original goals of the language were basically met. The de facto standard became Cfront 2.0, and in 1990, Stroustrup and Margaret A. Ellis wrote *The Annotated C++ Reference Manual* (known as the *ARM*), that still provides the final authority argument-splitter for many C++ implementations. Also in 1990, Stroustrup updated his *C++ Programming Language* 2nd Edition to bring it into modern times. The Cfront compiler is now in AT&T version 3, which will be supported almost in its entirety when the ANSI committee standardizes C++ sometime in the mid-1990s.

Now that the C++ fundamentals have been fairly standardized by the de facto AT&T standard, perhaps one of the major causes of C++ advantages, concerns, and debates is the input-output stream class library.

The Input-Output Stream Library

Borland C++ implements the input-output stream class library extremely well. Borland C++'s input-output stream library seems to correlate with most modern-day C++ compilers as well as the future ANSI C++ version, although nobody can really predict what the ANSI committee will finalize until their deed is done. As with C, ANSI's primary goal is to stay as compatible to currently installed programs as possible, so the odds of retaining the input-output stream class are high.

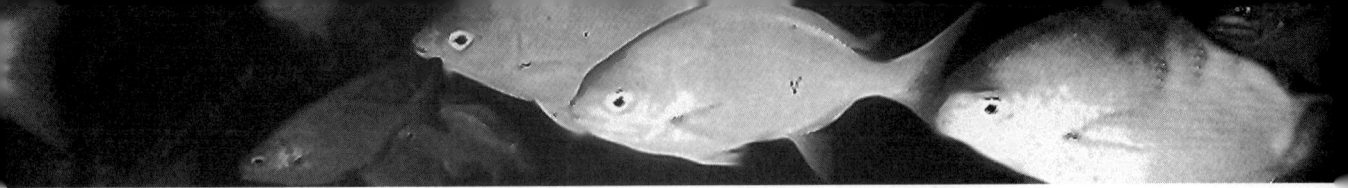

Figure 11.2 contains a general overview of the data flow in the input-output stream class. The data always flows from a *source* to a *sink*. Data is said to be *extracted* from an input source and *inserted* to an output sink.

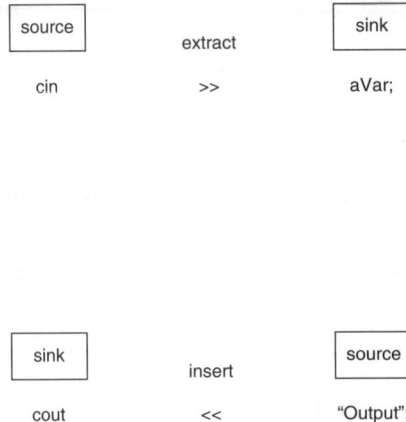

source	extract	sink
cin	>>	aVar;

sink	insert	source
cout	<<	"Output";

Fig. 11.2. Sources supply data sent to sinks

This section of the book gives you an overview of the input-output stream library in a pragmatic manner; using Borland C++, you'll read practical advice that expounds on Stroustrup's language and explains some of the areas of the input-output stream library that you may not have explored or thought much about. There is no way that a complete description of the input-output stream library can be discussed, and such a complete discussion would be out of place here anyway. The *Killer Borland C++ 4* programmer needs not a reference manual but some help and explanation in different areas that might add spice to his or her programming skills.

Overview of the Input-Output Streams

The SmallTalk programming language is a pure OOP language, as opposed to C++ which is known as a hybrid language due to its partial reliance on intrinsic data types in addition to derived object types. Nevertheless, SmallTalk is often considered to be the premiere *purest*

of the pure OOP languages and yet, SmallTalk supports only single inheritance. C++'s support for multiple inheritance garners C++ much pro and con criticism. SmallTalk programmers say they never miss multiple inheritance, and many C++ programmers say they can always substitute single inheritance for multiple inheritance.

One of the places that *all* C++ programmers use multiple inheritance (many times unknowingly) is when they use the input-output stream class library. The input-output stream class library derives from several overlapping multiply-derived classes (classes with more than one parent class). Figure 11.3 shows the mixed class inheritance hierarchy.

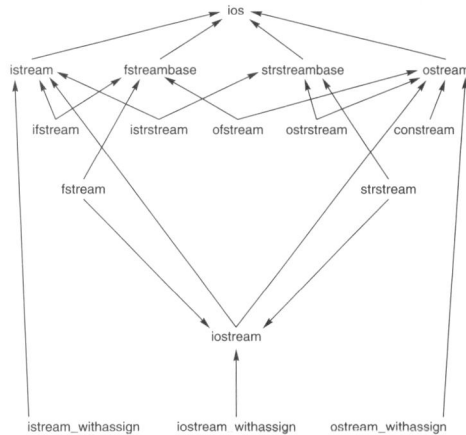

Fig. 11.3. The primary input-output stream class library.

Perhaps you've seen a similar multiply-derived, input-output stream class diagram. Many C++ programmers do not understand the entire diagram. The good news is that C++ programmers don't need to understand everything in the diagram. Data and implementation hiding is one of the strengths of C++, and the details of the input-output stream class can be hidden from view. Nevertheless, learning a little more about what goes on *under the hood* will give you more programming power. Table 11.1 explains each of the classes shown in figure 11.3.

Table 11.1. The Input-Output Stream Classes

Class Name	Description
ios	Specifies the ios (*input-output stream*) class family that performs input-output, error-checking, and formatting.
istream	The *input stream* class that provides the base class for all stream input.
fstreambase	The file stream class that provides the base class for all file stream operations.
strstreambase	The string buffer stream class that provides the base class for all memory buffering stream operations.
ostream	The *output stream* class that provides the base class for all stream output.
ifstream	Provides input operations for file streams.
istrstream	Provides for stream operations on input stream buffers. This class lets you perform input from a memory buffer that you've allocated.
ofstream	Provides output operations for file streams.
ostrstream	Provides for stream operations on output stream buffers. This class lets you perform output to a memory buffer that you've allocated.
constream	Supplies all console-related stream input-output capabilities.
fstream	Supplies input-output stream operations for file buffers. Commonly used to open files for both reading and writing.
strstream	Supplies both input and output support for stream buffer operations.
iostream	Supplies the base class for stream input-output providing functionality for the istream and ostream classes.
istream_withassign	Input stream functionality with the = overloaded to provide for assignment between streams.
iostream_withassign	Input and output stream functionality with the = overloaded to provide for assignment between streams.
ostream_withassign	Output stream functionality with the = overloaded to provide for stream assignment between streams.

From a practical standpoint, the classes at the bottom of the input-output hierarchy, namely, `iostream`, `ifstream`, `fstream`, `ofstream`, `ostrstream`, `strstream`, `constream`, are the most important classes to learn about because you will come across their use sometime in your programming. The nicest aspect of this inheritance structure is that the derived classes all share common characteristics such as being able to input, format, and output data automatically.

> **Caution:** Borland C++'s input-output class hierarchy does not necessarily match that of other C++ compiler stream classes. For example, not all C++ input-output stream classes contain the `constream` class. The `constream` class exists to support DOS-based text modes and not all vendors choose to implement such an input-output stream class.

Stream Functions or Classes?

Often, newcomers to C++ wonder why the `printf()` and `scanf()` stream functions were supplanted by the input-output classes described here. Although the stream functions, especially those related to `scanf()`, have syntactical problems for beginning programmers, these stream functions appear in countless lines of C code. Although C++ still supports the stream functions, C++ programmers are strongly encouraged to move to the input-output stream classes provided with C++.

From an application standpoint, the old stream functions simply no longer work well for today's common computing environments. Windows and OS/2 are not textual in nature. Borland C++'s EasyWin does support DOS-like textual style windows, and the input-output stream functions as well, but EasyWin is meant to be an intermediate vehicle for porting programs to the Windows environment. When you move to a strict Windows or OS/2 programming environment, `printf()` and `scanf()` do not provide practical programming input-output operations in the windowing environment because of their adherence to text modes.

There is, perhaps, a more pragmatic reason for using the input-output stream classes instead of the stream functions. Even if you still program in a text environment, the *safety* of the input-output stream classes is ample reason to begin using the input-output stream classes right away.

Most people reading this book will already be using C++'s input-output stream classes. Perhaps you love the classes and don't need to be convinced of their practical use. Nevertheless, you may or may not know how the input-output stream classes not only provide you with quicker programming speeds, but they also provide more debugging and even runtime efficiency than the input-output stream functions.

Before C++ came along, C programmers used the stream functions for all their textual input-output. The `printf()` function's prototype is rather simple, but that simplicity comes with a trade-off in efficiency. Here is the basic prototype for `printf()`:

```
int printf(char *format, ...);
```

The unspecified argument list means that, at runtime, C must determine exactly how to print the values in the list given the format string that you specify. In a way, a miniature `printf()` interpreter must be folded into your compiled runtime program to send the output to the output stream.

> **Note:** The C++ input-output stream classes, combined with the inserters (`>>`) and extractors (`<<`), produce much more efficient input-output because the C++ compiler fully compiles the statement at compile time and no runtime interpretation needs to be done.

In addition to their efficiency, the C++ input-output stream classes provide much better error-checking. The `printf()` functions can produce some hard to find bugs. Consider the program shown in Listing 11.1. The program compiles cleanly but it produces incorrect results.

Listing 11.1. An Incorrect Attempt at printf()

```
/* Produces a printf() runtime error */
#include <stdio.h>
main()
{
  int i = 10;
  long l = 20;
  float f = 30.0;

  /* Attempt to print the values */
  printf("%ld, %d, %.0f", i, l, f);
  return 0;
}
```

Here is Listing 11.1's output:

```
1310730, 0, 30
```

Obviously, something is wrong. The values should be 10, 20, 30 and the first two have major problems. The format string is incorrect. Although an int and long int values are printed first, their corresponding format string codes, %d and %ld are reversed.

The first format code, %ld, expects a long integer argument. When the printf() interpreter looks for the long int argument, the printf() looks on the stack for the values passed to printf(). (main() passes the three printf() arguments through the stack.) The first format code, %ld, makes printf() grab four bytes off the stack even though the i variable consumes only two bytes. The remaining two bytes come from the first half of l, hence the incorrectly printed value.

When printf() gets around to printing the second argument, only the last two bytes of the four-byte long integer l are left on the stack. The %d print code prints the long integer incorrectly, hence the 0 where a 20 should print. Finally, the float value f prints correctly. Figure 11.4 shows the arguments in memory and how the incorrect printf() format string grabs the wrong amount of memory.

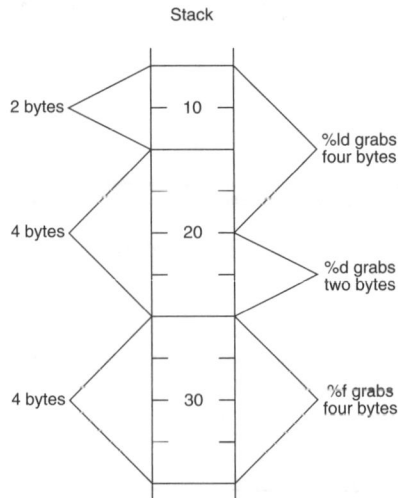

Fig. 11.4. The stack values don't match the `printf()` format string.

Perhaps you can see how the `f` would also print incorrectly had `%ld` been used for the first two argument format control codes; there would only be two bytes of the four-byte `float` value left to print by the time the third argument was printed.

Surely, you will never make the mistake shown here and reverse control codes in a `printf()` control string! The fact is, however, `printf()` offers no protection from bad argument lists. You can supply more data to print than you have `printf()` control codes for, more control codes than you have printed data, or mix up arguments without getting one compile error from a C compiler (or a C++ compiler compiling the C program).

The C++ input-output stream classes don't allow for such problems because the classes take care of selecting the appropriate format for the data you send to the stream. For example, the C++ program shown in Listing 11.2 prints the data correctly, and you don't have to worry about getting any control codes ordered properly. The C++ input-output are called *type-safe* because the data types print correctly every time.

Listing 11.2. The C++ Input-Output Streams Take Care of the Output for You

```
// Correctly prints the values
#include <iostream.h>
main()
{
  int i = 10;
  long l = 20;
  float f = 30.0;

  /* Fully type-safe */
  cout << i << ", " << l << ", " << f;
  return 0;
}
```

Here is the output from Listing 11.2:

```
10, 20, 30
```

The data types correctly streamed by the C++ input-output stream class are:

➤ `char`

➤ `short int`

➤ `int`

➤ `long int`

➤ `char *`

➤ `float`

➤ `double`

➤ `long double`

➤ `void *` (for printing pointer addresses)

Borland C++ formats these data types according to the rules of `printf()`, unless you override the formatting using manipulators.

The most important reason for using the C++ input-output stream classes is that you can extend the classes, unlike `printf()` and the other C input-output stream functions. For example, you cannot print your

class (or structure) data with `printf()`. You can print the individual members of a class, but you cannot print objects directly. For example, if you defined an inventory object named `item`, you cannot print `item` with `printf()`, but you can print `item` with `cout` like this:

```
cout << item;  // Prints an inventory item
```

To extend `cout` this way, you must first overload `<<` to print the `item` object exactly the way you want `item` printed, but once you overload `<<`, you never have to worry about the details again, and you won't have format string control codes getting in your way.

Overloading the inserter and extractor operators lets you take advantage of whatever kind of environment you program in. Overloading lets you output complete windows using simple statements such as this one:

```
cout << myWindow;  // Displays a window
```

Ending the Streams

Perhaps you have used one or more of the following items at the end of a `cout`:

➤ `'\n'`

➤ `endl`

➤ `flush`

Both `endl` and `flush` are input-output manipulators. (Input-output manipulators are discussed in the next section.) Most of the time, the first two perform the same function: Both `'\n'` and `endl` send a newline character to the output stream. The difference is the `endl` flushes the output buffer before sending the newline, whereas, the output buffer is not automatically flushed with `'\n'`. The difference is not critical unless there is an error during the output. If you use `cout` to display warnings and errors instead of `cerr`, you'll have a problem seeing some error message unless you consistently use the `endl` manipulator to end your output lines.

Listing 11.3 contains a short program that ends an output stream with the three characters. You see that `flush` does not send a newline to the output stream.

Listing 11.3. Using Three Different Terminating Characters

```
// End cout three different ways
#include <iostream.h>
main()
{
  cout << "One\n";
  cout << "Two" << endl;
  cout << "Three" << flush;
  cout << "Four\n";
  return 0;
}
```

Here is the program's output:

```
One
Two
ThreeFour
```

The purpose of the `flush` manipulator is to flush the output stream without sending a newline. `flush` leaves the cursor on its current line. You might use `flush` when you are outputting to a file or modem and you want to control exactly what kind of characters get sent without adding newlines.

Caution: Just because `endl` flushes the buffer in addition to outputting a newline doesn't mean that you should always use `endl` in place of `'\n'`. The extra flushing that `endl` performs takes time; if efficiency overrides your concern for flushing the buffer upon errors, end your `cout` insertions with `'\n'`.

The Manipulators

The header file named iomanip.h contains the header information for Borland C++'s input-output stream manipulators. Stroustrup defined the manipulators, and they have remained fairly constant since AT&T's version 2.0 of C++.

> **Tip:** When you include iomanip.h, don't also include iostream.h. The iomanip.h file includes the iostream.h for you. Although C++ won't include iomanip.h twice, the extra inclusion takes up your valuable typing time and the compiler's compilation time.

The input-output manipulators give you a chance to change the way that data behaves as it travels down the stream. There are two kinds of input-output manipulators:

➤ Nonparameterized manipulators

➤ Parameterized manipulators

Table 11.2 lists the input-output manipulators supported by Borland C++. These manipulators actually manipulate or change the stream, as well as sometimes sending additional data (such as a newline) down the stream as well.

Table 11.2. Borland C++'s Input-Output Manipulators

Manipulator	Description
dec	Output data in the base-10 numbering system.
hex	Output data in the base-16 numbering system.
oct	Output data in the base-8 numbering system.
ws	Extracts whitespace from the stream.
endl	Sends a newline and flushes the buffer.
ends	Sends null zero to the stream.
flush	Flushes an output stream without sending a newline.

Manipulator	Description
setbase(n)	Output data in the base-*n* numbering system. n can be 0, 8, 10, or 16. 0 resets the base back to decimal.
resetiosflags(n)	Clears the ios format flags.
setiosflags(n)	Sets the ios format flags.
setfill(n)	Sets the fill character for spaces left in the stream to n.
setprecision(n)	Sets the floating-point precision to n decimal places.
setw(n)	Determines the width of the field.

The last six manipulators in Table 11.2 are parameterized manipulators because they take an argument. By this time, you've no doubt used many or all of these manipulators, so this section will expand on just a few highlights of the manipulators.

Table 11.3 lists the format flags you can set and reset with setiosflags() and resetiosflags().

Table 11.3. Borland C++'s Format Flags

Format Flag	Description
ios::dec	Convert to decimal.
ios::left	Left-justify the output.
ios::fixed	Suppress scientific notation and always print with fixed decimal.
ios::hex	Convert to hexadecimal.
ios::internal	Pad with fill character after sign or base indicator and before number.
ios::oct	Convert to octal.
ios::right	Right-justify output.
ios::scientific	Display in scientific notation.
ios::showbase	Show base indicator (i.e., 0X8C).
ios::showpos	Display + on positive integers.
ios::showpoint	Always show decimal point.
ios::skipws	Skip whitespace.
ios::stdio	Flush stdout and stderr after insertion.
ios::unitbuf	Flush all streams after insertion.
ios::uppercase	Ensure uppercase letters in hexadecimal output.

All the input-output manipulators are sometimes called *sticky* manipulators except for `setw()`, which applies only to its current operation. As the program in Listing 11.4 shows, the field width value set with `setw()` lasts for one statement only.

Listing 11.4. setw( ) Lasts for its Current Operation Only

```
// Show stickiness of setw()

#include <iomanip.h>
main()
{
  int i = 123;
  cout << i << '\n';

  cout << setw(8) << i << '\n';  // Lasts for this line only

  cout << i << '\n';
  return 0;

}
```

Here is the output for Listing 11.4:

```
123
      123
123
```

If you want to output to a specific number of decimal places, `setprecision()` by itself will not work by itself. Sometimes, however, `setprecision()` *seems* to work for decimal precision as shown in Listing 11.5.

Listing 11.5. setprecision( ) Seems to Work Fine for Decimal Precision

```
// Show stickiness of setw()

#include <iomanip.h>
main()
{
  float f = 6.123456;
  cout << f << '\n';

  cout << setprecision(2) << f << '\n';
```

```
   cout << f << '\n';   // setprecision(2) still sticks
   return 0;

}
```

Here is the output for Listing 11.5:

```
6.123456
6.12
6.12
```

The problem is that `setprecision(2)` will not guarantee that two decimal places *always* prints; `setprecision(2)` guarantees that a *maximum* of two decimal places will print. Listing 11.6 shows that `setprecision(4)` ensures a maximum of four decimal places only.

Listing 11.6. setprecision( ) Controls Only the Maximum Number of Decimal Places

```
// Show that setprecision() ensures only maximum

#include <iomanip.h>
main()
{
  float f = 6.12;
  cout << f << '\n';

  cout << setprecision(4) << f << '\n';

  return 0;

}
```

Here is the output from Listing 11.6:

```
6.12
6.12
```

If you want four decimals printed (filled with zeros), you'll have to set the `ios::showpoint` and `ios::fixed` flags. Set the `ios::showpoint` and `ios::fixed` flags with the `setiosflags()` manipulator. Listing 11.7 contains a program that ensures four decimal places are printed for floating-point values once the appropriate `ios` values are set.

Listing 11.7. Control a Fixed Number of Decimal Places

```
// Print a fixed number of decimal places

#include <iomanip.h>
main()
{
  float f = 6.12;
  cout << f << '\n';

  cout << setprecision(4);
  cout << setiosflags(ios::showpoint) << setiosflags(ios::fixed);
  cout << f << '\n';  // Now prints with four places

  return 0;

}
```

Here is the output from Listing 11.7:

```
6.12
6.1200
```

If you do not specify the precision, Borland C++ will not print trailing zeros in float output unlike printf(). In other words, the following printf() call:

```
printf("%f\n", 100.000);
```

produces the following output because printf() automatically prints six decimal places unless you override the number of places with a format modifier:

```
100.000000
```

The Borland C++-equivalent code, however, shown here:

```
cout << 100.000 << '\n';
```

produces 100 on the stream. As mentioned before, you can modify the number of places sent to the stream. The lack of automatic trailing decimal zeros chosen by Borland seems to produce cleaner output without the trailing zeros. By the way, the action of printing or not printing trailing zeros on floating-point values is not defined by Stroustrup's standard; other compiler vendors may choose to display six trailing zeros on such floating-point numbers unless you override the trailing zeros with manipulators.

You might want to call the `setf()` or `unsetf()` member function applied to the `cout` object itself. In other words, these two statements are equivalent:

```
cout << setiosflags(ios::uppercase); // Uppercase hex letters
```

and

```
cout.setf(ios::uppercase);    // Uppercase hex letters
```

Write Your Own Manipulators

There might not be enough manipulators for your needs. One of C++'s strengths that Stroustrup strove to add to the language was the idea of extensibility. An earlier section explained how extensibility justifies the use of the input-output stream classes over their outdated input-output stream functions such as `printf()`. By adding your own input-output manipulators to C++, you can further extend the language. Once you write a manipulator, subsequent stream input-output can use that manipulator as if the manipulator were part of the language to begin with.

Tip: It is easy to write your own nonparameterized manipulators.

To write your own manipulator, you must supply a function that accepts a reference to an `ostream` object and that returns a reference to an `ostream` object. Your manipulator functions therefore take on the following prototype:

```
ostream & manipName(ostream & streamName);
```

Suppose that you wanted to write a manipulator that rang the PC's bell. ASCII 7 is the bell character. Listing 11.8 shows how such a bell-ringing manipulator is written.

Listing 11.8. Writing a Bell-Ringing Manipulator

```
// Contains a bell-ringing manipulator
#include <iomanip.h>

ostream & bell(ostream & out)
{
  out << '\a';
  return out;
}

main()
{
  int age;
  float dogYrs;
  cout << bell << "How old are you? ";
  cin >> age;
  dogYrs = (float)age / 7.0;
  cout << setprecision(2) << setiosflags(ios::showpoint);
  cout << "In dog years, that's only " << dogYrs
       << " years!";
  return 0;
}
```

If you compile and run Listing 11.8, the PC's speaker will beep right before the age question appears due to the manipulator. Borland C++ puts a function pointer in place of your manipulator and calls the function. For efficiency (although not necessarily code clarity), you can return the manipulator's `cout` object reference directly. You can replace the two-line body of Listing 11.8's manipulator function with this single line:

```
return out << '\a';
```

Some Thoughts on the Buffer Streams

The buffer classes, such as `ofstrstream`, provide input-output to and from memory, not unlike C's `sprintf()` and `sscanf()` functions. Unlike the C functions, however, the C++ buffer streams provide all the functionality of the stream classes because of their derivation from the stream classes. Therefore, you can use manipulators and overloaded input-output stream operators when sending data to memory buffers or when retrieving data from memory to a stream.

The program in Listing 11.9 demonstrates a stream-to-memory transfer. The memory is first allocated using `new` and then an output stream memory buffer object is instantiated using the `ofstrstream` class. The buffer then receives null zero-terminated stream information which is finally printed using `cout`.

Listing 11.9. Sending Data to an Allocated Memory Buffer

```
// Demonstrates output to buffer memory
#include <strstrea.h>
main()
{
  const int BUFSIZE = 100;
  char *memory = new char[BUFSIZE];
  ostrstream memBuf(memory, BUFSIZE);
  memBuf << "Hello, I have " << BUFSIZE
         << " bytes of memory allocated.\n" << ends;
  cout << "Here comes the memory:\n";
  cout << memory;
  delete [] memory;
  return 0;
}
```

Here is the output from Listing 11.9:

```
Here comes the memory:
Hello, I have 100 bytes of memory allocated.
```

The buffer stream classes provide you with an address-locator member function, `str()`. `str()` returns the address of a memory buffer. `str()` comes in handy when you want to let the stream's constructor handle the allocation of data. For example, you can instantiate an `ostrstream` object like this:

```
ostrstream memBuf;   // Construct a memory buffer object
```

Once instantiated, you can send data to the `memBuf` object using the inserter operator, `<<`, then output `memBuf` using the `str()` member function as shown in Listing 11.10.

Listing 11.10. Let ostrstream Allocate for You

```
// Demonstrates output to allocated buffer memory
#include <strstrea.h>
main()
{
  ostrstream memBuf;
  memBuf << "An automatically allocated buffer.\n" << ends;
  cout << "Here comes the buffer:\n";
  // You cannot print the contents of memBuf until
  // you have the address of memBuf ( returned by str() )
  cout << memBuf.str();
  return 0;
}
```

As you can see, letting the stream class allocate is a lot easier than doing it yourself. One of C++'s biggest strengths is taking burdens off the programmer's back. Here is the output from Listing 11.10:

```
Here comes the buffer:
An automatically allocated buffer.
```

> **Caution:** The ostrstream class allocates memory for you only if you can the constructor without any arguments.

In a like manner, you can grab incoming data from a memory buffer instead of another input device such as a file or keyboard. The `istrstream` class supports such formatted input-output stream input. Listing 11.11 shows a memory buffer being instantiated. There is no default constructor for the `istrstream` class; you must initialize the buffer at the time you construct it as shown here or allocate your own memory and specify the memory address and size as the `istrstream` constructor arguments.

Listing 11.11. Using istrstream to Grab Input from a Buffer

```
// Demonstrates input from buffer memory
#include <strstrea.h>
main()
{
  istrstream toMemBuf = "Hello there, I'm in memory.";
```

```
// Display the characters one at a time
for (char ch; toMemBuf >> ch; ) // Stop on null zero
{
  cout << ch;
}
return 0;
}
```

Here is the output from Listing 11.11:

```
Hellothere,I'minmemory.
```

Remember that all derived input-output stream classes share common properties with the others. The >> extractor operator skips stream whitespace by default. You must set a flag before Borland C++ knows that the whitespace is significant. Listing 11.12 fixes this input buffering problem and the output truly reflects all contents of the memory buffer.

Listing 11.12. Significant Whitespace on Buffer Input

```
// Demonstrates input from buffer memory
#include <strstrea.h>
main()
{
  istrstream toMemBuf = "Hello there, I'm in memory.";
  // Display the characters one at a time
  // but first, make whitespace significant
  toMemBuf.unsetf(ios::skipws);
  for (char ch; toMemBuf >> ch; ) // Stop on null zero
  {
    cout << ch;
  }
  return 0;
}
```

As you can see from the output that appears next, the unsetf(ios::skipws) ensured that Borland C++ did not ignore the whitespace coming from the input stream.

```
Hello there, I'm in memory.
```

Reference Counting

Although Borland C++ comes with a string class (described in the next chapter), Stroustrup did not originally intend to supply a string class with C++. Over the years, C++ programmers develop their own string classes. One of the most productive arguments C++ programmers get into are the benefits of one string class over another. Adding support for strings to a language that does not intrinsically support strings is a challenge that most newcomers to C++ hurdle while learning the language.

Many programmers will use Borland C++ 4.0 but not use Borland's string class. There are many advantages and disadvantages to the various approaches for string classes. Borland's implementation may not be as efficient for your application as a string class that you wrote and fine-tuned over the years. Therefore, many programmers continue using and honing their own string classes.

One of the ways you can improve a string class is by implementing *reference counting* in your string class. Reference counting is a simple process that keeps track of the number of string objects that refer to each defined string. The bottom-line advantage of reference counting over other string-storage approaches is that reference counting eliminates the need for duplicate strings in memory storage whenever there is assignment of one string to another. Reference counting also eliminates the need for inefficient string-length determination. When you call `strlen()`, C (and C++) must search from the string's beginning until a terminating zero is found. Reference counting offers the following advantages over other coding methods for strings:

➤ The string length is tracked instead of using the terminating zero for determining the string length at runtime.

➤ Strings can immediately be found to be unequal if their stored lengths differ instead of having to search tediously through the strings for a byte-by-byte comparison.

The first step in improving upon strings in C++ is to create a string class that contains at least two members, a length member, and a pointer to the string data like this:

```
class string {
  int length;
  char * sData;
// Other members follow
};
```

Strings are tracked via a pointer, and pointed-to data provoke special problems, such as when you create one string from another. Unlike other kinds of data, memberwise copying of data, from the current object to the new object being created, will not suffice for data pointed to. For example, consider the strings pointed to at the top of figure 11.5. s1's member pointer points to the first string and s2's member pointer points to the second string. Both strings are stored on the heap.

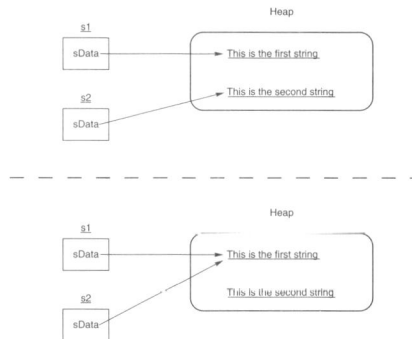

Fig. 11.5. Memberwise assignment loses a pointer.

If you do not supply an overloaded assignment operator, then attempt to assign one string to another like this:

```
s2 = s1;          // Lose a pointer
```

then you'll find yourself in the situation shown at the bottom of Figure 11.5. The same problem arises if you construct one string from another such as this:

```
string s3 = s1;  // Both pointers point to one occurrence of data
```

The following summarizes the problems that occur with memberwise assignment of strings:

➤ Heap memory is left unallocated.

➤ If the string pointed to by either s1 or s2 changes, *both* strings change.

➤ If only one string goes out of scope, the destructor will deallocate the data pointed to by *both* strings.

These problems arise simply because C++ performs memberwise assignment, assigning the pointer member of s1 to s2's pointer member but the heap data *pointed to* does not get copied. You must write an overloaded assignment (as well as a copy constructor for the same reason) to remove the string's heap data originally pointed to by s2, and then allocate a new string that is a copy of the original string. You then end up with the situation in figure 11.6 after the assignment.

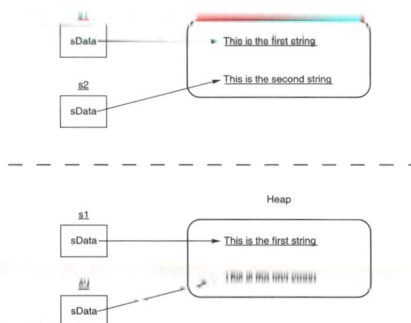

Fig. 11.6. An overloaded assignment and copy constructor fixes the situation.

So far, this discussion has probably been review for you. Most beginning C++ students study the following overloaded assignment member function to eliminate the problems just discussed:

```
String & String::operator=(const String & s2)
{
    if (this == &s2)   // If they're already
                       // equal, do nothing
```

```
          { return *this; }
      delete [] sData;  // Deallocate the old string
      // Allocate a copy of the data
      sData = new char[strlen(s2.sData) + 1];
      strcpy(sData, s2.sData);
      return *this;  // Allows for stacked assignments
  }
```

The copy constructor looks just like the overloaded assignment without the deletion of the right-hand string:

```
String::String(const String & s2)
{
    // Allocate a copy of the data
    sData = new char[strlen(s2.sData) + 1];
    strcpy(sData, s2.sData);
}
```

The problem with this generally accepted fix to a dangling string pointer problem is its efficiency. Also, the string class described so far does not use reference counting and, therefore, contains inefficiencies that can be cleared up. The copy constructor executes when one string object is created from another. This happens every time you pass or return a string object to or from a function. Therefore, if there are inefficiencies in the methods just shown for assignment and constructing, those inefficiencies can happen quite often.

The goal of reference counting is to duplicate strings whenever possible. That is, when assignment or construction takes place, the same data space will be shared among all pointers to that same string space. Unlike the code just shown, automatic duplication of strings will not take place. However, if any modification of a string is needed, then and only then does a new copy get created.

Reference counting in string class programming produces the situation shown in figure 11.7. There is only one copy of the string data and multiple string objects can point to that data. The first element of the data does not contain the first element of the string. Instead, the first element contains a *reference count* that describes the number of objects using the array as a string. The purpose of the reference count is threefold:

- When and only when the reference count becomes zero will a deallocation take place.

- If the reference count is 1, the data can safely be changed.

- If the reference count is more than one, and a string is changed, then and only then will a new string be allocated, copied, and *then* changed. Selectively allocating and copying a new string is much more efficient than allocating and copying a new string each time one is initialized or constructed from an existing string.

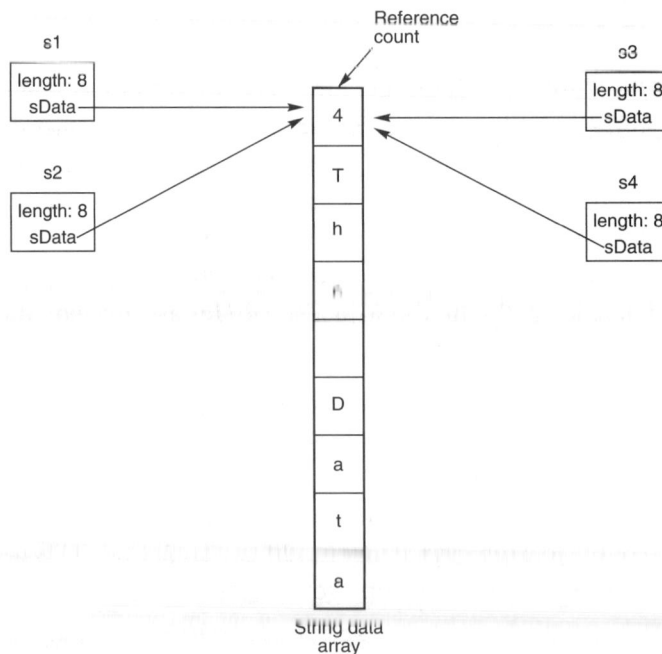

Fig. 11.7. Four string objects each point to the same string array.

Listing 11.13 contains the beginnings of a reference-counting string class. No operation is defined for string relational tests, input, or concatenation, but the class shown here is complete enough for initializing and creating strings. Concentrate on the three constructors, the overloaded assignment, and the destructor member functions for now.

Listing 11.13. Simple Implementation of a Reference Counting String Class

```cpp
// Demonstrates part of a reference counting string class
#include <iostream.h>
#include <string.h>
#include <stdlib.h>

class String {
  int length;
  char * sData;     // Point to the data array
public:
  String();                        // Default constructor
  String(String & str);            // Copy constructor
  String(char * sArray);           // Construct string from
                                   // null-terminated char array
  ~String();                       // Destructor
  String & operator= (const String & str);  // Overloaded assignment
  char & operator[] (int sub);  // Overload the subscript operator
  friend ostream & operator<< (ostream & out, String & str);
};

String::String() {
  length = 0;
  sData[0] = '\0';   // Just created an "empty" string
}

String::String(String & str) {  // Copy constructor
  length = str.length;
  // No copy needs to take place if rvalue string is null
  if (!str.length)
    { sData[0] = '\0'; }
  else    // Create a new string
    { sData - new char[length + 1];
      sData[0] = 1;
      strcpy(&sData[1], &str.sData[1]); // Copy the array only
      // The null zero also gets copied, but it's never used
    }
}

String::String(char * sArray) {  // Create a new string from old one
  length = strlen(sArray);
  if (!length)
    { sData = '\0'; }
  else
    { sData = new char[length + 1];
      sData[0] = 1;
      strcpy(&sData[1], sArray);  // Copy the char array
    }
}

String::~String()  { // Destructor
  if ((sData[0] != 0) && (-sData[0] == 0))
    { delete sData; }
```

continues

Reference Counting   **489**

Listing 11.13. Continued

```
    }

String & String::operator= (const String & str) {  // Overload the assignment
    length = str.length;
    if (!str.length)     // No data to copy
      { sData[0] = '\0'; }
    else
      // Delete the string only if need to
      { if ((sData[0] != 0) && (—sData[0] == 0))
          { delete sData; }
        sData = new char[length + 1];
        sData[0] = 1;
        strcpy(&sData[1], &str.sData[1]);
      }
    return *this;   // Allow for stacked assignments
}

char & String::operator[] (int sub) {
    // If the subscript is okay, and if the array exists,
    // create a new copy of the array to be changed so
    // as not to change others who share the array.
    // The implementation code bases the subscript at 1.
    if ((sub >= 1) && (sub <= length))
      {
        if (sData[0] > 0)
          { char * newS = new char[length + 1];
            newS[0] - 1;
            strcpy(&newS[1], &sData[1]);
            sData[0]—;
            sData = newS;   // Assign the pointers
          }
      }
    else
      { cerr << "Subscript error!" << endl;
        exit(-1);
      }
    return sData[sub];
}

ostream & operator<< (ostream & out, String & str) {
    int stCtr = 1;
    for (stCtr; stCtr <= str.length; stCtr++)
      { out << str.sData[stCtr]; }
    return out;   // Allow for stacked couts
}

main()
{
    String s1;
    s1 = "This is the first string";
    String s2 = s1;
    String s3;
    s3 = s1;
```

```
// All three constructed strings should have the same data
cout << "Contents of first string:\n " << s1 << endl;
cout << "Contents of second string:\n " << s2 << endl;
cout << "Contents of third string:\n " << s3 << endl;
s1[1] = 'X';  // Alter 1st element of s1
cout << "\n\nAfter changing the first string:\n" << endl;
cout << "Contents of first string:\n " << s1 << endl;
cout << "Contents of second string:\n " << s2 << endl;
cout << "Contents of third string:\n " << s3 << endl;

return 0;
}
```

Note: Even though the STRING.H header file is used in this class, the string functions are not used in the way they are for regular non-reference counting string classes.

Here is the output from Listing 11.13:

```
Contents of the first string:
 This is the first string
Contents of the second string:
 This is the first string
Contents of the third string:
 This is the first string

After changing the first string:

Contents of the first string:
 This is the first string
Contents of the second string:
 This is the first string
Contents of the third string:
 This is the first string
```

As you can see from the output, the first string is constructed, and then two more strings are constructed and initialized from the contents of the first string. Until the middle of `main()` where the first string's element is changed, there is only one copy of the string data as shown in figure 11.8.

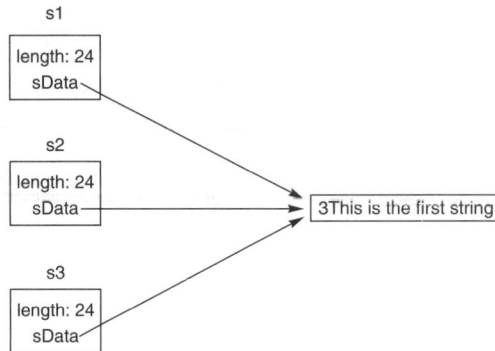

Fig. 11.8. One copy of the data is generated for the first part of `main()`.

The single copy of the string data keeps the memory and processing speed as fast as possible. Once the overloaded subscript operator executes when x is assigned to the first string's value, a copy of the string must be made so that the other strings' first element values don't change as well. The `operator[]()` creates the situation shown in figure 11.9.

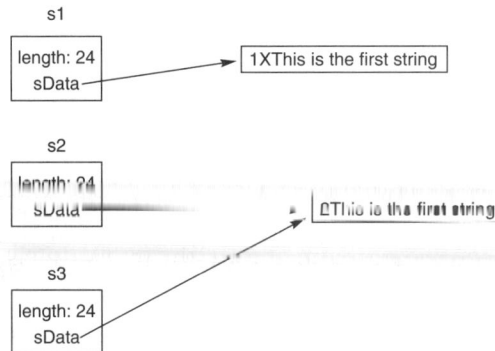

Fig. 11.9. A new first string (s1) must be generated.

Notice that a copy of the string is made only when a string must differ from the shared string data. Perhaps you now have the tools to add reference counting to your own string classes. If you have yet to write a string class, doing so will test your fundamental class knowledge. Implementing the reference counting algorithm described here will improve your string class considerably.

A C++ Mini-Tip Sheet

As you saw in the previous sections, there are many ways to take advantage of C++'s extensibility features and write programs that behave the way you want them to. With C++'s extensibility, you can expand and extend the language without resorting to nonstandard library functions or add-on language extensions.

In the next chapter, you see how Borland C++ improves upon the current C++ language standard by supplying nonstandard but helpful classes that decrease your programming time and (hopefully) increase your productivity. Nevertheless, there are many ways to improve your day-to-day C++ programming by taking advantage of shortcuts and by watching out for bug-prone code.

Although a complete library of books could be written on C++ tips and techniques, the following sections provide some tips and cautions that are practical but that still implement the C++ that Stroustrup intended. Each of the next small sections focuses on a specific part of the language that provides practical advice on using the C++ language.

Readability Usually Takes Priority

Just like C, and virtually every other programming language, you can write extremely cryptic code in C++ that runs efficiently but is difficult to maintain. In all but the most time-sensitive cases, you should code for readability over coding tricks.

C++ is a highly efficient language, close to C in its runtime speed and memory usage. Therefore, by using C++ instead of another language, you are improving your program's execution speed. It will rarely help your program to save a microsecond by writing cryptic code. Consider that computers get faster all the time so any code you write today will automatically get faster with each processor upgrade.

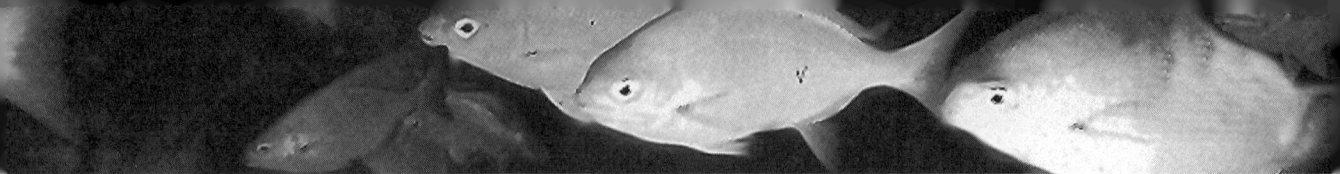

The following expression shows one such example. Can you describe what is going on here?

```
(i > j) ? ( (j > k) ? cout << "Yes" : cout << "Maybe" ) : cout <<
"No";
```

This nested conditional operator is probably efficient but each time someone has to maintain code around the conditional, that person will have to interpret the tedious nested conditional statement. Although nested `if` statements can sometimes be hard to read, the next nested `if` does the very same job as the nested conditional but is easier to understand and maintain:

```
if (i > j)
   { if (j > k)
       { cout << "Yes"; }
     else
       { cout << "Maybe"; }
   }
else
   { cout << "No"; }
```

Some Bug Eliminators

When testing for equality between constants and variables, get in the habit of putting the constant first in the relational expression. In other words, a habit of this

```
if (10==i)
```

eliminates more bugs than this

```
if (i==10)
```

simply because of the error that even C and C++ programming gurus still make: accidentally using the assignment in place of the equality operator. If you put the constant on the left side of the equality operator, the compiler will produce an error because the following statement would not be allowed:

```
if (10=i)
```

Borland C++ does tend to display a warning if you use an assignment in place of equality inside `if` statements like this:

```
if (i=10)   // Usually generates a warning
```

but you may turn off such warnings, or someone who might maintain your program later might turn the warning messages off.

Keep #define Only in C

If you eliminate the `#define` preprocessor directive from your C++ coding, the only thing you will lose is bugs. There are two problems with `#define`:

➤ `#define` does a blind search-and-replace without regard to data-type checking.

➤ #define often expands differently from the programmer's expectations.

As long as you use `#define` correctly, `#define` is safe. The problem is that using `#define` correctly is often easier to describe in theory than in practice.

A global `const` value is a variable that you cannot change. Being a variable means that a `const` value always has a data type, and type checking can be done on all uses of `const` values, whereas, such type checking is not always possible for `#define` constants. Additionally, `#define` is a preprocessor directive, not a language command, so a symbolic debugger cannot refer to a symbolic constant by its name, only by its defined constant value. The following `#define` at the top of a program:

```
#define AGE LIMIT 21
```

changes all occurrences of `AGE_LIMIT` to `21`. Therefore, if you run the debugger on the program, the debugger will always reference the value `21` and not `AGE_LIMIT` which is not as helpful as referring to the value by name. The following `const` statement, specified globally, produces the same result as `#define` without the side effects:

```
const int AGE_LIMIT = 21;
```

Another use for `#define` is macro coding. Using `inline` expands small functions and eliminates function call overhead without the side effects of `#define` macros. Consider the following simple macro:

```
#define NETSALES(g, f) g - (g * f)
```

If you were to use this macro in a simple assignment, you may or may not get the net sales that you expect. The following assignment assigns 80 to the netsales variable as you'd predict:

```
netsales = NETSALES(100.0, .2);
```

However, changing the assignment slightly produces an entirely different result. The following assignment

```
netsales = NETSALES(50.0+50.0, .2);
```

incorrectly stores 40, not 80, in netsales because the macro expands to this:

```
netsales = 50.0 + 50.0 - (50.0 + 50.0 * .2);
```

and the math precedence forces an unexpected result.

By the way, you do not need the inline keyword when you define member functions inside a class declaration. In other words, Borland C++ will always attempt to inline all functions that you specify inside a class. In the following class outline, Borland C++ will automatically attempt to expand fun1() inline but not fun2():

```
class Sample {
  // Private members
public:
  void fun1(int i) { cout << i << endl; }
  float fun2(void); // Defined later outside the class
  // Other class members go here
};
```

const Requires Care

As discussed in the previous section, you should begin to use const. const does produce a few programming considerations of which you should be aware.

Note: The ANSI committee added const to C *after* seeing the benefits of const in C++. const, just like prototypes, is an example of how C++ shaped the C language somewhat.

First of all, you should know that, unlike global constants in C, global constants in C++ have *file scope* (sometimes called *internal linkage*). If you need to compile together several source files and each needs to refer to one of the file's `const` values, you must qualify that `const` value with `extern` before the other files can reference the constant. If you were to define a global `const` value in C, any file linked with the `const` source file knows about the one file's `const` value without the need for `extern`.

When you combine `const` with a pointer, you can get into trouble if you're not extremely careful about the meaning of the relationship of `const` and the pointer. Consider the following possibilities:

➤ The following statements define a pointer to a constant variable named `fixed` and then assigns the address of a variable to `fixed`:

```
const int * fixed;
fixed = & anInt;
```

You can change the address stored in `fixed`. Therefore, you can assign other addresses to `fixed` throughout the program. You *cannot*, however, change any value pointed to by `fixed` because C++ knows that the pointer always points to a constant. `anInt` is not really a constant, but the `fixed` pointer will always act like `anInt` is constant. If you want to change the value in `anInt`, you can, but not through the `fixed` pointer.

➤ The following statement defines a constant pointer named `cPoint`:

```
int anInt = 15;
int * const cPoint = &anInt;
```

The address in the pointer cannot change but the value pointed to by `cPoint` can change. This is allowed:

```
*cPoint = 25;    // Increase anInt by 10
```

but this is not allowed:

```
cPoint = &anotherInt;    // Not allowed
```

➤ The following statement defines a constant pointer to a constant value:

```
const int aConstInt = 99;   // An integer constant
const int const * aConstPoint = &aConstInt;
```

The pointer and the value pointed to are locked together and you cannot change either one.

> **Tip:** When your program's definitions get confusing, read the definitions from right to left starting with the equal sign. The second line in the previous 2-line snippet of code says the following: *"Define a variable named* `aConstPoint`, *make it a pointer variable, be sure it is a constant pointer variable (cannot be changed), and make that pointer point only to an integer constant."*

References

A reference is easy for some people to understand and difficult for others. References are extremely easy to understand when you follow this definition:

"A reference is a pointer that is dereferenced for you."

In other words, when you declare a reference, you define a pointer to a value. However, you can use the reference variable without using the dereference, *, operator. The following statements define and print the value of a reference:

```
int & aVal = 5;
cout << "aVal is " << aVal << endl;
```

The following statements define a pointer and then print the value pointed to by the pointer:

```
int * aPtr;
*aPtr = 5;      // Notice that * is always needed
cout << "aPtr is " << *aPtr << endl;
```

Get used to using references, especially for converting C-based complicated pointer-to-pointer notation. Defining a reference to a pointer is simpler than using a double-dereference, **, to get the a double pointer's value.

If you return a reference from a function, be sure that the reference refers only to global variables. If you return references to automatic local variables, those variable values disappear when the function ends and you'll be stuck with a dangling reference.

Prototypes

As you already know, C++ requires that you prototype all functions. If you specify a prototype without any arguments, C++ assumes that you mean `void`. In other words, the following prototypes are identical to C++ (unlike C):

```
int aFunction();       // C++ assumes void argument list
```

and

```
int aFunction(void);
```

This can cause you problems when you convert your C programs to C++ because C treats empty argument lists as unspecified argument lists, not `void` argument lists. If you leave an argument list empty in a C program, C assumes that you don't want to prototype the argument list. C then lets you pass any kind of argument you want to the function. (In doing so, C also does no argument data-type checking.)

If you want to prototype an unspecified argument list in C++, you must use ellipses, ..., in the prototype's argument list.

When your program calls a function several times, and you pass the same set of arguments for most function calls, consider coding a default argument list so you don't have as much typing to do when calling the function. If you use default arguments for some of the function's argument list, be sure to specify those default arguments at the *right* of the argument list like this:

```
int aFun(int i, float f, char c='W', double d=.099345);
```

instead of incorrectly putting the default arguments on the left like this:

```
int aFun(char c='W', double d=.099345, int i, float f,);
```

main( ) May Not Return a Value

Unlike strict ANSI C, a C++ program's `main()` function does not
have to return a value. When K&R first developed C, they thought
that the operating system running a C program would need to
know the program's return value in case an error condition had to
be tested for.

C++ does not require that `main()` return an integer. Therefore, it is
fine to specify `main()` like this:

```
void main()
{   // Rest of main() follows
```

and then a simple `return;` is all you need.

By the way, you never have to prototype `main()`, although doing so
will not hurt anything. `main()` is *self-prototyping* because `main()`
executes first in your program and no other function calls `main()`.

Constructor Thoughts

If you do not supply a constructor, C++ will supply a default constructor for you. However, if you supply any constructor at all, C++ will *not*
supply a default constructor. Therefore, if you code a constructor
with arguments, you should *always* code a default constructor. For
example, the following class does not define a constructor:

```
class aClass {
    int i;
public:
    int iGet(void) { return i; }
};
```

C++ supplies a default constructor for `aClass`. You can define an `aClass`
object like this because a default constructor takes over and constructs
a simple `aClass` object:

```
aClass object1;
```

If you specify a constructor that requires an argument such as this:

```
class aClass {
  int i;
public:
  int iGet(void) { return i; }
  aClass(int I) { i = I; }
};
```

then you cannot define a simple `aClass` object like this:

```
aClass object1;
```

Therefore, if you ever specify any constructor, C++ decides that no default constructor is needed unless you supply your own.

If you do specify a default argument, be sure that you do not attempt to call the constructor like this:

```
aClass object1();  // Invalid!
```

Borland C++ will think that you were prototyping a function named `object1()` that takes no arguments and that returns an `aClass` object.

Name-Mangling and C Functions

C++ uses *name-mangling* when resolving function calls. When C++ encounters a function call or a function definition, C++ combines the function's name and argument list into a new name so that C++ can properly resolve overloaded function calls.

The problem with name-mangling is that a lot of C++ programmers still have libraries of compiled but unlinked C routines that they want to link to their C++ programs. If you link together a C++ program and a C routine, and the C++ program calls the C routine, the function call will be mangled (changed), but the C function name will not be mangled because it was compiled under a C compiler.

Be sure to tell any C++ program about C routines that it calls by adding a *linkage specification* that prohibits C++ from mangling any function calls to the functions described in the linkage specification. Here is such a linkage specification:

```
extern "C" {   // Let C++ know about all C function names
  void prNames(char * nameList[100]);
  int calcAge(int limit, float factor);
}
```

Allocating and Deallocating

Not only are `new` and `delete` easier to code than `malloc()` and `free()`, the automatic construction and destruction of objects by `new` and `delete` provides yet another reason to forget the C-style allocation and deallocation functions.

Do not mix the old with the *new* either. If you allocate with the `new` operator, always deallocate with the `delete` operator to ensure that any object that `new` constructs also gets destructed by `delete`. The reverse also is true; if you allocate with `malloc()`, be sure to deallocate with `free()` because `delete` might attempt to destruct an object that `malloc()` never constructed.

Newcomers to C++ often get confused with using brackets and `delete`. Which of the following do you use?

```
delete anObject;
```

or

```
delete [] anObject;
```

The answer depends on the constructor. The second `delete` line tells Borland C++ to remove both the object's pointer and all objects pointed to. You'll use the brackets if you allocated an array of several objects like this:

```
myClass * myObject = new myClass [45];  // Allocate 45 myClass objects
```

Without the brackets, `delete` would deallocate memory for `myClass[0]` only, not all 45 `myClass` objects.

Inheritance

When deriving classes from base classes, there may be times when you want to execute a base class function from within a derived class function. In other words, a base class function might print a message that a derived class function needs printing as well. You can repeat the base class function code inside the derived class, but it's much easier to use the scope resolution operator, `::`, to call the base class version from within the derived class.

For example, the derived class in the following code overrides the base class's `display()` function. However, the first thing the overridden `display()` function does is call the base class version of the `display()` function. The scope resolution operator used in this way eliminates duplication of code within your class hierarchies.

```
class aBase {
  // Private members
public:
  void display(void) { cout << "Initial message"; }
};
class aDerived : public aBase {
  // Private members
public:
  void display(void) { aBase::display();
                       cout << "Inside derived class." }
};
```

If you write a class that contains virtual functions, be sure to specify that the base class destructor is virtual as well. Making the destructor virtual ensures that C++ destructs any class object properly if the program uses a pointer or reference to the object.

Note: When you set up polymorphic virtual functions, you cannot virtualize a friend function or a regular program function.

From Here...

➤ Chapter 2, "Turbocharging Pointers," teaches you more pointer caveats and tricks in addition to those described in this chapter.

➤ Chapter 5, "Optimizing C++," gives you tips for writing the most efficient C++ programs.

➤ Chapter 12, "Extending Stroustrup's C++," explains how compiler vendors such as Borland C++ have gone well beyond Stroustrup's original intentions—for better or for worse. The chapter also shows how to get the most from the C++ language using many of the tools supplied with Borland C++.

➤ Chapter 18, "Exception Handling," discusses writing C++ code that does not fail when it encounters a common error. You learn how to identify potential errors and how to write code that works around these errors.

Extending Stroustrup's C++

by Greg Perry

Is Stroustrup's C++ language enough? C++ purists would say yes, and they can make a great case. Nevertheless, there is always room for improvements, perhaps not in the fundamental nature of Stroustrup's C++, but in the way compilers such as Borland C++ implement added classes and library routines.

This chapter discusses some of the ways that vendors such as Borland expand on the current basics of the C++ language. In the light of Stroustrup's intentions in the *ARM*'s specified language and the proposed ANSI C++ proposals, you will see how vendors will extend C++ to make your life as a programmer easier. (The last chapter explained the *ARM* (Stroustrup's *Annotated Reference Manual*) and its importance to C++'s beginnings.)

In this chapter, you learn about what makes a C++ standard. You also read about how the standards committee wrestles with these four important and sometimes difficult issues faced by the committee:

➤ Templates

➤ Exceptions

➤ Runtime Type Identification

➤ Namespaces

Finally, you will learn about some of the ways that Stroustrup and the rest of the committee go about deciding what to put in the standard language and what to leave out altogether.

What Is Standard Today?

Is Stroustrup's C++ the standard? Considering that the ANSI C++ committee working on its first C++ standard uses Stroustrup's C++ as its primary guide, a good case can be made that Stroustrup's C++, defined in his *ARM*, is still defining C++. Consider the following facts:

➤ In December 1989, an ANSI C++ committee was formed. Its fundamental design base was Stroustrup's *The C++ Programming Language*, published in 1985.

➤ Six months later, in May 1990, Stroustrup finished the *ARM*, which is considered the industry's current de facto standard and which the ANSI committee immediately began using as its authoritative C++ reference base.

Where is the ANSI C++ standard? As of mid-1994, there is not yet an official ANSI C++. There are leaks and the ANSI C++ committee members freely and openly discuss their problems, resolutions, and progress, but where is their final endorsed product? Language vendors wait around anxiously.

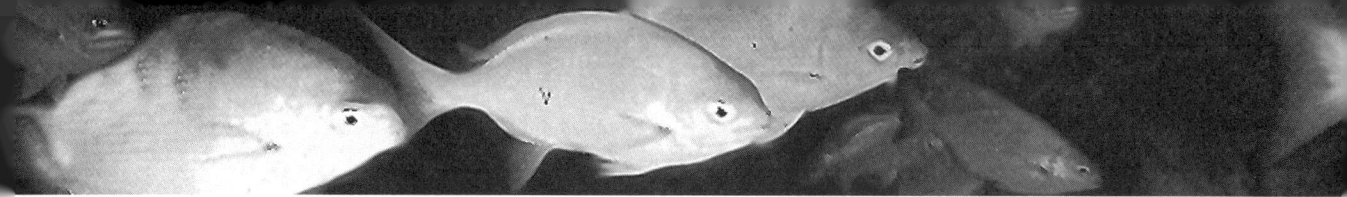

Although you will not veer too far off course by sticking with Stroustrup's *ARM*, Stroustrup himself has been overheard saying that he cannot carry the C++ torch by himself anymore and that the ANSI committee, despite its seeming slowness, is the only plausible way to standardize C++. (Stroustrup works with the ANSI C++ committee.)

Stroustrup has not updated the *ARM* since 1990. The ANSI C++ committee, however, has worked diligently, consistently, and continuously on its standard since its inception. It is currently agreed that the ANSI committee's *proposed* C++ is the most up-to-date and the one that vendors attempt to follow the most closely.

> **Caution:** Don't get too impatient with the ANSI C++ committee. It took the ANSI C committee around 10 years to solidify a C standard. If ANSI C++ can produce a standard by the mid-1990s, it will do so almost twice as fast as the ANSI C committee did!

If there is no ANSI C++ yet, how can vendors protect themselves by providing compilers that will *probably* match the final ANSI C++ document? The ANSI C++ committee has published its *X3J16 working paper,* which is a loose model of the C++ language it is working on. Throughout this chapter, you will hear the X3J16 working paper called simply the *working paper.* Language vendors spend much time studying the working paper and those vendors attempt to implement everything in the working paper, but many issues are still unresolved.

Four major issues still not completely resolved are:

➤ Exception handling

➤ Templates

➤ Runtime type information (*RTTI*)

➤ Namespace handling

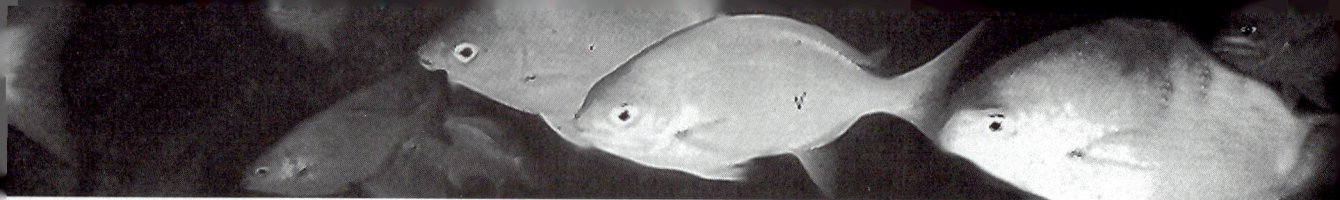

It is fairly agreed upon that the first two issues are close to being finalized and the committee is working heavily on the last two. Starting with version 4.0, Borland C++ supports exceptions and templates according to the current working paper's specifications as well as runtime type information. Borland C++ does not seem to support the C++ namespace handling, however. (Each of these issues and their impact on extending Stroustrup's and the committee's standard are discussed in the next few sections.)

There are, of course, many other details that the committee is working out, but the four mentioned in the previous list comprise what most consider of prime importance. The committee also has yet to finalize all its class libraries, virtual function return type handling, wide and European character sets, and multiple inheritance with virtual base classes.

> **Note:** When the ANSI committee does finalize its standard, there will be one single international ANSI C++ standard. An international standard is vital for those developers who write programs for other countries.

If all compiler vendors strive for the eventual ANSI C++ compatibility, will compiler vendors be able to differentiate their products enough to compete? Vendors such as Borland (Borland C++) and Microsoft (Visual C++) are competing by being as compatible to the working paper as possible while adding superset function libraries and class libraries to their fundamental C++ languages.

As chapters 9 and 10 presented, C compiler vendors often met the ANSI C compatibility requirements but strove to differentiate their products by adding library routines that went beyond ANSI C. In many ways, C++ compiler vendors are even more free to add libraries, and more importantly, classes, because the entire nature of C++ is its extensibility. C++ was a language designed to be expanded upon; the class mechanism is the perfect way for compiler vendors to add their personalized edge over the competition.

One of the ways that PC compilers gain a competitive edge is by providing an application framework class library that eases the programming of Windows programs. Both Borland's and Microsoft's application frameworks provide an object-oriented approach to Windows programming. Windows, although object-like, was designed to be written in C, not C++; many of the object-oriented advantages of programming were not available to Windows programmers until vendors began providing object-oriented programming wrappers around Windows calls. The frameworks available today let Borland and Microsoft programmers write powerful Windows programs in fractions of the time it took before the frameworks. The frameworks also provide OOP-like mechanisms for the programmers to use as well.

Borland C++ and other vendors also offer additional libraries that help you with many mundane programming tasks. Here are a few of the classes provided by Borland C++:

> *Container class library.* A template-based library, called the Borland International Data Structures (*BIDS*) library, that provides safe arrays (with bounds checking), binary trees, linked lists, hashtables, vectors, queues, sets, stacks, dictionaries, and dequeues.

> *Persistent streams library.* Lets you create an object, then store that object on the disk, send the object over modem lines, or pass the object back and forth between processes and applications.

> *Object Windows Libraries (OWL).* Borland's Windows application framework.

> *Mathematical classes.* Provides binary-coded decimal (*bcd*) and complex mathematical member functions.

> *Date class.* Support for date arithmetic and date conversion routines.

> *Time class.* Support for time manipulation and conversion.

> *File class.* Encapsulates standard file routines.

> ➤ *Thread class.* Provides class support for systems-level threaded programming algorithms.

> ➤ *String class.* Provides string functions for most common string operations such as creation, assignment, dynamic allocation and deallocation, and automatic resizing. Borland's string class is compatible to the string class being proposed by the ANSI C++ committee.

Most of today's C++ compiler vendors supply similar class libraries. As mentioned in the previous chapter, C++ programmers often write their own classes or purchase some that are fine-tuned to specific types of programming.

Perhaps someday, we'll all be able to buy a "plain vanilla" C++ compiler that is ANSI C++ compatible and simply has the standard input/output stream class library but nothing else. We'll then purchase only those additional class libraries that we need. The end result will be that each programmer will have a different set of compiler tools that is personalized to give each programmer the specific tools that he or she needs.

Standards and Templates

Chapter 17, "Mastering Templates," explains how to program with templates (sometimes called *parameterized types*). If you are unfamiliar with the way templates work, you'll want to study Chapter 17. The following sections analyze templates in light of ANSI C++ committee's solidifying C++. Some say that templates are not necessary, but the following sections show why templates are needed in ANSI C++'s final product.

The Necessity of Templates

Templates have been a part of Stroustrup's C++ language specification for several years now, but many C++ programmers view templates as something new. Templates were introduced to AT&T's version 2.1 of

C++ in 1990. Templates are still new components to many versions of C++, and there are still major C++ compiler vendors (the most notable is Microsoft) who have yet to implement templates in their products.

Although Borland began shipping templates with version 3.0 of Borland C++, Borland's first two versions of C++ did not ship with templates. Surely, one must wonder how useful the template language feature is for the major vendors not to mess with it in their early releases.

Given the lateness of compiler vendors, a question naturally arises at various conference debates: *Are templates really necessary?* The people at Microsoft certainly do not think that templates are necessary. The scores of programmers who now use Microsoft's Visual C++ don't seem to miss templates either.

You can program around simple function templates using `#define` macros or overloaded functions. Listing 12.1 contains a program that includes a simple function template that finds the minimum of two values while Listing 12.2 shows the very same program but uses macro to implement the template-like feature.

Listing 12.1. A Program that Uses a Function Template

```
#include <iostream.h>

// The following template function simply finds
// the minimum of two values. The first value
// is an integer (see main()) and the
// second is a floating-point value.

template <class Type>
Type min(Type first, Type second) {
  return (first < second) ? first : second;
}

main()
{
  cout << "The lowest integer is ";
  cout << min(45, 30) << endl;

  cout << "The lowest float is ";
  cout << min(45.67, 30.111) << endl;

  return 0;
}
```

Listing 12.2. A Macro-Based Function Template

```
#include <iostream.h>

// The following macro becomes inline code that
// finds the minimum of two values. The first value
// is an integer (see main()) and the
// second is a floating-point value.

#define MIN(first, second) (first < second) ? first : second

main()
{
  int lowi;
  float lowf;
  cout << "The lowest integer is ";
  lowi = MIN(45, 30);
  cout << lowi << endl;

  cout << "The lowest float is ";
  lowf = MIN(45.67, 30.111);
  cout << lowf << endl;

  return 0;
}
```

Here is the output of both listings:

```
The lowest integer is 30
The lowest float is 30.111
```

The first reaction of most C++ programmers is to discount the macro immediately, and rightly so. After all, Stroustrup, and virtually every other author on C++, can rarely begin a discussion of C++'s advantages over C, without describing the dangers of macro-based code. All C++ programmers learn early that const and inline replace #define and that #define should be buried very soon and very deeply.

Too many errors can find themselves in macro-based code. The macro expansion occurs before a program's compilation and this prepro-cessed expansion causes too many #define problems. Consider the subtle change to the Listing 12.2 shown in Listing 12.3.

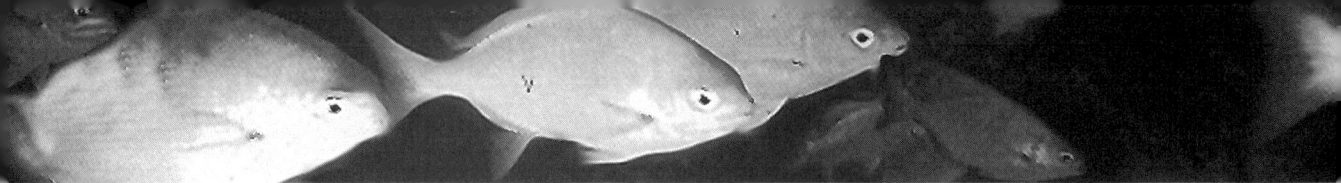

Listing 12.3. Introducing a Subtle Error Due to the Macro

```
#include <iostream.h>

// The following macro becomes inline code that
// finds the minimum of two values. The first value
// is an integer (see main()) and the
// second is a floating-point value.

#define MIN(first, second) (first < second) ? first : second

main()
{
  cout << "The lowest integer is ";
  cout << MIN(45, 30) << endl;

  cout << "The lowest float is ";
  cout << MIN(45.67, 30.111) << endl;

  return 0;
}
```

The `#define` no longer works when you insert the macro inside the `cout` output stream as Listing 12.1 did with template functions. The expanded conditional operator inside the streams produces these errors:

```
Illegal use of pointer
Illegal use of floating-point
```

The conditional operator's precedence interferes with the insertion operator, `<<`. If you enclose the `#define` macro inside parentheses like this:

```
#define MIN(first, second) ((first < second) ? first : second)
```

then Listing 12.3 would work. However, the case is proven that without templates, extra time and effort on your part (which backlogged programmers cannot afford) makes the case that begs compiler vendors to support templates. The problem is that you cannot easily write such simple template-like code without `#define` in languages that don't implement templates. Therefore, language programmers on platforms such as Visual C++ are left with this `#define` alternative.

`#define` does not provide the strong type-checking that templates offer. If you have the choice of using `#define` or a properly-implemented template mechanism such as that provided by Borland C++, you'll want to opt for the templates to ensure type safety.

Overloading without Templates

If a vendor does not support templates, you can achieve more type-checking by using overloading functions in place of #define but your functions are then too specific to extend very easily. For example, Listing 12.4 contains a function template that finds the minimum value in an array. With templates, you type only one version of the function. If you were to substitute overloaded functions for templates, you'd have to cut and paste a second version of the function, changing the data types, as done in Listing 12.5. Cutting and pasting code that *almost matches* what you need is not in the spirit of C++, whose extensibility and inheritance power attempts to eliminate such coding redundancy.

Listing 12.4. A Program that Uses a Longer Function Template Not Easily Implemented with *#define*

```
#include <iostream.h>

// The following template finds the minimum of
// an array of any data type. Pass the array
// and the number of elements in that array to
// this template function.
template <class Type>
Type minArray (Type ar[], int n ) {
  Type minVal;
  minVal = ar[0];  // Initialize with first array element
  for (int i=1; i<n; i++)
    {  if (ar[i] < minVal)
         { minVal = ar[i]; }
    }
  return minVal;
}

// main() implements the function template
// by passing an integer array and a floating-
// point array to the template
main()
{
  int array1[10] = {9, 4, 66, 2, 2, 55, 8, 53, 23, 12};
  int minArrVal1;
  float array2[5] = {8.765, 456.765, 23.21, 0.99, 0.1};
  float minArrVal2;

  // Find the minimum in each array
  minArrVal1 = minArray(array1, 10);
  minArrVal2 = minArray(array2, 5);

  cout << "The minimum in array1 is " << minArrVal1 << endl;
```

```
    cout << "The minimum in array2 is " << minArrVal2 << endl;
    return 0;
}
```

Listing 12.5. Two Overloaded Functions that Replace the Template

```cpp
#include <iostream.h>

int minArray (int ar[], int n );
float minArray (float ar[], int n );

// The following functions are a pair of overloaded
// functions. The first finds the minimum of
// an array of integers and the second floating-point.
// The array argument determines which function
// is called from main().
int minArray (int ar[], int n ) {
  int minVal;
  minVal = ar[0];  // Initialize with first array element
  for (int i=1; i<n; i++)
    {  if (ar[i] < minVal)
         { minVal = ar[i]; }
    }
  return minVal;
}

// Here is the second overloaded function that
// works with float arrays.
float minArray (float ar[], int n ) {
  float minVal;
  minVal = ar[0];  // Initialize with first array element
  for (int i=1; i<n; i++)
    {  if (ar[i] < minVal)
         { minVal = ar[i]; }
    }
  return minVal;
}

main()
{
  int array1[10] = {9, 4, 66, 2, 2, 55, 8, 53, 23, 12};
  int minArrVal1;
  float array2[5] = {8.765, 456.765, 23.21, 0.99, 0.1};
  float minArrVal2;

  // Find the minimum in each array
  minArrVal1 = minArray(array1, 10);
  minArrVal2 = minArray(array2, 5);

  cout << "The minimum in array1 is " << minArrVal1 << endl;
  cout << "The minimum in array2 is " << minArrVal2 << endl;
  return 0;
}
```

Standards and Templates   **515**

Here is the output of each listing of the previous listings:

```
The minimum in array1 is 2
The minimum in array2 is 0.1
```

If you wanted to implement a `double` array minimum function, you would have to write another overloaded function if you were left without template capabilities. With templates, you would not have to do any more than call the template function using the `double` array data type. (Again, if you need a full discussion of how to code templates, including template classes which are not discussed here, refer to Chapter 17, "Mastering Templates.")

Templates offer a strong argument for implementing the full features of ANSI's proposed language, despite the fact that you can "get by" without a full implementation. It is true that Visual C++ programmers might be extremely happy with Microsoft's product and never miss templates, but their programming lives really would be improved if and when Microsoft finally adds template capabilities to its C++ language. Besides, despite the fact that Stroustrup is no longer considered the final authority on C++, thanks to the ANSI C++ committee in the works, Stroustrup probably would not want to keep a feature such as templates in the language if there were no good reason to do so; Stroustrup *definitely* wants templates to remain in C++.

> **Note:** One of the most important reasons for Stroustrup's template handling desire was to support *container classes*. Container classes do just that: contain data. The container classes hold linked lists, binary trees, and so forth. The logic behind a container class sometimes gets complex. Once you write a container class for one data type, you must then write that same container class for another data type. Templates eliminate the need for writing a different container class for each data type your program requires.

Standards and Exception Handling

Chapter 18, "Exception Handling," explains programming with exception handling. If you are unfamiliar with the way exception handling works, you'll want to study Chapter 18. This section discusses exceptions in light of Stroustrup's and the ANSI C++'s language goals. Exception handling has been a part of Stroustrup's C++ language specification for several years now but, as with templates, many C++ programmers think that exceptions are something that's been recently added to C++ by the ANSI committee or by Stroustrup. In reality, both templates and exceptions have been a part of Stroustrup's C++ since before the *ARM* was published.

Until there is a final standard ANSI C++, the methods used by compiler vendors to design exceptions is open to change and interpretation. Although ANSI's working paper gives a good understanding of its direction, vendors such as Microsoft choose to implement exceptions in a fairly different manner from ANSI's working paper's specifications.

Fortunately, Borland C++ chose to stick with ANSI's proposal as Borland C++'s exception handling seems to be right in line with that of the proposed ANSI C++'s. To give you an idea of how compilers differ from one another in their support for exceptions, Table 12.1 lists a comparison between Borland C++'s and Visual C++'s exception handling to show you the direction that each uses to implement the same feature.

Table 12.1. Borland C++ and Visual C++ Exception-Handling Comparison

In Borland C++:	In Visual C++:
Exceptions are implemented in the OWL 2.0 classes.	Exceptions are implemented in the MFC 2.0 classes.
Supports ANSI C++'s working paper on exceptions.	Supports a non-ANSI C++ exception implementation.

continues

Table 12.1. Continued

In Borland C++:	In Visual C++:
Destructs objects where exceptions are thrown and caught through a process called *stack unwinding*. Borland C++ lets you change this default behavior if you need to ignore the destruction of certain objects when an exception is thrown.	Visual C++ implements exceptions through a series of macros.
The programmer can install his or her own try block.	Microsoft says that a future release of Visual C++ will support ANSI's proposed exceptions. Therefore, your current exception code may have to be changed.

As you can see from Table 12.1, Microsoft supports a modified exception handling through its MFC classes. Borland's exception handling follows the proposed ANSI C++'s exception handling design.

> **Note:** Chapter 18 explains the details of exceptions if you want to know how to code them. This chapter only explains the implementations of certain exception features in light of Stroustrup's and ANSI's intentions.

Neither Microsoft nor Borland introduced exceptions into their language products until 1992 (Microsoft) and 1994 (Borland). Therefore, as with the template discussion in the previous section, are exceptions really necessary? The answer is that in C++, exceptions are necessary if you want proper cleanup from error conditions. The `setjmp()` and `longjmp()` C library functions cannot handle the following situations:

> ➤ `longjmp()` does not automatically destruct objects. (Neither does Visual C++'s exceptions as currently implemented.)

- You cannot use `longjmp()` with overlaid DOS programs. There is no guarantee that the code to jump to is in memory when it is needed.

- A programmer's time is often taken returning through a series of intertwining function call links until the `longjmp()` returns program control to the proper error-handling condition.

- It is easy for a function that set a `setjmp()` to be resolved (already returned back to). When an error triggers a `longjmp()`, the `setjmp()` function will no longer be active to return to.

Unlike templates for which there were programming workarounds (discussed in the previous section and more fully in Chapter 17), it is amazing that *any* version of C++ was designed without exceptions! Controlling error conditions is too much of a laborious job for programmers; Stroustrup's initial exception-handling specifications should have been added to all C++ compilers written after Stroustrup went public with exceptions.

> **Note:** Exceptions are difficult for compiler vendors to implement. The difficulty involved probably explains why the vendors took so long to include exceptions in their products.

Standards and Runtime Type Identification

One of the newest features of the emerging C++ standard is the *runtime type identification (RTTI)* feature. The only PC-based C++ compiler that currently supports RTTI is Borland C++ version 4.0. Stroustrup did not even mention RTTI in the *ARM*. RTTI gives the programmer the ability to check information, especially data type information, of an object through a pointer to that object. RTTI is needed when you define pointers to several layers of inheritance and need to know what kind of data the pointer points to at any given time.

ANSI and RTTI

The ANSI C++ standards committee was initially reluctant to introduce RTTI for several reasons. The members felt that the overhead incurred would violate the nature of the efficient C-like superset language they were standardizing. Surely, one of the most important elements of C that a C++ language must maintain is efficiency. The committee decided that supporting RTTI for all data types, including `int`s, `float`s, and so on, would greatly hamper runtime performance. Therefore, if implemented, RTTI would apply only to polymorphic classes.

The committee members also saw RTTI as a mammoth addition to the language that was not necessary. RTTI would consume not only overhead, but RTTI also would require language extensions that replicate into several changes to C++ that might deteriorate C++ into something bigger than it should be.

One of the reasons that the committee decided to add RTTI to C++ is that, although C++ programmers could simulate RTTI in their own class libraries, such RTTI simulation is non-portable from one library to the next. The details of such RTTI support for a specific library are too ingrained in that class library's format for another class to use the RTTI effectively. If one class is to use objects of another class, runtime information must be made available, through the language itself, if the classes are going to work together.

Using RTTI

Figure 12.1 illustrates one reason that RTTI can be used to a programmer's advantage. In the figure, B is the base class and d1, d2, d3, d4, and d5 are derived classes coming from B.

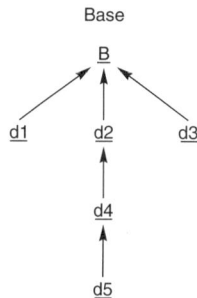

Fig. 12.1. Several classes derive from B.

If you wanted polymorphic access to figure 12.1's class hierarchy, you could define a base class pointer like this:

```
main()
{
  B * pObj;  // A pointer to the base class
```

As you know, a pointer defined to point to the base class can point to any class derived from the base class. You could not, however, define a pointer for one of the derived classes and expect to point to the base class.

The type of object pointed to by pObj can change as the program runs. What a program needs is to be able to find out exactly what kind of object is pointed to at any one time. In other words, in mid-execution, RTTI must be able to tell if pObj points to a B object, a d1 object, a d2 object, or another kind. You cannot use the data type of the pointer itself because the pointer is a base class pointer. If you were to define a different pointer for each data type in the inheritance hierarchy, you would lose the polymorphic advantages.

The programmer also might want to *downcast* a base pointer to one of the derived classes. The term *downcast* comes from the inheritance hierarchy representation that would require a cast *down* in the hierarchy if the base pointer were to convert to one of the derived classes. The program must ensure that a proper downcast is permissible and RTTI provides this information.

The goals of RTTI are:

➤ Allow for safe runtime-checked type conversions of a pointer. Borland C++ follows the ANSI-proposed specification of implementing the `dynamic_cast` operator.

➤ Identify the type of object pointed to. Borland C++ follows the ANSI-proposed specification of implementing the `typeid` operator.

The first and most important part of RTTI is the `dynamic_cast` operator, often referred to as the *downcast operator*. The format of `dynamic_cast` is somewhat strange. Here it is:

```
dynamic_cast<T*>(p)
```

The template-like notation makes sense when you realize that the `T` stands for a data type. The `p` argument stands for a pointer. Unlike many operators, the `dynamic_cast` operator performs two jobs. In a way, the `dynamic_cast` operator contains its own error-checking, a feature certainly not found in other operators. The `dynamic_cast` tells the compiler this:

"Cast the pointer, `p`, to the data type `T*`. If, however, the pointer `p` is not descended from `T*`. or if the downcast is not allowed, just return a `0`."

> **Note:** The use of a `dynamic_cast` operator instead of a function means that the programmer has to do less work to convert from one type to another.

You also can downcast to reference objects as long as `T` is a pointer and `p` is a reference to a non-base class.

Astute readers may wonder why Stroustrup and the ANSI C++ committee see the need for RTTI. Consider the class header in Listing 12.6 (the class is kept simple so you can better examine the details of RTTI). There is no need for RTTI in this situation because the normal virtual polymorphic actions take care of everything that's needed.

Listing 12.6. A Class Header without the Need for RTTI

```
// No need for a downcast because the polymorphic
// virtual functions take care of themselves.

class Machine {        // Base class
public:
  virtual void prPrice() = 0;
  virtual void prSpeed() {};
        // Assume nothing is available to you
};

class PC : public Machine {
  int numDisks;
  int speed;
  float price;
public:
  virtual void prPrice();
  virtual void prSpeed();
  PC(int N, int S, float P) : numDisks(N), speed(S),
                              price(P) {} // Initializer
};
void PC::prPrice()  {
  cout << "PC:" << endl;
  cout << "Number of disks: " << numDisks << endl;
  cout << "Price: $" << price << endl; }

void PC::prSpeed() {
  cout << "Speed: " << speed << "\n\n" << endl; }

class Typewriter : public Machine {
  int numKeys;
  float price;
  int ageYrs;
public:
  void prPrice();
  Typewriter(int N, float P, int A) : numKeys(N), price(P),
                                      ageYrs(A) {} // Initializer
};
void Typewriter::prPrice() {
  cout << "Typewriter:" << endl;
  cout << "Keys: " << numKeys << endl;
  cout << "Age: " << ageYrs << endl;
  cout << "Price: $" << price << "\n\n" << endl; }
```

Suppose that `main()` were to create an array of pointers to `PC` and `Typewriter` objects like this:

```
main()
{
  Machine * things[2];
  things[0] = new PC(2, 66, 2321.95);
  things[1] = new Typewriter(102, 265.99, 14);
```

Suppose `main()` wants to print the value of its pointed-to objects. `main()` can pass `things` to a `display()` function like this:

```
for (int i=0; i<2; i++)   // Pass each pointer
    {
      display(things[i]);
    };
```

The `display()` function will have no trouble printing the object pointed to correctly because of polymorphism. Here is a sample `display()` function:

```
// It is in the next function that virtualization takes
// the most importance. If item receives a pointer to PC,
// polymorphism makes sure that the PC's prPrice() executes.
// If item receives a pointer to Machine, polymorphism makes
// sure that the Typewriter's prPrice() executes.
void display(Machine * item)
{
  item->prPrice();
  item->prSpeed();
}
```

The problem arises when you derive from a class that you did not write. Suppose that you had no source access to the `Machine` class but you were to derive the `PC` and `Typewriter` objects from `Machine`. Assume that `Machine` does not supply `virtual` access to `prSpeed()`. You would have to rewrite `display()` using the `dynamic_cast` operator so that you only call `prSpeed()` when the passed pointer points to a `PC` object. Here is code that demonstrates the `dynamic_cast` usage:

```
void display(Machine * item)
{
  item->prPrice();               // Works on class
  // Attempt to downcast the item pointer
  // to a PC class pointer. If it works,
  // then you know that you have a PC pointer
  // and a 0 returned from dynamic_cast
  // means that the pointer was not pointing
  // to a PC object.
  PC * Pptr = dynamic_cast<PC*>(item);
  if ( Pptr )
  {
    item->PC::prSpeed();    // Okay to use prSpeed()
  }
}
```

If you wish, you can use the `dynamic_cast` directly and combine the `if` and `dynamic_cast` like this:

```
if (dynamic_cast<PC*>(item))
{
    item->PC::prSpeed();    // Okay to use prSpeed()
}
```

The `typeid` operator returns information about your data types and expressions. `typeid` returns a reference to an object of type `const Type_info`. Here is the class structure for `Type_info`:

```
class Type_info
{
private:
 Type_info(const Type_info _FAR &);
 Type_info & operator=(const Type_info _FAR &);
public:
    virtual ~Type_info();
    int operator==(const Type_info &) const;
    int operator!=(const Type_info &) const;
    int before(const Type_info &) const;
    const char * name() const;
};
```

As you can see, you can get the name of a type, compare two data types for equality, inequality, and compare whether one data type falls lexically before the other. The `before()` member function is not well-defined by Borland. Certain data types compare true or false against others when you perform `before` on them. The following statement compares true (returns a `1`):

```
cout << (typeid(double).before(typeid(float))) << "\n";
```

The lexical ordering of `before`'s return values is left up to the implementor of the language, according to the ANSI C++ working papers. It seems that Borland doesn't make consistent use of the `before` function but that ANSI C++ does not define `before`'s action very well either.

One of the nice things about `typeid` is that you can use `typeid` to find information about any data type, not just polymorphic pointer data types. The reason that ANSI C++ lets the `typeid` operate on both built-in data types as well as polymorphic data types is that the programmer controls when `typeid` is called and the runtime system does not have to continuously update type information as it would have to if the `dynamic_cast` operator worked on built-in types.

Caution: Be sure that you include the header file named typeinfo.h in all programs that use the `typeid` operator. The `typeinfo.h` header file contains structure descriptions needed by `typeid`.

Listing 12.7 offers a rather simplistic usage of the `typeid` operator. Notice that the member function `name()` returns the name of the data type that you pass to the `typeid` operator.

Listing 12.7. The typeid Operator Applied to Several Built-In Data Types

```
// Apply the typeid operator to several built-in
// data types
#include <typeinfo.h>
#include <iomanip.h>
main()
{
  cout << typeid(char).name() << "\n";
  cout << typeid(int).name() << "\n";
  cout << typeid(float).name() << "\n";
  cout << typeid(double).name() << "\n";
  cout << typeid(long double).name() << "\n";

  return 0;
}
```

Here is the output from Listing 12.7:

```
char
int
float
double
long double
```

The `typeid`'s `name()` member function returns the name of your own data types. If you were to define a class like this:

```
class aClass {
  int i;
public:
  display() { cout << i << endl; }
};
```

and then define a pointer to `aClass` like this:

```
main()
{
  aClass * classPtr;
```

You could display the data type using `typeid` like this:

```
cout << typeid(classPtr).name() << "\n";
```

Of course, such uses of `typeid` are good for discussing `typeid`, but printing data types is not the true power of `typeid`. With `typeid`, you can make sure that a cast is safe or check to see whether a function received a base class pointer or a derived class pointer.

The ANSI C++ committee admits that `typeid`, and all of RTTI for that matter, may not go as far as a lot of programmers would like but that RTTI is a good start. You'll find that templates and exceptions are much better thought out and documented than RTTI, not just because templates and exceptions have been proposed longer but because they are more complete. Over time, expect RTTI's power to increase as programmers become accustomed to its use and want more power from the operator.

Tell Borland C++ that You Want RTTI

Be sure that you have the correct compiler options set before using RTTI and Borland C++. The default Borland C++ 4.0 installation is ready for RTTI but through project file and compiler option changes, you may have unhooked RTTI.

If you run the command-line compiler, you can turn on RTTI by setting the `-RT` command-line switch. `-RT-` will turn off Borland C++'s RTTI ability if you want to eliminate RTTI for size considerations.

You also can set up individual classes for RTTI readiness. Use the `_rtti` class modifier to inform Borland C++ that you want the class and all derived classes to be RTTI aware. The following class named `rClass` is RTTI aware but `nClass` is not:

```
class __rtti rClass {
  // Rest of rClass class
};
class nClass {
  // rest of nClass
};
```

Standards and Namespaces

So far, you have read about how well Borland C++ supports most of Stroustrup's C++ and the proposed ANSI C++ specification. One area where Borland fails in providing compatibility is in the support of *namespaces*. Namespaces keep the global names from one class library from clashing (being the same and therefore causing compile problems) with global names from another class library.

As of version 4.0, Borland C++ does not address the namespace problem. Perhaps in a future release it will. In the meantime, you should familiarize yourself with some of the major namespace issues so that you will be ready to tackle them when vendors begin to add them to C++ compilers.

Borland's Limited Namespace

Borland C++ does support a limited namespace control, but the namespace control does not well support the use of class conflicts that arise in C++ programming. In a limited way, the scoping of a language helps define its namespace limits. There are currently five kinds of scope in Borland C++:

➤ Global scope

➤ File scope

➤ Block scope

➤ Prototype scope

➤ Class scope

Some scopes, such as prototype scope, do not affect identifiers. Therefore, additional namespace rules must be set up to ensure variable and function names do not conflict. There is already a namespace definition in Borland's C++, but that namespace is limited compared to ANSI's proposed C++ namespace addition. The following elements of Borland C++ are currently affected by a limited namespace:

➤ All `goto` label names must be unique within their function. You cannot have more than one label with the same name in the same function. Although using `goto` is fairly rare these days, understanding `goto`'s namespace helps you understand the entire namespace issue. The following code violates the `goto` label namespace:

```
int aFunction(int i)
{
  if (i == 2)
    { goto here; }
  else if (i <= 2)
      { here: return 1; }  // One label
    else { return 0; }
  { here: return 2; }      // Same label in
                           // a different block
}
```

Even though the label names appear in separate blocks, they both fall within the same function namespace so they violate the label namespace rules.

➤ Structure, class, union, and enumeration tags share a special namespace. The same block cannot contain duplicate tags. The following function violates the tag namespace rules:

```
void aFunction(int i)
{
  struct aStruct {
    int n;
    float * f;
  } a, b, c;  // Even though variables
              // are defined here...
  struct aStruct {
    long l;
    double d;
  } x, y, z;  // ... this struct's tag cannot
              // legally match the previous tag
}
```

If a structure (or class or union or enumeration) tag is defined globally outside a function, a local structure tag cannot have the same name as the global tag.

➤ Within a structure, class, or union, no two members can have the same name. The member namespace is violated in the following class:

```
class aClass {
public:
  char * name;
  int age;
  char name[];   // Oops! Same "name" as before
}
```

➤ Variables, typedefs, functions, and enumerations also share the same namespace. You cannot have two functions with the same name in the same program. Also, if you define an external variable or function, there can be no other external variable or function with that name.

Implementing Limited Namespaces

In place of class-oriented namespaces, various workarounds are available, but none of them seem to be adequate or reliable enough. A class vendor can supply a prefix or suffix to all class library names that would, in all probability, be unique and not clash with any other application. For example, if you were a class library vendor and you wrote a video rental check-out class, you could prefix your class names with a random sequence of characters such as this:

```
class p8L2_videoClass {
// Private members
public:
  int p8L2_getNumInInv();
  float p8L2_getPrice();
  void p8L2_checkOut();
  // And so on
};
```

The programmers who use your classes will tire very shortly of your classes. Programming requires enough typing without adding a strange prefix to every use of every class.

ANSI's Possible Solution

A better solution is to offer a space-naming extension to the language using, perhaps, the keyword `namespace`. The ANSI members are very reluctant to add new keywords and new standard library routines.

The namespace problem, however, is enough of a problem to warrant ANSI's attention. Also, the members know that adding a keyword does not make existing programs stop working as long as not using the new keyword keeps compatibility and that the programs change only when the keyword is used.

> **Tip:** To better understand class namespaces, consider the namespace scope as adding a sixth scope that is programmer-definable. As a matter of fact, namespaces are sometimes called *programmer-defined scopes*.

The following items can be scoped with a programmer-defined namespace:

➤ Structures

➤ Classes

➤ `typedef`S

➤ Globals (both variables and functions)

➤ Templates

Here is the format of the proposed `namespace` usage:

```
namespace nameSpaceName {
  // One or more identifiers
}
```

Here is an example of definitions that don't belong to a programmer-defined namespace:

```
int i;
float * f;
void prData(void);
double computeStats(double mean, double avg, double harmonic);
```

Here are the same identifiers defined as belonging to the `unique` namespace:

```
namespace unique {
  int i;
  float * f;
```

```
     void prData(void);
     double computeStats(double mean, double avg, double harmonic);
   }
```

This `namespace` is named `unique` and no other part of the program, even if a global or local variable is defined and named `i` or `f`, will conflict with any of the identifiers within the `unique` namespace. You can even define the same namespace throughout parts of a program (or across source files that might be compiled together). For example, `f` is not part of the `unique` namespace but the other three identifiers are in this code:

```
namespace unique {
   int i;
}
   float * f;  // Not part of unique
namespace unique {     // Continue the namespace definition
   void prData(void);
   double computeStats(double mean, double avg, double harmonic);
}
```

Once compiler vendors begin to support the namespace standard, class library writers can put their class headers into unique namespaces to avoid clashes with other libraries the user may later add.

> **Note:** There is a slight chance that two libraries might define namespaces with the very same name. The odds are great that this will not happen. Nevertheless, vendors will want to be creative with their namespace names to lower the chance that another may conflict. For example, `stringclass`, `strings`, and `stringlib`, might *not* be good namespace name candidates for a string class's namespace! There is a chance that someone else might choose the same namespace name for another class.

There is a usage problem associated with namespaces. One of the goals of ANSI is to make C++ as easy to use as possible while maintaining safety. Once namespaces are brought into a program, the program must, from then on, specify the namespace *and* the object whenever referring to an object from within the namespace. For example, in the

preceding namespace example, the programmer could not increment
the value of `i` without scoping `i` with the namespace like this:

```
unique::i++;  // Without namespace, C++ wouldn't know which i
```

The very idea of namespaces forces this extra resolution. After all, once
an object belongs to a namespace, a conflict cannot arise if that same
object's name is used in another context. The namespace ensures that
the two objects, despite their dual names, will not produce a conflict
but the programmer's burden increases by having to scope the
namespace object as well.

After a while, scoping the namespace to the object gets tiresome.
Therefore, the ANSI committee offers a solution called *namespace
aliasing* to help ease the namespace notation. Here is the general format of the proposed namespace aliasing:

```
namespace nsAlias = namespaceName
{ // One or more alias lines
}
```

The namespace alias works almost like a `typedef`. After the following
alias of `unique`:

```
namespace u = unique;
```

the rest of the program only needs to scope each `unique` namespace
member with `u` like this:

```
u::i++;  // Increments the unique namespace's i
```

There are several other namespace considerations in the works. The
ANSI C++ committee is proposing `using` directives and `using` declarations that will eliminate the need for scoping namespaces altogether.
The *overload resolution* lets all overloaded versions of a function appear in the namespace with only a single declaration. For example, the
following namespace declaration:

```
namespace functions3 {
  void prData(int);
  void prData(float);
  void prData(char *);
}
```

ensures that the three overloaded functions `prData(int)`, `prData(float)`, and `prData(char *)` all fall within the `functions3` namespace scope.

Now that exceptions, templates, and RTTI are finding a place in many C++ compilers, namespaces are almost assuredly the next ANSI C++ addition to be requested by programmers and added by vendors.

> **Note:** In fairness to Borland C++, which has continuously been on the leading edge in supporting ANSI C++-proposed language components, the committee may not have finalized namespaces in time for Borland to implement the namespace concept, or even a subset of namespaces, in time for the 4.0 version of Borland C++.

Possible Future Additions to C++?

Once the official ANSI C++ standard is released, what then? Can we all sit back and program in C++ knowing that the standard we have is written in stone? ANSI committees are not one-shot organizations. The ANSI C committee still works today, updating the C language with such issues as wide character sets. (Chapters 9 and 10 explained some of the issues with which the ANSI C standard deals.) Once a final ANSI C++ standard is written, you can be assured of the following:

➤ The programs you write under ANSI C++ will probably work with all future ANSI C++ standards.

➤ The programs you write under ANSI C++ are using a language debated and finalized by a group of experts who have your best programming interests in mind.

➤ The programs you write under ANSI C++ are fairly compatible to those written under previous pre-ANSI versions of C++, especially those compiled under an AT&T-approved C++ language.

There are many issues that the ANSI C++ committee has ruled out for current inclusion, but that the committee has left room for discussion in the future. The committee knows that C++ must be a living language and that the members must respond to the problems and requests offered by C++ programmers.

Consider the issue of garbage collection. *Garbage collection* is a term used for automatic dynamic memory defragmentation such as that shown in figure 12.2. There are many areas where garbage collecting may improve programs. Garbage collection has been left out of C and C++ and the committee has no plans for including it in the foreseeable future. Nevertheless, someday the committee may address garbage collection as an option or as a standard part of the language.

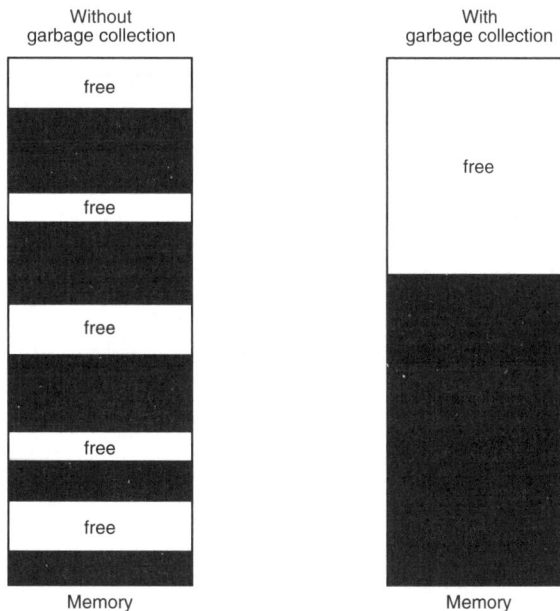

Without
garbage collection

free

free

free

free

free

Memory

With
garbage collection

free

Memory

Fig. 12.2. Without garbage collection, the heap gets fragmented.

The reason that garbage collection is now left out is to maintain the C-like efficiency of C++. One of the reasons that compiled BASIC languages are so much slower than C and C++ is that the BASIC runtime systems work furiously in the background, defragmenting string space

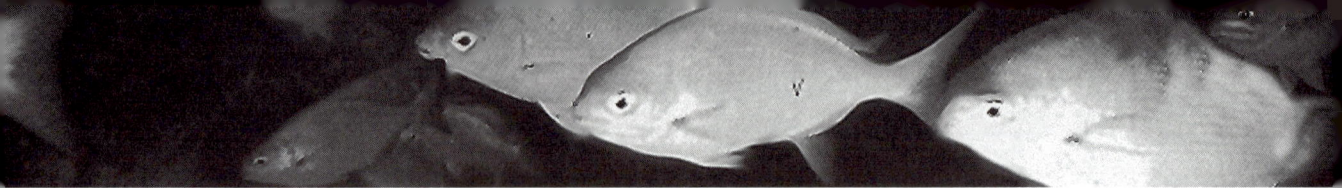

while your program executes. C and C++ programmers want efficiency. They don't want a behind-the-scenes helper defragmenting anything. If C and C++ programmers want garbage collection routines, they will write them and call those routines when they want to call them.

Despite its negative favor by C and C++ programmers, garbage collection is certainly a feature that would be useful if it were not inefficient. One of the reasons that BASIC-like languages are given to programming newcomers is because BASIC does so much for the programmer. Computers are supposed to be slaves of people, not the other way around. If C++ fragments memory, then C++ ought to be able to defragment that memory when needed.

Computers will always get faster with each new processor. Computers will never slow down. At the time of this writing, the magazines are touting 100 MHz PCs; at the time some readers read this, 100 MHz PCs will be offered for sale, used and cheap, in the backs of newspaper classifieds (and this book will still be considered new and as up-to-date as they come). Computers can get to a speed point where the garbage collection times simply will not matter to programmers and the committee will add the feature. Perhaps you will see garbage collection added as some kind of compiler option, or `#pragma` directive, but eventually, you will see it.

There is some talk about providing for overloaded functions that differ based on the return data type. Currently, the following functions are the same to C++:

```
int prData(void);
float prData(void);
```

If you attempted to put both these functions in a C++ program, you would violate one of the namespaces mentioned earlier. If the ANSI C++ committee approves overloading by return data types, these two functions will be considered separate and overloaded functions.

The committee also has thrown around the idea of supporting user-defined operators. If you want an operator that subtracts one and multiplies by 10, perhaps the language should support your wants. The user-defined operators may not find their way any time soon into a

C++ standard, however, because of the problems associated with precedence and program readability. Some think that defining your own operators will add complexity to programs. Of course, that did not stop Stroustrup from providing overloaded functions and overloaded operators. When a programmer can overload the minus sign to perform matrix addition, one must agree that the feature can be used for bad programming. There must be a common chord struck between difficulty in readability and ease of programming. The fact is that bad programs can be written using simple commands and regular operators, and good programs can be written using overloaded operators. The same can also be said for programmer-defined operators.

The committee feels, currently at least, that your functions should provide for any operations you desire and that giving the arbitrary ability to change /* to mean divide by 10 and multiply by 34 might render too many programs impossible to maintain. For now, ANSI has not ruled out user-defined operators, but user-defined operators will not appear any time soon.

From Here...

➤ Chapters 9 and 10, "K&R Implementation Secrets," and "Extending K&R's C," describe C++'s predecessor, C, in light of the language's original intentions and current standards. These chapters give you lots of background of what a standard means and what extending that standard implies for compiler vendors.

➤ Chapter 11, "Stroustrup Implementation Secrets," discusses several C++-related situations that Stroustrup did not originally directly address or explain in detail. You also will read about several practical techniques and tips that go one step beyond Stroustrup's language definition and explore the capabilities of the language.

➤ Chapter 17, "Mastering Templates," explains the ins and outs of templates giving you not only a template tutorial but also showing you how to best use templates in your programs to provide for your own parameterized types.

> ➤ Chapter 18, "Exception Handling," shows you how to write bullet-proof C++ applications by handling errors exactly the way you want them to be handled.

> ➤ Chapter 20, "C++ Style Tips," is one of the most important chapters in this book for meeting K&R and Stroustrup's common goal: the capability to write good, readable, maintainable code.

Mixed Language Programming

by Mark Davidson

While there are lots of books and magazine articles that cover programming with C and C++, very little attention is paid to the topic of Mixed Language Programming. You may not have many occasions in which you must link together code written in two different languages, yet the day will come where you have to tackle this somewhat thorny problem.

This chapter attempts to give you some insight into the kind of problems you can run into when mixing C++ with other languages. Combining C++ with C, Assembly Language, and Pascal will be discussed, under both DOS and Windows. Due to the complexity of this subject, this chapter only touches on the basics. However, there should be enough information here to get you started and at least point you in the right direction.

Why Use C++ with Other Languages?

Like it or not, one of these days you're going to run into the situation where you have to call a procedure or use some code that isn't written in C++. While it would be nice if everybody used C++ for everything, this just isn't the way the world works. You may have access to a lot of class libraries that provide tons of functionality for you, but what about that library of C code you or your company has developed over the past several years?

There are other reasons for using code not written in C++. For example, let's say you finish your application and determine that while everything works quite well, there are a few routines that need to be a little faster. In order to speed them up, you're going to have to rewrite them in assembler.

Let's say your company has a lot of code that provides capabilities you need, but it's not even written in C. It could be in Pascal. Or FORTRAN. Now what do you do? You could rewrite the code in C or C++, but then you are faced with the daunting task of testing this new code base (in addition to the code you've already written). In some cases, it may not even be feasible to convert the code yourself. You're just going to have to use it the way it is.

In fact, you've probably done some mixed language programming without realizing it. Something as simple as calling a function in the Borland C++ runtime library (such as `memcmp()` or `abs()`) involves mixed language programming simply because these functions are written in assembler, not C. Have you ever written a program in Microsoft's Visual Basic? Or Borland's Turbo Pascal for Windows? Programs written with these products are definitely not C programs, but you're calling routines defined in the Windows SDK, which is definitely not written in Pascal or Visual Basic. How about calling INT 21 from your program by using, say, `intdos()`? You're calling DOS, which is most definitely not written in C++. However, in all these cases, most of the work is done for you by the compiler vendors. There's no reason you can't do what they do; you just have to know how they do it.

Calling non-C++ code doesn't have to be that daunting. With a little thought (and a little code), you can easily call routines that are written in other languages from C++. However, there are some caveats to be aware of, and that is what this chapter is about. While calling C from C++ doesn't involve too much work, calling other languages throws several wrenches into the works that you need to be aware of, especially if you're developing DOS programs. Windows developers get a helping hand because, quite frankly, Windows encourages this practice. Thus, this chapter tackles the two environments separately.

However, before you see any actual code, there are several topics you need to be aware of. These pop up not only when you're doing mixed language programming, but also in several other circumstances, such as when you're developing a simple Windows program or invoking a DOS interrupt. First we take a look at these topics, and then we delve into calling non-C++ code from C++, covering not only C (which is supported by your friendly C++ compiler), but also Borland Pascal (which doesn't even use .OBJ files). After that, mixed language programming under Windows is discussed.

Please note that the subject of mixed language programming can be quite complicated and involved, so I just cover the basics here. However, I hope to give you enough information to get you started, and enough pointers to other documentation to answer any questions you might have.

Problems with Calling Other Languages

Calling other languages from C++ involves dealing with several details, many of which are usually handled for you by the compiler when you call C++ code from other C++ code. The details basically boil down to two subjects: *type differences* and *calling procedures.*

Different Native Types

When writing C++ (or C) code, you are provided with several basic types that are defined by the compiler (and the ANSI standard). These types are always available to you, and can be used to build other, more complex types and data structures. However, different languages have different ideas about basic types. C/C++ has `int`, `double`, pointers of all types, and so on, while Pascal has `INTEGER`, `REAL`, pointers, sets, etc. While the names may be similar, the amount of space each type uses in memory may or may not be the same, even if different types use the same amount of storage space in RAM. Table 13.1 covers the basic types for Borland C/C++, Table 13.2 covers Borland Pascal, and Table 13.3 covers Microsoft's Visual Basic. Table 13.4 attempts to compare some similar (and not so similar) types.

Table 13.1. C/C++ Types

Type Name	Size (in bits)	Range or Contents
char	8	Signed or unsigned, holds one ASCII character
int	16	Signed or unsigned integer
short	16	Either used alone or with int creates a 16-bit integer
long	32	By itself (or with int); creates a 32-bit integer
float	32	Floating point value
double	64	Floating point value; can be extended to 80 bits with the long modifier
enum	8/16	Size depends on compiler settings (the default is the same size as an int)
class	N/A	Varies with size of class definition
struct	N/A	Varies with size of struct definition
union	N/A	As large as the largest member of the union definition

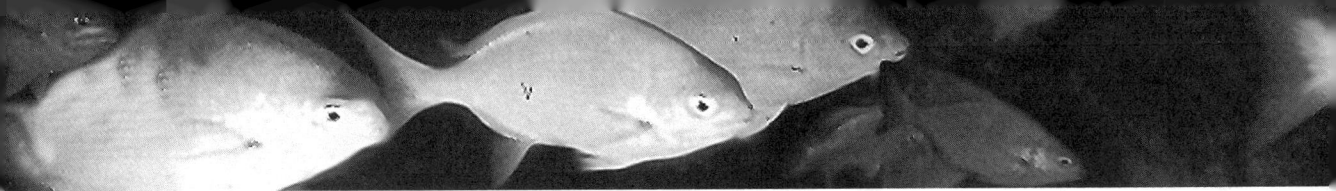

Type Name	Size (in bits)	Range or Contents
pointers	16/32	Size depends on memory model/type; it is 16-bits for the Small and Medium memory models, 32-bits for Compact, Large, and Huge. The size can be overridden with the "near" and "far" keywords.

Table 13.2. Pascal Types

Type Name	Size (in bits)	Range or Contents
Char	8	Holds one ASCII character
Shortint	8	128..127 (same as Char, except signed)
Integer	16	–32768..32767 (signed integer)
Longint	32	–2147483648..2147483647 (signed)
Byte	8	0..255 (unsigned byte)
Word	16	0..65535 (unsigned integer)
Boolean	8	Can be either False or True; All of the Bool types are sets with two possible values.
WordBool	16	(False, True)
LongBool	32	(False, True)
ByteBool	8	(False, True); (same as Boolean)
Pointer	32	Can point to any type
Real	48	2.9e-39..1.7e38 (floating point value)
Single	24	1.5e-45..3.4e38 (floating point value)
Double	64	5.0e-324..1.7e308 (floating point value)
Extended	80	3.4e-4932..1.1e4932 (floating point value)
Comp	64	–9.2e18..9.2e18
String	N/A	Varies with size of declaration
Structure Types	N/A	Varies with size of declaration

Table 13.3. Visual Basic Types

Type Name	Size (in bits)	Range or Contents
Integer	16	–32,768..32,767 (signed integer)
Long	32	–2,147,483,648..2,147,483,647. (signed long)
Single	32	–3.402823E38..-1.401298E-45 for negative values; 1.401298E-45..3.402823E38 for positive values
Double	64	–1.79769313486232E308..-4.94065645841247E-324 for negative values; 4.94065645841247E-324..1.79769313486232E308 for positive values
Currency	64	–922,337,203,685,477.5808.. 922,337,203,685,477.5807.
String	N/A	Depends on declaration (up to 64K)
Variant	N/A	Any numeric value up to the range of a Double or any character text
User-defined	N/A	Varies with size of declaration

Table 13.4. Similar Types between Languages

Contents	Type Size	C/C++	Pascal	Visual Basic
8-bit value	8	char	char	String[1]*
16-bit integer	16	short int	Shortint	Integer
32-bit integer	32	long	Long	Long
generic pointer	16/32	void *	Pointer	Long**
string	N/A	char[]	String	String
structures	N/A	struct	Record	User-defined
Boolean	8***	char	Boolean	Integer
sets	N/A****	enum	set types	User-defined

* Visual Basic does not have an 8-bit type for a single ASCII character; however, a one character string can be used.

** Visual Basic does not have an explicit pointer type; however, a `Long` integer can be used to hold a 32-bit value.

*** *For Boolean values, the size of the actual variable is greatly dependent on the language. Since Pascal is the only language that has a native Boolean type, C and Visual Basic must use other methods to create the same thing. In C's case, an* enum *type could be used instead, but many compilers treat* enums *as integers. Visual Basic uses integers to store Boolean values.*

**** *Again, this contrast greatly depends on the language. Only recently has C been given the capability to create "set types" through the* enum *construct. Pascal has "set types," which allow the programmer to create sets implicitly (no specific language keyword is used). Visual Basic can mimic C's* enum, *but it has no native type support for this kind of construct. Furthermore, while C's* enum *usually uses integers to represent set values (some compilers use char [8-bit] values if the set is small enough), some Pascal implementations use bit fields to implement sets and sub-range types.*

Notice that C and C++ are lumped together in the table because the compiler uses the same format and size for basic types, whether a C or C++ program is being compiled (with the exception of C++-specific types, such as `class`). However, on other platforms, this may not always be the case. For example, on the Macintosh using THINK C++, ints are 16 bits when compiling C code and 32 bits when compiling C++ code (unless you change the default compiler options).

When you look at Table 13.4, it's easy to see some correspondence between types. It is also easy to see how you can get into trouble if you aren't careful with the differences between language implementations. For example, both C and Pascal have a `char` type, which is an 8-bit value designed to hold one ASCII character. However, Visual Basic has no 8-bit native type. For character values, you would typically use an Integer type and ignore the high byte (or strip it off before passing the value to, say, a C procedure).

There is also the problem of types with similar names that don't look alike internally. As you might have surmised, floating-point values can suffer from this. A more common problem is the idea of a "string" type. In C, a string is defined as an array of `char`s terminated by a zero byte. This type is sometimes referred to as an "ASCIIZ" string. C strings can be almost any length, and are just stored as an array of bytes. Pascal also has a string type. However, a Pascal string can be no longer than 255 characters and is not terminated by a zero byte. Instead, Pascal strings store the length of the string as the first element. There is no terminating byte to signal the end of the string.

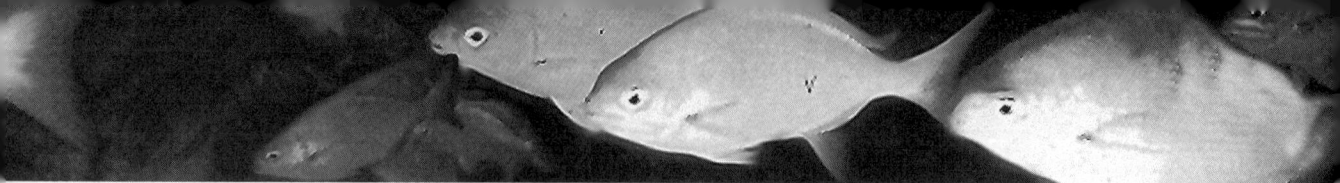

An example will make this a little more obvious. If you declare a string

```
char s[10]; /* C: a character array with room for no more than 10 characters */
s: String[10];     (* Pascal: a string of 10 characters *)
```

and store the string "Hello" in each variable, here's what is stored in memory:

```
      C:      H e l l o \0     In RAM: 0x48 0x65 0x6c 0x6c 0x6f 0x00
   Pascal:    5 H e l l o In RAM: $05 $48 $65 $6c $6c $6f
```

Because the C compiler doesn't know about Pascal's string format (and vice versa), you have to remember what kind of string you're dealing with.

As mentioned previously, not only do you have to worry about the size of types, you also have to worry about the format of different types. Perhaps the simplest example of this is the idea of *structure alignment* (or structure packing, as it's sometimes called). Structure alignment occurs when any type of compound data type is created. In C and C++, this is done with the `struct` keyword. However, `union` variables can also be affected. Here's an example:

```
struct abc {
     char aChar;
     short int anInt;
} myStruct;
```

In this case, you are allocating a structure `myStruct`, which contains two data items, an 8-bit character value, and a 16-bit integer.

Note: With Borland C++ 4.0, the `short` modifier gives you a 16-bit integer whether you're compiling for 16-bit code or 32-bit code. Under the ANSI C specification, a `short int` is guaranteed to not be longer than an `int`; furthermore, a `long int` is guaranteed to be at least as big as an `int`. While prior versions of Borland C++ went by the rule that a `short int` and an `int` are 16 bits and a `long int` was 32 bits long, this no longer is always true. It's still true if you're compiling 16-bit code. However, the 32-bit compiler considers `int` to be a 32-bit value and a `short int` to be a 16-bit value. This is definitely something to watch out for.

Given the above structure, how much space is allocated in memory? The answer is that it depends on what the compiler options are set to regarding structure alignment. Structure alignment controls whether structure types are "padded" to make them an integral size. Usually this means that if padding is turned on, structures have empty space added to make them more palatable for fast memory access. In the case of Borland C++, "integral size" means an even number of bytes.

`myStruct` contains two data items, an 8-bit signed value and a 16-bit signed value, making the total number of bytes used by the data items three bytes. However, if padding is turned on, an "empty" byte is added by the compiler between the space allocated for `aChar` and `anInt`, which would make the structure use four bytes of memory (see fig. 13.1). The reason this is done, again, is for speed. Earlier Intel processors (most notably the 8086) performed slightly better if whole words (16-bit values) were fetched at one time. You can't use the empty space for anything; it is completely transparent (or should be) to your program. If you want to find out how much space was allocated, C's `sizeof()` operator will tell you.

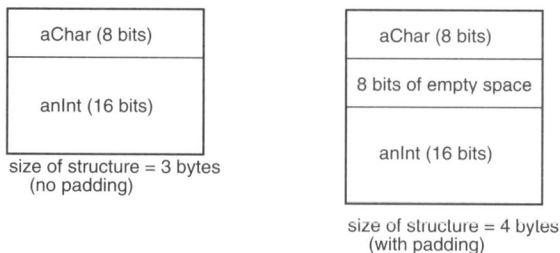

```
+------------------------+          +------------------------+
|   aChar (8 bits)       |          |   aChar (8 bits)       |
|                        |          +------------------------+
+------------------------+          |  8 bits of empty space |
|   anInt (16 bits)      |          +------------------------+
|                        |          |   anInt (16 bits)      |
+------------------------+          |                        |
  size of structure = 3 bytes       +------------------------+
       (no padding)                   size of structure = 4 bytes
                                           (with padding)
```

Fig. 13.1. The effects of structure alignment.

However, Borland Pascal doesn't even attempt to align structures by padding. ISO Pascal has the optional "packed" modifier to apply to variables that asks the compiler to pack structures for you. Borland Pascal recognizes the "packed" modifier, but it doesn't do anything. Borland Pascal *always* packs structures. Thus, when a structure type is defined in C/C++, it is important to make sure your corresponding Pascal definition matches exactly. Otherwise, you can end up with

parameters that get initialized in a C function correctly, but end up wrong on the Pascal side (or vice versa).

There are two ways to do this. The easiest is to turn off structure padding in the C compiler. Then all you have to worry about is making sure the types match. However, if for some reason this isn't viable, you must make sure the Pascal definition matches the C structure definition, padding and all. In this case, you have to do a little extra work to make sure your structure definitions align properly.

Given the above structure, how would you do the same thing in Visual Basic? Things start to get a little tricky, because Visual Basic has no native 8-bit type to match `aChar`. There are several approaches to take. You could redefine `aChar` to be an `int`. This way you would have two 16-bit values, instead of one 8-bit and one 16-bit. Another way would be to move the data items around:

```
struct abc {
      short int anInt;
      char aChar;
} myStruct;
```

This way, you could use a Visual Basic Integer to get to `aChar`, but you would only look at one byte of the Integer. In Visual Basic's case, you would be creating a structure that matched only the first three bytes of the structure, even though your Visual Basic type occupied four bytes. Another solution is to create a Visual Basic "user defined type":

```
Type myStruct
      aChar as String * 1
      anInt as Integer
End Type
```

This creates a user defined type `myStruct` that matches the original structure definition.

Generally, it isn't too difficult to make your data types match. You run into problems when you start using types that are difficult to "simulate" in other languages. One example that comes to mind is C's bitfields. Bitfields are extremely compiler-dependent and require great care if you are going to pass them to non-C code. However, you can use integral types in other languages to match groups of bitfields. Another

is floating-point values. Unless two compilers use the same format for floating point, you can end up having to take floating-point values apart and put them back together in a format understandable by the language to which you are passing them.

Different Calling Procedures

Another issue that you have to worry about is what calling convention the different languages you are attempting to link together use. *Calling convention* is a term used to describe the way a compiler calls, passes values to, and receives values from another routine. In normal C/C++ development, the only issue you have to worry about is whether you are passing the correct parameters in the correct order to a routine. Prodigious use of function prototypes virtually eliminates this as a concern because the compiler itself will perform the checking for you.

However, when using C/C++ with other languages, you can't depend on the compiler to do all your work for you because you are linking in code that is foreign to the compiler. In other words, the compiler didn't generate it, so it won't be checked by the compiler at compile time! Function prototypes don't solve the problem because they only tell the compiler what you intend to do, not what you did. If you write a Pascal procedure that takes two integers as parameters and then write a C prototype that says that function takes two real numbers, the C compiler will believe your prototype simply because that's all it has to work with.

There are three main calling conventions used today. The first, used by assembler programmers, I'll simply call the "assembler" convention. The second, popularized by Pascal compilers, is called the "Pascal" calling convention. Lastly, C compilers have their own, called, surprisingly enough, the "C" (or `cdecl`) calling convention. Each does things a little differently.

Additionally, using C++ with C code introduces the concept of "name mangling" (or "name decoration," as it is sometimes called). Because Borland C++ can use either the C or Pascal calling convention, name mangling is discussed in the section on calling C code from C++.

The calling convention used depends on the language used, but this does not mean that one language can only use one convention. Borland C++ supports two modifiers that determine what calling convention a function uses. If a function name is declared of type `cdecl` (or if no declaration is used), the standard C calling convention is used. If a function is declared to be of type `pascal`, the Pascal calling convention is used. Borland Pascal doesn't have explicit modifiers to change calling conventions. All functions use the Pascal calling convention. Visual Basic can use the Pascal calling convention, but it does so through declaring "library" functions.

Why are there different calling conventions? Simply put, they were developed because they solved a specific need. Each calling convention has plusses and minuses.

The "assembler" convention is the simplest, in that there really isn't any "convention," per se. While the C and Pascal conventions have very specific rules on how parameters are passed to subroutines and who cleans up the stack, assembler programmers have one rule: there are no rules. Generally, like all other decisions of this type, it is the code you are calling that determines what you do (although you could modify the source code if you wanted to). An assembler subroutine could have parameters it needs pushed on the stack in any order, or the parameters could be placed in registers, similar to the way you pass information to MS-DOS when making an INT 21h call.

For example, if you call C code from assembler, you use the C calling convention because that's what the C compiler wants you to do, and you can't alter too much what the compiler expects. Likewise, if you call a function in the Windows SDK, you use the Pascal calling convention, because Windows DLLs typically use the Pascal calling convention. However, if you call MS-DOS, you follow MS-DOS's rules.

The C Calling Convention

When you call a C function from another C function, the C calling convention is used (if the called function is not declared with the `pascal` modifier). This means three things:

1. The parameters in the function call are pushed on the stack from right to left.

2. It is up to the calling function to clean up the stack after the called function returns.

3. Function names are preserved in case and have an underscore prefixed to them.

One reason for this is that, because parameters are pushed onto the stack from right to left (i.e., the last parameter in the function call is the first pushed on the stack), it is easy for C code to handle functions that take a variable number of arguments. The best example of a function that accepts a variable number of arguments is the `printf()` family of functions. When you call `printf()`, you pass a formatting string as the first parameter, followed by however many variables are necessary to satisfy the requirements of the format string. The code in `printf()` can examine the first parameter to see how much data it needs to pop off the stack.

To make this a little clearer, let's look at an example of how this would be set up for a C function call. Consider this function call (assuming small memory model here):

```
int f(int a, int b);
    .
    .
    .
f(1, 3);
    .
    .
```

The compiler will generate code similar to the following:

```
    .
    .
    .
mov     ax, 3
```

```
push     ax
mov      ax, 1
push     ax
call NEAR PTR _f
add      sp, 4
         .
         .
         .
```

This code simply loads the value 3 (the second parameter) into a register, pushes it onto the stack, then pushes the value 1 (the first parameter) onto the stack, and calls the function. When the function returns, the stack space used for the two parameters (two 16-bit integers or four bytes) is removed from the stack.

The called function (in this case f()) uses the value of SP to access the parameters passed to it. The code for f() generated by the compiler looks something like this:

```
_f      PROC
        push    bp              ; save BP
        mov     bp, sp          ; copy the stack pointer to BP
                ; for now, let's assume that f() adds the two integers passed to it
        mov     ax, [bp + 4]    ; get the first parameter (1)
        add     ax, [bp + 6]    ; add the second parameter to it (3)
        pop     bp              ; restore BP's original value
        ret
_f      ENDP
```

The called function copies the stack pointer (SP) to BP (making sure to save BP before doing so), and uses BP to access the parameters on the stack. Since the return address was pushed on the stack by the CALL instruction (and we pushed BP onto the stack to save its value), the code looks four bytes "up" the stack to get the first parameter.

Before f() returns, the code restores BP. The RET instruction passes control back to the calling code, removing the calling address from the stack in the process. Finally, the calling code adds four bytes to SP to remove the passed parameters from the stack.

Figure 13.2 is an illustration of what the stack looked like while f() was executing.

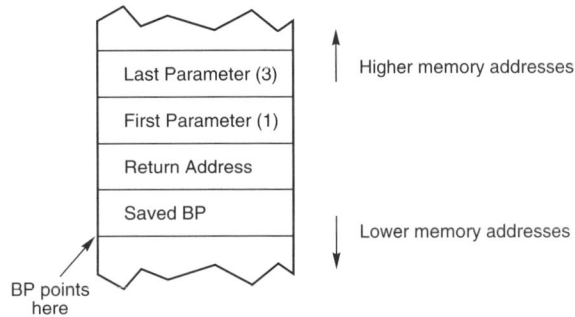

Fig. 13.2. The stack while `f()` is executing (C calling convention).

The Pascal Calling Convention

The `Pascal` convention was developed for Pascal compilers. It is also used by Microsoft Windows for almost all the Windows SDK functions. In addition, routines that you write in Windows programs that are called by Windows (otherwise known as "callback functions") are declared in C with the pascal directive so that the compiler uses the Pascal calling convention when generating code for that function.

The Pascal calling convention does things a little differently:

1. The parameters in the function call are pushed on the stack from left to right.

2. It is up to the called function to clean up the stack after the called function returns.

3. Function names are converted to uppercase.

Because the parameters are pushed from left to right, Pascal functions and procedures don't support open-ended argument lists. This is because it would be difficult for a called function to determine exactly where the first parameter occurred on the stack and would make the code to calculate the position of the first parameter rather slow and obtuse.

Again, let's look at an example of how this would be set up for a Pascal function call. Consider this function call (assuming a small memory model here):

```
int pascal f(int a, int b);
    .
    .
    .
f(1, 3);
    .
    .
```

The compiler generates code similar to the following:

```
        .
        .
        .
mov     ax, 1
push    ax
mov     ax, 3
push    ax
call NEAR PTR F
        .
        .
        .
```

Notice the difference between this code and the (hypothetical) code generated for the C example. The first parameter (1) is pushed on the stack, followed by the second parameter (3). Then, the function f() is called. Notice that the ADD instruction is no longer generated because it is up to f() to clean up the stack.

You probably noticed the difference in the CALL instruction, too. As mentioned above, Pascal function names are automatically converted to uppercase (and do not have an underscore prefixed onto their name).

The called function (in this case f()) again uses the value of SP to access the parameters passed to it. The code for the Pascal version of f() generated by the compiler looks something like this:

```
F       PROC
        push    bp              ; save BP
        mov     bp, sp          ; copy the stack pointer to BP
            ; for now, let's assume that f() adds the two integers passed to it
        mov     ax, [bp + 6]    ; get the first parameter (1)
```

```
add     ax, [bp + 4]    ; add the second parameter to it (3)
pop     bp              ; restore BP's original value
ret     4               ; remove the parameters from the stack
F       ENDP
```

Like the C version of `f()`, the Pascal version of `f()` copies the stack pointer (`SP`) to BP (making sure to save BP before doing so), and uses BP to access the parameters on the stack. This time, however, the first parameter is located six bytes up the stack and the second parameter is four bytes up the stack.

Again, before `f()` returns, BP is restored. However, the RET function has an additional parameter attached to it that causes the CPU to pop an additional four bytes from the stack.

The Pascal convention has a slight speed advantage over the C calling convention, because it is a little faster for the CPU to execute the RET 4 instruction instead of the ADD SP, 4 instruction.

Figure 13.3 is an illustration of what the stack looked like while `f()` was executing. This should visually illustrate the differences between the two conventions.

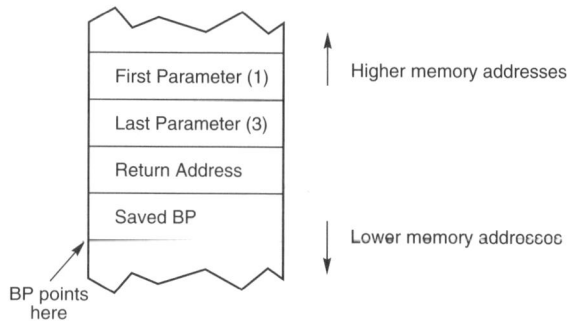

Fig. 13.3. The stack while `f()` is executing (Pascal calling convention).

Other Issues (Library Routines)

There are several other issues that pop up when dealing with mixed language programming. Some (such as register preservation) typically rear

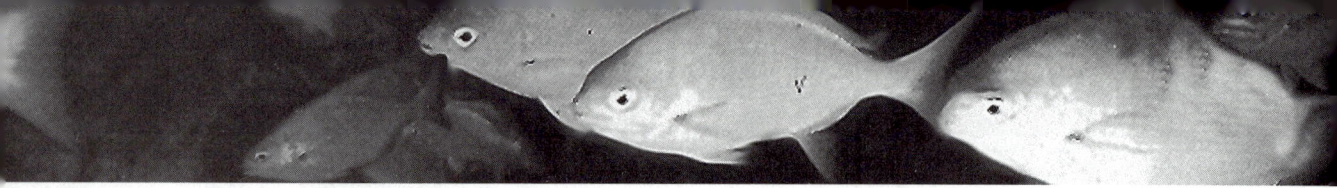

their heads only when calling assembler from a higher level language. However, one problem that must be dealt with is the problem of library routines.

Library routines provided by the compiler vendor are often very useful, but they can pose problems when dealing with multiple languages. First of all, if you're using Borland C++ and assembler, there is no problem because Turbo Assembler doesn't come with a library of routines. If you're using C++ and C in the same program, again, there is no problem, but this time it's because C and C++ use the same library. (With the exception of the iostream libraries; I'm limiting the discussion to the standard library, not ObjectWindows or any other C++-specific library shipped with Borland C++.) However, when it comes to mixing C/C++ and Pascal, the choice becomes a little murkier. This is discussed later in the chapter (in the section on calling Pascal from C++), but it turns out that you have to use the Pascal library when combining C/C++ and Pascal; the standard C library can't be easily used.

Finally, there is the problem of variables and procedures that are globally visible to other parts of your code. Pretty much all issues (besides calling conventions and data type conflicts) are determined by the tools used to create mixed language programs. This becomes apparent when discussing how different languages are hooked together.

Calling C from C++

So far, the problems that have been discussed have been dealing with somewhat theoretical issues. Let's start looking at some actual code and discuss the issues that arise when combining modules written with different languages together. First, let's look at combining C and assembler code with modules written in C++.

A Simple Example

Here's a simple example to start with. You have a small program consisting of two modules, main.c and sub.c. The code for main.c appears in Listing 13.1; sub.c appears in Listing 13.2.

Listing 13.1. Main.c

```c
#include <stdio.h>
#include <stdlib.h>

extern int sum(int, int);

int main(int argc, char **argv)
{
    int s;
    int n1, n2;

    if (argc != 3)
    {
        fprintf(stderr, "usage: %s <n1> <n2>\n");
        fprintf(stderr, "Calculates the sum of <n1> and <n2>\n");
        exit(-1);
    }
    n1 = atoi(argv[1]);
    n2 = atoi(argv[2]);

    s = sum(n1, n2);
    printf("The sum of %d and %d is %d\n", n1, n2, s);
    return(s);
}
```

Listing 13.2. Sub.c

```c
int sum(int a, int b)
{
    return (a + b);
}
```

This program simply pulls two numbers off the command line, adds them together (via sum()), and returns the sum to the environment. If you compile these two modules together,

```
D:\BC4>bcc main.c sub.c
Borland C++ Version 4.00 Copyright (c) 1993 Borland International
main.c:
sub.c:
Turbo Link  Version 6.00 Copyright (c) 1992, 1993 Borland International

D:\BC4>
```

you end up with main.exe, which you can execute from the DOS command line.

```
D:\BC4>main 3 4
The sum of 3 and 4  is 7

D:\BC4>
```

Because you're moving this code to the world of C++ and you want to take advantage of C++'s stricter type checking, you can rename the modules to have a .cpp extension and recompile them both.

```
D:\BC4>rename main.c main.cpp
D:\BC4>rename sub.c sub.cpp
D:\BC4>bcc main.cpp sub.cpp
```

Again, you end up with main.exe. So far, so good. However, let's say you weren't quite ready to move *sub.c* to the world of C++ yet, and so you didn't rename sub.c.

```
D:\BC4>rename sub.cpp sub.c
D:\BC4>bcc main.cpp sub.c
Borland C++ Version 4.00 Copyright (c) 1993 Borland International
main.cpp:
sub.c:
Turbo Link  Version 6.00 Copyright (c) 1992, 1993 Borland International
Error: Undefined symbol sum(int,int) in module main.cpp

D:\BC4>
```

This looks a little strange. We're getting an unresolved reference for sum(). But we declared sum() as an external in main.cpp! So why can't the linker find sum()?

The linker can't find sum() because C++ has done something akin to an "end run" around you when it compiled the code in main.cpp. This "end run" is what is commonly known as name mangling. Name mangling is done by C++ to implement the concept of *type-safe linkage.*

Type-Safe Linkage

Type-safe linkage allows, among other things, the compiler to make sure that a call to a member function in a C++ class actually has some code to call. In C++, you can have several functions with the same name that only differ in their arguments. If you have a function sum() that expects two

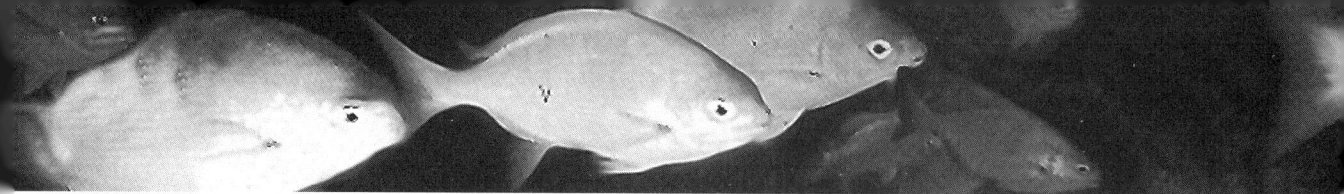

integers, along with another version of sum() that accepts two float arguments, the compiler has to be able to resolve the call to a unique function. Both functions can't be called _sum in the object code because this would confuse the linker and you would get an error due to a "multiply defined label." Sure, you could write a version of sum() that took some sort of identifier that told it what you wanted to add:

```
void sum(int type, void *n1, void *n2, void *result)
{
    switch (type)
    {
        case ADD_INT:
        {
            int a1,  a2;
            a1 = (int) *n1;
            a2 = (int) *n2;
            *result = a1 + a2;
            break;
        }
        case ADD_FLOAT:
        {
            float a1, a2;
            a1 = (float) *n1;
            a2 = (float) *n2;
            *result = a1 + a2;
            break;
        }
        .
        .
        .
```

But this kind of module is ugly and prone to error every time you change it. The C++ way to do this is to have multiple functions called sum(), each with different argument lists and return types:

```
int sum(int a1, int a2)
{
    return (a1 + a2);
}

float sum(float a1, float a2)
{
    return (a1 + a2);
}
```

and so on, with a version of sum for each different type you needed. Thus, you can just call sum() without worrying about maintaining the case statement used above.

```
int f;
float g;

f = sum(1, 3);
g = sum(1.0, 3.0);
```

The compiler makes sure the right version of `sum()` is called. How does it do this? Again, by using name mangling to generate different names for the different versions of `sum()`. The mangled name is usually a combination of the base name (sum, in this case) and some suffix generated by looking at the argument list and return type. Each version of `sum()` gets a unique name. This also means that if you issue a call to a version of `sum()` that doesn't exist (say, `sum(d, 'A')`, where `d` is of type `double`), you get a linker error to signal that you called a version of `sum()` you haven't written.

What does this have to do with the situation involving main.cpp and sub.c? By default, the C++ compiler always mangles names of functions, unless you tell it differently. Thus, it mangled the name of `sum()` in main.cpp when it was compiled, but it didn't mangle the definition of `sum()` in sum.c because Borland C++ assumed .c files are C programs, not C++ programs.

If we look at the code generated by Borland C++ when it compiled main.cpp, we can see what happened.

```
D:\BC4>bcc -S -c main.cpp
Borland C++ Version 4.00 Copyright (c) 1993 Borland International
main.cpp:

D:\BC4>type main.asm
     (code not relevant to this discussion was removed)
     .
     .
     .
   ;
   ;
   ;            s = sum(n1, n2);
   ;
       push    word ptr [bp-4]
       push    word ptr [bp-2]
       call    near ptr @sum$qii
       add     sp,4
       mov     di,ax
     .
     .
     .
```

You can see the compiler generated the standard C calling convention code, but instead of calling `sum`, it's calling `sum$qii`. `sum$qii` as the mangled name.

So, how do we get around this? There are two ways. The first way (which is not recommended) is to modify sum.c to have the mangled name produced by the compiler, so that the linker can correctly resolve the reference to `sum()`. However, this is more work than it's worth. For a simple example like this, it may not be hard, but what if you had 20 functions in sum.c? Or 100? It would be a major headache to figure out what mangled name the compiler was going to generate for each function and change your source code. Furthermore, there is no standard for mangling. Each compiler vendor is free to generate the name however he or she wants (for example, Microsoft's Visual C++ generates "?sum@@YAHHH@Z" for the preceding code). Thus, switching C++ compilers means figuring out the mangled names all over again.

No Mangling, Please!

Fortunately, there is a simple solution. Because C++ was meant to be used with older C code (in fact, the original implementations of C++ from AT&T are preprocessors that produce C code), C++ has a special construct to tell the C++ compiler that a function is written in C, not C++, and therefore should not have it's name mangled. Simply declare the function as being `extern "C"`.

So all we have to do is change our declaration of `sum()` in main.cpp and the linker error goes away (see Listing 13.3).

Listing 13.3. Main.cpp Modified to Fix Linker Error

```
#include <stdio.h>
#include <stdlib.h>

extern "C" int sum(int, int);

int main(int argc, char **argv)
{
    int s;
    int n1, n2;
```

continues

Listing 13.3. Continued

```
if (argc != 3)
{
        fprintf(stderr, "usage: %s <n1> <n2>\n");
        fprintf(stderr, "Calculates the sum of <n1> and <n2>\n");
        exit(-1);
}
n1 = atoi(argv[1]);
n2 = atoi(argv[2]);

s = sum(n1, n2);
printf("The sum of %d and %d is %d\n", n1, n2, s);
return(s);
}
```

You also can use the `extern "C"` construct to tell the C++ compiler that a whole list of functions are not to be mangled:

```
extern "C" {
    void func1(int, int);
    void func2(void);
    char *func3(char *);
};
```

or even all the functions declared in a header file:

```
extern "C" {
    #include "myInclude.h"
};
```

In fact, this is how the .h files included with Borland C++ handle this problem.

When mixing C and C++ code, you generally don't have to worry about type conversion, because the basic types are the same. The only exception to this is when you are dealing with types that are specific to C++. Generally, it is not a good idea to pass C++-specific types to C programs, because the C compiler doesn't know how to handle objects and classes. For example, when you create a class, the C++ compiler builds a *virtual function table*, which contains the addresses of the methods associated with this class. This table is passed around with each instance of a class and is generally invisible to the C++ programmer. However, if you pass a pointer to an object, you may not be

getting exactly what you expect. This is because a pointer to an instance of a class may not only have values specific to the class, but may also have values inherited from parent classes. In general, it is more trouble than it's worth to second-guess how the compiler is going to construct objects in memory. Instead, if you need to pass a member variable of a class to a C function, write a member function to do that. Don't pass the whole object to a C function. Besides, if you do compose some structure to match the layout of an object of the class, you'll end up having to change it if the hierarchy of the class changes (or Borland decides to change the format of classes).

> **Note:** The format of an object is another aspect of C++ programming that is completely up to the compiler developer. Borland has documented the format of an instance of a class in memory for Borland C++ 3.1 (and also its scheme for name mangling) in *The Borland Languages Open Architecture Handbook*. However, this manual is no longer available and, as of this writing, Borland has only released a preliminary version for Borland C++ 4.0, available in the Borland C++ forums on CompuServe.

Now let's look at this problem from a lower level. Mixing C and C++ code wasn't too difficult because the compiler does a lot for you. However, if you want to mix C++ and assembler, a few more problems pop up, because the compiler can't help you as much.

Calling Assembler from C++

Calling a function written in assembler is exactly like calling a C function, at least as far as the C++ compiler is concerned. In fact, it can be difficult to tell if a function is written in assembler, because there is no visible difference in the function invocation. Assembler functions are declared exactly like any other function, with a function prototype. However, all similarity disappears when you write the assembler function. This is because you have to handle several details that are normally handled by the C++ compiler.

For the purpose of this discussion, I'm assuming that you are linking together a C/C++ module and an assembler module that you are writing. If you are linking to someone else's assembler code, his or her code determines how parameters are passed and in what format those parameters should be.

There are four questions you need to consider before writing the assembler code. First, what calling convention will you use (C or Pascal)? Second, what parameters do you expect to pass to the assembler code and what format will they be? Third, do you expect to return any values to the calling routine? If so, will it be the normal "return value," or will your routine be expected to accept pointer values that the assembler routine can use to return values? Finally, what about memory models? Are you going to limit your code to work with only one memory model, or are you going to invest a little work and make your code work with a variety of memory models?

Let's tackle each of these questions one at a time.

Which calling convention you pick is largely arbitrary, although your code will be slightly faster if you use the Pascal calling convention. In your C/C++ code, you simply have to set up your function prototype correctly. However, if you plan on passing open-ended argument lists to your assembler code, remember that you should use the C calling convention.

The second and third questions go together because passing and returning values to assembler code involve similar problems. When you pass values to a subroutine in C/C++, you simply make sure that your function call and the function declaration match as far as types go. If they're not the same, the compiler will produce either a warning or an error (depending on how different the types are). If you know that a warning is going to be produced and you are sure that the code is correct, you can usually use a cast to stop the compiler from complaining.

However, when passing values to an assembler subroutine, you have to be more careful because the compiler has to rely on your prototype to tell it what is valid. As mentioned previously, there is nothing to

prevent you from writing a subroutine that wants a character while prototyping the same subroutine to accept a floating-point number.

Remember, there is nothing to prevent you from "lying" to the compiler. You can create a function that accepts one *char* as an argument, while prototyping this same function to accept a completely different type.

You can pass any type you like to an assembler subroutine; the trick is to know what to expect when your subroutine gets invoked. Table 13.1 gave an overview of the sizes of different types, but it doesn't cover their format or how they are passed to subroutines. The easiest way to look at this is to let the compiler tell us by writing a small program that passes arguments of various types to a "mythical" subroutine and looking at the code that gets generated. While Borland's manuals do cover this, it's always helpful to see what the compiler actually does. The arbitrarily simple program that does this is shown in Listing 13.4 (test.c). You can see that it simply declares several variables of different types and then uses them in a function call. I compiled this program and dumped out the assembler source code. Notice that all the variables are declared to be global to this module. This was done so that Borland C++ would not allocate them on the stack. Instead, they are allocated in the static data segment and are thus referenced with a readable name instead of stack offsets (see Listing 13.5).

Listing 13.4. Test.c

```
char aChar;
enum { value1, value2, value3 } anEnum;
int anInt;
long aLong;
float aFloat;
double aDouble;
long double aLongDouble;
void near *aNearPtr;
void far *aFarPtr;

void func();

void main(void)
{
    func(aChar);
```

continues

Listing 13.4. Continued

```
    func(anEnum);
    func(anInt);
    func(aLong);
    func(aFloat);
    func(aDouble);
    func(aLongDouble);
    func(aNearPtr);
    func(aFarPtr);
}
```

Listing 13.5. Test.asm—Variable Storage

```
_BSS       segment word public 'BSS'
_aChar     label     byte
    db      1 dup (?)
_anEnum    label     word
    db      2 dup (?)
_anInt     label     word
    db      2 dup (?)
_aLong     label     word
    db      4 dup (?)
_aFloat    label     dword
    db      4 dup (?)
_aDouble   label     qword
    db      8 dup (?)
_aLongDouble     label     tbyte
    db     10 dup (?)
_aNearPtr  label     word
    db      2 dup (?)
_aFarPtr   label     dword
    db      4 dup (?)
    ?debug      C E9
    ?debug      C FA00000000
_BSS       ends
```

Let's look at how variables of different types are passed to subroutines. Instead of printing the whole assembler listing, I show it in pieces because we are only interested in how the values are passed.

Variables of type int, enum, and char are passed in much the same fashion. They are all pushed on the stack as 16-bit values. Because chars are not 16 bits, they are placed in the AL register and then widened to 16 bits via the CBW instruction (see Listing 13.6). The POP CX instructions that follow the call are generated to put the stack back the way it was

before the CALL instruction executed. Because we didn't declare func() to be a Pascal function, it is up to the calling code to fix the stack, and because we pushed a value on the stack before calling func(), the compiler generated the POP to remove the parameter we passed. Although an ADD instruction could have been used, Borland C++ decided that the POP was faster for removing two bytes from the stack.

Listing 13.6. test.asm—int, enum, and char Being Passed to func()

```
;               func(aChar);
;
    mov     al,byte ptr DGROUP:_aChar
    cbw
    push    ax
    call    near ptr _func
    pop     cx
;
;               func(anEnum);
;
    push    word ptr DGROUP:_anEnum
    call    near ptr _func
    pop     cx
;
;               func(anInt);
;
    push    word ptr DGROUP:_anInt
    call    near ptr _func
    pop     cx
```

Variables of type long (and *unsigned* long) are more than two bytes in size, so they are broken up into pieces and passed on the stack. As Listing 13.7 shows, the upper two bytes are pushed on the stack first, followed by the lower two bytes. If you look at Listing 13.8, you can see that pointers whose size is over two bytes are also passed this way.

Listing 13.7. test.asm—long Being Passed to func()

```
;               func(aLong);
;
    push    word ptr DGROUP:_aLong+2
    push    word ptr DGROUP:_aLong
    call    near ptr _func
    add     sp,4
;
```

Listing 13.8. Pointers Being Passed to func()

```
;
;           func(aNearPtr);
;
  push      word ptr DGROUP:_aNearPtr
  call      near ptr _func
  pop       cx
;
;           func(aFarPtr);
;
  push      word ptr DGROUP:_aFarPtr+2
  push      word ptr DGROUP:_aFarPtr
  call      near ptr _func
  add       sp,4
;
```

Floating-point values are passed a little differently. As you can see in
Listing 13.9, BCC generated code to place the floating-point values
onto the numeric coprocessor stack. If the machine this code is running on doesn't have a numeric coprocessor, then the Borland C++
runtime library can emulate one. In each case, the compiler generated
code to load the floating-point value onto the coprocessor stack (FLD)
and then stored back onto the CPU stack (FSTP). This converts the
floating-point value to a known format. Finally, the compiler generated
an FWAIT instruction, which causes the CPU to synchronize with the
numeric coprocessor (if one is installed) or generate an interrupt to
invoke the Borland floating-point emulator (if no coprocessor is
present).

Listing 13.9. Floating-Point Values Being Passed to func()

```
;
;           func(aFloat);
;
  fld       dword ptr DGROUP:_aFloat
  sub       sp,8
  fstp      qword ptr [bp-8]
  fwait
  call      near ptr _func
  add       sp,8
;
;           func(aDouble);
;
  fld       qword ptr DGROUP:_aDouble
  sub       sp,8
```

```
        fstp    qword ptr [bp-8]
        fwait
        call    near ptr _func
        add     sp,8
;
;               func(aLongDouble);
;
        fld     tbyte ptr DGROUP:_aLongDouble
        sub     sp,10
        fstp    tbyte ptr [bp-10]
        fwait
        call    near ptr _func
        add     sp,10
;
```

Finally, pointer values are simply pushed on the stack like any other number (see Listing 13.8). As mentioned previously, far pointers (pointers that are 32 bits in size) are broken up into two pieces, just like a *long* value. Near pointers (16 bits) are pushed onto the stack just like an `int` value.

Returning values from a function is much easier. If you want your function to return a value of a certain type, you simply have to know which registers to use, because all return values from functions are returned in registers. Table 13.5 summarizes which registers to use.

Table 13.5. Return Value Locations

Return Value Type	Register to Use
`char` (signed/unsigned)	AX
`enum`	AX
`short` (signed/unsigned)	AX
`int` (signed/unsigned)	AX
`near` pointer	AX
`long` (signed/unsigned)	DX:AX
`far` pointer	DX:AX
floating-point values	8087 Top Of Stack Register (ST(0))

Finally, there is the question of memory models. Borland C++ (like almost all the C/C++ compilers for DOS) supports no less than six different memory models, each a little different. Table 13.6 summarizes the memory models supported by Borland C++.

Table 13.6. Comparison of Borland C++ Memory Models

Model	Code Size	Data Size	Comments
Tiny	64K	N/A	Used to generate .COM files (64K max)
Small	64K	64K	1 Code Segment, 1 Data Segment
Compact	64K	1M	1 Code Segment, > 1 Data Segment
Medium	1M	64K	>1 Code Segment, 1 Data Segment
Large	1M	1M	>1 Code Segment, >1 Data Segment
Huge	1M	1M	>1 Code Segment, >1 Data Segment

Different memory models are used for different purposes. The Tiny memory model is used to create .COM files for MS-DOS. .COM files are somewhat limited in that your program generally has one 64K segment for code, data, and the stack. The other memory models can be used for either DOS or Windows programs.

With the Small memory model, all pointers are 16 bits in size (otherwise known as near pointers). You have one segment for code and one segment for the data and stack.

The Compact memory model also has one code segment, but supports multiple data segments. Theoretically, you can have up to 1M of data, but the architecture of the PC limits the amount of data to less than that. Because data can exist in multiple segments, data pointers are 32 bits in size and code pointers are 16 bits. All functions are near functions because you only have one code segment.

Medium is the opposite of Compact. You have multiple code segments and one data segment. Thus, your data pointers are 16 bits and code pointers are 32 bits in size. Functions can be either near or far, depending on which segment the code is located in.

Large and Huge models are pretty much the same, with one exception. Both allow multiple code and data segments, with all pointers being 32 bits in size. However, no data item can be larger than 64K in Large model. The Huge memory model does allow data items over 64K. When compiling code with the Huge model, the compiler generates code to make sure pointers are *normalized* before they are used.

Normalizing is the process of changing the value of a pointer to allow the pointer to address as much memory as possible while preventing segment wrap-around. This is done because of the way the Intel 80x86 processors handle addresses.

Let's say you have a pointer that contains the address 13F8:FFF0. If you add one to that pointer, you'll get 13F8:FFF1. Now add one again. And again. What will happen when you get to 13F8:FFFF and add one? No, you won't get 13F9:0000. When incrementing addresses, the CPU doesn't automatically increment segments. Instead, the address will "wrap around" to the beginning of the segment again and you get 13F8:0000. Not exactly what you wanted.

In the Huge memory model, Borland C++ generates code that adjusts the value of a pointer to have as large a segment value as possible. This ensures that the pointer will not wrap around to a new segment when it is used.

Probably the best way to approach the problem of memory models is to think about what changes between memory models. The only thing that really changes (as far as variables go) is pointer size. Under the Small and Medium memory models, your (data) pointers are going to be 16 bits in size; under Large, Huge, and Compact, they are 32 bits in size. If you prepare your assembler code to handle 32-bit pointers, you can easily make it work with any memory model. However, you do have to tell the assembler what memory model you're building for.

There are some other things to keep in mind. First, when your assembler code is called, be careful that you don't change any registers that the compiler is assuming will stay unchanged while your code is executing. You should always make sure that the BP, SP, CS, DS, and SS registers are saved if you decide to change them in any way. As a matter of safety, it's also a good idea to save SI and DI, because Borland C++ uses them to store "register variables" (if the compiler is optimizing for register variables). Second, it helps to keep in mind that on every memory model except Huge, DS is pointing to the DGROUP segment, which is the static data segment for the program. This makes it convenient to access global values.

Given all this information, let's look at a simple example of a C/C++ program calling an assembler module. This example is used throughout the chapter. Listing 13.10 contains a simple C program that calls two functions, which will be written in assembler. As you can see, the program does nothing more than set up a test string and call the first functions (str2upper), which places the uppercase version of the string in the buffer passed as the second parameter. It then calls the second functions (strfind) to locate the letter "h" in the string.

Listing 13.10. Program to Test 2funcs.asm (Listing 13.11)

```c
#include <stdio.h>
#include <string.h>

void str2upper(char *s, char *d);
int strfind(char *s, char c);

void main(void)
{
    char s[30];
    char t[30];
    int i;

    strcpy(s, "This is a test.");
    str2upper(s, t);
    printf("Before: %s\n", s);
    printf("After: %s\n", t);
    i = strfind(s, 'h');
    printf("The letter 'h' occurs at position %d\n", i);
}
```

Listing 13.11 contains the assembler module called by the program in Listing 13.10. Both functions contain the standard prologue/epilogue code, where BP is pushed and SP is moved to BP so that we can get to the parameters passed to us on the stack. Notice that because both functions use the SI and DI registers, we save those too, because code generated by Borland C++ will use these two registers as part of its optimization.

Listing 13.11. 2funcs.asm (Assembler Module with 2 Functions To Be Called by C/C++)

```
; Small model assembler functions to be called from Borland C++
;
; For Killer Borland C++ - Chapter 14 (Mixed Language Programming)
;
; Functions:
;
; void str2upper(char *s, char *d)
;      Takes the string pointed to by s and converts it to uppercase
;      The resulting string is placed in the buffer pointed to by d
;
; int strfind(char *s, char c)
;      Looks for the first occurrence of 'c' in the buffer pointed to by
;      s.  Returns the offset or 0 if the character doesn't occur.
;

        .MODEL    small            ; small memory model
        .CODE
        PUBLIC    _str2upper       ; make these functions visible
        PUBLIC    _strfind          ; to the outside world

_str2upper      PROC

;      Standard function prologue - save BP and place SP into BP so we can
;      get to the parameters passed to us.
        push      bp
        mov       bp,sp

        push      si               ; save SI and DI since BCC uses them for
        push      di               ; register variables

        mov       si,word ptr [bp+4]    ; SI = source buffer
        mov       di,word ptr [bp+6]    ; DI = destination buffer
```

continues

Listing 13.11. Continued

```
;     Loop over the buffer, stopping when we hit a null byte
str2loop:

        mov     al, byte ptr [si]           ; Get the character into AL
        cmp     al, 0                   ; Are we pointing at a null byte?
        je      str2end                 ; If so, we're done

        cmp     al, 'a'                 ; Compare character to 'a'
        jl      contloop            ; It's less, continue loop
        cmp     al, 'z'                 ; Compare to 'z'
        jg      contloop            ; It's greater, continue loop

;     The character in AL is between 'a' and 'z'. Convert it to
;     uppercase.

        sub     al, 32d                 ; Convert it to upper case

contloop:

        mov     byte ptr [di],al            ; Move character to dest buffer
        inc     si              ; Move to the next position
        inc     di              ; (in both buffers)
        jmp     str2loop                ; Continue loop

str2end:
        mov     byte ptr [di],0             ; We're done; null-terminate dest

        pop     di              ; Restore registers and return
        pop     si
        pop     bp
        ret
_str2upper      ENDP


_strfind        PROC

;     Save BP and get SP into BP so we can get parameters
        push    bp
        mov     bp,sp

        push    si                  ; Save SI
        mov     si,word ptr [bp+4]      ; Put address of first char of string
                                ; into SI

        mov     dx,1                ; We'll use DX to hold our counter
```

```
;       Loop through the string, looking for the character in SI

strfloop:
        cmp     byte ptr [si],0         ; Are we at the end of the string?
        je      strfend                 ; Yes, get out

        mov     al,byte ptr [si]        ; Get char of string into AL
        cmp     al,byte ptr [bp+6]      ; Compare it to what we're looking for
        je      found                   ; If equal, we've found a match

        inc     si              ; Point to next char
        inc     dx              ; Increment our counter
        jmp     strfloop                ; Go through loop again

found:
        mov     ax,dx                   ; Move our counter to AX so it will
        jmp     done                    ; be our return value

strfend:
        xor     ax,ax                   ; No match; Zero out AX
done:
        pop     si              ; Restore registers and return
        pop     bp              ; (AX contains our return value)
        ret
_strfind        ENDP
        END
```

str2upper() starts by placing the address of the source buffer into SI and
the destination buffer into DI. Remember, this is Small model code so
the DS register points to the segment where these buffers are located,
and by default the system uses DS as the segment for pointer references.

str2upper() then loops over the source buffer, looking at each character
and seeing if it falls between a lowercase "a" and a lowercase "z." If so,
it is converted to uppercase by subtracting 32 (decimal) from the value;
otherwise, it is left alone. After this, the pointers to each buffer are
incremented to point to the next character.

When the loop encounters a NULL (0) byte, the loop is terminated and
a NULL byte is copied to the destination buffer. Finally, any registers
that were saved are restored and the function is returned.

`strfind()` goes through a similar process. However, it only uses the `SI` register, which again holds the address of the string we're looking at. The character we're searching for is directly referenced on the stack. `DX` is used to hold our counter of which position in the string we're looking at.

When `strfind()` returns, it needs to place it's return value in `AX`, because Borland C++ expects return values of type `int` to be in `AX`. So, `DX` (or 0 if no match occurred) is moved to `AX` before `strfind()` returns. Again, any registers that were saved are restored before returning.

This code works for Small model. Let's see what we would have to change for the Large memory model. Listing 13.12 contains the same assembler code, rewritten for Large model. The basic logic stays the same. However, the way we deal with the pointers passed to us is different.

Listing 13.12. Large Model Version of Assembler Functions

```
; Large model assembler functions to be called from Borland C++
;
; For Killer Borland C++ - Chapter 14 (Mixed Language Programming)
;
; Functions:
;
; void str2upper(char *s, char *d)
;     Takes the string pointed to by s and converts it to uppercase
;     The resulting string is placed in the buffer pointed to by d
;
; int strfind(char *s, char c)
;     looks for the first occurrence of 'c' in the buffer pointed to by
;     s.  Returns the offset or 0 if the character doesn't occur


        .MODEL    large          ; large memory model
        .CODE
        PUBLIC    _str2upper     ; make these functions visible
        PUBLIC    _strfind         ; to the outside world

_str2upper     PROC

;     Standard function prologue - save BP and place SP into BP so we can
;        get to the parameters passed to us.
```

```
        push    bp
        mov     bp,sp


;       Loop over the buffer, stopping when we hit a null byte
str2loop:

        les     bx, dword ptr [bp+6]        ; Make ES:BX -> source buffer
        mov     al, byte ptr es:[bx]        ; Get the character into AL
        cmp     al, 0                   ; Are we pointing at a null byte?
        je      str2end                 ; If so, we're done

        cmp     al, 'a'                     ; Compare character to 'a'
        jl      contloop                    ; It's less, continue loop
        cmp     al, 'z'                     ; Compare to 'z'
        jg      contloop                    ; It's greater, continue loop

;       The character in AL is between 'a' and 'z'. Convert it to
;       uppercase.

        sub     al, 32d                     ; Convert it to uppercase

contloop:

        les     bx, dword ptr [bp+10]       ; Make ES:BX -> destination buffer
        mov     byte ptr es:[bx],al         ; Move character to dest buffer
        inc     word ptr [bp+6]             ; Move to the next position
        inc     word ptr [bp+10]            ; (in both buffers)
        jmp     str2loop                    ; Continue loop

str2end:
        les     bx, dword ptr [bp+10]       ; Make ES:BX -> destination buffer
        mov     byte ptr es:[bx],0          ; We're done; null-terminate dest

        pop     bp                  ; Restore registers and return
        ret
_str2upper      ENDP


_strfind        PROC

;       Save BP and get SP into BP so we can get parameters
        push    bp
        mov     bp,sp

        les     bx, dword ptr [bp+6]        ; Make ES:BX -> our string
        mov     dx,1                    ; We'll use DX to hold our counter
```

continues

Calling Assembler from C++

Listing 13.12. Continued

```
;     Loop through the string, looking for the character in SI

strfloop:
        cmp     byte ptr es:[bx],0          ; Are we at the end of the string?
        je      strfend            ; Yes, get out

        les     bx, dword ptr [bp+6]     ; Make ES:BX -> current character
        mov     al,byte ptr es:[bx]           ; Get char of string into AL
        cmp     al,byte ptr [bp+10]      ; Compare it to what we're looking for
        je      found              ; If equal, we've found a match

        inc     word ptr [bp+6]            ; Point to next char
        inc     dx         ; Increment our counter
        jmp     short strfloop             ; Go through loop again

found:
        mov     ax,dx                 ; Move our counter to AX so it will
        jmp     done                  ; be our return value

strfend:
        xor     ax,ax                 ; No match; Zero out AX
done:
        pop     bp                    ; Restore BP and return value in AX
        ret
_strfind        ENDP
        END
```

In the Small memory model code, we could count on DS to point to the segment where our data and stack was, so we only needed to deal with the offset of the pointers we were passed. Here, we are being passed 32-bit pointers, so our approach changes slightly. In both functions, we don't use SI or DI anymore. Instead, we make ES:BX point to our buffers and index via that register pair. Each time we need to access one of the buffers (in either function), we have to use the LES BX instruction to load the pointer from the stack into ES:BX. Notice also that because the size of the parameters we are being passed changed, we had to alter the offsets we used to access the stack. Notice also that instead of loading the pointers into different registers and incrementing the registers to

get to the next position in a buffer, we're incrementing the offset of the pointer while it's still on the stack. This doesn't hurt our original pointer (in the C code) because we're dealing with a copy of that pointer on the stack.

Is it possible to keep from having to write this assembler code more than once? The answer is yes, if you're careful. We could use the Large model code and, with careful use of Turbo Assembler conditionals, make one piece of source code that can be recompiled for different memory models. An easier approach would be to assume that you'll always be passed 32-bit pointers, and change your C prototype so that Borland C++ will pass far pointers, even in Small memory model. You can place some of the burden on the C compiler by intelligent use of prototypes. Just be sure you don't try to pass a 32-bit pointer to a small model C runtime routine!

Calling Pascal from C++

So far, we've talked about fairly straightforward issues dealing with mixed language programming. When combining C++ with C or assembler, the techniques are easy to understand; you simply have to get the linkage right. Now let's look at something a little more esoteric: linking Borland Pascal and Borland C/C++ code together.

Earlier in this chapter, I mentioned that the tools you have to use make many of the decisions for you. If you're combining C++ and C, you're still using the same compiler; it just handles your code a little differently depending on whether you're compiling C or C++. Similarly, when linking assembler and C++, you are essentially writing code that the compiler could produce. However, you are doing it yourself, handling some of the details the compiler normally handles for you. If you think about it, Borland C++ can produce assembler source, which you can assemble yourself. You're just inserting code at the level of the linker.

However, when it comes to combining Borland Pascal and Borland C++ code, you're dealing with an entirely different situation. First of all,

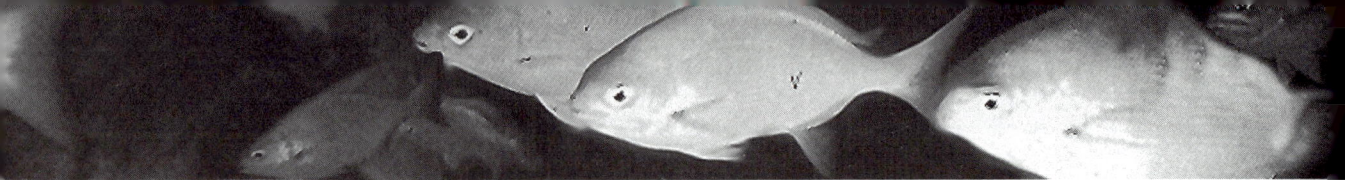

Borland Pascal doesn't normally produce stand-alone object files like Borland C++. Borland Pascal also doesn't use library files like Borland C++; instead, routines are typically compiled into *units*, which serve a similar purpose.

In fact, if you compile a Pascal program with Borland Pascal, you'll notice these things. If you use the command-line compiler, BPC.EXE, you'll see that it quickly compiles and links your program without a separate link step and with no intermediate .OBJ files.

So, given that no .OBJ files can be used and Borland C++ can't produce unit files, what can you do?

If we compare Borland Pascal to Borland C++, some interesting differences show up. Borland Pascal can't produce .OBJ files for TLINK.EXE, so we'll have to let its linker pull in our code. It also only understands the Pascal calling convention. There is also the problem of which compiler's library routines to use. Both compilers come with many routines to read and write files, allocate and manage memory, work with strings, and much more. We can't link in Borland C++'s .LIB files, because the Borland Pascal linker can only pull in units or single .OBJ files. Thus, we have to use the Borland Pascal Runtime library. Even if we could link in the C++ runtime library, some of its routines depend on the C++ compiler's *start-up code*. This code is linked to your C/C++ programs (unless you handle it yourself) by default. It is responsible for setting up the environment for your programs. It is the code that calls `main()` in your code. It also sets up the environment for the C++ library, which means that some C++ library routines will not work if the startup code is not present. All of this means that we will have to use Borland Pascal's Runtime library and linker, and somehow get our code in a format the Pascal compiler can be happy with.

Borland Pascal has the capability to link .OBJ files as part of a Pascal program by using a special compiler directive $L. With $L, you are telling Borland Pascal's integrated linker to include a separate object module when it builds the final executable. However, because you are using Pascal's special linker, you have to live by it's rules. In essence, you have to supply object files the Pascal linker understands and can deal with.

All the above details boil down to this. You can link together code from Borland C++ and Borland Pascal. However, Borland Pascal is the controlling environment. You cannot use any of the C/C++ library functions (because you can't link in the C runtime library). You also cannot declare any globals in your C code, for the simple reason that there is no way to tell the C compiler not to add an underscore to the variable name (remember that all C globals are case-sensitive and have an underscore prepended to their name; functions can be of type `pascal` to prevent this, but variables cannot). In fact, the Borland Pascal linker won't accept any .OBJ files that contain global declarations.

These restrictions limit you somewhat in what you can do in your C code. However, it does let you use C functions with very little translation. Let's look at a simple example. Listing 13.13 contains the source code for a simple Pascal program that calls an external C module. Listing 13.14 contains the C module.

Listing 13.13. Simple Pascal Program That Calls an External C Module

```
program Test;

var
   i : Integer;

{$L CP.OBJ}    { Link in the Borland C .OBJ module }

function add2(one, another : Integer) : Integer; external;

begin
   i := add2(1, 3);
   WriteLn(i);
end.
```

Listing 13.14. C Module Called by Program in Listing 13.13

```
int pascal add2(int one, int another)
{
    return (one + another);
}
```

On the C side, all functions need to be declared with the *pascal* modifier (or compile the source module with the -p option, which will force all functions to be of type Pascal). You also need to try and stick with the small memory model, because Borland Pascal and Borland C++ have different ideas about segment naming. Also, make sure that structure packing is turned on because Borland Pascal always packs structures. Finally, remember: NO GLOBALS.

On the Pascal side, make sure your function declarations match. Because Borland Pascal always converts variable and procedure names to all uppercase (as the Pascal calling convention requires), you cannot differentiate between functions solely on case (like you can in C).

Let's try something a little more complicated. This example will show up in the discussion of DLLs under Windows, but there's no reason not to try it here. Listings 13.15 and 13.16 contain the Pascal and C code for another program, this time dealing with strings.

Listing 13.15. Second Pascal Program

```
program test2;

var
s : String[30];
t : String[30];

{$L cp2.obj }

procedure str2upper(s, t : String); external;

begin
s := 'This is a test.';
str2upper(s, t);
WriteLn('Before: ', s);
WriteLn('After: ', t);
end.
```

Listing 13.16. Second C Module

```
void pascal str2upper(char far *s, char far *t)
{
    int c;

for (c = 1; c <= s[0]; c++)
{
    if (s[c] >= 'a' && s[c] <= 'z')
    {
        t[c] = 'A' + (s[c] - 'a');
    } else
    {
        t[c] = s[c];
    }
}
t[0] = s[0];
}
```

This second example shows how the C code has to deal with a Pascal native data type. Remember that Pascal strings are not null-terminated. Instead, the first byte of a Pascal string has the length of string. This is why Pascal strings are limited to 256 characters in length (only a byte is available to store the length). The C code expects a far character pointer (because Borland Pascal passes a 32-bit address) and looks at the length byte to determine the length of the string.

In this case, the Pascal code allocates space for the string to be returned. The C function str2upper() simply fills it in. Remember, we don't have access to the C runtime library, so we can't use malloc() to allocate space for the return string.

Two final things to keep in mind: First, it is possible to use some of the C runtime library if you can mimic any setup code the function you want to use needs. If you have the C runtime library source code, you can recompile functions for your use. However, keep in mind that the C compiler may generate calls to "helper" functions, which you have to provide if they are needed. In this case, there is no substitute for compiling the C code with the -S option to get a look at the assembler code; that way, you can see if any helper functions are going to be called.

While linking Pascal and C together seems quite restrictive, there's a lot you can do. Rumor has it that Quattro Pro for DOS is written mostly in Borland Pascal, with lots of assembler and C linked in.

Mixed Language Programming under Windows (DLLs)

So far, the examples that we've looked at have dealt with the problems of static linking. Static linking is the process you normally go through when you build an .EXE or .COM file (for example, if you've written a simple program like "hello, world!"):

```
#include <stdio.h>

void main(void)
{
    printf("hello, world!\n");
}
```

You usually invoke BCC.EXE to compile and link your program. BCC compiles your program (producing an .OBJ file) and invokes TLINK. It is TLINK's responsibility to resolve all *external references*, or references that one module makes to another. In this case, TLINK uses C0S.OBJ (assuming we're using the Small memory model), HELLO.OBJ (the object file generated by the program above), and CS.LIB (the C runtime library for the Small memory model).

TLINK will see that C0S.OBJ makes a call to a function called _main, which it can resolve from HELLO.OBJ. It will also see that HELLO.OBJ makes a reference to a function called _printf, which is located in CS.LIB. Additionally, the code in HELLO.OBJ might make other references to "helper" functions, which are also located in CS.LIB. If it is able to resolve all the external references (and encounters no other problems), TLINK will produce HELLO.EXE, which is your program, ready to run.

HELLO.EXE is a self-contained entity that needs no other code (except for DOS) to run. If you wrote another program, BCC and TLINK would go through the same process again. If this other program also used

`printf()`, this would mean that both .EXE files contain a copy of the code for `printf()`. If at some point in the future you develop a new version of `printf()`, you'd have to relink both programs for each program to have access to the new version of `printf()`.

Under DOS, this doesn't pose too many problems, because DOS is a single-task operating system. Normally, you only execute one program at a time under DOS. The only other "program" sitting in memory (besides device drivers and TSRs) is DOS. In normal C programming, you make calls to the C runtime library, which has been linked to your .EXE file by TLINK. The C runtime library, in turn, may make calls to DOS.

When Microsoft developed Windows, it introduced many programmers to the idea of *dynamic linking*, which lets a program load library modules at runtime instead of having all the necessary code bound to the .EXE file by a linker. In other words, when you reference a function in your code, you provide just enough information for the linker to resolve the reference. When your program is executed under Windows, Windows "magically" makes your program call the correct code in the Windows system. This "magic" is nothing more than Windows fixing the addresses that calls jump to when your program is loaded.

If you think about it, dynamic linking is really no more complicated than, say, what you go through when calling DOS. When you want to have DOS perform some operation for you, you simply place the right values in the 80x86's registers and issue an INT 21 instruction. You don't know where DOS is located in memory; you don't have to. DOS patches the interrupt table in low memory so that when you issue an interrupt 21, a chain of calls takes place that eventually has the code in DOS that handles the function you want to execute. You can consider this a crude form of dynamic linking.

For Windows, Microsoft took a somewhat more streamlined approach. If you think about it, Windows had to implement something like dynamic linking. Otherwise, every Windows program would have to have the code for the Windows API embedded in each .EXE file. This would leave developers with a lot of large .EXE files, each containing the code for a specific version of Windows.

Here's how dynamic linking works under the Windows operating environment. On the application side, you write your application as you normally would. The standard Windows include file, windows.h, which contains prototypes for all the Windows API functions, along with definitions for the many #defines and structures that Windows works with. When you link a Windows program, you link with IMPORT.LIB (under Borland C++), which is the Windows API *import library.* An import library is a library that contains just enough information for the linker to do its job, namely producing a valid .EXE file. IMPORT.LIB doesn't contain any actual code; it's only there so the linker can resolve all the external references you've made in your program (to functions like `GetMessage()`, `BeginPaint()`, `LoadCursor()`, etc.).

After TLINK has done its job, you are left with an .EXE file that only runs under Windows. When you execute your program under Windows, the Windows loader looks at the .EXE file to see if it references any code in dynamic link libraries. Your code will almost always reference at least a few Windows functions, so the loader goes about its job of setting up your program in memory. Part of this process involves fixing these calls to Windows functions so that they call the proper routines. After all, the code for `BeginPaint()` is somewhere in GDI.EXE, which is the Windows dynamic link library that handles graphical output for any device. Windows makes sure that when your code gets to the call for `BeginPaint()`, it actually calls the proper procedure in memory. If the code is not in memory, Windows goes and loads the dynamic link library automatically.

Dynamic Link Libraries (or DLLs as they are usually called) actually can make mixed language programming rather easy (or at least easier). As mentioned previously, if you call a Windows function, most likely you're doing mixed language programming without even knowing it. Let's look at two examples. Both examples use a simple DLL, which we call first from C and then from Visual Basic. To make things interesting, we'll write the DLL twice; once in Borland C and once in Borland Pascal.

There are several things to keep in mind. First, the development system you use has to be able to create DLLs, as they are a special type of executable file. For this reason, not all Windows development tools can be used to create a DLL. For example, Visual Basic can't be used to create a .DLL because it doesn't use a linker in the "normal" way. Second, a DLL doesn't have to have the extension .DLL. After all, Windows is nothing more than a large collection of DLLs, many of which don't have the .DLL extension. Instead, you see files with extensions like .DRV, .FON, .SYS, .CPL, and many more. All of these are DLLs. However, Windows will not automatically load a DLL for you unless it has the .DLL extension. If it has some other extension, you have to load it yourself via the `LoadLibrary()` function.

Let's get down to business. The DLL will have two exportable functions. One function takes a string and converts it to all uppercase (`str2upper`); the second function takes a string and searches for a character in that string (`strfind`). While this is a rather simple example, it covers the basics of writing a DLL.

When you write a Windows program in C, you normally have a function named `WinMain()`, which is the entry point for your program (similar to `main()` in a DOS C program). DLLs have a similar starting point called `LibMain()`. `LibMain()` is called when the .DLL is originally brought into memory and gives the DLL a chance to set itself up. The code for a DLL stays in memory until Windows determines that no other programs or DLLs are using that DLL, at which point it unloads the DLL from memory. When this happens, a special routine named `WEP()` (Windows Exit Procedure) is called so that the DLL can clean up after itself.

Listings 13.17, 13.18, and 13.19 contain the source files for the C version of the DLL. Listing 13.18 is the header file that you include in any source file that uses the DLL. It provides function prototypes for the functions in the DLL. Listing 13.19 is the module definition file (.DEF) that the linker uses when it builds the DLL.

Listing 13.17. Source Code for str.dll (str.c)

```c
/* str.c - source code for str.dll */

#include <windows.h>
#include <string.h>
#include "str.h"

extern "C" {



    int FAR PASCAL _export WEP(int);
}

int FAR PASCAL LibMain(HANDLE hInstance, WORD wDataSeg, WORD wHeapSize,
➥LPSTR lpszCmdLine)
{
    if (wHeapSize > 0)
        UnlockData(0);
    return (1);
}

int FAR PASCAL _export WEP(int nParam)
{
    return (1);
}

/* str2upper - copy string in "from" to "to" */

void FAR PASCAL _export str2upper(LPSTR from, LPSTR to)
{
    while (*from)
    {
        if (*from >= 'a' && *from <= 'z')
        {
            *to++ = 'A' + (*from++ - 'a');
        } else
        {
            *to++ = *from++;
        }
        *to = 0;
    }
    return;
}

/* strfind - looks for the first occurrence of "c" in "s"; returns 0 if */
/* not found                                                            */

int FAR PASCAL _export strfind(LPSTR s, char c)
{
    int i = 1;

    while (*s)
```

```
        {
            if (*s == c)
                return (i);
            s++;
            i++;
        }
        return (0);
    }
```

Listing 13.18. Header File for str.c (str.h)

```
/* str.h - header file for str.c/str.dll */

extern "C" {
    void FAR PASCAL _export str2upper(LPSTR, LPSTR);
    int FAR PASCAL _export strfind(LPSTR, char);
}
```

Listing 13.19. Module Definition File for str.dll (str.def)

```
;
;   str.def module definition file
;

LIBRARY STR

DESCRIPTION 'Simple string DLL for Killer Borland C++'
EXETYPE WINDOWS
CODE PRELOAD MOVEABLE DISCARDABLE
DATA PRELOAD MOVEABLE SINGLE
HEAPSIZE 1024
```

The first function in the source code is LibMain(), which is called by Windows when the DLL is brought into memory. LibMain()'s job is to make sure everything is set up correctly for the DLL, and to return a value to Windows saying whether or not everything is ready. LibMain() is actually called by startup code that is provided by Borland in a module called C0DS.OBJ. When you tell Borland C++ to build a DLL (via the -WD command-line option), it automatically tells TLINK to link in the proper startup code for a DLL. This startup code then calls LibMain().

`LibMain()` passes four parameters. The first, hInstance, is the instance handle for this DLL. This is similar to the instance handle that Windows programs are passed when they start up in `WinMain()`. Notice that there is no previous instance handle passed to `LibMain()`, because there is never more than one copy of a DLL in memory. The second parameter, `wDataSeg`, is the DLL's data segment, and is the value in the `DS` register. If the module definition file for the DLL specifies a value for `HEAPSIZE`, then that value is passed as the third parameter `wHeapSize`. The last parameter, `lpszCmdLine`, is of dubious value. It contains command-line information if there is any. Because DLLs are usually loaded automatically, they rarely have a command line.

It is `LibMain()`'s job to set up anything the DLL needs and to tell Windows whether the DLL can stay in memory. If everything is OK, `LibMain()` needs to return the value "1." If `LibMain()` returns "0," then the DLL is unloaded from memory and an error is returned to the program that attempted to load the DLL. In Listing 13.17, our DLL doesn't have any special requirements, so all it does is unlock our data segment (if there is one) and return "1" to signal that everything is OK. By default, the startup code that calls `LibMain()` locks the DLL's data segment, so `LibMain()` has to unlock it if it wants to move around.

The next function, `WEP()`, is the DLL's Windows Exit Procedure. By default, Borland C++ automatically includes a predefined `WEP()` for you. If you include `WEP()` in your source code, Borland's DLL code will call it for you. `WEP()` is passed one parameter that tells the DLL why it's being unloaded. If the parameter is `WEP_SYSTEM_EXIT`, then the DLL is being unloaded because Windows is shutting down. If the parameter is `WEP_FREE_DLL`, then all the applications that have been using the DLL have freed it, so Windows is unloading the DLL automatically. `WEP()` gives the DLL a chance to free any resources it allocated in `LibMain()`. `WEP()` should always return "1."

The last two functions are the ones provided by the DLL for use in other programs. They should be self-explanatory. `str2upper()` takes the address of two strings. The first string is copied to the second string,

with all alphabetic characters being converted to their uppercase equivalents. The second function, `strfind()`, returns the index of a character if it occurs in the string passed to `strfind()`. If the character doesn't occur, `strfind()` returns 0. Notice that both functions are declared as `FAR PASCAL`. While it is required that DLL functions be declared as `FAR` functions (because it's pretty much guaranteed that they won't be in the same segment as the program calling them), they don't have to be PASCAL functions. In fact, if they use variable argument lists, they must be `CDECL` functions.

After you have these three files (str.c, str.h, and str.def), building the DLL is simply a matter of invoking Borland C++ with the proper arguments. Here's the command line I used:

```
bcc -ms! -P -WD -2 str.c
```

The -ms! option tells the compiler to use small memory model, but not to assume that `DS == SS`. This is a common "gotcha" when writing DLLs. You must keep in mind that DLLs may have their own data segment, but they use the stack of the program that called them. Thus, parameters that are passed to the DLL have to be treated a little bit differently, because the data segment and stack segment are not the same.

The -P option tells Borland C++ to treat the code as C++ code, even though the source file has a .C extension. -WD tells the compiler that we are building a .DLL and to export all functions. Finally, the -2 option tells the compiler to generate 80286 instructions.

This command line will invoke Borland C++ and TLINK and produce STR.DLL. Next, we have to generate an import library for this DLL, so that when we compile and link programs that use this DLL, we have a .LIB file to satisfy the linker. The following command line does this:

```
implib str.lib str.dll
```

We can test this DLL by writing a simple Windows program that calls the functions in it. Instead of writing a full-blown Windows program, I used Borland's EasyWin library, which lets you use some of the standard input-output functions (like `printf()`) in a Windows program. This means that we don't have to write a lot of code to put up a window, handle the message loop, etc. Listing 13.20 contains the source code for this program; Listing 13.21 shows the module definition file for the test program. Notice that it IMPORTS the two functions from the DLL.

Listing 13.20. Program to Test STR.DLL (strtest.c)

```
/* strtect.c - Program to test str.dll */

#include <stdio.h>
#include <windows.h>
#include <string.h>
#include "str.h"

#pragma argsused

int PASCAL WinMain(HANDLE hInstance, HANDLE hPrevInstance, LPSTR
lpszCmdParam, int nCmdShow)
{
    char s[30], d[30];
    int i;

    _InitEasyWin();

    strcpy(s, "This is a simple string.");
    str2upper(s, d);
    printf("Before: %s\n", s);
    printf("After: %s\n", d);
    i = strfind(s, 'h');
    printf("The character 'h' occurs at position %d", i);
    return(0);
}
```

Listing 13.21. Module Definition File for strtest.c (strtest.def)

```
EXETYPE WINDOWS
CODE PRELOAD MOVEABLE DISCARDABLE
DATA PRELOAD MOVEABLE MULTIPLE
HEAPSIZE 4096
STACKSIZE 8192
IMPORTS STR.STR2UPPER
        STR.STRFIND
```

The test program #includes the header file for the DLL (so we can get prototypes for the functions). It then calls _InitEasyWin() to set up Borland's EasyWin library. Finally, it tests the two functions in the DLL. When executed, you get output similar to figure 13.4.

Fig. 13.4. Output from strtest.exe.

Now, let's take the same idea and write the DLL in Borland Pascal. Listing 13.22 contains the source code for the Pascal version.

Listing 13.22. Pascal Version of DLL (StrPascal.pas)

```pascal
library StrPascal;
{$X+}

uses Strings;

{ The export procedure directive prepares str2upper and strfind
for exporting}

procedure str2upper(from, t: PChar); export;
   var
      i : Integer;
   begin
      i := 0;
      while from[i] <> Char(0) do
        begin
          t[i] := UpCase(from[i]);
          Inc(i);
        end;
        t[i] := Char(0);
   end;
```

continues

Listing 13.22. Continued

```
function strfind(s : PChar; c : Char) : Integer; export;
  var
    i : Integer;
  begin
    i := 0;
    while s[i] <> Char(0) do
      begin
        if s[i] = c then
          begin
            strfind := i + 1;
            Break;
          end
        else
          begin
            strfind := 0;
          end;
        Inc(i);
      end;
  end;

exports
    str2upper index 1,
    strfind index 2;

begin
end.
```

DLLs in Borland Pascal begin with the `library` keyword, which tells Borland Pascal that you are building a DLL and not an EXE file. Then, each procedure (or function) follows, with the `export` keyword signaling that this procedure is to be exported to the outside world. In this case, we just rewrite the two procedures in Pascal. Borland Pascal provides a way to handle C type strings (null terminated) in a fairly standard way via the `PChar` type, which is just a pointer to a char (^char). Borland Pascal treats the string as an array of `char`s. It is important to remember that while `PChar`s allow Pascal programs to work with Windows C-style strings, the compiler cannot generate code to perform its normal, rigorous type-checking.

After the procedures and functions comes the exports section, which assigns ordinal identifiers to each exported procedure or function. Although previous module definition files have explicitly named the functions that they needed to import, you can also specify imports using these ordinal indexes.

Finally, any code that comes between the `begin` and `end` statements is considered to be initialization code for the DLL and takes the place of `LibMain()` in a C DLL. In our case, there isn't any, so only the `begin`/`end` statement pair is needed. Pascal DLLs do not have a WEP() procedure, but instead can hook into Borland Pascal's exit chain via the `ExitProc` variable declared in the System unit. Since this DLL doesn't have any exit code, this was not done.

Because this DLL (externally) looks like the previous C DLL we wrote, we can relink strtest.c with the import library (created with `IMPLIB`) from StrPas.DLL. Strtest.EXE will run exactly the same.

Similarly, we can call STR.DLL from Visual Basic, just by declaring the DLL procedures correctly. Execute Visual Basic and place the following declaration in the "(general) (declarations)" section of a form:

```
Declare Sub STR2UPPER Lib "Str.DLL" Alias "STR2UPPER" (ByVal from$, ByVal t$)
```

Then, create a button on the form and add the following code to the "`Click`" procedure for the button:

```
Sub Command1_Click ()
    Dim s As String * 30
    Dim t As String * 30
    s = "This is a test"
    Call STR2UPPER(s$, t$)
    Print "Before: "; s$
    Print "After: "; t$
End Sub
```

Visual Basic will dutifully call the DLL and pass it the strings.

This brings up two important points. First, it should be fairly obvious that mixed language programming under Windows is a little easier than mixed language programming under DOS, for the simple reason that Windows provides the linkage between an EXE file and a DLL. Also, most Windows development environments take care of the problem of different variable types. As was shown in the Borland Pascal DLL example, Borland Pascal provides you with a predefined type (and several library routines) that work with null-terminated strings. Similarly, Visual Basic knows how to convert its string format to a null-terminated string when it's being passed to a DLL. Second, while

programming with DLLs is somewhat easier under Windows, all sorts of perplexing problems can pop up. While you can pass "normal" data types from an EXE to a DLL, things can get complicated if you pass some "special" data types. For example, Visual Basic has many types of "objects" (such as Forms) that can be passed as variables to a DLL, but only a DLL written for Visual Basic knows about these types. Also, DLLs can be difficult to debug. If you've linked together a C and assembler module (or Pascal and C) under DOS, the debugger will debug it for you; the worst that can happen is that you drop into assembler code while debugging. However, Visual Basic's debugger doesn't know how to debug DLLs, so when a DLL dies during execution, tracking the cause of the problem can be somewhat problematic.

All in all, mixed language programming under Windows is much easier than under DOS, simply because you aren't working with as many limits and barriers. Because a DLL is really nothing more than a self-contained .EXE file, it really is a separate program, not a linked-in module.

From Here...

Linking code written in different languages is a learning experience, no matter whether it's for DOS or Windows. Each development environment brings both plusses and minuses into the picture, and you must be sure and think about what you are doing before you plunge into this subject. Unfortunately, there are a lot of gray areas that one single chapter in a book cannot cover. Here are some pointers on places to look for more information.

➤ If you are linking assembler code into your program, see Chapter 14, "Bare Metal Programming."

➤ The most obvious place to look is your compiler manuals. For DOS, Turbo Assembler comes with two chapters on mixing C++ and Pascal with assembler. Also, Borland Pascal's *Language Guide* has a chapter dealing with linking assembler and Pascal.

➤ For Windows, the manuals for Visual Basic, Borland Pascal for Windows, and Borland C++ have in-depth discussions on writing and using DLLs. There are whole books devoted to the topic of DLLs, including *The Windows Programmer's Guide to DLLs and Memory Management* from Sams Publishing.

➤ The most important thing to remember is this: The compiler has the final word in what's going on underneath your code. Don't be afraid to look at the code generated by the compiler!

Bare Metal Program- ming: Turbocharging C++ Programs with Assembly Language

by John M. Dlugosz

C++ is unusual in its extensive range: It has very abstract and powerful features at one end of the spectrum, and low-level bit twiddling at the other. This chapter takes a close look at the low end of the spectrum, and beyond. In the "infrared" range is bare metal programming using direct 80x86 assembly code. You may use assembly language because in some cases it is simpler than using C++, or you may use it because the compiler generates lousy code.

In this chapter, we cover the usage and quirks of inline assembly, interfacing C++ with external assembly language functions, and suggested uses of assembly language within C++ programs.

A First Look

To give you a feeling for the performance improvements possible with judicious use of assembly language, let's open the discussion by taking a look at BASM (the built-in assembler). Listing 14.1 shows how a couple of well placed lines of inline assembly code can make a substantial improvement in performance.

Listing 14.1. Demonstration on How a Minor Use of Assembly Code Can Make a Substantial Improvement in Performance

```
#if TEST == 1
int transform (int a, int b, int c)
{
int result= long(a)*b/c;      //original
}

#elif TEST==2
int transform (int a, int b, int c)
{
int result;                   //faster
asm {
   mov ax,a
   imul b
   idiv c
   mov result,ax
   }
}

#elif TEST==3
int transform (int a, int b, int c)
{
return 0;    //time overhead only
}
#endif

int main()
```

```
{
// simple test driver, to get timings
for (int loop= 100;  loop < 1100;  loop++) {
    for (int loop2= 100;  loop2 < 1100;  loop2++) {
        int dummy= transform (loop, loop2, 37);
        }
    }
return 0;
}
```

On a casual test, this takes 3.12 seconds with the inline assembly language code, 1.9 seconds stubbed out to just time the program loading and test bed overhead, and 46.7 seconds originally. The inline assembly speeds up the function computation by a factor of 36, and the overall program, including overhead, by a factor of almost 15.

The function multiplies two numbers and divides by a third. All inputs and the result are `int`s, but a `long` is needed for the intermediate result. Under Borland C++, this is rather inefficient. The details of why the speedup was so dramatic is covered in the section "`Long` Arithmetic." Next let's take a look at the syntax and details of BASM.

Using Inline Assembly

A program containing inline asm may be compiled via assembly, or may use BASM, the built-in assembler. Compiling via assembly gives more flexibility. Differences between compiling via assembly and BASM are mentioned throughout the discussion.

As seen in Listing 14.1, an `asm` block lets you mix assembly language and C++ in C++ program code. This has both advantages and disadvantages over functions written in an ASM source file.

The syntax of inline assembly language code can take two forms. The `asm` keyword can be followed by an assembly language statement, or the `asm` keyword can be followed by a `{` character, followed by lines of assembly language, which are terminated by a `}` on a line by itself. In both cases, the asm statements are *line-oriented*. Each must appear on a line by itself, and they are line delimited.

The ANSI/ISO form of inline asm (the keyword followed by a string literal in parentheses, which may be mixed with other statements without regard for line breaks) is not supported by Borland C++.

Inline asm is handy because it can be used within a function that is otherwise written in C++, and can access local variables, C/C++ labels, and parameters directly. Listing 14.1 showed the multi-line form of inline assembly language code referring to all three parameters and to a local variable.

Here is another example, Listing 14.2, where a library function is called to check to see if a keystroke is waiting. Originally, an animation loop was found to be slowed dramatically by a call to kbhit(). Amazingly, it slowed the loop to a crawl when used as the exit condition:

Listing 14.2. A Slow Loop

```
while (!kbhit()) {
    //... body of loop draws an animation
    }
```

The solution was to eliminate a function call and directly use the BIOS service. Here is the interesting part of the code, as shown in Listing 14.3.

Listing 14.3. The Improved Loop

```
int done= 0;
while (!done) {
    //... body of loop here
    asm {
        mov AH,1
        int 16h
        jz label3   //Z set if no keystroke available
        inc done
        }
    label3: ;
    }
```

The above example also shows a few more interesting points: If you compile via assembly, labels may be inside asm blocks. Using BASM,

a label may *not* be inside an `asm` block. Instead, labels must be C/C++ labels. This is easy to work around by breaking up `asm` blocks into multiple blocks with labels in between the blocks, like so:

```
asm {
    //statements here...
    jb lab_2
    //more statements...
    }
lab_2:
asm {
    //more statements...
    }
```

The other point is that C/C++ style comments are used within `asm` blocks, not `asm` style comments. If compiling via assembly, `asm` style comments will also work. Using BASM, they will not.

In inline assembly language code, the names of parameters and variables are replaced with `[bp+somevalue]` addresses. Using BASM, the result is then assembled. BASM is a *subset* of a full assembler, and all too often you will find some things it will not handle, or will find outright bugs. An alternative to BASM is to compile via assembly. You can enable this with the `-B` compiler switch or the use of `#pragma inline` at the top of the file. When enabled, the compiler generates an ASM file instead of an OBJ file, which is then passed to TASM to complete the process. In this mode, the contents of asm statements are copied to the output file after names are replaced, so the lines can contain anything that TASM would handle. This includes the use of macros and assembler pseudo-ops, as well as instructions and constructs on which BASM simply chokes.

> **Note:** Borland's Turbo Assembler, or TASM, complements their high level language products. TASM came bundled with Borland C++ 3.1, but was made a separate product with Borland C++ 4.0. If you have the older version of TASM, you can use it with the new C++ compiler without having to purchase an upgrade.

Inline Assembly Language Code and Symbols

In inline assembly language code, the names of parameters and variables are replaced with `[bp+somevalue]` addresses. This can be very handy, as it provides for transparent use of some names within the asm code. Inline assembly language can be valuable for this reason alone. However, there are a few caveats.

Consider address arithmetic. Say you want the segment word of a `far` pointer. In real assembly code, you can do this:

```
p dd ?  ;more likely, is a parameter
.....
mov si, p+2
```

This loads the high two bytes of `p` into `si`. Using inline assembly language, one might try something similar:

```
void foo()
{
void far* p;
//... use p for a while
asm {
   mov SI, p+2
   }
//...
}
```

But this raises the question, will the `+2` refer to an asm-like 2 bytes, or will `(p+2)` be taken as a C-like 2 times the size of the object, or 8 bytes?

The symbol `p` is treated like a dumb text macro. The line emitted if compiling to assembly is

```
MOV  SI,   [BP-4]+2
```

which works as expected (accessing `bp-2`) in the final code, but it chokes BASM. In general, the names of local variables and parameters expand like text macros, so any surrounding context is taken as it would be in assembly language. Meanwhile, BASM can't handle expressions or addressing forms of any complexity.

Global Variables

Global variables are similar. They expand into the C or C++ compiler's name for the item. The following use of `_x` expands to `DGROUP:_x` if compiling to assembly.

```
int x;
void foo()
{
asm mov SI,x      //  OK, works as expected
}
```

This works with external and file-scope global variables, but unfortunately does not work with static members.

```
class C {
public:
   int x;
   void foo();
   };
void C::foo()
{
asm mov SI, x    //  error
}
```

Using `_x` within a member function or referring to `C::x` from a non-member does the same thing: causes a compiler error. Borland C++ simply cannot handle static member names within inline assembly language code. Contrast this to what it does with names it does not recognize at all, which is to pass them unchanged to the asm file if compiling via assembly. If you need to refer to a static member, the work-around is to use its mangled name directly. Name mangling is discussed later under "Separate ASM Functions."

Members

If you have used variables in inline assembly language code, you may try using a member as well and find it does not work. In fact, variables can be used, but in a different way. Inline assembly language code will expand members into an offset, when used on the right hand side of a dot. The following example shows that you can indeed access members without getting compiler errors if you use the symbol in the correct context.

While global variables implicitly use DS, and local variables and parameters implicitly use SS and BP, for members you need to specify from what the member is offset. This is true even if implying `this`. The symbols of C/C++ members are offsets, and should be used with some kind of indexed addressing mode in assembly language.

```
class C {
public:
    int x;
    int y;
    void foo();
    };
void C::foo()
{
asm mov AX, [SI].y
}
```

The `asm` line expands to:

```
MOV  AX,  [SI]+2
```

Since members produce an offset, you will need an object of the proper type in order to use it. Using the same class c from the previous example,

```
void C::foo()
{
asm {
    mov SI, this
    mov AX, [SI].y
    }
}
```

To access a member name, a dot is used, in a way similar to its C use. The left hand side must be something that produces an address of an object of the proper type, in such a way that a +constant can be tacked onto the end. This includes primarily the index registers (SI, DI or BX) in square brackets.

Member names can be used from any structure or class type. This sheds light on the problems dealing with static members. Experiments indicate that the compiler does not treat static members any differently with respect to inline assembly language statements. It allows their use in the member syntax described above, and they expand to an offset of zero. Clearly, this is a compiler bug.

> **Note:** Complex programs have bugs. This applies to compilers as well. Don't be too shocked or horrified to discover one. See Chapter 7, "Debugging Tips and Tricks."

Functions

It is possible to call a function from inline assembly language code. However, there are a few traps to watch out for. Here is an example:

```
void bar (int i)
{
//foo (i);
asm {
    push i
//   call foo
    call near ptr foo
    pop CX
    }
}
```

The `asm` block will do the same thing as the C statement `foo(i);`. Be aware that this will not work in BASM in versions prior to Borland C++ 4.0. The compiler accepts the statement without error, but generates incorrect code for the `call`. It works correctly if compiling via assembly, and the bug appears to be fixed in version 4.0.

Notice that the line of assembly `call foo` does not work. This gives the error `invalid combination of opcodes and operands`, which is just the generic BASM error for anything it doesn't like. The cast is required, and `call near ptr foo` does work.

This is due to a problem in BASM. It thinks that function symbol names are actually pointers to functions. If you try treating the symbol as a data item, BASM will accept it without complaint. If you code the line

```
    asm mov AX,foo
```

then BASM will translate `foo` into `CS:[foo]`. You can see the similarity between this and global variables. This statement will not load the

offset address of `foo` into AX as you might expect, but will instead load the first two bytes of the function into AX, which is nonsense. BASM thinks that `foo` is a pointer, `void(*foo)(int)`, not a function.

If you compile via assembly, you get different results. The symbol `foo` will be translated into the name `_foo`, and the emitted line is `mov AX,_foo`. This causes an assembly error, since TASM does strong type checking on symbol types. It is expecting `mov AX, offset _foo`.

If you are using C++, matters are worse. If compiling via assembly, function names are not correctly translated into their "mangled" OBJ names, but always use the C mechanism of prepending an underscore. The symbol `foo` still becomes `_foo`, not `foo$qi` as is required. This causes the assembler to terminate with an `unknown symbol` error. Member functions are even more dismal. Use of a qualified function name produces a syntax error.

All things considered, it is best to avoid the use of function symbols in inline assembly language code. It is possible to call non-member functions if you watch for a couple of caveats, but for the most part the compiler is uncooperative.

Inline Assembly Language Code and Registers

One of the advantages of using inline assembly language code instead of C++ code is to make simple manipulations of some value much more efficient by using registers instead of local variables. Even for other uses, such as an INT call, it is necessary to get the proper values into specified registers.

If you use registers with inline assembly language code, what happens to the C++ code in which the statement is embedded? How can the compiler give you free rein of the registers yet still be able to generate correct code?

This section explores how you can use registers freely, and how to get values into registers prefatory to other work.

Getting Values into Registers

If you are using assembly language, values are naturally computed in registers and are easily moved from and to other registers or from and to memory. Using inline assembly language code, values may be more easily computed in C++, or found in places not easy to specify with the symbol uses described in the previous section.

It is easy to get a value out of a local variable, global variable, or parameter, and somewhat more difficult, but not impossible, to get a value out of a member. But if the value is to be computed, or is accessed with a lengthy expression, you would rather do the work in C++.

Register Pseudovariables

The most straightforward way to do this is with *register pseudovariables*. Borland C++ provides a syntax to refer to the 80x86 registers within C++ expressions. The reserved symbols _AX, _BX, _CX, _DX, and so on are available, and may be used for accessing or loading registers. A natural use is an alternative to a MOV instruction in inline assembly language code. For example, this will load a value into BH and then call an interrupt:

```
_BH = !get_settings().blink();
asm {
   mov AX, 1002h
   int 10h
   }
```

Suppose get_settings() was a virtual function. This simple-looking expression operates at much too high of a level to be reworked into assembly language, and is not the point of having asm code here. Instead of trying to put high level expressions in the asm code, we instead put low level register access into C++ code. The use of register pseudovariables allows the high-level expression to contain direct reference to processor registers.

As well as loading values before going into an assembly language block, this also is useful for getting values out after completing an assembly language block. If the result, found in a register, is to be stored someplace simple, you could use a mov instruction after the work is done.

Or, you might find it clearer to switch back to C++ as soon as possible and do the store with a register pseudovariable. The first example in this chapter might instead be written:

```
int result;
asm {
   mov ax,a
   imul b
   idiv c
   }
result= _AX;
return result;
```

Or even:

```
asm {
   mov ax,a
   imul b
   idiv c
   }
return _AX;
```

Using Extra Local Variables

The problem with register pseudovariables (which is explored in more detail in the next section) is that they may get overwritten by the actions of compiled code. While it is simple to store the result of one expression into a register immediately before doing some inline assembly language, this does not work so well if you have two such values. Consider:

```
_AX= (foo->bar() + 15) & ~15;
_DX= int (foo->size() / 16L);
asm {
   ...
```

The problem is that although the first line sets AX, the second line probably uses AX in the code generated by the expression, clobbering AX's value.

A better way would be to use local variables for the values, and then load them within the asm block.

```
int offset= (foo->bar() + 15) & ~15;
int segsize= int (foo->size() / 16L);
asm {
   mov AX, offset
   mov DX, segsize
   ...
```

The problem with this is that the code generated is not as good. The compiler stores the value in a stack-based variable, just to fish it out again. This negates some of the advantage of using inline assembly language code. For some purposes, the extra overhead is quite acceptable. In the preceding example, a compromise approach could be used: Compute one of the values and store in a local variable, then store the second directly into the register.

Encapsulate

Instead of assigning all the input parameters to local variables first, and doing similar work on the output values, it is usually cleaner to create a C++ wrapper. This is a function that has no other duties other than to contain your special asm code. The parameters to the wrapper function take the place of the extra local variables, and are easy to load from. Any complex work in generating the values is done by the caller, and does not complicate the code in the region of the asm block.

The previous example might be written as:

```
void wrapper (int offset, int segment)
{
asm {
    mov AX, offset
    mov DX, segsize
    ...
later...
wrapper ((foo->bar() + 15) & ~15, int (foo->size() / 16L));
```

Using Registers Freely

So how can you use registers freely within an asm block, when the compiler normally uses them for its own purposes? The answer is that most of the time the compiler will notice your use and allow for it. The bad news is that, in some cases, it *doesn't* work.

The good news is that the general purpose registers AX, BX, CX, and DX may be used freely. These are considered the "accumulator" and scratch registers, used for many purposes, and the compiler simply doesn't assume anything about their contents when an inline assembly language block is encountered. Furthermore, if you use SI and DI, then the compiler won't

use them for register variables, but still knows that they are "used" in the function and will generate code to save and restore them in the function prologue and epilogue. So, these six registers may be used freely.

However, you must make sure that the compiler knows you are using them. For example, if you make an INT call, and that call changes the value of registers, the compiler won't know that and hence cannot take steps to avoid the use of those registers. Furthermore, some instructions use registers implicitly, such as MUL, which uses DX. The compiler doesn't know about that, either. It does not read the code, but rather looks for explicit mention of the register's names.

> **Caution:** Only registers explicitly mentioned in asm code will be allowed for. If a function or INT changes a register, or if registers are implicitly changed by instructions, the compiler will not notice.

Now here is an interesting catch. If you realize, for example, that DX will be trashed by the contents of the asm block and the compiler won't take steps to protect DX, you would want to take precautions. The obvious solution is to insert a PUSH and POP DX around your code. However, this causes DX to be explicitly mentioned, and now the compiler will avoid using DX across the asm block, so you don't have to save it! The overhead of the PUSH and POP are wasted. A clever trick is to "use" the register even though you don't need to. XCHG DX,DX is a good candidate.

So much for the general purpose registers. What about the others? Here, the situation is not as nice. If you use a segment register, for example, the compiler takes no action. You must be careful, and put such registers back the way you found them. Here, PUSH-POP pairs are appropriate.

```
void write_ioctl (void far* data, int length, int channel)
{
asm {
   push DS
   lds DX, data
   mov BL, channel
   mov cx, length
   int 21h
   pop DS
   }
}
```

Inspecting the Results

When using inline assembly language, it is important to inspect the output to make sure that it assembled to what you had in mind, and that it interfaces correctly with the surrounding C or C++ code. On more than one occasion I've been glad I looked, as a register was getting trashed before I used it, or was not being saved, or the code generated was not what I expected.

In addition, looking at the generated code is helpful when trying to discover the details of how inline assembly language works, such as was done when preparing the earlier section on symbols.

The simplest way to get a look at the generated code is to compile via assembly, and look at the resulting ASM file. If you are compiling via assembly (instead of using BASM) anyway, this is perfectly natural.

To do this, use the -s switch on the compile line. You can compile a single file this way, without rebuilding the whole program in a multi-file project, and take a look at the results. Be sure to delete or rename the resulting ASM file afterwards, as in some situations it can confuse the (re)make process when you resume normal work.

However, as noted earlier, sometimes BASM and compiling via assembly can generate different results. For the most part this should not be an issue, but it is a reason to look at the assembled result. This means that looking at the output of compiling with -s may not be what BASM actually produces.

But sometimes BASM goofs and compiles, but generates an incorrect code sequence. Documented cases have tended to involve a bad fixup or incorrect instruction length. So when things don't work right, you might want to take a look at the output from BASM.

One of the simplest approaches to see what's going on is to take a look at the code with the debugger. Using the stand-alone Turbo Debugger program, you can position the cursor at the beginning of the ASM block and press Alt-V then C, for "View CPU." However, looking at the code with the

debugger is only applicable if you have a linkable program (it does not have to be runable). However, looking at the `-s` output is usually good enough, and re-inspecting with this method only needs to be done if you observe problems when actually running the program.

A more direct way, which does not require a complete program, is to use a program to disassemble the OBJ file. However, such a tool is not included with Borland C++.

Separate ASM Functions

Note: This section assumes more familiarity with the structure of assembly language source files. Besides the opcodes and argument addressing modes, you need to know about a few pseudo-ops and directives. Here is a quick overview. For more details, check the *Borland Turbo Assembler Quick Reference* or other documentation.

`STRUC ... ENDS`	Defines a structure type.
`EQU`	Defines a macro.
`PROC ... ENDP`	Used to define a function. As well as producing a labled entry point, high-level language features can be used to set up the stack frame and access arguments.
`ARG, LOCAL, USES`	Used within a `PROC` to describe arguments, local variables, and registers to be preserved.
`.MODEL`	Goes at the top of an ASM source file to declare details about how `PROC`s will work.
`.CODE, .DATA`	Open the code and data segments, respectively.

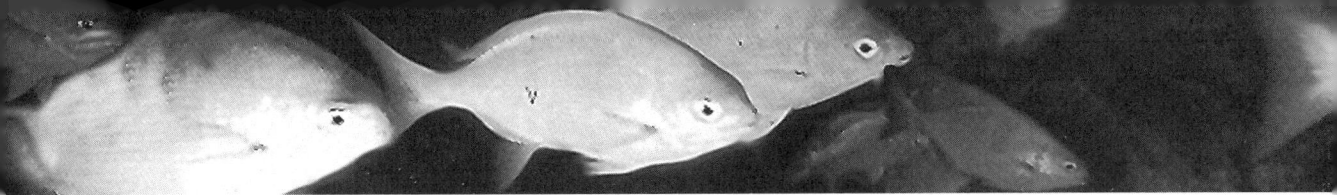

Inline assembly code within a C or C++ function is handy for some things, but also can be more trouble than it's worth. The compiler adds overhead for the function prolog and epilog, saves registers, and so forth. The work necessary to get the parameters into registers, and results out, may be inefficient. If you are coding in assembly in order to call some DOS or BIOS function, the overhead is not a consideration. However, if you are using assembly language to do something that is simply inefficient when compiled in C, the extra work to do something simple may be annoying and undesirable.

In such cases, it may be better to write the entire function in assembly language, in a separate assembly language source file. This can be called from C or C++ quite easily. When writing in real assembly language, you have complete control that inline assembly language just does not provide.

In addition, inline assembly language blocks are non-portable. Even on the same platform (CPU and operating system), different compilers may not implement `asm` blocks in the same way Borland C++ does. Although C++ has a defined syntax for inline assembly, Borland C++ does it differently, and other compilers also do it differently yet. Conversely, separate assembly language ASM files, if carefully written, can serve for all PC C++ compilers without modification or even reassembling.

Basics of Interfacing

The general idea is to write a function in assembly language, and then call that function from C or C++. When declared, the compiler will not care that the function is written in assembly language, but treats it as just another case of separate compilation. In reality, both C++ and assembly language files must cooperate in declaring and defining the function in order for this to work properly.

Let's start with plain C. TASM has built-in support for building functions that conform to C's calling conventions. Typically, it is a simple matter to use the language directive with `.MODEL`, or on the specific function. This will set up the proper stack frame for parameter passing, and add a leading underscore to the function's external name. In other cases, you will want better control and will prefer to do things manually.

Here is an example of an assembly language function that can be called from C:

```
mouse_call_setcursor proc
   uses ES
   param xhot:WORD, yhot:WORD, bitmap:FAR PTR
      mov AX,9
      mov BX,xhot
      mov CX,yhot
      les DX,bitmap
      int 33h
      ret
mouse_call_setcursor endp
```

The details of syntax of the high-level-language `proc` features used here can be found in the TASM documentation. This function will be compatible with C's declaration of:

```
void __cdecl __far mouse_call_setcursor (
   int xhot, int yhot, void __far* bitmap);
```

The `__cdecl` and `__far`'s are for increased compatibility. In Borland C, the normal function calling convention is compatible with the assembly language function as written. However, compiler options can be used to change the default calling convention. Using `__cdecl` will cause this function to be used correctly even if such switches were used when compiling. Furthermore, other compilers may use a different default, but they generally support `__cdecl` for compatibility.

In C, it is easy to compile for different memory models. In assembly language, it is more difficult. Whether functions are called with a near or far call instruction generally does not affect the body of the function, and is simple to change by using the `.MODEL` directive. Pointer parameters are more difficult. Whether a near or far pointer is passed will make a big difference as to the code you write within the function in order to use that parameter, and may make a difference in processing in general. At the very least, you will need conditional compilation, and in some cases you may have completely different versions of a function for different memory models.

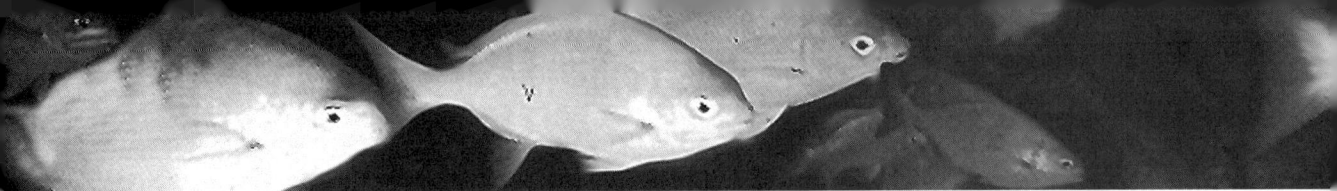

For cases where the additional overhead is not as important, you can write only the large model version and it will normally serve for all uses. Such is the case with the above listing. The ASM file opens with

```
.MODEL large, C
```

and all pointer parameters are declared as far pointers.

Because of this, the `__far` modifier is used on the function itself and on all pointer parameters on the C declaration. This lets the function work in any memory model, and is simply redundant if you are compiling in large model.

The last parameter is declared as a `void*`. You could, and most often would, declare it as a correctly typed pointer. When it gets to the assembly language function it is just another address, but it gives you stronger type checking in the C code.

C++ Function Calls

In C++, a non-member function would be written the same way. But the C++ declaration needs one more step. In C++, functions have a "linkage." A function's linkage was intended to address the issues of calling conventions, like the `__cdecl` does in most PC C compilers, and to address linker issues. In Borland C++, the linkage specification does not affect the calling convention, but is merely used to disable "name mangling," which is discussed in more detail later. So, you will need a mixture of new-style linkage specifications and the PC's unique keywords for calling convention. In short, the declaration becomes:

```
extern "C"  void __cdecl __far mouse_call_setcursor (
    int xhot, int yhot, void __far* bitmap);
```

Notice that the function has a rather long name. This is not out of the ordinary in C, but it is considered unnecessarily wordy and baroque in C++. Due to overloading, function names can be simpler, containing just a verb, with the parameters serving to indicate the subject and direct object of the command. If the above function were simply called `setcursor()`, there would be no conflict with other functions named `setcursor()` because the parameters are different.

You can recover this simpler name by using an inline function wrapper:

```
inline void setcursor (int xhot, int yhot, void* bitmap)
{
mouse_call_setcursor (xhot, yhot, bitmap);
}
```

Besides changing the name, this simple wrapper can be used to dress up the function and make it presentable in other ways. If there were any "uglies" in the parameters, they can be hidden in the wrapper.

The inline wrapper idea can be applied to member functions, too. Perhaps setcursor would not be global, but would be a static member of class mouse. The wrapper would become:

```
inline void mouse::setcursor (int xhot, int yhot, void* bitmap)
{
mouse_call_setcursor (xhot, yhot, bitmap);
}
```

and there is no change in the underlying assembly language function. For normal members, the hidden this parameter can be handled the same way. In order to write the member function c::foo(), you might have the following:

```
extern "C" int __cdecl __far asm_C_foo (C __far*, int, int);
inline int C::foo (int x, int y)
{
return asm_C_foo (this, int, int);
}
```

This moves the this pointer into an explicit parameter and calls the assembly language function in the standard C way. So what becomes of the instance variable in the assembly language code? In the assembly language file, the data part of the class can be declared as a STRUC. The assembly language code will receive a pointer to the struc, which has the same layout as the C++ struct or class.

C++ Classes

Writing an asm struc with the same layout as a C++ class is easy if there are only data members, as in a C-style structure. Even member functions can be simply ignored when translating the members. However, with more elaborate classes, there may be system information

included at unknown places within the data structure. A simple way to guarantee that the declarations in C++ and assembly language match is to separate the data "lump" being passed from the rest of the class with its virtual functions and other items.

Here is an example taken from a case where I wanted entire class members to be written in assembly language for efficiency. The class is called `pixarray`, and it manipulates bitmaps, or "pixel arrays."

First, the data part of the class was declared in a structure. The *FIXED* comment is my note to indicate that the layout of a structure is known by code that doesn't read this header, so it can't be freely changed. This includes structures used for calling DOS functions that I don't have any control over, and structures that must exactly match a STRUC in an assembly language file somewhere else.

```
struct pixarray_prim { //FIXED
    int height, width;          // in pixels
    // items omitted for the example...
    byte __far* data;
    };
```

This is a C-style structure, with no access modifiers (`public:`, `protected:`, `private:` keywords), no base classes, no member functions, no static members, and no members of exotic types such as classes or references. It is perfectly simple to duplicate this in assembly language:

```
pixarray_prim STRUC
    PA_Height      DW    ?    ; height of pixarray in pixels
    PA_Width       DW    ?    ; width of pixarray in pixels
    // items omitted for the example...
    PA_Data        DD    ?
ENDS
```

A C++ class is now written, using the simple struct as a starting point. Thanks to inheritance, you can simply add on all the fancy stuff, including virtual functions. The compiler will keep the data from the base class together in one contiguous structure, and make it easy to pass this to the assembly language code.

```
class pixarray : private pixarray_prim {
public:
    void write_pixel (int x, int y, pentype color, int page= 0);
    };
```

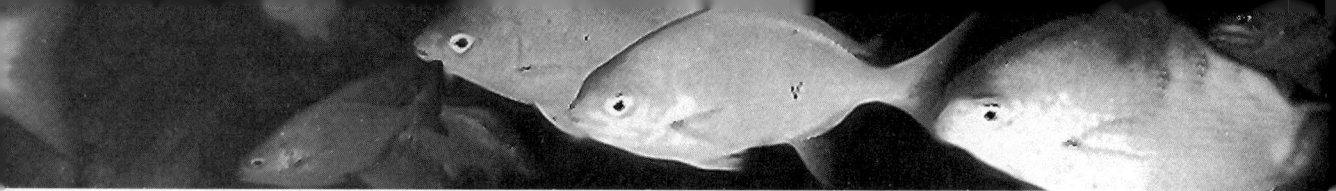

The implementation is simple. Only the base class, the `pixarray_prim` core, is passed.

```
extern "C" __cdecl __far pix_WritePixel (
   pixarray_prim __far*, int x, int y, pentype color, int page);
inline void pixarray::write_pixel (
   int x, int y, pentype color, int page)
{
pix_WritePixel (this, x,y,color,page);
}
```

Notice what happens when `this` is passed to the assembly language primitive. The assembly language function is declared as taking a pointer to the `pixarray_prim`. So the value of `this`, which is a `pixarray*`, is automatically converted. If the `pixarray_prim` part of the pixarray was located at some offset within the larger object, its location is computed and that is the address which is passed. The address `this` points to will be a valid object of type `pixarray_prim`, and there will be no influences due to the unique C++ parts of the `pixarray` class. The assembly code is none the wiser that the STRUC is the base of a more complex type.

Now the assembly language function would be defined as:

```
pix_WritePixel  PROC
   USES ds,es,si,di
   ARG  pix:FAR PTR pixarray_prim
   ARG  x:WORD,y:WORD, color:DWORD, page_n:WORD
   lds  si,pix          ; DS:SI -> pix
   ; the bulk of the function follows...
pix_WritePixel ENDP
```

Name Mangling

This interface mechanism works well, but there are still times when you want to know how C++ actually treats things, instead of avoiding the issue. Most often, you will want to access static member variables from within assembly language functions. This is simple. A more formidable task is writing a member function directly in assembly language without an inline wrapper. I have encountered one case where I had to do this.

In Borland C++, accessing a static data member from assembly language is as simple as knowing its name. Just declare it as such, and use that name. Better yet, hide the complex name with an `EQU`.

In Borland C++, the name of a static data member is encoded as an `@` character followed by the class name followed by another `@` character followed by the member's name. For example, `C::x` becomes `@C@x`. If a C++ file defined class `File` with static member `error`, you could reference it in assembly language by calling it `@File@error`. Notice that you have to suppress the generation of a leading underscore if using `LANGUAGE C` when assembling, by specifying `NOLANGUAGE` in the `extern` statement itself. In C++:

```
class File {
   // other members omited for example
   static int error;
   };
in ASM
      .DATA
extern NOLANGUAGE @File@error : word
```

Simple! In other compilers, the name may be different, or even impossible to represent in assembly language. You can still avoid the issue, and refer to the symbol with a simple name in assembly language by using a linker trick. As of version 4.0, you can create aliases for symbols.

Unlike static data members, the name of a function in C++ is considerably more complex. The class name and the types of all the parameters are encoded. For example, `C::foo(int)` comes out as `@C@foo$qi`. The parameter list is encoded following a `$` character. Details of the encoding scheme are presented in the Borland Open Architecture Handbook, though it is incomplete with respect to new features introduced in Borland C++ version 4.0. The best way to find the name of a C++ item for use in assembly language is to have the C++ compiler do it.

If you are writing a C++ function in assembly language, make a stub version in C++ first, and compile using the `-S` switch. Look at the resulting ASM file, or better yet, use your editor's *cut and paste* method to extract the `PROC` line. Use this as a starting point for your assembly language version, and delete your stub.

Once you know the name, you must make sure that TASM does not stick an extra underscore before it. Typically, you will be writing with the "C" language in the .MODEL directive of the source file. This adds leading underscores to the function names that are made PUBLIC, and sets up calling convention information. If you don't use "C" in the .MODEL directive, the ARG construct won't work. However, you can have it both ways. Use NOLANGUAGE on that symbol's PUBLIC line, and do not use any special modifiers on the PROC line. If you use NOLANGUAGE on the PROC line, the function will not have the right calling convention set up, and arguments will be tolerated but will generate incorrect code. Only put NOLANGUAGE on the PUBLIC line, which changes the exported name but does not affect anything else.

Again, notice that it is rarely necessary to actually write a C++ member in assembly language. The majority of the time, having an inline wrapper will be just as efficient.

Using '286 and '386 Code

For years, PC software was compiled for 8086 instructions even though AT class and better machines were commonplace. For complex applications that would be so impractical as to be unusable on an XT, you could probably compile to use '286 specific code and nobody would mind. But still, most people did not, because somebody someplace might want to run on an XT, and the compiler doesn't really do much better with -2 enabled anyway.

However, the backwards compatibility of only using instructions that are available on an XT is fading. In what some could consider a bold move, BC++ 4.0 generates '286 code by default. Now, you have to take special steps to produce code to run on an XT. Programs are now being produced that use '286 code.

In assembly language, the benefits of using '286 code are greater. When optimizing by hand to use registers to their fullest and avoid memory references, some new instructions are very handy. With '286 code you can PUSH an immediate value, rotate by an immediate, and

multiply by an immediate. Besides saving a line or two, such instructions are much more important in that they free up a register, which can be used for something else. It is possible to write tighter code.

In order to use these instructions in an assembly language file, simply use the `.286` directive at the beginning of the file.

While the '286 offers some nice new instructions, the '386 also offers new abilities. There are some new instructions, but they are of limited use for writing tighter, faster real-mode code. However, what it does offer is completely different: 32-bit arithmetic, and new addressing modes.

When writing an assembly language file that will contain '386 specific instructions, you use the `.386` directive at the beginning of the file. However, that is not sufficient. This also changes the defaults for other things, and the assembled file will be incompatible with real-mode DOS programs and won't link with your C++ code. To make it work properly, include the USE16 modifier in the MODEL directive. A typical file starts with these two statements:

```
; typical start of file that uses '386 instructions
        .386
        .MODEL USE16 LARGE,C
```

You can use 32-bit registers and 32-bit manipulations to dramatically speed up handling of long values. Also, use of 32-bit registers is required when using some of the new addressing modes. The new registers are named by prepending an E (for "extended") to the old names. So you have EAX for the 32-bit accumulator, for example.

If you use these extended registers, be sure to save and restore their values just as with the old 16-bit registers. If you use ESI, make sure you save and restore all 32 bits. This is simple: just use ESI instead of SI in the USES directive.

The new addressing modes can be handy, sparing the need to compute intermediate results and taking up another register. For example, I coded a tight binary search of 8-byte records with the key located in the second word. I used AX to hold the target key, CX and DX to hold the

high and low index values, and BX to hold the mid index value which is the current test candidate. DS:SI points to the array, and let us assume that DI also is otherwise engaged. To write tight code that keeps everything in registers, there is no room to calculate the array offset in bytes.

With '386 code, the compare line was:

```
cmp AX, [ESI+8*EBX+2]
```

The primitive addressing mode will multiply the index BX by 8, add this to the base address in SI, and add another 2 bytes. This resulting address is used to fetch the word of interest. No extra steps of shifting and adding were required, and no extra register was needed. The fancy addressing modes require the use of the 32-bit registers, and in this case I just zeroed out the high 16 bits and ignored them afterwards.

There also are more registers to use. A shortage of segment registers plagues the 8086 programmer. If you are processing data passed in with two far pointers and are sending the output to a third, you are in trouble. The need to switch segment registers around will put a kink in your quest to write tight code. On the 80386, FS and GS are available as well as DS and ES for general purpose data pointers. They will be welcomed for such purposes.

You may want to provide code that is optionally compatible with other processors. For example, a function may have two versions, one for general use and one that takes advantage of '386 instructions. This will give a speed boost on '386 capable machines, but still provide compatbilty with other processors.

What to Code

Now that you know how to use assembly language with C/C++, the question arises of what actually needs to be coded in assembly language. There are three categories of operations to consider:

> ➤ Something may be impossible in C. At the very least, you may need an assembly language primitive to code the library functions that other parts of the program use.

> Some things may be more convenient to write in assembly language than in C, even though it is possible. A line or two of inline assembly language might be far simpler than using the library functions for the same purpose, as you'll see later with DOS interrupts, discussed under "Hardware Interfacing." Also, consider the task of rotating a 16-bit register. It is certainly possible to do it in C, with several statements. But the underlying machine has a primitive instruction that can do it, so why not use it?

> Sometimes efficiency is a real issue. Profiling the program may indicate that particular parts are too slow, and you decide that rewriting those parts in assembly language is warranted.

Hardware Interfacing

Consider the low-level `write()` function which calls DOS. This needs to call `INT 21`, so inline assembly language is the simplest thing to do. You might say, "use `intdos()` or `geninterrupt()`," but the reply is the same: How could those functions be written in C? C and C++ have no primitives built in for input/output, but rely on a standard library. Ultimately, something not in C is required to interface with hardware.

This generally takes two forms. You can access the input/output ports using the `IN` and `OUT` instructions, or call DOS, BIOS, and other installable services through `INT` instructions.

Both of these are simple to do with a few lines of inline assembly language. Personally, I took a dislike to the INT86 set of library functions the first time I saw them. They are complex to use, and too much trouble compared to inline assembly language. You can call an interrupt function with a single line of asm, and easily set up the registers. For calling such a service, the overhead of one more function call is not an issue, and the best thing is to encapsulate the access in a wrapper function, as this example shows:

```
void write_ioctl (void far* data, int length, int channel)
{
asm {
  push DS
```

```
        lds DX, data
        mov BL, channel
        mov cx, length
        int 21h
        pop DS
        }
    }
```

Accessing the input/output ports is similar, and usually much simpler since only the `AX` and `DX` registers are needed. On the other hand, because of its simplicity, the `inport()` and `outport()` functions are not at all difficult or clumsy.

In addition to accessing `INT`'s and ports, other tasks concerning hardware interfacing include disabling interrupts, locking the bus, and dealing with other timing issues.

Exotic Instructions

Some things are just easier in assembly language than in C. Consider rotating an `int x` right one bit. It would take a bit of thought, several lines of code, and testing to do this in C, but what could be simpler than the single line below?

```
    asm  ror X
```

Other things that can be done in assembly language include checking of flags after doing arithmetic. It is possible to carefully test for overflow in advance when doing normal C arithmetic, but it is easier and more efficient to do it with a line of asm followed by a conditional jump.

Sometimes, business applications want to use BCD (binary coded decimal) arithmetic in order to prevent round off errors. The task of doing BCD arithmetic is simpler in assembly language, or at least with the help of a few well-chosen instructions such as `AAS` and `AAA`.

The 80386 offers a bit scan instruction, of which there is no counterpart in C. Sometimes, the right language for the job is not C, but assembly language. In such a case, mix languages.

Long Arithmetic

In Borland C++ generating 16-bit code, arithmetic with the `long` data type is particularly bad. For general use, there is no way around it. A 32-bit by 32-bit multiply requires multiple steps to break it into component 16-bit operations. Division is horrid, and the implementation is particularly bad: Besides reimplementing with a more efficient algorithm, someone familiar with assembly language and instruction timings could save a few hundred cycles with trivial changes. Addition and subtraction is conceptually simple, requiring two primitive 16-bit operations.

The big problem comes when you don't need the general case. Say you wanted to multiply a `long` by an `int`. The compiler would convert the `int` to a `long` and call the helper function for the general case. This is wasted effort, since just multiplying an `int` by a `long` can be done in fewer steps. For division, the savings are much bigger, since the CPU's divide instruction is designed to divide a 32-bit number by a 16-bit number. Even for simple addition and bit manipulation with constants, the compiler is not smart enough to eliminate instructions which add zero or perform a "logical or" with zero.

A similar problem exists when you multiply two `int`s such that you know a `long` is needed to hold the result. In C, the only thing you can do is do `long` multiplication. The CPU can do it directly! Why not let it do it? If you use explicit assembly code, you can harness this capability. The opening of this chapter showed an example where a number was multiplied by one value and then divided by a second. All values were `int`s, and the result was an `int`. But C requires `long` arithmetic to perform this, and doing it with inline assembly language provided a significant improvement.

The high-yield cases to look for are multiplying two `int`s to produce a `long`, multiplying an `int` by a `long`, and dividing a `long` by an `int` to produce an `int`.

From Here...

➤ For more information on mixing C++ with other languages, see Chapter 13, "Mixed Language Programming," and Chapter 15, "Interfacing With Database Languages."

➤ For a different look at the Bare Metal, see Chapter 19, "Writing Interrupt Handlers and TSR Programs."

➤ For the flip side, why this kind of code is bad in some cases, see Chapter 1, "Writing Portable Code."

Interfacing with Database Languages

by Steve Potts

In some applications, a requirement is that objects maintain their
identity beyond the end of the program's current execution. If your
sales figures for the year went to $0.00 because you turned off your
computer, you wouldn't be likely to use software to track your business. If your bank account disappeared every time the bank's computer system completed execution, you wouldn't be a customer for
long. These persistent objects form a large part of the information
world. Inventory, insurance, personnel, and accounting systems are a
few examples of persistent object systems. These programs must have
a way of saving their objects between invocations of the program.

Another attribute of these persistent systems is that they are not usually accessed by a single individual or program. It may be necessary for
the employee records to be accessed by a human resources program,
a payroll program, and a training program in the same day or even
at the same time. It may be accessed in the future by programs not yet

written. Some of this access might be from a C++ program that also contains hooks to the company e-mail system. Another may be from a manager doing ad hoc queries. Parts of the data may be sensitive, and therefore need to be encrypted. Some of this access may take place from branch offices via a wide-area network.

There may be rules associated with the data. An example of this could be, "No purchase orders may be written to companies that do not appear in our approved vendor table." At times the data from many different files must be brought together to produce critical reports. These files must be easy to change since new fields are added regularly. Some of the data is massive. Some of the data is not traditional text; it is spreadsheet data or a bit-mapped image.

This chapter explores the subject of persistent data management from two perspectives. One is from the viewpoint of a C++ programmer who wants to incorporate persistent data in a system under development. The second viewpoint is that of a database developer whose native language is PAL or SQL and who rarely writes in C++. They may be forced to move down in the "food chain" of programmers by a need to integrate their database application with others. Some applications like bar-code readers or forms-based mail systems can only be accessed by a C or C++ application programming interface (API).

In this chapter you explore:

➤ Using Databases in C++ Programs

➤ Using the Paradox Engine

➤ Using the Database Framework

➤ Using the ODBC

The goal of this chapter is to make you aware of the motivations for using database technology and some of the major technology choices available. Another goal is to show you how to develop a basic application using three different types of database systems. The DBMS offerings in this chapter are a sampling of the systems that would likely be the most interesting to a Borland C++ developer. There are more

products in this category that would have to be discussed if this were a buyer's guide for DBMS systems. The inclusion of a product does not represent an endorsement. They were selected to provide a variety of approaches. The Paradox Engine is implemented as a set of C function calls. The Database Framework is a C++ class library that provides access to databases in the Paradox format. ODBC is an interface that was put forth by Microsoft to allow the programmer to build an application that can access databases from a variety of vendors. With a good understanding of these products and approaches, you will be able to evaluate the competing products against your program's unique requirements.

Using C++ or a Commercial DBMS Language

Many DBMS power users have enjoyed a charmed life. Instead of working in the "bits and bytes" world of third-generation languages, they have had concurrent access, schema independence, referential integrity, interactive tools, and a host of other DBMS capabilities at their finger tips. Why would someone willingly leave this "Garden of Eden?" The reason is simple: limitations. As long as we are willing to live with the limitations that come with a user interface and query facility, there is no reason to program at a lower level. However, there are problems that are easier to solve by programming in C++. For example, if we need to integrate a magnetic-strip reader with an e-mail system and a database management system, C++ is the quickest (and often the only) solution.

A more personal reason is job security. The world of a computer professional is changing. Every year the borders around those people who are net consumers of computer technology (bankers, insurance agents, manufacturing engineers, and so on) expands to include more of what was once the province of the computer professional. These people once came to us for simple reports. Now they usually create their own. There was a time when they delegated all programming to us. They are

now very comfortable with fourth generation languages. They are better than we are at screen design (since they know their discipline better), and they manage their own network to a certain level. In short, they are doing things that they used to pay us to do.

Before you get too depressed, you should know that our province is getting larger also. For every province lost at our interior, four more open up on our outer border. This is why employment opportunities are expanding for computer professionals in spite of the encroaching hoards of computing "do-it-yourself" types. The problem is not a lack of demand for skilled people; it is one of demand in areas where we are not experienced. New provinces, by definition, never have experienced programmers in them. In these frontiers, just as in the frontiers of the last century, the rewards are great for those settlers who rush in and stake a claim to 80 acres of prime farming land. One of the best pieces of this "land" is in the area of software integration.

End-users will not often pay us to develop a database to track sales, but they will pay for a database on a network that dynamically combines the sales for the whole country and automatically sends e-mail versions of the reports to management. They often write simple forms interfaces themselves. They pay, however, for a mail-based forms system that automatically routes the results of a form-based request to the appropriate person and then tracks the movement of that form throughout the bureaucracy. They will pay for systems that give them access to a real spreadsheet program (for example, 1-2-3 and Excel), a real word processor (such as, WordPerfect and Word), and a real presentations graphics package (for example, CorelDRAW! and Aldus PageMaker) all from within their main application. In the future, these same users will pay for programs that let them control their copying machine and even the coffee pot from their computer.

What do all of these various systems have in common? They are based on application programming interfaces or APIs. These APIs are usually C/C++ libraries of function calls that give the programmer access to the functionality of a software package from within his or her own program. Borland has announced Borland Object Component

Architecture (BOCA), a set of APIs that will eventually make all of its flagship products available to programmers at the function call level. The Paradox Engine is a part of the BOCA strategy. Microsoft has announced its own Windows Open System Architecture (WOSA). This is a set of APIs for Microsoft's products. Third-party vendors are also producing products built around these and similar APIs. Hardware devices such as magnetic-strip readers and bar-code devices are shipped with C++ callable APIs as standard equipment.

What this means to the programmer on the street is that a whole new world of interoperating systems is on the horizon. The programmers who develop a level of comfort in this new order will find that they are in great demand. While fourth generation languages (4GLs) are being enhanced to provide some access to these APIs, the natural place for them to interact is at the C/C++ level. Many of these APIs are released with a class library that simplifies their use (after you peddle furiously up a steep learning curve). These class libraries will be very difficult to access from a 4GL. The flexibility of C++ is unlikely to be matched in any other widely used language.

The area of data storage and retrieval is a natural place to start moving into the world of APIs. Program access to commercial database management systems on large computers dates back at least 20 years. The API-based database products on the PC are more mature than their counterparts in the area of mail or telephone communication.

For those of you who are accustomed to developing in a 4GL, there are several things that you need to understand. The learning curve for an API is fairly steep and filled with frustration. Getting the very first trivial application to compile and run can take days. You will, over time, need to deepen your knowledge of C++ and the Microsoft Windows operating system. Be aware though, that after a brief introductory period of frustration, programming at this level can be very addictive. Programmers have been known to lose all interest in sports and all other forms of recreation (well, almost all). They also start babbling in a manner that is incomprehensible to all but their fellow C++ programmers— tossing acronyms around with the agility of an Olympic discus thrower.

After the initiation period ends, they become very productive. Systems written with the database APIs can be completed in a very short time compared to those done with traditional third-generation language development.

Using Database Access or C++ Files

As a C++ programmer, you may be wondering why you need a database management system at all. Many programmers sound like the grouchy old man on *Saturday Night Live*. They say things like "When I was a boy, we didn't have any sissy database management system software. All files were streams. They were a pain to code, but we were happy, and we liked it that way."

So, why use a database management system at all? Why don't we just act like the grouchy old man above and "roll our own."

➤ *Cost.* The database management system products of the class mentioned here sell for under $500. How much code can you write and debug for $500? It is a great benefit to productivity to have routines that have been "debugged" and distributed with a manual (though it will not seem so beneficial for the first few hours after you open the box). Most of these packages allow you to distribute your application built with their software without royalty. If you can save money by doing it yourself, we will all be impressed.

➤ *Customer Acceptance.* Many purchasers of your system will want access to their data in an ad hoc fashion. They will resist systems that are not open to other purchased tools. If your system uses the Paradox Engine, they know that a commercial version of Paradox can give them access to the data. They will not feel trapped. They will also know that you have followed at least a little discipline in developing the system. It is unbelievable what convoluted schemes for data management can be found when you *attempt* to gain access to the data in a proprietary file structure.

➤ *Schema Independence.* In a proprietary file layout, the data is accessed by its position in the record. We say that the "last name" is located from the 14th to the 28th bytes from the beginning of the record. If we want to add data fields to the record (and we will), we must put the data fields at the end or change our code to the new layout. If our fellow programmer has written his or her code to use the original layout, a shouting match of millennial proportions will be required also. Heaven forbid that anyone outside your company ever use that layout. If you don't even know who or where they are, you will find yourself locked into that format for the duration. Relational database management systems refer to their data by name, not by location in a record layout. If someone is accessing your data using the name, it does not matter what you do to the layout. Individual fields may be added without worry.

➤ *Concurrent Access.* If we follow the macho approach and do our own data management, we will have to handle the situation where two users or applications are accessing the data at the same time. Solving this problem consumed the best years of many programmers' lives in the late 70s and early 80s. Tomes have been published on how to make these concurrent systems work without completely killing performance. If you are going to solve this problem, you need to read these works.

➤ *Performance.* All programmers feel that they can move mountains when called upon. Challenge that belief when it pertains to mountains of data. It is easy enough to find a specific record when you have 2,000 of them. When that record is one of 20,000 or 200,000, you have a challenge. If you access the data sequentially and do an "if test" to find it, you will be lucky to be done by the end of the user's second cup of java, much less the first. PhDs have spent years developing algorithms to speed data access. Commercial DBMS vendors spent millions of dollars incorporating these algorithms into their products. A donation of a few hundred dollars is all that is required to obtain the benefits of this effort.

➤ *Security.* Many programs must deal with the problem of private or sensitive data. Every human resources person knows that the pay given to individuals is not completely rational. They are convinced that they will be hung from the yardarm if the workers knew how much others make. They must have a way to encrypt their data in a way that makes it impossible for anyone except them to see it. This is another area where "fools rush in." The science of encryption is an entire field of study in the academic world. If we want to protect our data from unauthorized access, we are going to need quite an education. Password protection of tables is another area where we could spend weeks developing a strategy and then coding it.

➤ *Transaction Processing.* Not all updates from the database take place in isolation. For example, imagine a program that changes an employee's health insurance from one provider to another. Suppose that this process requires a deletion of one record and the addition of another. Also suppose that system crashes after the deletion but before the addition. The database is not corrupted because the physical delete was completed. You have, however, an employee without any insurance. Commercial DBMS offerings have a "begin/commit" logic that allows the programmer to specify the start and end (commit) of a transaction. These systems automatically "roll back" to the "begin" if they crash before they see the "commit."

➤ *Non-Textual Data.* Modern DBMS systems support the storage and retrieval of non-textual data. This includes but is not limited to word processing documents, spreadsheets, and bit-mapped images. These objects can be huge, which makes processing them a nightmare.

➤ *Referential Integrity.* Your customer's data is not a set of independent tables. These tables are interconnected. The customer table is connected to the order table because it is a violation of company policy to ship to a company that is not in the customer table. In order to store this kind of knowledge, the commercial

DBMS vendors have implemented referential integrity. This is a set of logic that refuses to process certain transactions (like sending an order to a noncustomer) that causes an integrity problem. Failure to implement this processing requires it to be implemented (or ignored) in every application written against the data.

➤ *Events and Rules.* Some processing occurs as a result of a certain event taking place. An example of this would be an airplane maintenance system. If the supervisor assigns a number of mechanics to an airplane when it lands, it is logical that they should be unassigned when the plane flies off. Again, this could be done at the application level, but a lot of duplicated logic could result. The more advanced commercial offerings in the DBMS world provide this capability.

Hopefully, by now, you are completely converted to the virtues of commercial database offerings. Not all DBMS products contain all of the features listed above. However, they all contain much more than stream files are able to provide. You'll probably find it challenging to learn to use purchased software. There are always function calls that don't behave the way that you think they should. In the object-oriented world, some of the objects that developers give us to use are not very intuitive. In spite of this, the benefits of using a DBMS far outweigh the inconveniences. Let's examine several commercial offerings and example programs that use them.

Using the Paradox Engine

The Paradox Engine is a software library that allows a programmer to create and modify tables in the Paradox format. It supports development in C++ with a procedural approach. (There is an object-oriented version of the engine called the Paradox Database Framework, which is the subject of the next section, "Using the Paradox Database Framework.") The Engine, written to coexist with PAL applications but not replace them, allows programs to be written for both DOS and Windows targets. The Engine is composed of more than 90 functions that

allow programs to manipulate Paradox tables in single-user and multi-user environments. Normally, a programmer would develop reports using the traditional Paradox tools and would "drop down" into C++ and make API calls when necessary to integrate Paradox with other applications (such as, bar-code readers and e-mail systems). The developer's toolkit includes the rights to distribute run-time versions of your applications royalty-free.

The Engine is a function library that resembles the tools that C programmers have used for years. It is specifically written for Paradox applications. The section "Using ODBC" introduces us to the Open Database Connection (ODBC), which gives us access to the multiple databases via the Structured Query Language (SQL).

In order to use the Engine, you need to write a traditional C++ program and then embed the Engine's application programming interface (API) calls in it. Let's look at a simple example. Figure 15.1 shows the development environment in the correct configuration for running the Engine programs.

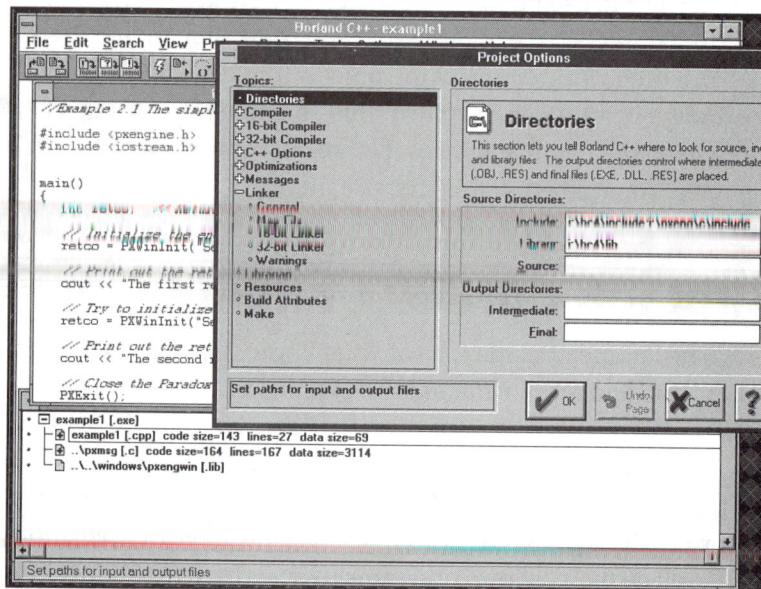

Fig. 15.1. Setting the IDE to run the Paradox Engine.

Listing 15.1 can be used to verify that you have set up the project correctly and that the linker can find all of the external references needed to run Engine programs.

Listing 15.1. The Simplest Paradox Engine Example

```
// Listing 15.1 The Paradox Engine
// The simplest Paradox Engine example

#include <pxengine.h>
#include <iostream.h>


main()
{
    int retco;  // Return code for the functions

    // Initialize the Engine for use under Windows
    retco = PXWinInit("Setup", PXSHARED);

    // Print out the return code
    cout << "The first return code is " << retco << "\n";

    // Try to initialize the Engine for the second time
    retco = PXWinInit("Setup", PXSHARED);

    // Print out the return code
    cout << "The second return code is " << retco << "\n";

    // Close the Paradox Engine
    PXExit();

    // Return the value of the return code
    return retco;
}
```

The first thing that you need do to get the application running is to make a reference to the `include` file:

```
#include <pxengine.h>
```

This file contains the prototypes for all of the Engine's routines and constant definitions. It is located in the ?\PXENG\C\INCLUDE directory; ? is the drive letter (for example, C:) where you installed the Paradox Engine.

Before you can use the Engine in the Windows environment, you must run `PXWinInit()`. If this is a DOS application, you use `PXInit()` instead.

However, you need the Windows version even though you are only doing text output because you are running this program as an EasyWin.

```
// Initialize the Engine for use under Windows
retco = PXWinInit("Setup", PXSHARED);
```

PXWinInit() initializes the Engine for concurrent operations under Windows. The first argument, "Setup", is an arbitrarily chosen name for the application. The second argument, PXSHARED, indicates that this application is willing to share all tables when necessary. If you print out the return code,

```
The first return code is 0
```

you see that it has the value of 0. This indicates that the connection was successfully established. For purposes of illustration, you can try and call PXWinInit() again. This time the printout you get is

```
The second return code is 82
```

The manual that comes with the product indicates that a return code of 82 is an error whose defined value is PXERR_ALREADYINIT. This means that the Engine is already initialized. This makes sense in this application. The last function that you need to call is PXExit().

```
// Close the Paradox Engine
PXExit();
```

PXExit() saves all buffered changes to disk, closes all tables, and removes all locks. It also clears and frees all buffers, data structures, and internal tables.

Now that you have tested the installation of the Engine and the configuration of the IDE, you're ready to do some work. In Listing 15.2, you create a table using the Engine.

Listing 15.2. Creating a Table with the Paradox Engine

```
//Listing 15.2 The Paradox Engine
//Creating a table

#include <pxengine.h>
#include <iostream.h>
```

```
main()
{
    int retco;  // Return code for the functions

    // Initialize the Engine for use under Windows
    retco = PXWinInit("Setup", PXSHARED);

    //Check the return code
    cout << "The return code for the PXWinInit() was " << retco << "\n\n";

    //Create an array of strings that contain the field names
    char *fields[] = {    "Last_Name",
                "First_Name",
                "Age" };

    //Create an array of strings that contain the field types
    char *types[] = {    "A30",
                "A30",
                "N" };

    //Create the handle for the table
    TABLEHANDLE tblHandle;

    //Create the table
    retco = PXTblCreate("Employee", 3, fields, types);

    //Check the return code
    cout << "The return code for the PXTblCreate() was " << retco << "\n\n";

    //Open the table
    retco = PXTblOpen("Employee", &tblHandle, 0, 0);

    //Print out the return code
    cout << "The return code for the PXTblOpen() was " << retco << "\n\n";

    //Close the table
     retco = PXTblClose(tblHandle);

    //Print out the return code
    cout << "The return code for the PXTblClose() was " << retco << "\n\n";

    // Close the Paradox Engine
    PXExit();


    // Return the value of the return code
    return 0;
}
```

After initializing the Engine, create two arrays:

```
//Create an array of strings that contain the field names
char *fields[]= {      "Last_Name",
                "First_Name",
                "Age" };

//Create an array of strings that contain the field types
char *types[] = {      "A30",
                "A30",
                "N" };
```

The first array contains the names of the columns in the new table. The second contains the field types of the new columns.

Having done this, you are ready to allocate the handle for the table.

```
//Create the handle for the table
TABLEHANDLE tblHandle;
```

`TABLEHANDLE` is a `typedef` for an unsigned integer. The `typedef` allows the declaration to be more readable and for very strict type checking in some applications. For the purposes of running the Engine, think of it as a datatype. The table handle is like your Social Security number. It uniquely identifies the table to the system. The exact value is not important, as long as the entire system uses the same handle when referring to this table. Now you can create the table.

```
//Create the table
retco = PXTblCreate("Employee", 3, fields, types);
```

`PXTblCreate()` creates the table's file and schema. You pass it four arguments. The name of the table is `"Employee"` in the current directory with 3 fields in it. The names of the fields are stored in an array called `fields`, and the datatypes are stored in an array called `types`. In order to verify that the table was created correctly, open it.

```
//Open the table
retco = PXTblOpen("Employee", &tblHandle, 0, 0);

//Print out the return code
    cout << "The return code for the PXTblOpen() was " << retco << "\n\n";
```

`PXTblOpen()` takes as its arguments the table name and the handle that you allocated earlier. This handle serves to identify the table for the duration of this program. The third argument, `0` in this case, indicates

that you access the data in its natural order. The fourth argument is set to 0, which indicates the desire to buffer writes before putting them to disk. Again, the return code should be 0.

```
//Close the table
retco = PXTblClose(tblHandle);

//Print out the return code
cout << "The return code for the PXTblClose() was " << retco << "\n\n";
```

PXTblClose() writes all unsaved changes to the disk and frees the table handle. Also, it unlocks all of the locks held by this program on this table and closes all indexes. All tables should be closed in this fashion.

Now that you have a valid table, you need to put some data into it. You do this in Listing 15.3.

Listing 15.3. Appending Data to an Existing Table

```
//Listing 15.3   The Paradox Engine
//Appending Data to an existing table

#include <pxengine.h>
#include <iostream.h>


main()
{
    int retco;   // Return code for the functions

    // Initialize the Engine for use under Windows
    retco = PXWinInit("Setup", PXSHARED);

    //Create the handles for the table and the record
    TABLEHANDLE tblHandle;
    RECORDHANDLE recHandle;

    //Open the table
    retco = PXTblOpen("Employee", &tblHandle, 0, 0);

    //Create a record buffer for this table
    retco = PXRecBufOpen(tblHandle, &recHandle);

    //Print out the return code
    cout << "The return code for the PXRecBufOpen() was " << retco << "\n\n";

    //Put data into the record buffer
```

continues

Listing 15.3. Continued

```
retco = PXPutAlpha(recHandle, 1, "Einstein");

//Check the return code
cout << "The return code for the PXPutAlpha() was " << retco << "\n\n";

rotco = PXPutAlpha(recHandle, 2, "Albert");
retco = PXPutDoub(recHandle, 3, 91);

//Append the new row to the table
retco = PXRecAppend(tblHandle, recHandle);

//Check the return code
cout << "The return code for the PXRecAppend() was " << retco << "\n\n";

//Put data into the record buffer
retco = PXPutAlpha(recHandle, 1, "Regan");
retco = PXPutAlpha(recHandle, 2, "Ronald");
retco = PXPutDoub(recHandle, 3, 81);

//Append the new row to the table
retco = PXRecAppend(tblHandle, recHandle);

//Put data into the record buffer
retco = PXPutAlpha(recHandle, 1, "Hun");
retco = PXPutAlpha(recHandle, 2, "Atilla");
retco = PXPutDoub(recHandle, 3, 55);

//Append the new row to the table
retco = PXRecAppend(tblHandle, recHandle);

//Close the record Buffer
 retco = PXRecBufClose(recHandle);

//Close the table
 retco = PXTblClose(tblHandle);

// Close the Paradox Engine
PXExit();

return 0;
}
```

This program uses the `"Employee"` table that was created earlier. Open the table in the manner of the previous example. Before you can store data in the table, you must create it locally and put it into a record buffer. A record buffer is an area of memory that is laid out with the

same data types as one row of the table. Declare it in a similar fashion to the table handle.

```
RECORDHANDLE recHandle;
```

No memory is allocated, however, until you open it.

```
//Create a record buffer for this table
retco = PXRecBufOpen(tblHandle, &recHandle);
```

In order to put the data into the table, put the data in the record buffer. You do this for character data by making calls to the PXPutAlpha() function.

```
//Put data into the record buffer
retco = PXPutAlpha(recHandle, 1, "Einstein");
```

The first argument is the record handle that you obtained by opening the buffer. The second argument is the field number in which to put the character data. Thirdly, you placed the data in a quoted string. The process is repeated for the first name.

```
retco = PXPutAlpha(recHandle, 2, "Albert");
retco = PXPutDoub(recHandle, 3, 91);
```

A similar call to PXPutDoub() is used to put the age into the third field of the record buffer. You're now ready to append the data in the buffer to the table.

```
//Append the new row to the table
retco = PXRecAppend(tblHandle, recHandle);
```

PXRecAppend() takes only the tblHandle and the recHandle as its arguments. It moves the data from the record into the write buffer where it will be written to disk by the Engine. In order to keep that record from being lonely, append two more.

Being naturally suspicious, read the data from the database just to prove to ourselves that it is really there. Listing 15.4 does just that.

Listing 15.4. Retrieving Data from an Existing Table

```
//Listing 15.4 The Paradox Engine
//Retrieving Data from an existing table

#include <pxengine.h>
#include <iostream.h>
```

continues

Using the Paradox Engine   **645**

Listing 15.4. Continued

```
main()
{
        int retco;  // Return code for the functions

        // Initialize the Engine for use under Windows
        retco = PXWinInit("Setup", PXSHARED);

        //Create the handles for the table and the record
        TABLEHANDLE tblHandle;
        RECORDHANDLE recHandle;
        FIELDHANDLE fldHandle;

        //Open the table
        retco = PXTblOpen("Employee", &tblHandle, 0, 0);

        //Create a record buffer for this table
        retco = PXRecBufOpen(tblHandle, &recHandle);

        //Get a handle for this field
        retco = PXFldHandle(tblHandle,"Last_Name", &fldHandle);

        //Print the field handle
        cout << "The value of the field handle is " << fldHandle << "\n\n";

        //Get a record from the table into the record buffer
        retco = PXRecGet(tblHandle, recHandle);

        //Get data from the record buffer
        char local_last_name[31];
        retco = PXGetAlpha(recHandle, fldHandle, 31, local_last_name);

        //Check the return code
        cout << "The return code for the PXGetAlpha() was " << retco << "\n\n";

        //Print the value of local_last_name
        cout << "The value of the variable local_last_name is " << local_last_name;
        cout << "\n\n";

        //Close the record buffer
         retco = PXRecBufClose(recHandle);

        //Close the table
         retco = PXTblClose(tblHandle);

        // Close the Paradox Engine
        PXExit();

        return 0;
}
```

In order for data to be really useful in a C++ program, it has to be stored in a local variable. In order to do this, declare a field handle.

```
FIELDHANDLE fldHandle;
```

In order to keep the application from becoming dependent on the order of fields in the row, make a call to `PXFldHandle()`. This routine takes, as its arguments, the table handle and the name of the field that you want to retrieve, reading the schema data in the table to determine the position of the desired field in the table at this time. It stores the value in the field handle. You could use your knowledge of the fact that the `"Last Name"` field is the first one in the record and hard-code the handle. If later, however, the order of the fields changed, the hard-coded value would be wrong, and the program would fail. It is recommended to always inquire as is done here.

```
//Get a handle for this field
retco = PXFldHandle(tblHandle,"Last_Name", &fldHandle);
```

Next, you move a record from the table into the record buffer. `PXRecGet()` does this.

```
//Get a record from the table into the record buffer
retco = PXRecGet(tblHandle, recHandle);
```

`PXRecGet()` always gets the current record. Immediately after opening the table, this is the first record.

Next, get the data out of the record.

```
//Get data from the record buffer
char local_last_name[31];
retco = PXGetAlpha(recHandle, fldHandle, 31, local_last_name);
```

At this point, the desired data is in the buffer. You move it into a local variable called `local_last_name` via the `PXGetAlpha()` function. In addition to the record and field handles, you pass a buffer size and the name of the variable to receive the data.

```
//Print the value of local_last_name
cout << "The value of the variable local_last_name is " <<
local_last_name;
    cout << "\n\n";
```

Finally, print out the value of the local variable to prove that the program succeeded.

```
The value of the variable local_last_name is Einstein
```

The final example deals with searching for a record based on the value of certain fields. Listing 15.5 illustrates how this is done.

Listing 15.5. Searching for Data in an Existing Table

```
//Listing 15.5 The Paradox Engine
//Searching for data in an existing table

#include <pxengine.h>
#include <iostream.h>


main()
{
    int retco;  // Return code for the functions

    // Initialize the Engine for use under Windows
    retco = PXWinInit("Setup", PXSHARED);

    //Create the handles for the table and the record
    TABLEHANDLE tblHandle;
    RECORDHANDLE recHandle;
    FIELDHANDLE fldHandle;

    //Open the table
    retco = PXTblOpen("Employee", &tblHandle, 0, 0);

    //Create a record buffer for this table
    retco = PXRecBufOpen(tblHandle, &recHandle);

    //Get a handle for this field
    retco = PXFldHandle(tblHandle, "Last_Name", &fldHandle);

    //Put a value in RecBuf
    retco = PXPutAlpha( recHandle, fldHandle, "Hun" );

    //Search for a record that matches the value in the RecBuf
    retco = PXSrchFld(tblHandle, recHandle, fldHandle, SEARCHFIRST);

    //Get the current record from the table and into the RecBuf
    retco = PXRecGet(tblHandle, recHandle);

    //Get a handle for the Age field
    retco = PXFldHandle(tblHandle, "Age", &fldHandle);

    //Get the age data from the record buffer and into a local variable
```

```
double local_age;
retco = PXGetDoub(recHandle, fldHandle, &local_age);

//Print the value of local_last_name
cout << "The value of the variable local_age is " << local_age;
cout << "\n\n";

//Close the record Buffer
 retco = PXRecBufClose(recHandle);

//Close the table
 retco = PXTblClose(tblHandle);

// Close the Paradox Engine
PXExit();

return 0;
}
```

In order to do a random search, allocate a record buffer and record handle as in the earlier examples. Call PXPutAlpha() to put a character string into the record buffer.

```
//Put a value in RecBuf
retco = PXPutAlpha( recHandle, fldHandle, "Hun" );
```

The fldHandle variable tells in which field the function should place the quoted string "Hun". Now call PXSearchFld(), which looks through the table to find the first row that matched "Hun" in the "Last Name" column.

```
//Search for a record that matches the value in the RecBuf
retco = PXSrchFld(tblHandle, recHandle, fldHandle, SEARCHFIRST);
```

When PXSearchFld() finds the correct row, it makes it the current row. This doesn't retrieve the row though. In order to do this, you must do a PXRecGet() as earlier in the listing.

```
//Get the current record from the table and into the RecBuf
retco = PXRecGet(tblHandle, recHandle);
```

Now that the row is in a record buffer, you need to get the data into a local variable. To do this, follow the same procedure as in the previous example.

```
//Get a handle for the Age field
retco = PXFldHandle(tblHandle,"Age", &fldHandle);

//Get the age data from the record buffer and into a local variable
```

```
double local_age;
retco = PXGetDoub(recHandle, fldHandle, &local_age);

//Print the value of local_last_name
cout << "The value of the variable local_age is " << local_age;
cout << "\n\n";
```

Finally, print it out to verify the correct execution.

```
The value of the variable local_age is 55
```

The Paradox Engine is a good product for a procedural program that can limit itself to one kind of database management system's tables. In the next section, see how to access the same tables using an object-oriented interface.

Using the Paradox Database Framework

The Paradox Database Framework, an object-oriented interface built as a class library, is distributed as part of the Database Engine product. It allows access to data stored in the Paradox format via a small number of objects and their public member functions. The Engine is built around four main objects:

➤ Engine objects

➤ Database objects

➤ Cursor objects

➤ Record objects

The engine object represents all of the code that makes up the purchased database management system. An instance of the engine object must be declared before any other work is done.

The database object represents all of the data in the database, as well as the functions that create and manage tables. The database object is normally declared immediately after the engine object. It too must be present in order to do work using the Database Framework.

The cursor object allows access to the tables. There is no such thing as a table object in the Database Framework. When you want access to a table, declare a cursor and open it on a certain table. This provides not only a handle to the table but also a navigation utility. Implicit in the creation of the cursor is the concept of a current row and a generic record. The current row is the one that would be retrieved if you request one at this moment. You can move the current row to the first, last, next, or previous row in the table via function calls.

The last type of object is the record object. A record is a buffer that holds data that has been read from the table. The way that the cursor object implements the generic record is by declaring an instance of the record class. The generic record is created automatically when the cursor is created. It serves as a buffer of exactly the right size to hold one record of the table pointed to by the cursor. In order to update the table, you update the generic record and write it to the file that contains the table data. In order to get data from the database into the program, read it into the generic record using one of several functions. You may then extract the fields that you want into local variables.

These classes, like most classes in C++, can provide valuable tools to the developer. Using the Database Framework to write database applications is much easier than using procedural function calls. This is true, however, only after you have learned how the Database Framework operates. The Framework is much harder to learn than the procedural interface. One reason for this is that the computer industry has not yet devised a way to describe a class library without confusing the reader. Most manuals that describe class libraries are a mishmash of abstract discussions and overly symbolic function prototypes.

The Database Framework is easier to understand in a set of simple examples. The following listings will help you grasp the role of the four main objects and the dozen or so member functions that are required to perform the basic storage and retrieval operations of most programs. The following listings were written with this in mind.

Before you can run the listings, you must install and build the Framework. Installing the Framework is a chore of its own. In order to use the product, it must be compiled and linked by using a MAKE file. Unfortunately for users of Borland 4.0, the documentation that accompanies version 3.0 of the Paradox Engine and Database Framework assumes that you are running a Borland 3.x compiler. Therefore, it is necessary to receive a new MAKE file from Borland before proceeding. The easiest way to do this is via the Borland Forum on CompuServe. If you go into the Borland Development Tools Forum and then into the "Pdox Eng. C/C++/Pas" library, you will find a selection called "DBF Makefile for BC4.0." Download and unzip this makefile. You can then move it into your database engine directory and run it, building the appropriate class library functions.

Next, set up your environment as shown in figure 15.2.

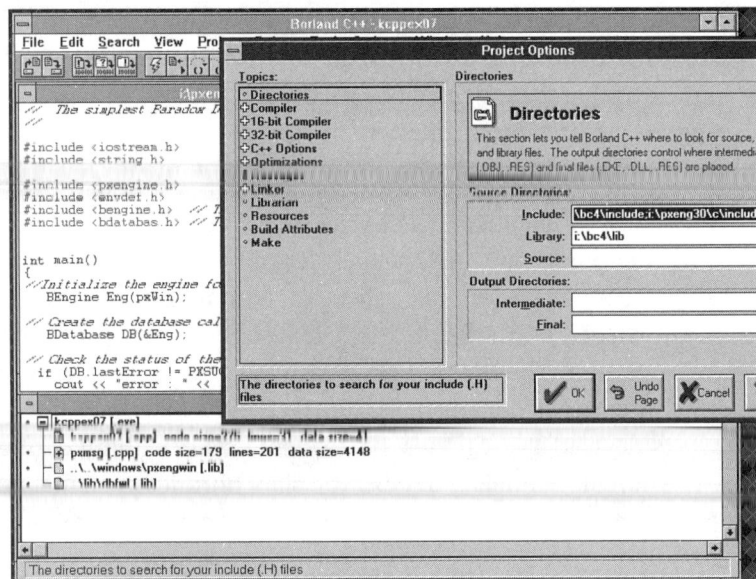

Fig. 15.2. Setting the IDE to run a Database Framework application.

The following is the simplest Database Framework example. If you enter and run it using the setup in figure 15.2, you can verify that your environment is correctly configured.

Listing 15.6. The Simplest Paradox Database Framework Example

```
//  Listing 15.6 Paradox Engine
//  The simplest Paradox Database Framework example
//

#include <iostream.h>
#include <string.h>

#include <pxengine.h>
#include <envdef.h>
#include <bengine.h>  // The BEngine class.
#include <bdatabas.h> // The BDatabase class.


int main()
{
//Initialize the Engine for use under Windows
     BEngine Eng(pxWin);

// Create the database called DB
     BDatabase DB(&Eng);

// Check the status of the creation
  if (DB.lastError != PXSUCCESS)
      cout << "error : " <<
          Eng.getErrorMessage(DB.lastError) << endl;
  else
      cout << "database" << "' created successfully";

  DB.close();
  Eng.close();
  return 0;


}
```

Before you can run a Database Framework application you must "start your Engine." You do this by declaring an object called `Eng`.

```
//Initialize the Engine for use under Windows
     BEngine Eng(pxWin);
```

`Eng` is an object of type `BEngine`, and you want to construct it to run under Windows, so use the argument `pxWin`. At this point, you're ready to declare a database object.

```
// Create the database object called DB
     BDatabase DB(&Eng);
```

The concept of a database is a loose one in a system that stores all of its entities as separate files as Paradox does. Neverthclcss, the database concept gives you a way of grouping tables together and reporting errors. After you open the database, check the value of the database's last error to see if it succeeded.

```
// Check the status of the creation
  if (DB.lastError != PXSUCCESS)
      cout << "error : " <<
         Eng.getErrorMessage(DB.lastError) << endl;
  else
      cout << "database" << "' created successfully";



  DB.close();
  Eng.close();
  return 0;
```

Having succeeded at setting up the environment and opening the database once, you're ready to create a table in it, as shown in Listing 15.7.

Listing 15.7. Creating a Table with the Paradox Engine Database Framework

```
//   Listing 15.7 Paradox Engine Database Framework
//   Creating a table
//

#include <iostream.h>
#include <string.h>

#include <pxengine.h>
#include <envdef.h>
#include <bengine.h>   // The BEngine class.
#include <bdbase.h>   // The BDatabase class.

int main()
{

//Initialize the Engine for use under Windows
    BEngine Eng(pxWin);

// Create the database called DB
    BDatabase DB(&Eng);

// Array of field descriptors for the table, needed for the
// createTable member function in the BDatabase class.
    FieldDesc fields[3];

// Create an array that contains the field info
    fields[0].fldNum = 1;
```

```
        strcpy( fields[0].fldName, "Last_Name");
        fields[0].fldType = fldChar;   // Create an alphanumeric field.
        fields[0].fldLen = 30;          // Specify the length of the field.

        fields[1].fldNum = 2;
        strcpy(fields[1].fldName, "First_Name");
        fields[1].fldType = fldChar;
        fields[1].fldLen = 30;

        fields[2].fldNum - 3;
        strcpy(fields[2].fldName, "Age");
        fields[2].fldType = fldShort;  // Create a short field.

// Create the table

    DB.createTable("Employee", 3, fields);

    // Check to see if there was an error.

    if (DB.lastError != PXSUCCESS)
        cout << "Error in Employee table create : " <<
            Eng.getErrorMessage(DB.lastError) << endl;
    else
        cout << "table " << "Employee" << " created successfully" << endl;


    DB.close();
    Eng.close();
    return 0;
}
```

In this example, you start off by creating the engine object and the
database object. Then in preparation for the table creation, you need
to declare an array of field description objects.

```
// Array of field descriptors for the table, needed for the
// createTable member function in the BDatabase class.
    FieldDesc fields[3];

// Create an array that contains the field info
    fields[0].fldNum = 1;
    strcpy( fields[0].fldName, "Last_Name");
    fields[0].fldType = fldChar;  // Create an alphanumeric field.
    fields[0].fldLen = 30;          // Specify the length of the field.

    fields[1].fldNum - 2;
    strcpy(fields[1].fldName, "First_Name");
    fields[1].fldType = fldChar;
    fields[1].fldLen = 30;

    fields[2].fldNum = 3;
```

```
        strcpy(fields[2].fldName, "Age");
        fields[2].fldType = fldShort;  // Create a short field.
```

The `FieldDesc` objects contain data about each field in the table. Having described the fields, you call a member function of the database object to create the table.

```
// Create the table
   DB.createTable("Employee", 3, fields);
```

Once again, you can check the database's last error to see if the operation succeeded.

```
// Check to see if there was an error.

if (DB.lastError != PXSUCCESS)
    cout << "Error in Employee table create : " <<
        Eng.getErrorMessage(DB.lastError) << endl;
else
    cout << "table " << "Employee" << " created successfully" << endl;
```

If it did, you want to print a message to that effect.

Having a properly created table, you can't wait to fill it with data, the purpose of Listing 15.8.

Listing 15.8. Putting Data into a Table

```
//  Listing 15.8 Paradox Engine Database Framework
//  Put Data into a table
//

#include <iostream.h>
#include <string.h>

#include <pxengine.h>
#include <envdef.h>
#include <bengine.h>   // The BEngine class.
#include <bdatabas.h>  // The BDatabase class.
#include <bcursor.h>   // Header file for the BCursor class.
#include <brecord.h>   // Header file for the BRecord class.

int main()
{

//Initialize the Engine for use under Windows
    BEngine Eng(pxWin);

// Open the Database
    BDatabase DB(&Eng);
```

```
// Create a BCursor object.  Use it to open the table

    BCursor *tblCursor = new BCursor(&DB, "Employee", 0, FALSE);

    if (tblCursor->lastError != PXSUCCESS)
      cout << "error '" << Eng.getErrorMessage(tblCursor->lastError) <<
              "' in opening BCursor 'tblCursor.'" << endl;
    else
      cout << "cursor created successfully" << endl;

// Go to the first record in the table.
tblCursor->gotoBegin();
tblCursor->gotoNext();

// Fill the genericRec member of the BCursor class
BRecord *genRec = tblCursor->genericRec;

Retcode pxErr;  //Return Code

pxErr = genRec->putField(1, "Walsh");
if (pxErr != PXSUCCESS)
    cout << "error in putField to field 1" << endl;

pxErr = genRec->putField(2, "Patrick");
if (pxErr != PXSUCCESS)
    cout << "error in putField to field 2" << endl;

pxErr = genRec->putField(3, 37);
if (pxErr != PXSUCCESS)
    cout << "error in putField to field 3" << endl;

// Insert the record.

tblCursor->insertRec(genRec);

// Check for errors.

if (tblCursor->lastError)
{
    cout << "Error inserting record: ";
    cout << Eng.getErrorMessage(tblCursor->lastError) << endl;
}
else
    cout << "Record inserted successfully" << endl;

// Close the cursor, which closes the table as well.

tblCursor >close();
DB.close();
Eng.close();
return 0;

return 0;
}
```

In order to put this data in the table, you need to declare an object of type `BCursor`. Remember that you didn't declare table objects in your system. You declare a cursor and pass to it the name of the table that you want it to navigate. The cursor is used instead of a table object.

```
// Create a BCursor object.  Use it to open the table
   BCursor *tblCursor = new BCursor(&DB, "Employee", 0, FALSE);
```

Once the cursor is active, position it at the start of the file. This you do with a couple of member functions in the class `BCursor`.

```
// Go to the first record in the table.
  tblCursor->gotoBegin();
  tblCursor->gotoNext();
```

In order to make your code easier to read, define a pointer to the generic record.

```
// Fill the genericRec member of the BCursor class
BRecord *genRec = tblCursor->genericRec;
```

At this point, you can put a few data values into a field in the generic record.

```
pxErr = genRec->putField(1, "Walsh");
if (pxErr != PXSUCCESS)
    cout << "error in putField to field 1" << endl;

pxErr = genRec->putField(2, "Patrick");
if (pxErr != PXSUCCESS)
    cout << "error in putField to field 2" << endl;

pxErr = genRec->putField(3, 37);
if (pxErr != PXSUCCESS)
    cout << "error in putField to field 3" << endl;
```

With the generic buffer filled, move the data out into the table via another member function of the `BCursor` class called `insertRec`.

```
// Insert the record.
  tblCursor->insertRec(genRec);
```

Having done this, you'll certainly want to verify that it worked. See Listing 15.9 for printing verification.

Listing 15.9. Getting Data from a Table

```cpp
//  Listing 15.9 Paradox Engine Database Framework
//  Get data from a table
//

#include <iostream.h>
#include <string.h>

#include <pxengine.h>
#include <envdef.h>
#include <bengine.h>   // The BEngine class.
#include <bdatabas.h>  // The BDatabase class.
#include <bcursor.h>   // Header file for the BCursor class.
#include <brecord.h>   // Header file for the BRecord class.

int main()
{
  Retcode pxErr;   //Return Code
  BOOL fnull;

//Initialize the Engine for use under Windows
     BEngine Eng(pxWin);

// Open the Database
     BDatabase DB(&Eng);

// Create a BCursor object.  Use it to open the table
     BCursor *tblCursor = new BCursor(&DB, "Employee", 0, FALSE);
     if (tblCursor->lastError != PXSUCCESS)
        cout << "error '" << Eng.getErrorMessage(tblCursor->lastError) <<
                "' in opening BCursor 'tblCursor.'" << endl;
     else
        cout << "cursor created successfully" << endl;

  // Go to the first record in the table.
  tblCursor->gotoBegin();
  tblCursor->gotoNext();

  // Declare a pointer to the generic record
  BRecord *genRec = tblCursor->genericRec;

// Retrieve the record into the generic record

     pxErr = tblCursor->getRecord();
     char local_last_name[31];

// Copy the last name field from the generic record into a local variable
     pxErr = genRec->getField(1, local_last_name, 31, fnull );
  if (pxErr != PXSUCCESS)
      cout << "error in getField to field 1" << endl;

// Print out the result
```

continues

Listing 15.9. Continued

```
        cout << "The value of the last name field is " << local_last_name;


    // Check for errors.

    if (tblCursor->lastError)
    {
        cout << "Error: ";
        cout << Eng.getErrorMessage(tblCursor->lastError) << endl;
    }


    // Close the cursor, which closes the table as well.

    tblCursor->close();
    DB.close();
    Eng.close();
    return 0;
}
```

In order to get this data, you need to call another BCursor function called
getRecord().

```
    // Retrieve the record into the generic record
        pxErr = tblCursor->getRecord();
```

This function copies data from the current cursor position into the
generic record. Now that the data is present in the generic record you
need to transfer it to a local variable for processing. Declare a variable
that is large enough to hold 30 characters plus a null.

```
        char local_last_name[31];
```

At this point, you can call getField to copy the value of the first field in
the buffer into the variable called local_last_name. You also specify that
the variable's length is 31.

```
    // Copy the last name field from the generic record into a local variable
        pxErr = genRec->getField(1, local_last_name, 31, fnull );
    if (pxErr != PXSUCCESS)
        cout << "error in getField to field 1" << endl;
```

Having done this, print it out to convince yourself that it worked.

```
// Print out the result
    cout << " The value of the last name field is " << local_last_name;
```

This is the output of the statement:

```
The value of the last name field is Walsh
```

The purpose of these exercises was to help you understand the fundamentals of using a class library to store and retrieve data. The Database Framework can be a powerful tool to use in developing applications once the learning curve has been traversed. This type of class library usage appears to be the way that we are going to be developing applications in the future. If this is going to become reality, vendors need to find better ways of documenting these libraries.

Using the ODBC

As stated earlier, computer users don't want database management systems, databases, or even computers. They just want the information needed to do their work. Users are frustrated by computer people who look them in the eye and tell them that something is impossible. The users know when they have made a reasonable request for information. If we tell them that we can't provide certain valuable information to them because it runs on a Unisys Mainframe or UNIX workstation, we frustrate them and lower their opinion of computer people in general—and us in particular.

On the other hand, we know that the barriers to data access are real. It is not easy to combine data that is in different formats, on different kinds of computers, running under different operating systems, and in different cities. This distributed heterogeneous database access is required, however, if we are going to run our governments and our businesses by computer. Consider the case of an international corporation. These companies are often composed of other smaller companies that can reside anywhere on the globe. They all have computer systems that have evolved as the companies grew. They are not likely to be running

the same operating system or the same brand of computers as their sister companies. If the president of this corporation calls you into his office and asks you to provide data on worldwide sales for the past three months, you had better not respond by babbling about wide-area networks and data-format problems. He knows that this request is reasonable and so do you.

In past decades, we solved the heterogeneous database problem with custom interfaces, redundant data entry, and import/export programs. They got us by (we are still in business, aren't we?), but at a higher price than is now required. Everyone who participated in building these kinds of systems felt that there had to be a better way to accomplish this. Figure 15.3 illustrates this complicated approach.

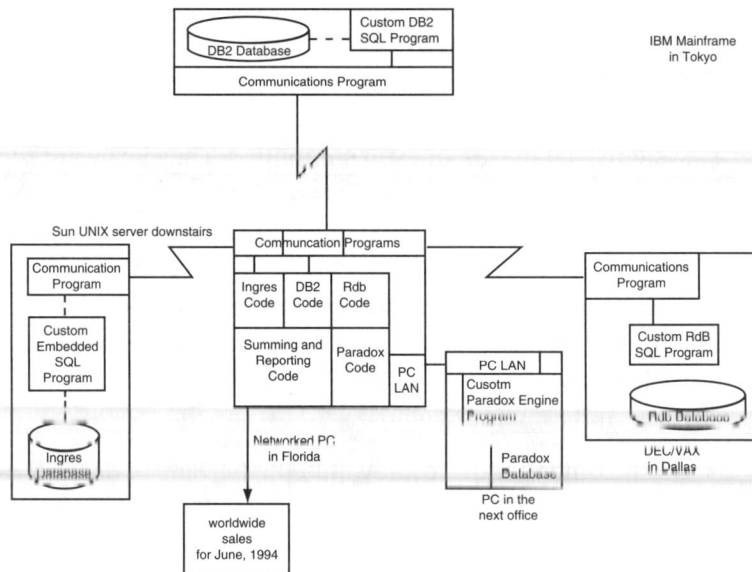

Fig. 15.3. Gathering data from multiple computers via a network.

Figure 15.3 illustrates the state of affairs in the early 90s. We normally write a program that knows the details of all of the different database management systems in the network. We have grown accustomed to having to allocate buffers, set up environment variables and control

blocks, and allocate handles for the different tables and records. These activities are different for each of the different DBMS systems. We then get to pass requests to each system in turn. The SQL-based databases allow us to shorten the learning curve a little, but there is still quite a bit of learning associated with each system. The non-SQL databases must be communicated with in a custom way.

We are starting to see more generalized solutions to the problems associated with accessing far-flung data. Instead of completely proprietary database access languages, SQL has become a widely supported standard. Even with its many dialects, it is a big step forward. Network technology has evolved to the point where almost every hardware platform can communicate via the network.

Given this, it should be possible to run an application on one computer that passes an SQL request to another computer running a different operating system. A program on the second computer can then open a database, pass the SQL request to it, and receive the results. It then can pass the results back to the first computer over the same network. The program on the first computer can then request similar data from other computers in the same manner. When all of the data is collected, the original requester program sums the figures and produces a report with the worldwide sales.

How could this situation be improved? We could send out a memo which standardizes the entire company on the same DBMS. Since all DBMSs don't all run on all brands of computers, we can standardize all of the hardware too. We must consider all of the other applications that run on each platform. We will simply rewrite them. After this is completed, we will pray that our standard computer vendor continues to be a good supplier of modern products. If he doesn't, we can repeat the whole process as we standardize on a different vendor. We can pay for this whole venture by simply raising the prices that we charge to our customers. We can then hope that our competitors don't tell them that we are charging too much. Sounds like a bad idea, doesn't it? As absurd as this plan is, there are thousands upon thousands of companies who are putting some form of it in place as you read this book. Fortunately for them, there are "narrow-minded" people in their respective organizations who foil their every attempt.

Because we can't afford to homogenize our computing equipment and software, we have to get it to interoperate if we are going to use the data. If we write custom interfaces between platforms, we will have to write a lot of them. But suppose that we asked every DBMS vendor to write an interface between its specific product and a neutral, generic application programming interface (API). Other programs could make calls to their DBMS using this API. If these interfaces could translate each of these API calls into their own embedded SQL or proprietary interface, programs could access the data without custom coding. This is the goal of the Microsoft Open Database Connection (ODBC).

The ODBC is not just a published standard, it is also a software development kit that allows programmers to develop these drivers. It is called the ODBC SDK. Figure 15.4 illustrates how the ODBC works.

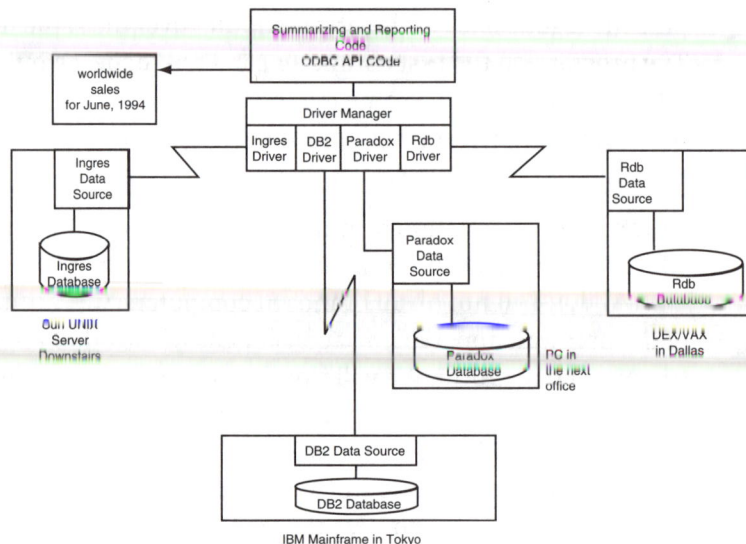

Fig. 15.4. Gathering data over the network using ODBC.

Using the ODBC we can wait until runtime to specify which DBMS and database to access. The same application can access one DBMS today and a different one tomorrow, without recompiling. The ODBC specification requires that these interfaces handle all network communications and make the database seem local to applications. We call these interfaces "ODBC database drivers." We need one of them for each brand of DBMS that we want to access.

We also need a vendor-independent way of specifying the name of each database, and the DBMS that manages it. We combine this information into a table and name each of the entries. ODBC calls these "data sources." We will need a program to connect our programs to the data sources upon request. This eliminates the need to hard-code instructions for a specific DBMS in our programs. This program is called the "driver manager." We need a way to create and name the data sources. This is called the "Administration Utility." Finally, we need an API specification so that all of the vendors can know what kind of commands that they must accept if they want to comply with the ODBC specification.

At first blush this figure is only marginally less complex than figure 15.3. There are important differences, though. Figure 15.3 is populated with boxes that represented custom code development. In figure 15.4, the only piece of code that has to be written is the main program that summarizes and prints the report. Everything else is purchased. This makes the cost of these pieces a tiny fraction of the cost required to do custom-code development. It also removes the risk of failure on these modules since they already exist. The custom code that must be written needs to contain only one API, the ODBC API. This means that the learning curve also has been reduced. Notice that all of the network considerations are solved between the driver and the data source. The API programmer can treat all of the data sources as if they were local. It is the responsibility of the driver writers and DBMS vendors to negotiate this area.

The only difficulty is in the setup and execution of the ODBC utilities. You step through that in the following pages. The first thing that you

do in this new scenario is to obtain the ODBC software development kit (ODBC_SDK) from Microsoft. This used to be available upon request, but it is now provided on the Microsoft Developer Network Level II CDs. This can be obtained by calling Microsoft Sales.

Next we need to obtain drivers for each of our target platforms. Some of the drivers like Paradox and Microsoft SQL server are available from Microsoft or one of its distributors. Other drivers like INGRES are sold by the vendor of the DBMS.

Now we are ready to install the different pieces that make up the ODBC. We are going to go into some detail about the installation and setup of these different pieces because most readers have no experience installing this kind of software. It is sometimes difficult to picture what should be done without detailed instructions.

First, install the ODBC drivers that you have purchased. Follow the directions included with them. This is normally trivial. The exact procedure varies depending upon the vendor of the driver. Some DBMSs have a number of drivers available for them by different vendors. There will be a difference in their performance since a driver is a non-trivial piece of code.

Install the ODBC software development kit next. This program was written to aid the programmer in developing both drivers and applications. It contains samples and tools, as well as a few drivers to help you get started. Put the first disk of the ODBC SDK in your A: drive, and click File Run. In the Run dialog box, type

    a:\setup

A screen that looks like figure 15.5 should appear.

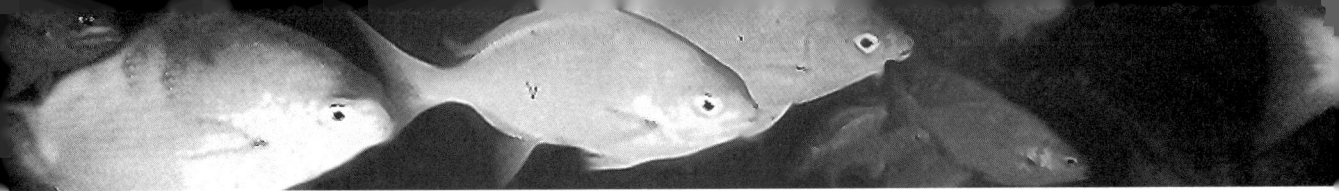

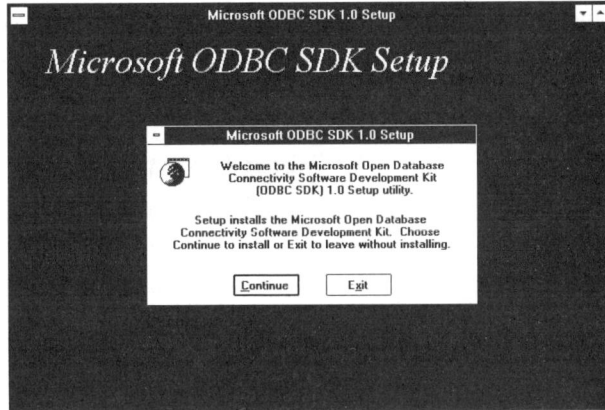

Fig. 15.5. The setup screen for the ODBC SDK.

If you click the Continue button, the Install Drivers dialog box appears (see fig. 15.6).

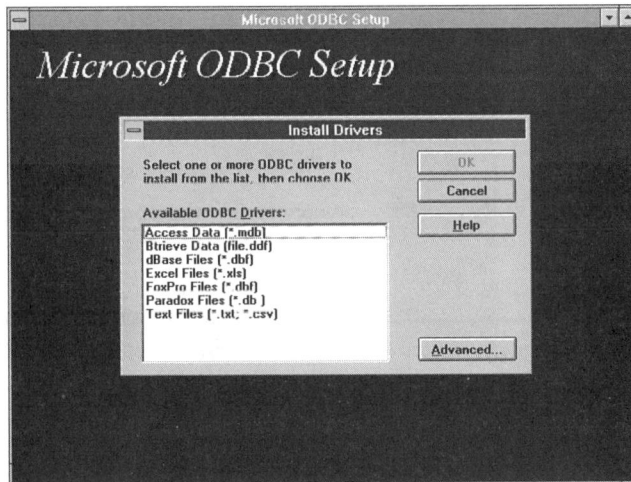

Fig. 15.6. The Install Drivers dialog box for the ODBC SDK.

The actual drivers that you see depend on what is installed on your system. Choose the drivers that you anticipate using, and click the OK button. Don't worry about setting up services yet. We'll configure them later. You now see the program group created and the icons added (see fig. 15.7).

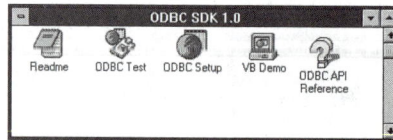

Fig. 15.7. The ODBC SDK 1.0 program group.

Now you want to add the ODBC Administrator program and icon. This allows you to add new services at any time. To do this, double-click the ODBC Setup icon. The Microsoft ODBC 1.0 Setup dialog box appears (see fig. 15.8).

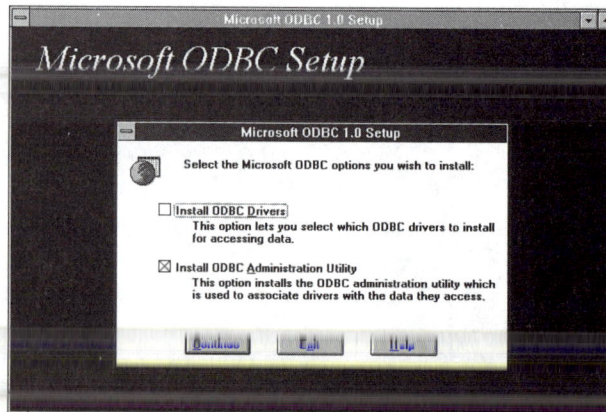

Fig. 15.8. Install the ODBC SDK administration utility.

Mark Install ODBC Administration Utility and click the Continue button. At this point, a new program group and icon appear on-screen. Drag the lone icon into the ODBC SDK program group, and delete the empty group. You can leave it, but it doesn't help to have many program groups. You should now have a program group like that in figure 15.9. You are now ready to add data sources.

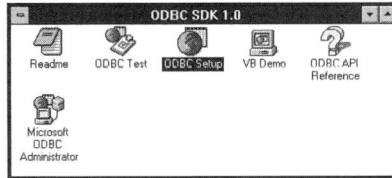

Fig. 15.9. The ODBC SDK program group with the administration icon added.

Double-click the Microsoft ODBC Administrator icon. The Microsoft ODBC Administrator dialog box appears (see fig. 15.10). Click the driver that you want to use in the Installed Driver box.

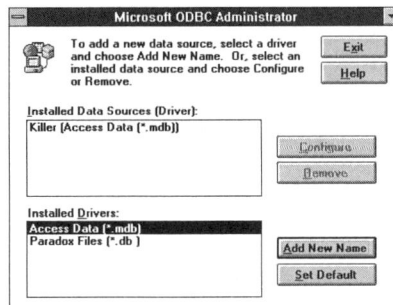

Fig. 15.10. Choosing a driver for a data source.

You can have many different drivers and many different data sources defined on your system. Having chosen the driver, click the Add New Name button. This leads you to the dialog appropriate to the driver you chose. Figure 15.11 is the ODBC Microsoft Access Setup dialog box. The others are similar.

The first thing you do is name the data source. This doesn't have to be the name of the database on the host system. It can be a completely different name. In figure 15.11, I called this new data source Killer because of this book. Since we want a totally clean database upon which to create examples, choose Create Database. This choice allows us to specify the name and path of the database on the host system. Click

OK. This creates the empty database. Notice that the data source is associated with a database and not a specific table. This is very important because we have ambitions of creating tables via the ODBC API and not just accessing data.

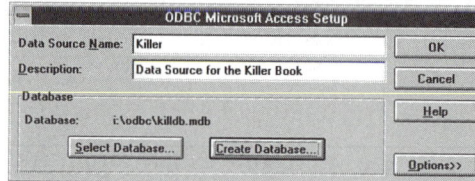

Fig. 15.11. Setting up an ODBC data source.

Now that we have a data source called Killer, we are ready to dive into the world of ODBC API programming. Before you get intimidated, be assured that there is nothing spooky or mystical about this or any other API. If you have ever called functions that were written by others, you will be comfortable with this API in a short time. Normally, the most difficult administrative task in any C++ program is resolving the external function references. This is especially true when the references are in a Dynamic Link Library written by someone else. Figure 15.12 shows where to resolve all required references.

In the Source Directories section of the project options window, you see a text box called Include. This is the path for the compiler to resolve references to the header (.h) files. It is imperative that you add the C:\ODBCSDK\INCLUDE (the one in the example is on the I: drive) to other directories already listed there. Several of the headers used in the following examples reside here.

Secondly, you must add the import library associated with the odbc.dll to the project. This library is called odbc.lib. You do this in the window at the bottom of the page. The import library is a special file that contains no code. It contains a map showing the exact location of the routines contained in a .dll file. All of the ODBC routines can be found in odbc.dll, so their location map will be in odbc.lib.

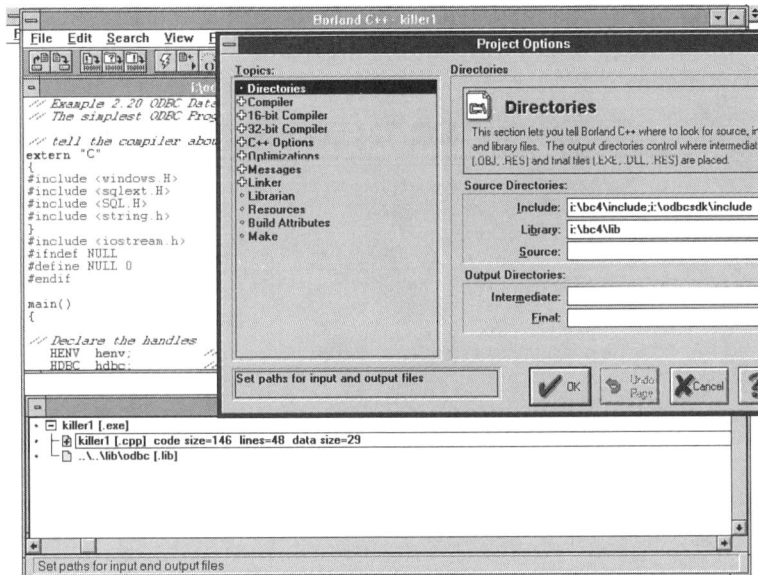

Fig. 15.12. The IDE for a successful program.

Last but not least, we need an actual program with some API calls in it. In figure 15.12, this file is called killer.cpp and is referred to in the project window near the bottom of the IDE window. The source code is also displayed in a window to the left of the figure.

So having read a dozen or so pages without seeing any code, you should be ready for some action. Let's compose a very simple ODBC program and build it up in subsequent examples. The goal is to demonstrate the basic flow and not to perform an acrobatic coding demonstration. All examples are kept simple so as not to detract from this goal. Listing 15.10 is a demonstration of how to perform the necessary housekeeping and connection to a data source. You'll connect to the Killer data source which is an Access database called killdb.mdb. It is stored locally on the computer. If we moved it to Tahiti, though, this program wouldn't even have to be recompiled. We would simply have to go into the ODBC administration utility and modify the data source description. Likewise, if we moved the application to an INGRES database on a DEC Alpha computer, we would still be able to use this same program unchanged, and without recompilation. The only work would be on the driver and ODBC Manager side.

Listing 15.10. The Simplest ODBC Program

```
// Listing 15.10 ODBC Database Drivers
// The simplest ODBC Program

// tell the compiler about the "C" routines that will be called
extern "C"
{
#include <windows.H>
#include <sqlext.H>
#include <SQL.H>
#include <string.h>
}
#include <iostream.h>
#ifndef NULL
#define NULL 0
#endif

main()
{

// Declare the handles
    HENV henv;            // Environment handle
    HDBC hdbc;            // Database connection handle
    HSTMT hstmt;          // Statement handle

// Declare the local Variables
    RETCODE rc;

// Allocate the control block for the environment
    rc = SQLAllocEnv(&henv);

// Allocate the control block for the database
    rc = SQLAllocConnect(henv, &hdbc);

// Connect to the "Killer" data source
    rc = SQLConnect(hdbc, "Killer", SQL_NTS, "", SQL_NTS, "", SQL_NTS);

// Verify that the connection was made by the return code = 0
    cout << "the Return Code is " << rc;

//  Free the handles and terminate
    rc = SQLFreeStmt(hstmt, SQL_DROP);
    rc = SQLDisconnect(hdbc);
    rc = SQLFreeConnect(hdbc);
    rc = SQLFreeEnv(henv);

        return(0);
}
```

Near the top of the program, there are several header files surrounded by French braces.

```
extern "C"
{
#include <windows.H>
#include <sqlext.H>
#include <SQL.H>
#include <string.h>
}
```

The extern "C" statement tells the compiler that the function prototypes that appear in between these braces have been compiled with a C compiler. C++ then looks for C style function names instead of the mangled C++ variety. Without this statement, your program would not be able to resolve some of the function calls.

Following these calls we see a few C++ include files and a definition of the constant NULL. Then we see a number of declarations:

```
// Declare the handles
     HENV  henv;          // Environment handle
     HDBC  hdbc;          // Database connection handle
     HSTMT hstmt;         // Statement handle
```

These probably look a little strange to you. The data types HENV, HDBC, and HSTMT are all typedefs that give a little more meaningful name to the type. The purpose of these is as follows:

HENV. The environment handle points to the memory storage for global information. It is a control block that contains information about all of the connection handles. An application only needs one of these no matter how many data source connections that it plans to make.

HDBC. The connection handle points to the memory storage for a connection. A connection is a "completed circuit" between your program, the driver manager, the driver, and a data source. Your application must declare a connection handle before it can query a data source.

HSTMT. The statement handle points to the memory storage for information about one SQL statement. Your application must declare a statement handle and then get the value for it before processing a statement with it. Each statement handle is associated with exactly one connection handle. It uses the connection to move the request to the data source and back.

Thus, each program has a HENV. This HENV can support multiple HDBCs. Each HDBC can support multiple HSTMTs. Figure 15.13 illustrates this.

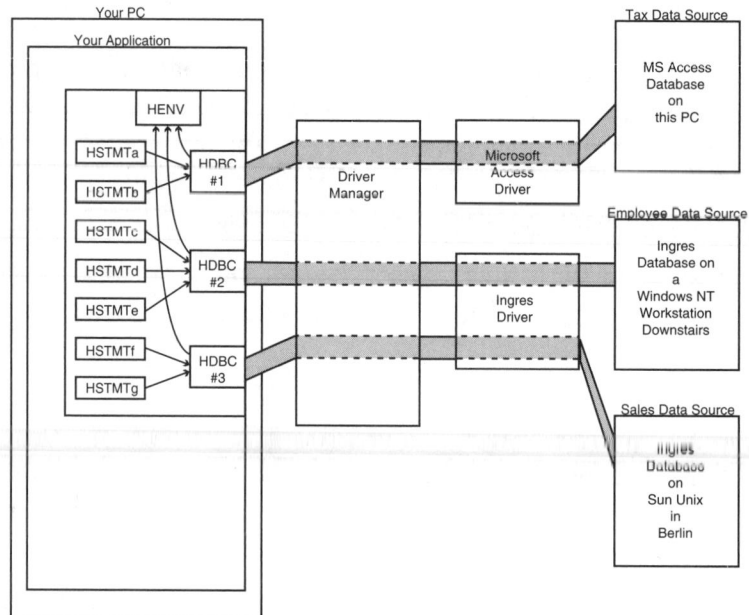

Fig. 15.13. Using the ODBC control block structure to process requests.

Thus, the connection can be viewed as a pipe that you push requests through. The driver manager finds the appropriate driver and data source to receive the requests. This complete connection looks like a set of local function calls to the application program.

```
// Declare the local Variables
    RETCODE rc;
```

Next you declare a return code that will be used to accept the value returned by an ODBC function upon completion.

You are ready to set up the "circuit" between your program and the data it needs to acquire. Do this by calling SQLAllocEnv().

```
// Allocate the control block for the environment
    rc = SQLAllocEnv(&henv);
```

Pass to it the address of the handle of type HENV called henv. (There is
nothing magic about the name henv. It could have been called xyz just
as easily.) The data source manager passes this address to the driver
which allocates the memory and fills the handle with the location. On
subsequent calls, the driver uses this handle to locate the application's
control block. This is needed since the driver is a DLL and can support
a number of applications simultaneously.

Having created the HENV, you are ready to allocate a connection. Call
SQLAllocConnect() to do this. The parameters that you give it are the location of the HENV, and the address of the local connection handle hdbc.

```
// Allocate the control block for the database
    rc = SQLAllocConnect(henv, &hdbc);
```

The driver manager can tell by the value of henv which application is to
create a connection control block. It allocates the memory, associates
it with the henv, and fills in the location into the variable hdbc. On subsequent function calls, you'll use the hdbc variable to tell the driver manager which connection you're talking about. You could easily have two
or three data sources open at the same time. This would require a
separate HDBC control block for each connection.

Now that you have the needed control blocks, you're ready to "complete the circuit." In order to do this, you associate a source name,
"Killer", with an HDBC, hdbc. If the data source is password protected, you
pass this information also.

```
// Connect to the "Killer" data source
    rc = SQLConnect(hdbc, "Killer", SQL_NTS, "", SQL_NTS, "", SQL_NTS);
```

SQLConnect() loads the appropriate driver into memory and establishes a
connection to the data source. For this to succeed, several components
must be ready. The data source must be able to use the network as
planned. Any problems with this will cause a failure. It must find a
serviceable driver to place in memory. It must also be able to locate the
database that you associated with the data source back during the
ODBC administrator setup. If all of this takes place, rc=0 appears. If rc=0

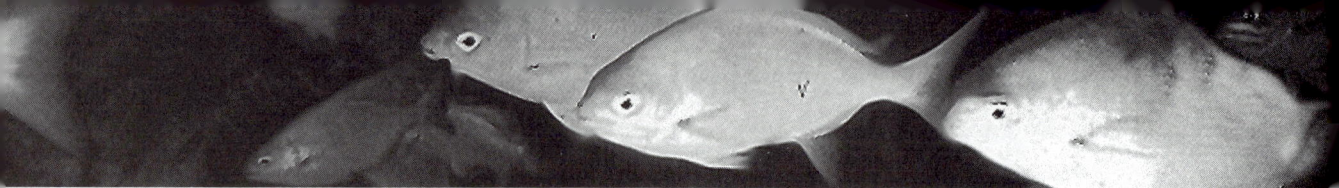

doesn't appear, don't despair. For this connection to work seamlessly requires that a lot of code be written by a lot of companies. If you have trouble, a call to the vendor of the driver might be the best place to start. At this point our sample program prints the return code to the screen.

```
// Verify that the connection was made by the return code = 0
      cout << "the Return Code is " << rc;
```

You can view it just as well using the debugger, but the first time that you get an `rc=0` is a moment to savor. It deserves a `cout` statement.

At this point, you have only one small rope across a pretty big gorge, but you do have one. With Listing 15.11, you'll build on it. Before we go, you should be a good citizen and return all of your handles to their rightful owners. Sure, some of you cowboys will just end the program and let other software clean up for you, but this is not wise. Your chances of developing a memory leak are greatly reduced if you practice good housekeeping.

```
//   Free the handles and terminate
    rc = SQLFreeStmt(hstmt, SQL_DROP);
    rc = SQLDisconnect(hdbc);
    rc = SQLFreeConnect(hdbc);
    rc = SQLFreeEnv(henv);

    return(0);
}
```

Now that you have successfully connected to a heterogeneous, possibly distributed database, you are ready to create a table. Often ODBC is thought of as a front-end API to existing data. This is true, but ODBC is also a highly functional specification, allowing you to create and delete tables and store and delete data.

Listing 15.11 is an example of how to create a simple table with one field.

Listing 15.11. The Simplest ODBC Create Table Program

```
// Listing 15.11 ODBC Database Drivers
// The simplest ODBC Create Table Program

// tell the compiler about the "C" routines that will be called extern "C"
```

```
{
#include <windows.H>
#include <sqlext.H>
#include <SQL.H>
#include <string.h>
}
#include <iostream.h>
#ifndef NULL
#define NULL 0
#endif


main()
{
// Declare the handles
    HENV  henv;          // Environment handle
    HDBC  hdbc;          // Database handle
    HSTMT hstmt;         // Statement handle

// Declare the local Variables

    RETCODE rc;

    rc = SQLAllocEnv(&henv);
    rc = SQLAllocConnect(henv, &hdbc);
    rc = SQLConnect(hdbc, "KILLER", SQL_NTS, "", SQL_NTS, "", SQL_NTS);
    if (rc != SQL_SUCCESS && rc!= SQL_SUCCESS_WITH_INFO)
        return(-99);
    rc =SQLAllocStmt(hdbc, &hstmt);


//Build up the SQL statement into a text string variable
    UCHAR create[] = "CREATE TABLE CHILDREN (NAME TEXT(30))";


// Execute the SQL statement.
    rc = SQLExecDirect(hstmt, create, SQL_NTS);

//Print out the return code
    cout << "The return code from the table create was " << rc;

// Commit the transaction
    rc = SQLTransact(henv, hdbc, SQL_COMMIT);

// Release all of the handle
    rc = SQLFreeStmt(hstmt, SQL_DROP);
    rc = SQLDisconnect(hdbc);
    rc = SQLFreeConnect(hdbc);
    rc = SQLFreeEnv(henv);

    return(0);
}
```

In order to create a table, you need to allocate a number of handles like you did in the last example. Follow the exact same procedure until you've successfully connected to the service. At that point, call `SQLAllocStmt()` to create a statement control block for your program.

```
rc =SQLAllocStmt(hdbc, &hstmt);
```

The application passes the address of an HSTMT to `SQLAllocStmt()`. The driver is responsible for allocating memory and putting in its location into &hstmt. Your program uses this value to communicate to the driver the identity of a statement to execute. The information stored in the HSTMT control block is very specific to the driver. It normally includes network information, error message translation tables, and other messages specific to the data source. The driver normally allocates space for a cursor name and status information.

You now have every control block allocated and connected with every other one. You can finally use it to get some work done. In order to do this, create a string that contains a valid SQL statement.

```
//Build up the SQL statement into a text string variable
    UCHAR create[] = "CREATE TABLE CHILDREN (NAME TEXT(30))";
```

This SQL statement says that it wants the data source to create a table named CHILDREN and to add one column to it. The column will be named NAME and will be of type TEXT with a length of 30. The data type issue can be confusing since all of the commercial DBMSs were developed with their own set of data types. The SQL-based systems generally support the SQL data types. Since you will be sending the array create[] down to the driver to parse and execute, it must satisfy the driver. At times only trial and error yields a correct result.

At this point, you are ready to send the SQL statement to the data source.

```
// Execute the SQL statement.
    rc = SQLExecDirect(hstmt, create, SQL_NTS);
```

The `SQLExecDirect()` function sends the SQL string to the driver. The driver then translates the request into the language of the data source (if necessary). It then passes the request to the data source. The data source completes the request and passes back an integer return code

to indicate whether it completed successfully. Capture the result and print it out.

```
//Print out the return code
    cout << "The return code from the table create was " << rc;
```

It is the responsibility of the application to decide when to commit the state of the database. A transaction is a logical entity, not a physical one. If you try to buy theater tickets online you would enter your credit card number. The ticketing program would then try to get the seats requested. If someone else purchases the seats a split second before you do, the credit card transaction must be "rolled-back" while you search for other seats. If you don't like any others, you certainly don't want to pay anything. If, however, you succeed in obtaining the seats, the transaction "commits" and becomes part of the database. To do this using the ODBC, use the SQLTransact() command. Pass the identifier for the HENV, so that the driver knows which application to commit. You must also pass a parameter for the HDBC to tell the driver which connection needs to be committed. The third parameter is the SQL_COMMIT which commits the transaction. You could have sent an SQL_ROLLBACK instead if you wanted to wipe out the application.

```
// Commit the transaction
    rc = SQLTransact(henv, hdbc, SQL_COMMIT);
```

Following this, simply close all of the connections and release all of the handles. If all of our return codes indicate success, you should be able to go into the DBMS for the data source that you chose and see a table named CHILDREN that has a column of width 30 called NAME.

Now that you have a table, you need to put some data into it. Do this by using the ODBC API in a similar fashion. Listing 15.12 does this.

Listing 15.12. A Simple ODBC Insert Program

```
// Listing 15.12 ODBC Database Drivers
// A simple ODBC insert program

// tell the compiler about the "C" routines that will be called extern "C"
{
#include <windows.H>
```

continues

Listing 15.12. Continued

```
#include <sqlext.H>
#include <SQL.H>
#include <string.h>
}
#include <iostream.h>
#ifndef NULL
#define NULL 0
#endif


main()
{

// Declare the handles
    HENV  henv;          // Environment handle
    HDBC  hdbc;          // Database handle
    HSTMT hstmt;         // Statement handle

// Declare the local Variables
    UCHAR   first_name[31];
    RETCODE rc;

// Allocate the control block for the environment
    rc = SQLAllocEnv(&henv);

// Allocate the control block for the database
    rc = SQLAllocConnect(henv, &hdbc);

// Connect to the "Killer" data source
    rc = SQLConnect(hdbc, "Killer", SQL_NTS, "", SQL_NTS, "", SQL_NTS);

// Verify that the connection was made by the return code = 0
    cout << "the Return Code is " << rc  << "\n\n";

// Allocate the control block for a statement
    rc =SQLAllocStmt(hdbc, &hstmt);


// Create a statement and put it into a character array
    UCHAR insert[] = "INSERT INTO CHILDREN VALUES (?)";


// Begin the process of building the SQL statement
    SQLPrepare(hstmt, insert, SQL_NTS);
    cout << "The return code from the prepare was " << rc  << "\n\n";

// Load the value of the parameter into the statement
    SQLSetParam(hstmt,1,SQL_C_CHAR, SQL_VARCHAR,
UDWORD)sizeof(first_name),0,first_name, NULL);
    strcpy(first_name, "Chris");
```

```
// Execute the statement that we have built
    rc = SQLExecute(hstmt);

// Check the return code to verify success (rc=0)
    cout << "The return code from the insert was " << rc  << "\n\n";


// Commit the transaction
    rc = SQLTransact(henv, hdbc, SQL_COMMIT);

//  Free the handles and terminate
    rc = SQLFreeStmt(hstmt, SQL_DROP);
    rc = SQLDisconnect(hdbc);
    rc = SQLFreeConnect(hdbc);
    rc = SQLFreeEnv(henv);

    return(0);
}
```

We will need a local variable so that we can load it with the data that we want to store in the database. This will be called first_name. Its length is 31 because it is a null terminated string.

```
// Declare the local Variables
    UCHAR    first_name[31];
    RETCODE rc;
```

Everything else about the declaration of variables and connection to the data source is identical to the previous example. The SQL statement is stored in a character string like the create example was (refer to Listing 15.11).

```
// Create a statement and put it into a character array
    UCHAR insert[] = "INSERT INTO CHILDREN VALUES (?)";
```

There is one important difference though. This string has a ? stored in it. This indicates the existence of a parameter. If there were two of them then you would look for two parameters. At this point, the program doesn't know anything about the parameter.

The next few statements fill in the missing information. SQLPrepare() prepares a statement for execution and sends it to the driver. The driver stores it in the HSTMT until it receives further instruction. The statement may be executed multiple times without "preparing" it again.

```
// Begin the process of building the SQL statement
    SQLPrepare(hstmt, insert, SQL_NTS);
        cout << "The return code from the prepare was " << rc  << "\n\n";
```

With the SQL statement in the HSTMT, you can now fill in the parameter. SQLSetParam() allows the application to describe the parameter in detail. You associate it with the insert via the variable hstmt. The parameter following hstmt has a value of "1." This signifies that this parameter definition corresponds to the first ? in the SQL statement.

```
// Load the value of the parameter into the statement
    SQLSetParam(hstmt,1,SQL_C_CHAR, SQL_VARCHAR,
(UDWORD)sizeof(first_name),0,first_name, NULL);
```

The SQL_C_CHAR indicates that the data type of the data being passed is character. The SQL_VARCHAR indicates that the ODBC data type is variable character. The 0 is the precision (mainly used for numeric types). Next follows the name of the C++ variable containing the value to be stored. The NULL indicates that first_name will be null-terminated.

After much ado, you are ready to put data into the first_name variable and pipe it over to the database. To do this, use the old reliable strcpy() library function.

```
        strcpy(first_name, "Chris");
```

Having now completed all preliminary activities, you're ready to store the data in the database. Do this via the SQLExecute() function.

```
// Execute the statement that we have built
    rc = SQLExecute(hstmt);
```

This function executes the statement identified by hstmt, expecting that all of the preparation has been done. SQLExecute() also issues an implicit "Begin transaction."

The return code confirms that you have succeeded.

```
// Check the return code to verify success (rc=0)
        cout << "The return code from the insert was " << rc  << "\n\n";
```

At this point, you have a pending transaction. By issuing a Commit statement, you can store it in the database permanently.

```
// Commit the transaction
        rc = SQLTransact(henv, hdbc, SQL_COMMIT);
```

After the usual disconnections and releasings, you are ready to inspect the data. If you go into the database via a user-interface, you should see a row with the word Chris stored in it.

You are now ready for the final leg of you ODBC journey. You need to retrieve data from the database using C++. Listing 15.13 does exactly that.

Listing 15.13. A Simple ODBC Select Program

```
// Listing 15.13 ODBC Database Drivers
// A simple ODBC select program

// tell the compiler about the "C" routines that will be called extern "C"
{
#include <windows.H>
#include <sqlext.H>
#include <SQL.H>
#include <string.h>
}
#include <iostream.h>
#ifndef NULL
#define NULL 0
#endif


main()
{
    HENV   henv;        // Environment handle
    HDBC   hdbc;        // Database handle
    HSTMT  hstmt;       // Statement handle

// Declare the local Variables
    UCHAR   kid_name[31];
    SDWORD  kidnamelen;
    RETCODE rc;


// Allocate the control block for the environment
    rc = SQLAllocEnv(&henv);

// Allocate the control block for the database
    rc = SQLAllocConnect(henv, &hdbc);

// Connect to the "Killer" data source
    rc = SQLConnect(hdbc, "Killer", SQL_NTS, "", SQL_NTS, "", SQL_NTS);

// Verify that the connection was made by the return code = 0
    cout << "the Return Code is " << rc  << "\n\n";
```

continues

Listing 15.13. Continued

```
// Allocate the control block for a statement
    rc =SQLAllocStmt(hdbc, &hstmt);

// Create a statement and put it into a character array
    UCHAR select[] = "SELECT NAME FROM CHILDREN";

// Execute the SQL statement
    rc = SQLExecDirect(hstmt, select, SQL_NTS);
    cout << "The return code from the SELECT was " << rc << "\n\n";

// bind the local variable kid_name to the SQL variable NAME
// This will cause the ODBC driver to load NAME's value into kid_name
    rc = SQLBindCol(hstmt, 1, SQL_C_CHAR, kid_name, (SDWORD)sizeof(kid_name),
➡&kidnamelen);
    cout << "The return code from the last name bind was " << rc << "\n\n";

//Fetch the data from the driver into local memory
    rc = SQLFetch(hstmt);
    cout << "The return code from the fetch was " << rc << "\n\n";

//Prove that it worked
    cout << "The value of the kid_name is " << kid_name << "\n\n";

//Commit the transactions
    rc = SQLTransact(henv, hdbc, SQL_COMMIT);


// Free all of the handles
    rc = SQLFreeStmt(hstmt, SQL_DROP);
    rc = SQLDisconnect(hdbc);
    rc = SQLFreeConnect(hdbc);
    rc = SQLFreeEnv(henv);

    return(0);
}
```

This listing resembles the other listings also. It is virtually identical to the previous one until you get to the SQL statement.

```
// Create a statement and put it into a character array
    UCHAR select[] = "SELECT NAME FROM CHILDREN";
```

Being a select statement, it returns data to you. Go ahead and execute the statement first, and then figure out how to get the data into a local variable. This seems backwards but it works.

```
// Execute the SQL statement
    rc = SQLExecDirect(hstmt, select, SQL_NTS);
    cout << "The return code from the SELECT was " << rc << "\n\n";
```

The `SQLExecDirect()` statement causes the driver to send the SQL statement to the data source. When the data source sends back the results, the driver stores them in its own memory.

You don't, at this point, have access to the data in your program. You need to tell the driver where in your application to put the results. You do this with a call to `SQLBindCol()`.

```
// bind the local variable kid_name to the SQL variable NAME
// This will cause the ODBC driver to load NAME's value into kid_name
    rc = SQLBindCol(hstmt, 1, SQL_C_CHAR, kid_name,
(SDWORD)sizeof(kid_name),&kidnamelen);
        ➥cout << "The return code from the last name bind was " << rc << "\n\n";
```

Please note that the `SQLBindCol()` call is on two lines for publishing reasons. Be sure to put it on the same line when you key in this example.

This `SQLBindCol()` tells the driver that the first variable in the `hstmt` is to be bound to a local variable named `kid_name` that is of `type` character. The `sizeof(kid_name)` tells the driver the maximum length of the data to be returned. After the `SQLFetch()`, the driver puts the actual length retrieved in the variable `kidnamelen`.

At this point, you need to tell the driver to get the data from the driver and put it in our local variables. Do this with `SQLFetch()`.

```
//Fetch the data from the driver into local memory
    rc = SQLFetch(hstmt);
    cout << "The return code from the fetch was " << rc << "\n\n";
```

`SQLFetch()` fetches a row of data from the result set in the driver. The driver looks to see which columns have been bound to local variables. It then moves the designated data into these variables.

At this point, you are ready to print the result.

```
//Prove that it worked
    cout << "The value of the kid_name is " << kid_name << "\n\n";
```

It is an interesting exercise to experiment with putting data into the database via the standard user interface and then retrieving it via ODBC. You should do this enough times to convince yourself that it works.

Microsoft provides a very useful utility called ODBC Test that is distributed with the ODBC SDK. It is accessible through an icon in the ODBC SDK group. It provides an interactive interface to the API. This sounds like a contradiction in terms, but it is true. Figure 15.14 shows what it looks like.

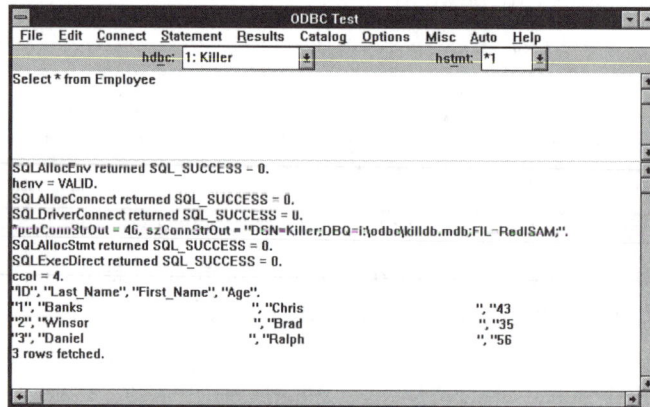

Fig. 15.14. The ODBC SDK's test program.

ODBC Test is very helpful in prototyping an application's SQL Calls. The menu bar contains categories of SQL calls. For example, all of the connection relate calls are under the Connect menu. Just under the menu bar are two combo boxes that are labeled hdbc and hstmt. These allow you to choose which connection and statement you want to work on if you have allocated several. The upper half of the window is for entering SQL statements. This corresponds to the character arrays that we used in the earlier programs to enter SQL text. The bottom half of the screen contains the data, return codes, and error messages that result from the commands that you run from the menu bar.

To obtain the window in figure 15.14, start up ODBC Test by double-clicking the icon. The window appears. Choose Connect and SQLAllocEnv. You get a message back in the lower half of the screen that looks like the one in the figure. Next, continue in this order and choose Connect and SQLAllocConnect, Connect and SQLDriverConnect, Statement and SQLAllocStmt. Next, enter the SQL that you want to run. Finally, Statement

and `SQLExecDirect` runs your SQL and puts the results on the lower half of the screen. Experiment with this and you may find it easier to debug your SQL using this interface before coding it into your program.

The ODBC is good way to write applications where you are not sure which DBMS will be used in production. It is also valuable for applications that need to pull data from a number of different sources. The fact that it hides the network complications from your applications makes it easier to cross platforms for access to data. This section has covered the basics of getting an ODBC application up and running.

The use of a commercial database application can provide a cost-effective way of storing and retrieving data in your programs. For programmers who make heavy use of the fourth-generation language front-ends provided with most DBMS packages, C++ programs can increase the integration of your applications with external devices and mail-based systems.

From Here...

This chapter has taught you the essentials of database access from within your C++ applications, but this information is only the beginning. Here are some other areas you might look into:

> There are several good books on the Paradox Database Engine, including *Paradox Developer's Guide* and *Paradox Power Programming* by Que, *What Every Paradox 4.5 for Windows Programmer Should Know* by Sams Publishing, and *Inside Paradox 4.5 for Windows* by New Riders Publishing.

> Sometimes Turbo Debugger just isn't enough for your power programs. That's where the independent debuggers on the market come in. For more information on these, see Chapter 8, "Third-Party Debugging Tools."

> For more power in your C++ programs, you can write routines directly in assembly language. For information on including assembler routines in your C++ programs, see Chapter 14, "Bare Metal Programming."

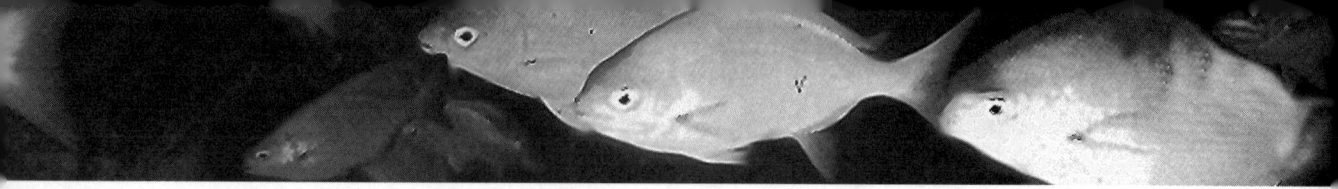

➤ At other times, you may want to include routines you (or others) have already written in another programming language. For more information on this, see Chapter 13, "Mixed Language Programming."

➤ You also might be interested in including VBX custom controls in your database programs. For more information on these custom controls, see Chapters 21-25, which discuss the communication, tab, gauge, alarm, and spin controls, which are included on the enclosed disk.

Runtime Type Identification

by Chris Corry

The Borland C++ 4.0 compiler provides full support for a recently adopted ANSI/ISO extension called runtime type identification (RTTI). Although RTTI is not widely used today, you will find that RTTI provides a variety of important services that can help make your code more robust and portable.

In this chapter we'll investigate the different components of RTTI, and then walk though the steps required to integrate RTTI features into your programs. As you will see, the most important aspects of RTTI involve the `dynamic_cast` and `typeid` operators, and the `Type_info` class.

What Can RTTI Do for Me?

Programs can use the features of RTTI for a number of different things. Specifically, using RTTI enables your programs to:

➤ Determine the precise type of an object instance, even if the pointer used to perform the query is of a type higher up in the class hierarchy.

➤ Safely cast a pointer up and down an inheritance hierarchy. This includes casting pointers to virtual base classes down to derived classes (a practice that has been illegal until now).

➤ Utilize object instance types in expressions.

At first glance, these features appear to be fairly uninspired; but, as you will see throughout the rest of this chapter, these simple and somewhat pedestrian language features, when correctly applied, can actually provide some important capabilities.

Portability and Compatibility Concerns

Runtime-type identification was accepted into the working draft of the X3J16 ANSI standard committee in March of 1993. To date, however, the number of compiler vendors supporting the RTTI extensions (particularly on Intel-based operating systems) has been small, and Borland is a standout in this regard.

The implications, at least for the time being, are pretty obvious. If you use RTTI features in your code, your programs may not compile on other operating systems or with other compilers. If portability is not of immediate concern to you, use these RTTI features with reckless abandon. After all, they are destined to be part of the final ANSI C++ specification anyway, and ultimately all C++ compiler vendors will have to support these features.

On the other hand, if portability is important to you, skip the rest of this chapter. Although RTTI provides useful services, its features are not absolutely essential. You are better off waiting until all of your compilers support these capabilities.

Knowing Your Fruit

C++ enables programmers to abstract complex problems and break them into descriptions about the relationships between different object classes. This arrangement is all well and good, but the C++ object model breaks down somewhat when compared to the tangible inter-action that takes place between humans and objects on a day-to-day basis.

When you pick up an apple, you are relatively certain that you are holding an apple, not a kiwi fruit. All human beings have a range of experiences that tell them what an apple looks and feels like, and there is little chance that they will confuse it with another fruit.

Things can get a little trickier when dealing with C++ objects. Generally C++ programs have a pretty good idea of what object types they are dealing with at any given time. If your code has done its job right, an initialized pointer to an `Apple` object actually points to an `Apple` object, and that object behaves as expected.

Assuming, however, that your `Apple` class is derived from a generic `Fruit` class, and a program is given a pointer to a `Fruit`, there is no easy way to determine if the pointer refers to an `Apple`, a `KiwiFruit`, or any other class derived from `Fruit`. To make matters worse, if `Fruit` is derived from a top-level `GenericObject` class (as is typical in many SmallTalk-like class libraries) and your code is given a pointer to a `GenericObject`, your code may be working with an `Apple`, a `KiwiFruit`, or a `Boeing747`. If you have ever tried to peel a 747, you know how undesirable such confusion can be.

Casting a `GenericObject` pointer to an `Apple` and then calling its `Peel()` method can have disastrous results if the pointer is actually pointing to a `Boeing747` object. This realization makes it clear that C++ classes could

benefit greatly from some mechanism that enables programs to identify the precise type of an object pointer. Unfortunately, knowing your fruit in C++ is not as straightforward as it is in real life.

There isA() Way

To a large degree, C++ programmers solved the problem of type identification back when the language was in its infancy. The most common solution is to declare a virtual function—sometimes named `isA()`—at the highest level of the class hierarchy that is responsible for returning the unique name of the class. As the class hierarchy evolves, each derived class is responsible for overloading `isA()`, so that it returns the name of the new class. This structure makes possible code similar to the following:

```
void MakeSalad(const GenericObject* pObject)
{
    switch(pObject->isA()) {

        case OBJ_APPLE:
        case OBJ_ORANGE:
        case OBJ_BANANA:
            pObject->Peel();
            break;

        case OBJ_LETTUCE:
            pObject->Chop();
            break;

        case OBJ_BOEING747:
            cout << "Very funny, wiseguy!\n";
            break;

    }
}
```

In this example, the `isA()` function is declared so that it returns a numerical value that can be checked in a `switch` statement. Each object class presumably has been assigned a unique class ID which corresponds to the appropriate `OBJ_*` constant or enumeration member.

Unfortunately, implementing `isA()` in this fashion can result in a number of problems. Returning a number implies that all classes are able to coordinate in such a manner so that there is no duplication of class

IDs. Using numerical constants for class ID constants is easily accomplished for smaller class libraries, where the developers have all of the library source code in their possession. In some cases, however, the programmers may not have access to all of the library sources. This lack of access, at the very least, precludes using an enumeration to store the class ID constants.

Using constant numerical values can be quite useful, but it can quickly become a maintenance and managerial nightmare. For that reason, programmers often prototype their `isA()` methods to return a character string representation of the class name. The code to check whether or not a `GenericObject` is an `Apple`, for example, is similar to the following:

```
// Is this pointer referencing an Apple?
if (!strcmp(pObject->isA(), "Apple")) {
    // Yes it is, do Apple stuff
}
else {
    // Nope, do otherwise
}
```

This code is a bit messier than it would be if `isA()` simply returned an integer, but it provides a little more flexibility. With `isA()` coded this way, the chance that two different class designers will inadvertently implement overlapping `isA()` return values is considerably less likely.

Problems with the `isA()` approach remain, however. What happens if a programmer forgets (or ignores) the requirement to provide an `isA()` method? An object instance of the new class will return the `isA()` value of its parent class, which is simply wrong. Even if the programmer implements the method, the possibility (albeit a slim one) remains that the programmer may return a value from `isA()` that is identical to a value already in use (talk about a hard bug to track down). Finally, what if you want to integrate one of your class libraries with someone else's, but they have called their type identification method `IsA()`? Or `GetTypeID()`? Or even worse, what if the other developer doesn't even use and implement a type identification method?

Ultimately the problem boils down to an issue of standard practices. *If* you always follow the rules, and *if* you're fortunate enough to avoid overlapping type IDs, and *if* you don't need to interface with third-party class libraries, then the `isA()` approach will probably work well for you. On the other hand, all of these "ifs" should probably make you feel a little nervous. Writing code on a foundation of "ifs" is just asking for trouble.

Enter the dynamic_cast

The runtime type identification system of the Borland compiler offers a better way to provide `isA`-type services (among other things) without worrying about politically charged development mandates, or relying on error-prone programmatic devices built into your class libraries.

dynamic_cast Basics

One way that RTTI provides improved `isA`-type services is through a new casting operator: the `dynamic_cast`. Essentially, a dynamic cast is designed to *safely* cast a pointer up and down an inheritance hierarchy. The operative word here is safely because a normal C++ cast usually enables you to cast pointers up and down inheritance trees as well.

A dynamic cast pointer uses the following syntax:

```
dynamic_cast<T*>(ptr)
```

`T`, as used here, refers to a valid C++ type, and `ptr` is the source pointer. The cast returns a pointer of type `T` if and only if `ptr` points to an object of type `T`. If `ptr` doesn't point to a `T`, the dynamic cast fails and returns `NULL`.

Keep these important caveats in mind when using the `dynamic_cast`; however, the `dynamic_cast` (and other RTTI constructs) are designed to be used only with polymorphic classes. A *polymorphic class* is a class that contains at least one virtual (or pure-virtual) function. Further, classes that inherit virtual functions from a superclass also qualify to use RTTI.

Note: Because integral types are not polymorphic, the compiler does not support (in effect, generate and store type information) RTTI operations and manipulations on these types. Only user-defined classes and structures are eligible for RTTI use. Notice that this rule does *not* exclude the ANSI string class or the `xalloc` exception class.

Using the dynamic_cast: Salad Anyone?

Listing 16.1 shows the `dynamic_cast` in action (your use of this language feature is certain to be more profound than this frivolous example). The program simulates the preparation of salad ingredients and, obviously, is not designed to be particularly useful. Take special note of the `dynamic_cast` used in the `ProcessIngredient()` function.

Listing 16.1. SALAD.CPP—Using the dynamic_cast to Discern an Object Instance Type

```
#include <iostream.h>

// Some miscellaneous definitions we will need
typedef enum {
    WHOLE,
    SHREDDED,
    GRATED,
    SLICED,
    CHOPPED
} FoodState;

// The top of the inheritance tree
class Food {
public:
    // Constructor
    Food(const FoodState = WHOLE);

    // Virtual methods — all food
    // must be able to set and return
    // its state. These functions also
    // ensure that Food is polymorphic
    // and can use RTTI.
    virtual FoodState GetState() const;
    virtual void SetState(const FoodState);
```

continues

Listing 16.1. Continued

```
private:
    // Private member data
    FoodState theFoodState;
};

// Food constructor
Food::Food(const FoodState newState)
{
    SetState(newState);
}

// Getter and setter virtual methods
FoodState Food::GetState() const
{
    return theFoodState;
}

void Food::SetState(const FoodState newState)
{
    theFoodState = newState;
}

// Overload << so we can display our state
ostream& operator<<(ostream& outstrm,
                    Food& theFood)
{
    switch(theFood.GetState()) {
        case WHOLE:     outstrm << "Whole";
                        break;
        case SHREDDED:  outstrm << "Shredded";
                        break;
        case GRATED:    outstrm << "Grated";
                        break;
        case SLICED:    outstrm << "Sliced";
                        break;
        case CHOPPED:   outstrm << "Chopped";
                        break;
        default:
                        outstrm << "Bad state!";
    }
    return outstrm;
}


// Individual food types
class Apple : public Food {
public:
    void Chop() { SetState(CHOPPED); }
    void Slice() { SetState(SLICED); }
};

class Cheese : public Food {
public:
```

```cpp
        void Grate() { SetState(GRATED); }
};

class Lettuce : public Food {
public:
        void Shred() { SetState(SHREDDED); }
};


// Process a single ingredient
void ProcessIngredient(Food* pIngredient)
{
        // Is this an Apple?
        Apple* pApple =
              dynamic_cast<Apple*>(pIngredient);
        if (pApple) {
              pApple->Chop();
              return;
        }
        // Is this a head of Lettuce?
        Lettuce* pLettuce =
              dynamic_cast<Lettuce*>(pIngredient);
        if (pLettuce) {
              pLettuce->Shred();
              return;
        }
        // Is this a piece of Cheese?
        Cheese* pCheese =
              dynamic_cast<Cheese*>(pIngredient);
        if (pCheese)
              pCheese->Grate();

        return;
}

// Let's prepare a salad
void main()
{
        Lettuce      MyLettuce;
        Apple        MyApple;
        Cheese       MyCheese;

        // Process the vegetables
        ProcessIngredient(&MyLettuce);
        ProcessIngredient(&MyApple);
        ProcessIngredient(&MyCheese);

        // Show what we've done
        cout << "The lettuce is ";
        cout << MyLettuce << "\n";
        cout << "The apple is ";
        cout << MyApple << "\n";
        cout << "The cheese is ";
        cout << MyCheese << "\n";
}
```

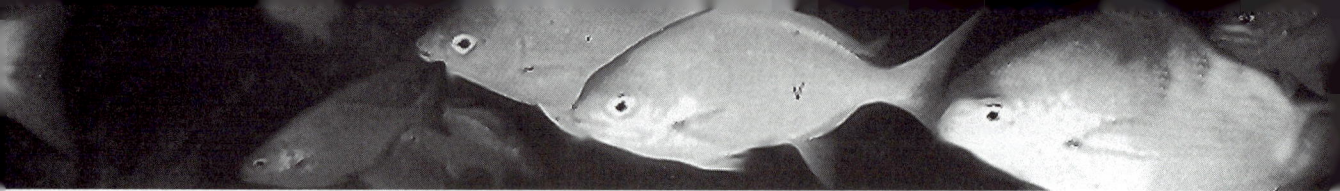

This program defines a high-level Food class that only knows that food always exists in a certain state. The Food class enables you to set, query, and display the food's state, but it is generally uninteresting. In fact, within a class hierarchy of any appreciable complexity and size, the Food class would probably have a number of pure virtual methods returning more detailed information about the specific type of food—an arrangement not included in our intention here.

Several specific food classes are derived from Food. Each of these classes makes methods available that correspond to different ways that these foods might be processed. No rocket science going on here!

The most interesting part of the program is the ProcessIngredient() function. The function accepts a pointer to an object of type Food; after all, you don't want to limit your programs to just using fruits and vegetables. Maybe you like cheese on your salads, and maybe someone else likes croutons or peanut butter (there's no accounting for taste!). The point is that ProcessIngredient() should not limit what types of objects can be processed, except to insist that they be foods and not wide-bodied aircraft (or something equally unappetizing).

ProcessIngredient() takes this Food pointer and proceeds to attempt casts to various object pointer types. Since a dynamic_cast is safe and will return NULL if the requested cast is inappropriate, each of these casting attempts will fail until the correct cast succeeds. Once a dynamic_cast has succeeded, the function knows what type of Food the pointer refers to and the object can be processed accordingly.

dynamic_cast versus Virtual Functions

Just because you can use the dynamic_cast to determine the identity of an ambiguous pointer doesn't mean you should. The dynamic_cast can be tremendously useful for ensuring that your pointers are referencing what you think they are and for providing a generalized mechanism for determining object types. On the other hand, dynamic_cast isn't intended to be used as a crutch when a design can accomplish the same thing through virtual functions.

Take the previous salad-making example. Assume that the classes depicted in that example are more concerned with making salad than they are with providing a generic Food class hierarchy. In this case, the program can be better written using virtual functions. Listing 16.2 shows how this program may look.

Listing 16.2. SALAD2.CPP—Using Virtual Functions to Create a Better Salad

```cpp
#include <iostream.h>

// Some miscellaneous definitions we will need
typedef enum {
    WHOLE,
    SHREDDED,
    GRATED,
    SLICED,
    CHOPPED
} FoodState;

// The top of the inheritance tree
class Food {
public:
    // Constructor
    Food(const FoodState = WHOLE);

    // Virtual methods — all food
    // must be able to set and return
    // its state. These functions also
    // ensure that Food is polymorphic
    // and can use RTTI.
    virtual FoodState GetState() const;
    virtual void SetState(const FoodState);

private:
    // Private member data
    FoodState theFoodState;
};

// Food constructor
Food::Food(const FoodState newState)
{
    SetState(newState);
}

// Getter and setter virtual methods
FoodState Food::GetState() const
{
    return theFoodState;
}
```

continues

Listing 16.2. Continued

```cpp
void Food::SetState(const FoodState newState)
{
    theFoodState = newState;
}

// Overload << so we can display our state
ostream& operator<<(ostream& outstrm,
                    Food&    theFood)
{
    switch(theFood.GetState()) {
        case WHOLE:      outstrm  << "Whole";
                         break;
        case SHREDDED:   outstrm << "Shredded";
                         break;
        case GRATED:     outstrm << "Grated";
                         break;
        case SLICED:     outstrm << "Sliced";
                         break;
        case CHOPPED:    outstrm << "Chopped";
                         break;
        default:
                outstrm << "Bad state!";
    }
    return outstrm;
}


// Intermediate class grouping
class SaladIngredient : public Food {
public:
    // Pure virtual function which any
    // salad ingredient class must
    // provide
    virtual void ProcessIngredient() = 0;
};


// Individual food types
class Apple : public SaladIngredient {
public:
    void ProcessIngredient() { SetState(CHOPPED); }
};

class Cheese : public Food {
public:
    void ProcessIngredient() { SetState(GRATED); }
};

class Lettuce : public Food {
public:
    void ProcessIngredient() { SetState(SHREDDED); }
};
```

```
// Let's prepare a salad
void main()
{
    Lettuce    MyLettuce;
    Apple      MyApple;
    Cheese     MyCheese;

    // Process the vegetables
    MyLettuce.ProcessIngredient();
    MyApple.ProcessIngredient();
    MyCheese.ProcessIngredient();

    // Show what we've done
    cout << "The lettuce is ";
    cout << MyLettuce << "\n";
    cout << "The apple is ";
    cout << MyApple << "\n";
    cout << "The cheese is ";
    cout << MyCheese << "\n";
}
```

In this salad-making variant you can see that RTTI use has been completely removed. This is because the `ProcessIngredient()` virtual function that is forced on any class derived from `SaladIngredient` assumes the responsibility for changing the object's state as appropriate. Using virtual functions in this case is much cleaner than having to rely on the cascading "if" statements and `dynamic cast`s found in the Listing 16.1 `ProcessIngredient()` function.

> **Tip:** Any time you are tempted to use a `dynamic_cast` to determine a pointer's type (as opposed to simply providing a safe cast), ask yourself if there is a way to accomplish the same thing using virtual functions. Leveraging polymorphism is superior to using the brute force capabilities of RTTI's `dynamic_cast`.

Of course, the program may want to use some of the specific food classes in a context separate from simply making salads. The class hierarchy, for example, can have a `PizzaIngredient` class. The `Cheese` class then can use multiple inheritance and be derived from both `SaladIngredient` and `PizzaIngredient`. Be careful, though; if a program adopts this approach, it must ensure that the `Food` class is a virtual base class. Additionally, the program must change the `ProcessIngredient()` method names found in `SaladIngredient` and `PizzaIngredient` to avoid any naming conflict. In some cases, you may decide to use the RTTI approach of Listing 16.1 because it alleviates the need for multiple inheritance and its messy problems.

dynamic_cast and References

You also can use the `dynamic_cast` operator to create a reference to a particular type. The syntax for this operation follows the following format:

```
dynamic_cast<T&>(ref)
```

`T`, as used here, refers to a valid C++ type and `ref` is the source reference. The cast returns a reference of type `T` only if `ref` refers to an object of type `T`. Because a `NULL` reference is not possible, you have no way to compare the result of a dynamic reference cast to determine whether or not it has failed. In the case of an invalid dynamic reference cast, a `Bad_cast` exception gets thrown. (For a thorough discussion of exception handling, see Chapter 18, "Exception Handling.") The following code snippets demonstrate the differences in checking for invalid dynamic pointer casts and invalid dynamic reference casts:

```
// Checking for errors with dynamic pointer cast
Derived* pDerived = dynamic_cast<Derived*>(pBase);
if (!pDerived) {
    // Whoops! This was an invalid cast
}

// Checking for errors with dynamic reference casts
try {
    Derived& MyDerived = dynamic_cast<Derived&>(MyBase);
}
catch (Bad_cast) {
    // Whoops! This was an invalid cast
}
```

In every other way, using the dynamic reference is just like using the dynamic pointer cast— except for the obvious differences implied by the returned result of the former being a reference as opposed to a pointer.

Boring Classes Need Not Apply (Usually)

The "polymorphic class only" RTTI limitation discussed in previous sections appears in the draft ANSI standard, but in some cases the Borland 4.0 compiler is a little more lenient. Examine the code sample presented in Listing 16.3.

Listing 16.3. DYNCAST1.CPP—Using the dynamic_cast() with Non-Polymorphic Classes

```cpp
#include <iostream.h>

class Base {
    // Do nothing (not a polymorphic class)
};

class Derived : public Base {
    // Do nothing (not a polymorphic class)
};

void main()
{
    Derived  MyDerived;
    Derived* pMyDerived = &MyDerived;

    // Successful upcast
    Base* pBaseTest = dynamic_cast<Base*>(pMyDerived);
    cout << "pMyDerived ";
    cout << (pBaseTest ? "is" : "is not");
    cout << " a Base*.\n";
}
```

This code compiles and runs as expected, although it does not follow the ANSI working draft to the letter. As it turns out, the Borland 4.0 compiler enables you to dynamic_cast *up* a class hierarchy (for example, from a derived class to a base class) even if the classes involved are not polymorphic. Listing 16.4, however, shows a change to this code that breaks the program.

```
#include <iostream.h>

class Base {
    // Do nothing (not a polymorphic class)
};

class Derived : public Base {
    // Do nothing (not a polymorphic class)
};

void main()
{
    Derived  MyDerived;
    Derived* pMyDerived = &MyDerived;

    // Successful upcast
    Base* pBaseTest = dynamic_cast<Base*>(pMyDerived);
    cout << "pMyDerived ";
    cout << (pBaseTest ? "is" : "is not");
    cout << " a Base*.\n";

    // Successful(??) downcast
    if (pBaseTest) {
        Derived* pDerivedTest =
                    dynamic_cast<Derived*>(pBaseTest);
        cout << "pBaseTest ";
        cout << (pDerivedTest ? "is" : "is not");
        cout << " a Derived*.\n";
    }
}
```

This program cannot even compile, because the second use of
dynamic_cast attempts to cast a base pointer down to a derived pointer,
and neither class is polymorphic. The Borland compiler complains
that "Type Base *is not a defined class with virtual functions*," just as we
would expect.

Changing Listing 16.4 so that it works is a simple matter of adding a
single line to the definition of Base:

```
class Base {
    // Do nothing
    void virtual Nothing() { } // Now polymorphic
};
```

This change rids you of the troublesome compiler error and enables the program to compile, link, and run as expected.

RTTI and Multiple Inheritance

Prior to the advent of RTTI, programmers often were frustrated in their attempts to construct a piece of code to cast a pointer down a class hierarchy that incorporated a virtual base class. This sort of coding is simply not supported by C++ using the normal casting syntax.

Listing 16.5 depicts a very simple class hierarchy composed of a Base class, two Middle classes derived from the base class, and then a main Derived class derived through multiple inheritance from both of the middle classes. The program itself simply tries to take a pointer to a Derived class instance and cast it down to the Base level and then cast it back up to the Derived level.

Listing 16.5. VRTBASE1.CPP—A Simple Multiple Inheritance Hierarchy

```
#include <iostream.h>

class Base {
public:
    // Do nothing (not a polymorphic class)
    void BaseFunc() { cout << "In Base.\n"; }
};

class Middle1 : public Base {
public:
    // Do nothing (not a polymorphic class)
    void Middle1Func() { cout << "In Middle1.\n"; }
};

class Middle2 : public Base {
public:
    // Do nothing (not a polymorphic class)
    void Middle2Func() { cout << "In Middle2.\n"; }
};

class Derived : public Middle1, public Middle2 {
public:
```

continues

Listing 16.5. Continued

```
        // Do nothing (not a polymorphic class)
        void DerivedFunc() { cout << "In Derived.\n"; }
};

void main()
{
    Derived  MyDerived;
    Base*    pBase = (Base*) &MyDerived;
    pBase->BaseFunc();
    Derived* pDerived = (Derived*) pBase;
    pDerived->DerivedFunc();
}
```

This program does not compile. The compiler gives you two main error messages: *"Cannot cast from 'Derived *' to 'Base *'"* and *"Cannot cast from 'Base *' to 'Derived *'."*

You easily can fix one of these error messages. Because Derived indirectly inherits from Base twice, you have the classic multiple-instance problem that often plagues users of multiple inheritance. Clearly, you must make Base a virtual base class. The following changes to the Middle1 and Middle2 classes accomplish this task:

Listing 16.6. VRTBASE2.CPP—Changes to Make Base a Virtual Base Class

```
// First part identical to VRTBASE1.CPP

class Middle1 : virtual public Base {
public:
        // Do nothing (not a polymorphic class)
        void Middle1Func() { cout << "In Middle1.\n"; }
};

class Middle2 : virtual public Base {
public:
        // Do nothing (not a polymorphic class)
        void Middle2Func() { cout << "In Middle2.\n"; }
};

// Rest of program identical to VRTBASE1.CPP
```

This works—almost. The program still doesn't compile, but now you get only a single error: *"Cannot cast from 'Base *' to 'Derived *'."* The fact that you can't cast from a virtual base class down to a derived class is simply a limitation of C++, and without RTTI there isn't an easy or safe way to get around this problem.

Of course, because the Borland compiler supports the dynamic_cast, you have a simple and safe solution to this problem. Listing 16.7 shows the changes that need to be made to the program in order to get everything working as desired.

Listing 16.7. VRTBASE3.CPP—Changes Needed to Incorporate RTTI and Make the Program Finally Work

```
#include <iostream.h>

class Base {
public:
        // Do nothing
    void BaseFunc() { cout << "In Base.\n"; }

    // Now polymorphic so we can use RTTI
    virtual void Nothing() { }
};

// Definitions of Middle1, Middle2, and Derived
// are the same as VRTBASE2.CPP

void main()
{
    Derived  MyDerived;
    Base*    pBase = dynamic_cast<Base*>(&MyDerived);
    pBase->BaseFunc();
    Derived* pDerived = dynamic_cast<Derived*>(pBase);
    pDerived->DerivedFunc();
}
```

This version of the program not only compiles but runs as expected. Although you may find that you rarely need to perform an operation as relatively esoteric as this, you certainly will appreciate the dynamic_cast on those occasions when this sort of casting manipulation is required.

As a final note on using the `dynamic_cast` operator with inheritance trees that utilize multiple inheritance, understand that RTTI enables programs to cast pointers and references *across* inheritance trees. Conceptually, this action is like casting a base pointer down to the lowest class in the inheritance tree and then casting the same pointer back up the tree, but through a different inheritance path. Listing 16.8 shows how the VRTBASE3.CPP example can be changed to demonstrate this lateral casting ability.

Listing 16.8. VRTBASE4.CPP—Hopping across a Multiple Inheritance Hierarchy

```
  // All class declarations and definitions the same as
  // VRTBASE3.CPP

1 void main()
2 {
3    Derived  MyDerived;
4    Middle1* pMiddle1 = dynamic_cast<Middle1*>(&MyDerived);
5    pMiddle1->Middle1Func();
6    Middle2* pMiddle2 = dynamic_cast<Middle2*>(pMiddle1);
7    pMiddle2->Middle2Func();
8 }
```

In this example, the `pMiddle1` pointer is set to point to a class in the middle of the inheritance tree (line 4). On line 6 the program uses the `dynamic_cast` operator to move across the inheritance tree to another class located between `Base` and `Derived`. Notice that the syntax makes absolutely no reference to `Derived` and that the compiler is responsible for "finding a path" from one class in the tree to another.

A Brief Aside: Valued Declarations

The ANSI C++ standards committee has adopted a language change called *valued declarations*. Valued declarations often are used in conjunction with the `dynamic_cast`. Unfortunately, the Borland compiler does not support this feature in the 4.0 compiler version.

Briefly, valued declarations refer to the fact that standard C++ enables a variable declaration to return a value and that this value is usable inside an expression evaluation. Take, for example, the following C++ declaration:

```
MyClass* pMyClass = new MyClass;
```

With valued declarations this syntax now yields a value that indicates whether or not pMyClass has been correctly initialized. A programmer could rewrite the declaration so that it was evaluated within an expression designed to trap memory allocation errors.

```
if (MyClass* pMyClass = new MyClass) {
    // Do something
}
else {
    // The call to new failed
}
```

A full-fledged discussion of the implications of using valued declarations is beyond the scope of this chapter—and somewhat pointless, considering the Borland compiler doesn't support the feature yet—but it is important that you can at least recognize the feature's use. The Borland compiler will support valued declarations sooner rather than later, and the feature's use will be appearing in code snippets that you may run into in books, magazines, and other users' code.

The most important use of valued declarations, at least with respect to RTTI and the dynamic_cast, is in conditionally creating variable instances with limited scope. Look closely at the following code snippet:

```
1 void DoNothing(Base* pBase)
2 {
3     Derived* pDerived = dynamic_cast<Derived*>(pBase);
4     if (pDerived) {
5         // Do something with the object
6         cout << "It's a Derived!\n";
7     }
8     // pDerived is still in scope and is accessible
9 }
```

On line 8 you can see that the variable pDerived is still in scope and is fully accessible to the rest of the function, even though pDerived has clearly been declared simply for the purpose of determining whether or not pBase is also a Derived instance.

This semantic problem can be solved by creating explicitly a new level of scope, in this way:

```
1   void DoNothing(Base* pBase)
2   {
3      { // Start of new scope
4        Derived* pDerived = dynamic_cast<Derived*>(pBase);
5        if (pDerived) {
6             // Do something with the object
7             cout << "It's a Derived!\n";
8        }
9      } // End of new scope
10       // pDerived is not in scope and is unaccessible
11 }
```

Lines 10 and on do not have access to `pDerived`, so technically this code does solve the problem—but it's not pretty. You can use valued declarations to solve the problem more elegantly.

```
void DoNothing(Base* pBase)
{
    if (Derived* pDerived =
            dynamic_cast<Derived*>(pBase)) {
       // Do something with the object
        cout << "It's a Derived!\n";
    }
    // pDerived is not in scope and is unaccessible
}
```

As you can see, with valued declarations we can combine the declaration of `pDerived`, its initialization, and the evaluation of the result into a single unit. This combination helps to avoid errors that often result from using variables before they have been validated. This approach also resolves those ugly scoping problems and makes the resulting function smaller and easier to understand.

Valued declarations soon will be appearing in compilers. Although the feature is hardly earth shattering, it is so convenient that programmers are sure to latch onto it and use it often. Be prepared.

Type_infos and the typeid Operator

Obviously the capability to determine whether or not a pointer or reference is of a particular type can be very useful. On some occasions, however, you want even more information about a particular class than can be obtained through the `dynamic_cast` operator.

The standard C++ implementation of RTTI includes a specification for a `Type_info` class that is used to describe various attributes of a particular type. Figure 16.1 shows the specific structure of Borland's `Type_info` class.

```
class Type_info {
public:
    virtual ~Type_info();
    int operator==(const Type_info&) const;
    int operator!=(const Type_info&) const;
    const char* name() const;
    int before(const Type_info&) const;

private:
    Type_info(const Type_info&);
    Type_info& operator=(const Type_info&);
};
```

Fig. 16.1. The `Type_info` class.

Take a brief look at some of things that you can do with a `Type_info`. As evidenced by the overloaded equality and inequality operators, `Type_info`s can be compared with each other. Using the `name` method, a program can retrieve the name of a type in the form of a character string. Finally, a program can determine the lexical order of two types (based on their name) using the `before` method.

Note: Because both the copy constructor and the assignment operator are declared as private, `Type_info`s cannot be copied.

So just how does a program create or otherwise get at these `Type_info` instances? RTTI provides an operator called the `typeid` operator that is designed expressly to return `Type_info`s. `typeid` takes a single argument that can be either a simple type name or an expression. The operator returns to the program a `Type_info` reference that corresponds to the requested type, or a `Type_info` reference that corresponds to the type of the supplied expression.

The `typeid` operator does not require that you feed it exclusively poly-morphic types. Consider, for example, the following code snippet:

```
// Show some integral type names
cout << typeid(int).name() << "\n";
cout << typeid(unsigned long).name() << "\n";
cout << typeid(char*).name() << "\n";
```

As you may expect, these three lines of code output "`int`," "`unsigned long`," and "`char *`" respectively.

Because the `typeid` operator can accept expressions, it is possible to pass in variable names to the operator and manipulate the resulting `Type_info` reference. As expected, the following code displays "`Apple`."

```
// Define our class
class Apple {
    // Do nothing
};

// Create an instance
Apple MyApple;

// Display the instance's name
cout << typeid(MyApple).name() << "\n";
```

In those cases where the expression being evaluated is an instance of a polymorphic type, the `typeid` operator looks at the actual object and returns an appropriate `Type_info` object. The following code displays "`Derived`":

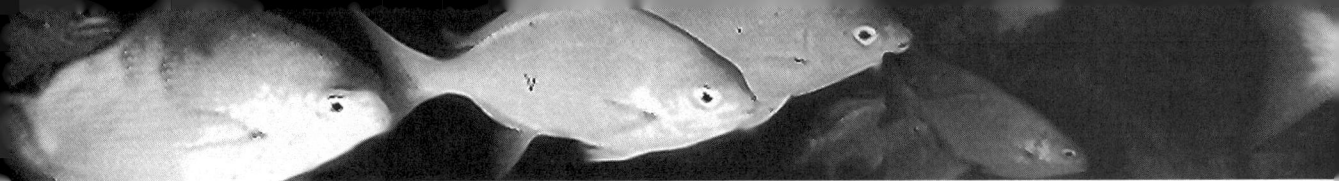

```
// Define our classes
class Base {
    // Do nothing
    // We have to make this class polymorphic
    // for this example to work correctly
    virtual void Nothing() { }
};

class Derived : public Base {
    // Do nothing
};

// Create an object instance
Derived  MyDerived;
Base*    pBase = dynamic_cast<Base*>(&MyDerived);

// Now show the "true" type of pBase
cout << typeid(*pBase).name() << "\n";
```

Notice that in this example the classes need to be polymorphic in order to get the correct behaviors. If you omit the stub definition of the *Nothing* method in class `Base`, this code snippet reports that the type name is "`Base`."

Caution: If RTTI features are disabled (using the `-RT-` switch discussed later in the chapter) the `typeid` operator will still function, but it may not return the results that your program expects. If RTTI is off and a program passes a polymorphic pointer or reference into `typeid`, `typeid` returns a reference to a `Type_info` instance that represents the declared type of the argument and not the `Type_info` for the actual object to which the pointer or reference is pointing.

Salad Making Revisited

You can use `Type_info`s in many of the same ways that you use the `dynamic_cast` operator. Recall that in the SALAD.CPP program (Listing 16.1), you used the `dynamic_cast` operator to query the type of a provided base pointer. If the base pointer was not of the correct type, `dynamic_cast` returned a NULL, and you could determine that the pointer needed to be processed in a different manner. Listing 16.9 shows how you can use the typeid operator to make the same sort of determination.

Listing 16.9. SALAD3.CPP—Using Typeid to Determine an Object's Type

```
#include <iostream.h>
#include <typeinfo.h>

// The definitions of FoodState, Food, Apple, Cheese,
// and Lettuce are the same as in SALAD.CPP

// Process a single ingredient
void ProcessIngredient(Food* pIngredient)
{
        // Is this an Apple?
        if (typeid(*pIngredient) == typeid(Apple)) {
                ((Apple*) pIngredient)->Chop();
                return;
        }
        // Is this a head of Lettuce?
        if (typeid(*pIngredient) == typeid(Lettuce)) {
                ((Lettuce*) pIngredient)->Shred();
                return;
        }
        // Is this a piece of Cheese?
        if (typeid(*pIngredient) == typeid(Cheese))
                ((Cheese*) pIngredient)->Grate();

        return;
}

// Let's prepare a salad
void main()
{
        Lettuce MyLettuce;
        Apple   MyApple;
        Cheese  MyCheese;

        // Process the vegetables
        ProcessIngredient(&MyLettuce);
        ProcessIngredient(&MyApple);
        ProcessIngredient(&MyCheese);
```

```
            // Show what we've done
            cout << "The ";
            cout << typeid(MyLettuce).name() << " is ";
            cout << MyLettuce << "\n";
            cout << "The ";
            cout << typeid(MyApple).name() << " is ";
            cout << MyApple << "\n";
            cout << "The ";
            cout << typeid(MyCheese).name() << " is ";
            cout << MyCheese << "\n";
        }
```

As you can see, SALAD3.CPP explicitly checks the Type_info of the passed in ingredient pointer with the Type_info of each of the possible food types. Because all of the classes are polymorphic, the Type_info returned by typeid(*pIngredient) will refer to the actual object, which makes this comparison possible.

So which way should it be written? It's a toss up. Using the Type_info method is a little easier to read and looks more obvious. However, the Type_info method also relies on dangerous and unprotected C-style typecasts, instead of the safer dynamic_cast. Because the dynamic_cast essentially performs two jobs simultaneously—checking for the correct pointer type and then safely performing the cast—you probably are safer using the dynamic_cast over the typeid solution in this case.

The Type_info::before() Enigma

Recall that the Type_info class contains a method called before() that is provided as a mechanism to help order a class hierarchy. This method is not mandated by the ANSI specification. This method is included in most discussions of Type_info, however, so apparently Borland felt compelled to provide some sort of implementation.

Unfortunately, the reality of the situation is that Borland's implementation of before() is of limited use (to say the least). Take a close look at Listing 16.10.

Listing 16.10. BEFORE.CPP—Using the Type_info before() Method

```cpp
#include <iostream.h>
#include <typeinfo.h>

// Define our classes
class Base {
    // Do nothing
    // Force polymorphism
    virtual void Nothing() { }
};

class Middle : public Base {
    // Do nothing
};

class Derived : public Middle {
    // Do nothing
};

// Show behind relationship
void ShowBefore(const Type_info& info1,
                const Type_info& info2)
{
    cout << info1.name();
    cout << (info1.before(info2) ? " is " : " is not ");
    cout << "before " << info2.name() << "\n";
}

void main()
{
    // Show the relationships
    ShowBefore(typeid(Base),    typeid(Middle));
    ShowBefore(typeid(Base),    typeid(Derived));
    ShowBefore(typeid(Middle),  typeid(Base));
    ShowBefore(typeid(Middle),  typeid(Derived));
    ShowBefore(typeid(Derived), typeid(Base));
    ShowBefore(typeid(Derived), typeid(Middle));
}
```

The most useful implementation of before() would enable us to tell whether one class is derived from another (for example, Base is before Derived). Using that definition, Listing 16.10 would output the following:

```
Base is before Middle

Base is before Derived
```

```
Middle is not before Base

Middle is before Derived

Derived is not before Base

Derived is not before Middle
```

This output, however, is not what the Borland compiler returns. Instead, the Borland product outputs what appears at first glance to be almost random ordering information:

```
Base is before Middle

Base is before Derived

Middle is not before Base

Middle is not before Derived

Derived is not before Base

Derived is before Middle
```

According to the compiler, the ordering of this class hierarchy can be described as Base, Derived, Middle. This ordering certainly does not describe the inheritance relationship. What's going on here?

When the *names* of the classes are changed from Base, Middle, Derived to A, B, C, the compiler returns the following results:

```
A is before B

A is before C

B is not before A

B is before C

C is not before A

C is not before B
```

By this point, you undoubtedly have realized that the compiler is just sorting the names of the classes in alphabetical order. If you don't understand what this order buys you, don't worry—neither does anyone else. Ultimately, Borland's implementation of the `before()` method appears to be of limited utility. If you can find a good use for it, more power to you.

> **Tip:** Even though the `before()` method probably doesn't strike you as being particularly interesting or useful, you still can use the `dynamic_cast` operator to get at the sort of information that you may have hoped `before()` would provide.

Setting the Borland RTTI Compiler Switch

The Borland 4.0 C++ compiler has only one command-line compiler switch that relates to runtime type identification. The `-RT` switch, which is on by default, controls whether or not RTTI information is created and stored for polymorphic classes. You effectively can turn off RTTI by placing `-RT-` on your compiler command line.

Notice that even if you have turned RTTI off, you can use the Borland C++ keyword `__rtti` to generate RTTI information on a per-class basis. This keyword is fully discussed in the following section.

Using the __rtti Keyword

A program can force the generation of RTTI information by placing the `__rtti` token immediately after the `class` or `struct` reserved word. For example:

```
class __rtti MyClass { // Do nothing };

struct __rtti MyStruct { // Do nothing };
```

This token ensures that even if the compiler has runtime type identification features turned off for the rest of the code, the RTTI information will be generated and maintained for these classes.

In an inheritance tree, it is important that any __rtti classes are themselves derived from an __rtti class. For example, the following code snippet shows an invalid declaration. Remember that "invalid" as used here is relative; this invalid condition works correctly if RTTI is turned on. The condition becomes invalid only when the -RT- option appears on the compiler command line, as shown here:

```
// Base needs __rtti
class Base {
    virtual void Nothing() { }
};
class __rtti Derived : public Base { };
```

Multiple inheritance conspires to complicate things even further. If a class inherits from more than one base class, and at least one of the base classes is __rtti, then all of the polymorphic base classes must be declared as __rtti, as follows:

```
// Base2 needs __rtti
class __rtti Base1 {
    virtual void Nothing() { } // Polymorphic
};
class Base2 {
    virtual void Nothing2() { } // Polymorphic
};
class __rtti Derived : public Base1, public Base2 { };
```

This example does not work because Base2 is polymorphic. The next example is fine, however, because Base2 is not polymorphic.

```
// This is OK
class __rtti Base1 {
    virtual void Nothing() { } // Polymorphic
};
class Base2 {
    // Not polymorphic
};
class __rtti Derived : public Base1, public Base2 { };
```

When you have a combination of polymorphic and nonpolymorphic base classes, such as the preceding example, the order that the base classes appear within the derived class's definition becomes important *if the derived class is not declared* __rtti. Consider this example:

```
// This is fine
class Derived : public Base1, public Base2 { };
```

```
// But this is not
class Derived : public Base2, public Base1 { };
```

The best strategy is to make it a habit to always make your derived class
`__rtti`, and then you can disregard the order of the base classes in the
definition.

```
// This is fine
class __rtti Derived : public Base1, public Base2 { };

// And now this one is too
class __rtti Derived : public Base2, public Base1 { };
```

From Here...

If you are interested in learning more about runtime type identification, check out the following publications.

➤ Stoustrup, B. and D. Lenkov. "Run-Time type Identification for
C++" (revised yet again), X3J16/92-0121 = WG21/N0198, 1992.

➤ Stoustrup, B. and D. Lenkov. "Run-Time Type Identification for
C++," *C++ Report* 4(3):32-42, 1992.

➤ Stoustrup, B. and D. Lenkov. "Run-Time Type Identification for
C++ (revised)," *Proceedings of the USENIX C++ Conference*,
Portland OR, August 1992.

➤ Lajoie, Josée. Standard C++ Update: "The New Language Extensions," *C++ Report* 5(6):47-52, 1993. (This list of supplementary
publications was taken from this article.)

You also might want to investigate some of the other chapters in this
book that discuss advanced C++ language extensions.

➤ Chapter 17, "Mastering Templates." Templates are probably the
most frequently used C++ extension. Templates allow programs
to build "class families" that function in a similar fashion, but
perform operations on a wide variety of different data types.

➤ Chapter 18, "Exception Handling." Exception handling allows programmers to localize error-processing logic and logically structure the way their programs deal with abnormal execution events.

Mastering Templates

by Chris Corry

Templates allow programs to create families of functions or classes, which is, of course, a rather dubious explanation. Programmers who are not familiar with templates often complain that there seems to be little intuitive need for a class "family" that cannot be handled by the standard C++ mechanisms of inheritance, polymorphism, and the like. This reaction, however, is usually based on a rather shaky understanding of exactly what class families are and how they can be used. It generally takes only a few well-chosen examples to demonstrate the value of the generic class concept.

There are several names for the problems that templates address. What one author refers to as *parameterized types*, another will refer to as *generic classes*, and yet another will call *class families*. This chapter will use the terms generic classes and class families interchangeably when talking about the abstract theoretical problems that templates address, and use the term templates (for obvious reasons) when referring to the

C++ solution to these problems. Still the question remains, what are class families and what is it about them that necessitates C++'s templates?

Templates Are Here to Stay

First of all, there is nothing inherent in the idea of generic classes and functions which absolutely requires the template language extensions. For that matter, however, there is nothing inherent in the tenets of object-oriented programming that required class extensions to C. Templates, like exception handling and runtime type information, are ultimately conveniences that make certain programming tasks easier and less error prone.

Although it is certainly possible to simulate class families in a variety of different ways (most relying on the C++ preprocessor), adding templates to the language proper has a number of distinct advantages. Most importantly, by accepting templates into the still evolving ANSI C++ standard, the user community creates a stable and dependable language extension that will be source code compatible across compilers and operating platforms. If programmers had to rely on their own implementations of generic classes, everyone would be forced to reinvent the wheel whenever they wanted to create a class family. Code written by one programmer would, in the best of cases, be difficult to maintain and be understood by other programmers without significant knowledge of the original author's generic class implementation.

Luckily, there is an emerging standard for templates, and most compiler vendors are scrambling to ensure that their compilers comply with the latest ANSI C++ standards draft. Borland helped pioneer the development of the template language extension when it provided template support with Borland C++ 2.0 in 1991. Templates have become a reasonably stable and persistent feature of the language, so there is little reason to resist using them on the grounds that the extensions are too young or immature.

The larger problem is convincing programmers—novice and expert alike—that there is a compelling use for templates. To many programmers, template syntax and use are just foreign enough to appear intimidating. They shouldn't be. The reality of templates is that once you've mastered a few of the basic abstractions and concepts, templates are as easy to use and understand as regular C++ classes.

Despite throwing around terminology like "generic classes" and "class families," you still don't have a good explanation of the template concept, so let's start with step one.

Why Do We Need Generic Functions and Classes?

C++ provides a powerful set of features that allows you to take complex programming problems and approach them using convenient abstractions. Well-designed classes can be used like a black box; you provide input data and concentrate on the output with little regard for how the class got there. This frees you from worrying about a host of compatibility and implementation issues, and, assuming you've done a good job designing your object interfaces, allows you to focus on tying objects together.

A frustrating problem arises in those situations where you want to take a potentially disparate collection of these different "black boxes" and do the same thing to all of them. For example, what do we do when we want to provide a function that, given three ordered objects of the same type, returns the object that is in the middle of the sort order? Listing 17.1 shows an implementation for integers.

Listing 17.1. Retrieving the "Middle" of Three Integers

```
#include <iostream.h>

int Middle(int a, int b, int c)
{
    return (a <= b ? (b <= c ? b : Middle(a, c, b)) :
```

continues

Listing 17.1. Continued

```
            Middle(b, a, c));
    }

    void main()
    {
        cout << "Middle(3, 12, 5) is " << Middle(3, 12, 5);
    }
```

When run, the program yields

```
    Middle(3, 12, 5) is 5
```

which is exactly what we would expect.

This is a nice enough solution to a pretty simple problem. Except what happens when you need to do exactly the same thing for three floating-point numbers? Ouch! Time to fire up the text editor and do a little bit of cut-and-paste. Listing 17.2 shows the new code needed to support floating-point numbers. Note that C++'s function overloading allows us to keep the function name identical to the original code. The compiler will decide which version of Middle will be called based on the function arguments.

Listing 17.2. Retrieving the "Middle" of Three Double Floating-Point Numbers

```
    double Middle(double a, double b, double c)
    {
        return (a <= b ? (b <= c ? b : Middle(a, c, b)) :
                Middle(b, a, c));
    }
```

This really does seem like a waste. Here we have two code snippets that do exactly the same thing, but to different data types. It should be sinking in now that in order to support an arbitrary number of integral and user-defined types, someone will have to write the same number of code snippets, most of which will be identical to Listing 17.2 except for the type names.

Depending on the amount of experience you've had with C and/or C++, you may be wondering if there is something that can be done with a preprocessor macro to solve the problem. The answer is yes and no.

Listing 17.3 shows a macro-based solution that appears to work. Note that our original implementation relied on recursion, which means that under certain circumstances the function had to call itself until a particular condition was met. Since C++ does not support recursive macros, the macro version is a little longer.

Listing 17.3. Using a Macro to Find the "Middle" of Three Ordered Objects of Arbitrary Type

```
#define _Middle(a, b, c)                                    \
    ((a) <= (b) ? ((b) <= (c) ? (b) : ((a) <= (c) ? \
    (c) : (a))) : ((a) <= (c) ? (a) : ((b) <= (c) ? \
    (c) : (b))))
```

The above listing does solve some of the problems inherent in applying `Middle()` to arbitrary types, but it ends up causing more problems than it solves. Yes, this code will allow you to call `_Middle` with a wide variety of integral and user-defined types (as long as the objects support `operator<=()`). However, this approach also causes the compiled source code to become bloated and inefficient, and the strict type checking that is one of the hallmarks of C++ is greatly compromised.

Source Code Reuse and Efficiency

One of the great promises of object-oriented programming relates to code reuse. Inheritance is based on the premise that the more behaviors you can push into the base classes of a class hierarchy, the less code has to be added to newly derived classes. The spirit of reuse is at the core of what C++ is all about. As you will see, the above example is not a very good example of tight, reusable code.

The code presented in Listing 17.3 appears to be relatively compact (readability is a completely different story). The operative word here is *appears*, because Listing 17.3 can potentially cause your programs to grow significantly. Remember that `_Middle` is a macro and that every occurrence of `_Middle` in your code will be expanded. Examine the following rather innocuous assignment:

```
float fMidValue = _Middle(34.23, 0.45, 396.27);
```

During compilation, this line is preprocessed and then passed onto the compiler. Look at what the preprocessor comes up with for this single line of code.

```
float fMidValue = ((34.23) <= (0.45) ? ((0.45) <= (396.27) ? (0.45) :
((34.23) <= (396.27) ? (396.27) : (34.23))) : ((34.23) <= (396.27) ?
(34.23) : ((0.45) <= (396.27) ? (396.27) : (0.45)))));
```

Now imagine this mess appearing in every place where your program calls the _Middle macro. An application wouldn't have to call this macro too many times before the size of the program is noticeably affected.

It's probably self-evident, but the above example is also pretty inefficient. The expanded block of code does represent a reasonable amount of processing to find the middle-ordered object. The biggest problem, however, is that the code is compiled everywhere it's used. You might be tempted to simply wrap the above expansion in a function declaration, but then you're back to where you started. Although placing this code in a function will prevent the program from getting bloated, the function's prototype would require explicitly typed arguments.

Type Safety

There is another problem with using macros to implement generic classes. C++ benefits from being strongly typed. Since the language catches many inadvertent errors related to type at compile time, a great number of bugs are resolved during development instead of at runtime.

> **Note:** C++ is a strongly typed language, as opposed to some object-oriented programming languages like SmallTalk. In most cases, this means that the compiler can determine at compile time whether your program contains typing-related errors (e.g., passing arguments of the wrong type into methods or calling methods that don't exist for a particular object class). It is only when programs take advantage of polymorphism and late-binding that C++ cannot do type checking until runtime.

The `_Middle` macro opens the door for a number of subtle bugs related to the types of its arguments. First and foremost, the compiler allows the `_Middle` macro to be called with arguments of different types. Depending on what you're trying to accomplish, this may or may not make sense, but in this context it seems unlikely. The macro also leaves the type of the result to be determined by the compiler. If you're lucky, the type will be appropriate; but if you're not, it might require a cast in order for the code to compile correctly.

Finally, there is the issue of certain expressions not correctly evaluating in a macro. Calling `_Middle` with arguments of 12, `MyVar++`, and 15 will not yield the desired result when the variable MyVar has a value of 14. This is because `MyVar` will have a value of 14 in some parts of the macro, but a value of 15 or 16 in others.

Templates as Function and Class Families

Without templates, there is no easy way to create implementations of function and class families that perform the same actions over a range of different data types. Although macros can work in some cases (and some uses of macros can get pretty elaborate and intricate), they suffer from the same problems of code size, efficiency, and type checking. There also are hybrid mechanisms for creating generic classes that rely on specialized C++ classes used in conjunction with macros. These solutions may be a little better, but ultimately suffer from many of the same failings of the pure-macro approach. Templates allow you to easily create generic classes without compromise.

As alluded to earlier, templates are useful for creating families of functions in addition to families of classes. The `Middle()` example is a perfect candidate for a function template, and the next section explains how to write such a template definition. As you will see, although function templates are very similar to class templates, there are a few differences in syntax and use.

Note: It is important to realize that the primary aim of templates is to help programmers do more while writing less code. A single template definition can cause the generation of many different C++ functions or classes "under the covers." However, templates do not purport to cut down on the sizes or amount of *object* code that gets generated. Don't expect your executable and DLL sizes to get smaller just because your programs make judicious use of templates (in fact, you might actually see them grow a little). You *can* expect the sizes of your sources (.CPP and .H files) to get smaller, which implies that you are spending less time writing code.

A class template definition (as opposed to a function template definition) is neither a class nor an object instance. Instead, a class template is a description of how to create a new class given a particular type (or types). In C++, a class is useless without declaring an object instance of that class. Similarly, a template is useless without declaring a class instance of that template. If you find this concept a little confusing, don't worry. The following sections will explain exactly how to write template definitions, and how to instantiate template classes and functions.

Note: With classes, you define the class and then declare an instance of the class. With templates, you define the template and then declare the type of class that you want to instantiate.

Function Templates

The `Middle` example is the perfect place to start the practical discussion of how to use templates. Carefully examine the elements of the `Middle` template, presented in Listing 17.4.

Listing 17.4. A Template Function for Finding the "Middle" of Three Ordered Objects

```
#include <iostream.h>

// This is the function template definition
template <class Type>
Type Middle(Type a, Type b, Type c)
{
    return (a <= b ? (b <= c ? b : Middle(a, c, b)) :
            Middle(b, a, c));
}

void main()
{
    cout << "Middle(3, 12, 5) is " << Middle(3, 12, 5);
}
```

Your first reaction might be that this listing looks very similar to Listing 17.1. Well, it should. After all, both pieces of code are trying to do exactly the same things. What makes Listing 17.4 interesting is in how it differs from the first listing. For convenience sake, Listing 17.5 compares the prototype of Middle() from Listing 17.1 with the declaration for the Middle template definition.

Listing 17.5. A Comparison of the Integer Middle Function Prototype with the Template Middle Declaration

```
1  // The "int" prototype of Middle
2  int Middle(int a, int b, int c);
3
4  // The template declaration
5  template <class Type>
6  Type Middle(Type a, Type b, Type c);
```

The most obvious difference can be found on line 5. This line tells the compiler to expect a template definition that will describe a family of functions that utilize an arbitrary type, referred to as *Type*. Following the "template" keyword is a list of arbitrary type declarations enclosed between angle brackets (< ... >). This list of types is referred to as the *template arguments list*.

Each type declaration in the arguments list begins with the reserved word `class` followed by a user-provided name. A program may use whatever name is most appropriate to represent its types, but by convention, "*Type*" or simply "*T*" are two of the more commonly used symbolic names. Once the generic type has been defined, it can be used throughout the function definition in the same way that any integral C++ type might be used. Although line 5 only includes a single parameter, a template argument list can contain as many type declarations as necessary.

Line 6 in Listing 17.5 provides the prototype for the function template. Instead of indicating explicit types for the arguments and return value, however, this line indicates that the function takes three arguments of the same arbitrary type and returns a value of the same type. Listing 17.6 shows examples of both legal and illegal function template declarations.

Listing 17.6. Some Sample Function Template Declarations

```
// Legal
template <class MyType>
int DoSomething(MyType AValue, char *str);

// Legal
template <class T1, class T2>
void PrintSomething(T1 page, T2 doc);

// Illegal -- the "class" keyword must precede every
// type argument (T2's is missing)
template <class T1, T2, class MyType>
void BlowSomethingUp(T1 target, T2 area, MyType val);

// Illegal -- a template must have at least one type in
// its argument list
template <>
char GetChar(unsigned char ch);

// Illegal -- argument names must be unique
template <class T, class T>
void OpenFile(T FileAlias);

// Illegal -- all arguments must appear in the function
// prototype (T2 does not)
template <class T1, class T2>
void WriteFile(T1 FileAlias, char *str);
```

Notice the difference between a template declaration and a template definition. A template declaration is the equivalent of a function prototype, except it describes a family of functions that will be defined later using a template definition. Lines 5 and 6 of Listing 17.5 show a template declaration. A template definition, on the other hand, contains the actual implementation of a function template. Listing 17.4, for example, shows a template definition.

The template definition is coded in virtually the same manner that a normal C++ function is written. The only difference, apart from the obvious syntactical discrepancies already discussed, is that any of the types defined in the template argument list may be used in the definition as generic types.

Why Templates Won't Work for Any Type

The fact that template definitions are by nature generic has some rather subtle implications. Take, for example, the code fragment presented in Listing 17.7.

Listing 17.7. The AddEquals Function Template

```
.
.
.
struct MyStruct {
    unsigned int a;
    unsigned int b;
};

template <class T>
unsigned int AddEquals(T val1, T val2, T compare)
{
    return (val1 + val2) == compare;
}

// Example 1 -- Legal
cout << "Does 4 + 5 = 9? ";
cout << (AddEquals(4, 5, 9) ? "Yes" : "No") << "\n";
```

continues

Listing 17.7. Continued

```
// Example 2 -- Legal
cout << "Does 7.0 + 5.5 = 12.0? ";
cout << (AddEquals(7.0, 5.5, 12.0) ? "Yes" : "No") << "\n";

// Example 3 -- Illegal
MyStruct  a = { 23, 43 }, b = { 11, 19 }, c = { 34, 62 };
cout << "Does a + b = c? ";
cout << (AddEquals(a, b, c) ? "Yes" : "No") << "\n"
    .
    .
```

This function will take two objects of a given type, add them, and then compare them for equality to a third object of the same type. The template is very simple and the first two examples work as expected. The third example, however, does not work. In fact, the third example does not even compile. Why?

The reason is simple. The third example will not compile because the compiler doesn't know how to add MyStructs or check them for equality. The AddEquals template function applies the addition operator on its first two arguments and then checks to see if the result of the addition is equal to the third argument. This works just fine for integral types that the compiler already knows how to add and compare, but for user-defined types like MyStruct, the compiler does not understand how to add them or check for equality.

To make things worse, the Borland compiler flags the error as being inside the AddEquals template, instead of being related to MyStruct. AddEquals, however, is just fine. The problem lies with calling AddEquals with MyStructs as arguments. This annoying compiler quirk is related to *template instantiation*, which will be discussed in detail a little later.

Listing 17.8 shows the changes to the MyStruct type needed to support the AddEquals template.

Listing 17.8. The Corrected MyStruct Type

```
struct MyStruct {
    unsigned int a;
    unsigned int b;

    // Operators
    MyStruct operator+(MyStruct &o) {
        MyStruct temp = { a + o.a, b + o.b };
        return temp;
    }

    unsigned int operator==(MyStruct &o) {
        return a == o.a && b == o.b;
    }
};
```

The third example in Listing 17.7 will work correctly with this version of the MyStruct type, displaying "Yes" when run.

> **Caution:** The main lesson to be learned from these examples is that templates are powerful constructs that can be used—potentially—with any integral or user-defined type. If, however, the type does not support the operations that the template needs, the type *cannot* be used with the template at all.
>
> At first glance, this limitation may be more problematic than it might seem. If, for example, you purchased a set of template-based class libraries from a third-party vendor, it is crucial that you know which operations need to be supported by types that will be used with the templates. This information can often be obtained by scanning header files or reading documentation, but it must be obtained somehow.

Building the Class Template

At this point you probably have a basic understanding of how function templates can be used to create generic functions that will accept a wide variety of type-independent arguments. Class templates are in

many ways very similar to function templates. However, there are a number of complications that arise when taking into account behaviors that are unique to classes, such as inheritance, member data, and class methods.

This section will focus on taking the concepts touched on in the function templates sections and applying them to the C++ class mechanism. This section will also explore in more detail some of the finer points of the general template syntax. Some of these details will also apply to function templates.

The Template Syntax

Let's start by satisfying the language lawyers and reviewing the "official" template syntax for functions and classes. Although the definition in figure 17.1 is not very intuitive, most of it has already been covered, and it will help later on to have at least a general feeling for the precise syntax.

The Borland C++ template syntax.

(a) template-declaration:

```
template < template-argument-list > declaration
```

(b) template-argument-list:

```
template-argument

template-argument-list, template-argument
```

(c) template-argument:

```
type-argument

argument-declaration
```

(d) type-argument:

```
class identifier
```

Fig. 17.1. The Borland C++ template syntax.

Ironically, the syntax is really simpler than the notation would suggest. This rather gruesome style is adopted from the Borland documentation (that is, in turn, adopted from *The C++ Annotated Reference Manual*) and while it's complete, it certainly isn't very easy to read.

Not to worry. The syntax is actually quite simple and is summarized by section **(a)**. As discussed previously in the function templates section, a template declaration (or definition) begins with the token "`template`" and is followed by an argument list enclosed in angled brackets. Nothing new here. The "declaration" found at the end of section **(a)** simply refers to a declaration or definition of a function or class.

Section **(b)** details exactly what makes up a template argument list. Not surprisingly, this section indicates that a template argument list is made up of one or more template arguments.

The next section, section **(c)**, tells us that a template argument is either a type argument or an argument declaration. The type argument is explained in section **(d)** and is just the "class identifier" syntax that you encountered when building the `Middle` and `AddEquals` template functions. The argument declaration, however, is something new. `Template` arguments also can be made up of constant types which will not be used as generic types at all. The idea of having nongeneric types in a template declaration, and why this might be desirable, will be covered in the "Constant Expression Template Parameters" section.

Defining the Template

It's time for some concrete examples. Suppose, for whatever reason, we wanted to build a class which represented a railroad car. One could, for example, create a base class called `RailroadCar` that knew everything about what it meant to be part of a train. Then, as the programmer happened along different types of `RailroadCar`s, she could inherit new classes from the original `RailroadCar` class.

The problem with this approach is that it requires a lot of specialized classes (for example, `CowRailroadCar`, `PassengerRailroadCar`, `CoalRailroadCar`), all of which are intrinsically linked to being a `RailroadCar`. In real life,

however, we don't have two different species of cow, the normal cow species and the cow-on-a-train species. Cows are just cows, regardless of whether or not they're on a train.

There also is the issue of taking new code and merging it with code that has already been written. Imagine a programmer has inherited a large inventory management class library from his predecessor. His boss has asked him to add a set of rail shipment classes to the preexisting class library. This library already contains classes for all of the products that the company produces, and each of these products can be shipped out by rail.

If the programmer were to use the inheritance method, he would have to take all of the existing objects and either insert the `RailroadCar` class high up in the class hierarchy (an object-oriented crime punishable by banishment to COBOL hell) or use multiple-inheritance to add the `RailroadCar` class functionality to each of the product classes (not much better).

To make things worse, let's assume that the programmer doesn't even have the source code for the class library. The library is a third-party product bundled up in some Windows DLLs and the programmer uses the classes by including header files and linking with the DLL's import libraries. In this case, inserting the `RailroadCar` class into the middle of the inheritance tree isn't even an option.

Templates provide an easy solution to the problem. Since trains can haul virtually any type of commodity, it is important that a `RailroadCar` class not make any immediate assumptions about what it is inside the car. Templates don't have to make any assumptions about the characteristics of their generic types unless the programmer deems it appropriate. It seems like a good match. Listing 17.9 shows what a simple `RailroadCar` class template might look like.

Listing 17.9. A RailroadCar Class Template

```cpp
#include <iostream.h>
#include <cstring.h>

// Things to put in a RailroadCar
class Cow {
public:
    // Public member functions
    string isA() { return "Cow"; }
    string Moo() { return "Moo!"; }
};

class Passenger {
public:
    // Constructors and destructor
    Passenger(string NewName) { Name = NewName; }

    // Public member functions
    string isA() { return "Passenger"; }
    string GetName() { return Name; }
    string Complain() { return "Oh my poor back!"; }

private:
    string Name;
};


// The RailroadCar class template
template <class T>
class RailroadCar {
public:
    // Constructors and destructor
    RailroadCar(int NewCarNumber, T& NewContents);
    ~RailroadCar();

    // Public member functions
    void ShowContents();
    T* Unload();

private:
    T* pContents;
    int CarNumber;
};

// Constructor
template <class T>
RailroadCar<T>::RailroadCar(int NewCarNumber,
                            T&  NewContents)
{
    CarNumber = NewCarNumber;
    pContents = &NewContents;
}
```

continues

Building the Class Template   **739**

Listing 17.9. Continued

```
// Destructor
template <class T>
RailroadCar<T>::~RailroadCar()
{
    Unload();
}

// Public member functions
template <class T>
void RailroadCar<T>::ShowContents()
{
    cout << "Railroad car #" << CarNumber;
    cout << " is filled with " << pContents->isA();
    cout << "s\n";
}

template <class T>
T* RailroadCar<T>::Unload()
{
    T* temp = pContents;
    pContents = NULL;
    return temp;
}
```

This example is actually a pretty complete, albeit silly, implementation of a template class. Although a lot of this program is self-explanatory, there are a number of new concepts presented here, and a few things that merit additional discussion.

The actual template definition is reprinted below, and as one would expect, it looks almost exactly the same as a regular class definition.

```
// The RailroadCar class template
template <class T>
class RailroadCar {
public:
    // Constructors and destructor
    RailroadCar(int NewCarNumber, T& NewContents);
    ~RailroadCar();

    // Public member functions
    void ShowContents();
    T* Unload();

private:
    T* pContents;
    int CarNumber;
};
```

There are a number of parallels to the declaration of a function template as well. As expected from our discussion of the formal template syntax, the first line uses the same syntax as the `Middle` and `AddEquals` examples encountered earlier in this chapter. This line tells the compiler that our template definition will use a single generic type, named `T`.

The rest of the definition describes the template class, and there are no surprises here. The constructor takes an integer identification number as its first argument and a reference to a `T` for its second. This reference will be stored within the class as a pointer to `T` and represents the railroad car's contents.

Other member functions include a method to display the contents of the car and a method to "unload" the car by returning a pointer to the car's contents. Not surprisingly, the template class's member data includes an integer for the car identification number, and, as already mentioned, a pointer of type `T` which will point to the car's cargo.

With the definition of the template class's constructor and member functions, a new syntax is introduced. Examine the following definition for the Unload method.

```
template <class T>
T* RailroadCar<T>::Unload()
```

For the most part, the definition of the method prototype is identical to a normal method declaration. However, instead of a simple class name, there is a template name with accompanying arguments.

```
// What you might expect
T* RailroadCar::Unload() ...

// The correct syntax
template <class T>
T* RailroadCar<T>::Unload() ...
```

There are actually several reasons why the `<T>` is placed between the template name and the double-colons (": :") but one of the most important reasons relates to something called specialization. *Specialization* allows a program to override the default template behaviors for specific types. We'll discuss specialization in later sections.

For the most part, everything that applies to the coding of normal C++ classes applies to the creation of template code. It is important that member functions are declared using the slightly different syntax, but apart from that, the functions are written like any other class methods. Don't forget that you can use your generic type anywhere you might use a normal integral or user-defined type. This is, after all, the real reason you are using templates in the first place.

Instantiating Templates

A template definition by itself does nothing. In order to use a template, a program needs to create an instance of it, in much the same way that programs create object instances of classes. This process, like its class counterpart, is called instantiation.

Instantiating Function Templates

Instantiation for function templates and class templates is handled a little differently. Unlike class templates, a function template instantiation has no special syntax. All that is required from a program is to declare a normal function prototype with the appropriate types filled in. Therefore, to create an instance of our `AddEquals` function template that would accept arguments of type `Cow` (found in Listing 17.9), all that is required is the following:

```
// Create an AddEquals template instance for Cows
unsigned int AddEquals(Cow val1, Cow val2, Cow compare);
```

Of course, you can't really do this since the `Cow` class doesn't have `operator+()` and `operator==()` defined, but that's beside the point.

Alternatively, a program can simply refer to a particular function template instance, and the compiler will realize that the instance needs to be generated. In Listing 17.7, the compiler understands that it needs to generate a version of `AddEquals` for integers and for floating-point numbers when it encounters the use of these functions. Still, it's good programming practice to explicitly declare your function template instances for purposes of readability and documentation.

Instantiating Class Templates

Although the syntax for instantiating a class template is quite similar to the syntax for instantiating an object instance, there are a couple of important differences. First and foremost, it is important to remember that the *process* of instantiating a template is very different than the process of instantiating an object instance. When the compiler encounters a template instance, it builds a whole new class definition custom-tailored to the type (or types) that the template instance will be using. Compare this to instantiating a new object, where the compiler simply looks up the appropriate class and creates a new object of that type. Luckily the generation of new classes from templates is performed at compile time so there are no runtime performance penalties. The class template instantiation syntax is detailed in figure 17.2.

```
The Borland C++ class template instantiation syntax.

(a) template-class-name:

        template-name < template-arg-list >

(b) template-arg-list:

        template-arg
        template-arg-list , template-arg

(c) template-arg:

        expression
        type-name
```

Fig. 17.2. The Borland C++ class template instantiation syntax.

Section **(a)** reveals that the instantiation begins with a template name and is followed by an argument list enclosed in the obligatory angled brackets. As indicated by section **(b)**, the argument list is composed of one or more arguments.

More interesting is section **(c),** which describes what an argument is. Remember that the program is creating a new class, so all of the generic type arguments specified in the template definition need to be filled in with specific types. It shouldn't, therefore, come as any surprise to see that when instantiating a template, the program needs to pass in type names. Section **(c)** also indicates that the program can pass in constant expressions where appropriate. This variation on the normal instantiating syntax will be explored in more detail in the section entitled "Constant Expression Template Parameters."

Since there's no better way to learn than by doing, Listing 17.10 shows how instantiation might be used with the `RailroadCar` template.

Listing 17.10. Using the RailroadCar Class Template

```
void main()
{
    // At Station 1
    Cow ACow;
    Passenger APassenger("Monty");

    RailroadCar<Cow> CarNumber1(1, ACow);
    RailroadCar<Passenger> CarNumber2(2, APassenger);

    CarNumber1.ShowContents();
    CarNumber2.ShowContents();

    // Go to Station 2...
    cout << "\n..Choo..Choo..\n\n";

    // At Station 2
    Cow* AtStation2Cow = CarNumber1.Unload();
    Passenger* AtStation2Passenger =
                        CarNumber2.Unload();

    cout << "How was the trip, ";
    cout << AtStation2Passenger->GetName() << "?";
    cout << " " << AtStation2Passenger->Complain();
    cout << "\n";
    cout << AtStation2Cow->Moo() << "\n";
}
```

The most important lines, from a template standpoint, can be found at the beginning of the listing.

```
RailroadCar<Cow> CarNumber1(1, ACow);
RailroadCar<Passenger> CarNumber2(2, APassenger);
```

These two lines are responsible for creating two railroad car classes: one that can be used with `Cows` and another that can be used with `Passengers`. The first part of each of these lines actually instantiates

the new class. Once the template class has been instantiated, it can be used just like any other class; this program proceeds to declare two object instances of the newly created classes.

The above code also could have been written like this:

```
// Create new types for template instantiations
typedef RailroadCar<Cow> CowRailroadCar;
typedef RailroadCar<Passenger> PassengerRailroadCar;

// Now instantiate the object instances
CowRailroadCar CarNumber1(1, ACow);
PassengerRailroadCar CarNumber2(2, APassenger);
```

This style is a little more verbose, and accordingly maybe even a little more readable. It also allows further instantiations of `CowRailroadCars` and `PassengerRailroadCars` without having to type in the cumbersome `RailroadCar<...>` syntax. Which mechanism you choose is really a matter of personal preference. Keep in mind that a template instantiation (e.g., `RailroadCar<Car>`, `RailroadCar<Passenger>`) can be used in the same way, and in the same places, as any other type.

One interesting thing to note when using the more verbose style is that the Borland compiler does not actually generate the `RailroadCar<Cow>` and `RailroadCar<Passenger>` classes when it encounters the `typedef` statements. The classes aren't generated until the compiler encounters an instantiation of a `CowRailroadCar` or `PassengerRailroadCar` object. Since there is little or no overhead associated with the `typedef`s, they can be declared liberally without concern about bloated object files or long compile times.

Using Static Template Member Data and Methods

Since the class generated by a template instantiation is really just a normal C++ class, static member functions and data are completely supported. The only tricky part is getting acclimated to the new syntax that the template definition requires, and even that's not so bad.

Take as an example a program that needs to implement a `GlobalValue` template. A `GlobalValue` is a global instance of some type that may be different for different programs (thus the template implementation). A `GlobalValue` class template has a static member function which returns the global value.

The `GlobalValue` example merits a quick digression about the values and dangers of using global data. Quite simply, global data is evil and programs shouldn't use it unless it's declared `const`. The main problem is that classes and functions can inadvertently modify global data in ways that might not have been anticipated by other objects in other parts of the program. These bugs are notoriously difficult to track down since it is very difficult to retroactively track the changes in an object's state and determine the parts of the program that were responsible for making those changes.

Things get even trickier when the program runs under an advanced operating system (such as Windows NT or OS/2) that supports multithreading. In these cases, the culprit responsible for the modification of global data could be running concurrently in another thread, and could be behaving differently from run to run depending on ambiguous and hard-to-reproduce factors like machine load.

That being said, there are a few good excuses for using global data (and a lot of bad ones). In some cases, performance requirements dictate a quick way to modify program-wide control objects. This is particularly true in multithreaded programs, where threads may need to communicate with each other as quickly as possible. This also may apply to programs that are concerned with communications or low-level network plumbing, or other programs that may have to meet real-time processing requirements. In other cases, the burden (from both a performance and a coding perspective) of passing data through many levels of functions and objects may be too great to justify.

The `GlobalValue` template presented in Listing 17.11 doesn't do much to alleviate the dangers of using global data, but it does suggest a more formalized mechanism for declaring and accessing global information. At the very least, a `GlobalValue` class provides a convenient place to

insert debugging routines used to help track down tricky global data bugs. A full-blown GlobalValue template used in multithreaded environments also could implement semaphore mechanisms that would prevent contention on shared objects across multiple threads. Finally, using a GlobalValue class means that global information does not have to actually reside in the global namespace. This makes inadvertent modification of global data much less likely, since a class or function has to specifically obtain access to the global data through a static function call before being able to modify it.

Listing 17.11. A GlobalValue Template Using Static Member Data and Functions

```
#include <iostream.h>

// Define our boolean type
typedef unsigned char Boolean;
const Boolean TRUE = 1;
const Boolean FALSE = 0;

// GlobalValue template definition
template <class T>
class GlobalValue {
public:
    // Constructors and destructor
    GlobalValue();
    GlobalValue(T* pNewGlobalValue);
    ~GlobalValue();

    // Public member functions
    static T* GetGlobalValuePtr();

private:
    static T* pGlobalValue;
     static Boolean ShouldDelete;
};

// Initialize static data
template <class T>
T* GlobalValue<T>::pGlobalValue = NULL;
template <class T>
Boolean GlobalValue<T>::ShouldDelete = FALSE;

// Constructors
template <class T>
GlobalValue<T>::GlobalValue()
{
    pGlobalValue = new T;
```

continues

Listing 17.11. Continued

```cpp
        ShouldDelete = TRUE;
}

template <class T>
GlobalValue<T>::GlobalValue(T* pNewGlobalValue)
{
        pGlobalValue = pNewGlobalValue;
        ShouldDelete = FALSE;
}

// Destructor
template <class T>
GlobalValue<T>::~GlobalValue()
{
        if (ShouldDelete && pGlobalValue)
            delete pGlobalValue;
}

// Public member functions
template <class T>
T* GlobalValue<T>::GetGlobalValuePtr()
{
        return pGlobalValue;
}


// Now demonstrate use of a GlobalValue
void AFarAwayFunc()
{
        cout << "The int GlobalValue is ";
        cout << *GlobalValue<int>::GetGlobalValuePtr() << endl;
}

void main()
{
    int AVeryImportantInt = 123;
    GlobalValue<int> GlobalInt(&AVeryImportantInt);

        // Show the current value
        AFarAwayFunc();

        // Change the value
        AVeryImportantInt++;
        AFarAwayFunc();
}
```

The template definition is found on lines 8 through 23. The static member function GetGlobalValuePtr and the static member data pGlobalValue and ShouldDelete are all declared in the same way that

they would be in a normal C++ class. In the constructors, destructor, and member function these data values are all manipulated just as one would expect. Similarly, the GetGlobalValuePtr method is defined just like any other class template member function.

As you can see in the code reprinted below, the syntax for initializing static member data is different than for normal classes because of the template relationship.

```
// Initialize static data
template <class T>
T* GlobalValue<T>::pGlobalValue = NULL;
template <class T>
Boolean GlobalValue<T>::ShouldDelete = FALSE;
```

Still, since the syntax is identical to the definition of class template member functions, there really is nothing new here that hasn't already been previously described.

There are a number of things worth mentioning about the parts of Listing 17.11 that actually use the GlobalValue template. The AFarAwayFunc function is named as such to reinforce the point that any function or class method has access to the global data through the GlobalValue class template, even if the class or function is defined in another source module. Since the AVeryImportantInt variable is declared only within the scope of main(), AFarAwayFunc can only access this value through the appropriate class template. Notice also the syntax used to call the static method. It is identical to a normal static member function call, except a template qualifier is used instead of a class name.

Constant Expression Template Parameters

The previous sections that addressed template definition and instantiation made references to certain declaration forms that allowed for placing nongeneric types within a template argument list. Instead, a program may opt to use a regular integral or user-defined type and pass in a constant expression for that parameter during template instantiation. This mechanism can be used to introduce a certain amount of flexibility in those classes that typically rely on fixed values.

The template declaration syntax allows for type parameters or constant expressions to appear in a template argument list. If a template uses an expression argument, it must be resolvable at compile time. Listing 17.12 shows examples of both legal and illegal uses of constant expressions in argument lists.

Listing 17.12. Using Constant Expressions in Template Argument Lists

```
const int MAX_NUM_BLAHS = 23;
const char* A_STR_NUM = "356";

template <int AnInt>
class BlahBlahBlah {
    Template definition omitted...
};

// All legal
BlahBlahBlah<22*4> Blahs1;
BlahBlahBlah<MAX_NUM_BLAHS>  Blahs2;
BlahBlahBlah<(MAX_NUM_BLAHS ? MAX_NUM_BLAHS : 1)> Blahs3;

// Illegal
BlahBlahBlah<atoi(A_STR_NUM)> Blah4;

// Illegal
void MyFunc(int NumBlahs)
{
    BlahBlahBlah<NumBlahs> InFuncBlah;
    ...
}
```

Constant expression template arguments are particularly useful in those cases where fixed-size data structures are used. Take a template that typically declares an array of a constant size.

```
template <class T>
class MyClass {
    ...
private:
    T AnArray[A_CONST_VALUE];
    ...
};
```

This same template class can be made more flexible by declaring it with a constant expression argument and passing in the size of the array during template instantiation.

```
template <class T, int ArraySize>
class MyClass {
    ...
private:
    T AnArray[ArraySize];
    ...
};

MyClass<double, A_CONST_VALUE> ADoubleMyClass;
```

Although the same general effect is achieved, the latter approach allows for instantiations that may vary the size of the array. Although there may not be any immediate need for such flexibility, other programs that use the same template may benefit from this sort of foresight. Since this approach does not affect runtime performance and has only minimal effects on object code size, it is an easy change to justify.

Some Syntactical Gotchas

Due to some subtleties in the argument list syntax, special care has to be taken in those cases where a constant expression in a template argument list uses the greater-than operator (such as `operator>()`). Without parentheses, some expressions can prematurely close a template argument list.

```
MyClass<float, A_CONST > ANOTHER_CONST> AMyClass;
```

These sort of errors are easily resolved (and avoided) by simply enclosing all template argument list expressions inside parentheses.

```
MyClass<float, (A_CONST > ANOTHER_CONST)> AMyClass;
```

A similar case arises when a template class is instantiated using a nested template syntax. As an example, look at the following two classes.

```
template <class T>
class FirstClass {
    Template definition omitted...
};
```

```
template <class T>
class SecondClass {
    Template definition omitted...
};

SecondClass<FirstClass<char *>> MySecondClass;
```

In this example the two right-angled brackets ("`>>`") in the `MySecondClass` declaration could be interpreted as being a right-shift operator. However, the Borland 4.0 compiler is intelligent enough to realize that a nested template declaration is probably intended and returns the warning "*Use '> >' for nested templates instead of '>>'.*" This is good advice. The following declarations for `MySecondClass` compile without warnings or errors.

```
// This works fine
SecondClass<FirstClass<char *> > MySecondClass;

// As does this
SecondClass< FirstClass<char *> > MySecondClass;
```

How Generic Is a Template?

C++ templates are based on the idea of building (relatively) type-independent class families that all rely on a single definition. Unfortunately, there are certain cases where it is simply not possible to describe a set of behaviors for every conceivable type. There really are two issues here: What should be done when a template needs to make assumptions about the generic types it manipulates? What should be done when a template makes assumptions about its generic types, and the type you want to use doesn't conform to these assumptions?

Type-Dependent Templates

Although templates can be useful for manipulating data in a generic fashion, they become even more valuable if you can make a few well-chosen assumptions about the generic types with which they will be working. In some respects, a certain amount of assuming cannot be helped. In the `AddEquals` example (refer to Listing 17.7), the template function assumed that the types that would be passed to it could be added and compared for equality. These two assumptions were of

paramount importance for the function to accomplish its task. On the downside, the template broke when passed the `MyStruct` type that could not be added or compared.

In a similar manner, the `RailroadCar` example also makes an assumption. In the `ShowContents` method the template calls the `isA` method of the item that the object is storing. Of course there are many types of objects that won't have an `isA` method to call. In fact, the mere requirement of an `isA` method precludes the use of any integral types as the template's generic type.

There is a certain "Catch-22" in this logic. The more assumptions made about a template's generic type, the more capably the template can manipulate its data and the more useful the template becomes. On the other hand, the more assumptions made about a template's generic type, the fewer types can be used and the whole argument for using templates is weakened.

The reality is that a *truly* generic class is seldom a useful class. Since a truly generic template cannot make any assumptions about its data—about its `T`—there is only so much that can be expected from it. Without framing its data in a useful context, a template is restricted from performing its most useful functions.

The ideal goal, of course, is to find a middle ground between making the template too dependent on its types, and making the template too generic to be very useful. In some cases a truly generic (or close to it) template may be appropriate. Both the `Middle` and `AddEquals` template functions probably meet this criteria, although even these simplistic examples make some basic assumptions about their parameterized types. The `RailroadCar` class, on the other hand, would be severely limited by such a generic implementation. After all, what good is a railroad car that you can't look inside of and determine its contents?

Specialization

Regardless of what sort of compromises need to be struck between functionality and generic approachability, you will eventually encounter a situation where a template that you want to use will not work with

a desired type. Luckily, a program can address these cases by using a template feature called *specialization.*

A template specialization allows you to overload a template function, a template class, a template class method, or template class static data member for a particular type. We'll return to the `AddEquals` example of Listing 17.7 to demonstrate how and why this might be done.

You will recall that the `AddEquals` function template took two arguments of the same generic type, added them together, and then compared the sum for equality with a third argument of the same type. But what happens when you try to use the `AddEquals` template with character pointers?

```
char *pBig = "Big ";
char *pDog = "Dog";
char *pBigDog = "Big Dog";

unsigned int result = AddEquals(pBig, pDog, pBigDog);
```

This code will not compile. The Borland compiler complains that the template definition contains code that performs an "Invalid pointer addition." This makes sense, since it is illegal to take two character pointers and add them together. What really needs to be done is to concatenate the strings that the character pointers refer to.

This is a case, like the `MyStruct` example in Listing 17.7, of the type not supporting the operations that the template needs to perform on it. Unlike the `MyStruct` example, however, it is not possible to add the `operator+()` semantic to character pointers, since character pointers are an integral type. Even if we could add the addition semantic, the equality operation for character pointers compares only the pointer addresses and not the strings pointed to. So, even if we could add character pointers, the template still wouldn't operate as expected.

The answer to this problem is to write a specialization that understands how to work with character pointers and provides the same sort of behaviors with a type-specific implementation. This specialization is detailed in Listing 17.13.

Listing 17.13. The AddEquals Function Template with a Character Pointer Specialization

```cpp
#include <iostream.h>
#include <stdio.h>
#include <string.h>

template <class T>
unsigned int AddEquals(T val1, T val2, T compare)
{
    return (val1 + val2) == compare;
}

// Specialization for character pointers
unsigned int AddEquals(char *val1,
                       char *val2,
                       char *compare)
{
    char Temp[512];
    sprintf(Temp, "%s%s", val1, val2);
    return !strcmp(Temp, compare);
}

// OK -- Uses template
cout << "Does 4 + 5 = 9? ";
cout << (AddEquals(4, 5, 9) ? "Yes" : "No") << "\n";

// OK -- Uses template
cout << "Does 7.0 + 5.5 = 12.0? ";
cout << (AddEquals(7.0, 5.5, 12.0) ? "Yes" : "No") << "\n";

// OK -- Uses specialization
cout << "Does \"Big \" + \"Dog\" = \"Big Dog\"? ";
cout << (AddEquals("Big ", "Dog", "Big Dog") ? "Yes" : "No")
     << "\n";
```

Apart from the obvious criticisms (the specialization uses a fixed-size character array that can be overflowed), this code will now work as expected with character strings. It is interesting to note that with regard to function templates, a specialization makes no direct reference to template syntax at all. Instead, the function is written the way it would normally be without regard to whether or not there may be a function template that tries to accomplish the same thing.

In a similar manner, we can specialize the ShowContents member function from Listing 17.9's RailroadCar template to support types that may not have an isA member function. Listing 17.14 shows how this is accomplished.

Listing 17.14. Specializing the RailroadCar Template's ShowContents Member Function for Integers

```
#include <iostream.h>
#include <cstring.h>

Definition of Cow class omitted...

Definition of Passenger class omitted...

Definition of RailroadCar template omitted...

// ShowContents specialization for integers
void RailroadCar<int>::ShowContents()
{
    cout << "Railroad car #" << CarNumber;
    cout << " is filled with an integer (" << *pContents;
    cout << ")\n";
}

void main()
{
    int IntegerCargo = 456;
    Cow Bessie;
    RailroadCar<int> CarNumber1(1, IntegerCargo);
    RailroadCar<Cow> CarNumber2(2, Bessie);

    // Calls the int specialization
    CarNumber1.ShowContents();

    // Calls the normal template member function that
    // relies on isA
    CarNumber2.ShowContents();
}
```

Unlike the `AddEquals` function template specialization, the `RailroadCar` class specialization for `int`s *does* use template notation, although a `"template <...>` line does not precede the member function definition. Apart from this slight discrepancy, the syntax and implementation is standard with respect to other member function definitions.

Static member functions can be specialized in the same manner as normal member functions. In addition, static member data can be specialized. A class that initialized a static class integer to one value for a particular generic type can initialize the same static integer to another value for a different generic type. For example, in the following class, the static integer `BufferSize` is normally initialized to 4K:

```
template <class T>
class NetworkCard {
    ...
    static int BufferSize;
    ...
};

// Initialize the static member data
template <class T>
int NetworkCard<T>::BufferSize = 4 * 1024; // 4 Kbytes
```

If, however, the program needs a larger buffer size when the generic type T is a character pointer, the application only needs to initialize a specialization.

```
// Initialize the static member data for char*
// specialization
int NetworkCard<char*>::BufferSize = 16 * 1024; // 16 Kbytes
```

If the program instantiates a NetworkCard template with a generic type of char*, the BufferSize will be 16K instead of the default 4K.

If all of this specialization flexibility still isn't enough to meet a program's demands, it is possible to specialize an entire class definition.

```
template <class T>
class MyClass {
    ...
    void DoSomething() { cout << "Apples\n"; }
    ...
};

// Class specialization for ints
class MyClass<int> {
    ...
    void DoSomething() { cout << "Oranges\n"; }
    ...
};

MyClass<char> ACharMyClass;
MyClass<int> AnIntMyClass;
```

In this case, the ACharMyClass object will use the normal class template. If the program calls ACharMyClass.DoSomething(), the object will write "Apples" to cout. The AnIntMyClass object, on the other hand, will use the specialization class for integers. If the program calls AnIntMyClass.DoSomething(), the object will write "Oranges" to cout.

Specializations provide enough flexibility to accommodate most of the situations where a template definition appears to be either incomplete or inadequate to support the types that you want to use.

Inheritance and Templates

Since the classes that are generated when a template is instantiated are simply normal C++ classes, it should come as no surprise that templates can be full and equal players in inheritance trees. Templates also can be mixed with regular classes in the inheritance tree, either as base classes or derived classes.

This being the case, it means that there are three potential types of inheritance that can involve templates. A template class can inherit from a normal C++ class, a normal C++ class can inherit from a template class, and a template class can inherit from another template class.

Inheriting a Template Class from a Non-Template Class

Take the case of a normal base class A, and a derived template `BTemplt`. Each of these definitions can be coded in the following manner:

```
// Base class definition
class A {
public:
    A(int aval) { Construct something for A }
    void FuncA() { Do something }
};

template <class T>
class BTemplt : public A {
public:
    BTemplt(int val1, int val2);
    ...
};

// Derived template definition
template <class T>
BTemplt<T>::BTemplt(int val1, int val2) :
                A(val2)
{
    Construct something for BTemplt
}
```

```
// Create an instance and use it
BTemplt<int> MyStuff(1, 5);
MyStuff.FuncA();
```

This type of inheritance is straightforward. In this example, no matter what type is passed into the class template, all of the public class A behaviors are available to MyStuff.

Inheriting a Non-Template Class from a Template Class

A little more interesting is the case of a template ATmplt and a derived normal class B.

```
// Base template definition
template <class T>
class ATemplt {
public:
    ATemplt(int aval);
    void FuncA() { Do something }
    ...
};

template <class T>
ATemplt<T>::ATemplt(int aval)
{
    Construct something for ATemplt
}

// Derived class definition
class B : public ATemplt<int> {
public:
    B(int val1, int val2);
};

B::B(int, int val2) : ATemplt<int>(val2)
{
    Construct something for B
}

// Create an instance and use it
B MyStuff(1, 5);
MyStuff.FuncA();
```

Again, most of this example is pretty straightforward. However, one item of note stands out. Since the class being inherited from the template is a normal class, the specific instance of ATemplt must be specified when declaring class B. In this case, the class B is not really derived from template ATemplt; it is derived from class ATemplt<int>.

Since the generic type for `ATemplt` is hard-coded into the definition of class `B`, users of class `B` do not have to use any sort of template-specific syntax. In fact, it should be possible for programmers to use objects of class `B` without ever being aware of the fact that some of its behaviors are implemented using a base template.

Inheriting a Template Class from Another Template Class

In the final case, a template class can be inherited from another template class. This allows the generic types of one template to be intrinsically linked to the generic types of its base class.

```
// Base template definition
template <class T>
class ATemplt {
public:
    ATemplt(int aval);
    void FuncA() { Do something }
    ...
};

template <class T>
ATemplt<T>::ATemplt(int aval)
{
    Construct something for ATemplt
}

// Derived template definition
template <class T>
class BTemplt : public ATemplt<T> {
public:
    BTemplt(int val1, int val2);
    ...
};

template <class T>
BTemplt<T>::BTemplt(int val1, int val2) :
        ATemplt<T>(val2)
{
    Construct something for BTemplt
}

// Create an instance and use it
BTemplt<int> MyStuff(1, 5);
MyStuff.FuncA();
```

When one template class is derived from another, as in this example, the base class is able to receive its generic types from the derived class, which in turn receives its generic types from a template instantiation.

It is not necessary for the derived template to actually use a generic type that is used only by a base template. It is required, however, that the derived template at least declare the generic type and pass it down to the base template. To demonstrate this, the following example depicts a derived class that requires two generic types, T1 and T2. The derived class, however, only uses T1 and accepts T2 only so that it can instantiate a base class that accepts a T2 generic type.

```cpp
// Base template definition
template <class T2>
class BaseTemplt {
public:
    BaseTemplt(int aval);
    void FuncA() { Do something }
    T2 AnInstanceOfT2;
};

template <class T2>
BaseTemplt<T2>::BaseTemplt(int aval)
{
    Construct something for BaseTemplt
}

// Derived template definition
template <class T1, class T2>
class DerivedTemplt : public BaseTemplt<T2> {
public:
    DerivedTemplt(int val1, int val2);
    T1 AnInstanceOfT1;
};

template <class T1, class T2>
DerivedTemplt<T1, T2>::DerivedTemplt(int val1, int val2) :
                    BaseTemplt<T2>(val2)
{
    Construct something for DerivedTemplt
}

// Create an instance and use it
DerivedTemplt<int, char*> MyStuff(1, 5);
MyStuff.FuncA();
```

Building Containers with Templates

A *container* is a programming construct designed to facilitate the storage, organization, and manipulation of objects. Programmers typically use containers throughout the run of a program to hold onto objects they know they will need later.

The range of container types can be mind-boggling. Data structures like stacks, queues, trees, lists, vectors, bags, sets, dictionaries, associative arrays, hash tables, and the like are all specialized examples of containers (with new types emerging from academia every year). Each of these different container types has compromises and tradeoffs related to performance, ease of use, implementation size, and so on.

C++ provides a myriad of different ways to create and implement container objects. Before templates came along, most of these implementations depended on inheritance to provide the flexibility needed to build containers capable of storing arbitrary data types. It should come as no surprise, however, that with the advent of templates, the creating of container classes has become easier and has removed a lot of the disadvantages of using an inheritance-based approach. It is for these reasons that Borland has completely replaced its inheritance-based container classes and replaced them with the template-based BIDS container classes.

Container Philosophy

To those unfamiliar with containers, a typical question is "Why?" What is it that can be accomplished with containers that cannot be accomplished with, say, a standard C++ array?

The big problem with arrays is that they need to be declared with a fixed size. Regardless of whether an array is declared on the stack or off the heap using new, its subscript limits the array from growing or shrinking. If a subscript is selected that is too small, the program runs the risk of overflowing the array. If a subscript is selected that is too large, the program is wasting memory and both efficiency and speed are compromised.

Containers are typically implemented as dynamic data structures, which means that memory for their use is allocated off the heap as it is needed. If an item is added to a container, memory for a reference or copy of that item (depending on implementation) is allocated with new. When items are removed from the container, this memory can be freed up for use by other areas of the program.

Dynamic memory allocation/deallocation is certainly slower than using statically declared data structures, but the flexibility gained from a dynamic container usually makes up for the performance penalty. Sophisticated containers can play games with preallocating a certain number of items and allocating new items only when they are needed. Of course, caching schemes like this suffer from some of the same problems as fixed-sized arrays if the initial number of created items is larger than will ever be used, but this is more of an implementation concern than a reason not to use containers.

A full-fledged treatment of containers is beyond the scope of this chapter (indeed it would very easy to write a long book just about implementing containers). Still, one of the most valuable uses of templates is in creating container classes. For this reason, the next few sections will walk through the creation of a simple list container.

The Inheritance-Based List Class

We'll start by building a linked-list class that relies on an inheritance approach to give you a feel for some of the reasons why a template approach is superior. The list class presented here is by no means the definitive word on how to build a linked-list container. In fact, this is a fairly low-powered implementation that has serious performance problems and only supports the most rudimentary of operations. However, our goal is to demonstrate how a template implementation is superior to an inheritance-based implementation and not to provide instruction on how to best build containers in general. In this capacity, the linked-list class presented here will serve our needs quite nicely.

The List Class Implementation

A linked list is a container made up of a list of nodes. Each of these nodes is connected to each other with link pointers in a linear fashion. The last node has a NULL link pointer.

Our linked-list implementation will rely on three different classes: the linked-list class, a node class, and a base object class. Listing 17.15 shows the code for a node class.

Listing 17.15. A Linked-List Node Class

```
class ListNode {
public:
    ListNode(int NewKey, BaseObject& NewObject);
    void SetNext(ListNode* pNewNext);
    BaseObject* GetContents() const;
    int GetKey() const;
    ListNode* GetNext() const;

private:
    ListNode* next;
    BaseObject* value;
    int key;
};

// Constructor
ListNode::ListNode(int NewKey, BaseObject& NewObject) :

        // Initialize member data
        next(NULL),
        value(&NewObject),
        key(NewKey)
{ }

// Public member functions
void ListNode::SetNext(ListNode* pNewNext)
{
    next = pNewNext;
}

BaseObject* ListNode::GetContents() const
{
    return value;
}

int ListNode::GetKey() const
{
    return key;
}

ListNode* ListNode::GetNext() const
{
    return next;
}
```

The `ListNode` is not a very sophisticated object, which is just fine.
Sophistication generally means larger objects and slower performance, which are not things that we want to sacrifice when building
containers.

A `ListNode` is composed of a key, a value, and a pointer to the next `ListNode` in the list. The key is an integer that will be provided by the application that inserts items into the list. This key will be used when the application wants to find things in the list or remove items from the list. The fact that the key is hard-coded as an integer is a potential problem, since an application may very well want to use a key other than a simple `int`. Our template implementation will take care of that, however.

The contents of the node are stored in the value pointer which is a pointer to an instance of our `BaseObject` class. Our `BaseObject` class is essentially an empty class definition and looks like this:

```
class BaseObject {
      // Empty
};
```

Since our linked-list class only knows how to store `BaseObject`s, a user needs to derive anything that is put into the list from the `BaseObject` class.

The final element of the linked list is the `List` class itself. It is presented in Listing 17.16.

Listing 17.16. The Main List Class

```
// Boolean type
typedef unsigned char Boolean;
const Boolean TRUE = 1;
const Boolean FALSE = 0;

class List {
public:
    List();
    ~List();
    Boolean Add(int NewKey, BaseObject& NewObject);
    Boolean Remove(int SearchKey);
    BaseObject* Find(int SearchKey) const;
    BaseObject* operator[](int OrderKey);
    int GetListSize() const;

private:
    ListNode* head;
    unsigned int NumItems;
};
```

continues

Listing 17.16. Continued

```
// Constructor
List::List() :

        // Initialize member data
        head(NULL),
        NumItems(0)
{ }

// Destructor
List::~List()
{
    // Delete all of the nodes in the list
    while (head) {
        ListNode* pTemp = head->GetNext();
        delete head;
        head = pTemp;
    }
}

// Public member functions
Boolean List::Add(int NewKey, BaseObject& NewObject)
{
    // Allocate memory for our new node
    ListNode* pNewNode = new ListNode(NewKey, NewObject);
    if (!pNewNode)
        return FALSE;

    // Insert the node into the list
    pNewNode->SetNext(head);
    head = pNewNode;
    NumItems++;
    return TRUE;
}

Boolean List::Remove(int SearchKey)
{
    ListNode* pCursor = head;

    // Is there a list?
    if (!pCursor)
        return FALSE;

    // Check the head first
    if (pCursor->GetKey() == SearchKey) {
        head = pCursor->GetNext();
        delete pCursor;
        NumItems--;
        return TRUE;
    }

    // Scan the list
    while (pCursor->GetNext()) {
        if (pCursor->GetNext()->GetKey() == SearchKey) {
```

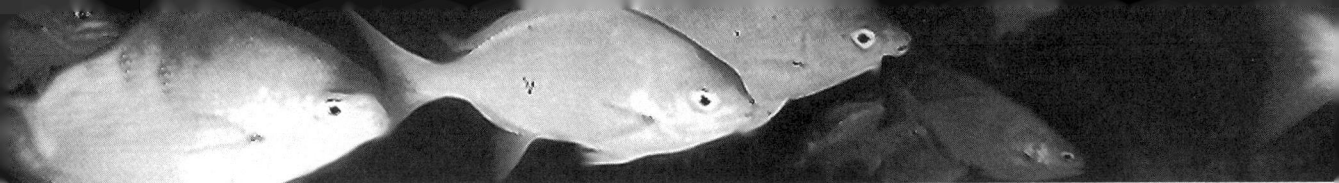

```
                      ListNode* pTemp = pCursor->GetNext();
                      pCursor->SetNext(pTemp->GetNext());
                      delete pTemp;
                      NumItems--;
                      return TRUE;
                 }
            }
            return FALSE;
      }

      BaseObject* List::Find(int SearchKey) const
      {
            ListNode* pCursor = head;
            while (pCursor) {
                 if (pCursor->GetKey() == SearchKey)
                      return pCursor->GetContents();
                 else
                      pCursor = pCursor->GetNext();
            }
            return NULL;
      }

      int List::GetListSize() const
      {
            return NumItems;
      }

      // Operators
      BaseObject* List::operator[](int OrderKey)
      {
            ListNode* pCursor = head;
            int Count = 1;
            while (pCursor) {
                 if (Count++ == OrderKey)
                      return pCursor->GetContents();
                 pCursor = pCursor->GetNext();
            }
            return NULL;
      }
```

The List class is a little more exciting because there are so many things
going on. As indicated by the class declaration, this class supports the
insertion and deletion of nodes, the searching for a node based on its
key, querying the list size, and retrieving a node based on its order in
the list (as opposed to by its kcy).

The List constructor does nothing but initialize some local member
data. The destructor moves through the list and deletes any nodes
remaining in the list.

The Add method allocates storage for a new ListNode object and sets the appropriate fields in the object through the ListNode constructor. The new node is then placed at the head of the list.

The Remove method first checks to make sure that there is at least one node in the list, and if there is, it then checks to see if the list has only one node. If there is only one node (the head), this node is removed separately. Otherwise, a cursor moves through the list, looking one node ahead of its current position. If the List finds the node that needs to be removed, the next pointer of the current node is set equal to the next pointer of the next node (try saying that 10 times fast). The List then removes the appropriate node using the delete operator.

The Find method simply moves through the list until it finds a ListNode whose key is equal to the search key. When it does, it returns the ListNode's value pointer back to the calling application.

The overloaded operator[] returns the value pointer of the Nth ListNode in the list. Note that this operation is independent of any node's key value. This means that MyList.Find(5) is not necessarily the same node as MyList[5]. The operator[] accomplishes this by moving through the list and maintaining a count of its current position. When the appropriate node is reached, its value pointer is returned back to the calling application.

To show the list in action, Listing 17.17 shows a program that adds three items to a list and then removes them one at a time.

Listing 17.17. Using the Inheritance-Based List

```
struct IntClass : public BaseObject {
    IntClass(int NewInt) { theInt = NewInt; }
    int theInt;
};

void ShowList(List& theList)
{
    int Loop;
    cout << "The list: ( ";
    for (Loop = 0; Loop < theList.GetListSize(); Loop++) {
        if (Loop) cout << ", ";
```

```
            IntClass* pIntClass = (IntClass*) theList[Loop+1];
            cout << pIntClass->theInt;
        }
        cout << " )\n";
    }

    void main()
    {
        List theList;
        IntClass Int1(34), Int2(22), Int3(675);

        theList.Add(1, Int1);
        theList.Add(2, Int2);
        theList.Add(3, Int3);
        ShowList(theList);
        theList.Remove(2);
        ShowList(theList);
        theList.Remove(1);
        ShowList(theList);
        theList.Remove(3);
        ShowList(theList);
    }
```

Problems with the List Class

The `List` class is a complete and usable implementation of a linked list, but it has some serious flaws. Although none of these flaws are fatal, they certainly make the `List` less desirable to use.

The biggest problem with this implementation is that everything that is placed into the list has to be derived from the `BaseObject` class. Many programmers will not want to pick up the additional overhead of inheriting from `BaseObject`, even though in its current form the class does nothing. In reality, though, a class like `BaseObject` would probably implement a whole range of behaviors that are common to an entire object inheritance tree. This could include things like a virtual `isA` method that returns the name of the class, support to traps errors, and the like.

There also are problems with merging different code bases together. If a programmer needs to integrate her code with a third-party class library, it becomes virtually impossible to place any of the third-party objects into this `List` class.

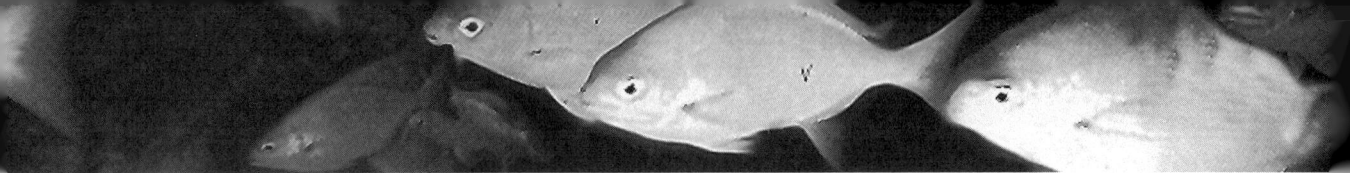

Finally, this sort of inheritance dependency makes it impossible to store integral types and simple standard user-defined classes in the `List` without the help of a wrapper class. Listing 17.17 demonstrates the sort of hoops that have to be jumped through just to store a series of integers. If a program wanted to store a wide variety of integral types in a `List`, each type would have to be wrapped in a class that was derived from `BaseObject`.

Of course, one alternative is to have our `ListNode` value pointer simply be a void pointer. But this is C++, not the dark and dangerous world of C! Using a void value pointer, the `List` sacrifices any sort of type checking and requires the application to rely on intricate casting. With a void pointer implementation, there really is no way to be completely sure that the item returned from `Find` or `operator[]` is what you expect it to be. If a void pointer is cast to a particular object type, and the pointer doesn't really point to an instance of that object, a call to one of that object class's methods is almost certain to lead to a horrible program (or worse, system) crash.

As if things weren't bad enough, this `List` class requires that all of the application keys be integers. This is a pretty arbitrary decision, considering that some applications are sure to want to use strings, while others will want to use user-defined types.

The answer to all of these problems is to use a template-based container.

A Better Way with Templates

The great thing about porting the inheritance-based `List` class over to templates is that none of the core logic has to change. The code that actually performs operations remains almost completely intact, while only the definitions and declarations change. Even better, ugly constructs like `BaseObject` and `IntClass` disappear completely.

Listing 17.18 shows the entire list template and a program that uses it in a manner similar to Listing 17.17. The name has been changed to `ListT` to reflect the fact that the list has been implemented using templates.

Listing 17.18. The ListT Template

```cpp
#include <iostream.h>
#include <cstring.h>

// Boolean
typedef unsigned char Boolean;
const Boolean TRUE = 1;
const Boolean FALSE = 0;


// LIST NODE
template <class KeyType, class ValType>
class ListNodeT {
public:
    ListNodeT(KeyType NewKey, ValType& NewObject);
    void SetNext(ListNodeT* pNewNext);
    ValType* GetContents() const;
    KeyType GetKey() const;
    ListNodeT* GetNext() const;

private:
    ListNodeT* next;
    ValType* value;
    KeyType key;
};

// Constructor
template <class KeyType, class ValType>
ListNodeT<KeyType, ValType>::ListNodeT(KeyType  NewKey,
                                       ValType& NewObject) :

        // Initialize member data
        next(NULL),
        value(&NewObject),
        key(NewKey)
{ }

// Public member functions
template <class KeyType, class ValType>
void
ListNodeT<KeyType, ValType>::SetNext(ListNodeT* pNewNext)
{
    next = pNewNext;
}

template <class KeyType, class ValType>
ValType* ListNodeT<KeyType, ValType>::GetContents() const
{
    return value;
}

template <class KeyType, class ValType>
KeyType ListNodeT<KeyType, ValType>::GetKey() const
```

continues

Listing 17.18. Continued

```
{
    return key;
}

template <class KeyType, class ValType>
ListNodeT<KeyType, ValType>*
ListNodeT<KeyType, ValType>::GetNext() const
{
    return next;
}


// LIST
template <class KeyType, class ValType>
class ListT {
public:
    ListT(),
    ~ListT();
    Boolean Add(KeyType NewKey, ValType& NewObject);
    Boolean Remove(KeyType SearchKey);
    ValType* Find(KeyType SearchKey) const;
    ValType* operator[](int Position);
    int GetListSize() const;

private:
    ListNodeT<KeyType, ValType>* head;
    unsigned int NumItems;
};

// Constructor
template <class KeyType, class ValType>
ListT<KeyType, ValType>::ListT() :

        // Initialize member data
        head(NULL),
        NumItems(0)
{ }

// Destructor
template <class KeyType, class ValType>
ListT<KeyType, ValType>::~ListT()
{
    // Delete all of the nodes in the list
    while (head) {
        ListNodeT<KeyType, ValType>* pTemp =
                                head->GetNext();
        delete head;
        head = pTemp;
    }
}

// Public member functions
template <class KeyType, class ValType>
```

```
Boolean ListT<KeyType, ValType>::Add(KeyType  NewKey,
                                     ValType& NewObject)
{
     // Allocate memory for our new node
     ListNodeT<KeyType, ValType>* pNewNode =
             new ListNodeT<KeyType, ValType>(NewKey,
                                             NewObject);
     if (!pNewNode)
          return FALSE;

     // Insert the node into the list
     pNewNode->SetNext(head);
     head = pNewNode;
     NumItems++;
     return TRUE;
}

template <class KeyType, class ValType>
Boolean ListT<KeyType, ValType>::Remove(KeyType SearchKey)
{
     ListNodeT<KeyType, ValType>* pCursor = head;

     // Is there a list?
     if (!pCursor)
          return FALSE;

     // Check the head first
     if (pCursor->GetKey() == SearchKey) {
          head = pCursor->GetNext();
          delete pCursor;
          NumItems-;
          return TRUE;
     }

     // Scan the list
     while (pCursor->GetNext()) {
          if (pCursor->GetNext()->GetKey() == SearchKey) {
               ListNodeT<KeyType, ValType>* pTemp =
                                   pCursor->GetNext();
               pCursor->SetNext(pTemp->GetNext());
               delete pTemp;
               NumItems-;
               return TRUE;
          }
     }
     return FALSE;
}

template <class KeyType, class ValType>
ValType*
ListT<KeyType, ValType>::Find(KeyType SearchKey) const
{
     ListNodeT<KeyType, ValType>* pCursor = head;
     while (pCursor) {
          if (pCursor->GetKey() == SearchKey)
```

continues

Building Containers with Templates   **773**

Listing 17.18. Continued

```
                        return pCursor->GetContents();
               else
                        pCursor = pCursor->GetNext();
        }
        return NULL;
}


template <class KeyType, class ValType>
int ListT<KeyType, ValType>::GetListSize() const
{
        return NumItems;
}


// Operators
template <class KeyType, class ValType>
ValType* ListT<KeyType, ValType>::operator[](int Position)
{
        ListNodeT<KeyType, ValType>* pCursor = head;
        int Count = 1;
        while (pCursor) {
                if (Count++ == Position)
                        return pCursor->GetContents();
                pCursor = pCursor->GetNext();
        }
        return NULL;
}


// Now use it all
template <class T>
void ShowList(T& theList)
{
        int Loop;
        cout << "The list: ( ";
        for (Loop = 0; Loop < theList.GetListSize(); Loop++) {
            if (Loop) cout << ", ";
            cout << *theList[Loop+1];
        }
        cout << " )\n";
}


void main()
{
        int Int1 = 34, Int2 = 22, Int3 = 675;
        ListT<int, int>  theIntList;
        theIntList.Add(1, Int1);
        theIntList.Add(2, Int2);
        theIntList.Add(3, Int3);
        ShowList(theIntList);
        theIntList.Remove(2);
        ShowList(theIntList);
        theIntList.Remove(1);
```

```
    ShowList(theIntList);
    theIntList.Remove(3);
    ShowList(theIntList);

    string Str1("Here we are"), Str2("There you go"),
        Str3("What's up?");
    ListT<string, string> theStrList;
    theStrList.Add("Bob quote", Str1);
    theStrList.Add("Frank quote", Str2);
    theStrList.Add("Sally quote", Str3);
    ShowList(theStrList);
    theStrList.Remove("Frank quote");
    ShowList(theStrList);
    theStrList.Remove("Bob quote");
    ShowList(theStrList);
    theStrList.Remove("Sally quote");
    ShowList(theStrList);
}
```

This version of our linked list provides the same capabilities, without the liabilities of the inheritance-based list. Since both the types of the key and the value are filled in by the application, this template allows for the creation of containers that can hold anything, and that are indexed on almost any type of value.

One potential problem is that the key type has to support `operator==()`. If you want to use the `ListT` template with a key type that doesn't have an `operator==()`, you will have to either add one, or specialize `ListT::Remove`, `ListT::Find`, and `ListT::operator[]` to support the desired type. Still, the level of key flexibility in `ListT` compared to the plain `List` class is quite dramatic.

Since `ListT` no longer relies on `BaseObject`, any type can be stored in a `ListT` class. This includes all of the integral types and standard user-defined types that come with the Borland class libraries (e.g., `string`, `TTime`, `TDate`, `TFile`, `TThread`). Even better, integrating third-party objects with `ListT` is trivial, since there are no inherent dependencies on the inheritance tree. All of this has been accomplished without compromising the built-in C++ type-checking mechanisms.

Template Compiler Switches

Most of the discussion of templates has so far focused on the broader issues of philosophy of use, syntax, and implementation subtleties. However, from a purely pragmatic standpoint, you will eventually have to sit down at the computer and write the code that will implement and use templates. Whether you are using the integrated development environment (IDE) or the command-line compiler, whether you are developing code for DOS, 16-bit Windows, Win32s, or Win32, and whether your operating environment is Windows or Windows NT, eventually you will have to interact with the template options in a settings notebook or with compiler options from a makefile.

Figure 17.3 shows the notebook settings in the IDE that you will need to modify in order to effectively use the Borland C++ 4.0 template features. If you plan on using the IDE as your primary development environment, pay special attention to this figure as the different template options are discussed in the following sections.

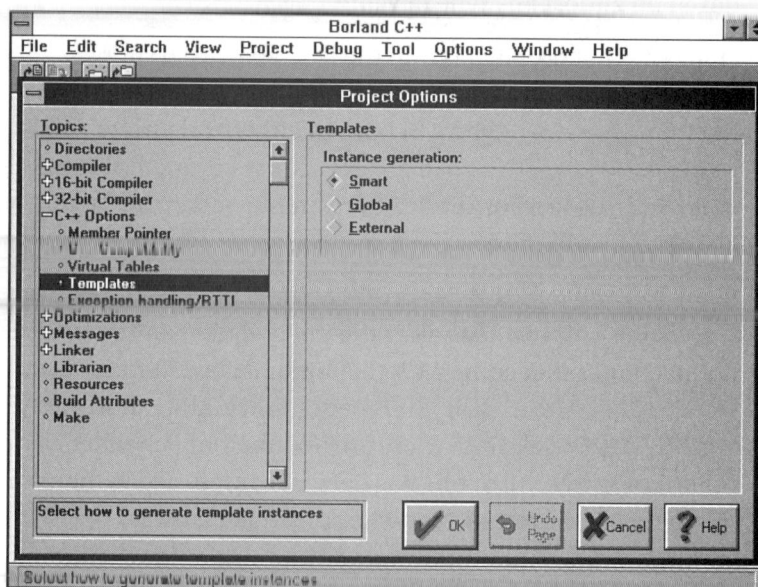

Fig. 17.3. The IDE notebook settings page for template options.

Smart Templates

The default template implementation used by the Borland compiler is called *smart templates*. If you build your programs using makefiles and you want to use smart templates, the command-line compiler switch to activate smart templates is `-Jg`. This option is the default, however, so you do not need to explicitly include it in your makefile if you don't want to.

When using smart templates, the compiler scans each source module for template instantiations and generates class instances as needed. These classes are then placed in the object file for that module. At link time, all of the object files are combined and any duplicate class instantiations are discarded.

There are a number of advantages and disadvantages to using templates in this manner. The best aspect of this strategy is that it requires the lowest maintenance. The compiler does all the work of generating templates as needed and sorting through duplicates at link time. In fact, the programmer doesn't need to be concerned with tracking template instantiations at all.

The biggest problem with smart templates is that, since every source file that uses templates may need to generate a template class, the entire template definition needs to be compiled in with every module. This has two profound implications.

First, this suggests that templates cannot be segregated into separate template modules. Instead, the entire template needs to be defined in an `include` file that is then read into any source file that may need to use that template.

Second, the fact that all of the templates are defined in `include` files suggests that your entire template is a public entity. If your template utilizes some amazing and proprietary computing algorithm, every nuance of its implementation will be open to public scrutiny. Even if your template doesn't contain any earth-shattering code, the fact remains that every aspect of the template will be viewable by anyone who has access to the appropriate header file. If you don't believe it,

look in your compiler's \BC4\INCLUDE\CLASSLIB directory. All of the template implementations for the Borland BIDS class library are contained in .H files!

The painful truth of the matter is that if you don't want users of your templates to see how you get things done, you can't use smart templates.

Global and External Templates

The alternative to smart templates is to use a combination of global and external templates. If you build your programs using makefiles and you want to compile a module using global or external templates, the command-line compiler switches are -Jgd and -Jgx, respectively.

Global templates allow you to place template instantiations into a source module and compile them together. Duplicate instantiations are not resolved, so you need to be careful that a given instantiation does not appear more than once, or the linker will complain with a long litany of duplicate symbol warning messages.

Modules compiled with the global templates option are used in conjunction with modules compiled with the external template option. When source code is compiled using external templates, every instantiation is simply recorded as a reference to an external class definition. The compiler does not generate a new class, even if the instantiation is the first of that type that the compiler has encountered.

At link time, the linker takes all of the references to class templates from the modules compiled with the external template option and tries to match those references with template instantiations contained in modules compiled with the global templates option.

This approach has the inverse advantages and disadvantages of smart templates. Clearly, this method of template compilation requires a lot more effort in managing program template use. Specific template instantiations need to be carefully tracked and included in the globally

compiled modules. If, at some later time, a source module is changed to use a new instantiation of an existing template, the new instantiation needs to be added to a globally compiled module. This is a tedious and error prone process.

Additionally, since the provider of the template needs to anticipate all of the template instantiations that will be required by a program, this technique becomes unrealistic for programmers planning on providing shrink-wrapped class libraries. In order to meet every user's potential demands, the programmer would need to include an object module that contained instantiations for every and all types. This is clearly impossible, especially if the templates are to interact with user-defined object types.

Class library developers who depend on templates are caught between a rock and a hard place. Most commercial developers will want to keep their source code hidden and proprietary, which rules out using smart templates. However, they clearly cannot use global/external templates because they cannot anticipate or limit the potential template instantiation demand. Most programmers facing this dilemma will either have to bite the bullet and use the smart templates, or shy away from using templates all together.

The upside is that the source code modules that use the templates only have to have access to the template declaration, as opposed to the entire template definition. This means that template header files can get away with containing only declarations, while the actual implementation of the templates can be hidden away in those modules that are compiled using the global templates option. Proprietary algorithms and programming techniques used in the implementation of the templates can be safely hidden from prying eyes.

As a demonstration of how this rather cumbersome task is accomplished, Listing 17.19 shows how the RailroadCar example (refer to Listing 17.9) can be modified to use global and external templates.

Listing 17.19. The RailroadCar Example Using Global and External Templates

```
// TEMPLTS.H
// The RailroadCar class template
template <class T>
class RailroadCar {
    Template definition omitted...
};


// CONTENTS.H
#include <cstring.h>

// Things to put in a RailroadCar
class Cow {
    Class definition omitted...
},
class Passenger {
    Class definition omitted...
};


// TEMPLTS.CPP — Compile with global templates (-Jgd)
#include <iostreams.h>
#include "templts.h"
#include "contents.h"

// Constructor
template <class T>
RailroadCar<T>::RailroadCar(int NewCarNumber,
                              T&  NewContents)
{ ... }

// Destructor
template <class T>
RailroadCar<T>::~RailroadCar()
{ ... }

// Public member functions
template <class T>
void RailroadCar<T>::ShowContents()
{ ... }

template <class T>
T* RailroadCar<T>::Unload()
{ ... }

// Force generation of our template instances
Cow AnUnusedCow;
RailroadCar<Cow> AnUnusedCowCar(1, AnUnusedCow);
Passenger AnUnusedPassenger((char*) NULL);
RailroadCar<Passenger> AnUnusedPassengerCar(1, AnUnusedPassenger);
```

```
// LIST19.CPP -- Compile with external templates (-Jgx)
#include <iostream.h>
#include "templts.h"
#include "contents.h"

void main()
{
      // At Station 1
      Cow ACow;
      Passenger APassenger("Monty");

      RailroadCar<Cow> CarNumber1(1, ACow);
      RailroadCar<Passenger> CarNumber2(2, APassenger);

      CarNumber1.ShowContents();
      CarNumber2.ShowContents();

      // Go to Station 2...
      cout << "\n..Choo..Choo..\n\n";

      // At Station 2
      Cow* AtStation2Cow = CarNumber1.Unload();
      Passenger* AtStation2Passenger =
                        CarNumber2.Unload();

      cout << "How was the trip, ";
      cout << AtStation2Passenger->GetName() << "?";
      cout << "  " << AtStation2Passenger->Complain();
      cout << "\n";
      cout << AtStation2Cow->Moo() << "\n";
}
```

Perhaps the most noteworthy part of this listing is the instantiations of
the dummy templates in TEMPLTS.CPP. These declarations ensure
that the appropriate template classes get generated for use by the
LIST19.CPP source file.

Notice that in Listing 17.19, the classes that represent items placed into
railroad cars have to be separated into a header file. This is because the
dummy instantiations that are used in TEMPLTS.CPP rely on these
classes.

If you are starting to believe that using global/external template generation is a painful process that is probably not worth the effort, you
are not alone. Most users of Borland templates will probably choose to
use smart templates.

Using Specializations with Smart Templates

A unique situation arises when you try to add a specialization to a template that is contained in a header file and used in modules that are compiled with the smart template option. Remember that in Listing 17.3, we took the `AddEquals` template and added a specialization for character pointers. If you were to place the template and its specialization in a header file and include the header file in every module that needs the template, all your code would compile without problems.

Unfortunately, at link time (and assuming that the template header file is included in at least two modules), the linker complains with the following message: `AddEquals(char far*,char far*,char far*)` defined in module FILE1.CPP and is duplicated in module FILE2.CPP. Because all the code for the specialization is contained in the header file, the specialization gets duplicated in every module. Function template specializations, however, really aren't any different from regular old C++ functions. This means that every source file that includes the template header file gets its own identical copy of the specialization, and the linker ends up choking when it finds multiple copies of a function with exactly the same argument signatures.

Fine, you might say. Why not simply replace the specialization with a prototype and include the actual code for the specialization in another file? This would make sense if it weren't for one big problem: It doesn't work.

The Borland 4.0 compiler instead ignores our specialization prototype and tries to create a template instance for `AddEquals` where T is `char*`. This doesn't work, of course; the whole reason we wrote a specialization in the first place was because the function template doesn't work for `char*`!

The trick to getting this to work is to use a combination of smart and global/external templates. This is done by wrapping the specialization prototype in pragma definitions that turn external templates on and then turn smart templates back on after the specialization prototype. This is depicted in Listing 17.20. Don't forget to actually create and link with a module that contains the specialization code.

Listing 17.20. Template Header File for AddEquals with char* Specialization

```
// ADDEQ.H -- Compile modules that use this header file
//            with smart templates (-Jg)

template <class T>
unsigned int AddEquals(T val1, T val2, T compare)
{
    return (val1 + val2) == compare;
}

// Turn on external templates
#pragma option -Jgx

// Specialization prototype
unsigned int AddEquals(char*, char*, char*);

// Turn back on smart templates
#pragma option -Jg
```

With this header file, when the compiler encounters a situation in which it normally would instantiate a version of `AddEquals` that uses `char*`, it now understands that this code is already available but in another module.

Using Templates in Dynamic Link Libraries

Placing templates into a Windows or Windows NT dynamic link library (DLL) is a good news/bad news scenario. The good news is that yes, it can be done. The bad news is that in order to do it one has to use global/external template generation. This will probably be unacceptable for many users since the template instantiations stored in the DLL will have to be predetermined by the template programmer.

The entire process is actually quite straightforward and is virtually identical to Listing 17.15. If we were to place the `RailroadCar` template into a DLL, the TEMPLT.CPP file would be the only source file to actually appear in the library. The client program, LIST19.CPP, would have to link with an import library generated from the DLL, but the LIST19.CPP source code would not have to change at all. In fact, the

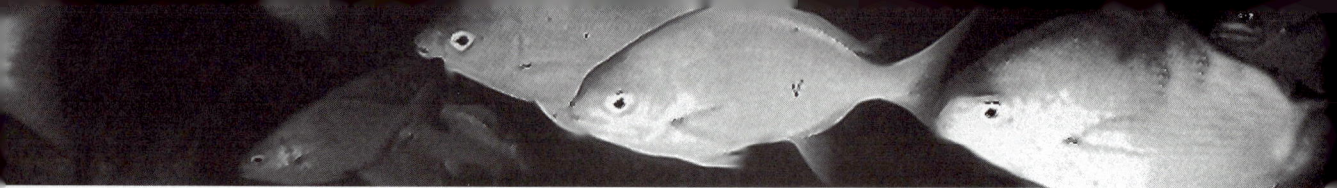

only source code change would have to be made to TEMPLT.H, where the declaration of the template class would need to be changed from

```
template <class T>
class RailroadCar {
    Template definition omitted...
};
```

to

```
template <class T>
class _export RailroadCar {
    Template definition omitted...
};
```

The _export statement added to the declaration ensures that the template classes generated and placed in the DLL will be made publicly available to client programs that need to use them.

From Here...

This chapter covered a lot of ground and introduced a good number of new concepts. The following chapters will aid you in your further explorations and experimentations with C++ templates:

➤ An excellent example of template programming is shipped with the Borland compiler. The BIDS container classes are exclusively template based and provide a rich environment for learning the more subtle and advanced aspects of template programming. The source code is well documented and provides plenty of room for exploration.

➤ Bjarne Stroustrup laid the foundation for the templates' language extension in his book *The C++ Programming Language* (Addison-Wesley, 1992) and in his collaboration with Margaret A. Ellis on the *Annotated C++ Reference Manual* (Addison-Wesley, 1990). Although they are not the easiest books to get through, both are required reading for programmers who want to become proficient in template programming.

➤ In James Coplien's book *Advanced C++ Programming Styles and Idioms* (Addison-Wesley, 1992), the author presents a variety of advanced programming techniques. Many of these concepts are template based and give the reader an excellent feel for some of the advanced capabilities of this language extension. Be fore-warned, however, that this book is advanced and not everything that Coplien espouses is considered good programming style or C++ gospel.

Exception Handling

by John M. Dlugosz

Exception handling (EH) is a new feature of C++, and Borland C++ supports it as of version 4.0. EH is more than just a language feature—it is a major cornerstone of the philosophy behind C++, which is finally available to us.

EH is necessary to C++ because of how constructors work. A constructor is automatically called to create objects. There is no way a constructor can fail. The constructor must construct a valid object. If something does go wrong during a constructor, what can be done in pre-EH compilers? The most common work-around is to construct the object to an error state. The code which uses the object checks to make sure construction was successful before using it. Extreme care must be taken, as constructors automatically construct subobjects, and nothing can be done in pre-EH compilers to abort the process.

Exception handling is the proper mechanism for making constructors fail. If an exception is thrown during a complex object's construction process, it automatically backs out, destructing those parts that had been constructed, and canceling the rest.

Besides its use in constructors, EH is the error handling mechanism of choice. It is a powerful mechanism that makes traditional forms of coping with errors obsolete.

A First Look

Consider a simple program that reads an input file, does some processing, and writes an output file. The top level of such a program might look something like this:

Listing 18.1.

```
int main (int argc, char* argv[])
{
file infile (argv[1]);
file outfile (argv[2]);
string buffer;
while (!infile.eof()) {
   infile.read(buffer);
   process (buffer);
   outfile.write (buffer);
   }
return 0;   //normal exit
}
```

A few notes about the hypothetical program: class `file` is a hypothetical class which does simple file IO; `string` is a string class; `process` is a function which is not shown in this excerpt.

Even though this program is simple and easy to read, it only works in an ideal world. In reality, almost every statement needs some kind of explicit error checking. The files might not open. The read-and-write operations might fail. The `process()` function might encounter an error, due to bad input data.

A more realistic function might look like this:

Listing 18.2.

```
int main (int argc, char* argv[])
{
file infile (argv[1]);
if (!infile.ok()) {
   cout << "error opening input file " << argv[1] << endl;
   return 1;   //abnormal exit
   }
file outfile (argv[2]);
if (!outfile.ok()) {
   cout << "error opening output file " << argv[2] << endl;
   return 1;
   }
string buffer;
while (!infile.eof()) {
   if (!infile.read(buffer)) {
      cout << "error reading from infile\n";
      return 2;
      }
   int errcode= process (buffer);
   if (errcode != 0) {
      diagnose_error (errcode);
      return 2;
      }
   if (!outfile.write (buffer)) {
      cout << "error writing to outfile\n";
      return 2;
      }
   }
return 0;   //normal exit
}
```

This function is much longer and more difficult to understand. The first listing was clean and succinct. Reading it, you clearly see the steps to be performed. The second listing is long and wordy. The actual algorithm is completely buried in the error checking code. The steps to perform are difficult to discern. It is as if the main point of the function is to do a bunch of testing; and, of secondary importance, is to process the file.

Listing 18.2 shows three styles of error checking.

```
file infile (argv[1]);
if (!infile.ok()) {...
```

A test is made on the object, using the class's preprogrammed error function `ok()`, to see if the constructor was successful.

```
if (!infile.read(buffer)) {...
```

Here, the `read(buffer)` call returns True or False, depending upon whether or not it was successful.

```
int errcode= process (buffer);
if (errcode != 0) {
```

Here, the call to `process(buffer)` returns an error code. Zero means no error, and nonzero values indicate different errors.

One problem with using an error flag for a return value is that the user of the function has to know what the success condition is. One function is false (zero) on failure. Another is zero on success. Getting these mixed up can really ruin your day.

Second, both functions are using the return value of the function to indicate an error code. This is fine for a function that has nothing better to return, but what if the function requires a meaningful return value? There are several ways to go.

You can add a special error value to the normal domain. For example, a function returns either the number of words counted normally, or -1 for an error.

You can employ a different mechanism to return an error code. Either pass in the error code variable as a reference parameter, or reverse them, pass the normal return value by reference, and return the error code. Either way, the function is now returning two distinctly different logical values to the caller.

You can use a variable, not mentioned in the function call, to indicate an error. This is convenient for member functions, as the error flag can be another member.

Adding a special error value to the domain means that you have to remember what to test for. Adding secondary return values makes the function more awkward to use. In all cases, you have to remember to test for errors, and do the correct test. Clearly, the lessons in Chapter 7,

"Debugging Tips and Tricks," show you that a better design would use antibugging techniques in place of the user of the function having to test for errors. That way he can't accidentally leave it out or get it wrong.

Exception handling is such a mechanism. The program, written to use EH, would look something like this (the original program's content is bold faced):

Listing 18.3.

```
int main (int argc, char* argv[])
{
try {
   file infile (argv[1]);
   file outfile (argv[2]);
   string buffer;
   while (!infile.eof()) {
      infile.read(buffer);
      process (buffer);
      outfile.write (buffer);
      }
   return 0;   //normal exit
   }
catch (xmsg& error) {
   cout << error.why() << endl;
   return 2;
   }
}
```

The code added to support error checking is much smaller. One construct serves the entire function. More important, it is not mixed in with the statements describing the main work of the function. The original clean implementation is uninterrupted. It also is much more resistant to misuse. More on that later.

Here, the `try` keyword introduces the block of code to run in the normal case. The `catch` keyword introduces the block of code to be run in an exceptional case. If an error occurs anywhere in the `try` block, execution is transferred to the `catch` block. `xmsg` is a standard class, and `why()` is a function that returns the text of the error message.

Syntax of a try Block

According to the official grammar, the syntax is:

```
try-block:       try compound-statement handler-seq
handler-seq:        handler handler-seq_opt
handler:       catch ( exception-declaration ) compound-statement
exception-declaration:
    type-specifier-seq declarator
    type-specifier-seq abstract-declarator
    type-specifier-seq
    ...
```

This means that the `try` keyword is followed by a compound statement; the braces are required. You can't just have a single unbracketed statement after the `try`, as you can with `if` and `while`.

The try block must be immediately followed by one or more catch handlers. Each catch handler is the keyword `catch` followed by a parameter list containing one parameter or ellipsis (...), followed by a compound statement.

Semantics of a try Block

Now that you can write try blocks, catch handlers, and throw expressions, what does it all mean, and what does it do for you?

A *try block* establishes protection for the enclosed block of statements. The *catch handler* holds code to run if something within that try block goes wrong. The *throw expression* is how you signal that something has gone wrong.

The meaning of this is that any error occurring within the scope of the try block (signaled by using a `throw` expression) will cause execution to be transferred to one of the catch handlers. The catch handlers take a parameter. This is how information about the error is transmitted from the throw point to the catch point.

The general idea may be best explained with an example.

```
void foo (int x)
{
if (x < 0)  throw 4;
//... rest of function goes here
```

```
    }
void bar()
{
try {
    int x= get_input_from_user();
    foo(x);
    cout << "process complete." << endl;
    }
catch (int error) {
    cout << "an error occured. error code " << error << endl;
    }
catch (const char* error) {
    cout << "an error occured.  " << error << endl;
    }
}
```

In this example, function `foo()` throws the number 4. The `try` block in `bar()` is triggered because a throw occurred while it is active. Note the dynamic nature of the try/throw mechanism: Any throw that occurs will search back through the callers for the first active try block. The matching is done at runtime, based on the calling sequence, *not* at compile time, based on scope. The search process is described in more detail in the next section.

The throw expression will throw some value, which will be information about the error. Anything can be thrown. The thrown value is bound to the parameter in the catch handler. This is described in greater detail in the upcoming section on "Throw and Catch Arguments."

The Search for a Matching Catch

When you throw something, the runtime system looks for a matching catch by using dynamic scoping. This is important to understand, since it is different from the way scope normally works in C++. As the runtime system searches, it checks each catch handler's parameter definition against the type of thing being thrown and stops at the first one that is found to be suitable.

Let's take a closer look at the dynamic scoping. A `throw` will first check for an enclosing `try` block.

```
void test_function()
{
try {
```

```
    do_something();
    throw 4;
    do_somethingelse();
    }
catch (int x) {
    cout << "I caught a " << x << endl;
    }
cout << "this is after the try block\n";
    }
```

In the above example, the `throw 4` will jump to the catch that follows. The call to `do_somethingelse()` will never be done. Here, the `throw` behaves as an exotic form of `goto`.

But, the try block doesn't just extend to the statement within it. The protection of the `try` extends to the called functions, as well. More typically, we will have this situation:

```
void foo()
{
throw 4;
}
void test_function()
{
try {
    do_something();
    foo();
    do_somethingelse();
    }
catch (int x) {
    cout << "I caught a " << x << endl;
    }
cout << "this is after the try block\n";
    }
```

This works the same way, even though the exception is thrown from a called function and is not actually in the lexical scope of the try block.

The interesting thing to note here is that `foo()` may be called from many places. There is no magic compile-time tie between `foo()` and `test_function()`. Instead, when the throw is made, the runtime system looks at the actual caller to locate catch blocks. This is what is meant by *dynamically scoped.*

Whenever the program flow enters a try block, the system notes that a try block was entered. When the block is exited, the system likewise has to pop the record. So when a `throw` takes place, the system checks its list

of enclosing `try`'s. You can see that it doesn't matter if the enclosing `try` block is in a calling function or immediately surrounding the `throw`. It tracks "enclosing" at runtime.

When a `throw` is made, the system checks the first enclosing `try` and sees if it has a suitable `catch` to match the object being thrown. If a suitable `catch` is found, execution is transferred to it. If not, the next outer `try` is checked. This progresses until there are no more enclosing `try` blocks, at which time the program is aborted.

Unwinding the Stack

When an exception causes execution to be transferred to the catch handler, the block containing the `throw` is exited. This implies that destructors are called. Listing 18.4 is a simple case that demonstrates this:

Listing 18.4. Stack Unwinding Spy

```
#include <iostream.h>

class scope_spy {
   const char* s;
public:
   scope_spy (const char* s);
   ~scope spy();
   };
scope spy::scope spy (const char* s)
: s(s)
{
cout << "constructing " << s << endl;
}
scope_spy::~scope_spy()
{
cout << "destructing " << s << endl;
}
// the above class is generally useful for watching
// constructor and destructor behavior.
void testfunc1 (int choice)
{
cout << "entering testfunc1()\n";
scope_spy spy1 ("spy 1 - main body of function");
try {
   scope_spy spy2 ("spy 2 - inside try block");
   if (choice == 1) throw 4;
   scope_spy spy3 ("spy 3 - also inside try block");
   }
```

continues

Listing 18.4. Continued

```
catch (int dummy) {
    cout << "now in catch block\n";
    }
cout << "back in main block of function\n";
}
int main()
{
testfunc1 (0);   //no error
testfunc1 (1);   //error case
return 0;
}
```

Inside the `try` block, which controls the scope of contained variables just like any other block, `spy2` and `spy3` are defined. When the program flow reaches the closing brace and drops out, the destructors for these variables are called. You should know that even if the block were exited in a different way, such as with a `break`, `continue`, `goto`, or `return`, that any variables that had been constructed will be destructed. The `throw` is no different. If the `throw` causes the block to be exited between the definitions of `spy2` and `spy3`, then the destructor for `spy2` will be executed.

Here is the output of the program:

```
entering testfunc1()
constructing spy 1 - main body of function
constructing spy 2 - inside try block
constructing spy 3 - also inside try block
destructing spy 3 - also inside try block
destructing spy 2 - inside try block
back in main block of function
destructing spy 1 - main body of function
entering testfunc1()
constructing spy 1 - main body of function
constructing spy 2 - inside try block
destructing spy 2 - inside try block
now in catch block
back in main block of function
destructing spy 1 - main body of function
```

This is no different than how a `goto` functions in a similar situation. But, it also works with the dynamic scoped nature of `try` blocks. Even if an exception propagates back through several called functions, destructors will be called for local variables. This is a very important concept. Exceptions are more than C's `longjmp()` in a fancy new syntax. Exceptions will clean up in their path.

Listing 18.5. More Unwinding Spying

```cpp
#include <iostream.h>

// note:  class scope_spy, same as in 18.4, should be pasted here.

void bar ()
{
cout << "entering bar()\n";
scope_spy spy ("bar");
throw 4;
cout << "leaving bar()\n";
}
void foo()
{
cout << "entering foo()\n";
scope_spy spy ("foo");
bar();
cout << "leaving foo()\n";
}
void testfunc2()
{
cout << "entering testfunc2()\n";
scope_spy spy1 ("spy 1 - main body of function");
try {
    scope_spy spy2 ("spy 2 - inside try block");
    foo();
    }
catch (int dummy) {
    cout << "now in catch block\n";
    }
cout << "back in main block of function\n";
}
int main()
{
testfunc2();
return 0;
}
```

Here, the exception thrown in `bar()` will not only destroy the local variables from `bar()`, but those of `foo()` as well, and those in the try block itself. This process is known as "stack unwinding," and is a cornerstone of EH. The output of the above example is:

```
entering testfunc2()
constructing spy 1 - main body of function
constructing spy 2 - inside try block
entering bar()
constructing foo
entering foo()
constructing bar
```

```
destructing bar
destructing foo
destructing spy 2 - inside try block
now in catch block
back in main block of function
destructing spy 1 - main body of function
```

Backing out of Constructors

If you understand that exiting a block destructs variables that are constructed in that block, no matter how the exit takes place, then the behavior of exceptions as the stack is unwound is no surprise. Implementing it is not easy, but it should be easy to understand what is supposed to happen.

Besides destroying local variables in called functions, exception handling backs out of constructors if an exception is thrown while the constructor is in progress.

If an exception takes place during a constructor, then all fully constructed subobjects are destructed. Consider a simple case where an exception is thrown from the body of a constructor:

```
void kaboom()
{
throw 4;
}
class testclass : public B {
    C member1;
    C member2;
public:
    testclass();
    ~testclass();
};
testclass::testclass()
{
kaboom();
}
```

Assume that B and C are classes that have constructors and destructors. The constructor for testclass first constructs the base class by invoking B::B(), then constructs member1 by calling C::C(), then constructs member2 similarly. Finally, it executes the body of testclass::testclass().

When the body of the constructor runs into a problem and throws an exception, the system does *not* call `testclass`'s destructor, as you first might think. In general, things are not considered to be constructed until after their constructors return. An error during a constructor is an error of the construction process itself; the object is not considered to have been constructed yet.

However, various parts of the object have been constructed. These parts will be destructed. In this example, destructors are called for `member2`, `member1`, and, finally, for the base (in that order).

Finally, execution is transferred to a catch handler belonging to a try block, which encloses the statement that tried to create the `testclass`. It might be something like this:

```
try {
   testclass xx;  //define one
   xx.foo();  //use it
   }
catch (int) {
   //handle errors
   }
```

The point is, try blocks catch problems in constructors during data-item definitions, as well as problems with function calls. The two are handled in an identical way.

If an exception is thrown, not in the constructor body, but in the construction of one of the subobjects, then the same rule applies: The system backs out of the constructor by calling destructors for those subobjects that have already been fully constructed.

In the above `testclass`, suppose an exception was thrown while in the constructor for `member2`. Then, only `member1` and the base would have their destructors called. If the exception were thrown from the constructor for `member1`, then only the base would be destructed. If the exception were thrown from the constructor of the base, then nothing would get destructed.

The rule is applied recursively. If class `c` has base classes or members with constructors, then every sub-subobject is counted among the subobjects that have been constructed and will be destructed.

throw and catch Arguments

We have seen that a throw expression throws some*thing*, and, likewise, a catch handler will accept the thrown object. We will now look into the subject in more detail.

You have seen that a throw keyword is followed by a value. This is the object that is being thrown and is used to communicate information about the error to the catch point.

Syntax of a Throw Expression

In many ways the syntax of a throw expression is like that of a return statement. But, there are some important differences, because a throw expression is an *expression*, while a return statement is a *statement*. Recall that statements are complete entities in C++, while expressions build up into more complex expressions. In this way, throw is like + and *; it may be used as part of a larger expression. Because of this, there are rules as to how it relates to other expressions, including its level of precedence.

The return keyword can be followed by any expression, without ambiguity. The throw keyword, because of its level of precedence, is followed by an assignment-expression. That is, it is one level above assignment in the order of precedence.

A throw expression may be used in a ?: expression, without additional parentheses. However, the reverse is not true.

```
x= y>0 ? y-1 : throw y;    //correct and useful
throw y>0 ? y-1 : 0;       //not correct
```

Because of the level of precedence, the second case would be taken as

```
(throw y>0) ? y-1 : 0;
```

which is an error, as the throw has no return value and so can't be used as the first argument to a ?:. The line would need to be written as

```
throw (y>0 ? y-1 : 0);
```

with parentheses around the expression to be thrown.

Another significant difference between a `throw` and a `return` is that temporary values can be thrown and bound to a reference. A throw expression will copy the value to an internal temporary and transport that internal value, rather than transporting the actual object in the throw expression.

```
void foo()
{
int local= 4;
throw local;
}
void bar()
{
try {
   foo();
   }
catch (int& error) {
   cout << error;
   }
```

This may seem fishy, but it is perfectly correct. The catch parameter `error` is not bound to a local variable in `foo()` (which has since gone out of scope). Instead, the system provides a temporary variable for this purpose. Note that although it is referred to as a temporary, it may be bound to a non-const parameter, as shown.

Argument Matching and Derived Types

Once a `throw` takes place, the thrown object is transported to the proper catch clause. The type of thing thrown determines which catch will snag it. The runtime system checks each one in turn, and passes them by until it finds a handler with a compatible type that can accept the relevant value object.

The catch statement syntax is modeled after a function call. But, unlike an overloaded function, the system will not provide for all kinds of conversions. Instead, only simple matching is used, and it will stop at the first compatible match found, even if there is a better match later on.

Obviously, an exact match will do. As in the example, if the type of the thing thrown matches the catch expression, it is considered a match.

```
void f1()
{
try {
    //statements...
    foo();
    //more statements...
    }
catch (int x) {
    cout << "I caught an int!  Value is: " << x << endl;
    }
catch (char* s) {
    cout << "I caught a c-string!  Value is: " << s << endl;
    }
}
```

If `foo()` throws an `int`, the first handler will be used. If `foo()` throws a `char*`, the second handler will be used. If neither matches, both of them will be passed by and the search will continue in `f1`'s caller.

A special form can be used as a "catch all." An ellipsis argument for the catch statement will catch anything. If the function were written as below, then the function would catch all exceptions, and not let any exception continue searching into `f2`'s callers.

```
void f2()
{
try {
    //statements...
    foo();
    //more statements...
    }
catch (int x) {
    cout << "I caught an int!  Value is: " << x << endl;
    }
catch (char* s) {
    cout << "I caught a c-string!  Value is: " << s << endl;
    }
catch (...) {
    cout << "I don't know what I caught, but it wasn't"
            "an int or a char*.\n";
    }
}
```

Now, what if `foo()` throws an `unsigned`? It will *not* be stopped by the `int` handler. Only a very simple set of conversions can be used. Besides an exact match, a handler for a base class can catch a derived class, and if a pointer is thrown, the standard pointer conversions can be used.

A catch parameter may be a reference, and it may be `const`. This does not affect the parameter matching, but the usual meanings of those modifiers apply to the parameter once caught.

Here are some more examples. Suppose that class `C` is derived from class `B`. The very cranky function `bar()` will throw objects of type `B`, pointers to `B`, character pointers, and various other things.

```
int bar (int name_your_poison)
{
switch (name_your_poison) {
    case 0:  throw B(1);
    case 1:  throw new B(1);
    case 2:  throw "hello there!";
    case 3:  throw C(1);
    case 4:  throw new C(1);
    case 5:  throw 22;
    default:  return name_your_poison;
    }
```

You can use this to see how different sets of `catch`'s will respond to it. You are encouraged to write sample `try` blocks and actually run them.

If you have the following catch handlers in this order:

```
catch (int)  { }
catch (B&)   { }
catch (C&)   { }
catch (void*) { }
```

then here is what will happen. Case 0 will be caught by the `B&` handler. Case 1 will be caught by the `void*` handler. A `void*` handler will catch any non-const pointer type, since that is a standard pointer conversion. A const `void*` handler will catch all pointer types thrown its way. Cases 2 and 4 also will be caught by the `void*` handler.

Case 3 will be caught by the `B&` handler. Yes, the `C&` handler is a better fit, but the handlers are checked in order of occurrence. The `B&` fits, so it stops looking.

One last thing to note: The type of the object thrown is determined at compile time, based on the static type of the expression. It is not polymorphic. Here is what that means:

```
B* beanball()
{
return new C(1);  //derived type
```

```
}
void bar()
{
throw beanball();
}
void f3()
{
try {
   bar();
   }
catch (C* p) {
   cout << "caught a C*\n";
   }
catch (B* p) {
   cout << "caught a B*\n";
   }
}
```

Which catch will be used? The second. The runtime system treats the thrown object as a B*, and does not know or care that it is really pointing to a derived type instance. It is the static type of the expression that is used in the search, as the logic must be known at compile time.

How the Argument Is Passed

The way the argument to `throw` is transmitted to the catch point is designed to resemble a function call. But, it needs to be a little more complex than that, in order to get it to work right. As soon as the search for the catch starts, the stack is unwound, and this process destroys stack-based variables. So, it can't just push the parameter as in a function call!

Instead, the argument of the `throw` is copied to some kind of "safe place" provided by the runtime system. Then, the stack is unwound, the proper `catch` is found, and the internal copy is used to initialize the argument of the `catch`, in exactly the same way as a function call.

Re-Throwing

You can use `throw;` by itself, with no argument. This will re-throw the current exception. It is the internal copy that is continued upstream, not the argument of the catch clause.

This is handy for catches that need to do a little work and then pass on, acting as way stations. This is discussed in greater detail later.

Exception Specifications

The `throw` keyword, besides appearing in an expression to initiate an exception, may be used as part of a function declaration. When so used, it appears after the parameter list and is followed by a possibly empty list of type names. This clause is called an *Exception Specification*. The following excerpts show how the exception specification appears among the other items in various function declarations and definitions.

```
void foo (int x) throw (int);
void foo (int x) throw (int,char*) { //...
void C::bar() const
 throw (xalloc)
{ //...
C::C (int x)
 throw (xalloc)
: B(x)
{ //...
```

The purpose of an exception specification is to document the function's behavior as it relates to exceptions. When the user sees a function declared as

```
void foo (int x)  throw(xalloc);
```

then he knows to expect this function to throw `xalloc` objects (note: `xalloc`, as discussed later, is used to indicate an out-of-memory condition) and can plan accordingly. More important, the user of this function knows that it cannot throw any other exception type.

The list of types following `throw` means that the function can only throw objects of those types, or things derived from those types. If the exception specification listed `c`, then the function bearing it could throw anything derived from `c`. If the exception specification listed `c*`, then the function could throw pointers to anything derived from `c`.

One fact, that is particularly worth noting, is that a function with an empty specification list, `throw()`, cannot throw anything.

A function's exception specification is not part of its signature. That is, the exception specification does not contribute to the function's type and is not considered during overloading. In fact, the exception specification for a function in a declaration and its definition in another compilation unit do not have to agree.

This was done intentionally, to prevent undue problems with revisions in library code. For example, if your code makes a call to a function that was declared in a header to be

```
void sample_function (int) throw (xmsg);
```

and the library is updated so that the function is now defined as

```
void sample_function (int x)
  throw ()
{
//...
```

then your code will not need to be recompiled and should still link and call it correctly.

This implies that the exception specification on a function's declaration is nothing more than a comment. In fact, if you use functions in such a way that these functions appear to violate your own exception specification, the compiler will still allow it without error, as follows:

```
void foo() throw (xmsg);
void bar() throw()
{
foo();
}
```

The function `bar()` certainly looks suspicious, but it is legal. The compiler trusts that you know that `foo()`, although it may throw an `xmsg`, will not do so under the circumstances. If `foo()` does throw an exception, this will cause `bar()` to violate its exception specification. Such a condition is caught at runtime, not at compile time. The system will transfer execution to the `unexpected()` function, as detailed in the next section.

The above function would be better written as:

```
void bar() throw()
{
try {
   foo();
   }
catch (...) {}
}
```

With the `catch` in place, all exceptions will be caught and will not try to propagate out of `bar()`.

Generally, exception specifications should be used sparingly. They are intended for interfaces to major subsystems and an occasional recovery function that should not, itself, throw exceptions. Overuse of exception specifications will make a program suffer from excessive `unexpected`'s, and, therefore, force the users of the functions to overplan their exception handling. This defeats the purpose of the exception handling mechanism.

Special Functions

The details of exception handling are administered at runtime. The whole idea is that binding is not known at compile time, but that exceptions follow the runtime calling sequence of the program. The calling sequence, and hence the binding, is only known at the time an exception is actually thrown.

So, sometimes things go wrong. In particular, what happens if an exception is thrown and there is no suitable catch handler for it? Normally, exceptions are used to indicate errors. So, what can be done with errors in the exception handling system itself? In general, nothing can be done. The action taken in cases like this is simple and final; the system calls `terminate()`.

By default, `terminate()` simply calls `abort()`. The action taken by `terminate()` is configurable. You can write your own termination function and register it with a call to `set_terminate()`. Then, subsequent calls to `terminate()` will be directed to your function. The call to `set_terminate()` returns a pointer to the current handler, so that you can remember and restore it later. The declarations of `terminate()` and `set_terminate()` are

```
void terminate();
typedef void(*_PFV)();
_PFV set_terminate (_PFV);
```

If you do write your own termination function, it is very limited in what it may do. In particular, it must terminate the program and not return or throw an exception. It can't shut down the program normally (with a call to `exit()`); it must do an emergency shutdown with `abort()` or cruder means. The function should be written very conservatively, as it is only called when the program is in *very* deep trouble. It may be out of memory, for example. In general, it is not intended to perform an orderly shutdown of the program. It can be used to do some kind of clean up, such as freeing EMS memory or returning to text mode. But whatever it does, it must do so carefully. A second uncaught exception will crash the program.

The `terminate()` function is called in response to throwing an exception, if a suitable catch handler is not found. The `terminate()` function also is used if the system finds the stack corrupted, or otherwise runs into trouble when looking for a catch handler. The third condition is more complicated to explain. When an exception is thrown, the stack is unwound back to the catch point. This calls destructors. If one of those destructors throws an exception, there is nothing to catch it. In this case, `terminate()` is also employed.

The `unexpected()` function is similar in character to the `terminate()` function. The `unexpected()` function is called by the system. You may specify your own handler with a call to `set_unexpected()`. The arguments of both are the same, as with the `terminate()` functions.

```
void unexpected();
PFV set_unexpected (_PFV);
```

By default, `unexpected()` calls `terminate()`. Unlike `terminate()`, `unexpected()` has another way out besides terminating the program. The `unexpected()` handler may throw an exception.

The system calls `unexpected()` when the stack unwinding process discovers that the object being thrown is propagating out of a function whose exception specification prohibits an exception of this type. Your code can veto the exception specification by supplying an `unexpected()` function that throws another exception.

Applied Use of EH in Programming

Exception handling can be wonderful to have in a major program or library. However, using any language feature well is hard to do without experience. There are things you will learn over time, such as what blind alleys to avoid, and lots of little ways in which it affects your program. This section is intended to help you get started, by giving you a little expert advice so that you don't have to start out making all the same mistakes as others have already made.

Guiding Principles

First of all, you should know what the role of EH is in your program or library. When will it be used, and what will it be used for?

As explained in the section "A First Look," EH is specifically good for two main applications: getting out of constructors, and getting out of nested expressions. But, what about other uses? Should exceptions be used for more general purpose error conditions, and if so, how far should you go?

Careful study and experimentation offers the conclusion that EH should be used everywhere, as the fundamental mechanism of choice for dealing with errors.

What to Do Once You Catch Something

Stroustrup notes that the C++ exception handling mechanism supports a number of common options from which a program may choose when an exception is caught: Fix something and try again, calculate something differently and return a result, propagate the error up to the caller unchanged, turn the error into a different kind of error, cancel the operation and continue, or terminate the program.

Here are examples of each of these, so that you can see what kind of syntax is used to achieve the effect, and a discussion of when the technique might be used.

Cancel the Operation

It is simple to use `try`/`catch` to protect a passage of code, and do nothing if the protected passage fails.

```
try {
    line1();
    }
catch (...) { /* nothing */ }
line2();
```

Here, if `line1()` fails, execution resumes with `line2()`. This can be used when an operation is optional, and you can't tell in advance if it will work or not. Remember, if exception handling is used uniformly in a program, a reusable library function won't return a success/failure code. That would force the user to check such a code with each use, in cases where it does matter if the operation failed. Instead, the library function throws an exception if it fails, and the exception will find code that will deal with it. So, when you *do* want to ignore the failure, use a block like this.

Do Something Else

It is very straight forward to use a `try`/`catch` block in a manner similar to an `if`/`else` block. If one operation fails, do something else instead.

```
try {
    line1();
    }
catch (...) {
    line2();
    }
line3();
```

Here, if `line1()` fails for any reason whatsoever, `line2()` is performed. In either case, `line3()` is done next. For an example, consider a function which moves a file. First, the function tries to rename the file. If the source and destination are on the same physical volume, this works. If that doesn't work, then the function does it the hard way, copying the file and then deleting the original. If the primitives did not use EH, this function would probably be written to use an `if`/`else` function based on the status codes produced by the primitives.

Try Again

There are two forms this can take. The first is really a special case of "Do something else." A function may take an action that is a repair of some kind, and then redo the original operation.

```
try {
    foo();
    }
catch (...) {
    fixit();
    foo();
    }
```

Or, a try block may be used inside a loop. This allows an action to be retried however many times it takes. Here is one form that such a function may take:

```
void get_it_right()
{
for (;;) {
    try {
        // the entire body of the function goes inside this
        // try block, which is inside an infinite loop
        foo();
        return;
        }
    catch (...) {
        fixit();
        }
    }
}
```

Propagate the Error

A function may decide whether or not to handle an error only after looking at it. Or, a function may have additional cleanup work that is not automatic. In either case, a special no-argument form of the throw expression may be used to continue propagating an exception.

```
void pizza (crust_t crust)
{
try {
    for (int loop= 0;  loop < max;  loop++)
        toss (crust);
    if (crust == thick) proof();
    get_toppings();
    bake();
    }
catch (pizza_error& p) {
    if (p.xx == 5)  throw;  //can't handle that here
    // ... code to recover from error
    }
}
```

The need for additional cleanup during an exception is discussed in greater detail, in the section "Caveats" later in this chapter.

Throw a Different Error

When an error is detected during an operation, the function performing the operation may want to show an error more specific to the operation, rather than an error detailing the primitive that caused the actual problem.

```
void invert (Matrix& m)
{
try {
   // ...details of inverting a matrix go here.
   // it may try to divide by zero or something nasty like that.
   // if something goes wrong, the caller doesn't care as to the
   // details, just that the matrix could not be inverted.
   }
catch (math_error) {
   throw matrix_error (Inversion);
   }
}
```

Terminate the Program

If something serious goes wrong, and the program cannot repair the error or properly continue propagating the error to a higher level, then the only way out is to terminate the program.

The best way to do this is by calling `terminate()`. This is preferred over `abort()`, in cases where `exit()` would not be appropriate. A case where termination might be the only option is when errors are detected in the error-processing functions.

```
void foo()
{
try {
   // ... stuff goes here
   }
catch (...) {
   // give up.
   terminate();
   }
}
```

Organization of Exception Types within a Program

The exception handling mechanism does two things: It moves the point of execution of the program away from an error, and it transmits information from the place where the error occurred to the place where the error is handled.

Information is transmitted in two ways. The kind of error may be indicated simply by the type of object thrown. This automatically selects a proper catch handler for the error. Or, the thrown object may contain additional information. In practice, a combination of the two forms is used.

The type of the object thrown indicates a gross type of error, such as a range error, file error, math error, and so on. Additional information may be placed in the class to provide more information about the specific error.

Simple Programs Need Simple Handling

Even in a program that is two pages long, EH might still be used. In a simple command-line utility, error handling may be very simple— display a message and quit. Such a program can effectively use very simple exceptions. After all, providing a rich system, as described in the next section, may be considerably larger than the main part of the program. The minimal case would be to simply throw character strings. To bail out, just throw the error message. The program would use library-provided exception types where applicable, and plain strings everywhere else.

```
int main (int argc, char* argv[])
{
try {
   // main code goes here.
   setup();
   process();
   shut_down();
   }
```

```
catch (char* s) {
    cout << "Error: " << s << endl;
    return 3;
    }
catch (xmsg& e) {
    cout << "Error: " << e.why() << endl;
    return 3;
    }
return 0;  //normal exit
}
```

In addition to error messages, a program can throw whatever it happens to have handy. If the simple program uses a few structures, it can throw the offending object when it runs into trouble. The catch handler can report on the condition of the object, or just use the type as an indicator of what the program is doing.

Larger Programs Need Hierarchical Error Classes

In general, a hodgepodge of error types will not do. There are good reasons for organizing errors, which are detailed in the next section. Any time a piece of code may be reused so that the point causing the error and the point catching the error may change with future reuse of either part, a disciplined and generic approach is needed for exception types.

It is a good idea to have all exceptions derive from a common type. From here, you have major classes of errors. Within the major error types, more specific errors may be specified, with further derived types or with instance data within that type.

There are no hard and fast rules for when to make the transition from new types to instance data. However, there are considerations and guidelines to help you plan. Consider a few examples. If you have an overall `math_error` exception, should you derive new types to signal `overflow`, `div_by_zero`, and `domain_error`? If you have an overall `file_error` exception, should you derive new types for `open_error`, `read_error`, `write_error`, and `critical_error`?

There is no question that the `file_error` would contain instance data specifying the details of the operation that failed. This is something that could not be indicated with unique error types. But, should there be different types for each error or a single structure that described any operation in detail? The choice weighs in favor of different types because the information you want to transmit is different for each error. For `open_error`, you want the file's name and modes. For read and write errors, you can give the size of the request. For critical errors, there would be additional status information. So, it makes sense that error types that hold different instance data should be different classes.

Second, you can anticipate the user of the code. Would the catcher want to do something totally different based on different kinds of errors? If so, making the catcher different types would be handy, as it would initially be routed to different catch handlers. If the catchers would do the same thing and just use the extra information for reporting, then it would be annoying to have different catch handlers that duplicated their code.

The bottom line is to be sure to arrange error classes (anything that is thrown) into a hierarchy, without overdoing the divisions. How your decisions here react with the program's error-handling code is discussed in the next section.

Organization of a Program that Uses Exception Handling

Low-level code will throw exceptions when detecting conditions that prevent normal operation. It is, and always has been, a good idea to make such tests at a suitably low level in a program. However, the problem has always been what to do if a test turns up an error. The function would need to be written in such a way as to provide error information back to the caller, and the design would need to include details of errors. Because it is so much trouble, what usually happens is that the error checking does not get performed.

With exceptions, this is no longer a problem. Code anywhere can perform error checking and, when an error is detected, get out of the current situation simply by using `throw`. The system takes care of canceling pending operations, and execution is transferred to a point where the error can be dealt with. Instead of having to build in a mechanism for error handling, it is only necessary to use a standard mechanism to report the error. The other half of the process, responding to the error, is provided by other code.

So, errors are thrown by low-level code, and it is so simple that you should build error checking into functions as a matter of course. Meanwhile, error catching is done at a high level.

At a high level, try blocks can be written to field any errors that occur within them. The important thing is that the middle layers need not consider error handling. The error goes directly from the point it was detected to the point where code is willing to deal with it, with no need for considerations and extra logic in the intermediate layers.

There are three general things you can do with a try block. You can protect major operations, field specific errors, and isolate a single possible error.

When protecting a major function, you don't really tend to care about the details of the error. You're more concerned with the fact that whatever you were trying to do did not work. For example, a function to copy a file will open a pair of files, allocate memory, read from and write to files, and finally clean up. Exception handling can make the implementation clean by not needing individual tests for open failure, out of memory, read failure, write failure, and whatever else can go wrong. In the end, a caller may only care that the file could not be copied. The details of what went wrong will go into a report for the user, but as far as recovery and taking action, the handler does not distinguish between different kinds of errors.

This is when the error base class comes in handy. A single `catch (xmsg& e)` can trap all the errors coming out of that block of code, and the virtual `why()` function can report the details to the user, even though the catch point doesn't care about the exact type of object caught.

On the other hand, sometimes code will want to distinguish between different kinds of errors and take different actions based on what the error was. Here, it is important that each kind of error has its own type, so that different catch handlers, possibly in different places, can handle them. This kind of handling will generally take action to try something else or to repair it, rather than reporting a blanket failure to the user.

When implementing delicate functions like the file copy above, it can be beneficial to prevent something that is normally an error from being an error in this case. For example, running out of memory allocating the buffer could be repaired by trying a smaller buffer size. In this case, a try block can surround a single statement, and watch for a specific error.

Caveats

Generally, the middle layers of a program, the code between the `throw` and the eventual `catch`, was handled automatically and need not consider error handling. However, some constructs can't be handled automatically. Many existing programming habits will prove hostile to automatic cleanup during exception handling.

Consider the humble pointer.

```
int foo (char* s)
{
char* tcmp= new char [size];
//... other code here
bar();
//... more code
delete[] temp;
return retval;
}
```

What happens if `bar()` throws an exception? You have a memory leak, since `temp` is a pointer and its value is never freed, as intended.

In cases like this, you need to provide cleanup code because you are doing things that the compiler will not do automatically. This "way station" idiom looks like this:

```
int foo (char* s)
{
char* temp= 0;
try {
   temp= new char [size];
   //... other code here
   bar();
   //,.. more code
   delete[] temp;
   return retval;
   }
catch (...) {
   delete[] temp;
   throw;
   }
}
```

There are several things to understand here. Although the bulk of the
function is moved into a protective try block, the definition of the
pointer temp is left outside and initialized to null. This is necessary so
that the catch block can refer to it. If `temp` were defined inside the try
block, it would not be visible within the catch. It is preinitialized to
null so that an exception that takes place before memory is allocated
(perhaps the error is in `new` itself?) does not cause trouble when the
"way station" catch handler trys to free It. Deleting a null pointer is
harmless.

Similar considerations should be taken for constructors. If an exception is thrown during a constructor, the destructor will not be called.
So, a try block around the body of the constructor can provide a catch
handler to undo any memory allocation done by the constructor.

This problem is not just for memory, but for any "resource." A good
idiom to follow is "resource acquisition is initialization." That is, every
use of a resource is encapsulated into a class, and the constructor and
destructor perform resource acquisition and release. This not only
makes EH work in a fully automated way, but prevents other mistakes
in usage as well.

If, instead of a pointer, there was a simple buffer class that did what
was needed, the above example would become:

```
int foo (char* s)
{
buffer temp (size);
```

```
//... other code here
bar();
//... more code
return retval;
}
```

Notice that no action is taken to free the memory now—the destructor of temp takes care of that. This works no matter how the function is exited, so not only does EH work right unassisted, but there also is no possibility of a mistake, such as a second `return` that is not preceded by the proper `delete`.

Another example is the use of files. A high-level file class can close files when the object goes out of scope, so you can't accidentally leave files open.

Details of Borland's Implementation

This section gives details on exceptions and exception handling as found in the Borland C++ 4.0 compiler.

Use of EH in the Runtime Library

Borland C++ 4.0 uses exceptions in library functions. They are used in free-store management and the new `string` class. The manuals purport to use EH in debug versions of the container classes, but the template definitions in the headers and other sources, contain no `throw` statements.

As explained earlier, BC++ 4.0 has a class that is designed to be the base of all exceptions. This is class `xmsg`. It is similar to the class, by the same name, that will be part of the eventual ANSI C++ standard. However, it differs in some important ways.

The header `<except.h>` contains the definitions for class `xmsg`, and a derived class `xalloc`. `xmsg` has a function `why()` which returns a `string` (it uses the new `string` class) that was specified when the `xmsg` was constructed.

Exceptions and the Free-Store

The derived class `xalloc` is used by the heap. This is an *important difference* between BC++ 4.0 and all other versions (and all other current DOS compilers). Historically, you were supposed to check the return value of `new` for 0, which was returned if the memory could not be allocated.

Not so anymore. Now, `new` will not return 0 on failure, but will throw an exception. This can be used in a manner similar to the old form, but it is more powerful.

A direct translation would be:

```
// before
p= new C;
if (!p)  //...take some action
// after
try {
   p= new C;
   }
catch (xalloc& e) {
   //...take some action
   }
```

That is, you can still test the result of a single statement for success. But, it can be used in a more powerful way, doing one test for an entire collection of statements. Effective use of this technique is explained more in the section "Organization of a Program that Uses Exception Handling."

```
// 3 new's, one test for failure.
try {
   p= new C;
   q= new D;
   r= new E;
   }
catch (xalloc& e) {
   //...take some action
   }
```

You can revert to the old behavior of `new` if you wish. If you register a `new_handler` of a null pointer, the old behavior of returning 0 on failure will be switched on. Do this by calling `set_new_handler (0);`.

The New String Class

BC++ 4.0 also comes with a `string` class. This is based on an early draft of what went into the ANSI C++ Draft Working Paper, so it is similar to, but different than, what will be found on other compilers. The class uses exceptions to indicate errors. You have already noted that the `xmsg` class uses the `string` class.

Within the string class (defined in `<cstring.h>`), there are two nested classes. To indicate errors, the members and friends of class `string` will throw objects of type `string::lengtherror` and `string::outofrange`.

Bugs in EH Implementation

Exception handling may be a terrific new feature, and a cornerstone of modern C++, but there are certain problems with the implementation in Borland C++, version 4.0. Even if you do everything right, your code still may not work right. Rather then be confused and think you did something wrong, keep these implementation bugs in mind. A related issue has to do with bloated EXE sizes that are caused by exception handling.

Incorrect Destructor Calls

There are two distinct, but related, major bugs in the code generated by the compiler that cause exceptions to malfunction. To see if your version still has the bug that existed in BC++ 4.0 when this book was written, try the test program in Listing 18.6. It malfunctions by calling a bogus destructor.

Listing 18.6. EH Sanity Test

```
#include <stdio.h>

class A {
   int val;
public:
   A (int x);
   ~A();
```

continues

Listing 18.6. Continued

```
    };

A::A (int x)
: val(x)
{
printf ("constructing at %p with %d\n", this, val);
}

A::~A()
{
printf ("destructing at %p with %d\n", this, val);
}

int main()
{
static A a_static(20);
try {
    A a1(1);
    A a2(2);
    throw 4;
    A a3(3);
    A a4(4);
    }
catch (int) {
    printf ("catching");
    }
return 0;
}
```

To implement EH, the compiler must keep track of the current state of the program with respect to constructors and destructors. If an exception occurs during a block, it must know which objects have been initialized and cause destructors to be called on just those objects, ignoring those that have not yet been constructed. Likewise, construction of a complex object with many subobjects must track which parts have been completed, so that an exception can destroy just those parts that have been completed.

To this end, BC++ uses a global variable as a counter. Within a try block, a list of cleanup actions is registered. If an exception unwinds past this block, the list of actions is performed, using a counter to perform just those actions that are needed. When executing normal code within the try body, the counter is incremented each time an object or subobject is constructed. Likewise, the global counter is decremented

during the block exit code and in destructors, as each object is destructed. In this way, a thrown exception should know exactly what needs cleaning up.

If that counter gets messed up, very bad things happen. In particular, the system calls destructors for objects that don't exist. When the destructor is presented with a garbage object, you can imagine what kind of chaos will result. Most likely, it will corrupt the heap or crash the system. Code written to do aggressive error checking within destructors will probably throw another exception, which will result in a call to `terminate()`. If you get the message `Abnormal program termination`, this is what is happening.

There are two things that do, in fact, cause the counter to get out of sync with reality. The first is static local variables. A local variable that is static will cause the counter to be incremented during initialization. However, the proper action is somewhat more complex and requires altering the housekeeping information, once the static variable is complete. The compiler neither stores correct cleanup information for an exception thrown during construction of the static variable, nor accounts for the counter's value being incremented.

It is easy to avoid the use of static local variables. However, the other bug is nearly impossible, and quite impractical, to work around: The counter also has problems with temporary objects.

If, in an expression, a temporary object is created under certain circumstances (such as due to an implicit conversion), the construction process will increment the counter. However, there is some question as to when the temporary is destroyed. Sometimes temporaries are destroyed shortly after use. Sometimes they are destroyed at the end of the block in which they were created. The latter case causes problems. When the destruction of a temporary is delayed until later, and a try block is subsequently encountered during execution, the counter will be in an incorrect state. Any exception will cause bogus destructors to be called.

Missing try Blocks

The optimization flags `-Obe` (`b` and `e` are supposed to be used together) performs dead code elimination. However, sometimes the compiler thinks that the setup required for a try block is dead code and eliminates it. The symptom is that the attached catch clauses are bypassed, and the search looks at the caller as if this `try`/`catch` construct were never put into place.

Note that since `-O1` (smallest code) expands to `-o -Ob -Oe -Os -k- -z` and `-O2` (fastest code) expands to `-o -Ob -Oe -Og -Oi -Ol -Om -Op -Ot -Ov -k- -z`, you should not use either of them as they contain the dreaded `-Obe` sequences. Note that several of the other flags also cause problems in other contexts (`-O1` can corrupt the stack, for example); however, a full discussion is beyond the scope of this chapter.

Memory Problems

Recall that the transport of a thrown object to its catch point requires copying it to a safe place that is not part of the stack. BC++ 4.0 apparently uses the heap for this purpose.

The direct problem is that throwing an exception will use the heap. This causes serious problems if the exception was thrown because the heap has problems or is already full.

Under normal circumstances, the only problems you will notice is that EH won't recover if the heap is really full. If you tried to request a large block, and that failed, it may not be a problem because other blocks do exist. But, if a request for a fairly small block fails, the throwing of the `xalloc` object also will run into memory problems, both with the construction of the contained string object and with the throw process itself. This will cause `terminate()` to be called.

Excessive EXE File Sizes

It has been observed that EXE files produced by BC++ 4.0 are rather large. Generally, this is blamed on the increase in the size of the

runtime library to provide RTTI (runtime type information) and EH features. In truth, the helper functions and data come to 13,594 bytes in large model.

In addition, more code is generated to support these features. You would not be surprised to know that code is generated to call helper functions to support try blocks, but in addition more code is generated for normal activities that do not involve try blocks at all. In particular, there is housekeeping to increment and decrement a counter for each object created and extra overhead for every polymorphic type you define.

Inside a class's virtual table, besides pointers to all the virtual functions, is a pointer to another data item that encodes the runtime type information for that class. The size of this structure starts out at around 35 bytes and goes up from there. Every polymorphic class you define will have this overhead.

The real killer, though, is the incrementing and decrementing of the counter that is used to track the construction of subparts of a complex object. Every constructor will contain an instruction to increment a `long`, and every destructor will contain code to decrement the counter. You may think that a simple `counter++` and `counter-` is trivial, right?

Actually, they are 12 bytes each. For a serious constructor (or destructor), this is in fact small. But, for a trivial and inline constructor, it becomes significant. When a destructor calls other destructors for its component subobjects, and those destructors are inline, then multiple counter sequences are generated. This happens even if the destructor doesn't do anything!

Here is the punchline. If a destructor for a class is not explicitly declared, the compiler supplies one anyway, to call the destructors of all its subobjects. Since you did not define one and supply a body, the only thing the compiler-supplied destructor does is call other destructors. The compiler-supplied destructor is inline. If the same is true for the component object's types as well, when an object of the derived type goes out of scope, the compiler will generate a massive block of

consecutive SUB instructions with no real work done. Further derived types make the size of this block increase exponentially.

In short, classes without explicitly defined constructors and destructors cause massive bloating of the generated object code. This was not observed in earlier versions of the compiler, so the difference in EXE sizes between other versions and 4.0 can be striking.

The remedy is to always define a destructor for a class, even if the body is empty, and not to make it inline. Likewise, avoid inline constructors like the plague. Also, if compiling with '386 code generation, a different instruction is used for the counter code, which is half the size.

Disabling EH Support

The extra overhead of exceptions exists even when writing C programs with Borland C++. Since C programs presumably do not use exceptions, you can cut out the additional overhead.

First, compile every file with the -RT- and -x- options, to remove the extra code generated to support RTTI and EH.

However, this will still link in the library routines for dealing with exception handling. You can trick the linker into leaving it out by including a dummy definition for a function that is called by the startup code.

```
void __ExceptInit(void) {}
```

This will prevent the startup code from dragging in the EH code, and if EH truly is not used anywhere in the program or libraries, the program size will decrease by up to 17K.

Exceptions in Turbo Debugger

If you run a program under the debugger, you will find that throwing an exception automatically breaks the program execution. This is because TD automatically sets a breakpoint on the library routine _RaiseException. However, TD is friendlier than that. If the code that threw the exception was compiled with debug info enabled, then the debugger will show your cursor over the throw statement.

Note that the debugger did not break *at* the `throw` statement. You will find that you cannot inspect variables to see what went wrong. The breakpoint is actually inside a library function, and the throw is in progress.

If the throw point did not have debug info, then the cursor in TD is left at the actual breakpoint position, the internal function, `_RaiseException`. If you do not have debug info switched on for the entire program, it may prove difficult to find out just where the throw point is.

One way to get more information on an exception, while in the debugger, is to set your own breakpoint. Instead of setting it deep inside the library code, set it in a more useful place. Set a breakpoint on the constructor for your exception base type. If all the exceptions in your program are derived from a common base, then it will be tripped for each exception thrown. Furthermore, you can continue single-stepping the program, and get back to the `throw` statement, before the object is actually thrown. The compiler generates code to construct the object, then throw it. Between these two steps, the trace of the program will return to the original line. You *can* at this point inspect variables in the function that will do the throwing.

There also are a couple global variables that may be of use. If you compile a module with the `-xp` switch (or "Enable exception location info" in the IDE), then the following values will be set when an exception is thrown:

```
char* __throwExceptionName;
char* __throwFileName;
unsigned __throwLineNumber;
```

These are declared in <except.h> (note that the Library Reference Manual is incorrect for `__throwLineNumber`), and may be useful to print diagnostics in the catch block. But, they are not global variables—they are macros which call functions to access the EH housekeeping information.

There are global variables by these same names, though, and they are unrelated to the above macros. They are normally not accessible in a running program, but are useful in the debugger. They do not require the use of `-xp`, but they are always set.

In the debugger, these variables can be viewed with an inspector window, but you will have to cast the result since TD consistently gets the type wrong. If you inspect `__throwExceptionName`, the debugger shows it as an `int`, which is a garbage value. Immediately press Ctrl-T (for typecast) and give the correct type, `char*`, at the prompt. Likewise, `__throwLineNumber` comes up as a `void*`, and needs to be cast back to an `unsigned`. The value of `__throwFileName` is unreliable, and often points to an empty string.

From Here...

➤ For another treatment on exception handling in C++, by the chief designer of the EH features himself, see Chapter 9 in *The C++ Programming Language*, Second Edition by Bjarne Stroustrup.

➤ For the definitive, formal specification on the C++ EH constructs, see the ANSI X3J16 "Working Paper for Draft Proposed International Standard for Information Systems-Programming Language C++" (updated quarterly).

➤ If your program contains assembly code, look at Chapter 14, "Bare Metal Programming," for information on writing the most efficient C++ programs containing assembler code.

➤ If database programming is more your style, see Chapter 15, "Interfacing with Database Languages," for information on writing the most efficient C++ and database programs.

➤ If you include code written in languages other than C, C++, and assembler, see Chapter 13, "Mixed Language Programming."

Writing Interrupt Handlers and TSR Programs

by Clayton Walnum

These days, the word *multitasking* gets a lot of attention. Products such as Microsoft Windows and IBM's OS/2 boast multitasking capability, which enables you to run more than one program simultaneously. But you may be surprised to learn that your computer has always been capable of multitasking, although in a very limited way. Without this capability, in fact, your computer is little more than a big paperweight. Think about what goes on inside your computer. Data travels its data buses, clocks tick, keystrokes are gathered from the keyboard, the screen is continually refreshed, and so on. All this activity apparently happens simultaneously, thanks to *interrupts.*

The keyword in the preceding sentence is *apparently*. The truth is that a computer with only a single CPU can never do more than one thing at a time. Because the CPU operates so quickly, however, it can divide its attention among several tasks, switching between them so quickly that it seems as though the tasks run simultaneously. This way Windows and OS/2 perform their magic and interrupts keep your computer running.

In this chapter, you learn how to use interrupts to change the way the operating system responds to certain events. Your knowledge of interrupts enables you to write TSR (terminate and stay resident) programs, which sit in the background, unaffected by any other program you run. You put this knowledge to the test by writing a TSR clock for DOS that displays the time in the corner of the screen.

What's an Interrupt?

As mentioned, computers must do a great deal of work to keep the operating system active and responsive to input. For example, what good is a word processor if the computer's operating system doesn't have a way to gather keystrokes from the keyboard without interfering with the word processor? Likewise, if the computer's monitor were not continually refreshed with new information, you couldn't see your keystrokes. That would be a tough way to produce a document! Thanks to interrupts, the computer's operating system can perform dozens of these little tasks without affecting the currently running program.

Because a single CPU can work on only one task at a time, it must be continually interrupted to perform all operating system tasks. Each operating system task has its own interrupt. For example, when you press a key, a keyboard interrupt is sent to the CPU. The CPU stops what it's doing, grabs the keystroke, and picks up where it left off with the task that was interrupted. These interrupts occur constantly. A timer interrupt alone occurs about 18 times a second. When you consider that the CPU can service hundreds of different interrupts, it's a wonder that your programs run.

You may wonder how the CPU knows what to do when it receives an interrupt. A small program called an *interrupt handler* processes it. When the CPU receives a keyboard interrupt, for example, it runs the keyboard handler, which gets the keystroke. Although every interrupt has a handler, some interrupt handlers do nothing. Later, you see how such an apparently pointless handler can perform a useful task.

Each interrupt in the system owns an entry in a table of addresses, or vectors, in low memory. When the CPU must find an interrupt handler, it uses the interrupt number to index the interrupt vector table, using the address it finds there to run the handler. Luckily for people who write interrupt handlers and TSR programs, the addresses in the interrupt vector table can be changed to point anyplace in memory. By changing a vector to point to your custom-written interrupt handler, you can change the way the operating system responds to a specific interrupt.

Writing an Interrupt Handler

You can take over an interrupt in two ways: by *hooking* an interrupt and by *chaining* to an interrupt. Chaining, which allows many interrupt handlers to run off the same interrupt, is discussed later in this chapter because it's a complicated method. Hooking an interrupt is a fairly straightforward process: You simply place the address of your custom interrupt handler into the interrupt vector table. When the interrupt occurs, the CPU runs your handler rather than the original one.

This may sound high-tech, but modifying the interrupt vector table is a snap because Borland C++ provides many handy functions for dealing with interrupts. Listing 19.1 contains an interrupt handler that takes over the control-break interrupt, which occurs when you try to exit a program by pressing Ctrl-C. When you run the program, it installs the interrupt handler and then continually prints the message `Waiting...` on-screen. When you press Ctrl-C, the interrupt handler takes over and prints the message.

Listing 19.1. CTRLC.CPP—Control-C Interrupt Program

```cpp
//////////////////////////////////////////////////////
// CTRLC.CPP: A simple interrupt handler.
//////////////////////////////////////////////////////

#include <dos.h>
#include <iostream.h>
#include <string.h>

// Constant for Ctrl-C interrupt.
#define CTRLC 0x23

// Function prototypes.
void interrupt (*old_ctrlc)(...);
void interrupt ctrlc(...);

//////////////////////////////////////////////////////
// main()
//////////////////////////////////////////////////////
void main(void)
{
    long int y;

    // Get address of the old interrupt.
    old_ctrlc = getvect(CTRLC);

    // Set vector to the new handler.
    setvect(CTRLC, ctrlc);

    // Let the user test the new handler.
    for (int x=0; x<300; ++x)
    {
        cout << "Waiting...\n";
        for (y=0; y<60000L; ++y);
    }

    // Restore the old handler.
    setvect(CTRLC, old_ctrlc);
}


//////////////////////////////////////////////////////
// ctrlc()
//
// This function is the new CTRL-C interrupt handler.
//////////////////////////////////////////////////////
void interrupt ctrlc(...)
{
    char s[] = {"*** Ctrl-C caught! ***\r\n"};

    // Output the message string.
    for (int i=0; i<strlen(s); ++i)
    bdos(0x02, s[i], 0);
}
```

Ordinarily, when a control-break interrupt occurs, its handler terminates the running program and exits to the DOS prompt. This interrupt, however, is often disabled in commercial programs so that users don't accidentally exit the application. Remember the mention of interrupt handlers that do nothing? Handlers that hook the control-break interrupt are often in this category because they are comprised of nothing more than the IRET (return from interrupt) instruction. With this type of handler, the Ctrl-C keystroke does nothing. The handler above, however, prints a message to the screen when Ctrl-C is pressed and shows that the handler is working.

How does the program work? First, near the top, is this line:

```
#define CTRLC 0x23
```

The value 0x23 is the control-break interrupt number. Every interrupt is identified by a unique interrupt number that you use when you change the interrupt vector table. The CPU uses this number to index the interrupt vector table and find the right address. After the interrupt number definition is this line:

```
void interrupt (*old_ctrlc)(...)
```

This line declares old_ctrlc as a pointer to an interrupt function. The address of the old control-break handler is stored in this pointer. Now examine main():

```
void main(void)
{
   long int y;

   // Get address of the old interrupt.
   old_ctrlc = getvect(CTRLC);

   // Set vector to the new handler.
   setvect(CTRLC, ctrlc);

   // Let the user test the new handler.
   for (int x=0; x<300; ++x)
   {
      cout << "Waiting...\n";
      for (y=0; y<60000L; ++y);
   }

   // Restore the old handler.
   setvect(CTRLC, old_ctrlc);
}
```

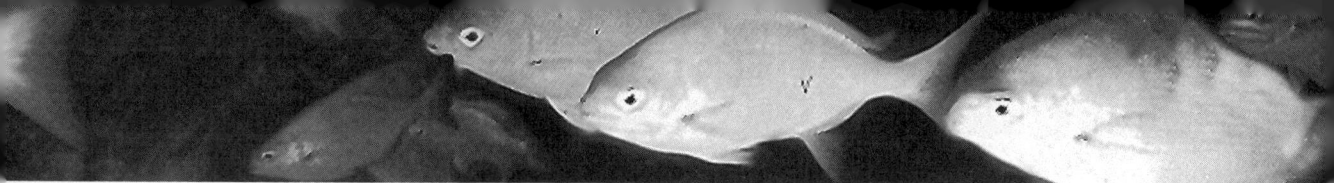

First, Borland's `getvect()` function gets the address of the old control-break interrupt handler. Notice that `getvect()` needs the interrupt number used by the CPU to index the interrupt vector table. After saving the address of the old interrupt handler, Borland's `setvect()` function installs the new handler. The function's parameters are the interrupt number and the address of your interrupt handler. Believe it or not, after these two simple calls, the new handler is installed and ready to go.

In the `for` loop, the message `Waiting...` is printed and another `for` loop acts as a delay. After printing the message 300 times (to give you plenty of time to experiment with the Ctrl-C key), `setvect()` is called to reinstall the old handler, using the address saved in `old_ctrlc`. (Actually, the old handler is supposedly reinstalled automatically when the program terminates, but why take a chance?)

You can see that the message `*** Ctrl-C caught! ***` is nowhere in the main program, nor is there any call in the program to any function containing the message. The message is, instead, in the interrupt handler, which is called by the CPU whenever it detects a Ctrl-C keystroke:

```
void interrupt ctrlc(...)
{
    char s[] = {"*** Ctrl-C caught! ***\r\n"};

    // Output the message string.
    for (int i=0; i<strlen(s); ++i)
    bdos(0x02, s[i], 0);
}
```

First, notice the `interrupt` keyword used in this function's declaration. When programmers wrote interrupt handlers in the old days, they had to write assembly-language code that saved the contents of all the registers before their handler ran. They had to do this to restore the machine to its original state after the handler exited. (An interrupt doesn't care what a program is doing when it takes over. The interrupted program's state is represented only by the contents of the registers. Changing those registers without restoring them to their original state leads to disastrous results when the interrupted program tries to take up where it left off.) To avoid all this assembly-language programming,

Borland created a special type of function for interrupt handlers. When the Borland compiler sees the `interrupt` keyword in a function's definition, it automatically generates the code needed to save and restore the registers.

Now look at the body of the function. In the first line, the function declares and initializes a string for the message. Then, in the `for` loop, the 0x02 DOS function prints the message to the screen, one character at a time. When you run the program and press Ctrl-C, notice the interrupt handler's message interrupts whatever the main program is printing to the screen. Such is the nature of an interrupt: It takes over immediately and returns control to the main program only after it has finished.

In a real program, you wouldn't print a message when the user presses Ctrl-C. Instead, you would probably ignore the keystroke. You can do this by creating a control-break interrupt handler that does nothing:

```
void interrupt ctrlc(...)
{
}
```

Writing a TSR Program

A TSR program is a lot like an interrupt handler because it relies on interrupts to interact with the user and the system. When a user loads a TSR, it first runs like any other program, executing the code in `main()`, which usually contains the TSR's initialization. After `main()` ends, however, the program doesn't terminate in the same way a conventional program does. Instead, it stays in memory, waiting to be reactivated by the user or by a system interrupt. When the TSR receives its appropriate signal, it "wakes up," does what it is designed to do, and goes dormant until it's needed again.

Some TSR programs, like the on-screen clock in this chapter, require no user input. The user runs the program and forgets about it. This type of TSR, like any TSR, gets its wake-up call through an interrupt. (For example, the clock TSR presented later in this chapter is activated by the timer interrupt.) Other TSR programs, like Borland's famous

SideKick, are activated when the user types a specific hot key. This type of TSR works by chaining to the keyboard interrupt, which occurs when a key is struck. This interrupt actually takes place twice for every keystroke, once when the key is pressed and once when the key is released. A TSR can look for its own hot key by examining the keys that are pressed.

Listing 19.2 contains an interrupt handler that chains to the keyboard interrupt. After you run this program, you hear a beep when you press a key and when you release it. This magical, yet annoying, special effect continues until you reboot your computer.

Listing 19.2. TSR1.CPP—Key Beep Program, Version 1

```
/////////////////////////////////////////////////////////
// TSR1.CPP: A simple TSR program.
/////////////////////////////////////////////////////////

#include <dos.h>
#include <iostream.h>
#include <string.h>

// The keyboard interrupt number.
#define KEYBRD 0x09

// Function prototypes.
void interrupt (*old_keybrd)(...);
void interrupt keybrd(...);

/////////////////////////////////////////////////////////
// main()
/////////////////////////////////////////////////////////
void main(void)
{
    // Get the address of the old handler.
    old_keybrd = getvect(KEYBRD);

    // Set address to the new handler.
    setvect(KEYBRD, keybrd);

    // Make the handler a TSR program.
    keep(0, (_SS + (_SP/16) - _psp));
}
```

```
///////////////////////////////////////////////////////
// keybrd()
//
// This function is the new keyboard interrupt.
///////////////////////////////////////////////////////
void interrupt keybrd(...)
{
    // Call old keyboard handler.
    old_keybrd();

    // Generate a key sound.
    sound(500);
    delay(30);
    nosound();
}
```

Look at main():

```
void main(void)
{
    // Get the address of the old handler.
    old_keybrd = getvect(KEYBRD);

    // Set address to the new handler.
    setvect(KEYBRD, keybrd);

    // Make the handler a TSR program.
    keep(0, (_SS + (_SP/16) - _psp));
}
```

Here, the program first gets the old keyboard interrupt vector and
saves it in old_keybrd. Then it changes the interrupt vector table to point
to the new handler. You saw this in Listing 19.1, so you should know
what's going on here. One big difference between Listings 19.1 and
19.2 is that, in Listing 19.1, main() prints messages, but main() in Listing
19.2 only sets up the new interrupt. The second difference is that
strange last line in main(), the one that calls the keep() function.

The keep() function is the magician that allows TSRs to be written with
Borland C++. It's the command that informs DOS to keep your program in memory when main() has terminated, which is what is meant
by "terminate and stay resident." When you call keep(), the first argument should be 0, which is the status code returned by DOS. The
second argument is the size of the program. This is calculated by the
formula (_SS + (_SP/16) - _psp).

This formula finds the program's highest address by determining the address of the end of the stack (using the ss and sp pseudovariables, which contain the contents of the stack-segment and stack-pointer registers). It then subtracts the address of the program segment prefix (stored in the psp global variable) from the address of the top of the stack. Because the address of the PSP also is the starting address of the program, this subtraction yields the size of the program. If all this has your head spinning, don't worry—simply use the formula as it's shown.

Now look at the interrupt handler:

```
void interrupt keybrd(...)
{
    // Call old keyboard handler.
    old_keybrd();

    // Generate a key sound.
    sound(500);
    delay(30);
    nosound();
}
```

First, the old keyboard handler is called. (Remember: old_keybrd is defined as a pointer to an interrupt function; you can call it like any other function.) This calling of the old interrupt is what is meant by chaining to the interrupt. You have to do this because the keyboard interrupt must be allowed to perform its usual function, unlike the control-break interrupt, which performs no essential services for the operating system. If the regular keyboard interrupt doesn't run, your computer stops responding to the keyboard, a predicament to which the only solution is a reboot.

> **Note:** When writing an interrupt handler for an interrupt that performs essential services, you must chain to the interrupt—that is, you must allow the old interrupt handler to run either before or after your own handler. You can hook an interrupt (take it over completely) only when the old interrupt handler can be ignored.

After the old keyboard handler runs, it returns control to the new interrupt handler, which makes a short beep sound and exits. In this case, it doesn't matter whether you call the original interrupt handler before or after the beep. But with critical interrupts such as the keyboard handler, it's usually a good idea to let them run first.

Chaining to an interrupt is important for interrupts that perform critical operating system functions. But it also is a good idea for most other types of interrupts. Why? Suppose a user loads a TSR that chains to the timer interrupt. Now suppose the user loads another TSR that also uses the timer interrupt, but it only hooks the interrupt, rather than chains to it. The second TSR disables the first TSR, because the first TSR's entry in the interrupt vector table was wiped out by the second TSR. By chaining to an interrupt, you ensure that critical operating system functions work properly and that other custom interrupt handlers and TSR programs continue to run properly.

In the "key beeper," you can see that the chaining is working because the keyboard continues to work along with the beeps. You can test this further by running yet another TSR that chains to the keyboard interrupt. Listing 19.3 is a version of the key beeper TSR that produces a higher beep. Run the first beeper and then run the second. Every time you press a key, you hear both types of beeps, which proves that all three interrupts—beep one, beep two, and the original keyboard handler—are running from the single keyboard interrupt.

Listing 19.3. TSR2.CPP—Key Beep Program, Version 2

```cpp
///////////////////////////////////////////////////////////
// TSR2.CPP: A simple TSR program.
///////////////////////////////////////////////////////////

#include <dos.h>
#include <iostream.h>
#include <string.h>

// The keyboard interrupt number.
#define KEYBRD 0x09

// Function prototypes.
void interrupt (*old_keybrd)(...);
void interrupt keybrd(...);
```

continues

Listing 19.3. Continued

```
/////////////////////////////////////////////////////////
// main()
/////////////////////////////////////////////////////////
void main(void)
{
   // Get the address of the old handler.
   old_keybrd = getvect(KEYBRD);

   // Set address to the new handler.
   setvect(KEYBRD, keybrd);

   // Make the handler a TSR program.
   keep(0, (_SS + (_SP/16) - _psp));
}


/////////////////////////////////////////////////////////
// keybrd()
//
// This function is the new keyboard interrupt.
/////////////////////////////////////////////////////////
void interrupt keybrd(...)
{
   // Call old keyboard handler.
   old_keybrd();

   // Generate a key sound
   sound(1000);
   delay(30);
   nosound();
}
```

An On-Screen Clock

Now that you know the basics of writing interrupt handlers and TSR programs, how about writing something useful? Listing 19.4 puts together everything you've learned to produce an on-screen clock. When you run the clock TSR, the clock display appears in the upper right corner of your DOS screen. It's a tenacious little critter; as long as the computer stays in DOS text mode, the clock should stay on-screen.

Listing 19.4. CLOCK1.CPP—On-Screen Clock TSR Program

```
/////////////////////////////////////////////////////
// CLOCK1.CPP: On-screen clock TSR, version 1
/////////////////////////////////////////////////////

#include <dos.h>
```

```
// Define some constants.
#define CLOCK 0x1c
#define ATTR 0x7900
#define FALSE 0
#define TRUE 1

// Define pointer to hold old vector.
void interrupt (*oldclock)(...);

// Define a pointer to screen memory.
unsigned int (far *screen);

// Define some global data.
struct time t;       // Struct for gettime().
int hour, min, sec;  // Counters for time.
int count,           // Interrupt counter.
    tick,            // Another interrupt counter.
    colon;           // Flag for colon visibility.
char clockstr[] = {"00:00"}; // Clock display string.

// Function prototypes.
void FormatClockStr();
void HandleColon();
void HandleTime();
void interrupt ClockIntr(...);

//////////////////////////////////////////////////////////
// main()
//////////////////////////////////////////////////////////
void main(void)
{
  // Get old vector and set new vector.
  oldclock = getvect(CLOCK);
  setvect(CLOCK, ClockIntr);

  // Initialize time counters and colon flag.
  gettime(&t);
  min = t.ti_min;
  hour = t.ti_hour;
  count = t.ti_sec * 18;
  tick = 0;
  colon = FALSE;

  // Initialize display string.
  FormatClockStr();

  // Go TSR.
  keep(0, (_SS + (_SP/16) - _psp));
}


//////////////////////////////////////////////////////////
// FormatClockStr()
//
// This function uses the hour and minute counters to
// construct the clock's display.
```

continues

Listing 19.4. Continued

```
///////////////////////////////////////////////////////
void FormatClockStr()
{
  // Format hour portion of string.
  if (hour < 10)
  {
    clockstr[0] = '0';
    clockstr[1] = hour + '0';
  }
  else
  {
    clockstr[0] = hour/10 + '0';
    clockstr[1] = hour%10 + '0';
  }

  // Format minute portion of string.
  if (min < 10)
  {
    clockstr[3] = '0';
    clockstr[4] = min + '0';
  }
  else
  {
    clockstr[3] = min/10 + '0';
    clockstr[4] = min%10 + '0';
  }
}


///////////////////////////////////////////////////////
// HandleColon()
//
// This function is responsible for the blinking colon
// in the clock display. Every 9 ticks (1/2 second), the
// colon is added to or deleted from the string, which
// causes the colon to blink in 1-second intervals.
///////////////////////////////////////////////////////
void HandleColon()
{
  // Increment counter
  ++tick;

  // If a half second has passed, set counter back
  // to zero, and then add or remove the colon.
  if (tick == 9)
  {
    tick = 0;

    // If colon is in the string, remove it.
    if (colon)
    {
      clockstr[2] = ' ';
      colon = FALSE;
    }
```

```c
    // If colon is not in the string, add it.
    else
    {
      clockstr[2] = ':';
      colon = TRUE;
    }
  }
}

////////////////////////////////////////////////////////
// HandleTime()
//
// This function calculates when a minute has passed,
// at which time it updates the time counters to
// reflect the current time.
////////////////////////////////////////////////////////
void HandleTime()
{
  // Increment timer.
  ++count;

  // If count == 1092, a minute has passed.
  // (18.2 ticks per second times 60.)
  if (count == 1092)
  {
    // Reset counter.
    count = 0;

    // Increment minutes.
    ++min;

    // If min == 60, reset min and increment hour.
    if (min == 60)
    {
      min = 0;
      ++hour;

      // If hour == 24, recycle back to 0 to
      // simulate 24-hour clock.
      if (hour == 24)
      hour = 0;
    }
    // Create new display string from new times.
    FormatClockStr();
  }
}

////////////////////////////////////////////////////////
// ClockIntr()
//
// This is the interrupt handler. It displays the
// current clock string, checks the counters, and
// finally chains to the old interrupt.
////////////////////////////////////////////////////////
```

continues

Listing 19.4. Continued

```
void interrupt ClockIntr(...)
{
  // Get the screen address.
  screen = (unsigned int far *) MK_FP(0xb800,0);

  // Get address of clock position on first screen line.
  screen += 75;

  // Write clock display string directly to screen memory.
  for (int x= 0; x<5; ++x)
    *screen++ = clockstr[x] + ATTR;

  // Update counters.
  HandleColon();
  HandleTime();

  // Chain to old handler.
  _chain_intr(oldclock);
}
```

Although the clock TSR is a bit more sophisticated than the keyboard beeper, you'll be delighted to know that it's still a fairly simple program. The program is discussed function by function, starting with `main()`:

```
void main(void)
{
  // Get old vector and set new vector.
  oldclock = getvect(CLOCK);
  setvect(CLOCK, ClockIntr);

  // Initialize time counters and colon flag.
  gettime(&t);
  min = t.ti_min;
  hour = t.ti_hour;
  count = t.ti_sec * 18;
  tick = 0;
  colon = FALSE;

  // Initialize display string.
  FormatClockStr();

  // Go TSR.
  keep(0, (_SS + (_SP/16) - _psp));
}
```

In a TSR, most program initialization takes place in `main()`, which executes once when the program is first loaded. Here, the program first gets and saves the old timer vector, and installs the new handler. Next,

a call to `gettime()` gets the current time, which is saved in the `min`, `hour`, and `count` time counters. Because `count` counts timer ticks (each timer interrupt represents one tick and occurs 18.2 times a second), `count` is initialized by multiplying `t.ti_sec` times 18. After initializing the remaining variables and the starting clock string, the program calls `keep()` to exit the program and leave it resident in memory.

After `main()` finishes its tasks, it's finished forever (or at least until the next time the program is loaded). The TSR, which is represented by the interrupt handler and the functions it calls, stands ready to spring into action whenever it detects a timer interrupt, which is 18.2 times a second:

```
void interrupt ClockIntr(...)
{
  // Get the screen address.
  screen = (unsigned int far *) MK_FP(0xb800,0);

  // Get address of clock position on first screen line.
  screen += 75;

  // Write clock display string directly to screen memory.
  for (int x= 0; x<5; ++x)
    *screen++ = clockstr[x] + ATTR;

  // Update counters.
  HandleColon();
  HandleTime();

  // Chain to old handler.
  _chain_intr(oldclock);
}
```

The handler first calculates the address of screen memory. It then adds 75 to the resulting address, yielding an address near the end of the first screen line (80 characters to a line). After calculating the screen address, the handler writes the clock display string directly into screen memory.

Why print directly to screen memory? First, if the handler prints to the screen using standard stream input-output (`cout`) or a string-display function like `cputs()`, it changes the location of the text cursor, which messes up the user's screen. (You can get around this problem by saving the location of the cursor, printing your string, and restoring the cursor's location.)

There's another, more important reason why the handler must write directly to screen memory. When the handler wants to print your clock display, MS-DOS may be busy with another task, and the handler cannot call MS-DOS safely. Remember, your TSR is running in the background; a foreground application, or even another TSR, may be running too. MS-DOS can handle only one task at a time; to ask it to do more is courting disaster. Imagine, for example, trying to save two files to disk simultaneously. Ouch!

Unless you know what you're doing, calling MS-DOS from a TSR can yield unpredictable behavior, anything from locking up the keyboard to destroying data on a hard disk. The next section shows some ways to determine whether MS-DOS is busy. For now, however, let's keep things simple.

(Notice that the program can call the MS-DOS `gettime()` function in `main()` because, when `main()` is running, the program is not yet a TSR program. When `main()` is running, the clock program is like any other program. There can be no conflict with MS-DOS, because no other program can call MS-DOS until `main()` is finished.)

After the handler displays the clock string, it calls the `HandleColon()` and `HandleTime()` functions, which implement the blinking colon in the display and update the time counters, respectively. Finally, the handler chains to the old timer interrupt by calling `_chain_intr()` with the address of the old handler. This function turns control over to the old handler without returning to the handler that called it. For this reason, call `_chain_intr()` only as the last line of a handler. If you must call the original handler before executing your own, use the method shown in Listing 19.3.

The `HandleColon()` function implements the blinking colon that marks the passing seconds:

```
void HandleColon()
{
  // Increment counter.
  ++tick;

  // If a half second has passed, set counter back
```

```
// to zero, and then add or remove the colon.
if (tick == 9)
{
  tick = 0;

  // If colon is in the string, remove it.
  if (colon)
  {
    clockstr[2] = ' ';
    colon = FALSE;
  }

  // If colon is not in the string, add it.
  else
  {
    clockstr[2] = ':';
    colon = TRUE;
  }
}
}
```

This function first increments the tick counter. Because the timer interrupt occurs 18.2 times a second, a half second has passed when this counter reaches 9. In that case, the counter is set back to 0, and then the colon character is added to or removed from the string. Which is done depends on the value of the colon flag. By adding or removing the colon every half second, the colon appears to blink.

The next function, HandleTime(), is responsible for keeping the clock up to date:

```
void HandleTime()
{
  // Increment timer.
  ++count;

  // If count == 1092, a minute has passed.
  // (18.2 ticks per second times 60.)
  if (count == 1092)
  {
    // Reset counter.
    count = 0;

    // Increment minutes.
    ++min;

    // If min == 60, reset min and increment hour.
    if (min == 60)
    {
      min = 0;
      ++hour;
```

```
          // If hour == 24, recycle back to 0 to
          // simulate 24-hour clock.
          if (hour == 24)
        hour = 0;
      }
      // Create new display string from new times.
      FormatClockStr();
    }
  }
```

This function works similarly to `HandleColon()`, except its counter is allowed to count up to 1092, which is the number of timer interrupts per
minute (60 * 18.2). When the counter reaches 1092, it's time to update
the clock string with a new minute, and maybe even a new hour. After
resetting the counter, `min` is incremented. If `min` is 60, another hour has
passed, so `min` is reset to 0 and `hour` is incremented. If `hour` is 24, it's reset
to 0, which simulates a 24-hour clock. Finally, `FormatClockStr()` builds
the clock's display string:

```
void FormatClockStr()
{
  // Format hour portion of string.
  if (hour < 10)
  {
    clockstr[0] = '0';
    clockstr[1] = hour + '0';
  }
  else
  {
    clockstr[0] = hour/10 + '0';
    clockstr[1] = hour%10 + '0';
  }

  // Format minute portion of string.
  if (min < 10)
  {
    clockstr[3] = '0';
    clockstr[4] = min + '0';
  }
  else
  {
    clockstr[3] = min/10 + '0';
    clockstr[4] = min%10 + '0';
  }
}
```

This function simply uses the values in `min` and `hour` to construct the
display string.

The MS-DOS Busy Flag

When the designers of MS-DOS knew that folks like you and I would be writing interrupt handlers and TSR programs, they provided a way for these programs to find out whether MS-DOS is busy. After all, if MS-DOS isn't servicing some other program, there's no reason why you can't call it in your interrupt handlers and TSR programs. To provide this extra service, the designers of MS-DOS added the InDos flag.

The InDos flag is nothing more than a location in memory that marks whether MS-DOS is currently servicing a function request. When MS-DOS is busy, this flag is set to 1. When MS-DOS is idle, the InDos flag is cleared to 0. So, to use MS-DOS in your TSR programs, you need only check the value of InDos. If it's 0, you can go ahead and do what you like. Right?

Well, 99.9% of the time you would be right. Unfortunately, MS-DOS' critical error handler (that's the handler that displays the infamous Abort, Retry, Fail? prompt) complicates matters. The details of this complication are beyond the scope of this book; simply put, to safely call MS-DOS, you must check both the InDos flag and another flag called CritErr (Critical Error). If both these flags are clear, you can use MS-DOS without worry.

Listing 19.5 is a new version of the clock TSR that relies on the InDos and CritErr flags to determine whether it can call MS-DOS. In this version, the call to gettime() is moved from main() to the interrupt handler. Doing this means the handler can get the current time at every timer interrupt, without keeping track of minute and hour counters. Because the handler no longer needs the time counters, the entire HandleTime() function has been deleted.

Listing 19.5. CLOCK2.CPP—On-Screen Clock TSR Program, Version 2

```
/////////////////////////////////////////////////////////
// CLOCK2.CPP: On-screen clock TSR, version 2
/////////////////////////////////////////////////////////

#include <dos.h>
```

continues

Listing 19.5. Continued

```
// Define some constants.
#define CLOCK 0x1c
#define ATTR 0x7900
#define FALSE 0
#define TRUE 1

// Define pointer to hold old vector.
void interrupt (*oldclock)(...);

// Define a pointer to screen memory.
unsigned int (far *screen);

// Define some global data.
struct time t;          // Struct for gettime().
int tick,               // Interrupt counter.
    colon;              // Flag for colon visibility.
char clockstr[] = {"00:00"}; // Clock display string.

// Declare pointers to InDOS and CritErr flags.
char far *indos;
char far *criterr;

// Function prototypes.
void FormatClockStr();
void HandleColon();
void interrupt ClockIntr(...);

//////////////////////////////////////////////////////////
// main()
//////////////////////////////////////////////////////////
void main(void)
{
  // Get address of inDOS flag.
  _AH = 0x34;
  geninterrupt(0x21);

  // Initialize InDOS and CritErr pointers.
  unsigned int seg = _ES;
  unsigned int off = _BX;
  indos = (char far *) MK_FP(seg, off);
  criterr = indos - 1;

  // Get old vector and set new vector.
  oldclock = getvect(CLOCK);
  setvect(CLOCK, ClockIntr);

  // Initialize time counters and colon flag.
  tick = 0;
  colon = FALSE;

  // Go TSR.
  keep(0, (_SS + (_SP/16) - _psp));
}
```

```
/////////////////////////////////////////////////////////
// FormatClockStr()
//
// This function uses the hour and minute counters to
// construct the clock's display.
/////////////////////////////////////////////////////////
void FormatClockStr()
{
  // Format hour portion of string.
  if (t.ti_hour < 10)
  {
    clockstr[0] = '0';
    clockstr[1] = t.ti_hour + '0';
  }
  else
  {
    clockstr[0] = t.ti_hour / 10 + '0';
    clockstr[1] = t.ti_hour % 10 + '0';
  }

  // Format minute portion of string.
  if (t.ti_min < 10)
  {
    clockstr[3] = '0';
    clockstr[4] = t.ti_min + '0';
  }
  else
  {
    clockstr[3] = t.ti_min / 10 + '0';
    clockstr[4] = t.ti_min % 10 + '0';
  }
}


/////////////////////////////////////////////////////////
// HandleColon()
//
// This function is responsible for the blinking colon
// in the clock display. Every 9 ticks (1/2 second), the
// colon is added to or deleted from the string, which
// causes the colon to blink in 1-second intervals.
/////////////////////////////////////////////////////////
void HandleColon()
{
  // Increment counter.
  ++tick;

  // If a half second has passed, set counter back
  // to zero, and then add or remove the colon.
  if (tick == 9)
  {
    tick = 0;

    // If colon is in the string, remove it.
    if (colon)
```

continues

Listing 19.5. Continued

```
    {
      clockstr[2] = ' ';
      colon = FALSE;
    }

    // If colon is not in the string, add it.
    else
    {
      clockstr[2] = ':';
      colon = TRUE;
    }
  }
}


////////////////////////////////////////////////////////
// ClockIntr()
//
// This is the interrupt handler. It displays the
// current clock string, checks the counters, and
// finally chains to the old interrupt.
////////////////////////////////////////////////////////
void interrupt ClockIntr(...)
{
  // Handle the blinking colon.
  HandleColon();

  // Is it safe to call MS-DOS?
  if (!*indos && !*criterr)
  {
    // Use MS-DOS to get current time.
    gettime(&t);

    // Build clock display string.
    FormatClockStr();

    // Get the screen address.
    screen = (unsigned int far *) MK_FP(0xb800,0);

    // Get address of clock position on first screen line.
    screen += 75;

    // Write clock display string directly to screen memory.
    for (int x= 0; x<5; ++x)
      *screen++ = clockstr[x] + ATTR;
  }

  // Chain to old handler.
  _chain_intr(oldclock);
}
```

Now let's see what else has changed in this version, starting with `main()`:

```
void main(void)
{
  // Get address of inDOS flag.
  _AH = 0x34;
  geninterrupt(0x21);

  // Initialize InDOS and CritErr pointers.
  unsigned int seg = _ES;
  unsigned int off = _BX;
  indos = (char far *) MK_FP(seg, off);
  criterr = indos - 1;

  // Get old vector and set new vector.
  oldclock = getvect(CLOCK);
  setvect(CLOCK, ClockIntr);

  // Initialize time counters and colon flag.
  tick = 0;
  colon = FALSE;

  // Go TSR.
  keep(0, (_SS + (_SP/16) - _psp));
}
```

First, the program gets the address of the `InDos` flag by calling the MS-DOS function 34 (Int 21). This function call returns the segment portion of the address in ES and the offset portion of the address in BX. To create a far pointer from these values, use Borland's `MK_FP()` macro. The `CritErr` flag is a little easier to calculate. In MS-DOS version 3.0 or greater, it's located at `InDos-1`.

After getting these all-important pointers, the program chains into the timer interrupt, initializes a few variables, and exits, leaving the program resident in memory. Because more of the work is done in the interrupt handler, `main()` is much smaller, and does little more than get the TSR going.

As with the first version of the clock program, after `main()` finishes, the interrupt handler is installed and starts responding to timer interrupts:

```
void interrupt ClockIntr(...)
{
  // Handle the blinking colon.
  HandleColon();
```

```
// Is it safe to call MS-DOS?
if (!*indos && !*criterr)
{
    // Use MS-DOS to get current time.
    gettime(&t);

    // Build clock display string.
    FormatClockStr();

    // Get the screen address.
    screen = (unsigned int far *) MK_FP(0xb800,0);

    // Get address of clock position on first screen line.
    screen += 75;

    // Write clock display string directly to screen memory.
    for (int x= 0; x<5; ++x)
        *screen++ = clockstr[x] + ATTR;
}

// Chain to old handler.
_chain_intr(oldclock);
}
```

Here, the program first calls `HandleColon()`, which updates the interrupt count and then modifies the clock display string each half second (9 ticks). This is done before anything else to ensure that the counter remains accurate. The colon in the display string does not blink at the proper interval if the counter is not kept up to date.

After taking care of the colon, the handler checks the `indos` and `criterr` flags to determine whether it's safe to call MS-DOS. If MS-DOS is busy, the bulk of the handler is skipped, and control is given to the old handler. (This is why the `HandleColon()` call wasn't placed here. When MS-DOS is busy, the interrupt counter would not be updated properly.) If it's safe to request MS-DOS services, the handler calls `gettime()` to get the current time and uses the values it returns to format the clock display string. Finally, the clock's display string is written to the screen.

After the code inside the `if` statement concludes, the program chains to the old handler. Note that whether MS-DOS is busy or not, the old timer handler is always called. If the program didn't do this, results would be unpredictable and other TSR programs chained to the interrupt might not run properly.

The other functions in version 2 of the clock program (Listing 19.5) are similar or identical to version 1 (Listing 19.4). The only difference is that the `FormatClockStr()` function no longer uses the values of the timer counters to construct the display string; it uses the time data in the `t` structure, which contains the values returned from `gettime()`.

To see that the `indos` and `criterr` flags are really doing their job, try this experiment: After resetting your machine (to be sure that all versions of the clock TSR are erased from memory), run CLOCK1 (Listing 19.4). Now, watching the clock display, copy a file to a disk. Although MS-DOS is busy copying the file, the clock continues to function. Now, after resetting your machine again, load CLOCK2 (Listing 19.5) and repeat the experiment. This time when you copy a file, the clock stops working until MS-DOS finishes its task. This proves that your TSR now knows when to leave MS-DOS alone.

One final note about the `InDos` flag: When you're at the DOS prompt, your computer calls an MS-DOS function to poll the keyboard for input, so the `InDos` flag is continually set and cleared as your computer looks for keystrokes. You can see this in action by modifying the interrupt handler in Listing 19.5 so the `HandleColon()` function call comes after the `if` statement. When you run the clock, the colon blinks about half as fast because the interrupt counter isn't properly updated when the `InDos` flag is set.

This can be a problem for a TSR that relies on the `InDos` flag to accomplish its work. Luckily, there's a solution. When your computer is polling for keystrokes, it continually generates interrupt 0x28, which is the idle loop interrupt. By chaining to this interrupt, you can determine when MS-DOS is polling for keystrokes. Moreover, this interrupt is issued only when it's safe to call MS-DOS, regardless of the `InDos` flag's state. When you detect interrupt 0x28, you can safely call MS-DOS functions from your TSR.

Detecting Whether a TSR Is Loaded

One thing you may have noticed about the clock TSR is that it has no way of knowing whether it's already loaded. Because of this, you can accidentally load the TSR repeatedly, which eats up memory that can be used for other programs. To avoid this problem, the clock TSR needs some way of checking its status. But how? You can't use a flag in the main program, because each time you run the TSR, a new instance of the TSR is created, and each instance has its own data. The answer to this dilemma, as you may have guessed, is an interrupt handler.

The interrupt 0x2F is traditionally used for communicating between TSR programs. In fact, an entire standard for the use of this interrupt with TSR programs has been developed (the TesSeRact standard, information about which is provided at the end of this chapter). There are many commands implemented in the standard, one of which, CHECK_INSTALL, is demonstrated in the third version of the clock TSR program, shown here in Listing 19.6. This version of the program does not allow you to load the TSR if it's already in memory. If you try, you get the message The clock TSR is already installed.

Listing 19.6. CLOCK3.CPP—On-Screen Clock TSR Program, Version 3

```
////////////////////////////////////////////////////////
// CLOCK3.CPP: On-screen clock TSR, version 3
////////////////////////////////////////////////////////

#include <dos.h>
#include <iostream.h>

// Define some constants.
#define CLOCK 0x1c
#define ATTR 0x7900
#define FALSE 0
#define TRUE 1
#define CLOCK_ID 0xEB
#define CHECK_INSTALL 0x00

// Declare pointers to hold old vectors.
void interrupt (*old2f)(...);
void interrupt (*oldclock)(...);

// Declare a pointer to screen memory.
```

```
unsigned int (far *screen);

// Declare some global data.
struct time t;      // Struct for gettime().
int    tick,        // Interrupt counter.
       colon;       // Flag for colon visibility.
char clockstr[] = {"00:00"}; // Clock display string.

// Declare pointers to InDOS and CritErr flags.
char far *indos;
char far *criterr;

// Function prototypes.
void FormatClockStr();
void HandleColon();
void interrupt ClockIntr(...);
void interrupt New2f(unsigned, unsigned, unsigned, unsigned,
                unsigned, unsigned, unsigned, unsigned,
                unsigned, unsigned, unsigned, unsigned);

/////////////////////////////////////////////////////////
// main()
/////////////////////////////////////////////////////////
void main(void)
{
  _AH = CLOCK_ID;
  _AL = CHECK_INSTALL;
  geninterrupt(0x2f);
  if (_AL == 0xff)
    cout << "The clock TSR is already installed.\n";
  else
  {
    // Get address of inDOS flag.
    _AH = 0x34;
    geninterrupt(0x21);

    // Initialize InDOS and CritErr pointers.
    unsigned int seg = _ES;
    unsigned int off = _BX;
    indos = (char far *) MK_FP(seg, off);
    criterr = indos - 1;

    // Get old vectors and set new vectors.
    oldclock = getvect(CLOCK);
    setvect(CLOCK, ClockIntr);
    old2f = getvect(0x2f);
    setvect(0x2f, (void interrupt(*)(...)) New2f);

    // Initialize time counters and colon flag.
    tick = 0;
    colon = FALSE;

    // Go TSR.
    keep(0, (_SS + (_SP/16) - _psp));
  }
```

continues

Detecting Whether a TSR Is Loaded **857**

Listing 19.6. Continued

```
}

#pragma argsused
///////////////////////////////////////////////////////
// New2f()
//
// This is the interrupt handler used for communicating
// between TSRs. In this case, the handler notifies the
// caller that the CLOCK_ID TSR is loaded.
///////////////////////////////////////////////////////
void interrupt New2f(unsigned bp, unsigned di, unsigned si,
                unsigned ds, unsigned es, unsigned dx,
                unsigned cx, unsigned bx, unsigned ax,
                unsigned ip, unsigned cs, unsigned flags)
{
  // Check for the TSR's ID. If this request is not
  // for this clock TSR, chain to the old 2f.
  if (_AH != CLOCK_ID)
    _chain_intr(old2f);

  // If the caller is requesting whether the
  // clock TSR is loaded, tell it yes.
  if (_AL == CHECK_INSTALL)
  {
    ax = 0xFFFF;
    bx = _psp;
  }
}


///////////////////////////////////////////////////////
// FormatClockStr()
//
// This function uses the hour and minute counters to
// construct the clock's display.
///////////////////////////////////////////////////////
void FormatClockStr()
{
  // Format hour portion of string.
  if (t.ti_hour < 10)
  {
    clockstr[0] = '0';
    clockstr[1] = t.ti_hour + '0';
  }
  else
  {
    clockstr[0] = t.ti_hour / 10 + '0';
    clockstr[1] = t.ti_hour % 10 + '0';
  }

  // Format minute portion of string.
  if (t.ti_min < 10)
  {
    clockstr[3] = '0';
```

```
    clockstr[4] = t.ti_min + '0';
  }
  else
  {
    clockstr[3] = t.ti_min / 10 + '0';
    clockstr[4] = t.ti_min % 10 + '0';
  }
}

/////////////////////////////////////////////////////////
// HandleColon()
//
// This function is responsible for the blinking colon
// in the clock display. Every 9 ticks (1/2 second),
// the colon is added or deleted from the string, which
// causes the colon to blink in one second intervals.
/////////////////////////////////////////////////////////
void HandleColon()
{
  // Increment counter.
  ++tick;

  // If a half second has passed, set counter back
  // to zero, and then add or remove the colon.
  if (tick == 9)
  {
    tick = 0;

    // If colon is in string, remove it.
    if (colon)
    {
      clockstr[2] = ' ';
      colon = FALSE;
    }

    // If colon is not in string, add it.
    else
    {
      clockstr[2] = ':';
      colon = TRUE;
    }
  }
}

/////////////////////////////////////////////////////////
// ClockIntr()
//
// This is the interrupt handler. It displays the
// current clock string, checks the counters, and
// finally chains to the old interrupt.
/////////////////////////////////////////////////////////
void interrupt ClockIntr(...)
{
  // Handle the blinking colon.
  HandleColon();
```

continues

Detecting Whether a TSR Is Loaded **859**

Listing 19.6. Continued

```
// Is it safe to call MS-DOS?
if (!*indos && !*criterr)
{
  // Use MS-DOS to get current time.
  gettime(&t);

  // Build clock display string.
  FormatClockStr();

  // Get the screen address.
  screen = (unsigned int far *) MK_FP(0xb800,0);

  // Get address of clock position on first screen line.
  screen += 75;

  // Write clock display string directly to screen memory.
  for (int x= 0; x<5; ++x)
    *screen++ = clockstr[x] + ATTR;
}

// Chain to old handler.
_chain_intr(oldclock);
}
```

Look at main() first, because it's in main() that the program generates the request to check whether the TSR is already loaded:

```
void main(void)
{
  _AH = CLOCK_ID;
  _AL = CHECK_INSTALL;
  geninterrupt(0x2f);
  if (_AL == 0xff)
    cout << "The clock TSR is already installed.\n";
  else
  {
    // Get address of inDOS flag.
    _AH = 0x34;
    geninterrupt(0x21);

    // Initialize InDOS and CritErr pointers.
    unsigned int seg = _ES;
    unsigned int off = _BX;
    indos = (char far *) MK_FP(seg, off);
    criterr = indos - 1;

    // Get old vectors and set new vectors.
    oldclock = getvect(CLOCK);
    setvect(CLOCK, ClockIntr);
    old2f = getvect(0x2f);
```

```
        setvect(0x2f, (void interrupt(*)(...)) New2f);

        // Initialize time counters and colon flag.
        tick = 0;
        colon = FALSE;

        // Go TSR.
        keep(0, (_SS + (_SP/16) - _psp));
    }
}
```

Here, the program first sends a CHECK_INSTALL request to the 0x2f interrupt. This is accomplished by placing the TSR program's ID in AH,
placing the command value (0x00 for CHECK_INSTALL) in AL, and generating a 0x2f interrupt. The results of the request are returned in AL. If the
clock TSR is already loaded, the value in AL is -1. In this case, the program need do nothing more than report that the TSR is already loaded,
and exit. Otherwise, the program can install the TSR.

In order for the CHECK_INSTALL request to work properly, the TSR must
install its own 0x2f interrupt handler:

```
void interrupt New2f(unsigned bp, unsigned di, unsigned si,
                unsigned ds, unsigned es, unsigned dx,
                unsigned cx, unsigned bx, unsigned ax,
                unsigned ip, unsigned cs, unsigned flags)
{
  // Check for the TSR's ID. If this request is not
  // for this clock TSR, chain to the old 2f.
  if (_AH != CLOCK_ID)
    _chain_intr(old2f);

  // If the caller is requesting whether the
  // clock TSR is loaded, tell it yes.
  if (_AL == CHECK_INSTALL)
  {
    ax = 0xFFFF;
    bx = _psp;
  }
}
```

When the clock TSR is not loaded, this interrupt handler is not active.
The 0x2f interrupt generated in main(), is handled by whatever handler
is installed at that time. It can be the system's default handler, or it
might be a handler installed by another TSR. In any case, that handler
doesn't recognize (hopefully) the clock TSR's ID and so does not respond with a -1 to the CHECK_INSTALL request.

Note: Because it's possible for two TSR programs to use the same ID, it also is possible for the CHECK_INSTALL request (and other commands) to return erroneous information. For example, if you try to load a TSR with the same ID as your clock TSR, the clock TSR may capture that TSR's CHECK_INSTALL request and not allow it to load. To help avoid this type of problem, Microsoft Corporation keeps a list of registered TSRs to which you can refer when choosing your TSR's ID number. When your TSR is complete, you can then register it with Microsoft, too, so that other developers are aware of your TSR's ID.

When the clock TSR is installed, however, its 0x2f interrupt handler can respond to `main()`'s CHECK_INSTALL request. First, this function checks the ID in AH. If AH doesn't contain the clock TSR's ID, the handler passes the buck, as it were, by chaining to the old 0x2f handler. If AH does contain the TSR's ID, the handler checks AL for the CHECK_INSTALL command value. If it finds this value, the program loads AX with -1 and loads BX with the TSR's PSP, which is found in the global variable _psp. (To be compliant with the TesSeRact standard, you must return the PSP in BX.)

Note: PSP stands for *program segment prefix*. The PSP is built by DOS when you run an executable file, and it contains 256 bytes of data that DOS needs when running your program. A complete discussion of the PSP is beyond the scope of this book, but it's helpful to know that the beginning of the PSP marks the beginning of your program in memory.

As you've already seen, the return values from the handler are easily checked by the program that generated the request, allowing any TSR to determine whether the clock TSR is loaded. In this way, you can make sure your TSR programs aren't loaded more than once, as well as communicate with other TSR programs with known IDs.

Note: Notice that, in some instructions, the 0x2f handler uses the register pseudovariables (_AH and _AL), and in others (where values are changed), it uses the register variables passed to the handler. It does this because, when the handler exits, the values in the register parameters are the ones used to restore the registers. If you try to make a change to a register using the pseudovariables, your change is overwritten by the values in the register parameters.

Caution: It's imperative that your 0x2f interrupt handlers chain to the old handler if the ID passed in AH does not belong to your TSR. This way you can pass requests targeted for other TSR programs. If you fail to do this, other TSR programs loaded into the system might not function properly.

In this chapter, you explored the basics of writing interrupt handlers and TSR programs. However, this chapter didn't cover advanced topics, such as how to unload a TSR from memory, how to avoid TSR stack overflows, or how to communicate with your or other TSR programs. These and other advanced topics are best left to highly experienced programmers with a good knowledge of assembly-language programming.

Such advanced topics cannot be overlooked by any programmer who plans to distribute his TSR programs. Because this chapter is meant as only an introduction to TSRs for intermediate-level programmers, it does not confront many of the critical topics that a competent TSR programmer must know. Writing TSR programs is a complex subject that requires much study to master.

From Here...

If you want to write TSR programs for general distribution, here are a few additional resources.

➤ A TSR standard has been developed by a group known as the TesSeRact Development Team. The TSR specifications included in this standard dictate a consistent way for TSR programs to communicate through interrupt `0x2f`. For a copy of this standard, write to:

> TesSeRact Development Team
> 1657 The Fairways, Suite 101
> Jenkintown, PA 19046

➤ Two books you might want to check out are *Advanced MS-DOS Programming* by Ray Duncan (published by Microsoft Press) and *Secrets of the Borland C++ Masters* by Ed Mitchell (published by Sams Publishing).

➤ Source code for several working TSR programs is available from Borland's BBS at (408) 439-9096. One example program, TSR_C.ZIP, includes code for unloading a TSR from memory.

➤ For more information on pointers to functions, see Chapter 2, "Turbocharging Pointers."

➤ For a discussion on using the memory heap effectively, see Chapter 9, "K&R Implementation Secrets."

➤ For information on writing C++ programs (including TSRs) that include code written in other languages (including assembly language), see Chapter 13, "Mixed Language Programming," and Chapter 14, "Bare Metal Programming."

C++ Style Tips

by Clayton Walnum

When the C language was first developed, the goal was to create a minor language that was portable between systems. To keep the language as concise as possible, special symbols were used to represent operators and other language elements. For example, rather than use the ubiquitous BEGIN and END statements found in languages like Pascal, the C designers chose the open and close braces ({ and }) to identify program blocks. Similarly, keywords like INTEGER were shortened to int.

While C's designers were successful in their task, the resulting language is somewhat cryptic. When programmers don't follow good style rules, C source code becomes almost unreadable. Even today, C (and C++) programmers are infamous for their muddy code, seeming to delight in creating programs that are as incomprehensible as possible. It's as if they think unreadable code is somehow evidence of a programmer's skill and intelligence.

However, programmers who insist on writing obscure code are programmers who will soon find themselves in the unemployment line. Just as no one wants to read a novel filled with ten-syllable words and two-page paragraphs, no one wants to muddle through source code that looks like it was created by pasting together random character sequences.

If you're one of those programmers who thinks that hard-to-understand source code is sophisticated, it's time to rethink your position. Your source code should be as crystal clear as a cool mountain stream. Often that means resorting to what you might currently think of as C++ baby talk—for example, avoiding the nesting of function calls—but as you develop new code-writing skills, you'll appreciate how clear code makes your job easier.

The first section of this chapter presents a number of style rules to help you write more understandable code. Not only will you learn to create clear code, but you'll also learn some tricks for organizing code into modules. Remember, though, that these are general rules that can be applied differently in different situations. For example, the coding style you'd use when working with a team of programmers designing a database application would be very different from the style you'd use for source code in a book. You need to use some judgment.

In the second section of this chapter, you will look at coding style from a more lofty viewpoint, learning how to properly use such C++ tools as classes, virtual functions, overloaded functions, and overloaded operators.

Formatting Your Code

The first step toward writing understandable programs is to adopt a standard way of formatting statements and functions. C++ allows for many types of code formats, but, over time, programmers have come

up with formats that work well for most situations. By adopting these tried-and-true format styles, your programs will be more understandable not only to yourself, but also to other programmers.

Below are some general rules for formatting statements and functions in a C++ program. Again, these rules are not cast in stone; there may be times when breaking a rule makes more sense than following it. The bottom line is that your source code must be as understandable as possible. Anything that obscures the code should be avoided.

Use Comments

Comments are a valuable tool for documenting your programs. They enable you to provide clear descriptions for C++ source code. Every function in your program should have a comment header that gives the function's name and explains what the function does. The actual format of this header varies from programmer to programmer and may be dictated by the programming team with which you're working. In any case, though, the function header comments should give the information other programmers need to understand how to use the function. This information usually includes descriptions of all the function's parameters, as well as any values returned from the function.

This chapter uses informal function comments. This is because program listings in a book must be as short as possible. In addition, the source code is usually thoroughly explained in the book's text. An example of one of my function comments follows:

```
/////////////////////////////////////////////////////
// DispatchEvent()
//
// This function checks the current event message and
// branches to the function chosen by the user.
/////////////////////////////////////////////////////
```

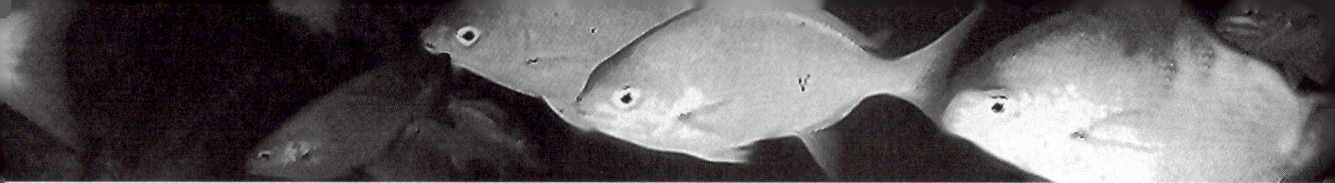

If programming is your hobby, this style of function comment is probably good enough. Programmers working in a professional atmosphere, however, must use more formal comment styles:

```
////////////////////////////////////////////////////////
// DispatchEvent()
//
// This function checks the current event message and
// branches to the function chosen by the user.
//
// PARAMETERS: eventMsg — Structure containing the
//                        current message data.
//
// RETURNS: Nothing.
////////////////////////////////////////////////////////
void DispatchEvent(EventMsg eventMsg)
```

Here, the function's parameter and return value are fully described in separate comment sections. By using a formal function header like this one, you and other programmers know exactly where to look to find the information you need to use the function.

You also should use comments throughout your program code wherever the code itself is not obvious. Source code that can be easily interpreted need not be commented. For example, the following line of code requires no comment:

```
profit = sellingPrice - cost;
```

These lines of code, however, should be commented:

```
// Translate mouse-click coordinates
// to column and row coordinates.
int x = (eventMsg.mx - XOFF) / 33;
int y = (eventMsg.my - YOFF) / 22;
```

While comments are a powerful tool for documenting your programs, be careful not to overdo them. When working on a program, no one wants to wade through large blocks of text. Make your comments clear and concise.

> **Caution:** Make sure all your comments are accurate. An inaccurate comment is worse than no comment at all. When you modify program code, be sure to update any associated comments, too.

> **Tip:** Add comments to your code as you're writing it, rather than try to comment a completed program. If you wait until later, you may forget exactly what a piece of code accomplishes. Also, if you wait until the end of a project to write your comments, the task may be so large that you just won't bother.

Use Meaningful Variable Names

Comments help you document your program's code. By using meaningful variable names, however, you can often make your code self-documenting to avoid adding extra comments. For example, I recently had a question about how OWL's transfer mechanism worked with a modeless dialog box. Specifically, I wondered whether the contents of a modeless dialog box were transferred to the transfer buffer when the dialog was closed. I loaded up the OWL source code and found the following:

```
void
TDialog::CloseWindow(int retValue)
{
  if (IsModal) {
    if (CanClose()) {
      TransferData(tdGetData);
      Destroy(retValue);
    }

  } else {
    TWindow::CloseWindow(retValue);
  }
}
```

Thanks to the well-named `IsModal` flag, a quick glance told me that only a modal dialog box transfers its contents when closed. But, suppose when I found Borland's `TDialog::CloseWindow()` function, it looked like this:

```
void
TDialog::CloseWindow(int retValue)
{
  if (var1) {
    if (CanClose()) {
      TransferData(tdGetData);
      Destroy(retValue);
    }

  } else {
    TWindow..CloseWindow(retValue);
  }
}
```

As you can see, by changing the name of only one variable, the entire function is now incomprehensible. What's `var1`? Who knows?

Use Meaningful Function Names

Just as using meaningful variable names helps you to create clear code, so too do meaningful function names. Often, a well chosen function name is all you need to understand how a program works. For example, look again at Borland's `TDialog::CloseWindow()` function. Notice, this time, the poorly chosen function names in the body of the function:

```
void
TDialog::CloseWindow(int retValue)
{
  if (IsModal) {
    if (func1()) {
      func2(tdGetData);
      func3(retValue);
    }

  } else {
    TWindow::CloseWindow(retValue);
  }
}
```

This version of the function is about as clear as a handful of Mississippi mud. If you look at the original version of the function, you can see that the function names `CanClose()`, `TransferData()`, and `Destroy()` make the `TDialog::CloseWindow()` function easier to understand.

Write Only One Statement Per Line

Although there are a few instances where you might want to bend this rule, in general you should never place more than one program statement on a line. When you place more than one statement on a line, you begin to obscure how the code works. For example, could you imagine having to maintain a program written like this:

```
setlinestyle(SOLID_LINE,0,THICK_WIDTH);
setcolor(RED); int sx = (c * 22) + XOFF;
int sy = (r * 22) + YOFF; circle(sx + 10, sy + 10, 8);
moveto(sx + 4, sy + 4); lineto(sx + 16, sy + 17);
```

Because the statements that make up the above example have very little visual organization, they look like a jumble of random text. The following revision of the above code is much easier to read:

```
setlinestyle(SOLID_LINE,0,THICK_WIDTH);
setcolor(RED);
int sx = (c * 22) + XOFF;
int sy = (r * 22) + YOFF;
circle(sx + 10, sy + 10, 8);
moveto(sx + 4, sy + 4);
lineto(sx + 16, sy + 17);
```

As mentioned previously, there are times when the one-statement-per-line rule can—and should—be broken. That's when writing one statement per line actually obscures some pattern in the code that would make the program easier to understand. For example, suppose you need to initialize an array that represents a 3x3 matrix. The following code style obscures the organization of the matrix:

```
matrix[1][1] = 1;
matrix[1][2] = 0;
matrix[1][3] = 0;
matrix[2][1] = 0;
matrix[2][2] = c;
```

```
matrix[2][3] = -s;
matrix[3][1] = 0;
matrix[3][2] = s;
matrix[3][3] = c;
```

However, when you organize the program statements to reflect the structure of the matrix, the code's purpose is much clearer. You can see the code not only as a series of initialization statements, but also as a matrix of values:

```
matrix[1][1] = 1; matrix[1][2] = 0; matrix[1][3] = 0;
matrix[2][1] = 0; matrix[2][2] = c; matrix[2][3] = -s;
matrix[3][1] = 0; matrix[3][2] = s; matrix[3][3] = c;
```

Use Spaces to Separate Statement Elements

When you read a book, your eyes don't see every letter of every word. Instead, you see words and phrases as complete units. It is the spaces between the words that enable your brain to distinguish the patterns that make reading possible. Look at this sentence:

```
Jamiehasawartonhisnose.
```

How long did it take you to figure it out? Now look at the sentence with spaces separating the words:

```
Jamie has a wart on his nose.
```

Chances are, you could read the above sentence with only two eye movements, grabbing the phrases "Jamie has a wart" and "on his nose" as complete units.

The same rules apply to program code. You should consider each statement as a sentence and use spaces and punctuation accordingly. In most cases, you should place spaces before and after each operator.

Following this rule, the statement

```
int sx=(c*22)+XOFF;
```

becomes

```
int sx - (c * 22) + XOFF;
```

which is much easier on the eyes. Each "word" of the statement stands out, making it easier for your eyes to understand the statement. Spacing a statement properly also helps you avoid some types of syntax errors. For example, look at this statement:

```
*numBoxes = *numItems / *capacity;
```

After removing the spaces, you get the following:

```
*numBoxes=*numItems/*capacity;
```

Although, at first glance, this looks like the same statement, it's not. In fact, the preceding statement won't compile. By placing the slash (/) and the asterisk (*) next to each other, you've created the beginning of a C comment.

You should also place spaces after each comma in your source code, which makes variable declarations and function parameters easier to see. A code segment like

```
int x,y,z;

moveto(sx+4,sy+4);
lineto(sx+16,sy+17);
```

is much easier to read when it's formatted like this:

```
int x, y, z;

moveto(sx + 4, sy + 4);
lineto(sx + 16, sy + 17);
```

Some programmers even go one step further and add spaces before and after parentheses:

```
moveto ( sx + 4, sy + 4 );
lineto ( sx + 16, sy + 17 );
```

The above code is very readable. However, use common sense, as well as the rules, when formatting a line of code. Adding too many spaces can make code hard to read. Too many spaces can also leave you with lines that are too long to fit on-screen, forcing you to scroll the window to see the whole line.

Use Blank Lines to Separate Functions into Logical Units

Although functions are often kept short (usually a maximum of one page of code), it's still helpful to divide a function into logical chunks. Processing performed in a loop, for example, might be separated from the rest of the code, as might a series of calculations that work together to determine a single value. For example, look at this function:

```
int CalcBox(void)
{
    int x = GetX();
    int y = GetY();
    int col = (x - XOFF) / 22;
    int row = (y - YOFF) / 22;
    int box = row * 8 + col;
    return box;
}
```

CalcBox() actually performs three main tasks. It gets values for x and y, it calculates the value of box based on x and y, and then returns the value of box from the function. The function would be much easier to read if these three main tasks were separated by blank lines:

```
int CalcBox(void)
{
    // Retrieve x and y.
    int x = GetX();
    int y = GetY();

    // Calculate the box number.
    int col = (x - XOFF) / 22;
    int row = (y - YOFF) / 22;
    int box = row * 8 + col;

    return box;
}
```

As you can see by the above example, when you group lines of code logically, you also make adding comments easier because you can comment several lines at once.

Indent Lines at Each Level of Logic

The Borland C++ compiler (and every other C++ compiler ever made) doesn't care whether code lines are indented logically. The compiler simply scans the code looking for the symbols that define the syntax of the language. The human mind, however, works better visually than analytically. People like pictures. By using proper indentation, you can make your source code clearly illustrate the code's structure.

For example, Borland C++ will be delighted to compile the following function:

```
void GetStr(void)
{
char s[81];
int strOkay;

if (file)
{
ReadStr(file, s);
strOkay = ParseStr(s);
if (!strOkay)
ShowError(s);
else
ShowStr(s);
}
}
```

People who look at that function, however, will struggle to determine its logical structure and thus how it works. Using indentation, the function becomes much easier to understand:

```
void GetStr(void)
{
   char s[81];
   int strOkay;

   if (file)
   {
      ReadStr(file, s);
```

```
            strOkay = ParseStr(s);
            if (!strOkay)
                ShowError(s);
            else
                ShowStr(s);
        }
    }
```

No real hard-and-fast rule dictates how many spaces you should indent for each level of logic. Three or four spaces works pretty well, giving the code an obvious structure, while not pushing the code too far to the right. No matter how many spaces you choose to indent, use the same number of spaces for each indentation. For example, don't indent one level three spaces and the next four.

Avoid Nested Function Calls

C++'s powerful syntax rules allow programmers to create extremely complex statements. Unfortunately, for the programmer who has to maintain the resultant code, these complex statements are difficult to figure out. One trick that few C++ programmers can resist is the nesting of function calls. For example, the following is a construction C and C++ programmers use all the time:

```
FILE *file;
if ((file = fopen(filename, "rb")) == NULL)
{
    // Generate an error.
}
```

Although common, this code is more obscure than it needs to be. By nesting the call to `fopen()` inside the `if` statement, only an experienced programmer is likely to see at a glance what the code accomplishes. By avoiding the nesting of the function call, the above example becomes much easier to understand:

```
FILE *file = fopen(filename, "rb");
if (file == NULL)
{
    // Generate an error.
}
```

Here, every step required to complete the task is clear. You don't need to try and untangle a nest of statements in order to see that, if opening the file returns a null pointer, the program must generate an error message. In addition, by not nesting function calls, you can avoid logic errors that result from misinterpreting the code. The more complex a line of code becomes, the more likely it is that you will misinterpret it. Debugging a well-written program is hard enough. Why make it harder than it needs to be?

Organizing Code into Modules

These days, even a relatively unambitious application is liable to comprise thousands of lines of code. And when you start talking about full-featured, commercial applications, the sky is the limit! Obviously, when confronted with thousands, and even hundreds of thousands, of lines of code, it can be difficult to find what you're looking for. For this reason, it's important to separate source code into logical modules that group functions and classes so that you know immediately where to look for a particular piece of code. Much like the chapters in a book, modules organize a program's source code into coherent units.

How do you decide what code to put into what module? And how do you make sure that the functions that make up a module are available to any other module that needs them? The answers to these questions vary from program to program, and depend greatly on the coding style you use. For example, a conventional C program would be organized very differently from a C++ program that takes advantage of object-oriented programming. The following rules will help you better organize both C and C++ source code.

Put General-Purpose Functions in Their Own Module

As you write more and more programs, you'll find yourself building up a collection of functions that you use regularly from program to program. These functions probably perform such general tasks as initializing a graphics display, reading words from a text file, sorting an array of values, and so on. By placing such functions in their own module, you can add them to your programs quickly and easily. After adding the module to your project, you can strip out the functions your current program doesn't need, to reduce the size of the source code, as well as the size of the resulting executable file.

To make the functions included in the general-purpose module accessible to other modules in your programs, you must create a header file containing function prototypes for the functions you want to access. You can then include the header file in any other module that needs to use the functions.

For example, suppose you've got a general-purpose module named PROCS.CPP that contains the functions `StartGraphics()`, `InitMouse()`, and `DefinePalette()`. Your header file should look something like this:

```
#indef __PROC_H
#define __PROCS_H

int StartGraphics(void);
void InitMouse(void);
void DefinePalette(void);

#endif
```

You would then include this file in any module that needs to use the functions in PROCS.CPP:

```
#include "procs.h"

int main(void)
{
    error = StartGraphics();
    if (!error)
    {
        InitMouse();
        DefinePalette();
        // Other program code.
    }
    return 1;
}
```

Because you might include the header file in more than one module, you need a way to avoid multiple declarations. That's what the `#ifndef`, `#define`, and `#endif` compiler directives enable you to do. The first time the PROCS.H header file is included in a module, the constant `__PROCS_H` is not yet defined. (Notice how the constant is formed from the header file's file name.) The compiler defines `__PROCS_H` and compiles the function prototypes. If PROCS.H is included in another module in the project, when the compiler tries to include it, `__PROCS_H` is already defined, which causes the compiler to skip ahead to the `#endif`. The function prototypes are not compiled a second time, yet they are still available to the module that included the header file.

Place Related Functions into the Same Module

Suppose you're working on a telecommunications program. This program includes a text editor and a file manager, and also supports X-Modem and Z-Modem file-transfer protocols. If you were to place the functions that make up this program into a single code module, you'd have a difficult time finding specific functions. In addition, you'd have to recompile the entire program every time you made even a small change to one of the functions.

The solution is to group related functions into a single module. That is, all the code related to the text editor could be placed into a module called EDITOR.CPP. Likewise, all the code that's related to Z-Modem file transfer could be placed into a module called ZMODEM.CPP. The other source code could be similarly categorized. Of course, you'd also need to create header files for each module, so that you can include the function prototypes in whatever module that needs them. For your telecommunications program, you'd probably end up with a main code module named something like TELECOM.CPP, as well as other modules and header files with names like FILEMANG.CPP, FILEMANG.H, EDITOR.CPP, EDITOR.H, XMODEM.CPP, XMODEM.H, ZMODEM.CPP, and ZMODEM.H.

By separating your source code into modules, you know exactly where to look for a particular function. As a bonus, only modules that you modify need to be recompiled, which speeds up the compilation process considerably.

Use Header Files to Declare Public Data and Functions

A well-written module comprises two parts; the first is the *.CPP* (or .C) file, which contains the module's implementation, and the second is the *header file*, which provides the information needed to use the module with other modules. You can think of the .CPP file as the private part of the module, the code that other modules and programmers need not look at. Conversely, you can think of the header file as the public part of the module, the code that tells other modules and programmers how to use the private part.

Your header file should contain no source code that generates object code. This means that all data, function, and class definitions should be placed in the .CPP file, not in the header file. By organizing your header file this way, you can take advantage of Borland's precompiled headers, which speeds up program compilation. If your module must allow access to data defined in the .CPP file, declare those data items as extern in the header file. This tells the compiler that those data items are defined elsewhere.

Listings 20.1 through 20.3 show how to organize your programs into modules and header files.

Listing 20.1. TEST.CPP—Tests the TESTMODL Module

```
/////////////////////////////////////////////////////////////
// TEST.CPP — A mini-application that demonstrates the
//            use of modules and header files.
/////////////////////////////////////////////////////////////

#include <iostream.h>
#include "testmodl.h"
```

```
//////////////////////////////////////////////////////////
// main()
//
// SetXY(), SetTS(), x, y, and ts are declared in
// TESTMODL.H and defined in TESTMODL.CPP. The constant
// MAX is defined in TESTMODL.H.
//////////////////////////////////////////////////////////
int main(void)
{
   int z;

   SetXY();
   SetTS();
   z = x + y + MAX;

   cout << "z = " << z << endl;
   cout << "ts.var1 = " << ts.var1 << endl;
   cout << "ts.var2 = " << ts.var2 << endl;

   return 1;
}
```

Listing 20.2. TESTMODL.H—Header File for TESTMODL.CPP

```
//////////////////////////////////////////////////////////
// TESTMODL.H - An example header file.
//////////////////////////////////////////////////////////

#ifndef __TESTMODL_H
#define __TESTMODL_H

// Define constants.
const MAX = 50;

// Declare data structures.
struct testStruct
{
   int var1;
   int var2;
};

// Declare public data.
extern int x, y;
extern testStruct ts;

// Declare functions.
void SetXY(void); // Sets the value of x and y.
void SetTS(void); // Initializes the ts structure.

#endif
```

Listing 20.3. TESTMODL.CPP—Implementation File for the TESTMODL Module

```cpp
//////////////////////////////////////////////////////////
// TESTMODL.CPP - An example module implementation.
//////////////////////////////////////////////////////////

#include "testmodl.h"

// Define public data.
int x = 0;
int y = 0;
testStruct ts;

// Define private data.
int t = 0;

// Prototypes for private functions.
void SetT(void);

//////////////////////////////////////////////////////////
// SetXY()
//////////////////////////////////////////////////////////
void SetXY(void)
{
    x = 3;
    SetT();
    y = 3 + t;
}

//////////////////////////////////////////////////////////
// SetTS()
//////////////////////////////////////////////////////////
void SetTS(void)
{
    ts.var1 = 10;
    ts.var2 = 20;
}

//////////////////////////////////////////////////////////
// SetT()
//////////////////////////////////////////////////////////
void SetT(void)
{
    t = 2;
}
```

When you run the program created by Listings 20.1 through 20.3, you see the following output:

```
z = 58
ts.var1 = 10
ts.var2 = 20
```

As you can see, although the functions `SetXY()` and `SetTS()` are defined in a separate module, the main program has full use of them. The same is also true of `x`, `y`, `ts`, and `MAX`, all of which are also defined in the TESTMODL module.

Look at the top of the main program, TEST.CPP. You see the line

```
#include "testmodl.h"
```

It is this line that gives TEST.CPP access to some of the functions and data defined in TESTMODL.CPP. None of the lines in the header file generate object code. They only inform another module what parts of TESTMODL.CPP are available for its use.

Now look at the header file, TESTMODL.H. It begins with the compiler directive

```
#ifndef __TESTMODL_H
```

which, along with the `#endif`, prevents the body of the header file from being compiled more than once. Then, the file defines a constant, declares a structure, and declares public data:

```
// Define constants.
const MAX = 50;

// Declare data structures.
struct testStruct
{
    int var1;
    int var2;
};

// Declare public data.
extern int x, y;
extern testStruct ts;
```

The `extern` keyword tells the compiler that the data is defined in another file (in this case, TESTMODL.CPP). By declaring the data this way, other modules that include TESTMODL.H can access these data items.

Finally, TESTMODL.H lists function prototypes for the public functions—those functions that need to be available to other modules—declared in TESTMODL.CPP:

```
// Declare functions.
void SetXY(void); // Sets the value of x and y.
void SetTS(void); // Initializes the ts structure.
```

Private functions—those that are used internally by TESTMODL.CPP—should not be listed in the header file. Their prototypes are in TESTMODL.CPP.

Now look at TESTMODL.CPP, which is where all data and functions are actually defined. First, the line

```
#include "testmodl.h"
```

brings in the data declarations and function prototypes for the module, without which the module would not compile. Next, TESTMODL.CPP defines the public data that was declared in the header file:

```
// Define public data.
int x = 0;
int y = 0;
testStruct ts;
```

These definitions generate object code that sets aside space for the data, whereas the data declarations in the header file only inform the compiler of the data items' names and types.

Next, the file defines a private variable, `t`:

```
// Define private data.
int t = 0;
```

Because this integer is not declared in the header file, it is private to TESTMODL.CPP—that is, no other module can access `t`, which keeps it safe from accidental meddling.

TESTMODL.CPP then lists prototypes for its private functions, of which there is only one, `SetT()`:

```
// Prototypes for private functions.
void SetT(void);
```

Just as with the private variable, `t`, the private function `SetT()` is accessible only from within TESTMODL.CPP.

Finally, TESTMODL.CPP defines all its functions, both public and private. Although the public functions are defined in this separate module, any other module that includes TESTMODL.H can call those functions.

Organize Classes into Header and Implementation Files

One big advantage of C++ is the ability to employ object-oriented programming techniques. Although object-oriented programs add an additional level of complexity to source code, they can still be easily organized into modules—modules not unlike those you learned to design in the previous section. Each class should be divided into two files. The first file contains the class declaration, which declares all the class's data and functions. The second file contains the class's implementation, in which the class's functions are defined.

Listings 20.4 through 20.6 make up an object-oriented program that shows how a class is organized into header and implementation files. Listing 20.4 tests the class, and Listings 20.5 and 20.6 are the class's header and implementation files, respectively.

Listing 20.4. TESTCAR.CPP—A Program that Tests the Car Class

```cpp
////////////////////////////////////////////////////////
// TESTCAR.CPP—An object-oriented program that simulates
//                a car ride.
////////////////////////////////////////////////////////

#include <iostream.h>
#include <stdlib.h>
#include <conio.h>
#include <time.h>
#include "car.h"

const HOME = 6;

// Function prototype.
int FindObstacle(void);

////////////////////////////////////////////////////////
// main()
////////////////////////////////////////////////////////
void main()
{
    int obstacle, at_destination = 0;
    Car car(HOME);

    randomize();
    car.StartCar();

    while (!at_destination)
    {
        at_destination = car.SteerCar();
        obstacle = FindObstacle();
        if (obstacle && !at_destination)
        {
            cout << "Look out! There's something ";
            cout << "in the road!" << endl;
            getch();
            car.BrakeCar();
            car.ReverseCar();
            car.ReverseCar();
        }
    }

    cout << "Ah, home at last." << endl;
    car.TurnOffCar();
}

////////////////////////////////////////////////////////
// FindObstacle()
//
// This function determines whether the car has come upon
// an obstacle in the road.
////////////////////////////////////////////////////////
```

```
int FindObstacle(void)
{
    int r = random(4);
    if (r) return 0;
    return 1;
}
```

Listing 20.5. CAR.H—Header File for the Car Class

```
//////////////////////////////////////////////////////////
// CAR.H—The Car class's header file.
//////////////////////////////////////////////////////////

#include <iostream.h>
#include <conio.h>

class Car
{
private:
    int test, position, forward;

public:
    Car(int destination);
    void StartCar(void);
    int SteerCar(void);
    void BrakeCar(void);
    void ReverseCar(void);
    void TurnOffCar(void);
};
```

Listing 20.6. CAR.CPP—Implementation File for the Car Class

```
//////////////////////////////////////////////////////////
// CAR.CPP—Implementation of the Car class.
//////////////////////////////////////////////////////////

#include "car.h"

//////////////////////////////////////////////////////////
// Car::Car()
//
// This is the class's constructor.
//////////////////////////////////////////////////////////
Car::Car(int destination)
{
```

continues

Organizing Code into Modules   **887**

Listing 20.6. Continued

```cpp
    test = destination;
    forward = 1;
    position = 0;
}


///////////////////////////////////////////////////////////
// Car::StartCar()
//
// This function starts the car.
///////////////////////////////////////////////////////////
void Car::StartCar(void)
{
    cout << "Car started." << endl;
    getch();
}


///////////////////////////////////////////////////////////
// Car::SteerCar()
//
// This function drives the car.
///////////////////////////////////////////////////////////
int Car::SteerCar(void)
{
    cout << "Driving..." << endl;
    getch();
    if (++position == test) return 1;
    return 0;
}


///////////////////////////////////////////////////////////
// Car::ReverseCar()
//
// This function backs up the car when the car reaches an
// obstacle.
///////////////////////////////////////////////////////////
void Car::ReverseCar(void)
{
    if (forward)
    {
        cout << "Backing up." << endl;
        getch();
        --position;
        forward = 0;
    }
    else forward = 1;
}


///////////////////////////////////////////////////////////
// Car::BrakeCar()
//
// This function puts on the brakes when the car reaches
// an obstacle.
```

```
////////////////////////////////////////////////////////////
void Car::BrakeCar(void)
{
    cout << "Braking." << endl;
    getch();
}


////////////////////////////////////////////////////////////
// Car::TurnOffCar()
//
// This function turns off the car after the trip is
// complete.
////////////////////////////////////////////////////////////
void Car::TurnOffCar(void)
{
    cout << "Turning off car." << endl;
    getch();
}
```

When you run this program, it simulates a car trip. To take the trip, press Enter after each message. A typical program run looks like this:

```
Car started.
Driving...
Look out! There's something in the road!
Braking.
Backing up.
Driving...
Driving...
Driving...
Driving...
Driving...
Driving...
Ah, home at last.
Turning off car.
```

As you can see by examining the listings, the `Car` class is declared in the header file. The class's declaration is the only thing another module needs to access the class, which it can do by including the CAR.H file.

The class's member functions are declared in the header file, but are defined in the CAR.CPP file. You can use the `Car` class without ever seeing this implementation file. You only need the object file created by compiling CAR.CPP. The header file tells you which functions and data members are available to you. (Of course, you must add either the CAR.CPP or CAR.OBJ file to your project.)

Other Style Considerations

Now that you've got your code nicely formatted and organized into modules, it's time to look at a few C++ style considerations with which programmers often have difficulty. In this section, you learn how to create C++ classes that take advantage of encapsulation, inheritance, and polymorphism. In addition, you'll learn about using overloaded functions and overloaded operators in logical ways.

Classes: From General to Specific

Starting with object-oriented programming can be a daunting experience; it's unlike other programming methods and requires adherence to a new set of principles. The process of designing a class is rarely easy because classes are often based on hard-to-understand abstractions. It's often difficult to know which parts of a program belong in the class and which don't. Moreover, a complex program has many classes, many of which are derived from classes that may have been derived from still other classes. And, each class may have many data and function members. Obviously, designing classes requires some thought and careful application of the object-oriented philosophy.

The first step in designing a class is to determine the most general form of an object in that class. For example, suppose you're writing a graphics program, and you need a class to organize the types of shapes it can draw. (In this new class, you'll draw only points and rectangles, to keep things simple.) Determining the most general class means determining what the objects in the class have in common. Two things that come to mind for graphical shapes are color and position. These attributes become data members in the base class. Now, what functions must a shape perform? Each shape object needs a constructor and a way to draw itself on-screen. Because drawing a point is different from drawing a square, you'll need to put polymorphism to work and use a virtual function for the drawing task.

Listing 20.7 is the header file for the Shape class. This class needs no implementation file because the class is fully implemented in the header file. The constructor is implemented inline, and the pure virtual function DrawShape() requires no implementation, because it is only a placeholder for derived classes. (Pure virtual functions contain no actual code and must be implemented in the derived class. You can easily recognize a virtual function because of the = 0 following the function's declaration.)

Listing 20.7. SHAPE.H—The Header File for the Shape Class

```
///////////////////////////////////////////////////////////////
// SHAPE.H—Header file for the Shape class.
///////////////////////////////////////////////////////////////

#ifndef __SHAPE_H
#define __SHAPE_H

class Shape
{
protected:
   int color, sx, sy;

public:
   Shape(int x, int y, int c)
      { sx = x; sy = y; color = c; }
   virtual void DrawShape(void) = 0;
};

#endif
```

As you can see in Listing 20.7, Shape does nothing but initialize the data members color, sx, and sy, which are the color and x and y coordinates of the object. To do anything meaningful with the class, you must derive a new class for each shape that you want to draw. Start with the point. Listings 20.8 and 20.9 are the header and implementation files for this new class.

Listing 20.8. POINT.H—The Header File for the Point Class

```
//////////////////////////////////////////////////////////
// POINT.H—Header file for the Point class.
//////////////////////////////////////////////////////////

#ifndef __POINT_H
#define __POINT_H

#include <graphics.h>
#include "shape.h"

class Point: public Shape
{
public:
    Point(int x, int y, int c): Shape(x, y, c) {};
    virtual void DrawShape(void);
};

#endif
```

Listing 20.9. POINT.CPP—The Implementation File for the Point Class

```
//////////////////////////////////////////////////////////
// POINT.CPP—Implementation of the Point class.
//////////////////////////////////////////////////////////

#include "point.h"

void Point::DrawShape(void)
{
    putpixel(sx, sy, color);
}
```

The constructor for this class does nothing but pass parameters to the base class's constructor. Because it is so short, it is implemented inline. The DrawShape() function, however, must draw the shape. In this case, the function draws a dot on-screen, at the coordinates specified by the sx and sy data members, and in the color specified by the color data member. This function is also short; you could implement it inline as well. However, to keep the program construction parallel with the next example, the Point class has a separate implementation file.

Listing 20.10 is the test program for the shape classes. Because poly-morphism is used to create shapes, and because each class derives from the Shape base class, the program can test a new shape class simply by changing the type of object created by the new statement. Run the program now. A dot should appear in the middle of your screen.

Listing 20.10. TSTSHAPE.CPP—The Test Program for the Shape Classes

```
//////////////////////////////////////////////////////////
// TSTSHAPE.CPP-this program tests the shape classes.
//////////////////////////////////////////////////////////

#include <graphics.h>
#include <iostream.h>
#include <conio.h>
#include "point.h"
// #include "rectngle.h"
// #include "barrec.h"

//////////////////////////////////////////////////////////
// main()
//////////////////////////////////////////////////////////
int main(void)
{
    int gdriver = VGA, gmode = VGAHI, errorcode;
    Shape *shape;

    initgraph(&gdriver, &gmode, "");
    errorcode = graphresult();

    if (errorcode != grOk)
    {
        cout << "Graphics not initialized: ";
        cout << errorcode << endl;
    }
    else
    {
        int maxx = getmaxx();
        int maxy = getmaxy();
        shape = new Point(maxx/2, maxy/2,  WHITE);
        shape->DrawShape();
        getch();
    }

    delete shape;
    closegraph();

    return 1;
}
```

Note: When you create a project for TSTSHAPE.CPP, make sure that you check the BGI check box in the New Project dialog box. This option links the Borland Graphics Interface library to the program. Also, before you run the program, be sure that the EGAVGA.BGI file is in the same directory. You can find this file in your BC4\BGI directory.

To make things interesting, let's add a second shape, Rectngle, to the classes. Rectngle also derives from Shape. Listings 20.11 and 20.12 show the files for this new class.

Listing 20.11. RECTNGLE.H—The Header File for the Rectngle Class

```
/////////////////////////////////////////////////////////////
// RECTNGLE.H—Header file for the Rectngle class.
/////////////////////////////////////////////////////////////

#ifndef __RECTNGLE_H
#define __RECTNGLE_H

#include <graphics.h>
#include "shape.h"

class Rectngle: public Shape
{
protected:
    int x2, y2;

public:
    Rectngle(int x1, int y1, int w, int h, int c);
    virtual void DrawShape(void);
};

#endif
```

Listing 20.12. RECTNGLE.CPP—The Implementation File for the Rectngle Class

```
/////////////////////////////////////////////////////////////
// RECTNGLE.CPP—Implementation of the Rectngle class.
/////////////////////////////////////////////////////////////
```

```
#include "rectngle.h"

Rectngle::Rectngle(int x1, int y1, int w, int h, int c):
        Shape(x1, y1, c)
{
    x2 = sx + w;
    y2 =  sy + h;
}

void Rectngle::DrawShape(void)
{
    setcolor(color);
    rectangle(sx, sy, x2, y2);
}
```

To test this new class, in the main program, change the line

```
shape = new Point(maxx/2, maxy/2, WHITE);
```

to

```
shape = new Rectngle(maxx/2, maxy/2, 100, 100, WHITE);
```

Thanks to polymorphism, this is the only change that you need in the main program (except, of course, for including the RECTNGLE.H file and adding RECTNGLE.CPP to your project list) to draw a rectangle.

The class Rectngle is more complicated than the Point class. To draw a rectangle, the program needs the rectangle's width and height, as well as its x,y coordinates. Therefore, Rectngle's constructor does more than send parameters to the base class. It also initializes two extra data members: x2 and y2. Rectngle's DrawShape() function, too, is more complicated than Point's, because drawing a rectangle takes more work than drawing a dot.

You started with an abstract shape that did nothing but initialize a couple of data members and, now, you can draw two simple shapes on-screen. Now you can move down another level, from the general shape of a rectangle to a more specific type: a rectangle with a colored bar at the top. This type of rectangle might, for example, be the starting point for a labeled window. Listings 20.13 and 20.14 are the source code for the BarRec class.

Listing 20.13. BARREC.H—The Header File for the BarRec Object

```
///////////////////////////////////////////////////////////
// BARREC.H—Header file for the BarRec class.
///////////////////////////////////////////////////////////

#ifndef __BARREC_H
#define __BARREC_H

#include <graphics.h>
#include "rectngle.h"

class BarRec: public Rectngle
{
public:
    BarRec(int x1, int y1, int w, int h, int c):
            Rectngle(x1, y1, w, h, c) {}
    virtual void DrawShape(void);
};

#endif
```

Listing 20.14. BARREC.CPP—The Implementation File for the BarRec Class

```
///////////////////////////////////////////////////////////
// BARREC.CPP—Implementation of the BarRec class.
///////////////////////////////////////////////////////////

#include "barrec.h"

void BarRec::DrawShape(void)
{
    setcolor(color);
    rectangle(sx, sy, x2, y2);
    setfillstyle(SOLID_FILL, RED);
    bar(sx+2, sy+2, x2+-2, sy+15);
}
```

To test this new shape, change the new statement in the main program as follows:

```
shape = new BarRec(maxx/2, maxy/2, 100, 100, WHITE);
```

Also, include the BARREC.H file in the main program and add BARREC.CPP to your project file list. Now, when you run the program, the new type of rectangle object appears on-screen.

You could easily continue creating new types of rectangles. For example, if you want a rectangle with both a bar at the top and a double-line border, you can derive from `BarRec` a new type of rectangle, with the new type using its own shape-drawing function to override `BarRec`'s virtual `DrawShape()` function. (This new function would probably need to call its base class's `DrawShape()` function to draw the bar at the top and then do the extra drawing required for the double border.)

By using the general-to-specific method of creating classes, you end up with extremely flexible code. When you need to derive a new class, you have many classes from which to choose. Moreover, the classes are less complex than they would be if you tried to cram a lot of extra functionality into them. Remember, the more general you make your classes, the more flexible they are.

Knowing When to Use Classes

Object-oriented programming means power. When programmers first experience this power, they often find it irresistible. They soon begin to use objects for everything in their programs, without considering whether each use is appropriate. Remember that C++ is both an object-oriented language and a procedural language. In other words, C++ programmers get the best of both worlds; they can develop a strategy for a particular programming problem that best suits the current task. That strategy may or may not include an object-oriented approach.

Classes are most powerful when used as the basis for many instances. For example, an object-oriented string class can help overcome C++'s limited string-handling capabilities. After developing the class, you're likely to have many instances of strings in your programs, each inheriting all the functionality of its class.

Nothing comes free, however. There is always a price. For example, to call an object's member functions, you must use a more complicated syntax than you need for ordinary function calls; you must supply the object and function name. Moreover, creating classes is a lot of work.

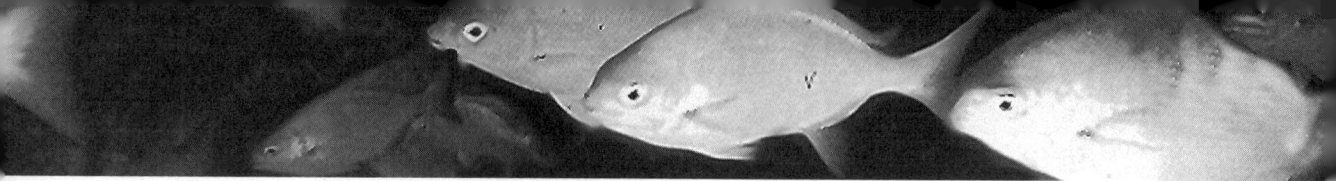

Why go through all the extra effort if the advantages don't outweigh the disadvantages?

Although classes are most appropriate when used to define a set of objects, sometimes creating a single-instance class is a reasonable strategy. For example, although you'll never have more than one mouse operating simultaneously, writing mouse functions into a single-instance class enables the programmer to conveniently package and organize routines that he'll need often.

Generally, a single-instance class is appropriate for wrapping up a big idea, like a screen display, a mouse driver, or a graphics library. It may not, however, be appropriate for smaller uses that would suffer from the overhead inherent in using classes. Remember that although you're programming in C++, you can still use simpler data structures, such as structures and arrays. When you need to create a new data type, don't automatically assume that the object-oriented approach is best. Often, it's not.

Responsible Overloading

One of the things that differentiates C from C++ is *function and operator overloading*. Overloading is the ability to create several versions of a function or operator, with each version having an identical name but requiring different arguments. For example, in C++, you can have two functions named Sum(), one that adds integers and another that adds floating-point numbers. When you call Sum() in a program, the compiler can tell which function you mean by checking the function's parameters.

The capability of C++ to overload functions and operators offers immense flexibility. You no longer have to come up with different names for functions that, although they take different parameters, perform virtually identical operations. You can simply write several versions of the function, using the same name, each version with its own set of arguments. As you've already learned, however, powerful techniques are often misused.

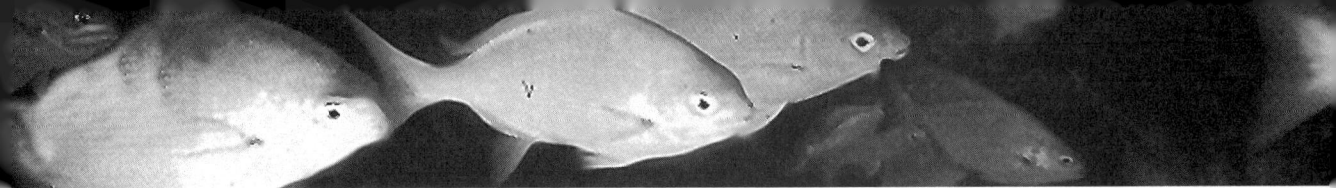

Overloading versus Default Arguments

There's no question that function overloading is a great feature of C++ programming. When overused, however, it can make code more difficult to understand. If nothing else, having several versions of a function considerably increases program maintenance. The solution? Default arguments also enable you to call functions with different parameters, but without resorting to overloading. For example, consider these prototypes for an overloaded function:

```
int Example(int x);
int Example(int x, int y);
```

Because of overloading, you can call the function `Example()` with one or two integer arguments:

```
Example(1);
Example(1,2);
```

This change adds much to the function's flexibility. However, do you really need two copies of the function to get this flexibility? Not really. By using default arguments, you can create one version of `Example()` that accepts either one or two integer arguments:

```
int Example(int x, int y = 0);
```

This new function retains the flexibility of the overloaded function, but without the extra baggage. Of course, you can't always replace overloaded functions with default arguments. For example, if the parameter types of overloaded functions are different, the default argument technique won't work. The following overloaded function cannot be written using default arguments:

```
int Example(int x);
float Example(float x);
```

You can't have a default type, only a default value. When you get the urge to overload a function, first consider whether it would be more expedient to use default arguments.

Using Operator Overloading Logically

You've seen how function overloading can be both bounty and bane. Operator overloading, too, requires thought before you use it. Although the use of default arguments doesn't apply here, there are still important considerations. The most important is using overloaded operators logically—in other words, using them as they were originally designed to be used.

Using operator overloading, you can make any of C++'s operators perform whatever task you want. For example, the + operator sums two values. Without operator overloading, this operator can be used only on C++'s built-in data types—in other words, types like `int`, `float`, and `long`. Suppose, however, you want to add two arrays and assign the result to a third array? You can then overload the + and = operators in an array class so that they can take arrays as arguments. Assuming you've done this, what do you suppose the following line would do (where `a`, `b`, and `c` are objects of your array class)?

```
c = a + b;
```

You would expect that the equal sign acts as an assignment operator, because that is normally its purpose. Similarly, you'd expect that the + operator summed the elements of each array. (You can find the code that performs this overloading in Listing 20.15.) What you wouldn't expect is for the sum operator to take, for example, two two-element arrays and combine them into a four-element array. This type of operation would not be consistent with the operator's conventional usage.

Listing 20.15 demonstrates how the previously discussed operator overloading might be implemented for an array class. For the sake of simplicity, the `Array` class has not been divided into separate header and implementation files.

Listing 20.15. OVERLOAD.CPP—A Program that Uses the + Operator to Sum the Elements of Two Arrays

```cpp
///////////////////////////////////////////////////////////
// OVERLOAD.CPP—Demonstrates operator overloading.
///////////////////////////////////////////////////////////

#include <iostream.h>
#include <conio.h>

// Array class declaration.
class Array
{
private:
    int a[2];

public:
    Array(int x=0, int y=0);
    void Print(void);
    Array operator=(Array b);
    Array operator+(Array b);
};

///////////////////////////////////////////////////////////
// Array::Array()
//
// The Array class's constructor.
///////////////////////////////////////////////////////////
Array::Array(int x, int y)
{
    a[0] = x;
    a[1] = y;
}


///////////////////////////////////////////////////////////
// Array::Print()
//
// This function prints out the contents of an Array
// object.
///////////////////////////////////////////////////////////
void Array::Print(void)
{
    cout << a[0] << ' ' << a[1] << endl;
}


///////////////////////////////////////////////////////////
// Array::operator=
//
// This function overloads the assignment operator to
// assign the contents of one Array object to another.
///////////////////////////////////////////////////////////
Array Array::operator=(Array b)
{
```

continues

Listing 20.15. Continued

```
        a[0] = b.a[0];
        a[1] = b.a[1];

        return *this;
}

/////////////////////////////////////////////////////////////
// Array::operator+
//
// This function overloads the addition operator to sum
// the contents of two Array objects.
/////////////////////////////////////////////////////////////
Array Array::operator+(Array b)
{
        Array c;

        c.a[0] = a[0] + b.a[0];
        c.a[1] = a[1] + b.a[1];

        return c;
}


/////////////////////////////////////////////////////////////
// main()
/////////////////////////////////////////////////////////////
int main(void)
{
        Array a(10, 15);
        Array b(20, 30);
        Array c;

        a.Print();
        b.Print();
        c.Print();
        c = a + b;
        c.Print();
        getch();

        return 1;
}
```

Operators should perform as expected. This means more than just
using them for the expected operation. It also means performing that
operation in a way that is consistent with the language's implementation. For example, look at the code for the + operator in the array class
(Listing 20.15). Notice that the source arrays are unchanged by the

operation. Instead, a third array is used to hold the results of the addition. This third array is returned from the function. This is how you expect the addition operator to work in C++. Contrast this with the way an addition instruction works in assembly language, by storing the result of the operation into one of the two operands. In most assembly languages, one of the operands is changed by the operation. In C++, it is not.

In summary, overloading functions and operators is a powerful technique. Like all powerful features of a language, however, it must be used with thought and style. Don't use overloading when a simpler method will do, and ensure that overloaded operators perform in the expected way.

When to Use Virtual Functions

Using virtual functions, you can create classes that, like the simple graphics demonstration earlier in the chapter, perform the same general functions, but perform those functions differently for each derived class. Like overloading, however, virtual functions are often misused.

Before using a virtual function, consider how the classes in the hierarchy differ. Do they need to perform different actions? Or do the classes require only different values?

For example, in the shapes demonstration, the program used virtual functions so that each class could draw its shape properly. Every shape object must know how to draw itself; however, every object needs to do it differently. Drawing a shape is an action.

It's inappropriate, however, to use a virtual function to assign a color to an object. Although each shape object has its own color attribute, the color attribute is a value rather than an action. So, it is best represented by a data member in the base class. Using polymorphism to set an object's color is like trying to kill a mosquito with a machine gun. Make sure that when you use virtual functions you are creating classes that differ in action rather than value.

Armed with the information in this chapter, you're well-prepared to produce nicely formatted and logically organized source code—code that can be easily modified and maintained. Always remember: style, as much as skill, separates the good programmers from the mediocre.

From Here...

➤ For tips on writing the best C code possible, see Chapter 4, "Optimizing C."

➤ For tips on writing the best C++ code possible, see Chapter 5, "Optimizing C++."

➤ For tips on debugging, and getting the most out of the Turbo Debugger, see Chapter 7, "Debugging Tips and Tricks."

➤ For information on templates, see Chapter 17, "Mastering Templates."

➤ For information on writing code that works around common errors, see Chapter 18, "Exception Handling."

The Sax VBX Communication Control

by Namir Shammas

This chapter looks at the Sax VBX communication control. This control supports a miniature communication application. In this chapter, you learn about the following topics:

➤ The relevant properties of the communication control

➤ The relevant VBX event for the communication control

➤ An example that demonstrates the use of the communication control

The Communication Control Properties

The Sax communication control has 37 properties. The following sections describe the relevant properties of the communication control. These properties support the communication-related operations of the control. The other irrelevant properties are related to the communication control as a general VBX control.

The AutoReceive Property

The Boolean `AutoReceive` property is a flag that indicates whether or not incoming characters are automatically read from the communication port. When the setting for this property is `True`, the Receive property explicitly reads incoming characters. The `AutoReceive` property has values that are compatible with the `BOOL` type. You can get the state of the auto-receive by using the member functions `TVbxControl::GetProp()` or `VbxsaxComm::GetPropAutoReceive()`. The declaration for the latter function is:

```
BOOL GetPropAutoReceive(BOOL& v);
```

The function `GetPropAutoReceive()` returns a Boolean value to indicate success or failure. In fact, all of the `GetPropXXXX()` member functions of the Sax communication control class return `BOOL` values. The function passes the `AutoReceive` setting to the caller via the reference parameter *v*. Here are examples for using the above functions.

```
OK = aSaxComm.GetPropAutoReceive(hasAutoReceive);
OK = aVbxCtl.GetProp("AutoReceive", hasAutoReceive);
```

To set the auto-receive state, you can use the member functions `TVbxControl::SetProp()` or `TVbxsaxComm::SetPropAutoReceive()`. The declaration for the latter function is:

```
BOOL SetPropAutoReceive(BOOL v);
```

The following examples use the preceding functions:

```
hasAutoReceive = TRUE;
 OK = aSaxComm.SetPropAutoReceive(hasAutoReceive);
  hasAutoReceive = FALSE;
  OK = aVbxCtl.SetProp("AutoReceive", hasAutoReceive);
```

The AutoSend Property

The Boolean AutoSend property is a flag which indicates whether or not keyboard input characters are automatically sent to the communication port. The AutoSend property has values that are compatible with the BOOL type. You can get the state of the auto-receive by using the member functions TVbxControl::GetProp() or VbxsaxComm::GetPropAutoSend(). The declaration for the latter function is:

```
BOOL GetPropAutoSend(BOOL& v);
```

The function GetPropAutoSend() returns a Boolean value to indicate success or failure. The function passes the AutoSend setting to the caller via the reference parameter v. Here are examples for using the above functions:

```
OK = aSaxComm.GetPropAutoSend(isAutoSend);
OK = aVbxCtl.GetProp("AutoSend", isAutoSend);
```

To set the AutoSend state you can use the member functions TVbxControl::SetProp() or TVbxsaxComm::SetPropAutoSend(). The declaration for the latter function is:

```
BOOL SetPropAutoSend(BOOL v);
```

These examples demonstrate the use of the preceding functions:

```
isAutoSend = TRUE;
OK = aSaxComm.SetPropAutoSend(isAutoSend);
isAutoSend = FALSE;
OK - aVbxCtl.SetProp("AutoSend", isAutoSend);
```

The BytesTransferred Property

The BytesTransferred property provides the number of bytes that are transferred while uploading or downloading a file. The BytesTransferred property has values that are compatible with the long type. You can

access the `BytesTransferred` property by using the member functions `TVbxControl::GetProp()` or `VbxsaxComm::GetPropBytesTransferred()`. The declaration for the latter function is:

```
BOOL GetPropBytesTransferred(long& v);
```

The function `GetPropBytesTransferred()` returns a Boolean value to indicate success or failure. The function passes the number of bytes transferred to the caller via the reference parameter *v*. Here are examples for using the above functions:

```
OK = aSaxComm.GetPropBytesTransferred(theBytesTrans);
OK = aVbxCtl.GetProp("BytesTransferred", theBytesTrans);
```

To set the `BytesTransferred` property you can use the member functions `TVbxControl::SetProp()` or `TVbxsaxComm..SetPropBytesTransferred()`. The declaration for the latter function is:

```
BOOL SetPropBytesTransferred(long v);
```

These examples use the preceding functions:

```
theBytesTrans = 0;
OK = SaxComm.SetPropBytesTransferred(theBytesTrans);
theBytesTrans = -1;
OK = aVbxCtl.SetProp("BytesTransferred", theBytesTrans);
```

The CtsRts Property

The Boolean property `CtsRts` is a flag that indicates whether or not the communication control uses the Cts/Rts hardware handshaking. The default setting for this property is `False`. The `CtsRts` property has values that are compatible with the `BOOL` type. You can get the state of the hardware handshake by using the member functions `TVbxControl::GetProp()` or `VbxsaxComm::GetPropCtsRts()`. The declaration for the latter function is:

```
BOOL GetPropCtsRts(BOOL& v);
```

The function `GetPropCtsRts()` returns a Boolean value to indicate success or failure. The function passes the hardware handshake setting to the caller via the reference parameter *v*. Here are examples for using the above functions:

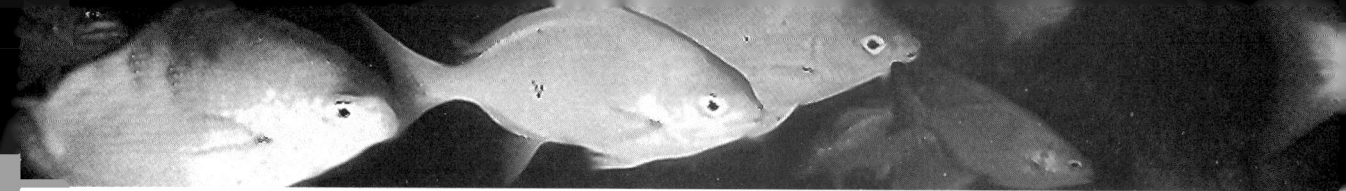

```
OK = aSaxComm.GetPropCtsRts(isCtsRts);
OK = aVbxCtl.GetProp("CtsRts", isCtsRts);
```

To set the hardware handshake state you can use the member functions `TVbxControl::SetProp()` or `TVbxsaxComm::SetPropCtsRts()`. The declaration for the latter function is:

```
BOOL SetPropCtsRts(BOOL v);
```

These examples demonstrate the preceding functions:

```
isCtsRts = TRUE;
OK = aSaxComm.SetPropCtsRts(isCtsRts);
isCtsRts = FALSE;
OK = aVbxCtl.SetProp("CtsRts", isCtsRts);
```

The DataBits Property

The `DataBits` property provides the number of bits that are used in transferring data. The default setting is 8, and can have the values 5, 6, 7, or 8. The `DataBits` property has values that are compatible with the `int` type. You can access the `DataBits` property by using the member functions `TVbxControl::GetProp()` or `VbxsaxComm::GetPropDataBits()`. The declaration for the latter function is:

```
BOOL GetPropDataBits(int& v);
```

The function `GetPropDataBits()` returns a Boolean value to indicate success or failure. The function passes the number of data bits to the caller via the reference parameter *v*. Here are examples for using the preceding functions:

```
OK = aSaxComm.GetPropDataBits(theDataBits);
OK = aVbxCtl.GetProp("DataBits", theDataBits);
```

To set the `DataBits` property, you can use the member functions `TVbxControl::SetProp()` or `TVbxsaxComm::SetPropDataBits()`. The declaration for the latter function is:

```
BOOL SetPropDataBits(int v);
```

These examples use the preceding functions:

```
theDataBits = 8;
OK = SaxComm.SetPropDataBits(theDataBits);
theDataBits = 7;
OK = aVbxCtl.SetProp("DataBits", theDataBits);
```

The Download Property

The `Download` property represents the name of the file to download using the XModem file transfer protocol. The `Download` property has values that are compatible with the `string` class. You can access the `Download` property by using the member functions `TVbxControl::GetProp()` or `VbxsaxComm::GetPropDownload()`. The declaration for the latter function is:

```
BOOL GetPropDownload(string& v);
```

The function `GetPropDownload()` returns a Boolean value to indicate success or failure. The function passes the name of the downloaded file to the caller via the reference parameter *v*. While the transfer is under way, you cannot access the `Download` property. Here are examples for using these functions:

```
OK = aSaxComm.GetPropDownload(DownloadStr);
OK = aVbxCtl.GetProp("Download", DownloadStr);
```

To set the `Download` property, you can use the member functions `TVbxControl::SetProp()` or `TVbxsaxComm::SetPropDownload()`. The declaration for the latter function is

```
BOOL SetPropDownload(string v);
```

Here are examples that use the preceding functions:

```
DownloadStr = "C:\\DOOM.ZIP";
OK = SaxComm.SetPropDownload(DownloadStr);
DownloadStr = "WOLF.ZIP";
aVbxCtl.SetProp("Download", DownloadStr);
```

The Echo Property

The `Echo` property is a flag which indicates whether or not to echo the keyboard input characters that are sent to the communication port. The `Echo` property has values that are compatible with the `BOOL` type. You can get the state of the keyboard input echo by using the member functions `TVbxControl::GetProp()` or `VbxsaxComm::GetPropEcho()`. The declaration for the latter function is:

```
BOOL GetPropEcho(BOOL& v);
```

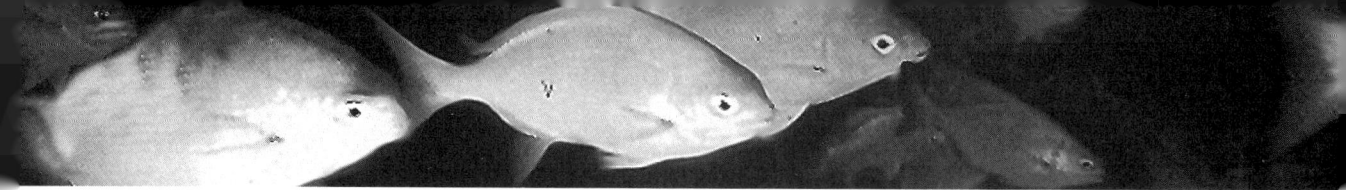

The function `GetPropEcho()` returns a Boolean value to indicate success or failure. The function passes the `Echo` setting to the caller via the reference parameter *v*. Here are examples for using the preceding functions:

```
OK = aSaxComm.GetPropEcho(hasEcho);
OK = aVbxCtl.GetProp("Echo", hasEcho);
```

To set the character echo state, you can use the member functions `TVbxControl::SetProp()` or `TVbxsaxComm::SetPropEcho()`. The declaration for the latter function is:

```
BOOL SetPropEcho(BOOL v);
```

These examples use the preceding functions:

```
hasEcho = TRUE;
OK = aSaxComm.SetPropEcho(hasEcho);
hasEcho = FALSE;
OK = aVbxCtl.SetProp("Echo", hasEcho);
```

The MaxReceiveLen Property

The `MaxReceiveLen` property provides the number of bytes that can be received using the `Receive` property. When the setting for the `MaxReceiveLen` property is 0, the `Receive` property has no limits for the number of bytes to retrieve. The `MaxReceiveLen` property has values that are compatible with the `int` type. You can access the `MaxReceiveLen` property by using the member functions `TVbxControl::GetProp()` or `VbxsaxComm::GetPropMaxReceiveLen()`. The declaration for the latter function is:

```
BOOL GetPropMaxReceiveLen(int& v);
```

The function `GetPropMaxReceiveLen()` returns a Boolean value to indicate success or failure. The function passes to the caller the maximum number bytes to receive, via the reference parameter *v*. The following examples demonstrate the use of these functions:

```
OK = aSaxComm.GetPropMaxReceiveLen(theMaxReceiveLen);
OK = aVbxCtl.GetProp("MaxReceiveLen", theMaxReceiveLen);
```

To set the `MaxReceiveLen` property, you can use the member functions `TVbxControl::SetProp()` or `TVbxsaxComm::SetPropMaxReceiveLen()`. The declaration for the latter function is:

```
BOOL SetPropMaxReceiveLen(int v);
```

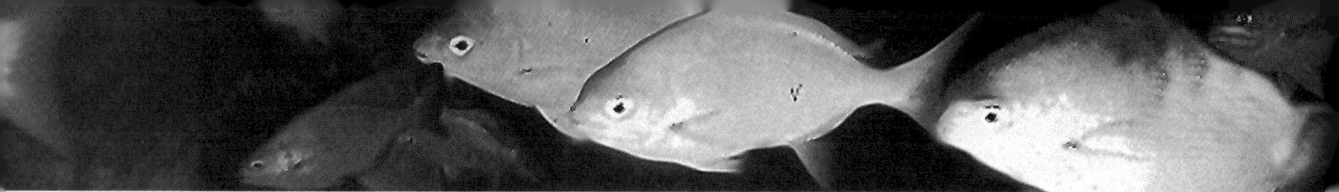

The use of these functions is demonstrated in the following examples:

```
theMaxReceiveLen = 16384;
OK = SaxComm.SetPropMaxReceiveLen(theMaxReceiveLen);
theMaxReceiveLen = 23767;
OK = aVbxCtl.SetProp("MaxReceiveLen", theMaxReceiveLen);
```

The Parity Property

The `Parity` property provides the kind of parity checking used in transferring data. The `Parity` property has values that are compatible with the ENUM enumerated type. Table 21.1 shows the enumerated values for the ENUM type. The default setting for this property is 0.

Table 21.1. The Values for the Parity Property

Value	Meaning
0	no parity
1	even
2	odd
3	mark
4	space

You can access the `Parity` property by using the member functions `TVbxControl::GetProp()` or `VbxsaxComm::GetPropParity()`. The declaration for the latter function is:

```
BOOL GetPropParity(ENUM& v);
```

The function `GetPropParity()` returns a Boolean value to indicate success or failure. The function passes the parity to the caller via the reference parameter *v*. Here are examples for using the preceding functions:

```
OK = aSaxComm.GetPropParity(theParity);
OK = aVbxCtl.GetProp("Parity", theParity);
```

To set the `Parity` property, you can use the member functions `TVbxControl::SetProp()` or `TVbxsaxComm::SetPropParity()`. The declaration for the latter function is:

```
BOOL SetPropParity(ENUM v);
```

These member functions are demonstrated in the following examples:

```
theParity = 1; // even parity
OK = SaxComm.SetPropParity(theParity);
theParity = 2; // odd parity
OK = aVbxCtl.SetProp("Parity", theParity);
```

The Port Property

The `Port` property represents the name of the currently used COM port. The `Port` property has values that are compatible with the `string` class. You can access the `Port` property by using the member functions `TVbxControl::GetProp()` or `VbxsaxComm::GetPropPort()`. The declaration for the latter function is:

```
BOOL GetPropPort(string& v);
```

The function `GetPropPort()` returns a Boolean value to indicate success or failure. The function passes the name of the communication port to the caller via the reference parameter *v*. If no port is open, the property contains an empty string. Here are examples for using the preceding functions:

```
OK = aSaxComm.GetPropPort(thePort);
OK = aVbxCtl.GetProp("Port", thePort);
```

To set the `Port` property you can use the member functions `TVbxControl::SetProp()` or `TVbxsaxComm::SetPropPort()`. If the attempt fails, the `Port` property is set to an empty string. Therefore, examine the `Port` property to determine whether or not the attempt to set a new COM port succeeded. The declaration for the latter function is:

```
BOOL SetPropPort(string v);
```

Here are examples for using the preceding functions:

```
thePort = "COM1";
OK = SaxComm.SetPropPort(thePort);
thePort = "COM2";
OK = aVbxCtl.SetProp("Port", thePort);
```

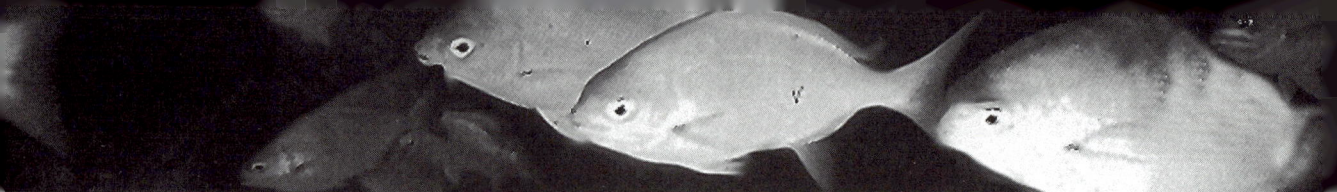

The Receive Property

The `Receive` property contains the characters received from the communication port. The `Receive` property has values that are compatible with the `string` class. You can access the `Receive` property by using the member functions `TVbxControl::GetProp()` or `VbxsaxComm::GetPropReceive()`. If the transfer fails, the `Receive` property contains an empty string. The property `MaxReceiveLen` determines if there is a limit for receiving characters and also determines the maximum number of input characters. The declaration for the latter function is:

```
BOOL GetPropReceive(string& v);
```

The function `GetPropReceive()` returns a Boolean value to indicate success or failure. The function passes the input characters to the caller via the reference parameter `v`. These examples use the preceding functions:

```
OK = aSaxComm.GetPropReceive(ReceiveStr);
OK = aVbxCtl.GetProp("Receive", ReceiveStr);
```

To set the `Receive` property you can use the member functions `TVbxControl::SetProp()` or `VbxsaxComm::SetPropReceive()`. The declaration for the latter function is:

```
BOOL SetPropReceive(string v);
```

Here are examples for using these functions:

```
ReceiveStr = "";
OK = SaxComm.SetPropReceive(ReceiveStr);
ReceiveStr = "";
aVbxCtl.SetProp("Receive", ReceiveStr);
```

The Send Property

The `Send` property contains the characters sent to the communication port. The `Send` property has values that are compatible with the `string` class. You can access the `Send` property by using the member functions `TVbxControl::GetProp()` or `VbxsaxComm::GetPropSend()`. The declaration for the latter function is:

```
BOOL GetPropSend(string& v);
```

The function GetPropSend() returns a Boolean value to indicate success or failure. The function passes the output characters to the caller via the reference parameter *v*. The following examples demonstrate the use of these functions:

```
OK = aSaxComm.GetPropSend(SendStr);
OK = aVbxCtl.GetProp("Send", SendStr);
```

To specify the output characters, you can use the member functions TVbxControl::SetProp() or TVbxsaxComm::SetPropSend(). The declaration for the latter function is:

```
BOOL SetPropSend(string v);
```

These examples use the preceding functions:

```
SendStr = "There goes the neighborhood";
OK = SaxComm.SetPropSend(SendStr);
SendStr = "Bye Bye Birdie";
OK = aVbxCtl.SetProp("Send", SendStr);
```

The Speed Property

The Speed property provides the baud rate for uploading or downloading a file. The Speed property has values that are compatible with the long type. The default setting is 2400. Settings for this property can be 300, 600, 1200, 4800, 9600, or 19200. You can access the Speed property by using the member functions TVbxControl::GetProp() or VbxsaxComm::GetPropSpeed(). The declaration for the latter function is:

```
BOOL GetPropSpeed(long& v);
```

The function GetPropSpeed() returns a Boolean value to indicate success or failure. The function passes the baud rate to the caller via the reference parameter *v*. Here are examples for using the above functions:

```
OK = aSaxComm.GetPropReceive(ReceiveStr);
OK = aVbxCtl.GetProp("Receive", ReceiveStr);
```

To set the baud rate, you can use the member functions TVbxControl::SetProp() or TVbxsaxComm::SetPropSpeed(). The declaration for the latter function is:

```
BOOL SetPropSpeed(long v);
```

These examples use the preceding functions:

```
theSpeed = 1200;
OK = SaxComm.SetPropSpeed(theSpeed);
theSpeed = 2400;
OK = aVbxCtl.SetProp("Speed", theSpeed);
```

The StopBits Property

The `StopBits` property provides the kind of parity checking used in data transfer. The default setting is 1, and can have the values 0 (1.5 stop bits), 1 (1 stop bit), or 2 (2 stop bits). The `StopBits` property has values that are compatible with the `int` type. You can access the `StopBits` property by using the member functions `TVbxControl::GetProp()` or `VbxsaxComm::GetPropStopBits()`. The declaration for the latter function is:

```
BOOL GetPropStopBits(int& v);
```

The function `GetPropStopBits()` returns a Boolean value to indicate success or failure. The function passes the stop bits to the caller via the reference parameter `v`. Here are examples for using the above functions:

```
OK = aSaxComm.GetPropStopBits(theStopBits);
OK = aVbxCtl.GetProp("StopBits", theStopBits);
```

To set the `StopBits` property, you can use the member functions `TVbxControl::SetProp()` or `TVbxsaxComm::SetPropStopBits()`. The declaration for the latter function is:

```
BOOL SetPropStopBits(int v);
```

The following examples demonstrate the use of the preceding functions:

```
theStopBits = 1;
OK = SaxComm.SetPropStopBits(theStopBits);
theStopBits = 2;
OK = aVbxCtl.SetProp("StopBits", theStopBits);
```

The Upload Property

The `Upload` property represents the name of the file to upload using the XModem file transfer protocol. The `Upload` property has values that are

compatible with the `string` class. You can access the `Upload` property by using the member functions `TVbxControl::GetProp()` or `VbxsaxComm::GetPropUpload()`. The declaration for the latter function is:

```
BOOL GetPropUpload(string& v);
```

The function `GetPropUpload()` returns a Boolean value to indicate success or failure. The function passes the name of the uploaded file to the caller via the reference parameter *v*. While the transfer is under way, you cannot access the `Upload` property. The use of these functions is demonstrated in the following examples:

```
OK = aSaxComm.GetPropUpload(UploadStr);
OK = aVbxCtl.GetProp("Upload", UploadStr);
```

To set the `Upload` property you can use the member functions `TVbxControl::SetProp()` or `TVbxsaxComm::SetPropUpload()`. The declaration for the latter function is:

```
BOOL SetPropUpload(string v);
```

The following examples demonstrate the use of these functions:

```
UploadStr = "C:\\MYDATA.ZIP";
OK = SaxComm.SetPropUpload(UploadStr);
UploadStr = "BOOK1.ZIP";
OK = aVbxCtl.SetProp("Upload", UploadStr);
```

The XonXoff Property

The Boolean property `XonXoff` is a flag that indicates whether or not the communication control uses the Xon/Xoff (software-related) handshaking. The default setting for this property is FALSE. The `XonXoff` property has values that are compatible with the `BOOL` type. You can get the state of the software handshake by using the member functions `TVbxControl::GetProp()` or `VbxsaxComm::GetPropXonXoff()`. The declaration for the latter function is:

```
BOOL GetPropXonXoff(BOOL& v);
```

The function `GetPropXonXoff()` returns a Boolean value to indicate success or failure. The function passes the software handshake setting to the caller via the reference parameter *v*. Here are examples for using the above functions:

```
OK = aSaxComm.GetPropXonXoff(hasXonXoff);
OK = aVbxCtl.GetProp("XonXoff", hasXonXoff);
```

To set the software handshake state, you can use the member functions
`TVbxControl::SetProp()` or `TVbxsaxComm::SetPropXonXoff()`. The declaration for
the latter function is:

```
BOOL SetPropXonXoff(BOOL v);
```

Here are examples of using these functions:

```
hasXonXoff = TRUE;
OK = aSaxComm.SetPropXonXoff(hasXonXoff);
hasXonXoff = FALSE;
OK = aVbxCtl.SetProp("XonXoff", hasXonXoff);
```

The Sax Communication Control Events

The Sax communication control can respond to the events `Click`,
`DragDrop`, `DragOver`, `GotFocus`, `KeyDown`, `KeyPress`, `KeyUp`, `LostFocus`, `MouseDown`,
`MouseMove`, and `MouseUp`. You can create applications that use the Sax communication control and need not respond to the above events. On the
other hand, if you want to create a communication application with
special features, you can make your application's class respond to the
above events.

The Communication Control Example

We have included a sample terminal application that uses the Sax
communication control. Figure 21.1 shows a sample session with the
terminal application TERMAPP.EXE. The program has a menu bar with
the File, Phone, and Help menu commands. In addition, the program
has a toolbar and a status bar. The toolbar buttons enable you to load a
new session, load an existing session, save the current session, upload
a file, and download a file. The commands for these toolbar buttons
also are available in the File menu. The Phone menu has two commands: Settings and Disconnect. When you invoke the Settings

command, the program displays the Communications dialog box, shown in figure 21.2.

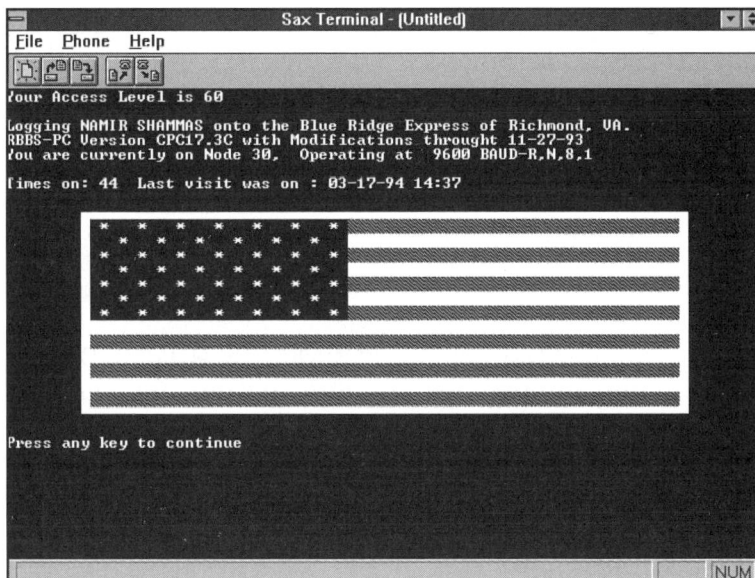

Fig. 21.1. A sample session with the TERMAPP.EXE program.

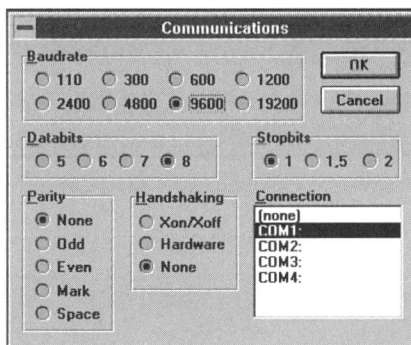

Fig. 21.2. The Communications dialog box.

For the complete code listings of this sample application, and a discussion of each code listing, see the SAMPLE21.DOC file in the archived file for Chapter 21, on the enclosed disk. SAMPLE21.DOC is a Microsoft Word for Windows 2.0 file that can be read from Word for Windows or any major word processor or text editor.

Summary

This chapter presented the VBX Sax communication control and discussed the following topics:

➤ You learned about the relevant properties of the communication control. These properties, such as the DataBits, Download, Upload, StopBits, and Parity, fine-tune the communication operations of the control. The control's properties specify how it communicates via the modem, how fast the control sends data, how much data to transfer, and the name of the uploaded or downloaded files.

➤ You learned about the relevant VBX event for the communication control which drives that control. The Sax communication control is really a window with built in menus which can operate without explicit event-handlers. The control can also respond to the events `Click`, `DragDrop`, `DragOver`, `GotFocus`, `KeyDown`, `KeyPress`, `KeyUp`, `LostFocus`, `MouseDown`, `MouseMove`, and `MouseUp`.

The Sax VBX
Tab Control

by Namir Shammas

This chapter looks at the Sax VBX tab control. The tab control allows you to select different sets of controls or data to be viewed or edited. This kind of control is becoming more popular in new applications, such as Microsoft Word and Excel. You will learn about the following topics:

➤ The relevant properties of the tab control

➤ The relevant VBX events for the tab control

➤ An example that uses the tab control to display system files

The Tab Control Properties

Let's look at the relevant properties of the tab control. The Sax tab control has 31 properties. The following subsections present some of these properties.

The ActiveTab Property

The `ActiveTab` property designates the index of the active tab—there can be only one active tab at a time. The index of the first tab is 0. The `ActiveTab` property has values that are compatible with the `int` type. You can get the index of the active tab by using the member functions `TVbxControl::GetProp()` or `TVbxSaxTab::GetPropActiveTab()`. The declaration for the latter function is:

```
BOOL GetPropActiveTab(int& v);
```

The function `GetPropActiveTab()` returns a Boolean value to indicate its success or failure. In fact, all of the `GetPropXXXX()` member functions of the Sax tab control class return `BOOL` values. The function passes the index of the active tab to the caller via the reference parameter *v*. Here are examples for using these functions:

```
OK = aSaxTab.GetPropActiveTab(theActiveTab);
OK = aVbxCtl.GetProp("ActiveTab", theActiveTab);
```

To select a tab you can use the member functions `TVbxControl::SetProp()` or `TVbxSaxTab::SetPropActiveTab()`. The declaration for the latter function is:

```
BOOL SetPropActiveTab(int v);
```

Here are examples for using these functions:

```
// select the next tab
theActiveTab = (theActiveTab + 1) % MAX_TABS
OK = aSaxTab.SetPropActiveTab(theActiveTab);
// select the next tab
theActiveTab = (theActiveTab + 1) % MAX_TABS
OK = aVbxCtl.SetProp("ActiveTab", theActiveTab);
```

The Visible Property

The Boolean property `Visible` indicates whether the tab control is visible. The `Visible` property has values that are compatible with the `BOOL` type. You can get the `Visible` setting of the tab control by using the member functions `TVbxControl::GetProp()` or `TVbxSaxTab::GetPropVisible()`. The declaration for the latter function is:

```
BOOL GetPropVisible(BOOL& v);
```

The function `GetPropVisible()` returns a Boolean value to indicate its success or failure. The function returns the setting of the `Visible` property to its caller using the parameter *v*. Here are examples for using these functions:

```
OK = aSaxTab.GetPropVisible(isVisible);
OK = aVbxCtl.GetProp("Visible", isVisible);
```

To hide or show a tab control you can use the member functions `TVbxControl::SetProp()` or `TVbxSaxTab::SetPropVisible()`. The declaration for the latter function is:

```
BOOL SetPropVisible(BOOL v);
```

Here are examples for using these functions:

```
// toggle the visibility of the tab control
    OK = aSaxTab.GetPropVisible(isVisible);
OK = aSaxTab.SetPropVisible(!isVisible);
// toggle the visibility of the tab control
    OK = aVbxCtl.GetProp("Visible", isVisible);
OK = aVbxCtl.SetProp("Visible", !isVisible);
```

The Enabled Property

The Boolean property `Enabled` denotes whether the tab control is enabled. The `Enabled` property has values that are compatible with the `BOOL` type. You can access the `Enabled` setting of the tab control by using the member functions `TVbxControl::GetProp()` or `TVbxSaxTab::GetPropEnabled()`. The declaration for the latter function is:

```
BOOL GetPropEnabled(BOOL& v);
```

The function `GetPropEnabled()` yields a Boolean value to denote its success or failure. The function yields the setting of the `Enabled` property to its caller using the parameter *v*. Here are examples for using these functions:

```
OK = aSaxTab.GetPropEnabled(isEnabled);
OK = aVbxCtl.GetProp("Enabled", isEnabled);
```

To disable or enable a tab control you can employ the member functions `TVbxControl::SetProp()` or `TVbxSaxTab::SetPropEnabled()`. The declaration for the latter function is:

```
BOOL SetPropEnabled(BOOL v);
```

Here are examples for using these functions:

```
// toggle the enabled state of the tab control
    OK = aSaxTab.GetPropEnabled(isEnabled);
OK = aSaxTab.SetPropEnabled(!isEnabled);
// toggle the enabled state of the tab control
    aVbxCtl.GetProp("Enabled", isEnabled);
aVbxCtl.SetProp("Enabled", !isEnabled);
```

The TabStop Property

The Boolean property `TabStop` indicates whether you can tab to the Sax tab control. The `TabStop` property has values that are compatible with the `BOOL` type. You may obtain the `TabStop` setting of the tab control by utilizing the member functions `TVbxControl::GetProp()` or `TVbxSaxTab::GetPropTabStop()`. The declaration for the latter function is:

```
BOOL GetPropTabStop(BOOL& v);
```

The function `GetPropTabStop()` returns a Boolean value to indicate its success or failure. The function returns the setting of the `TabStop` property to its caller using the parameter *v*. Here are examples for using these functions:

```
OK = aSaxTab.GetPropTabStop(theTabStop);
OK = aVbxCtl.GetProp("TabStop", theTabStop);
```

To disable or enable the tab stop feature of a tab control you may employ the member functions `TVbxControl::SetProp()` or `TVbxSaxTab::SetPropTabStop()`. The declaration for the latter function is:

```
BOOL SetPropTabStop(BOOL v);
```

Here are examples for using these functions:

```
// toggle the TabStop property of the tab control
    OK = aSaxTab.GetPropTabStop(isTabStop);
OK = aSaxTab.SetPropTabStop(!isTabStop);
// toggle the TabStop property of the tab control
    OK = aVbxCtl.GetProp("TabStop", isTabStop);
OK = aVbxCtl.SetProp("TabStop", !isTabStop);
```

The TabIndex Property

The `TabIndex` property specifies the tab index of the tab control. The `TabIndex` property has values that are compatible with the `int` type. You may obtain the index of the active tab by calling the member functions `TVbxControl::GetProp()` or `TVbxSaxTab::GetPropTabIndex()`. The declaration for the latter function is:

```
BOOL GetPropTabIndex(int& v);
```

The function `GetPropTabIndex()` yields a Boolean value to signal its success or failure. The function passes the tab index of the tab control to the caller through the reference parameter *v*. Here are examples for using these functions:

```
OK = aSaxTab.GetPropTabIndex(theTabIndex);
OK = aVbxCtl.GetProp("TabIndex", theTabIndex);
```

To set the tab index of a tab control you can use the member functions `TVbxControl::SetProp()` or `TVbxSaxTab::SetPropTabIndex()`. The declaration for the last function is:

```
BOOL SetPropTabIndex(int v);
```

Here are examples for using these functions:

```
OK = aSaxTab.SetPropTabIndex(theTabIndex);
OK = aVbxCtl.SetProp("TabIndex", theTabIndex);
```

The Caption Property

The `Caption` property establishes the captions for the tabs. The `Caption` property has values that are compliant with the `string` class. You may recall the caption of the tabs by using the member functions

`TVbxControl::GetProp()` or `TVbxSaxTab::GetPropCaption()`. The declaration for the latter function is:

```
BOOL GetPropCaption(string& v);
```

The function `GetPropCaption()` yields a Boolean value to denote its success or failure. The function passes the caption of the tab control to the caller by way of the reference parameter *v*. Here are examples for using these functions:

```
OK = aSaxTab.GetPropCaption(theCaption);
OK = aVbxCtl.GetProp("Caption", theCaption);
```

To assign a value for the caption of a tab control you can employ the member functions `TVbxControl::SetProp()` or `TVbxSaxTab::SetPropCaption()`. The declaration for the latter function is:

```
BOOL SetPropCaption(string v);
```

Here are examples for using these functions:

```
theCaption = "Grammar|Spelling|Thesaurus|AutoCorrect"
OK = aSaxTab.SetPropCaption(theCaption);
OK = aVbxCtl.SetProp("Caption", theCaption);
```

Note: The string which supplies the Caption property must include text for each tab, separated by the vertical bar character (as shown in the above example).

The FontName Property

The FontName property designates the name of the font used to display the tabs of the tab control. The FontName property has values that are compatible with the `string` class. You may obtain the caption of the tabs by using the member functions `TVbxControl::GetProp()` or `TVbxSaxTab::GetPropFontName()`. The declaration for the last function is:

```
BOOL GetPropFontName(string& v);
```

The function `GetPropFontName()` yields a Boolean value to indicate its success or failure. The function passes the font name of the tab control

to the caller through the reference parameter *v*. Here are examples for using these functions:

```
OK = aSaxTab.GetPropFontName(theFontName);
OK = aVbxCtl.GetProp("FontName", theFontName);
```

To set the font of a tab control you may use the member functions `TVbxControl::SetProp()` or `TVbxSaxTab::SetPropFontName()`. The declaration for the latter function is:

```
BOOL SetPropFontName(string v);
```

Here are examples for using these functions:

```
theFontName = "Arial";
OK = aSaxTab.SetPropFontName(theFontName);
theFontName = "Arial";
OK = aVbxCtl.SetProp("FontName", theFontName);
```

The FontSize Property

The `FontSize` property specifies the size of the font used to display the tabs of the tab control. The `FontSize` property has values that are compatible with the `float` type. You may obtain the font size of the tabs by using the member functions `TVbxControl::GetProp()` or `TVbxSaxTab::GetPropFontSize()`. The declaration for the latter function is:

```
BOOL GetPropFontSize(float& v);
```

The function `GetPropFontSize()` yields a Boolean value to signal its success or failure. The function passes the font size of the tab control to the caller via the reference parameter *v*. Here are examples for using these functions:

```
OK = aSaxTab.GetPropFontSize(theFontSize);
OK = aVbxCtl.GetProp("FontSize", theFontSize);
```

To assign the font size of a tab control you may utilize the member functions `TVbxControl::SetProp()` or `TVbxSaxTab::SetPropFontSize()`. The declaration for the last function is:

```
BOOL SetPropFontSize(float v);
```

Here are examples for using these functions:

```
theFontSize = 10;
OK = aSaxTab.SetPropFontSize(theFontSize);
theFontSize = 10;
OK = aVbxCtl.SetProp("FontSize", theFontSize);
```

The FontBold Property

The FontBold property specifies whether the text for the tabs appears in a bold font style. The FontBold property has values that are accordant with the BOOL type. You can get the font bold state of the tabs by using the member functions TVbxControl::GetProp() or TVbxSaxTab::GetPropFontBold(). The declaration for the last function is:

```
BOOL GetPropFontBold(BOOL& v);
```

The function GetPropFontBold() yields a Boolean value to indicate its success or failure. The function passes the bold style state of the tab control to the caller by way of the reference parameter *v*. Here are examples for using these functions:

```
OK = aSaxTab.GetPropFontBold(isFontBold);
OK = aVbxCtl.GetProp("FontBold", isFontBold);
```

To set the bold font style of a tab control you may employ the member functions TVbxControl::SetProp() or TVbxSaxTab::SetPropFontBold(). The declaration for the last function is:

```
BOOL SetPropFontBold(BOOL v);
```

Here are examples for using these functions:

```
isFontBold = TRUE;
OK = aSaxTab.SetPropFontBold(isFontBold);
isFontBold = FALSE;
OK = aVbxCtl.SetProp("FontBold", isFontBold);
```

The FontItalic Property

The FontItalic property specifies whether the text for the tabs appears in an italic font style. The FontItalic property has values that are compatible with the BOOL type. You can get the font italic state of the tabs by

using the member functions `TVbxControl::GetProp()` or `TVbxSaxTab::GetPropFontItalic()`. The declaration for the latter function is:

```
BOOL GetPropFontItalic(BOOL& v);
```

The function `GetPropFontItalic()` returns a Boolean value to indicate its success or failure. The function passes the italic style state of the tab control to the caller by way of the reference parameter v. Here are examples for using these functions:

```
OK = aSaxTab.GetPropFontItalic(isFontItalic);
OK = aVbxCtl.GetProp("FontItalic", isFontItalic);
```

To set the italic font style of a tab control you can use the member functions `TVbxControl::SetProp()` or `TVbxSaxTab::SetPropFontItalic()`. The declaration for the latter function is:

```
BOOL SetPropFontItalic(BOOL v);
```

Here are examples for using these functions:

```
isFontItalic = TRUE;
OK = aSaxTab.SetPropFontItalic(isFontItalic);
isFontItalic = FALSE;
OK = aVbxCtl.SetProp("FontItalic", isFontItalic);
```

The FontUnderline Property

The `FontUnderline` property indicates whether the text for the tabs appears in an underline font style. The `FontUnderline` property has values that are compatible with the `BOOL` type. You may recall the font underline state of the tabs by using the member functions `TVbxControl::GetProp()` or `TVbxSaxTab::GetPropFontUnderline()`. The declaration for the latter function is:

```
BOOL GetPropFontUnderline(BOOL& v);
```

The function `GetPropFontUnderline()` yields a Boolean value to signal its success or failure. The function passes the underline style state of the tab control to the caller through the reference parameter v. Here are examples for using these functions:

```
OK = aSaxTab.GetPropFontUnderline(isFontUnderline);
OK = aVbxCtl.GetProp("FontUnderline", isFontUnderline);
```

To set the underline font style of a tab control you may employ the member functions `TVbxControl::SetProp()` or `TVbxSaxTab::SetPropFontUnderline()`. The declaration for the latter function is:

```
BOOL SetPropFontUnderline(BOOL v);
```

Here are examples for using these functions:

```
isFontUnderline = TRUE;
OK = aSaxTab.SetPropFontUnderline(isFontUnderline);
isFontUnderline = FALSE;
OK = aVbxCtl.SetProp("FontUnderline", isFontUnderline);
```

The FontStrikethru Property

The `FontStrikethru` property indicates whether the text for the tabs appears in a strikethrough font style. The `FontStrikethru` property has values that are compatible with the `BOOL` type. You can recall the font strikethrough state of the tabs by using the member functions `TVbxControl::GetProp()` or `TVbxSaxTab::GetPropFontStrikethru()`. The declaration for the latter function is:

```
BOOL GetPropFontStrikethru(BOOL& v);
```

The function `GetPropFontStrikethru()` returns a Boolean value to indicate its success or failure. The function passes the font strikethrough style state of the tab control to the caller by way of the reference parameter *v*. Here are examples for using these functions:

```
OK = aSaxTab.GetPropFontStrikethru(isFontStrikethru);
OK = aVbxCtl.GetProp("FontStrikethru", isFontStrikethru);
```

To set the strikethrough font style of a tab control you can apply the member functions `TVbxControl::SetProp()` or `TVbxSaxTab::SetPropFontStrikethru()`. The declaration for the latter function is:

```
BOOL SetPropFontStrikethru(BOOL v);
```

Here are examples for using these functions:

```
isFontStrikethru = TRUE;
OK = aSaxTab.SetPropFontStrikethru(isFontStrikethru);
isFontStrikethru = FALSE;
OK = aVbxCtl.SetProp("FontStrikethru", isFontStrikethru);
```

The ActiveTabColor Property

The `ActiveTabColor` property specifies color for the active tab. The `ActiveTabColor` property has values that are compatible with the COLORREF type. You can get the active tab color of the tabs by using the member functions `TVbxControl::GetProp()` or `TVbxSaxTab::GetPropActiveTabColor()`. The declaration for the latter function is:

```
BOOL GetPropActiveTabColor(COLORREF& v);
```

The function `GetPropActiveTabColor()` returns a Boolean value to signal its success or failure. The function passes the color of the active tab to the caller by way of the reference parameter v. Here are examples for using these functions:

```
OK = aSaxTab.GetPropActiveTabColor(theActiveTabColor);
OK = aVbxCtl.GetProp("ActiveTabColor", theActiveTabColor);
```

To asssign the color of the active tab you may apply the member functions `TVbxControl::SetProp()` or `TVbxSaxTab::SetPropActiveTabColor()`. The declaration for the latter function is:

```
BOOL SetPropActiveTabColor(COLORREF v);
```

Here are examples for using these functions:

```
theActiveTabColor = RGB(255, 0, 0);
OK = aSaxTab.SetPropActiveTabColor(theActiveTabColor);
theActiveTabColor = RGB(0, 255, 0);
OK = aVbxCtl.SetProp("ActiveTabColor", theActiveTabColor);
```

The InactiveTabColor Property

The `InactiveTabColor` property specifies color for the inactive tabs. The `InactiveTabColor` property has values that are compatible with the COLORREF type. You may obtain the colors of the inactive tabs by using the member functions `TVbxControl::GetProp()` or `TVbxSaxTab::GetPropInactiveTabColor()`. The declaration for the latter function is:

```
BOOL GetPropInactiveTabColor(COLORREF& v);
```

The function `GetPropInactiveTabColor()` yields a Boolean value to indicate its success or failure. The function passes the color of the inactive tabs to the caller using the reference parameter *v*. Here are examples for using these functions:

```
OK = aSaxTab.GetPropInactiveTabColor(theInactiveTabColor);
OK = aVbxCtl.GetProp("InactiveTabColor",
                     theInactiveTabColor);
```

To set the color of the inactive tabs you can apply the member functions `TVbxControl::SetProp()` or `TVbxSaxTab::SetPropInactiveTabColor()`. The declaration for the latter function is:

```
BOOL SetPropInactiveTabColor(COLORREF v);
```

Here are examples for using these functions:

```
theInactiveTabColor = RGB(255, 0, 0);
OK = aSaxTab.SetPropInactiveTabColor(theInactiveTabColor);
theInactiveTabColor = RGB(0, 255, 0);
OK = aVbxCtl.SetProp("InactiveTabColor",
                     theInactiveTabColor);
```

The ActiveTextColor Property

The `ActiveTextColor` property specifies color for the text in the active tab. The `ActiveTextColor` property has values that are compatible with the `COLORREF` type. You may obtain the color of the text in the color tab by employing the member functions `TVbxControl::GetProp()` or `TVbxSaxTab::GetPropActiveTextColor()`. The declaration for the latter function is:

```
BOOL GetPropActiveTextColor(COLORREF& v);
```

The function `GetPropActiveTextColor()` returns a Boolean value to denote its success or failure. The function passes the color of the text in the active tab to the caller using the reference parameter *v*. Here are examples for using these functions:

```
OK = aSaxTab.GetPropActiveTextColor(theActiveTextColor);
OK = aVbxCtl.GetProp("ActiveTextColor",
                     theActiveTextColor);
```

To assign the color of text in the active tab you can use the member functions `TVbxControl::SetProp()` or `TVbxSaxTab::SetPropActiveTextColor()`. The declaration for the latter function is:

```
BOOL SetPropActiveTextColor(COLORREF v);
```

Here are examples for using these functions:

```
theActiveTextColor = RGB(255, 0, 0);
OK = aSaxTab.SetPropActiveTextColor(theActiveTextColor);
theActiveTextColor = RGB(0, 255, 0);
OK = aVbxCtl.SetProp("ActiveTextColor",
                     theActiveTextColor);
```

The InactiveTextColor Property

The InactiveTextColor property specifies color for the text in the inactive tabs. The InactiveTextColor property has values that are compatible with the COLORREF type. You can get the colors of the text in the inactive tabs by using the member functions TVbxControl::GetProp() or TVbxSaxTab::GetPropInactiveTextColor(). The declaration for the latter function is:

```
BOOL GetPropInactiveTextColor(COLORREF& v);
```

The function GetPropInactiveTextColor() returns a Boolean value to indicate its success or failure. The function passes the color of the text in the inactive tabs by way of the reference parameter *v*. Here are examples for using these functions:

```
OK = aSaxTab.GetPropInactiveTextColor(dInactiveTextColor);
OK = aVbxCtl.GetProp("InactiveTextColor",
                     dInactiveTextColor);
```

To set the color of the text in the inactive tabs you can use the member functions TVbxControl::SetProp() or TVbxSaxTab::SetPropInactiveTextColor(). The declaration for the latter function is:

```
BOOL SetPropInactiveTextColor(COLORREF v);
```

Here are examples for using these functions:

```
dInactiveTextColor = RGB(0, 0, 255);
OK = aSaxTab.SetPropInactiveTextColor(dInactiveTextColor);
dInactiveTextColor = RGB(0, 255, 255);
OK = aVbxCtl.SetProp("InactiveTextColor",
                     dInactiveTextColor);
```

The Tab Control Event

The Sax tab control supports the events `Click`, `DragDrop`, and `DragOver`. Handling the `Click` event enables your application to respond to clicking the various tabs.

The Tab Control Example

We have included a sample application that uses the Sax tab control to view the system files WIN.INI, SYSTEM.INI, NDW.INI (related to the Norton Desktop for Windows), AUTOEXEC.BAT, and CONFIG.SYS. Figure 22.1 shows a sample session with the SYSVIEW.EXE program. This sample program has a window with a read-only edit box and the tabs for the system files. In addition, there are two tabs labeled About and Exit. If you click a tab for one of the system files, the edit box control displays the contents of the selected file. If you do not have Norton Desktop for Windows you will see the message `unable to read file` appear in the first line of the edit box control. If you click the About tab, the program displays an About dialog box. If you click the Exit tab, you close the window and end the program. Compile and run the SYSVIEW.EXE program and experiment with clicking the various tabs. The SYSVIEW.IDE project file includes the SYSVIEW.DEF, SYSVIEW.RC, SYSVIEW.CPP, and TABVIEW.CPP. These files also use the SYSVIEW.H and SAXTABS1.H header files. The next subsections discuss the header and implementation files.

For the complete code listings of this sample application, and a discussion of each code listing, see the SAMPLE22.DOC file in the archived file for Chapter 22, on the enclosed disk. SAMPLE22.DOC is a Microsoft Word for Windows 2.0 file that can be read from Word for Windows or any major word processor or text editor.

Fig. 22.1. A sample session with the SYSVIEW.EXE program.

Summary

This chapter presented the Sax VBX tab control and discussed the following topics:

➤ You learned about the relevant properties of the tab control. These properties are set and query, index of the active tab, the visibility of a tab, the colors of the active and inactive tabs, the colors of the active and inactive tab's text, and the font name, size, and style of the text in a tab.

➤ You also learned that the Click event for the tab control is the most relevant event for that control. Handling the Click event allows you to respond to the user's selection of a new tab page.

The MicroHelp VBX Gauge Control

by Namir Shammas

This chapter looks at the MicroHelp gauge control. This control supports a gauge that is typically used to monitor the progress of time-consuming tasks, such as copying files or installing new programs. The Borland C++ and Turbo C++ installation programs use the gauge control. This chapter presents the following topics:

➤ The relevant properties of the gauge control

➤ The relevant VBX events for the gauge control

➤ A example which uses the gauge control

The Gauge Control Properties

The MicroHelp gauge control has many properties which specify the appearance and behavior of the control. The next subsections discuss the ones that are relevant.

The Value Property

The property `Value` yields the indicator position on the gauge. The `Value` property has values that are compatible with the `int` type. The setting of the `Value` property must be in the range specified by the `Min` and `Max` properties. You can get the `Value` setting of the gauge control by using the member functions `TVbxControl::GetProp()` or `TVbxMhGauge::GetPropValue()`. The declaration for the latter function is:

```
BOOL GetPropValue(int& v);
```

The function `GetPropValue()` returns a Boolean value to indicate its success or failure. The function returns the setting of the `Value` property to its caller using the parameter `v`. Here are examples for using the above functions:

```
OK = anMhGauge.GetPropValue(theValue);
OK = aVbxCtl.GetProp("Value", theValue);
```

To set the indicator position of gauge control you can use the member functions `TVbxControl::SetProp()` or `TVbxMhGauge::SetPropValue()`. The declaration for the latter function is:

```
BOOL SetPropValue(int v);
```

Here are examples for using the above functions:

```
theValue = 50;
OK = anMhGauge.SetPropValue(theValue);
theValue = 40;
OK = aVbxCtl.SetProp("Value", theValue);
```

The Min Property

The property `Min` defines the minimum position on the gauge. The `Min` property has values that are compatible with the `int` type. You can obtain the `Min` setting of the gauge control by utilizing the member functions

`TVbxControl::GetProp()` or `TVbxMhGauge::GetPropMin()`. The declaration for the last function is:

```
BOOL GetPropMin(int& v);
```

The function `GetPropMin()` yields a Boolean value to indicate its success or failure. The function returns the setting of the `Min` property to its caller through the parameter `v`. Here are examples for using the above functions:

```
OK = anMhGauge.GetPropMin(theMin);
OK = aVbxCtl.GetProp("Min", theMin);
```

To assign the minimum position of gauge control you may employ the member functions `TVbxControl::SetProp()` or `TVbxMhGauge::SetPropMin()`. The declaration for the latter function is:

```
BOOL SetPropMin(int v);
```

Here are examples for using the above functions:

```
theMin = 0;
OK = anMhGauge.SetPropMin(theMin);
theMin = 10;
OK = aVbxCtl.SetProp("Min", theMin);
```

The Max Property

The property `Max` specifies the maximum position on the gauge. The `Max` property uses values that are compatible with the `int` type. You can recall the `Max` setting of the gauge control by calling the member functions `TVbxControl::GetProp()` or `TVbxMhGauge::GetPropMax()`. The declaration for the latter function is:

```
BOOL GetPropMax(int& v);
```

The function `GetPropMax()` yields a Boolean value to signal its success or failure. The function returns the setting of the `Max` property to its caller by way of the parameter `v`. Here are examples for using the above functions:

```
OK = anMhGauge.GetPropMax(theMax);
OK = aVbxCtl.GetProp("Max", theMax);
```

To set the maximum position of gauge control you can utilize the member functions `TVbxControl::SetProp()` or `TVbxMhGauge::SetPropMax()`. The declaration for the last function is:

```
BOOL SetPropMax(int v);
```

Here are examples for using the above functions:

```
theMax = 100;
OK = anMhGauge.SetPropMax(theMax);
theMax = 90;
OK = aVbxCtl.SetProp("Max", theMax);
```

The ScaleMode Property

The property `ScaleMode` specifies scale of measurement for the gauge control. The `ScaleMode` property has values that are compatible with the ENUM type. The valid setting for this property is 1 (twips) or 3 (pixels). The default setting is 2. You may obtain the `ScaleMode` setting of the gauge control by calling the member functions `TVbxControl::GetProp()` or `TVbxMhGauge::GetPropScaleMode()`. The declaration for the latter function is:

```
BOOL GetPropScaleMode(ENUM& v);
```

The function `GetPropScaleMode()` returns a Boolean value to indicate its success or failure. The function yields the setting of the `ScaleMode` property to its caller using the parameter `v`. Here are examples for using the above functions:

```
OK = anMhGauge.GetPropScaleMode(theScaleMode);
OK = aVbxCtl.GetProp("ScaleMode", theScaleMode);
```

To set the scale of measurement for the gauge control, you can use the member functions `TVbxControl::SetProp()` or `TVbxMhGauge::SetPropScaleMode()`. The declaration for the latter function is:

```
BOOL SetPropScaleMode(ENUM v);
```

Here are examples for using the above functions:

```
theScaleMode = 1;
OK = anMhGauge.SetPropScaleMode(theScaleMode);
theScaleMode = 3;
OK = aVbxCtl.SetProp("ScaleMode", theScaleMode);
```

The Style Property

The property `Style` defines the style of the gauge control. The `Style` property uses values that are compatible with the ENUM type. Table 23.1 shows the valid settings for the `Style` property. The default setting is 0.

You can obtain the `Style` setting of the gauge control by employing the member functions `TVbxControl::GetProp()` or `TVbxMhGauge::GetPropStyle()`. The declaration for the last function is:

```
BOOL GetPropStyle(ENUM& v);
```

The function `GetPropStyle()` returns a Boolean value to denote its success or failure. The function yields the setting of the `Style` property to its caller using the parameter `v`. Here are examples for using the above functions:

```
OK = anMhGauge.GetPropStyle(theStyle);
OK = aVbxCtl.GetProp("Style", theStyle);
```

To assign the style of the gauge control you may use the member functions `TVbxControl::SetProp()` or `TVbxMhGauge::SetPropStyle()`. The declaration for the last function is:

```
BOOL SetPropStyle(ENUM v);
```

Here are examples for using the above functions:

```
theStyle = 1;
OK = anMhGauge.SetPropStyle(theStyle);
theStyle = 3;
OK = aVbxCtl.SetProp("Style", theStyle);
```

Table 23.1. The Settings for the Style Property

Setting	Meaning
0	Horizontal bar
1	Vertical bar
2	Semi-circular gauge with needle
3	Circular gauge with needle
4	Horizontal fill with bitmap
5	Vertical fill with bitmap

The Picture Property

The property `Picture` specifies the image used to display the gauge. The `Picture` property has values that are compatible with the `HPIC` type. You can get the `Picture` setting of the gauge control by using the member functions `TVbxControl::GetProp()` or `TVbxMhGauge::GetPropPicture()`. The declaration for the latter function is:

```
BOOL GetPropPicture(HPIC& v);
```

The function `GetPropPicture()` returns a Boolean value to indicate its success or failure. The function returns the setting of the `Picture` property to its caller using the parameter `v`. Here are examples for using the above functions:

```
OK = anMhGauge.GetPropPicture(thePicture);
OK = aVbxCtl.GetProp("Picture", thePicture);
```

To set the handle of gauge's picture, you can use the member functions `TVbxControl::SetProp()` or `TVbxMhGauge::SetPropPicture()`. The declaration for the latter function is:

```
BOOL SetPropPicture(HPIC v);
```

Here are examples for using the above functions:

```
PICTURE temp1, temp2;
// initialize temp1
thePicture = VBXCreatePicture(&temp1);
OK = anMhGauge.SetPropPicture(thePicture);
// initialize temp2
thePicture = VBXCreatePicture(&temp2);
OK = aVbxCtl.SetProp("Picture", thePicture);
```

The NeedleWidth Property

The property `NeedleWidth` defines the width of the needle in the gauge. The `NeedleWidth` property uses values that are compatible with the `int` type. The width is expressed in the control's setting of the `ScaleMode` property. The setting for the Style property must be 2 or 3. You may recall the `NeedleWidth` setting of the gauge control by utilizing the member functions `TVbxControl::GetProp()` or `TVbxMhGauge::GetPropNeedleWidth()`. The declaration for the last function is:

```
BOOL GetPropNeedleWidth(int& v);
```

The function `GetPropNeedleWidth()` yields a Boolean value to indicate its success or failure. The function returns the setting of the `NeedleWidth` property to its caller through the parameter `v`. Here are examples for using the above functions:

```
OK = anMhGauge.GetPropNeedleWidth(theNeedleWidth);
OK = aVbxCtl.GetProp("NeedleWidth", theNeedleWidth);
```

To set the needle width of the gauge control, you can use the member functions `TVbxControl::SetProp()` or `TVbxMhGauge::SetPropNeedleWidth()`. The declaration for the latter function is:

```
BOOL SetPropNeedleWidth(int v);
```

Here are examples for using the above functions:

```
theNeedleWidth = 1;
OK = anMhGauge.SetPropNeedleWidth(theNeedleWidth);
theNeedleWidth = 2;
OK = aVbxCtl.SetProp("NeedleWidth", theNeedleWidth);
```

The ControlBox Property

The Boolean property `ControlBox` indicates whether or not a control box is available on the gauge control. The `ControlBox` property has values that are compatible with the `BOOL` type. You may obtain the `ControlBox` setting of the gauge control by utilizing the member functions `TVbxControl::GetProp()` or `TVbxMhGauge::GetPropControlBox()`. The declaration for the latter function is:

```
BOOL GetPropControlBox(BOOL& v);
```

The function `GetPropControlBox()` returns a Boolean value to signal its success or failure. The function yields the setting of the `ControlBox` property to its caller using the parameter `v`. Here are examples for utilizing the above functions:

```
OK = anMhGauge.GetPropControlBox(hasControlBox);
OK = aVbxCtl.GetProp("ControlBox", hasControlBox);
```

To assign a value to the ControlBox property, you may use the member functions `TVbxControl::SetProp()` or `TVbxMhGauge::SetPropControlBox()`. The declaration for the latter function is:

```
BOOL SetPropControlBox(BOOL v);
```

Here are examples for using the above functions:

```
    hasControlBox = TRUE;
OK = anMhGauge.SetPropControlBox(hasControlBox);
    hasControlBox = FALSE;
aVbxCtl.SetProp("ControlBox", !isControlBox);
```

The Visible Property

The Boolean property `Visible` specifies whether or not the gauge control is visible. The `Visible` property has values that are compatible with the `BOOL` type. You may obtain the `Visible` setting of the gauge control by calling the member functions `TVbxControl::GetProp()` or `TVbxMhGauge::GetPropVisible()`. The declaration for the latter function is:

```
BOOL GetPropVisible(BOOL& v);
```

The function `GetPropVisible()` returns a Boolean value to flag its success or failure. The function yields the setting of the `Visible` property to its caller through the parameter `v`. Here are examples for using the above functions:

```
OK = anMhGauge.GetPropVisible(theVisible);
OK = aVbxCtl.GetProp("Visible", theVisible);
```

To show or hide a gauge control you can apply the member functions `TVbxControl::SetProp()` or `TVbxMhGauge::SetPropVisible()`. The declaration for the latter function is:

```
BOOL SetPropVisible(BOOL v);
```

Here are examples for using the above functions:

```
// toggle the visibility of the gauge control
    OK = anMhGauge.GetPropVisible(isVisible);
OK = anMhGauge.SetPropVisible(!isVisible);
// toggle the visibility of the gauge control
    OK = aVbxCtl.GetProp("Visible", isVisible);
OK = aVbxCtl.SetProp("Visible", !isVisible);
```

The Enabled Property

The Boolean property `Enabled` indicates whether or not the gauge control is enabled. The `Enabled` property has values that are compatible

with the `BOOL` data type. You may obatin the `Enabled` setting of the gauge control by using the member functions `TVbxControl::GetProp()` or `TVbxMhGauge::GetPropEnabled()`. The declaration for the latter function is:

```
BOOL GetPropEnabled(BOOL& v);
```

The function `GetPropEnabled()` yields a Boolean value to indicate its success or failure. The function returns the setting of the `Enabled` property to its caller through the parameter `v`. Here are examples for employing the above functions:

```
OK = anMhGauge.GetPropEnabled(theEnabled);
OK = aVbxCtl.GetProp("Enabled", theEnabled);
```

To disable or enable a gauge control you can apply the member functions `TVbxControl::SetProp()` or `TVbxMhGauge::SetPropEnabled()`. The declaration for the last function is:

```
BOOL SetPropEnabled(BOOL v);
```

Here are examples for using the above functions:

```
// toggle the enabled state of the gauge control
   OK = anMhGauge.GetPropEnabled(isEnabled);
OK = anMhGauge.SetPropEnabled(!isEnabled);
// toggle the enabled state of the gauge control
   OK = aVbxCtl.GetProp("Enabled", isEnabled);
OK = aVbxCtl.SetProp("Enabled", !isEnabled);
```

The Gauge Control Events

The MicroHelp gauge control responds to various events. The relevant events are `Change`, `Click`, `Move`, and `Resize`. The other methods which are typical of common VBX controls include `Close`, `DblClick`, `DragDrop`, `DragOver`, `GotFocus`, `KeyDown`, `KeyPress`, `KeyUp`, `LostFocus`, `MouseDown`, `MouseMove`, `MouseUp`, `Move`, and `Resize`.

The Gauge Control Example

We have included a sample program which tests the gauge control. The MDI-compliant program VBX.EXE displays a gauge control and the pushbuttons Add Percent, Sub Percent, and Auto Test (see fig. 23.1).

When you click the pushbutton Add Percent, you increase the value of the gauge by 1. When you click the pushbutton Sub Percent, you decrease the value of the gauge by one. Either button causes the needle of the gauge to move slightly. The program displays the current value of the gauge in the upper left corner of the MDI child window. When you click the Auto Test button the program resets the gauge's value to 0 and then systematically increases the value of the gauge to 100 percent using the internal clock of Windows. The program displays the elapsed number of seconds and the percentage in the upper left corner of the current MDI child window. This test lasts for 15 seconds. The systematic increase in the gauge's value also moves the needle. When this test is finished, the program restores the gauge's value to its original position.

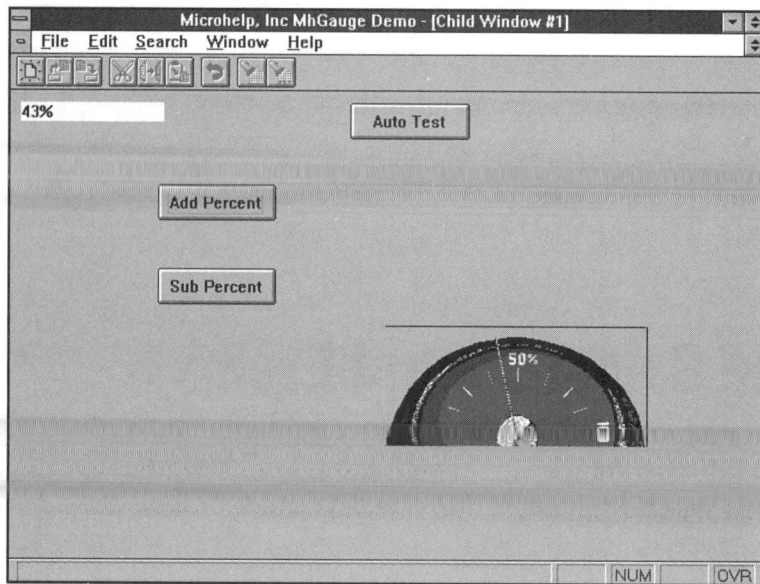

Fig. 23.1. A sample session with the program VBX.EXE.

For the complete code listings of this sample application, and a discussion of each code listing, see the SAMPLE23.DOC file in the archived file for Chapter 23, on the enclosed disk. SAMPLE23.DOC is a Microsoft Word for Windows 2.0 file that can be read from Word for Windows or any major word processor or text editor.

Summary

This chapter presented the MicroHelp gauge control which supports a gauge that is typically used to monitor the progress of time-consuming tasks. You learned about the following topics:

➤ The relevant properties of the gauge control which empower you to specify the appearance and behavior of the control.

➤ The relevant VBX events for the gauge control, which include `Change`, `Click`, `Move`, and `Resize`. The event Change is the most significant one since it allows the gauge control to respond to changing the value of its needle.

The MicroHelp VBX Alarm Control

by Namir Shammas

This chapter looks at the MicroHelp alarm control. This control supports an alarm control with three predefined pictures: the phone, the alarm clock, and the wrist alarm.

In this chapter, you learn the following:

➤ The relevant properties of the alarm control

➤ The relevant VBX event for the alarm control

➤ An example that uses the alarm control

The Alarm Control Properties

The MicroHelp alarm control has many properties which fine-tune the operations (such as ring type and frequency) and appearance (such as the bitmap image) of the control. The following sections discuss the control's relevant properties.

The Style Property

The property `Style` specifies the style of the alarm control. The `Style` property has values that are compatible with the `ENUM` type. Table 24.1 shows the valid settings for the `Style` property. The default setting is 0 which displays the telephone picture. You can get the `Style` setting of the alarm control by using the member functions `TVbxControl::GetProp()` or `TVbxMhIAlarm::GetPropStyle()`. The declaration for the latter function is:

```
BOOL GetPropStyle(ENUM& v);
```

The function `GetPropStyle()` returns a Boolean value to indicate success or failure. The function returns the setting of the `Style` property to its caller using the parameter `v`. These examples demonstrate the use of the preceding functions:

```
OK = anMhAlarm.GetPropStyle(theStyle);
OK = aVbxCtl.GetProp("Style", theStyle);
```

To set the style of the alarm control you can use the member functions `TVbxControl::SetProp()` or `TVbxMhIAlarm::SetPropStyle()`. Each style value has a default value for the properties `Interval`, `RingTime`, `PauseTime`, `RingTone`, `RingFreq`, and `RingLength`. The declaration for the latter function is:

```
BOOL SetPropStyle(ENUM v);
```

These examples use the preceding functions:

```
theStyle = 1;
OK = anMhAlarm.SetPropStyle(theStyle);
theStyle = 2;
OK = aVbxCtl.SetProp("Style", theStyle);
```

Table 24.1. The Settings for the Style Property

Setting	Meaning
0	Telephone
1	Alarm clock
2	Wrist alarm
3	User-defined bitmap

The RingMode Property

The property `RingMode` specifies the ringing mode of the alarm control. The `RingMode` property has values that are compatible with the `ENUM` type. Table 24.2 shows the valid settings for the `RingMode` property. The default setting is 0. You can get the `RingMode` setting of the alarm control by using the member functions `TVbxControl::GetProp()` or `TVbxMhIAlarm::GetPropRingMode()`. The declaration for the latter function is:

```
BOOL GetPropRingMode(ENUM& v);
```

The function `GetPropRingMode()` returns a Boolean value to indicate success or failure. The function returns the setting of the `RingMode` property to its caller using the parameter *v*. These examples demonstrate the use of the preceding functions:

```
OK = anMhAlarm.GetPropRingMode(theRingMode);
OK = aVbxCtl.GetProp("RingMode", theRingMode);
```

To set the ringing mode of the alarm control you can use the member functions `TVbxControl::SetProp()` or `TVbxMhIAlarm::SetPropRingMode()`. The declaration for the latter function is:

```
BOOL SetPropRingMode(ENUM v);
```

Here are examples for using the preceding functions:

```
theRingMode = 1;
OK = anMhAlarm.SetPropRingMode(theRingMode);
theRingMode = 3;
OK = aVbxCtl.SetProp("RingMode", theRingMode);
```

Table 24.2. The Settings for the RingMode Property

Setting	Meaning
0	Normal
1	Legato
2	Staccato

The RingOn Property

The property `RingOn` specifies whether or not the alarm control is active. If the control is active, this property specifies the frequency of the alarm rings. The `RingOn` property has values that are compatible with the ENUM type. Table 24.3 shows the valid settings for the `RingOn` property. The default setting is 0. You can get the `RingOn` setting of the alarm control by using the member functions `TVbxControl::GetProp()` or `TVbxMhIAlarm::GetPropRingOn()`. The declaration for the latter function is:

```
BOOL GetPropRingOn(ENUM& v);
```

The function `GetPropRingOn()` yields a Boolean value to indicate success or failure. The function returns the setting of the `RingOn` property to its caller by way of the parameter `v`. Here are examples for using the preceding functions:

```
OK = anMhAlarm.GetPropRingOn(theRingOn);
OK = aVbxCtl.GetProp("RingOn", theRingOn);
```

To set the RingOn property of the alarm control you can use the member functions `TVbxControl::SetProp()` or `TVbxMhIAlarm::SetPropRingOn()`. The declaration for the last function is:

```
BOOL SetPropRingOn(ENUM v);
```

These examples use the preceding functions:

```
theRingOn = 1;
OK = anMhAlarm.SetPropRingOn(theRingOn);
theRingOn = 3;
OK = aVbxCtl.SetProp("RingOn", theRingOn);
```

Table 24.3. The Settings for the RingOn Property

Setting	Meaning
0	Ring off
1	Flash ring (single ring only)
2	Ring on (continuous ring)
3	No flash ring

The RingLength Property

The property `RingLength` specifies the length of the note sent to the computer's speaker. The `RingLength` property has values that are compatible with the `int` type. The valid settings for this property range from 1 to 64. You can get the `RingLength` setting of the alarm control by using the member functions `TVbxControl::GetProp()` or `TVbxMhIAlarm::GetPropRingLength()`. The declaration for the latter function is:

```
BOOL GetPropRingLength(int& v);
```

The function `GetPropRingLength()` returns a Boolean value to indicate its success or failure. The function returns the setting of the `RingLength` property to its caller using the parameter `v`. Here are examples for using the preceding functions:

```
OK = anMhAlarm.GetPropRingLength(theRingLength);
OK = aVbxCtl.GetProp("RingLength", theRingLength);
```

To assign a value to the `RingLength` property of the alarm control you can use the member functions `TVbxControl::SetProp()` or `TVbxMhIAlarm::SetPropRingLength()`. The declaration for the latter function is:

```
BOOL SetPropRingLength(int v);
```

These examples demonstrate the use of the preceding functions:

```
theRingLength = 41;
OK = anMhAlarm.SetPropRingLength(theRingLength);
theRingLength = 55;
OK = aVbxCtl.SetProp("RingLength", theRingLength);
```

The RingTime Property

The property `RingTime` specifies the time duration (in milliseconds) during which the control sends tones to the speaker. The `RingTime` property uses values that are compatible with the `int` type. You can get the `RingTime` setting of the alarm control by using the member functions `TVbxControl::GetProp()` or `TVbxMhIAlarm::GetPropRingTime()`. The declaration for the last function is:

```
BOOL GetPropRingTime(int& v);
```

The function `GetPropRingTime()` returns a Boolean value to indicate success or failure. The function yields the setting of the `RingTime` property to its caller using the parameter `v`. Here are examples for calling the above functions:

```
OK = anMhAlarm.GetPropRingTime(theRingTime);
OK = aVbxCtl.GetProp("RingTime", theRingTime);
```

To set the ring duration of the alarm control you may employ the member functions `TVbxControl::SetProp()` or `TVbxMhIAlarm::SetPropRingTime()`. The declaration for the latter function is:

```
BOOL SetPropRingTime(int v);
```

The following examples demonstrate the use of the above functions:

```
theRingTime = 100;
OK = anMhAlarm.SetPropRingTime(theRingTime);
theRingTime = 300;
OK = aVbxCtl.SetProp("RingTime", theRingTime);
```

The RingTone Property

The property `RingTone` defines the musical note number that the control sends to the sound driver. The `RingTone` property has values that are compatible with the `int` type. The valid settings for this property range from 1 to 84. You can obtain the `RingTone` setting of the alarm control by using the member functions `TVbxControl::GetProp()` or `TVbxMhIAlarm::GetPropRingTone()`. The declaration for the latter function is:

```
BOOL GetPropRingTone(int& v);
```

The function `GetPropRingTone()` yields a Boolean value to signal success or failure. The function returns the setting of the `RingTone` property to its caller using the parameter *v*. Here are examples for using the above functions:

```
OK = anMhAlarm.GetPropRingTone(theRingTone);
OK = aVbxCtl.GetProp("RingTone", theRingTone);
```

To set the ring tone of the alarm control you can use the member functions `TVbxControl::SetProp()` or `TVbxMhIAlarm::SetPropRingTone()`. The declaration for the latter function is:

```
BOOL SetPropRingTone(int v);
```

These examples demonstrate the use of the above functions:

```
theRingTone = 6;
OK = anMhAlarm.SetPropRingTone(theRingTone);
theRingTone = 12;
OK = aVbxCtl.SetProp("RingTone", theRingTone);
```

The PauseTime Property

The property `PauseTime` specifies the pause duration (in milliseconds) between rings. The `PauseTime` property has values that are compatible with the `int` type. The valid settings for this property range from 0 to 32767. You can get the `PauseTime` setting of the alarm control by using the member functions `TVbxControl::GetProp()` or `TVbxMhIAlarm::GetPropPauseTime()`. The declaration for the latter function is:

```
BOOL GetPropPauseTime(int& v);
```

The function `GetPropPauseTime()` returns a Boolean value to indicate success or failure. The function yields the setting of the `PauseTime` property to its caller using the parameter *v*. These examples demonstrate the use of the preceding functions:

```
OK = anMhAlarm.GetPropPauseTime(thePauseTime);
OK = aVbxCtl.GetProp("PauseTime", thePauseTime);
```

To set the pause duration of the alarm control you may apply the member functions `TVbxControl::SetProp()` or `TVbxMhIAlarm::SetPropPauseTime()`. The declaration for the latter function is:

```
BOOL SetPropPauseTime(int v);
```

Here are examples for using the preceding functions:

```
thePauseTime = 1000;
OK = anMhAlarm.SetPropPauseTime(thePauseTime);
thePauseTime = 3000;
OK = aVbxCtl.SetProp("PauseTime", thePauseTime);
```

The Interval Property

The property `Interval` specifies the interval (in milliseconds) between changes in the alarm bitmap display when the setting for property `RingOn` is 0. The `Interval` property has values that are compatible with the `long` type. The valid settings for this property range from 1 to 2147483647. You can get the `Interval` setting of the alarm control by using the member functions `TVbxControl::GetProp()` or `TVbxMhIAlarm::GetPropInterval()`. The declaration for the latter function is:

```
BOOL GetPropInterval(long& v);
```

The function `GetPropInterval()` returns a Boolean value to indicate success or failure. The function returns the setting of the `Interval` property to its caller using the parameter `v`. Here are examples for using the preceding functions:

```
OK = anMhAlarm.GetPropInterval(theInterval);
OK = aVbxCtl.GetProp("Interval", theInterval);
```

To set the Interval property of the alarm control you can use the member functions `TVbxControl::SetProp()` or `TVbxMhIAlarm::SetPropInterval()`. The declaration for the latter function is:

```
BOOL SetPropInterval(long v);
```

These examples demonstrate the use of the above functions:

```
theInterval = 10000;
OK = anMhAlarm.SetPropInterval(theInterval);
theInterval = 30000;
OK = aVbxCtl.SetProp("Interval", theInterval);
```

The PictureX Properties

The properties `Picture1`, `Picture2`, and `Picture3` specify the bitmaps used to display the alarm control. You can use the `PictureX` properties only

when the `Style` property is set to 3. The `PictureX` properties have values that are compatible with the `HPIC` type. You can get the `PictureX` settings of the alarm control by using the member functions `TVbxControl::GetProp()` or `TVbxMhGauge::GetPropPictureX()`. The declarations for the latter functions are:

```
BOOL GetPropPicture1(HPIC& v);
BOOL GetPropPicture2(HPIC& v);
BOOL GetPropPicture3(HPIC& v);
```

The functions `GetPropPictureX()` return Boolean values to indicate their success or failure. The functions return the setting of the `PictureX` property to its caller using the parameter `v`. Here are examples for using these functions:

```
OK = anMhIAlarm.GetPropPicture1(thePicture);
OK = aVbxCtl.GetProp1("Picture", thePicture);
```

To set the control's pictures you can use the member functions `TVbxControl::SetProp()` or `TVbxMhGauge::SetPropPictureX()`. The declarations for the latter functions are:

```
BOOL SetPropPicture1(HPIC v);
BOOL SetPropPicture2(HPIC v);
BOOL SetPropPicture3(HPIC v);
```

Here are examples for using the preceding functions:

```
PICTURE temp1, temp2;
// initialize temp1
thePicture = VBXCreatePicture(&temp1);
OK = anMhIAlarm.SetPropPicture1(thePicture);
// initialize temp2
thePicture = VBXCreatePicture(&temp2);
OK = aVbxCtl.SetProp("Picture2", thePicture);
```

The PictureMaskX Properties

The properties `PictureMask1`, `PictureMask2`, and `PictureMask3` specify the mask pictures used to display the background of the alarm control. You can use the `PictureMaskX` properties only when the `Style` property is set to 3. The `PictureMaskX` properties have values that are compatible with the `HPIC` type. You can get the `PictureMaskX` settings of the alarm control by using the member functions `TVbxControl::GetProp()` or

`TVbxMhGauge::GetPropPictureMask`*X*`()`. The declarations for the latter functions are:

```
BOOL GetPropPictureMask1(HPIC& v);
BOOL GetPropPictureMask2(HPIC& v);
BOOL GetPropPictureMask3(HPIC& v);
```

The functions `GetPropPictureMask`*X*`()` return Boolean values to indicate their success or failure. The functions yield the setting of the `PictureMask`*X* property to their caller using the parameter *v*. Here are examples for using the above functions:

```
OK = anMhIAlarm.GetPropPictureMask1(thePictureMask);
OK = aVbxCtl.GetProp1("PictureMask", thePictureMask);
```

To set the control's pictures you can use the member functions `TVbxControl::SetProp()` or `TVbxMhGauge::SetPropPictureMask`*X*`()`. The declarations for the latter functions are:

```
BOOL SetPropPictureMask1(HPIC v);
BOOL SetPropPictureMask2(HPIC v);
BOOL SetPropPictureMask3(HPIC v);
```

Here are examples for using the preceding functions:

```
PICTURE temp1, temp2;
// initialize temp1
thePictureMask = VBXCreatePictureMask(&temp1);
OK = anMhIAlarm.SetPropPictureMask1(thePictureMask);
// initialize temp2
thePictureMask = VBXCreatePictureMask(&temp2);
OK = aVbxCtl.SetProp("PictureMask2", thePictureMask);
```

The WindowState Property

The property `WindowState` specifies whether or not the alarm bitmap is used when the window is minimized. The `WindowState` property has values that are compatible with the `int` type. Table 24.4 shows the valid settings for the `WindowState` property. The default setting is 0. You can get the `WindowState` setting of the alarm control by using the member functions `TVbxControl::GetProp()` or `TVbxMhIAlarm::GetPropWindowState()`. The declaration for the latter function is:

```
BOOL GetPropWindowState(int& v);
```

The function `GetPropWindowState()` returns a Boolean value to indicate success or failure. The function returns the setting of the `WindowState` property to its caller using the parameter `v`. Here are examples for using the above functions:

```
OK = anMhAlarm.GetPropWindowState(theWindowState);
OK = aVbxCtl.GetProp("WindowState", theWindowState);
```

To set the WindowState property of the alarm control you can use the member functions `TVbxControl::SetProp()` or `TVbxMhIAlarm::SetPropWindowState()`. The declaration for the latter function is:

```
BOOL SetPropWindowState(int v);
```

The preceding functions are used in these examples:

```
theWindowState = 1;
OK = anMhAlarm.SetPropWindowState(theWindowState);
theWindowState = 0;
OK = aVbxCtl.SetProp("WindowState", theWindowState);
```

Table 24.4. The Settings for the WindowState Property

Setting	Meaning
0	Normal display
1	Alarm bitmap used when window is minimized

The Visible Property

The Boolean property `Visible` indicates whether or not the alarm control is visible. The `Visible` property has values that are compatible with the `BOOL` type. You may obtain the `Visible` setting of the alarm control by using the member functions `TVbxControl::GetProp()` or `TVbxMhIAlarm::GetPropVisible()`. The declaration for the last function is:

```
BOOL GetPropVisible(BOOL& v);
```

The function `GetPropVisible()` yields a Boolean value to signal success or failure. The function returns the setting of the `Visible` property to its caller using the parameter *v*. Here are examples for using the above functions:

```
OK = anMhIAlarm.GetPropVisible(theVisible);
theVisible = aVbxCtl.GetProp("Visible");
```

To show or hide an alarm control you can use the member functions `TVbxControl::SetProp()` or `TVbxMhIAlarm::SetPropVisible()`. The declaration for the latter function is:

```
BOOL SetPropVisible(BOOL v);
```

Here are examples for using the preceding functions:

```
// toggle the visibility of the alarm control
    OK = anMhIAlarm.GetPropVisible(isVisible);
OK = anMhIAlarm.SetPropVisible(!isVisible);
// toggle the visibility of the alarm control
    aVbxCtl.GetProp("Visible", isVisible);
aVbxCtl.SetProp("Visible", !isVisible);
```

The Enabled Property

The Boolean property `Enabled` indicates whether or not the alarm control is enabled. The `Enabled` property has values that are compatible with the `BOOL` type. You can get the `Enabled` setting of the alarm control by using the member functions `TVbxControl::GetProp()` or `TVbxMhIAlarm::GetPropEnabled()`. The declaration for the latter function is:

```
BOOL GetPropEnabled(BOOL& v);
```

The function `GetPropEnabled()` returns a Boolean value to indicate success or failure. The function returns the setting of the `Enabled` property to its caller using the parameter *v*. Here are examples for using the preceding functions:

```
OK = anMhIAlarm.GetPropEnabled(theEnabled);
OK = aVbxCtl.GetProp("Enabled", theEnabled);
```

To disable or enable an alarm control you can use the member functions `TVbxControl::SetProp()` or `TVbxMhIAlarm::SetPropEnabled()`. The declaration for the latter function is:

```
BOOL SetPropEnabled(BOOL v);
```

These examples demonstrate the use of the preceding functions:

```
// toggle the enabled state of the alarm control
   OK = anMhIAlarm.GetPropEnabled(isEnabled);
OK = anMhIAlarm.SetPropEnabled(!isEnabled);
// toggle the enabled state of the alarm control
   OK = aVbxCtl.GetProp("Enabled", isEnabled);
OK = aVbxCtl.SetProp("Enabled", !isEnabled);
```

The Alarm Control Events

The MicroHelp VBX alarm control supports the event `Ring` in addition to the typical VBX control events `Change`, `Click`, `DblClick`, `GotFocus`, `KeyDown`, `KeyPress`, `KeyUp`, `LostFocus`, `MouseDown`, `MouseMove`, and `MouseUp`.

The Alarm Control Example

The following sections examine a simple program that tests the alarm control. The sample involves the MDI-compliant program VBX.EXE, that displays an alarm control and the pushbuttons Style and Ring State (see fig. 24.1). You click the Style button to change the style of the alarm control. The program switches between the three predefined bitmaps for the alarm control. When you click the Ring State button you toggle the alarm.

The program displays text in the upper-left corner of the window to indicate whether the alarm is continuous or off. If you click with the left mouse button on the alarm when it is off, the alarm rings once and then displays a message dialog box. If you click with the right mouse button on the alarm when it is off, the alarm just displays a message dialog box. If you click the alarm while it is continuously ringing, the program displays a message dialog box. Figure 24.1 shows a sample session with the program VBX.EXE displaying the phone icon. Figure 24.2 shows a sample session with the program VBX.EXE displaying the clock icon. Figure 24.3 shows a sample session with the program VBX.EXE displaying the wrist alarm icon.

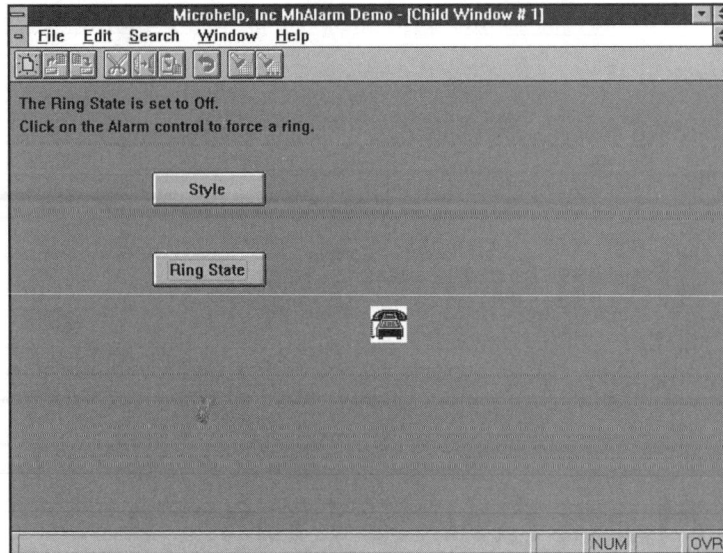

Fig. 24.1. A sample session with the program VBX.EXE showing the phone icon.

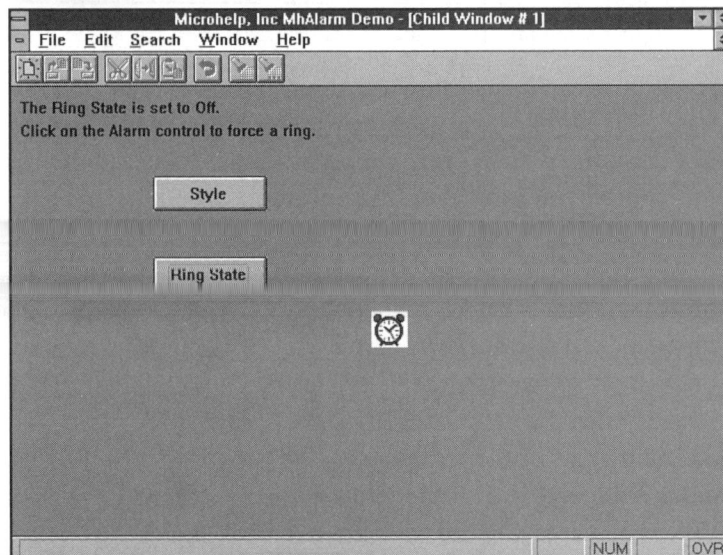

Fig. 24.2. A sample session with the program VBX.EXE showing the clock icon.

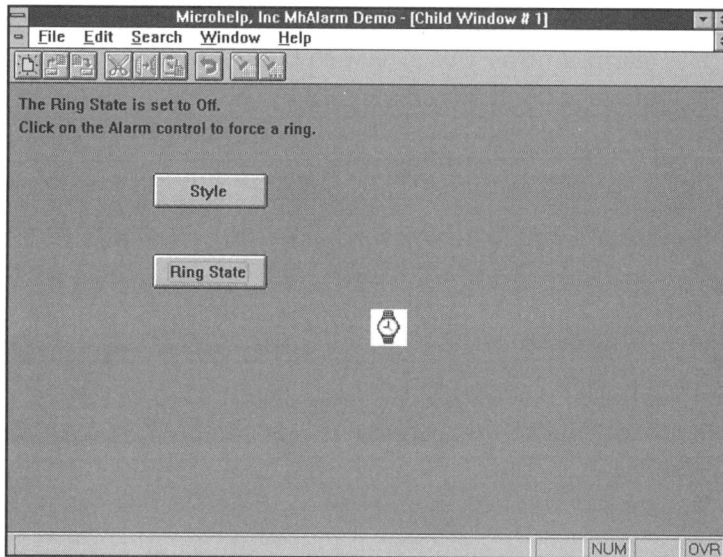

Fig. 24.3. A sample session with the program VBX.EXE showing the wrist alarm icon.

For the complete code listings of this sample application, and a discussion of each code listing, see the SAMPLE24.DOC file in the archived file for Chapter 24, on the enclosed disk. SAMPLE24.DOC is a Microsoft Word for Windows 2.0 file that can be read from Word for Windows or any major word processor or text editor.

Summary

This chapter presented the MicroHelp alarm control. This control supports an alarm control with three predefined pictures: the phone, the alarm clock, and the wrist alarm. You learned about the following topics:

➤ The relevant properties of the alarm control. These properties allow you to determine the appearance of the control as well as define its operations: frequency of alarm, duration of ring, type of ring, and so on.

➤ You learned that the event Ring is the most relevant event for the alarm control. This event allows the alarm control to sound an alarm at the interval specified by the control's properties.

The MicroHelp VBX Spin Control

by Namir Shammas

This chapter looks at the MicroHelp spin control. This control supports a spin control with an optional caption and 3-D appearance. The term *spin* comes from the fact that the control resembles the arrow portion of a scroll bar which, when combined with a caption, can be used to increase or decrease integer values. In this chapter, you learn about the following topics:

➤ The relevant properties of the spin control

➤ The relevant VBX event for the spin control

➤ An example that uses the spin control

The Spin Control Properties

The MicroHelp spin control has many properties which affect the appearance and operations of the control. The following sections discuss the relevant properties of the spin control.

The Style Property

The `Style` property specifies the style of the spin control. The `Style` property has values that are compatible with the ENUM type. Table 25.1 shows the valid settings for the `Style` property. The default setting is 0 and displays the control using the 3-D vertical style. You can obtain the `Style` setting of the spin control by calling the member functions `TVbxControl::GetProp()` or `TVbxMhSpin::GetPropStyle()`. The declaration for the latter function is:

```
BOOL GetPropStyle(ENUM& v);
```

The function `GetPropStyle()` returns a Boolean value to indicate success or failure. The function returns the setting of the `Style` property to its caller using the parameter `v`. Here are examples for using these functions:

```
OK = anMhSpin.GetPropStyle(theStyle);
OK = aVbxCtl.GetProp("Style", theStyle);
```

To set the style of the spin control you can use the member functions `TVbxControl::SetProp()` or `TVbxMhSpin::SetPropStyle()`. The declaration for the latter function is:

```
BOOL SetPropStyle(ENUM v);
```

Here are examples for using the preceding functions:

```
theStyle = 1;
OK = anMhSpin.SetPropStyle(theStyle);
theStyle = 2;
OK = aVbxCtl.SetProp("Style", theStyle);
```

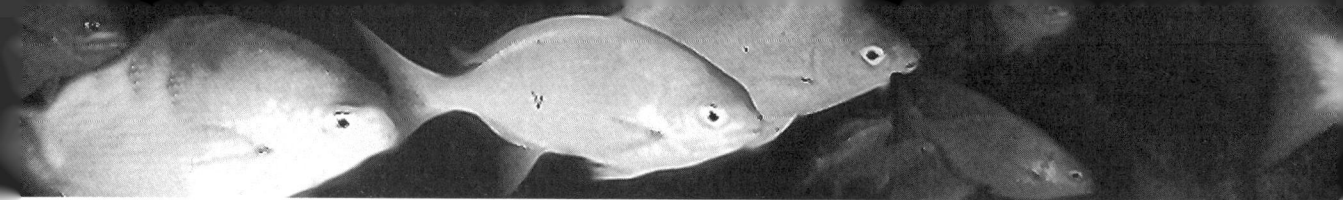

Table 25.1. The Settings for the Style Property

Setting	Meaning
0	3-D Vertical
1	3-D Horizontal
2	Normal Vertical
3	Normal Horizontal

The Arrows Property

The Boolean property `Arrows` indicates whether the spin control auto-matically draws the arrows. The `Arrows` property uses values that are compatible with the `BOOL` type. You may recall the `Arrows` setting of the spin control by using the member functions `TVbxControl::GetProp()` or `TVbxMhSpin::GetPropArrows()`. The declaration for the last function is:

```
BOOL GetPropArrows(BOOL& v);
```

The function `GetPropArrows()` returns a Boolean value to indicate success or failure. The function yields the setting of the `Arrows` property to its caller using the parameter `v`. Here are examples for using the preceding functions:

```
OK = anMhSpin.GetPropArrows(theArrows);
OK - aVbxCtl.GetProp("Arrows", theArrows);
```

To show or hide the arrows of a spin control you may apply the member functions `TVbxControl::SetProp()` or `TVbxMhSpin::SetPropArrows()`. The declaration for the latter function is:

```
BOOL SetPropArrows(BOOL v);
```

Here are examples for using the preceding functions:

```
// toggle the visibility of the arrows of the spin control
   OK = anMhSpin.GetPropArrows(hasArrows);
OK = anMhSpin.SetPropArrows(!hasArrows);
// toggle the visibility of the arraos of the spin control
   OK = aVbxCtl.GetProp("Arrows", hasArrows);
OK = aVbxCtl.SetProp("Arrows", !hasArrows);
```

The AutoSize Property

The Boolean property `AutoSize` indicates whether the spin control automatically sizes the picture area according to the size of the bitmap specified by the property `Picture1Up`. The `AutoSize` property has values that are compatible with the `BOOL` type. You may obtain the `AutoSize` setting of the spin control by using the member functions `TVbxControl::GetProp()` or `TVbxMhSpin::GetPropAutoSize()`. The declaration for the last function is:

```
BOOL GetPropAutoSize(BOOL& v);
```

The function `GetPropAutoSize()` returns a Boolean value to signal success or failure. The function returns the setting of the `AutoSize` property to its caller through the parameter `v`. Here are examples for using the preceding functions:

```
OK = anMhSpin.GetPropAutoSize(theAutoSize);
OK = aVbxCtl.GetProp("AutoSize", theAutoSize);
```

To set the `AutoSize` property of a spin control you can use the member functions `TVbxControl::SetProp()` or `TVbxMhSpin::SetPropAutoSize()`. The declaration for the latter function is:

```
BOOL SetPropAutoSize(BOOL v);
```

Here are examples for using the preceding functions:

```
    hasAutoSize = TRUE;
OK = anMhSpin.SetPropAutoSize(!hasAutoSize);
    OK = FALSE;
OK = aVbxCtl.SetProp("AutoSize", !hasAutoSize);
```

The BorderColor Property

The property `BorderColor` specifies the color of the outer border for the spin control. The `BorderColor` property has values that are compatible with the `COLORREF` type. You may access the `BorderColor` setting of the spin control by calling the member functions `TVbxControl::GetProp()` or `TVbxMhSpin::GetPropBorderColor()`. The declaration for the last function is:

```
BOOL GetPropBorderColor(COLORREF& v);
```

The function `GetPropBorderColor()` yields a Boolean value to indicate success or failure. The function returns the setting of the `BorderColor` property to its caller using the parameter `v`. Here are examples for using the preceding functions:

```
OK = anMhSpin.GetPropBorderColor(theBorderColor);
OK = aVbxCtl.GetProp("BorderColor", theBorderColor);
```

To assign the border color of a spin control you can use the member functions `TVbxControl::SetProp()` or `TVbxMhSpin::SetPropBorderColor()`. The declaration for the latter function is:

```
BOOL SetPropBorderColor(COLORREF v);
```

Here are examples for using the preceding functions:

```
      BorderColor = RGB(255, 129, 128)
OK = anMhSpin.SetPropBorderColor(BorderColor);
      BorderColor = RGB(129, 255, 129);
OK = aVbxCtl.SetProp("BorderColor", !hasBorderColor);
```

The BorderStyle Property

The property `BorderStyle` specifies border style of the spin control. The `BorderStyle` property has values that are compatible with the ENUM type. Table 25.2 shows the valid settings for the `BorderStyle` property. The default setting of 2 displays the control using single-line and rounded-corner boder style. You can get the `BorderStyle` setting of the spin control by calling the member functions `TVbxControl::GetProp()` or `TVbxMhSpin::GetPropBorderStyle()`. The declaration for the latter function is:

```
BOOL GetPropBorderStyle(ENUM& v);
```

The function `GetPropBorderStyle()` returns a Boolean value to signal success or failure. The function yields the setting of the `BorderStyle` property to its caller using the parameter `v`. Here are examples for using the preceding functions:

```
OK = anMhSpin.GetPropBorderStyle(theBorderStyle);
OK = aVbxCtl.GetProp("BorderStyle", theBorderStyle);
```

To set the border style of the spin control you can use the member functions `TVbxControl::SetProp()` or `TVbxMhSpin::SetPropBorderStyle()`. The declaration for the latter function is:

```
BOOL SetPropBorderStyle(ENUM v);
```

Here are examples for using the preceding functions:

```
theBorderStyle = 1;
OK = anMhSpin.SetPropBorderStyle(theBorderStyle);
theBorderStyle = 2;
OK = aVbxCtl.SetProp("BorderStyle", theBorderStyle);
```

Table 25.2. The Settings for the BorderStyle Property

Setting	Meaning
0	No border
1	Single line
2	Single line with rounded corners

The FillColor Property

The property `FillColor` specifies the background color of the spin control. The `FillColor` property has values that are compatible with the COLORREF type. You can get the `FillColor` setting of the spin control by using the member functions `TVbxControl::GetProp()` or `TVbxMhSpin::GetPropFillColor()`. The declaration for the latter function is:

```
BOOL GetPropFillColor(COLORREF v);
```

The function `GetPropFillColor()` yields a Boolean value to indicate success or failure. The function returns the setting of the `FillColor` property to its caller through the parameter `v`. Here are examples for using the preceding functions:

```
OK = anMhSpin.GetPropFillColor(theFillColor);
OK = aVbxCtl.GetProp("FillColor", theFillColor);
```

To set the background color of a spin control you can use the member functions `TVbxControl::SetProp()` or `TVbxMhSpin::SetPropFillColor()`. The declaration for the latter function is:

```
BOOL SetPropFillColor(COLORREF v);
```

Here are examples for using the preceding functions:

```
    theFillColor = RGB(255, 129, 128);
OK = anMhSpin.SetPropFillColor(theFillColor);
    theFillColor = RGB(129, 255, 129);
OK = aVbxCtl.SetProp("FillColor", theFillColor);
```

The FontBold Property

The Boolean property `FontBold` indicates whether the caption of the spin control has bold characters. The `FontBold` property uses values that are compatible with the `BOOL` type. You can recall the `FontBold` setting of the spin control by calling the member functions `TVbxControl::GetProp()` or `TVbxMhSpin::GetPropFontBold()`. The declaration for the last function is:

```
BOOL GetPropFontBold(BOOL& v);
```

The function GetPropFontBold() yields a Boolean value to signal success or failure. The function returns the setting of the FontBold property to its caller using the parameter v. Here are examples for using the preceding functions:

```
OK = anMhSpin.GetPropFontBold(isFontBold);
OK = aVbxCtl.GetProp("FontBold", isFontBold);
```

To use bold characters in a spin control's caption, you can apply the member functions `TVbxControl::SetProp()` or `TVbxMhSpin::SetPropFontBold()`. The declaration for the latter function is:

```
BOOL SetPropFontBold(BOOL v);
```

Here are examples for using the preceding functions:

```
    isFontBold = TRUE;
OK = anMhSpin.SetPropFontBold(isFontBold);
    isFontBold = FALSE;
OK = aVbxCtl.SetProp("FontBold", isFontBold);
```

The FontItalic Property

The Boolean property FontItalic indicates whether the caption of the spin control has italic characters. The FontItalic property has values that are compatible with the BOOL type. You can get the FontItalic setting of the spin control by using the member functions TVbxControl::GetProp() or TVbxMhSpin::GetPropFontItalic(). The declaration for the latter function is:

```
BOOL GetPropFontItalic(BOOL& v);
```

The function GetPropFontItalic() returns a Boolean value to indicate success or failure. The function returns the setting of the FontItalic property to its caller using the parameter v. Here are examples for using the preceding functions:

```
OK = anMhSpin.GetPropFontItalic(isFontItalic);
OK = aVbxCtl.GetProp("FontItalic", isFontItalic);
```

To use italic characters in a spin control's caption you can use the member functions TVbxControl::SetProp() or TVbxMhSpin::SetPropFontItalic(). The declaration for the latter function is:

```
BOOL SetPropFontItalic(BOOL v);
```

Here are examples for using the preceding functions:

```
    isFontItalic = TRUE;
OK = anMhSpin.SetPropFontItalic(isFontItalic);
    isFontItalic = FALSE;
OK = aVbxCtl.SetProp("FontItalic", isFontItalic);
```

The FontName Property

The Boolean property FontName specifies the name of the font used for the caption's text. The FontName property has values that are compatible with the string type. You can get the FontName setting of the spin control by using the member functions TVbxControl::GetProp() or TVbxMhSpin::GetPropFontName(). The declaration for the latter function is:

```
BOOL GetPropFontName(string& v);
```

The function `GetPropFontName()` returns a Boolean value to indicate success or failure. The function returns the setting of the `FontName` property to its caller using the parameter v. Here are examples for using the preceding functions:

```
OK = anMhSpin.GetPropFontName(theFontName);
OK = aVbxCtl.GetProp("FontName", theFontName);
```

To select a new font for a spin control's caption you can use the member functions `TVbxControl::SetProp()` or `TVbxMhSpin::SetPropFontName()`. The declaration for the latter function is:

```
BOOL SetPropFontName(string v);
```

Here are examples for using the preceding functions:

```
    theFontName = "Arial";
OK = anMhSpin.SetPropFontName(theFontName);
    theFontName = "Courier";
OK = aVbxCtl.SetProp("FontName", theFontName);
```

The FontSize Property

The Boolean property `FontSize` specifies the size of the font used for the caption's text. The `FontSize` property has values that are compatible with the `float` type. You may recall the `FontSize` setting of the spin control by using the member functions `TVbxControl::GetProp()` or `TVbxMhSpin::GetPropFontSize()`. The declaration for the latter function is:

```
BOOL GetPropFontSize(float& v);
```

The function `GetPropFontSize()` returns a Boolean value to indicate success or failure. The function returns the setting of the `FontSize` property to its caller using the parameter v. Here are examples for using the preceding functions:

```
OK = anMhSpin.GetPropFontSize(theFontSize);
OK = aVbxCtl.GetProp("FontSize", theFontSize);
```

To select a new font for a spin control's caption you can use the member functions `TVbxControl::SetProp()` or `TVbxMhSpin::SetPropFontSize()`. The declaration for the latter function is:

```
BOOL SetPropFontSize(float v);
```

Here are examples for using the preceding functions:

```
    theFontSize = 12.000;
OK = anMhSpin.SetPropFontSize(theFontSize);
    theFontSize = 11.000;
OK = aVbxCtl.SetProp("FontSize", theFontSize);
```

The FontStrikeThru Property

The Boolean property FontStrikeThru indicates whether the caption of the spin control has strikethrough characters. The FontStrikeThru property has values that are compatible with the BOOL type. You can get the FontStrikeThru setting of the spin control by using the member functions TVbxControl::GetProp() or TVbxMhSpin::GetPropFontStrikeThru(). The declaration for the latter function is:

```
BOOL GetPropFontStrikeThru(BOOL& v);
```

The function GetPropFontStrikeThru() returns a Boolean value to indicate success or failure. The function returns the setting of the FontStrikeThru property to its caller using the parameter v. Here are examples for using the preceding functions:

```
OK = anMhSpin.GetPropFontStrikeThru(isFontStrikeThru);
OK = aVbxCtl.GetProp("FontStrikeThru",isFontStrikeThru);
```

To use strikethrough characters in a spin control's caption you can call the member functions TVbxControl::SetProp() or TVbxMhSpin::SetPropFontStrikeThru(). The declaration for the latter function is:

```
BOOL SetPropFontStrikeThru(BOOL v);
```

Here are examples for using the preceding functions:

```
    isFontStrikeThru = TRUE;
OK = anMhSpin.SetPropFontStrikeThru(isFontStrikeThru);
    isFontStrikeThru = FALSE;
OK = aVbxCtl.SetProp("FontStrikeThru",isFontStrikeThru);
```

The FontStyle Property

The `FontStyle` property specifies font style of the spin control. The `FontStyle` property has values that are compatible with the `ENUM` type. Table 25.3 shows the valid settings for the `FontStyle` property. The default setting of 0 displays the control's text with no special 3-D effects. You can get the `FontStyle` setting of the spin control by using the member functions `TVbxControl::GetProp()` or `TVbxMhSpin::GetPropFontStyle()`. The declaration for the latter function is:

```
BOOL GetPropFontStyle(ENUM& v);
```

The function `GetPropFontStyle()` yields a Boolean value to signal success or failure. The function returns the setting of the `FontStyle` property to its caller using the parameter v. Here are examples for using the preceding functions:

```
OK = anMhSpin.GetPropFontStyle(theFontStyle);
OK = aVbxCtl.GetProp("FontStyle", theFontStyle);
```

To set the font style of the spin control you can use the member functions `TVbxControl::SetProp()` or `TVbxMhSpin::SetPropFontStyle()`. The declaration for the latter function is:

```
BOOL SetPropFontStyle(ENUM v);
```

Here are examples for using the preceding functions:

```
theFontStyle = 1;
OK = anMhSpin.SetPropFontStyle(theFontStyle);
theFontStyle = 2;
OK = aVbxCtl.SetProp("FontStyle", theFontStyle);
```

Table 25.3. The Settings for the FontStyle Property

Setting	Meaning
0	None
1	Raised text
2	Raised text with more shading
3	Lowered text
4	Lowered text with more shading

The FontTransparent Property

The Boolean property `FontTransparent` indicates whether the caption of the spin control has transparent characters. The `FontTransparent` property has values that are compatible with the BOOL type. You can get the `FontTransparent` setting of the spin control by using the member functions `TVbxControl::GetProp()` or `TVbxMhSpin::GetPropFontTransparent()`. The declaration for the latter function is:

```
BOOL GetPropFontTransparent(BOOL& v);
```

The function `GetPropFontTransparent()` returns a Boolean value to indicate success or failure. The function yields the setting of the `FontTransparent` property to its caller using the parameter v. Here are examples for using the preceding functions:

```
OK = anMhSpin.GetPropFontTransparent(isFontTransparent);
OK = aVbxCtl.GetProp("FontTransparent",isFontTransparent);
```

To use transparent characters in a spin control's caption you can call the member functions `TVbxControl::SetProp()` or `TVbxMhSpin::SetPropFontTransparent()`. The declaration for the latter function is:

```
BOOL SetPropFontTransparent(BOOL v);
```

Here are examples for using the preceding functions:

```
    isFontTransparent = TRUE;
OK = anMhSpin.SetPropFontTransparent(isFontTransparent);
    isFontTransparent = FALSE;
OK = aVbxCtl.SetProp("FontTransparent",isFontTransparent);
```

The FontUnderline Property

The Boolean property `FontUnderline` indicates whether the caption of the spin control has underlined characters. The `FontUnderline` property uses values that are compatible with the BOOL type. You may obtain the `FontUnderline` setting of the spin control by calling the member functions `TVbxControl::GetProp()` or `TVbxMhSpin::GetPropFontUnderline()`. The declaration for the latter function is:

```
BOOL GetPropFontUnderline(BOOL& v);
```

The function `GetPropFontUnderline()` returns a Boolean value to indicate success or failure. The function returns the setting of the `FontUnderline` property to its caller using the parameter v. Here are examples for using the preceding functions:

```
OK = anMhSpin.GetPropFontUnderline(theFontUnderline);
OK = aVbxCtl.GetProp("FontUnderline", theFontUnderline);
```

To use underlined characters in a spin control's caption, you can use the member functions `TVbxControl::SetProp()` or `TVbxMhSpin::SetPropFontUnderline()`. The declaration for the latter function is:

```
BOOL SetPropFontUnderline(BOOL v);
```

Here are examples for using the preceding functions:

```
    isFontUnderline = TRUE;
OK = anMhSpin.SetPropFontUnderline(isFontUnderline);
    isFontUnderline = FALSE;
OK = aVbxCtl.SetProp("FontUnderline", isFontUnderline);
```

The LightColor Property

The `LightColor` property specifies the *light* color of the spin control. The `LightColor` property has values that are compatible with the `COLORREF` type. The default light color is white. You can get the `LightColor` setting of the spin control by using the member functions `TVbxControl::GetProp()` or `TVbxMhSpin::GetPropLightColor()`. The declaration for the latter function is:

```
BOOL GetPropLightColor(COLORREF& v);
```

The function `GetPropLightColor()` returns a Boolean value to indicate success or failure. The function returns the setting of the `LightColor` property to its caller using the parameter v. Here are examples for using the preceding functions:

```
OK = anMhSpin.GetPropLightColor(theLightColor);
OK = aVbxCtl.GetProp("LightColor", theLightColor);
```

To set the light color of a spin control you can use the member functions `TVbxControl::SetProp()` or `TVbxMhSpin::SetPropLightColor()`. The declaration for the latter function is:

```
BOOL SetPropLightColor(COLORREF v);
```

Here are examples for using the preceding functions:

```
        theLightColor = RGB(255, 129, 128);
OK = anMhSpin.SetPropLightColor(theLightColor);
        theLightColor = RGB(129, 255, 129);
OK = aVbxCtl.SetProp("LightColor", theLightColor);
```

The Max Property

The `Max` property specifies the maximum value for the property `Value`. The `Max` property has values that are compatible with the `int` type. You may obtain the `Max` setting of the spin control by using the member functions `TVbxControl::GetProp()` or `TVbxMhSpin::GetPropMax()`. The declaration for the latter function is:

```
BOOL GetPropMax(int& v);
```

The function `GetPropMax()` returns a Boolean value to signal success or failure. The function yields the setting of the `Max` property to its caller using the parameter `v`. Here are examples for using the preceding functions:

```
OK = anMhSpin.GetPropMax(theMax);
OK = aVbxCtl.GetProp("Max", theMax);
```

To assign the maximum value for a spin control's caption, you can use the member functions `TVbxControl::SetProp()` or `TVbxMhSpin::SetPropMax()`. The declaration for the latter function is:

```
BOOL SetPropMax(int v);
```

Here are examples for using the preceding functions:

```
        theMax = 100;
OK = anMhSpin.SetPropMax(theMax);
        theMax = 144;
OK = aVbxCtl.SetProp("Max", theMax);
```

The Min Property

The `Min` property specifies the minimum value for the property `Value`. The `Min` property has values that are compatible with the `int` type. You can get the `Min` setting of the spin control by using the member functions

`TVbxControl::GetProp()` or `TVbxMhSpin::GetPropMin()`. The declaration for the latter function is:

```
BOOL GetPropMin(int& v);
```

The function `GetPropMin()` returns a Boolean value to indicate success or failure. The function returns the setting of the `Min` property to its caller using the parameter `v`. Here are examples for using the preceding functions:

```
OK = anMhSpin.GetPropMin(theMin);
OK = aVbxCtl.GetProp("Min", theMin);
```

To set the minimum value for a spin control's caption you can use the member functions `TVbxControl::SetProp()` or `TVbxMhSpin::SetPropMin()`. The declaration for the latter function is:

```
BOOL SetPropMin(int v);
```

Here are examples for using the preceding functions:

```
    theMin = 1;
OK = anMhSpin.SetPropMin(theMin);
    theMin = 7;
OK = aVbxCtl.SetProp("Min", theMin);
```

The PictureXDown Properties

The properties `Picture1Down` and `Picture2Down` specify the pictures that appear in the up/right or down/left arrow position when you depress the arrow. The `PictureXDown` properties have values that are compatible with the `HPIC` type. You can get the settings of the `PictureXDown` properties by using the member functions `TVbxControl::GetProp()` or `TVbxMhSpin::GetPropPictureXDown()`. The declaration for the latter function is:

```
BOOL GetPropPicture1Down(HPIC& v);
BOOL GetPropPicture2Down(HPIC& v);
```

The functions `GetPropPictureXDown()` return Boolean values to indicate their success or failure. The functions return the setting of either `PictureXDown` property to their caller using the parameter `v`. Here are examples for using the preceding functions:

```
OK = anMhSpin.GetPropPicture1Down(thePicture1Down);
OK = aVbxCtl.GetProp("Picture2Down", thePicture2Down);
```

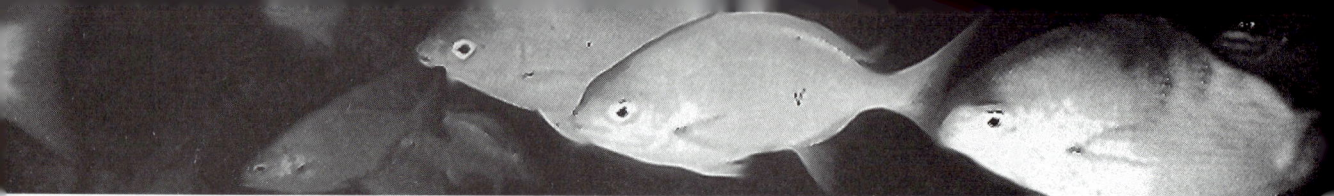

To set the `PictureXDown` properties, use the member functions `TVbxControl::SetProp()` or `TVbxMhSpin::SetPropPictureXDown()`. The declaration for the latter function is:

```
BOOL SetPropPicture1Down(HPIC& v);
BOOL SetPropPicture2Down(HPIC v);
```

Here are examples for using the preceding functions:

```
PICTURE temp1;
// initialize temp1
   thePicture1Down = VBXCreatePicture(&temp1);
OK = anMhSpin.SetPropPicture1Down(thePicture1Down);
PICTURE temp2;
// initialize temp2
thePicture2Down = VBXCreatePicture(&temp2);
OK = aVbxCtl.SetProp("Picture2Down", thePicture2Down);
```

The PictureXUp Properties

The properties `Picture1Up` and `Picture2Up` specify the pictures that become visible in the up/right or down/left arrow position when you are not depressing the arrow. The `PictureXUp` properties have values that are compatible with the `HPIC` type. You may obtain the settings of the `PictureXUp` properties by using the member functions `TVbxControl::GetProp()` or `TVbxMhSpin::GetPropPictureXUp()`. The declaration for the latter function is:

```
BOOL GetPropPicture1Up(HPIC& v);
BOOL GetPropPicture2Up(HPIC& v);
```

The functions `GetPropPictureXUp()` return Boolean values to indicate their success or failure. The functions return the setting of either `PictureXUp` property to their caller through the parameter `v`. Here are examples for using the preceding functions:

```
OK = anMhSpin.GetPropPicture1Up(thePicture1Up);
OK = aVbxCtl.GetProp("Picture2Up", thePicture2Up);
```

To set the `PictureXUp` properties use the member functions `TVbxControl::SetProp()` or `TVbxMhSpin::SetPropPictureXUp()`. The declaration for the latter function is:

```
BOOL SetPropPicture1Up(HPIC& v);
BOOL SetPropPicture2Up(HPIC v);
```

Here are examples for using the preceding functions:

```
PICTURE temp1;
// initialize temp1
    thePicture1Up = VBXCreatePicture(&temp1);
OK = anMhSpin.SetPropPicture1Up(thePicture1Up);
PICTURE temp2;
// initialize temp2
thePicture2Up = VBXCreatePicture(&temp2);
OK = aVbxCtl.SetProp("Picture2Up", thePicture2Up);
```

The ShadowColor Property

The property `ShadowColor` specifies the *shadow* color of the spin control. The `ShadowColor` property has values that are compatible with the `COLORREF` type. The default shadow color is medium gray. You can get the `ShadowColor` setting of the spin control by calling the member functions `TVbxControl::GetProp()` or `TVbxMhSpin::GetPropShadowColor()`. The declaration for the latter function is:

```
BOOL GetPropShadowColor(COLORREF& v);
```

The function `GetPropShadowColor()` yields a Boolean value to signal success or failure. The function returns the setting of the `ShadowColor` property to its caller using the parameter `v`. Here are examples for using the preceding functions:

```
OK = anMhSpin.GetPropShadowColor(theShadowColor);
OK = aVbxCtl.GetProp("ShadowColor", theShadowColor);
```

To set the shadow color of a spin control you can apply the member functions `TVbxControl::SetProp()` or `TVbxMhSpin::SetPropShadowColor()`. The declaration for the latter function is:

```
BOOL SetPropShadowColor(COLORREF v);
```

Here are examples for using the preceding functions:

```
    theShadowColor = RGB(255, 129, 128);
OK = anMhSpin.SetPropShadowColor(theShadowColor);
    theShadowColor = RGB(129, 255, 129);
OK = aVbxCtl.SetProp("ShadowColor", theShadowColor);
```

The SmallDown Property

The property `SmallDown` specifies the value for decreasing the property `Value`. The `SmallDown` property has values that are compatible with the `int` type. You can get the `SmallDown` setting of the spin control by using the member functions `TVbxControl::GetProp()` or `TVbxMhSpin::GetPropSmallDown()`. The declaration for the latter function is:

```
BOOL GetPropSmallDown(int& v);
```

The function `GetPropSmallDown()` returns a Boolean value to indicate success or failure. The function returns the setting of the `SmallDown` property to its caller using the parameter `v`. Here are examples for using the preceding functions:

```
OK = anMhSpin.GetPropSmallDown(theSmallDown);
OK = aVbxCtl.GetProp("SmallDown", theSmallDown);
```

To set the `SmallDown` property for a spin control's caption, you can use the member functions `TVbxControl::SetProp()` or `TVbxMhSpin::SetPropSmallDown()`. The declaration for the latter function is:

```
BOOL SetPropSmallDown(int v);
```

Here are examples for using the preceding functions:

```
    theSmallDown = 1;
OK = anMhSpin.SetPropSmallDown(theSmallDown);
    theSmallDown = 2;
OK = aVbxCtl.SetProp("SmallDown", theSmallDown);
```

The SmallUp Property

The property `SmallUp` specifies the value for increasing the property `Value`. The `SmallUp` property has values that are compatible with the `int` type. You may obatin the `SmallUp` setting of the spin control by using the member functions `TVbxControl::GetProp()` or `TVbxMhSpin::GetPropSmallUp()`. The declaration for the latter function is:

```
BOOL GetPropSmallUp(int& v);
```

The function `GetPropSmallUp()` yields a Boolean value to signal success or failure. The function returns the setting of the `SmallUp` property to its

caller using the parameter v. Here are examples for using the preceding functions:

```
OK = anMhSpin.GetPropSmallUp(theSmallUp);
OK = aVbxCtl.GetProp("SmallUp", theSmallUp);
```

To set the SmallUp property for a spin control's caption you can use the member functions TVbxControl::SetProp() or TVbxMhSpin::SctPropSmallUp(). The declaration for the latter function is:

```
BOOL SetPropSmallUp(int v);
```

Here are examples for using the preceding functions:

```
    theSmallUp = 1;
OK = anMhSpin.SetPropSmallUp(theSmallUp);
    theSmallUp = 2;
OK = aVbxCtl.SetProp("SmallUp", theSmallUp);
```

The TextColor Property

The property TextColor specifies the text color of the spin control's caption. The TextColor property uses values that are compatible with the COLORREF type. The default shadow color is black. You can get the TextColor setting of the spin control by using the member functions TVbxControl::GetProp() or TVbxMhSpin::GetPropTextColor(). The declaration for the latter function is:

```
BOOL GetPropTextColor(COLORREF& v);
```

The function GetPropTextColor() yields a Boolean value to indicate success or failure. The function returns the setting of the TextColor property to its caller using the parameter v. Here are examples for using the preceding functions:

```
OK = anMhSpin.GetPropTextColor(theTextColor);
OK = aVbxCtl.GetProp("TextColor", theTextColor);
```

To set the text color of a spin control, you can use the member functions TVbxControl::SetProp() or TVbxMhSpin::SetPropTextColor(). The declaration for the latter function is:

```
BOOL SetPropTextColor(COLORREF v);
```

Here are examples for using the preceding functions:

```
    theTextColor = RGB(205, 129, 128);
OK = anMhSpin.SetPropTextColor(theTextColor);
    theTextColor = RGB(129, 155, 129);
OK = aVbxCtl.SetProp("TextColor", theTextColor);
```

The Value Property

The property `Value` specifies the value for the spin control. The `Value` property has values that are compatible with the `int` type. The setting for the `Value` property is in the range defined by the properties `Min` and `Max`. You can get the `Value` setting of the spin control by using the member functions `TVbxControl::GetProp()` or `TVbxMhSpin::GetPropValue()`. The declaration for the latter function is:

```
BOOL GetPropValue(int& v);
```

The function `GetPropValue()` returns a Boolean value to indicate success or failure. The function returns the setting of the `Value` property to its caller using the parameter `v`. Here are examples for using the preceding functions:

```
OK = anMhSpin.GetPropValue(theValue);
OK = aVbxCtl.GetProp("Value", theValue);
```

To set the value of a spin control's caption, you can use the member functions `TVbxControl::SetProp()` or `TVbxMhSpin::SetPropValue()`. The declaration for the latter function is:

```
BOOL GetPropValue(int v);
```

Here are examples for using the preceding functions:

```
    theValue = 100;
OK = anMhSpin.SetPropValue(theValue);
    theValue = 123;
OK = aVbxCtl.SetProp("Value", theValue);
```

The ValueBorderStyle Property

The property ValueBorderStyle specifies whether the spin control displays a border around its value. The ValueBorderStyle property has values that are compatible with the ENUM type. Table 25.4 shows the valid settings for the ValueBorderStyle property. The default setting of 0 displays no border around the control's value. You can get the ValueBorderStyle setting of the spin control by using the member functions TVbxControl::GetProp() or TVbxMhSpin::GetPropValueBorderStyle(). The declaration for the latter function is:

```
BOOL GetPropValueBorderStyle(ENUM& v);
```

The function GetPropValueBorderStyle() yields a Boolean value to signal success or failure. The function returns the setting of the ValueBorderStyle property to its caller using the parameter v. Here are examples for using the preceding functions:

```
OK = anMhSpin.GetPropValueBorderStyle(dValueBorderStyle);
OK = aVbxCtl.GetProp("ValueBorderStyle",
dValueBorderStyle);
```

To set the value for the border style of the spin control, you can use the member functions TVbxControl::SetProp() or TVbxMhSpin::SetPropValueBorderStyle(). The declaration for the latter function is:

```
BOOL SetPropValueBorderStyle(ENUM v);
```

Here are examples for using the preceding functions:

```
dValueBorderStyle = 1;
OK = anMhSpin.SetPropValueBorderStyle(dValueBorderStyle);
dValueBorderStyle = 0;
OK = aVbxCtl.SetProp("ValueBorderStyle",
dValueBorderStyle);
```

Table 25.4. The Settings for the ValueBorderStyle Property

Setting	Meaning
0	None
1	Thin Border

The ValueBottom and ValueLeft Properties

The properties `ValueBottom` and `ValueLeft` specify the offset (in twips) from the control's bottom and left margins, respectively, where the the control's value appears. The `ValueBottom` and `ValueLeft` properties have values that are compatible with the `int` type. You can get the `ValueBottom` and `ValueLeft` settings of the spin control by using the member functions `TVbxControl::GetProp()`, `TVbxMhSpin::GetPropValueBottom()`, or `TVbxMhSpin::GetPropValueLeft()`. The declaration for the latter function is:

```
BOOL GetPropValueBottom(int& v);
BOOL GetPropValueLeft(int& v);
```

The functions `GetPropValueBottom()` and `GetPropValueLeft()` return Boolean values to indicate their success or failure. The functions return the setting of the `Value` property to its caller using the parameter `v`. Here are examples for using the preceding functions:

```
OK = anMhSpin.GetPropValueBottom(theValueBottom);
OK = aVbxCtl.GetProp("ValueBottom", theValueBottom);
OK = anMhSpin.GetPropValueLeft(theValueLeft);
OK = aVbxCtl.GetProp("ValueLeft", theValueLeft);
```

To set the properties `ValueLeft` and `ValueBottom` you can use the member functions `TVbxControl::SetProp()`, `TVbxMhSpin::SetPropValueBottom()`, and `TVbxMhSpin::SetPropValueLeft()`. The declarations for the latter functions are:

```
BOOL SetPropValueBottom(int v);
BOOL SetPropValueLeft(int v);
```

Here are examples for using the preceding functions.

```
    theValueBottom = 10;
OK = anMhSpin.SetPropValueBottom(theValue);
    theValueBottom = 15;
OK = aVbxCtl.SetProp("ValueBottom", theValueBottom);
    theValueLeft = 10;
OK = anMhSpin.SetPropValueLeft(theValue);
    theValueLeft = 15;
OK = aVbxCtl.SetProp("ValueLeft", theValueLeft);
```

The ValueDisplay Property

The Boolean property `ValueDisplay` indicates whether the spin control displays the `Value` property in the area defined by the properties `ValueBottom`, `ValueLeft`, `ValueRight`, and `ValueTop`. The `ValueDisplay` property has values that are compatible with the `BOOL` type. You can get the `ValueDisplay` setting of the spin control by using the member functions `TVbxControl::GetProp()` or `TVbxMhSpin::GetPropValueDisplay()`. The declaration for the latter function is:

```
BOOL GetPropValueDisplay(BOOL& v);
```

The function `GetPropValueDisplay()` returns a Boolean value to indicate success or failure. The function returns the setting of the `ValueDisplay` property to its caller using the parameter `v`. Here are examples for using the preceding functions:

```
OK = anMhSpin.GetPropValueDisplay(theValueDisplay);
OK = aVbxCtl.GetProp("ValueDisplay", theValueDisplay);
```

To show or hide the `Value` property of the spin control, you can use the member functions `TVbxControl::SetProp()` or `TVbxMhSpin::SetPropValueDisplay()`. The declaration for the latter function is:

```
BOOL SetPropValueDisplay(BOOL v);
```

Here are examples for using the preceding functions:

```
    hasValueDisplay = TRUE;
OK = anMhSpin.SetPropValueDisplay(hasValueDisplay);
    hassValueDisplay = TRUE;
OK = aVbxCtl.SetProp("ValueDisplay", !isValueDisplay);
```

The ValueRight and ValueTop Properties

The properties `ValueTop` and `ValueRight` specify the offset (in twips) from the control's top and right margins, respectively, where the the control's value appears. The `ValueTop` and `ValueRight` properties have values that are compatible with the `int` type. You can get the `ValueTop` and `ValueRight` settings of the spin control by using the member

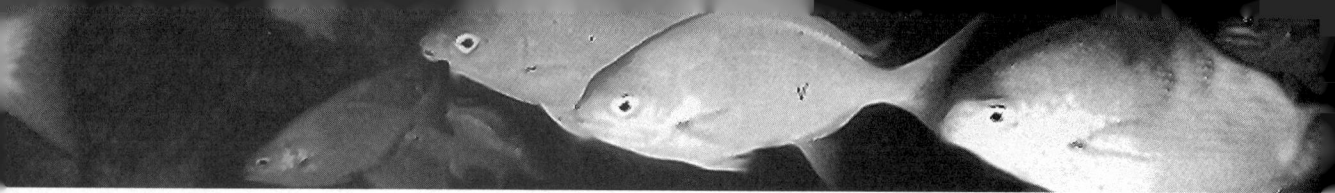

functions `TVbxControl::GetProp()`, `TVbxMhSpin::GetPropValueTop()`, or `TVbxMhSpin::GetPropValueRight()`. The declaration for the latter function is:

```
BOOL GetPropValueTop(int& v);
BOOL GetPropValueRight(int& v);
```

The functions `GetPropValueTop()` and `GetPropValueRight()` return Boolean values to indicate their success or failure. The functions return the setting of the `Value` property to its caller using the parameter `v`. Here are examples for using the preceding functions:

```
OK = anMhSpin.GetPropValueTop(theValueTop);
OK = aVbxCtl.GetProp("ValueTop", theValueTop);
OK = anMhSpin.GetPropValueRight(theValueRight);
OK = aVbxCtl.GetProp("ValueRight", theValueRight);
```

To set the properties `ValueRight` and `ValueTop`, you can use the member functions `TVbxControl::SetProp()`, `TVbxMhSpin::SetPropValueTop()`, and `TVbxMhSpin::SetPropValueRight()`. The declarations for the latter functions are:

```
BOOL SetPropValueTop(int v);
BOOL SetPropValueRight(int v);
```

Here are examples for using the preceding functions:

```
     theValueTop = 10;
OK = anMhSpin.SetPropValueTop(theValue);
     theValueTop = 15;
OK = aVbxCtl.SetProp("ValueTop", theValueTop);
     theValueRight = 10;
OK = anMhSpin.SetPropValueRight(theValue);
     theValueRight = 15;
OK = aVbxCtl.SetProp("ValueRight", theValueRight);
```

The Visible Property

The Boolean property `Visible` indicates whether the spin control is visible. The `Visible` property has values that are compatible with the `BOOL` type. You can get the `Visible` setting of the spin control by using the member functions `TVbxControl::GetProp()` or `TVbxMhSpin::GetPropVisible()`. The declaration for the latter function is:

```
BOOL GetPropVisible(BOOL& v);
```

The function `GetPropVisible()` returns a Boolean value to indicate success or failure. The function returns the setting of the `Visible` property to its caller using the parameter `v`. Here are examples for using the preceding functions:

```
OK = anMhSpin.GetPropVisible(theVisible);
OK = aVbxCtl.GetProp("Visible", theVisible);
```

To show or hide a spin control you can use the member functions `TVbxControl::SetProp()` or `TVbxMhSpin::SetPropVisible()`. The declaration for the latter function is:

```
BOOL SetPropVisible(BOOL v);
```

Here are examples for using the preceding functions:

```
// toggle the visibility of the spin control
    OK = anMhSpin.GetPropVisible(isVisible);
OK = anMhSpin.SetPropVisible(!isVisible);
// toggle the visibility of the spin control
    OK = aVbxCtl.GetProp("Visible", isVisible);
OK = aVbxCtl.SetProp("Visible", !isVisible);
```

The Enabled Property

The Boolean property `Enabled` indicates whether the spin control is enabled. The `Enabled` property has values that are compatible with the `BOOL` type. You can get the `Enabled` setting of the spin control by using the member functions `TVbxControl::GetProp()` or `TVbxMhSpin::GetPropEnabled()`. The declaration for the latter function is:

```
BOOL GetPropEnabled(BOOL& v);
```

The function `GetPropEnabled()` returns a Boolean value to indicate success or failure. The function returns the setting of the `Enabled` property to its caller using the parameter `v`. Here are examples for using the preceding functions:

```
OK = anMhSpin.GetPropEnabled(theEnabled);
theEnabled = aVbxCtl.GetProp("Enabled");
```

To disable or enable a spin control, you can use the member functions `TVbxControl::SetProp()` or `TVbxMhSpin::SetPropEnabled()`. The declaration for the latter function is:

```
BOOL SetPropEnabled(BOOL v);
```

Here are examples for using the preceding functions:

```
// toggle the enable state of the spin control
   OK = anMhSpin.GetPropEnabled(isEnabled);
OK = anMhSpin.SetPropEnabled(!isEnabled);
// toggle the enable state of the spin control
   aVbxCtl.GetProp("Enabled", isEnabled);
aVbxCtl.SetProp("Enabled", !isEnabled);
```

The Spin Control Events

The MicroHelp spin control responds to various events. The relevant event is `Change1`. Other events include `DragDrop`, `DragOver`, `GotFocus`, `KeyDown`, `KeyPress`, `KeyUp`, and `LostFocus`.

The Spin Control Example

The following sections present a simple program that tests the spin control. The MDI-compliant program, VBX.EXE, displays a spin in an MDI child window (see fig. 25.1). When you click on the up arrows of the spin control you increase the value of the spin control. Likewise, when you click on the down arrows of the spin controls you decrease its value. The program displays a caption that shows the current value of the spin control. The program also echoes the control's value in the upper-left corner of the MDI child window.

For the complete code listings of this sample application, and a discussion of each code listing, see the SAMPLE25.DOC file in the archived file for Chapter 25, on the enclosed disk. SAMPLE25.DOC is a Microsoft Word for Windows 2.0 file that can be read from Word for Windows or any major word processor or text editor.

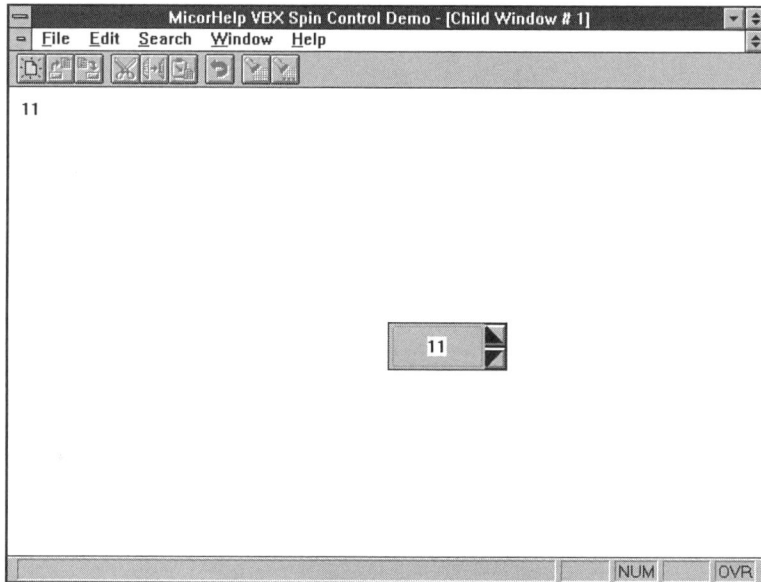

Fig. 25.1. A sample session with the program VBX.EXE.

Summary

This chapter presented the MicroHelp spin control, which supports a spin control with an optional caption and 3-D appearance. The chapter discussed the following topics:

➤ The relevant properties of the spin control that define the appearance and operations of the control. The spin control has a surprisingly large number of properties, despite its simple appearance.

➤ The chapter presented the relevant VBX event `Change1` that updates the spin control when you click the control or when the control is redrawn.

Index

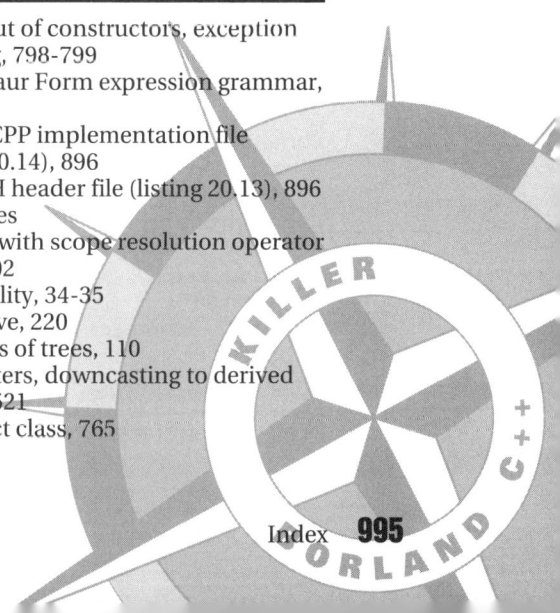

C

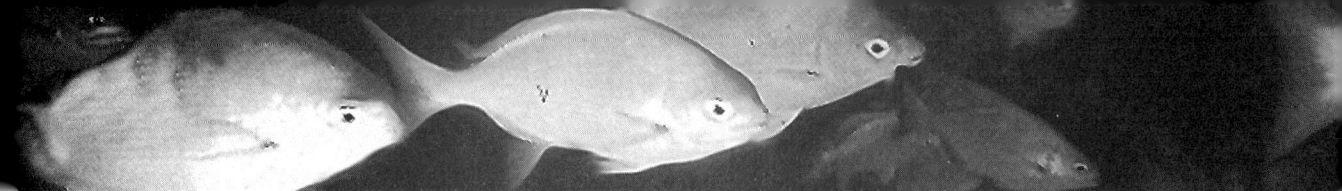

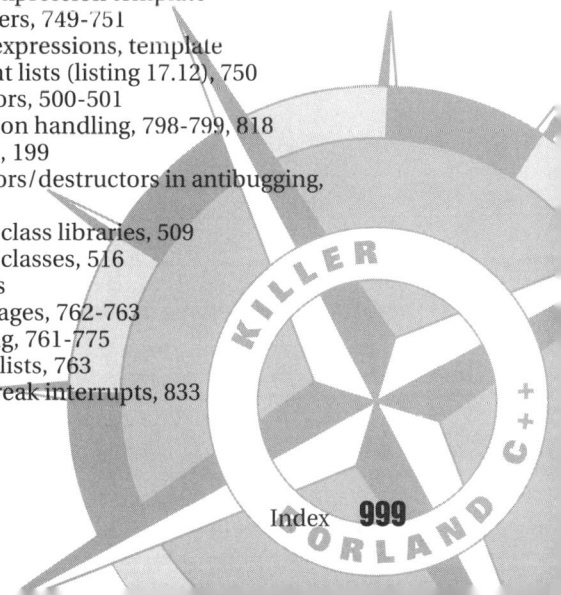

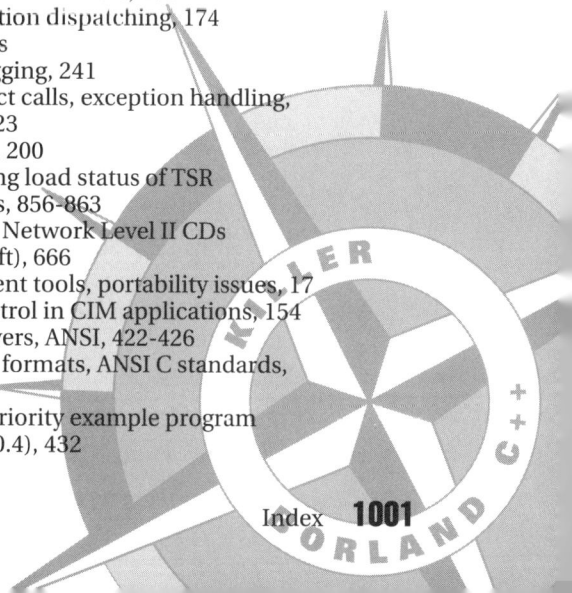

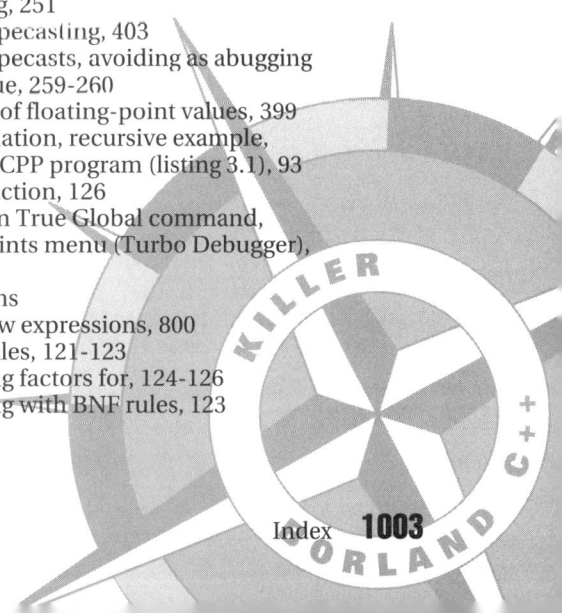

KILLER
BORLAND C++

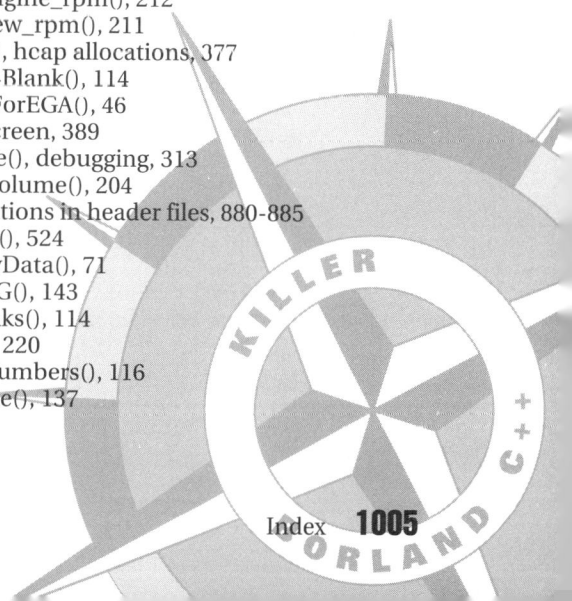

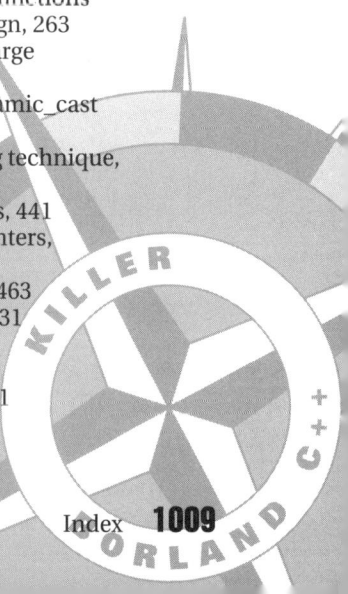

I

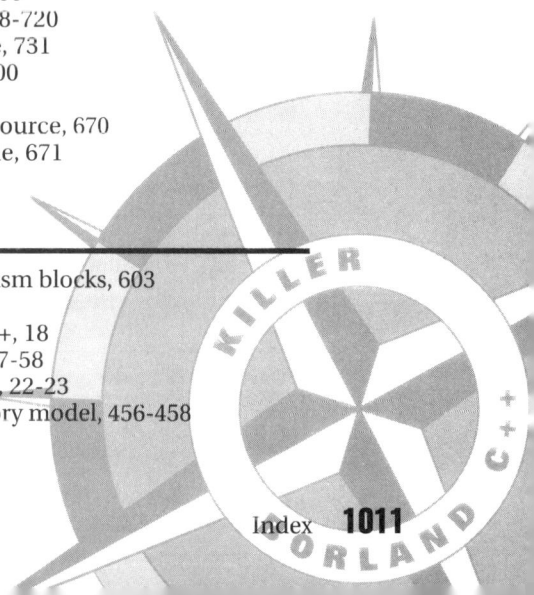

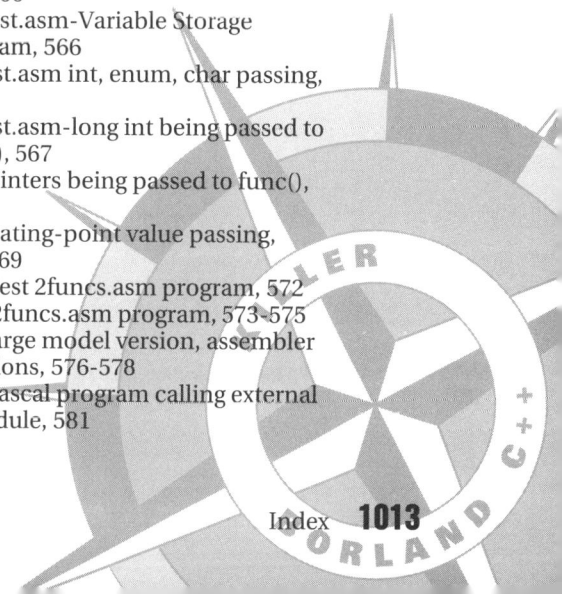

M

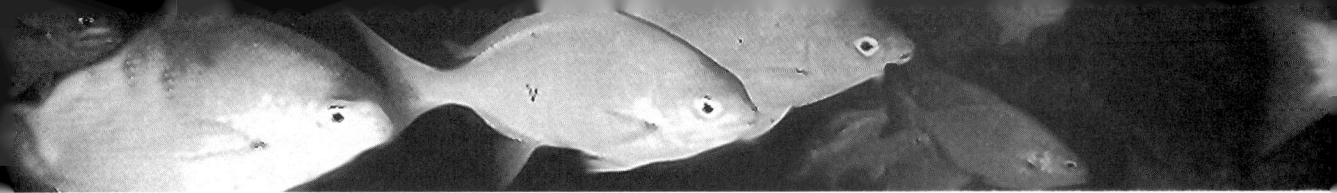

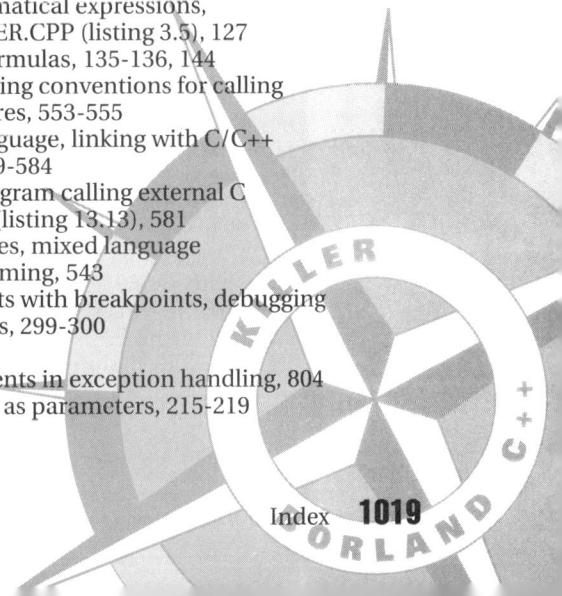

Q-R

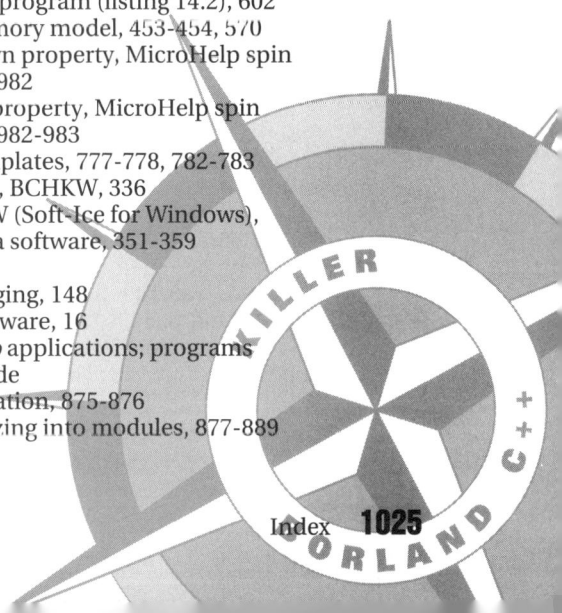

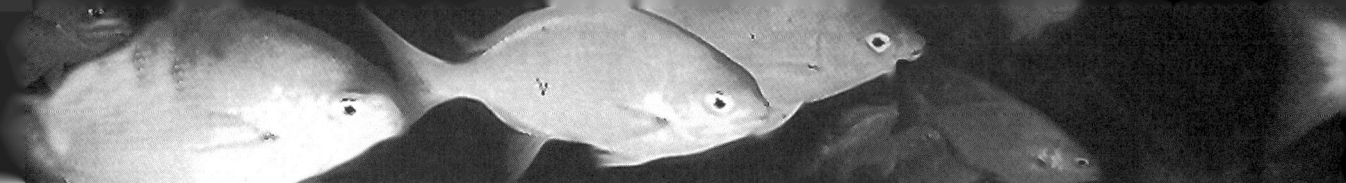

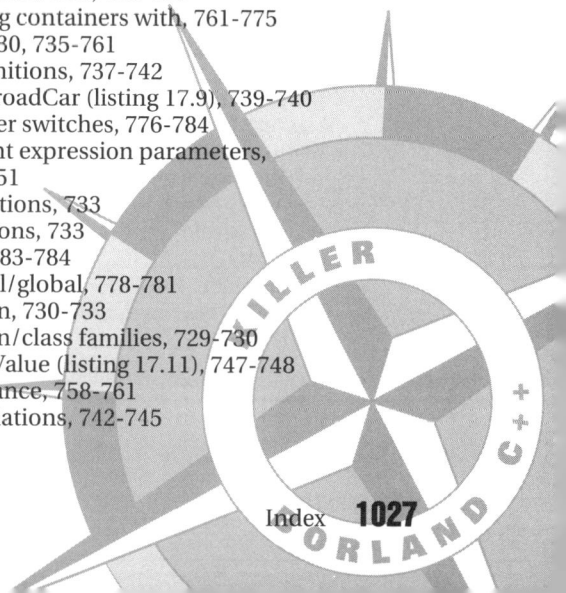

W

X–Y–Z

FarPoint Technologies Leads The Way
with custom controls for visual programming

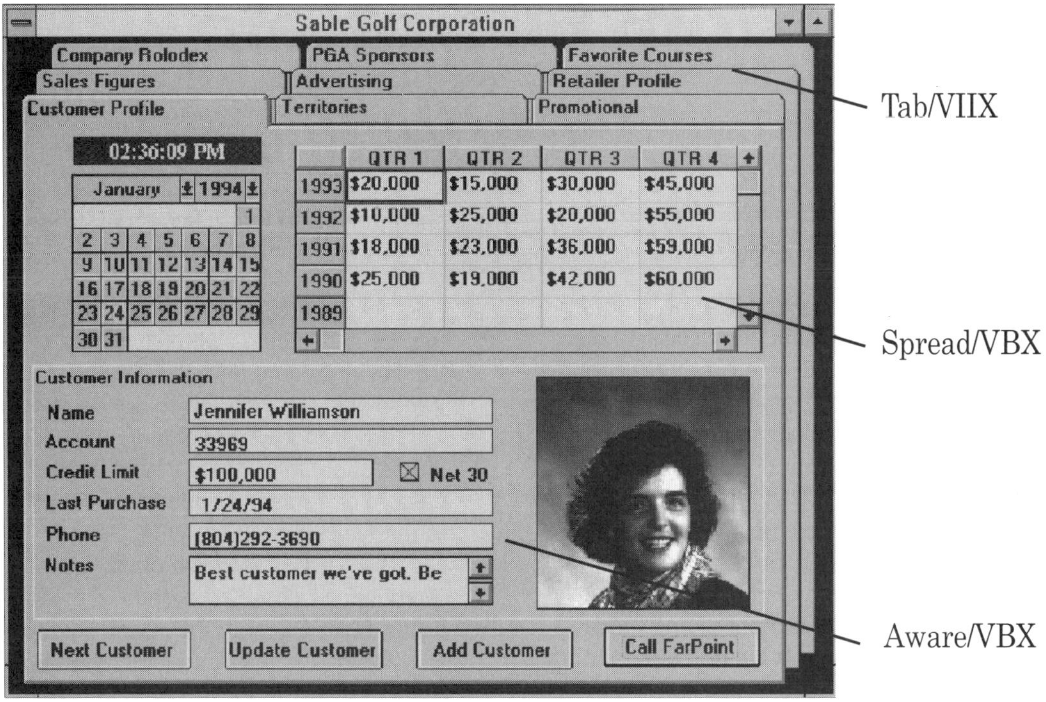

Put the experience of the VBX market leader to work for you by taking advantage of FarPoint's award winning Spread/VBX, Tab/VBX and Aware/VBX, all of which are pictured above. Spread/VBX is the full featured version of the control offered with this book. The new version 3 will feature a new calc engine, Excel 4 read/write capabilities, enhanced printing features and much, much more. Tab is a container control that offers the functionality found in the tab controls in Word and Excel. It features a drag'n drop design interface, the ability to insert, delete and move tabs, and also includes a free copy of Imprint/VBX, a 3-D container control that you'll find hundreds of uses for. Aware/VBX is a comprehensive set of formatted edit controls, multi-column combo and listbox, calendar control and more.

Special Offer for Que Customers

Product	Suggested Retail	Que Special
Spread/VBX	$245	$199
Tab/VBX	$ 49	$ 39
Aware/VBX	$149	$ 99

To Order Your Copies Call FarPoint Technologies at: (800) 645-5913 or (804) 378-0432
or fax your order to (804) 378-1015

FarPoint Technologies, Inc. • 569 Southlake Blvd. • Richmond, Virginia 23236

Visual Programming Tools from MicroHelp

VBTools 4

The Ultimate Visual Basic Add-On !

You get over 50 controls that no programmer should be without. You'll find 19 data aware controls, 3-D controls, Input controls (Masked, Integer, Real and Date), Container controls (including our new Tab control), a Calendar control, enhanced Picture controls, a Histograph control, enhanced Button controls, a Callback control, a Toolbox control, a Tree control, a Stretch control, a Gauge and a Slider control, a File Viewer control and more than 20 other controls we don't have room to mention.

Extra special bonus: Every copy of VBTools 4 includes a version of FarPoint's Grid.VBX, a data aware grid that features virtual data management and in-cell editing. It's the perfect complement to VBTools 4. Compatible with Visual Basic, Visual C++ and Borland C++. VBTools 4 - It's the best VBX control pack - anywhere, at any price! $129

MicroHelp Muscle 2

Faster, Smaller, More Functional Programs

600+ ASM routines for power programmers. All routines are invoked exactly like SubPrograms and Functions, so you don't need to know anything about assembly! Compatible with Visual Basic. $129

MicroHelp VBViewer

Supports Over 20 File Formats

Add drag 'n drop file viewing capabilities to your applications with MicroHelp's VBViewer, a custom control for Microsoft® Windows™ 3.x. VBViewer can be used with any Windows development language that is capable of using Visual Basic custom controls. It supports over 20 file formats including ASCII, HEX, PCX, TIF, GIF, BMP, ICON, Microsoft Word, WordPerfect®, AmiPro®, xBase, Paradox®, Lotus 123®, Excel™, ZIP, LZH, Quattro® Pro, MetaFiles, Q&A and Microsoft Works (documents). VBViewer automatically determines the file format and there's no limit on the file size. We've even included a Search function for text files. Compatible with Visual Basic, Visual C++ and Borland C++. $99

MicroHelp SpellPro™

Add Spell Checking capabilities to your Visual Applications

Contains a 50000+ word American English Dictionary and support for custom dictionaries. Features a built-in dialog box that offers the options to Ignore, Change, Change All, Ignore All, or Add to custom dictionary when a misspelled word is found. Compatible with Visual Basic, Visual C++ and Borland C++. $129

Optional Legal and Medical dictionary available. $59 each

MicroHelp Report Generator

WYSIWYG Reports, Labels, Barcodes and More!

The easiest and fastest way to design reports, mailing labels and lists. Because we're database independent, you're not locked into a particular format. Includes 9 barcodes. Compatible with Visual Basic. $189

Optional end user design module. $99

MicroHelp VBXRef™ 2

Cross-Reference and Project Management Tool for VB Applications

- Compatible with Visual Basic versions 1.0, 2.0 and 3.0.
- Create reports that display the names and scope of all variables, functions and subprograms.
- Move and remove modules, forms, DLL's and individual procedures between projects using drag 'n drop if you're using Visual Basic 2.0 or later.

Compatible with Visual Basic. $99

3-D Gizmos, VBTools, VBXRef and SpellPro are trademarks of MicroHelp, Inc. Windows and Visual Basic are trademarks and Microsoft is a registered trademark of Microsoft Corp. All other products and company names are trademarks and/or registered trademarks of their respective holders.

MicroHelp Network Library

Easy-To-Use Node and Admin Routines

Designed to provide easy access to network interface routines, the product currently supports Novell, Lantastic and NETBios-compatible networks. Compatible with Visual Basic. $99

MicroHelp Communications Library

Reliable, Easy-to-Use Communications Routines

Simultaneously access up to eight serial ports. Includes XMODEM, YMODEM, YMODEM-G, ZMODEM and CompuServe B+ protocols for automatic background file transfers. Compatible with Visual Basic. $149

MicroHelp HighEdit

A Full-Blown Word Processor in a Custom Control!

Now your programs can have built-in professional word processing capabilities. Edit multiple documents. Print with True Type or Postscript fonts. HighEdit supports multiple fonts, multiple colors, search and replace and more. Compatible with Visual Basic, Visual C++ and Borland C++. $495

1-800-922-3383

Credit card and COD orders, call toll free (M-F, 9-6 EST). In Georgia, call 404-516-0899. Fax 404-516-1099.

MicroHelp, Inc.

4359 Shallowford Industrial Parkway • Marietta, GA 30066-1135

We'd Like to Hear from You!

In a continuing effort to produce the highest-quality books possible, Que would like to hear your comments. As radical as this may sound for a publishing company, we **really** want you, the reader and user, to let us know what you like and dislike about this book, and what we can do to improve this book and future books.

In order to provide the most service to you, Macmillan Computer Publishing now has a forum on CompuServe (type **GO QUEBOOKS** at any prompt) through which our staff and authors are available for questions and comments. In addition to visiting our forum, feel free to contact me personally on CompuServe at 75230,1556. Or send your comments, ideas, or corrections to me by fax at (317) 581-4663, or write to me at the address below. Your comments will help us to continue publishing the best books on the market.

Bryan Gambrel
Product Development Specialist
Que
201 W. 103rd Street
Indianapolis, IN 46290